MW01121445

CANADA IN THE WORLD

In this volume marking the Sesquicentennial of Confederation in Canada, leading scholars and jurists discuss the evolution of the Canadian Constitution since the British North America Act 1867; the role of the Supreme Court in interpreting the Constitution as a "living tree" capable of application to new legal issues; and the growing influence of both the Constitution, with its entrenched Charter of Rights and Freedoms, and the decisions of the Court on other constitutional courts dealing with a wide range of issues pertaining to human rights and democratic government. The contributors assess how the Canadian Constitution accommodates the cultural diversity of the country's territories and peoples while ensuring the universal applicability of its provisions; the role of the Court in interpreting and applying the Constitution; and the growing global influence of the Constitution and decisions of the Court on legislatures and courts in other countries.

Richard Albert is Professor of Law at Boston College Law School, with visiting appointments at Yale University, Externado University of Colombia, University of Toronto, and IDC Herzliya. A graduate of Yale, Harvard and Oxford, he formerly served as law clerk to the Chief Justice of Canada. As of January 1, 2018, he is Professor of Law at the University of Texas at Austin.

David R. Cameron is Professor of Political Science at Yale and the Director of the Yale Program in European Union Studies. He has written extensively in the field of comparative political economy and the impact on states of globalization, including a book, co-edited with Gustav Ranis and Annalisa Zinn, entitled *Globalization and Self-Determination: Is the Nation-State under Siege?*

Comparative Constitutional Law and Policy

Series Editors

Tom Ginsburg
University of Chicago
Zachary Elkins
University of Texas at Austin
Ran Hirschl
University of Toronto

Comparative constitutional law is an intellectually vibrant field that encompasses an increasingly broad array of approaches and methodologies. This series collects analytically innovative and empirically grounded work from scholars of comparative constitutionalism across academic disciplines. Books in the series include theoretically informed studies of single constitutional jurisdictions, comparative studies of constitutional law and institutions, and edited collections of original essays that respond to challenging theoretical and empirical questions in the field.

Books in the Series

Canada in the World: Comparative Perspectives on the Canadian Constitution Richard Albert and David R. Cameron

Constitutions, Religion and Politics in Asia: Indonesia, Malaysia and Sri Lanka Dian A. H. Shah

Proportionality: New Frontiers, New Challenges edited by Vicki Jackson and Mark Tushnet

Constituents Before Assembly: Participation, Deliberation, and Representation in the Crafting of New Constitutions Todd A. Eisenstadt, A. Carl LeVan, and Tofigh Maboudi

Assessing Constitutional Performance Tom Ginsburg and Aziz Huq

Buddhism, Politics and the Limits of Law: The Pyrrhic Constitutionalism of Sri Lanka Benjamin Schonthal

Engaging with Social Rights Brian Ray

Constitutional Courts as Mediators Julio Ríos Figueroa

Perils of Judicial Self-Government in Transitional Societies David Kosař

Making We the People Chaihark Hahm and Sung Ho Kim

Radical Deprivation on Trial Cesar Rodríguez-Garavito and Diana Rodríguez-Franco

Unstable Constitutionalism edited by Mark Tushnet and Madhav Khosla

Magna Carta and its Modern Legacy edited by Robert Hazell and James Melton

Constitutions and Religious Freedom Frank Cross

International Courts and the Performance of International Agreements: A General Theory with Evidence from the European Union Clifford Carrubba and Matthew Gabel

Canada in the World

COMPARATIVE PERSPECTIVES ON
THE CANADIAN CONSTITUTION

Edited by

RICHARD ALBERT

Boston College Law School

DAVID R. CAMERON

Yale University

CAMBRIDGE
UNIVERSITY PRESS

CAMBRIDGE
UNIVERSITY PRESS

University Printing House, Cambridge CB2 8BS, United Kingdom

One Liberty Plaza, 20th Floor, New York, NY 10006, USA

477 Williamstown Road, Port Melbourne, VIC 3207, Australia

314–321, 3rd Floor, Plot 3, Splendor Forum, Jasola District Centre, New Delhi – 110025, India

79 Anson Road, #06–04/06, Singapore 079906

Cambridge University Press is part of the University of Cambridge.

It furthers the University's mission by disseminating knowledge in the pursuit of education, learning, and research at the highest international levels of excellence.

www.cambridge.org
Information on this title: www.cambridge.org/9781108419734
DOI: 10.1017/9781108333436

© Cambridge University Press 2018

First published 2018

Printed in the United Kingdom by Clays, St Ives plc

A catalogue record for this publication is available from the British Library.

Library of Congress Cataloging-in-Publication Data
NAMES: Albert, Richard (Law professor), editor. | Cameron, David R., editor.
TITLE: Canada in the world : comparative perspectives on the Canadian Constitution / edited by
    Richard Albert, Boston College; David R. Cameron, Yale University, Connecticut.
DESCRIPTION: Cambridge [UK] ; New York : Cambridge University Press, 2017. |
    Series: Comparative constitutional law and policy
IDENTIFIERS: LCCN 2017024133| ISBN 9781108419734 (hardback : alk. paper) |
    ISBN 9781108414753 (pbk. : alk. paper)
SUBJECTS: LCSH: Constitutional law–Canada. | Rule of law–Canada. | Civil rights–Canada.
CLASSIFICATION: LCC KE4219 .C33 2017 | DDC 342.7102–dc23 LC record available
    at https://lccn.loc.gov/2017024133

ISBN 978-1-108-41973-4 Hardback

Contents

Contributors

Richard Albert is Professor of Law at Boston College Law School; as of January 1, 2018, at the University of Texas at Austin.

David R. Cameron is Professor of Political Science, Director of the Program in European Union Studies and a member of the Canadian Studies Committee at Yale University.

Jamie Cameron is Professor of Law at Osgoode Hall Law School at York University.

Wen-Chen Chang is Professor of Law at the College of Law at National Taiwan University.

Alain-G. Gagnon is Professor of Political Science at L'Université du Québec à Montréal. He is a member of the Royal Society of Canada.

Lech Garlicki is Professor of Constitutional Law at Warsaw University and former Judge on the Constitutional Court of Poland and European Court of Human Rights.

Jeffrey Goldsworthy is Emeritus Professor of Law at Monash University and Adjunct Professor of Law at the University of Adelaide.

Ran Hirschl is Professor of Political Science and Law at the University of Toronto and holder of the Alexander von Humboldt Professorship in Comparative Constitutionalism at the University of Göttingen. He is a member of the Royal Society of Canada.

Hon. Grant Huscroft is a Justice on the Court of Appeal for Ontario.

Heinz Klug is the Evjue-Bascom Professor in Law at the University of Wisconsin Law School.

Catharine A. MacKinnon is the Elizabeth A. Long Professor of Law at the University of Michigan Law School and the James Barr Ames Visiting Professor of Law (long-term) at the Harvard Law School.

Patrick Macklem is the William C. Graham Professor of Law at the University of Toronto Faculty of Law. He is a member of the Royal Society of Canada.

Rt. Hon. Beverley McLachlin, P.C., is the Chief Justice of Canada.

Kent Roach is Professor and Prichard Wilson Chair in Law and Public Policy at the University of Toronto Faculty of Law. He is a member of the Royal Society of Canada and of the Order of Canada.

Michel Rosenfeld is University Professor of Law and Comparative Democracy and the Justice Sydney L. Robins Professor of Human Rights at the Benjamin N. Cardozo School of Law at Yeshiva University.

Ayelet Shachar is Professor of Law and Political Science at the University of Toronto and Director of the Max Planck Institute for the Study of Religious and Ethnic Diversity. She is a member of the Royal Society of Canada.

Adrienne Stone is Professor of Constitutional Law and Kathleen Fitzpatrick Australian Laureate Fellow and Director of the Centre for Comparative Constitution Studies at the University of Melbourne Law School.

Stephen Tierney is Professor of Constitutional Theory at the University of Edinburgh Law School.

Mark Tushnet is the William Nelson Cromwell Professor of Law at Harvard Law School.

Alison L. Young is Professor of Public Law at the University of Oxford Faculty of Law.

Acknowledgements

Today, as co-editors of this volume commemorating the Sesquicentennial of Confederation, we approach an anniversary of our own: we met nearly twenty years ago when David Cameron served as Richard Albert's senior thesis advisor at Yale University – on the subject of Canadian politics no less! When Richard returned to Yale as the 2015–16 Canadian Bicentennial professor, we picked up where we had left off years before and began to plan a major conference to mark the Sesquicentennial. We had one overriding objective in mind: to gather leading scholars in comparative public law to reflect collaboratively, provocatively and imaginatively on the Constitution of Canada. This volume memorializes the papers – since revised and refined – presented at the Yale Law School on April 12, 2016, in a conference organized under the theme "Comparative Perspectives on the Constitution of Canada."

This project was made possible by the generous support of the MacMillan Center for International and Area Studies at Yale and the Oscar M. Ruebhausen Fund at the Yale Law School.

We thank Lisa Brennan, Lina Chan, Rahima Chaudhury, George Joseph, Lourdes Haynes, Ian Shapiro and Marilyn Wilkes at the MacMillan Center.

We thank Joseph Crosby, Renee Dematteo, Debra Krosner, Susan Levesque, Jennifer Marshall, Brian Pauze, Tyson Streeter, Mike Thompson and Adrienne Webb at the Yale Law School.

We also thank our students Dhruv Aggarwal, Chintan Chandrachud, Dayo Gbadamosi, Sameer Jaywant and Mariana Velasco Rivera.

Owen Fiss, David Schleicher, Reva Siegel and Jim Whitman have earned our thanks for so ably and fluently moderating the panels on which the papers in this volume were presented and debated. We are likewise grateful to Bruce Ackerman for giving closing remarks at the conference, and to Guido Calabresi for introducing our keynote speaker, the Right Honourable Chief Justice

Beverley McLachlin, to whom we are appreciative for attending this conference accompanied by her husband Frank McArdle.

We thank the team at Cambridge University Press for the privilege of publishing this volume with them.

We have not forgotten the contributors to this volume. Each of them made considerable efforts to prepare and revise their own papers, to comment on other papers and to travel to the conference. It is not easy to get to New Haven when traveling from almost anywhere but the Northeast, and even then the weather often fails to cooperate. It was a pleasure of the highest order to collaborate with them on this volume – a book we hope will become a useful resource for those interested in learning about Canada since Confederation and as it marches toward its Bicentennial.

David Cameron wishes to thank Cynthia Horan for her support throughout the project, and Richard Albert is grateful to his late father for encouraging him to choose Yale for college.

Introduction

The Values of Canadian Constitutionalism

RICHARD ALBERT

In an interview on Al-Hayat television in Egypt on 30 January 2012, US Supreme Court Justice Ruth Bader Ginsburg stirred some controversy in America. She remarked that "I would not look to the US Constitution, if I were drafting a constitution in the year 2012."[1] Where would she look instead? To two countries, she said: Canada and South Africa.

Justice Ginsburg's revelation did not come as a surprise to scholars of comparative public law. For years, the US Constitution has declined in its global influence, due in no small part to its exceptionalism on matters of rights and liberties.[2] In its place, Canada has risen to prominence on the strength of its modern *Constitution Act, 1982*, which after years of failed attempts finally entrenched a domestic amending formula as well as the now-celebrated *Canadian Charter of Rights and Freedoms*.[3] Admired abroad for its constitutional success, Canada has since become a model for the promise and possibilities of constitutionalism in the democratic and democratizing world.

A CONSTITUTIONAL MODEL FOR THE WORLD?

The global importance of the Constitution of Canada has grown as we have approached 2017. Since Confederation began with the *British North America*

---

[1] Adam Liptak, '*We the People' Loses Appeal with People around the World*, NY TIMES, 6 Feb. 2012, *available at*: www.nytimes.com/2012/02/07/us/we-the-people-loses-appeal-with-people-around-the-world.html (last visited 1 August 2016).

[2] *See* David S. Law & Mila Versteeg, *The Declining Influence of the United States Constitution*, 87 N.Y.U. L. REV. 762 (2012).

[3] *Canadian Charter of Freedoms*, Part I of the *Constitution Act, 1982*, being Schedule B to the *Canada Act 1982*, 1982, c. 11 (UK).

Act, 1867,[4] Canada has evolved into a global economic, cultural and now constitutional force. The country has survived the Great Wars, the Great Depression, the internal challenges of regionalism, bilingualism, bijuralism and secession, and it has successfully managed the national security era in which we now find ourselves. By its resilient example, the Constitution of Canada has influenced the design of the South African Bill of Rights, the Israeli Basic Laws, the New Zealand Bill of Rights and the Hong Kong Bill of Rights.[5] The Constitution of Canada was perhaps fated to occupy this role in global constitutionalism given that the drafters of the *Charter* went to great lengths to incorporate international human rights principles.[6]

The 150th anniversary of Confederation in Canada offers an occasion both to reflect and to look ahead. There is of course much to celebrate about Canada and its Constitution, but triumphalism is not the spirit in which the scholars assembled for this volume have approached this project. We have taken an evaluative perspective on how the Constitution of Canada has influenced the world around it and how it has itself been influenced, with a view to examining the first 150 of Confederation through a distinctively comparative lens. Our collective effort to map and evaluate Canada's reach beyond its borders is therefore anchored in a critical approach, not a congratulatory one, although the group has not shied away from highlighting where a Canadian doctrine, practice or theory has been proven to work well.

THREE CANADIAN VALUES

The authors in this volume gathered at the Yale Law School to present early drafts of their chapters in a conference held to mark the Sesquicentennial. Our point of departure for the program was the following except from a speech given a few years earlier by The Rt. Hon. Beverley McLachlin, Chief Justice of Canada, who observed at the time, as she looked ahead to the year 2017, that the story of Canada's Constitution was one of peculiarly *Canadian* values:

> In 2017, not so far off, we will celebrate the 150th anniversary of the Canadian Constitution. As I mused on the up-coming date, it occurred to me that our constitution can be understood as a series of stories that together recount our

[4] Since renamed to "Constitution Act, 1867": Constitution Act, 1867, 30 & 31 Victoria, c. 3 (UK) [*Constitution Act, 1867*].
[5] Sujit Choudhry, *Globalization in Search of Justification: Toward a Theory of Comparative Constitutional Interpretation*, 74 IND. L.J. 819, 821–22 (1999).
[6] Claire L'Heureux-Dubé, *The Importance of Dialogue*, 34 TULSA L.J. 15, 24 (1998).

national odyssey. It is a story of how this country moved from a collection of colonies, to a dominion, to a fully sovereign nation. And it is a story of the gradual emergence of a unique mélange of values that we – and the world – see as distinctly Canadian.[7]

What are these Canadian values and how do we identify them? For the heralded sociologist Seymour Martin Lipset, the answer lies somewhere in Canada's beginnings. Born of counterrevolution, Canada has been engaged in "a long struggle" to reconcile its deeply rooted traditions of monarchy and responsible government inherited from Britain with the modern vanguard of constitutional democracy and popular sovereignty entrenched south of its border in the United States.[8] Yet what Canada has struggled to reconcile since Patriation is not only its external British and American influences but also a more complex interaction of internal forces that simultaneously pull and push Canada toward the particularistic political commitments of Confederation and the universalist aspirations of the *Charter*.[9] Keeping one eye on global norms and another on the local context is the challenge of modern constitutionalism – and the Canadian constitutional experience can help the countries of the world take steps toward meeting the demands of both.

Back to the question: what are these distinctly Canadian values? In her address years ago, the Chief Justice identified three values that defined Canada at Confederation and that continue to endure today: "[C]anada's first and defining moment, Confederation, grounded the nation in three values that were to prove lasting – democracy, federalism, and respect for difference and diversity."[10] Representative and responsible government are of course the democratic foundations of the country, just as federalism was the only possible construction for the new union of colonies, each of them different yet united in a federalist arrangement under a national government. And diversity being a political and sociological fact at Confederation, the new constitutional arrangements had to offer a way to accommodate those differences, at the time principally linguistic and religious ones. Whether Canadian federalism has succeeded in managing the country's diversity consistent with the demands of democracy depends on what we measure and how. But these

---

[7] The Right Honourable Beverley McLachlin, P.C., Chief Justice of Canada, *Defining Moments: The Canadian Constitution*, Remarks before the Canadian Club of Canada, 5 February 2013.

[8] Seymour Martin Lipset, CONTINENTAL DIVIDE: THE VALUES AND INSTITUTIONS OF THE UNITED STATES AND CANADA (New York: Routledge, 1990) at 1.

[9] *See* Benjamin L. Berger, *Children of Two Logics: A Way into Canadian Constitutional Culture*, 11 INT'L J. CONST. L. 319, 321–22.

[10] McLachlin, *supra* note 7.

three values form a distinctly Canadian foundation for the Constitution of Canada, and together they tell the story of Canadian constitutionalism from Confederation through Patriation to the present day.

IDENTIFYING CONSTITUTIONAL VALUES

Constitutional values are often discernible in the procedures of formal amendment. There being no part of a constitution more important than the rules that authorize changes to its highest political commitments,[11] we can mine the design of formal amendment procedures for outright declarations or subtle hints about what is foundational in a constitutional community. In multinational polities, the rules of amendment are the place to look for the legal recognition of multinationality because these rules reveal the agents of legal change.[12] The amending formula in the Constitution of Canada reflects the country's multinationality, albeit imperfectly as the failures of the Meech Lake and Charlottetown accords and the resulting 1995 Quebec referendum show so clearly. Nonetheless in its design and in the attempts to improve it, the Constitution's amending formula suggests that these three values – democracy, federalism and respect for difference and diversity – sit at the base of the Canadian project of Confederation, so far an experiment that has endured for 150 years, more than 130 years longer than the average lifespan of the world's national constitutions.[13]

For over a century, Canada did not have the power to amend its own Constitution. With some limited exceptions, the power of formal amendment belonged to the Parliament of the United Kingdom. The provinces could amend their own provincial constitutions, and the Parliament of Canada could amend a narrow class of matters concerning courts and the purely federal subjects in the Constitution.[14] All other matters had to be amended at the request of Canada by the Parliament in London. These included matters of the first importance including the admission of new provinces, the administration of territories and changes affecting federal-provincial relations such as the transfer of jurisdiction over employment insurance and

---

[11] See John Burgess, I POLITICAL SCIENCE AND COMPARATIVE CONSTITUTIONAL LAW, 137 (1891).
[12] Sujit Choudhry, *Does the World Need More Canada? The Politics of the Canadian Model in Constitutional Politics and Political Theory*, 5 INT'L J. CONST. L. 606, 638 (2007).
[13] See Zachary Elkins et al., THE ENDURANCE OF NATIONAL CONSTITUTIONS 2 (Cambridge: Cambridge University Press, 2009) (noting that the average lifespan of a national constitution has been 19 years).
[14] See *British North America Act, 1867*, ss. 92(1) [repealed], 101; *British North America (No. 2) Act, 1949*, 13 Geo. VI, c. 81 (UK).

pensions as well as changes to judicial tenure. It is unusual for one sovereign country to rely on another for amendments to its constitution. Yet this was the basic arrangement in Canada from 1867 until 1982, when Canada finally entrenched its own fully deployable domestic amending formula.

DEMOCRACY IN CONSTITUTIONAL AMENDMENT

In those 125 years, Canadian political actors tried but failed over one dozen times to sever their reliance on London for amendments to the Constitution. In every instance but the last they could not agree on how to structure the rules of formal amendment, hitting an impasse when the time came to decide which parts of the constitution would be amendable by whom and with what threshold of provincial agreement. The default rule therefore remained in place: amendments would be made by the Parliament of the United Kingdom at the request of Canada in a joint address of both houses of Parliament.[15] By 1965, however, it had become an ordinary practice for the Parliament of the United Kingdom to enact any amendment requested by Canada and it had also become common for Canada to consult with provinces and secure their consent prior to requesting an amendment affecting federal-provincial relations with specific regard to provincial powers.[16] The *Patriation Reference* in 1981 would later recognize that this practice of securing provincial consent had over the years matured into a constitutional convention.[17]

Canada's long search for a domestic amending formula was a quest not only for legal independence but for democracy as well. At their core, the rules of constitutional amendment are necessary procedures for democratic constitutionalism. They are legal rules that authorize a formal process to alter the constitutional text. They are also political rules that can confer sociological legitimacy on the legal changes made by amendment. Their entrenchment into a codified constitution reflects a choice of constitutional design to enable the people and their representatives to exercise the democratic right to rewrite their basic rules of self-government when the required majorities coalesce behind a proposed change. The political struggle for an amending formula was an exercise in democracy and its culmination in the patriation of the Constitution with an entrenched amendment formula was a vindication of democracy as a constitutional value in Canada.

---

[15] Peter W. Hogg, *Formal Amendment of the Constitution of Canada*, 55 L. & CONTEMP. PROBS 253, 254 (1992).

[16] *See* Guy Favreau, THE AMENDMENT OF THE CONSTITUTION OF CANADA 11–16 (1965).

[17] *See Reference Re Resolution to Amend the Constitution*, [1981] 1 SCR 753.

FEDERALISM IN CONSTITUTIONAL AMENDMENT

The *Constitution Act, 1982* establishes five different procedures in its amending formula. Each procedure is expressly designated for use in connection with a specific part, provision or principle in the Constitution. None has comprehensive application as a matter of law to all parts of the Constitution. One, for example, can be used only for the amendable matters assigned to it, and the others are legally disabled as to those matters. What is worth noting about these five procedures is the influence of federalism in their design both in the construction of each individual procedure and in their collective structure as an architectural whole across the entire amending formula.

The unilateral provincial procedure authorizes a majority of a provincial assembly to amend its own constitution to the extent the amendment does not affect matters of federal or federal-provincial interest.[18] There is a federal analogue to this procedure: the federal unilateral procedure authorizes a majority of Parliament to pass a law amending the Constitution in relation to the executive government or either house of Parliament, provided the subject of the amendment is not assigned to another procedure.[19] A third procedure – the bilateral amendment procedure – authorizes Parliament and a concerned province or provinces to amend the Constitution where the amendment affects "one or more, but not all, provinces."[20] The general amendment procedure applies to amendments that have national scope; it requires both houses of Parliament to agree along with seven out of ten provinces whose total population equals at least half of the entire provincial population.[21] The fifth – the unanimity procedure – requires both houses of Parliament and each of the provincial assemblies to agree on the amendment,[22] something that the two major amendment failures in modern Canadian history have proven is much easier said than done.[23]

Canada's commitment to federalism is reflected in this escalating structure of constitutional amendment. Each procedure in the amending formula is harder to satisfy than the previous, hence its escalation in terms of difficulty, the theory behind this design being that the more important or politically salient a subject, the greater should be the degree of political support for making changes to it. What makes a constitutional amendment more difficult as the subject of amendment rises in importance is the quantum of provincial

[18] See *Constitution Act, 1982*, s. 45.   [19] *See id*, s. 44.   [20] *See id*, s. 43.   [21] *See id*, s. 38.
[22] *See id*, s. 41.
[23] See Michael Lusztig, *Constitutional Paralysis: Why Canadian Constitutional Initiatives Are Doomed to Fail*, 27 Can. J. Pol. Sci. 747, 748 (1994).

consent required across the five procedures in the amending formula. The unilateral provincial procedure requires nothing beyond a vote in the relevant provincial assembly. But the role of provinces rises steadily from little to large beginning with the federal unilateral procedure. Only indirect provincial approval is needed to use the federal unilateral procedure, since parliamentarians voting on the amendment may take into account their provincial interests to the extent the amendment affects in some way the provinces, even though the procedure is not supposed to be deployed but for narrow federal matters. The bilateral amendment procedure requires the affected province or provinces to approve the amendment in order for it to become valid. The general amendment procedure, for use in amendments of national interest, raises the degree of provincial agreement to a supermajority, while the unanimity procedure brings it to its highest level.

The central point of distinction among these five procedures is the involvement of provinces. As the amendable subject moves from involving strictly provincial interests to matters of national interest, the influence of provinces increases in two ways: first, the number of provinces whose approval is needed jumps from zero to unanimity; second, provinces are given the power to veto important amendments passed using the general or unanimity procedures.[24] This feature of escalation in the amending formula is only one of the federalist commitments evident in the rules of constitutional amendment. The *Constitution Act, 1982* also gives provinces the right in some cases to dissent and to opt-out from successful amendments.[25] These two features join with the escalating structure of the amending formula to reinforce the federalist values of the Constitution – the second of three distinctly Canadian values highlighted by the Chief Justice.

DIFFERENCE AND DIVERSITY IN CONSTITUTIONAL AMENDMENT

The amending formula also reflects the respect for difference and diversity upon which the Chief Justice observed Confederation was built. Beyond the federalist foundations of the amending formula – which represent nothing if

---

[24] The Regional Veto Law, passed in 1996, supplements Part V. It requires Ministers to first secure the consent of each of Canada's regions before introducing a motion to amend the Constitution using the general amendment formula. *See* An act respecting constitutional amendments, S.C. 1996, c. 1 (1996). I have argued elsewhere that this law is unconstitutional. *See* Richard Albert, *The Difficulty of Constitutional Amendment in Canada*, 53 ALBERTA L. REV. 85, 111 (2015).

[25] *See Constitution Act, 1982*, ss. 38(3)-(4), 40.

not the recognition of differences among the various regions of Canada – there is an underappreciated provision in the *Constitution Act, 1982* located outside of the amending formula itself that nonetheless forms an integral part of the rules of constitutional change. Section 35.1 commits the Government of Canada and provincial governments to invite representatives of the aboriginal peoples of Canada to a constitutional conference of first ministers, convened by the Prime Minister, when a proposed amendment affects the rights of aboriginal peoples. The Constitution identifies three classes of provisions that trigger this commitment: a proposed amendment to Class 24 of section 91 of the *Constitution Act, 1867*, or to section 25, or to Part II of the *Constitution Act, 1982*. This commitment springs from the Canadian constitutional value of respect for difference and diversity. Yet there is reason to argue that the Constitution does not go far enough to bring aboriginal peoples to the table. First Ministers are required only to "invite" representatives of the aboriginal peoples when a proposed amendment is thought relevant. Well intentioned though it may be, this constitutional provision and others like it have the potential to further sharpen the divisions among the many peoples of Canada.

A LAND OF MANY PEOPLES

Yet the success of the Canadian model derives more from the aspiration of accommodation that shapes its constitutional politics than from its constitutional design. There is a reason rooted deeply in history why the will to accommodate difference is baked into Canada's DNA as a country: the diversity of Canada requires it. For all of its successes, the Constitution has yet to constitute Canadians into one people. Instead, it accommodates and recognizes different peoples, and in some cases even creates new categories of peoples. Many of these peoples continue to challenge of the legitimacy of the very Constitution that binds them under law. The Constitution of Canada therefore defies the conventional theory of democratic constitutionalism that a constitution, in order to endure, should concretize a political settlement that is seen as legitimate and is in fact legitimated in a single democratic moment by the consent of the governed.

The remarkable endurance of the Constitution of Canada suggests that its legitimacy derives neither from a founding moment nor from sociological veneration but rather from its continued contestability. The Canadian commitment to the living constitution entails the political reality that the Constitution is both an unfinished and an unfinishable project of self-government. It is a political arrangement that is not quite settled nor perhaps ever will be. This unsteady state invites both challenges and opportunities.

In the public imagination, modern constitution-making has become deeply interconnected with revolution, the former consolidating the achievements and ideals of the latter. Hannah Arendt twinned the two concepts of constitution and revolution as "correlative conjunctions."[26] The moment of constitutionalization that follows revolution is a triumph for challengers over incumbents in a contest for control, often a violent struggle.[27] There is, in the path to revolutionary victory, a cataclysmic character to the "sweeping, sudden and violent" change that attends the formation of a new constitutional order. For some revolutions, the transformation may be totalizing, embracing all manner of law and society, resulting in what Samuel Huntington has defined as a "violent domestic change in the dominant values and myths of a society, in its political institutions, social structure, leadership, government activity and policies."[28]

A revolution, then, marks a new beginning, the end of a prior regime and the installation of new leaders who bring with them new values to be marshalled in the creation of a new constitutional order. In the conventional theory of constitutionalism, what legitimates this new regime is the consent of the governed. The people, acting through their constitution-making representatives,[29] reject the old and embrace the new, authorizing their agents in the constituted branches of government to act in their name.

This Lockean formation of the constitutional consensus required to legitimate the new order concretizes a settlement among the people. The people, as Locke understands it, "enter into society to make one people, one body politic, under one supreme government,"[30] and though "there remains still in the people a supreme power to remove or alter the legislative, when they find the legislative act contrary to the trust reposed in them,"[31] they strike an agreement that repudiates difference or accommodates it, but in either case it is an agreement that constitutes one new people. Nowhere is this Lockean theory of constitutional settlement more evident than the people's

---

[26] Hannah Arendt, ON REVOLUTION (London: Penguin Books, rep. ed. 1990), 126.

[27] Harold J. Berman, LAW AND REVOLUTION: THE FORMATION OF THE WESTERN LEGAL TRADITION (Cambridge: Harvard University Press, 2009), 21.

[28] Samuel P. Huntington, POLITICAL ORDER IN CHANGING SOCIETIES (New Haven: Yale University Press, rev. ed. 2006), 264.

[29] *See* Andrew Arato, *Forms of Constitution Making and Theories of Democracy*, 17 CARDOZO L. REV. 191, 197–201 (1995) (outlining models of democratic constitution-making).

[30] John Locke, SECOND TREATISE OF GOVERNMENT AT 47–48 (§89) (Indianapolis: Hackett Publishing Co., C.B. MacPherson ed. 1980).

[31] *Id.* at 77–78 (§149).

charter written by Locke himself in 1669,[32] *The Fundamental Constitutions of Carolina*, which committed the people of North Carolina to a settlement that "shall be and remain the sacred and unalterable form and rule of government of Carolina forever."[33]

The US Constitution is born of a revolutionary democratic moment. Since its adoption, it has been the battleground for the formation of a new constitutional settlement, or for the defence of the old. The Constitution, deeply imbedded within a tradition of revolutionary constitutionalism, has been transformed by dialogic interactions among the constituted branches of government, civil society groups and movement parties that have struck a new agreement, whether at the founding, the Reconstruction, the New Deal or the Civil Rights era. Each of these "constitutional moments" has resolved an open question of polity and identity, concretizing though not necessarily formalizing in a new written constitutional text a new constitutional settlement that has governed subsequent generations of constitutional politics.[34]

The Canadian Constitution, however, is something of a departure from the conventional theory of constitution-making. Neither prompted nor attended by revolution, nor rooted in a tradition of revolutionary constitutionalism, the Constitution of Canada is not the product of the kind of settlement we commonly associate with constitutions,[35] and indeed has spent much of its life in search of one. For Canada's leading scholar of constitutional politics, this is the story of the country's "constitutional odyssey," a journey that has taken its peoples through multiple rounds of mega constitutional politics that have on each occasion failed to bring constitutional peace.[36] Worse still, these recurring periods of mega constitutional politics have hardened the differences that define the many peoples of Canada and indeed have deepened the fault lines that divide them.

[32] For a careful study of Locke's involvement in writing the North Carolinian Constitution, see David Armitage, *John Locke, Carolina, and the "Two Treatises of Government,"* 32 POL. THEORY 602 (2004).

[33] FUNDAMENTAL CONSTITUTION OF CAROLINA, art. 120 (1669).

[34] *See generally* Bruce Ackerman, WE THE PEOPLE – VOLUME 1: FOUNDATIONS (Cambridge, MA: Harvard University Press, 1991) (introducing theory of "constitutional moments"); Bruce Ackerman, WE THE PEOPLE – VOLUME 2: TRANSFORMATIONS (Cambridge, MA: Harvard University Press, 1998) (illustrating two major constitutional moments: Reconstruction and the New Deal); Bruce Ackerman, WE THE PEOPLE – VOLUME 3: THE CIVIL RIGHTS REVOLUTION (Cambridge, MA: Harvard University Press, 2014) (arguing that the Civil Rights movement created a constitutional moment).

[35] Jon Elster, *Forces and Mechanisms in the Constitution-Making Process*, 45 DUKE L.J. 364, 370 (1995).

[36] Peter H. Russell, *Constitutional Odyssey: Can Canadians Become a Sovereign People?* (Toronto: University of Toronto Press, 1992).

A MISSED DEMOCRATIC MOMENT?

The aspiration for the peoples of Canada to consent to a single peoplehood within the crucible of constitutional politics is what urged Bruce Ackerman and Robert Charney to suggest, some thirty years ago, that Canadians should forge a Lockean end to their constitutional odyssey. Observing that Canada has found itself "at the constitutional crossroads for some time,"[37] Ackerman and Charney urged Canadians to embrace their "emerging dualistic foundations"[38] to finally "elaborate the will of We the People through extraparliamentary processes."[39] The US Constitution is the model of a dualistic system of lawmaking: it authorizes two tracks of lawmaking – normal and higher – in which the constituted forms of government speak for the people in the former and the People speak for themselves through the constituted powers in a special lawmaking path in the latter.[40] But rooted as it was in its inherited traditions of British parliamentarism, the Canadian Constitution was a single-track model – until the events surrounding Patriation opened the door to new possibilities for higher lawmaking.[41]

Canada missed its opportunity for a truly democratic moment of popular higher lawmaking when, according to Ackerman and Charney, Pierre Trudeau declined to press ahead on his plan for a national referendum to legitimate the new constitution.[42] A referendum circumventing the convention of substantial provincial consent to any major constitutional change would have defied the Court's *Patriation Reference*,[43] though a successful outcome in the referendum might have ultimately legitimated what would certainly have been a controversial choice to hold a referendum to begin with. There is precedent, however, for this constitutional power-play: the Philadelphia Convention that proposed the US Constitution resorted to a similar strategy, only the drafters of the Constitution required the several states to vote to approve the proposed text in separate state conventions, in the face of the rigid Articles of Confederation that were amendable only with the unanimous agreement of the states.[44] The ratification of the Constitution in these extraordinary assemblies of the people therefore served retrospectively to legitimate what had been an unconstitutional constitution.[45]

---

[37] Bruce A. Ackerman & Robert E. Charney, *Canada at the Constitutional Crossroads*, 34 U. TORONTO L.J. 117, 117 (1984).

[38] *Id.* at 124.   [39] *Id.* at 125.   [40] *Id.* at 118.   [41] *Id.* at 124–30.   [42] *Id.* at 129–30.

[43] *Re: Resolution to amend the Constitution*, [1981] 1 SCR 753.

[44] *See* Gordon S. Wood, THE CREATION OF THE AMERICAN REPUBLIC, 1776–1787 (Chapel Hill: University of North Carolina Press, 2d ed. 1998), 532.

[45] Bruce Ackerman & Neal Katyal, *Our Unconventional Founding*, 62 U. CHI. L. REV. 475, 562–63 (1995).

No such legitimating constitutional referendum appears likely in the near term in Canada. There is simply no political will nor any public appetite at the moment for what observers describe as the risk of "re-opening" the Constitution. Yet rather than lamenting Canada's missed democratic moment, perhaps it is better to reflect on what Canada's democratic settlement might look like if not a large-scale referendum. It may well be that today in the period of normal politics and lower lawmaking, Canadians are living the kinds of moments in which they may, and perhaps should, anchor their perception of the Constitution's democratic legitimacy.

UNITY IN DISSIMILARITY

Some constitutional states manage difference in the construction of cultural homogeneity but this has never been the Canadian way.[46] As Lipset has argued, Canada has chosen instead "to work out agreements among disparate cultures rather than assimilate them into one."[47] Since the founding of the dominion of Canada by British and French settlers, Canada has self-consciously understood and governed itself as a union of different peoples.[48]

The Canadian polity and its peoples constitute a multinational state composed of what Kenneth McRoberts has described as "internal nations."[49] Canada is not a binational state, nor perhaps ever was despite the founding myth of Canada's English and French negotiated beginnings; it is rather an agglomeration of peoples whose shared interests bind them first to themselves, and also, though loosely, to Canada, the result being that we are a nation of nations.

The consequences of Canada's multinationality were evident in the outcome of the Charlottetown Accord in 1992. The package of comprehensive constitutional reforms may have been doomed to failure in light of the varied and competing demands of Canada's diverse peoples. As Michael Behiels explains, "virtually every dimension of the Charlottetown deal had its staunch

---

[46] Eva Mackey, THE HOUSE OF DIFFERENCE: CULTURAL DIFFERENCE AND NATIONAL IDENTITY IN CANADA (Toronto: University of Toronto Press, 2002), 16.

[47] Lipset, *supra* note 8, at 79.

[48] For a discussion of the dimensions of difference in Canada, *see* Daiva Stasiulis & Radha Jhappan, *The Fractious Politics of a Settler Society: Canada, Unsettling Settler Societies: Articulations of Gender, Race, Ethnicity and Class* (DAVIA STASIULIS & NIRA YUVAL-DAVIS eds., 1995), 95–131.

[49] Kenneth McRoberts, *Canada and the Multinational State*, 34 CAN. J. POL. SCI. 683, 688 (2001).

defenders and its vociferous critics,"[50] making the package unlikely ever to be accepted. In addition to the complexity of the package – complexity occasioned by the need to speak to the interests held by many of the peoples of Canada – there was an additional problem, writes Richard Johnston:

> The package Canadians rejected was formidably complex. It became so by a decade's accretion of elements, each calculated to appeal to, or to offset concessions to, groups excluded at an earlier stage – Quebec, the western provinces, and aboriginal peoples. Negotiators hoped that by 1992 they had finally found an equilibrium, a logroll sufficiently inclusive to survive referral to the people. Instead they seem to have gotten the logic of the logroll upside down: they may have overestimated both how much each group wanted what it got and how intensely some groups opposed key concessions to others.[51]

There is another observation worth making. Canada's Constitution has not only recognized a multiplicity of peoples but it has also created the possibility of recognizing new peoples, a group that Behiels identifies as "Charter Canadians" – peoples different from those historically recognized:

> [T]he Charlottetown Acord was so heavily burdened with innately incommensurate, competing interests – provincial and territorial governments, four national Aboriginal organizations, and Charter Canadians – that the odds of its rejection were extremely high.[52]

English and French Canada have always been the dominant actors in constitutional politics, and so too the provinces. But Aboriginal Canadians, territories and the "Charter Canadians" whom Behiels identifies in passing have not traditionally had a seat at the table. That changed in 1982, when the *Charter* constitutionalized their rights, and it changed once again ten years later in 1992 with the demise of the Charlottetown Accord, when these groups gathered alongside traditionally empowered groups to negotiate the future of Canada. The Charlottetown negotiations included the federal government, nine provincial governments, territorial governments and four major national Aboriginal organizations; Quebec joined in late and women's groups were consulted throughout.[53] All told, the Special Joint Committee of the House of

---

[50] Michael D. Behiels, *Charlottetown: The Anatomy of Mega-Constitutional Politics*, POLICY OPTIONS 65, 66 (Dec. 2002–Jan. 2003).

[51] Richard Johnston, *An Inverted Logroll: The Charlottetown Accord and the Referendum*, 26 POL. SCI & POL. 43, 43 (1993).

[52] Behiels, *supra* note 50, at 65.

[53] *See* Kathy L. Brock, *Learning From Failure: Lessons from Charlottetown*, 4 CONST. FORUM 29, 29 (1993); Richard Albert, *The Conventions of Constitutional Amendment in Canada*, 53 OSGOODE HALL L.J. 399, 404–12 (2016).

Commons and the Senate responsible for shepherding the proposals for
reform heard testimony from 700 individuals and received 3,000 submissions.[54] It is hard to imagine such broad consultation without the impetus of
the *Charter*.

The enactment of the *Canadian Charter of Rights and Freedoms* brought
with it recognition and accommodation for many of the peoples of Canada.[55]
In addition to affirming language rights,[56] the *Charter* recognizes Aboriginal
rights and freedoms,[57] as well as gender equality,[58] territorial rights and
privileges,[59] and it insists that the *Charter* "shall be interpreted in a manner
consistent with the preservation and enhancement of the multicultural heritage of Canadians."[60] The Supreme Court's recent recognition of Métis and
non-status Indians is a step in this direction.[61]

The freedoms entrenched in the *Charter* also created new groups of
Canadians bound neither by geography nor language nor culture but rather
by interest and commitment. For example, the fundamental freedoms of
conscience and religion have served as a focal point for the mobilization
of religious groups.[62] The same is true of the entrenchment of the "freedom
of the press and other media of communication," which has given the Fifth
Estate a textual referent in which to ground its claims.[63] These are some of the
"Charter Canadians" to which Behiels referred as groups that now have
constitutional rights to protect and indeed to seek to expand. The same may
be said of the interests of criminal defendants, now entrenched in the *Charter*.[64] Just as important is the recognition of rights and freedoms that are not
currently entrenched in the *Charter* but that may in the future be enforced.[65]
The most generative source of new protected classes of Canadians, however,
each of whom now has interests to defend in the context of any effort
to comprehensively reform the Constitution, is section 15, the locus of equality
rights.[66]

The *Charter* has therefore entrenched, expanded and revolutionized the
meaning of citizenship in Canada, giving rights and recognition to classes
of Canadians, old and new. As Alain Cairns has observed, the Canadian

---

[54] *Consensus Report on the Constitution*, 28 August 1992, at Preface.
[55] *Canadian Charter of Rights and Freedoms*, Part I of the *Constitution Act, 1982*, being
Schedule B to the Canada Act 1982 (UK), 1982, c 11 (the "Charter").
[56] *See id.* at ss. 16–23.   [57] *See id.* at s. 25.   [58] *See id.* at s. 28.   [59] *See id.* at s. 30.
[60] *See id.* at s. 27.
[61] *See Daniels v. Canada (Indian Affairs and Northern Development)*, 2016 SCC 12.
[62] *See Charter*, s. 2(a).   [63] *See id.* at s. 2(b).   [64] *See id.* at ss. 7–14.   [65] *See id.* at s. 26.
[66] *See id.* at s. 15.

Constitution is a "citizens' constitution" that identifies and empowers the peoples of Canada:

> The Charter brought new groups into the constitutional order or, as in the case of aboriginals, enhanced a pre-existing constitutional status. It bypassed governments and spoke directly to Canadians by defining them as bearers of rights, as well as by according specific constitutional recognition to women, aboriginals, official language minority populations, ethnic groups through the vehicle of multiculturalism, and to those social categories explicitly listed in the equality rights section of the Charter. The Charter thus reduced the relative status of governments and strengthened that of the citizens who received constitutional encouragement to think of themselves as constitutional actors.[67]

All of these peoples, established and nascent both, makes it is no surprise that the grand political settlement that drives the march to constitutionalism has continued to elude Canada. And yet it is in this very unsettled state that we may find the core of the legitimacy that sustains the Constitution.

CONSTITUTION AS NOUN AND ACTION

In Canada, "constitution" is a verbal noun that reflects "the action or activity of constituting."[68] Constitution, in this sense, never ends, is never complete, and no final settlement is attainable, nor perhaps even desirable since it could entail the extinguishment of the equally valid claims of others. The peoples of Canada constitute and reconstitute themselves in their daily interactions and in the intermediated politics of normal lawmaking. Though Canada may one day return to mega constitutional politics, today Canada remains in the necessary yet unsettled state of recognized and unrecognized difference, sometimes celebrated sometimes not, but always at the foreground of the peoples' conscious self-understanding as a polity.

Canadian constitutional politics are therefore open to possibilities that are not always available in states bound by a final settlement. The Constitution of Canada is a constitution ever in constitution, in which the people remain in conversation, contested to be sure, with each other, looking ahead to what shape an eventual political settlement might take but feeling that it

---

[67] Alan C. Cairns, *Citizens (Outsiders) and Governments (Insiders) in Constitution-Making: The Case of Meech Lake*, 14 CAN. PUB. POL. SUPP: MEECH LAKE ACCORD S121, S122 (1988).

[68] Hanna Fenichel Pitkin, *"The Idea of a Constitution,"* 37 J. LEG. ED. 167, 168 (1987); *see also* Richard Albert, *Counterconstitutionalism*, 31 DALHOUSIE L.J. 1, 3 (2008) (comparing constitution as both "noun" and "verb").

may perhaps remain as elusive as ever before. This conversation and the contestability of the Constitution is what gives its peoples validation as participants in the project of constitution and reconstitution, and also what breathes legitimacy into the constitutionalized agreements that to this day remain unfinished. Perhaps the future will bring some resolution or some settlement, however difficult this may be to envision in the present day.

Of course no constitution is ever finished, not even the paradigmatic Lockean constitution that was made unalterable. Even where its text does not change, the meaning of a constitution evolves over time through judicial interpretation, the enactment of statutes, the accretion of political practices, and the evolution of societal norms. All of these change constitutions in ways that may be stronger than a formal amendment. In Canada, judicial interpretation has been the most common way – and by comparison to the stringency of the amending formula, the easiest as way as well – to update the meaning of the Constitution.[69] The Supreme Court of Canada has been the subject of criticism for what is labelled its judicial activism,[70] yet it is important to remember that it is through its politically deft if sometimes purposefully ambiguous judgments that Canada has most clearly advanced its ethic of accommodation, and with it, the country's reputation as a constitutional model for the world.

THREE THEMES

Three major themes strike us as important in this volume to evaluate the Constitution of Canada in comparative perspective. In the chapters that constitute each Section of this volume, we often see recurrence of the Canadian constitutional values identified by the Chief Justice: democracy, federalism and respect for diversity and difference. The role of Court – an institution respected the world over for its elaboration of the Constitution – features prominently in our volume with a Section devoted all to itself.

---

[69] Allan C. Hutchinson, *Constitutional Change and Constitutional Amendment: A Canadian Conundrum*, ENGINEERING CONSTITUTIONAL CHANGE: A COMPARATIVE PERSPECTIVE ON EUROPE, CANADA AND THE USA 51 at 57 (Xenophon Contiades ed., 2013); Richard Albert, *The Theory and Doctrine of Unconstitutional Constitutional Amendment in Canada*, 41 QUEEN'S L.J. 143, 167–76 (2015).

[70] *See, e.g.*, Rory Leishman, AGAINST JUDICIAL ACTIVISM: THE DECLINE OF FREEDOMS AND DEMOCRACY IN CANADA (Montreal: McGill-Queen's Press, 2006); Robert Ivan Martin, THE MOST DANGEROUS BRANCH (Montreal: McGill-Queen's University Press, 2003); F.L. Morton & Rainer Knopff, THE CHARTER REVOLUTION AND THE COURT PARTY (Toronto: University of Toronto Press, 2000).

Another Section focuses on federalism and pluralism, both ideas joined together to appraise how Canada has managed the richness of its diversity. The third Section on the global impact of the Constitution examines how the laws, doctrines and theories of the Constitution have travelled elsewhere in the world and have sometimes been adopted in whole cloth by foreign legal systems and at other times been adapted to local needs and specificities. Each of these three themes forms a self-standing Section in this collection.

We begin first with *Federalism and Pluralism in Canadian Constitutionalism*. This Section opens with the remarks-as-delivered of Chief Justice McLachlin, who gave the keynote address at the conference we convened at the Yale Law School to mark the Sesquicentennial of Confederation. In her remarks entitled *Diversity and the Rule of Law: A Canadian Perspective*, the Chief Justice reminds us that Canada is built on a diversity that sustains and strengthens it. It is in the way that Canada manages its diversity that there is something to learn about the country and its foundational constitutional principles. The Canadian approach to managing its diversity, explains the Chief Justice, is rooted in three tenets: a commitment to accommodating difference, an embrace of living constitutionalism as reflected in the living tree doctrine, and a deep respect for and resort to foreign legal materials to better understand Canada's own values. It is useful to begin the volume with the Chief Justice's remarks as her reflections offer insights that inform our understanding of each of the three themes in this book: the role of the Court in Canadian constitutionalism, how the Constitution manages difference, and how the ideas and jurisprudence of the Constitution have migrated outside Canada.

Stephen Tierney then delves into the theory of federalism in his chapter on *Misconceiving Federalism: Canada and the Federal Idea*. He draws from the Canadian example to explore what federalism is and also more specifically what it is in its Canadian variation. He shows how Canadian federalism represents a specific model of government that has influenced other multilevel systems of government and that continues to serve as a working template for how a state can manage a multiplicity of cultural, linguistic and national identities. The plurinational political and constitutional character of Canada, Tierney shows, has implications for how Canadian federalism is understood and how it should operate. In the end, Tierney explains what makes the Canadian model of federalism unique and also how it fits into the larger canvass of federal design around the world today.

It is against this theoretical backdrop that we then move to four subjects of controversy and contestation in Canada, some older than others but all central to the success or failure of the Constitution in matters of federalism and pluralism. Alain-G. Gagnon's chapter on *Political Dynamics in Quebec: Charting Concepts and Imagining Political Avenues* takes on a question older than Confederation and answers it with a comparative twist: how should we understand Quebec's relationship with Canada? Gagnon suggests five competing models, each of which entails different implications for power-relations between Quebec and Canada, for Quebec within Canada and for the communities that constitute Quebec itself. Gagnon also looks to the world for comparisons and contrasts for the Quebec-Canada relationship.

In *Indigenous Peoples and the Canadian State: The Prospects of Constitutionalism Pluralism*, Patrick Macklem asks "how receptive is the Canadian constitutional order to conceiving of Indigenous-Canadian relations in accordance with an ethos of constitutional pluralism?" Macklem begins by inquiring why constitutional pluralism did not take root between Indigenous nations and colonial legal orders at the point of contact or thereafter, and why relations between Indigenous peoples and the Canadian state have continued all of these years without a "common normative language." He brings us with him on a search for possible openings to constitutional pluralism today in Canada's constitutional landscape, along the way evaluating the potential barriers to it. He concludes with thoughts on what might follow from constitutionalism pluralism, the principal consequence being that Canada would become a tri-federal state with powers divided among federal, provincial and Indigenous institutions of governance.

We close this first Section with a third subject of controversy in connection with federalism and pluralism: constitutional amendment. Patriation did not fix the problems created by Canada's lack of a domestic amending formula – amendment remains a point of contention in Canada, as evidenced by the failures of the Meech Lake and Charlottetown accords, and recent Supreme Court references on the amendment rules themselves. In her chapter on *Legality, Legitimacy and Constitutional Amendment in Canada*, Jamie Cameron offers an explanation for Canada's difficulties with constitutional amendment. Unlike other works that focus separately on the path to Patriation and the struggles since then, Cameron draws from theories of constitutional change to explain how both periods are connected: the Constitution's original design flaw created a legitimacy deficit that Patriation could not cure; on the contrary, she writes, the Constitution's new amending formula may have exacerbated that deficit.

The second Section of this volume focuses on *The Court in Canadian Constitutionalism*. We begin with an inquiry into the role of Supreme Court of Canada in questions of high political salience. In his chapter on *The Judicial Constitutionalization of Politics in Canada and Other Contemporary*

Democracies, Michel Rosenfeld explores the constitutionalization of politics in Canada, Israel, South Africa and the United States. Drawing from the *Secession Reference* in Canada, the creation of Basic Laws in Israel, the *Makwanyane* death penalty case in South Africa and the *Bush v. Gore* decision in the United States, Rosenfeld cautions us to pause "before issuing any wholesale condemnation of constitutional review by unelected judges." Rosenfeld takes the view that the constitutionalization of politics "is certainly worrisome" but he distinguishes two kinds of politics – judicial politics and ordinary politics – that invites a reconsideration of the proper judicial function.

Jeffrey Goldsworthy and Grant Huscroft also invite an important reconsideration in their chapter on *Originalism in Australia and Canada: Why the Divergence?* What they suggest requires our reconsideration is the commonly held view that Canada has rejected originalist constitutional interpretation, a method of interpretation that has become associated with conservative constitutionalism in the United States. They show that the living tree interpretation popularized by judicial constitutional interpretation in Canada has fewer differences from public meaning originalism than is usually thought. This will no doubt come as a surprise to many, perhaps even as a shock. Goldsworthy and Huscroft contrast the Canadian approach with the Australian one, and explain why the judicial interpretative methods of the latter appear to show more of an interest in the original meanings of constitutional rules than the former.

In his chapter on *Rights Inflation in Canada and the United States*, Mark Tushnet seeks to identify and subsequently evaluate in comparative perspective the doctrinal and jurisprudential sources of rights inflation in Canada and the United States. Tushnet contrasts proportionality review in Canada with the US approach under the Due Process Clause to identifying constitutional limits on the regulation of relatively minor interests, or of relatively minor adverse effects on important interests. The upshot of his chapter is that we have seen rights inflation in both Canada and the United States but within different frameworks of constitutional doctrine – and that concerns about rights inflation are less about doctrine or results than about constitutional, legal and political cultures.

Our Section on *The Court in Canadian Constitutionalism* turns next to specific rights. In *Substantive Equality Past and Future: The Charter Experience*, Catharine MacKinnon reminds us that the Sesquicentennial of Confederation coincides with the 35th anniversary of the *Charter*. MacKinnon observes that Canada's pioneering jurisprudential theory of substantive equality has yet to reach its full potential. Rooted in the idea of dignity, substantive equality would be more profitably anchored in the rejection of hierarchy, argues MacKinnon, whose chapter draws upon law and doctrine in Europe, South Africa and the United States.

Adrienne Stone focuses on free speech law in her chapter on *Canadian Constitutional Law of Freedom of Expression*. Stone identifies the three fundamental commitments she sees as having shaped freedom of expression in Canada – equality, multiculturalism and the state as a positive agent in rights protection – and shows how they have generated a distinctively Canadian freedom of expression. Comparing Canada and the United States, Stone explains her choice of this comparator: "[t]he Supreme Court of Canada deliberately sought a distinctive Canadian approach and in doing so rejected core elements of First Amendment law." By examining those elements of US free speech law rejected by the Supreme Court, we can more fully understand the Canadian approach to freedom of expression, suggests Stone, who also draws from Australia, Germany and Europe.

We then feature a chapter by Ayelet Shachar entitled *Constituting Citizens: Oaths, Gender, Religious Attire*. Shachar's inquiry is about diversity and equality: what does and should the *Charter* say about the face-covering ban during the swearing-in ceremony for citizenship – a ban that became the focus of heated political disagreement during the 2015 Canadian general federal elections? Neither of the legal challenges to the ban were resolved as a constitutional matter, whether as to claims of breach of religious freedom or violations of gender equality. Shachar situates the Canadian case in comparative perspective and explores how Canada's twin commitments to diversity and equality would have driven the outcome of this case on constitutional grounds had the Court addressed the question.

We close this Section with Kent Roach's chapter on *The Judicial, Legislative and Executive Roles in Enforcing the Constitution: Three Manitoba Stories*. Roach examines the comparative strengths and weaknesses of executive, judicial and legislative enforcement of the Constitution using a case study of efforts to enforce the rights of Francophones, Roman Catholics and the Métis in Manitoba. In his chapter, which explores principally the variable success of enforcement strategies in Canada, Roach makes comparative reference to the congressional enforcement power in the Civil War Amendments of the US Constitution and the suspended declaration of invalidity in the South African Constitution – a Canadian innovation.

The third and final Section of this volume contains five chapters on the theme of *The Global Impact of Canadian Constitutionalism*. The Section begins with Ran Hirschl's chapter entitled *Going Global? Canada as Importer and Exporter of Constitutional Thought*. Hirsch identifies not only what has been imported and exported but he explores also why: which of Canada's constitutional innovations have been adopted in other constitutions, and why did countries look to Canada when they did; what has Canada imported from other constitutional states, and what does this tell us about the stability of Canada's internal constitutional arrangements; and what can Canada learn from the world beyond its borders to brainstorm and ultimately implement solutions for the enduring constitutional and political challenges facing the country? Hirschl sets the stage in his chapter for the chapters to follow on how, when, where and why Canadian constitutional law, doctrine and theory have migrated abroad.

Alison Young continues our analysis of Canada's constitutional exports in her chapter on *Exporting Dialogue: Critical Reflections on Canada's "Commonwealth" Model of Human Rights Protections*. Young evaluates how the Canadian variation on the "Commonwealth" model of rights protection has been adopted in the United Kingdom, though without the impact that may have been hoped. But rather than ascribing failure to the exportation or the model itself, Young suggests that at least some of the weaknesses of the model are attributable both to misunderstanding how the model can and actually does facilitate institutional dialogue and also to underappreciating that inter-institutional interactions may in fact serve two purposes: constitutional collaboration and constitutional counter-balancing. Young compares the Canadian *Charter* and *Bill of Rights 1960* experiences with the United Kingdom's own experiment with the *UK Human Rights Act 1998*.

Moving from comparative political practice to comparative judicial reasoning, we arrive at Lech Garlicki's chapter on *The European Court of Human Rights and Canadian Case-Law*. Garlicki sets out to examine whether and how often the European Court of Human Rights has cited Supreme Court of Canada cases. Highlighting several examples, Garlicki concludes that the Canadian Supreme Court is cited more frequently than any other foreign jurisdiction, including the US Supreme Court, though references to Canada occur mostly in connection with cases arriving at the European Court of Human Rights from the United Kingdom. Garlicki closes with thoughts on whether and why citation might also go in the opposite direction: the Canadian Supreme Court citing the European Court of Human Rights.

Switching our focus from Europe to Asia, Wen-Chen Chang's chapter on *Canadian Rights Discourse Travels to the East* is a systematic analysis of instances when the Hong Kong Court of Final Appeal and Taiwan's Constitutional Court have referenced Canadian *Charter* cases. Chang looks at references by both judges and litigants in each court, and also the reasons why the references were made, for instance whether to support the protection or restriction of rights. Concluding that the *Charter*'s influence has not been substantial in either case, Chang nonetheless uncovers important findings to better understand the influence of the Canadian Constitution abroad.

Heinz Klug takes us finally to South Africa in his chapter on *The Canadian Charter, South Africa and the Paths of Constitutional Influence*. Klug's chapter investigates the influence not only of the Canadian Constitution but also of the US Constitution on South Africa's democratic transition and its jurisprudence under its post-apartheid Constitution. Klug shows that Canada's influence on South Africa was much broader than a few individual influences that resulted in the adoption of certain constitutional provisions. Canada's influence on the South African Constitution and on its transition from apartheid to democracy was driven by Canada's Constitution and also by Canadian professors, politicians and civil society more generally. Klug's analysis is therefore contextual, not strictly legal. Klug goes on to show that Canada remained influential after the drafting of the Constitution and into the new Constitutional Court's jurisprudential infancy and growth. The Court, Klug notes, referenced and discussed foreign law in roughly half of its judgments over the course of its first twenty years, with the United States and Canada being referenced 182 and 173 times, respectively. Klug thereafter explores the why question: why did South Africa seek to learn and borrow from Canada?

In his concluding chapter, David Cameron discusses the role of the Canadian Constitution, with its entrenched *Charter of Rights and Freedoms*, and the Court, with its view of the Constitution as a "living tree" – a Constitution that, as Chief Justice McLachlin explained, "lives and adapts through its application to new situations" – in the transnational dialogue that occurs today among constitutional courts throughout the world. He concludes with thoughts on Canada's path to the present over the past 150 years, and about what the country can rightly celebrate about its Court and Constitution in this Sesquicentennial moment of reflection. Cameron also highlights the constitutional challenges – some of them long-standing, others more recent in origin – that remain today.

THE RISK AND REWARD OF ANNIVERSARY SPECIALS

There is risk in a project like ours to mark the anniversary of Confederation in Canada. We risk being seen as insensitive to the reality that the union of peoples and places that we know today as Canada did not begin in 1867, or worst still complicit in what many see as an occupation of territory that was illegitimately taken from others. The stakes are high in this anniversary project just as they are in many anniversary specials. In the Bicentennial year of the US Constitution, Supreme Court Justice Thurgood Marshall observed that the object of their celebration had grown "vastly different from what the framers barely began to construct two centuries ago."[71] Justice Marshall declined the invitation to join the chorus of good cheer for a document that had been enacted to exclude many persons from the rights and privileges of citizenship:

> The focus of this celebration invites a complacent belief that the vision of those who debated and compromised in Philadelphia yielded the "more perfect Union" it is said we now enjoy. I cannot accept this invitation, for I do not believe that the meaning of the Constitution was forever "fixed" at the Philadelphia Convention. Nor do I find the wisdom, foresight, and sense of justice exhibited by the framers particularly profound. To the contrary, the government they devised was defective from the start, requiring several amendments, a civil war, and momentous social transformation to attain the system of constitutional government, and its respect for the individual freedoms and human rights, that we hold as fundamental today.[72]

There is nuance in Justice Marshall's words. His message was not that the Constitution is not worth celebrating. It was that the Constitution as designed in 1787 was intrinsically unjust, but through war and sacrifice it had earned its status as a national symbol worthy of pride. The true miracle, he stressed, "was not the birth of the Constitution, but its life, a life nurtured through two turbulent centuries of our own making, and a life embodying much good fortune that was not."[73] For Justice Marshall, it was the transformation of the Constitution, not its founding text, that the Bicentennial anniversary ought to celebrate. Rather its adaptative capacity to accommodate profound social change than its inegalitarian foundations. Justice Marshall saw something to celebrate in the redemptive possibilities of a constitution that would have been unrecognizable to those who had written it two hundred years prior. I take another message from Justice Marshall's reflections: that we must understand what it is we are doing when we mark an anniversary and also how our marking of it will be perceived. For us, as we mark the Sesquicentennial of Confederation in Canada, the task is no different.

I am reminded of a powerful exchange between Mary Ellen Turpel-Lafond and Patricia Monture in the aftermath of the failure of the Meech Lake

---

[71] Thurgood Marshall, *Reflections on the Bicentennial of the United States Constitution*, 101 HARV. L. REV. 1, 1 (1987).
[72] *Id.* at 1–2.   [73] *Id.* at 5.

Accord in 1990.[74] Turpel-Lafond (then Turpel) suggested as they opened their public conversation that they start by identifying a period of time or a year to trace aboriginal history in the land now identified as Canada. One option was "first contact 500 years ago," suggested Turpel-Lafond, or "if not there, at least we have to mention 1867, a date which I hate to use."[75] Monture responded in no uncertain terms that the year 1867 was not one she believed was worth celebrating:

> I do *not* want to start with 1867. Canada's birth is not something I celebrate; anymore than I believe the history of the country dates back to 1763 and the *Royal Proclamation*, or when the first European stepped onto the shores of what First Nations know to be Turtle Island.[76]

And yet here we are in this volume starting with the year 1867. We have chosen this date for a reason we hope will bear fruit for scholars of public law: to examine in detail and in broad strokes the evolution of the Constitution from a distinctly comparative perspective, beginning from the point of its creation by an imperial statute at Confederation to the present day. In the intervening decades, Canada has grown from a colony to a dominion and now to a sovereign state whose constitutional law has influenced and been influenced by the world around it. It is on these terms that we begin at 1867 – to study the Constitution of a country that has become a constitutional superpower. Yet despite the accolades Canada has earned abroad for the theory and doctrine of its constitutional law, the lived experience of many of the peoples of Canada remains one of misgiving, disenchantment and also of anger for a past that remains unreconciled with the present. This anniversary presents an opportunity for the stewards of Canada's Constitution to reach righteous and just resolutions to long-standing internal challenges – both because the time is long past and because the world is now watching. How and whether public law succeeds in repairing what remains broken in Canada may well determine whether the Constitution of Canada will continue to be as influential in the world when we gather again to mark its Bicentennial.

---

[74] *See* M.E. Turpel and P.A. (Trisha) Monture, *Ode to Elijah: Reflections of Two First Nations Women on the Rekindling of Spirit at the Wake for the Meech Lake Accord*, 15 QUEEN'S L.J. 345 (1990).
[75] *Id.* at 346.   [76] *Id.*

Federalism and Pluralism in Canadian Constitutionalism

PART I

Federalism and Pluralism in
Canadian Constitutional...

1

Diversity and the Rule of Law

A Canadian Perspective

THE RIGHT HONOURABLE BEVERLEY MCLACHLIN, P.C.

As delivered at Yale Law School on 12 April 2016.

INTRODUCTION

I am delighted to be at this prestigious law school, and to have the opportunity to address students and faculty on a subject dear to my heart: the relationship between Canada and the United States. My thanks to Richard Albert for arranging this conference and inviting me here. My special thanks to Justice Calabresi for his kind introduction. Ever since I listened to his brilliant lecture on torts at the Cambridge Lectures, I have stood in awe of Justice Calabresi. His presence here today is an honour that leaves me feeling both humbled and privileged.

Canada and the United States share many things. Both countries are mature democracies. Both countries are committed to the rule of law. And both countries are built on a diverse amalgam of people of different races, religions and historic backgrounds. Each country has found its own way to deal with that diversity. Today, I would like to talk about Canada's way.

Hence my topic – the nexus between diversity and the rule of law in my country, Canada.

I begin with a story. Many years ago, my husband and I found ourselves at a conference of the Vail Institute, in Vail, Colorado. Diversity was on the academic menu. The distinguished American historian, Arthur Schlesinger Jr., was there. Dr. Schlesinger had just published a book, entitled *The Disuniting of America*. The topic of the book was the growing Hispanic population in America, and the consequences this was having and would have on the fabric of American life. Dr. Schlesinger spoke of growing enclaves where the dominant language was Spanish. Left unchecked, he argued, this could lead to the "disuniting of America."

In support of his argument, Dr. Schlesinger pointed north, to Canada. Canada had just come off a Québec referendum, in which the option of sovereignty-association had been narrowly rejected. Beware, he argued – the same could happen in the United States if Spanish was accepted. Separatism. In a phrase, the disuniting of America.

Dr. Schlesinger referred *en passant* to a quip of a former Canadian Prime Minister that "Canada has too much geography and too little history." In fact, Canada has quite a lot of history – a history that has produced its own unique take on diversity and such things as language rights. To suggest that Canada made the wrong political choice in allowing French to be spoken in Québec is to forget Canada's history and the simple truth that no nation can escape its history.

In fact, as I (humbly I hope) explained after the lecture, when England took over the former French colony of New France after the Battle of the Plains of Abraham in 1763, it was faced with a settled population, who spoke French, attended the Catholic Church and regulated their affairs by the French Civil Code. The French vastly outnumbered the few Anglo colonials and the trickle of United Empire Loyalists that was starting to come from the south. England had little appetite for yet another American Revolution, this one to the north. So in the end the 1774 Québec Act was passed, giving the colony the right to retain its language, religion and civil code.

In 1867 these arrangements were constitutionalized in Canada's first constitution, the *British North America Act, 1867*, and confirmed and strengthened in the *Constitution Act, 1982*, which repatriated Canada's constitution and introduced a constitutional bill of rights, the *Canadian Charter of Rights and Freedoms*.

My point is simple: Canada, like the United States, is built on diversity. But our two countries have, by dint of history, managed their diversity in different ways. In both countries, diversity is accepted, indeed prized. But differences remain.

The metaphor of the melting pot is associated with the United States. Many different ingredients go into the pot. They are stirred around and left to simmer until the individual ingredients lose their original savour. The product is a rich broth with a new flavour all of its own.

Canada, by contrast, is often described by the metaphor of the mosaic. Different pieces, each with their own character, are laid onto a single landscape. The overall picture is very different from any of the pieces. But if you look closely, you see that each piece retains its unique identity.

In both Canada and the United States, the courts have played an important role in managing diversity. In both countries, constitutional interpretation has been at the centre of the exercise. In the United States, the Supreme Court over the centuries has worked to define relations with diverse groups – the Indians; the descendants of slaves; the plethora of cultures and religions that have come to the country over the past century and a half. In discharging this task, the Court has enunciated new precepts of liberty, equality and freedom of religion. The same has happened in Canada.

But once again, for all the commonalities, each country has developed its own approach. The Canadian approach to managing diversity under the Constitution is marked by three central tenets: (1) the ethic of accommodation of difference; (2) the value of comparative law; and (3) the view of the constitution as a living tree, capable of growth and expansion. In the time that remains, let me say a few words on each of these tenets.

RESPECTFUL ACCOMMODATION

First, the ethic of accommodation of difference. Canada's history has fostered an attitude of respectful accommodation of different races, religions and creeds. Of course, one can find notable examples that show the opposite. But by and large, we are viewed by others and we view ourselves as not only tolerant of difference, but capable of embracing it. This is what the Aga Khan, speaking about Canada, calls a culture of cosmopolitanism.[1]

John Ralston Saul, in his book, *A Fair Country*, traces the early origins of this attitude of respectful accommodation. The early explorers who came to Canada's shores found a vast land of forests, lakes, rivers and interminable winters. To survive, they were forced to learn from the indigenous population. This need of the other bred respect of the other and set the dominant tone for the country. Sadly, in more modern times, discrimination against indigenous people may have been more dominant than respectful accommodation. But still it was there, in our roots.

Respectful accommodation was again the order of day in the late eighteenth century, when the English conquerors passed the *Québec Act* and granted the French of what is now Quebec, French linguistic rights, Catholic religious rights and the right to use the Civil Code. Again, subsequent centuries have witnessed difficult times – times of tension and dissent – but so far we have overcome the difficulties. Differences have been resolved peacefully. Violence has been rare. Even at the height of separatist sentiment, the need to respect minorities was conceded by all. And the Supreme Court of Canada's

[1] *Address of His Highness the Aga Khan to Both Houses of the Parliament of Canada in the House of Commons Chamber, Ottawa*, February 27, 2014, available at: www.akdn.org.

decision on the *Secession Reference*,[2] which set forward the fundamental constitutional norms of the democratic principle, the federal principle, the principle of protection of minorities and the rule of law, was praised on all sides.

The ethos of respectful accommodation continues to mark the Court's jurisprudence. Time and time again, the Court has confirmed the duty to accommodate difference to the point of undue hardship. It has issued rulings that protect minority religious practices, like the right of a student to wear an encased kirpan in a school with a no-weapons policy,[3] the right of a Jewish person to erect a sukka on his condo balcony,[4] and the right of a Muslim woman to wear a niqab when testifying in Court, provided it is not shown to interfere with the right of effective cross-examination and a fair trial.[5] This reasonable accommodation of difference has become a fundamental plank of Canadian jurisprudence. It does not seek to erase difference, nor to impose conformity. Like the pieces of a mosaic, each group is allowed to maintain its distinctions, provided it does not impinge on other important interests or threaten the greater public good.

The same ethic holds for the rights of indigenous people. In defining rights to lands and resource use, the Supreme Court of Canada has stressed the importance of recognizing aboriginal rights in a fulsome and generous way. But it has also said that those rights can be limited if the state can justify this in the broader public interest.[6] Not all or nothing solutions, but reconciliation. As former Chief Justice Antonio Lamer stated at the end of his landmark judgement on land rights in *Delgamuukw*, "Let's face it, we are all here to stay."[7]

THE VALUE OF COMPARATIVE LAW

Canadian lawyers are comparative lawyers; Canadian judges are comparative judges. It's not a matter of debate; it's simply the way we are, the way our history has made us.

It is sometimes said that while the United States was born of revolution, Canada was born of evolution. The United States fought a bitter war that resulted in throwing out England and beginning anew. English common law was retained as the basis of the new country's legal system – there was no other

2   *Reference Re Secession of Quebec*, [1998] 2 SCR 217.
3   *Multani v. Commission scolaire Marguerite-Bourgeoys*, [2006] 1 SCR 256.
4   *Syndicat Northcrest v. Amselem*, [2004] 2 SCR 551.   5   *R. v. NS*, [2012] 3 SCR 726.
6   *R. v. Sparrow*, [1990] 1 SCR 1075.
7   *Delgamuukw v. British Columbia*, [1997] 3 SCR 1010, at para. 186.

option – but henceforth it would be American law. The idea grew up that to look at the law of other courts in other countries might sully the unique and pristine nature of American law.

Canada, on the other hand, kept the law of England as its basic law (apart from the Civil Code in Quebec governing private law) until the second half of the twentieth century. Until 1949, the Judicial Committee of the Privy Council, sitting in London, was Canada's final court of appeal. Think of it – our law was not our own law; it was another country's law. The thought gives comparative law a whole new twist.

Things have changed. Canada now has its own unique jurisprudence, and the decisions of its courts are often cited abroad in countries like Israel,[8] South Africa,[9] by the European Court of Human Rights[10] – and yes, by the Supreme Court of the United Kingdom.[11] But Canada remains committed to the idea that we can gain insights and ideas from jurists in countries that possess similar values to our own.

To be sure, we do not simply slap foreign law on a Canadian problem. We approach the rulings of other courts on problems we face with respectful caution, and with attention to the different history and social context that shaped those decisions. Each nation's law must be true to its own history, context and jurisprudential traditions. Using comparative law involves sophisticated, high-level judging. But used appropriately it produces richer, better decisions. That, in any event, is our belief.

THE CONSTITUTION AND CHANGING REALITIES

The third central tenet of Canadian constitutional interpretation – a tenet that has been of great assistance in coming to grips with the tensions and disputes inevitable in a diverse society – is the principle of constitutional interpretation that recognizes the ability of constitutional jurisprudence to be applied to changing social realities of Canadian society. In Canada, this is referred to as the "living tree" principle.

In the late 1920s, a group of determined Canadian women challenged a law in force throughout the British Commonwealth that denied women the right to hold public office. Under accepted constitutional interpretation, only "persons"

---

[8]   H.C. 721/94, *El-Al Israel Airlines Ltd. v. Danielowitz*, [1992–94] IsrLR 478 (Israel High Court of Justice).

[9]   *S. v. Williams*, [1995] (3) S.A. 632 (S. Afr. Const. Ct.).

[10] *O'Halloran and Francis v. The United Kingdom* [GC], No. 15809/02 and No. 25624/02, ECHR 2007-III, [2007] ECHR 545.

[11] *Various Claimants v. Catholic Child Welfare Society*, [2012] UKSC 56, [2013] 2 A.C. 1.

could hold public offices, like judging, or serving on the Senate. Women were deemed not to be "persons" and therefore could not hold public office.

The women in question, now referred to as "The Famous Five," refused to accept this restriction. They demanded redress in what is referred to as the *"Persons Case."* They lost at the Supreme Court of Canada, but took their case to London. Against all odds, they succeeded before the Judicial Committee of the Privy Council, which was then, as I have mentioned, Canada's final Court of Appeal.[12] Writing for the Court, Viscount Sankey noted the evolving position of women in society and held that despite prior precedent, the time had come to change the law and recognize that women were indeed "persons" and hence capable of holding public office. The fundamental question was this: Was constitutional interpretation cast in stone, or could it be modified to reflect changing social conditions? In holding that constitutional interpretation should be capable of adapting to changing social realities, Viscount Sankey likened the constitution to "a living tree capable of growth and expansion within its natural limits."[13]

The metaphor of the living tree continues to guide Canadian constitutional interpretation to this day. The tree of the constitution stands firm and fixed, rooted in the national soil of the country. But it is capable, from time to time, of sprouting a new leaf or even growing a new branch. The constitution lives and adapts through its application to new situations.

I have spoken of three tenets of Canadian constitutional jurisprudence – respectful accommodation of difference; acceptance of the value of comparative law; and the view of the Constitution as a living tree, capable of growth and expansion. These tenets have guided Canadian courts as they grapple with the tensions inherent in a diverse society. Together, they have provided a mechanism for balancing conflicting interests and goals in Canadian society in a way that comports with the rule of law. I, for one, would argue that the result has been to improve Canadians' lives, and bring Canadian society closer to the ideal of the "just society" that Prime Minister Pierre Elliott Trudeau, the present Canadian Prime Minister's father, articulated more than thirty-five years ago.

CONCLUSION

I have described the Canadian Constitution as a "living tree." Let me leave you with a second metaphor for the Canadian Constitution, this one proposed by contemporary Canadian philosopher James Tully. Tully likens the Canadian Constitution to "The Spirit of Haida Gwaii," the masterpiece of Haida

---

[12] *Edwards v. Canada (Attorney General)*, [1930] A.C. 124.   [13] *Id.* at 136.

artist Bill Reid. You have perhaps seen it in the Vancouver airport terminal or outside the Canadian embassy in Washington, DC – a large, dark bronze, traditional Haida canoe, carrying a motley crew: the Raven, the Grizzly bear, his wife and their cubs, the Eagle and the Frog. In the middle sits a quiet figure, the Human Shaman. Tully explains his constitutional metaphor as follows:

> The passengers are squabbling and vying for recognition and position each in their culturally distinct way. They are exchanging their diverse stories and claims as the chief appears to listen attentively to each, hoping to guide them to reach an agreement.[14]

Throughout my life as a judge, I have witnessed many diverse passengers in the Canadian ship of state vie and squabble for position. And I have seen the passengers listen in return, and accept the judgments of the courts, sometimes grudgingly, but always with the understanding that a commitment to fair treatment and fair process through the courts is necessary to maintain the values that bind the people together as a society.

The result is an overarching story that is quintessentially Canadian – a story of the rights and limits enshrined in our Constitution and preserved by our legislatures and our courts. The constitutional boat moves forward, often by fits and starts, sometimes unsure of its ultimate goal, but thus far, always forward. Sometimes the process is difficult; often, it is imperfect. One person wants this; the other wants that. They key is to listen – to each other directly and to each other through our modern shaman, the rule of law. There is no other way forward for, as Tully reminds us, diverse as we are, we are all in the same boat.

Let me end this chapter with the words of a great Canadian artist: Bill Reid himself, the indigenous artist behind "The Spirit of Haida Gwaii" and a man who understood profoundly the value of inclusion and diversity:

> Here we are at last, a long way from Haida Gwaii, not too sure where we are or where we're going, still squabbling and vying for position in the boat, but somehow managing to appear to be heading in some direction. At least the paddles are together, and the man in the middle seems to have some vision of what's to come.[15]

Thank you very much for your attention.

---

[14] James Tully, Strange Multiplicity: Constitutionalism in an Age of Diversity (Cambridge: Cambridge University Press, 1995), 24.

[15] Bill Reid, Gallant Beasts and Monsters (Vancouver: Buschlen Mowatt, 1992), 15.

2

Misconceiving Federalism
Canada and the Federal Idea

STEPHEN TIERNEY

INTRODUCTION: CANADA AND THE FEDERAL IDEA

The Canadian model of federalism is unique. When we consider it in comparative perspective, and appreciate the widely different polities across the globe that are each supported by the idea of federalism, inevitably we come back to questions about the federal model itself: what is it – if anything - that unites so many disparate systems of government, including Canada, within one common genus? In this chapter, I address this question by taking federalism to be at root an idea, or more precisely, a constitutional idea, rather than a detailed institutional paradigm. The history of federalism in Canada is an ideal case study with which to consider this question. Canada was one of the world's first federal systems. It made a self-conscious turn towards federalism in 1867 but the constitutional origins of the system long pre-date this. Another important factor, however, is that Canada's commitment to federalism has faced considerable challenges over the past forty years, passing through a controversial period of constitutional reform from 1980 to 1982, experiencing failure in efforts to reform the constitution in 1987 and 1992, and surviving secessionist challenges in 1980 and 1995. Given the distinctive nature of the Canadian system of government and this troubled recent history, it seems that the Canadian constitutional story, as well as being interesting in itself, also offers a prism through which to consider the wider question: What is federalism?

What are the distinguishing features of Canadian federalism? The nineteenth century constitution emerged within the British Empire structure as a Dominion and was therefore built upon the Westminster model of government. Although it gradually developed a written constitutional form, it did so against the backdrop of a wider, unwritten framework of constitutional authority that characterized the Westminster parliamentary system itself as Canada's ultimate rule of recognition until 1982. This normative background stands in contrast with, for example, the American model of federalism which emerged (as did to some extent Australia's) with a clean break from the United Kingdom, leading in each of these cases to forms of constitutional codification very different from Canada's. In fact, until 1982 the nature of Canada's federation, although governed by a written constitution in the form of the British North America Act 1867, relied heavily upon informal channels of constitutional convention and practice even at the level of constitutional amendment, and it was this degree of informality which would come under such dramatic strain during the patriation process of the early 1980s.[1]

Another distinguishing feature is the cultural and linguistic diversity of Canada which the Canadian turn to federalism was specifically modelled to respect and accommodate. Canada over time took on a more overtly *plurinational* political and constitutional character as the cultural and linguistic specificity of Quebec as a province passed through its own nation-building process in the twentieth century. This again has implications for how we think about federalism as a transferable form of government; in particular, one that is able to embrace multinational as well as uninational models – Germany, Australia and Switzerland being obvious examples of the latter.

The considerable societal and institutional differences that attend the federal model, particularly as it continues to diversify in a range of new and troubled settings such as South Africa, Ethiopia, Bosnia-Herzegovina and Iraq, suggest that a reconsideration of the nature of the federal idea is needed. Only by rethinking federalism as being at root a constitutional idea can we elicit the core *constitutional* purposes and principles which can both unite the radically new directions which the federal idea is taking today and still offer a coherent narrative that also explains the specifics of the Canadian model and other older federal systems such as Australia and Germany. Existing theoretical accounts of federalism tend to elide political and constitutional theory, superimposing upon the inherent constitutional essence of federalism substantive ideological commitments, in particular commitments derived from the liberal tradition. Such a conflation misconceives federalism. Federalism is not a political ideology, it is a form of constitutionalism. As such, its essence needs to be understood in constitutional rather than ideological terms. It is only by stripping federalism down and examining its inherent structure through a

---

[1]   S. Tierney, *Le formalisme constitutionnel strict: la toxine britannique, l'antidote canadien?*, in F. Rocher and B. Pelletier (eds.); *Le nouvel ordre constitutionnel canadien: du rapatriement de 1982 à nos jours* (Montreal, Presses de l'Université du Québec (PUQ), 2013), 291–313.

constitutionalist lens that we can reconstruct the common conceptual thread that runs through federal practice both old and new, uninational and plurinational, and made manifest in radically different constitutional forms today. The conceptual and purposive confusion and disagreement that have beset Canadian federal history exemplify the imperative of such a study.

FEDERALISM: AN EXERCISE IN CONSTITUTIONAL THEORY

Constitutional theory is itself a relatively new and still-developing area of enquiry. It is a discrete discipline which is concerned with analysing and evaluating a particular area of social activity: the framing, founding, practice and changing of constitutions, operational through internationally comparable institutions and rules. Constitutional theory differs from political philosophy which is an exercise in ideal theorising from first, abstract principles. By contrast, constitutional theory is an attempt both to understand constitutionalism as a form of political practice, and to frame evaluations of how this practice works against its own internal logic.[2] The core methodological claim I am making in this chapter is that since federalism is a subset of the specific area of social activity we call constitutionalism, federal theory needs to be reconceived through the method of constitutional theory.

This leads to three arguments: first, federalism as an idea, while informed by political theory and political science, must be understood through the particular lens of constitutional theory as shaping a specifically *constitutional*, rather than merely *political*, form of practice. Second, that constitutional theory as a discrete discipline helps us to understand the federal idea as in some sense a normative concept; I use the term "normative functionalism" to explain the link between the instrumental and the normative dimensions of the federal idea. This helps illuminate how the idea of federalism and its practice operate in symbiotic ways: the normative value of federalism as a form of "good" or "prudential" government deriving from the success of the idea in practice as the fulfilment of its core theoretical goals. Third, that normative functionalism as a methodology directs us to a set of purposes and principles which underpin these goals as a theoretical template for the federal form.

What we need to develop is an idea of the federal constitution to explain the anatomy of this model of government as rooted in a particular set of constitutional purposes and informed by a particular set of constitutional principles. This is an approach with which we are now familiar in relation to unitary

---

[2] M. Loughlin, *Constitutional Theory: A 25th Anniversary Essay*, OXFORD JOURNAL OF LEGAL STUDIES, 25, 183 (2005).

constitutionalism. There is an extensive literature that has served to explain how concepts such as constituent power, democracy, government, sovereignty, rights and citizenship are institutionalized in the creation of constitutions designed to serve one undifferentiated territorial people. But the same systematic analysis has not been undertaken in relation to federalism, addressing the specificities of a system of government designed to accommodate territorial pluralism, and assessing how the institutional manifestation of these same elements – constituent power, democracy, government, etc. – ought to be constructed in recognition of this discrete context.

It is not possible in this chapter to construct a systematic constitutional theory of federalism in any detailed way, but I will seek speculatively to re-explore the federal idea in the context of Canadian constitutionalism by identifying the building blocks which together can be used to constitute the essence of the federal idea. The key conceptual categories I adopt are Origins, Purposes, Subjects, Design and Dynamics. These categories characterize any model of constitutionalism and can therefore be applied to federalism. I will consider each in turn, arguing that it is in the misconception of federalism as the bearer of specifically constitutional purposes that so many of the disagreements and misunderstandings in the recent Canadian constitutional past have arisen.

ORIGINS

Constitutional theory requires us to focus upon the "federal moment" as a specific and discrete constituent event resulting in a particular constitutional form. The federal pact that emerges may have sprung from political motives and will continue to be conditioned by these, but it is in essence a constitutional act, producing legal commitments that take on their own character, legitimacy and normative force. Therefore, in time the constitution also develops its own path dependency, conditioning and potentially changing in radical ways the political power balance that brought it into being. The question for the constitutional theorist is not simply the *how* of the federal moment or the political *why* of the political moment, but rather *what*, in constitutional terms, was done at that moment in terms of creating a new normative framework of rights and duties.

I would submit that such an approach can help us to cut through a lot of the debate about the political conditions prevailing at the point of origin of the federation, the founders' intent, etc. An approach that focuses more upon contemporaneous political power and intention can lose traction. For example, as the state develops, the relative influence of the sub-state territories can change considerably. They may have been influential in the origins of the state but that political power can diminish; an observation that is often made about the transition over time within American federalism.[3] The opposite situation can arise, as it arguably did in Canada, where the provinces became more powerful, making Canada one of the most decentralized federations despite the initial imperative of confederation which, for many of the founders, was to avoid the centrifugal experience of the American union. Similarly, federal states might be founded as voluntary unions in a "coming together" way, but the federation may become more fractious over time, with the maintenance of the state becoming the key job for federalism; the American experience in the first half of the nineteenth century bears this out.

Let us briefly explore the history of the formation of Canadian federalism. The British colonies of North America, Canada, Nova Scotia and New Brunswick, were federally united into one Dominion of Canada on July 1, 1867.[4] Canada itself had been an earlier creation through the British North America Act, 1840,[5] which merged the legislatures of Lower Canada and Upper Canada into the Province of Canada (Upper Canada now being known as Canada West and Lower Canada as Canada East). The confederal move in 1867 served to re-divide Canada into the provinces of Ontario and Quebec, recognising Nova Scotia and New Brunswick also as provinces. In time Canada would expand to include within its confederation ten provinces and three territories.

Another dimension of the constitutional story is the country's binational reality. This can be traced back to the imperial competition between Great Britain and France in North America. New France was acquired by Britain in the Treaty of Paris (1763), which ended the Seven Years' War. New France became the Province of Quebec, a status it held from 1763 to 1791. The Constitutional Act of 1791 recognized the ongoing reality of French Canadian culture, and it was in this Act that the Province was separated into Upper Canada, which was predominantly English, and Lower Canada with its largely French-speaking population.

There are different interpretations of the ideological imperatives (if any) that lay behind confederation and the steps that led to it.[6] There is a convincing

---

[3] M. Feeley and E. Rubin, ON FEDERALISM: POLITICAL IDENTITY AND TRAGIC COMPROMISE (Ann Arbor: University of Michigan Press, 2008).

[4] Constitution Act, 1867, 30 & 31 Victoria, c. 3 (UK), RSC 1985, App. II, No. 11.

[5] 3 & 4 Victoria, c. 35, The Short Titles Act 1896, section 1 and Schedule 1, known as the Act of Union 1840.

[6] Peter Smith helped begin a new debate in the 1980s challenging the idea that the motivation for confederation had been essentially pragmatic and non-ideological. P. J. Smith, *The Ideological Origins of Canadian Confederation*, CANADIAN JOURNAL OF POLITICAL SCIENCE / REVUE CANADIENNE DE SCIENCE POLITIQUE, 20, 3–29 (1987).

narrative that posits the purpose of confederation to have been one of central-ization.[7] Certainly this argument does fit with the sense at the time that a primary cause of the American Civil War was the failure to settle the states' rights debate. The distribution of authority between the US federal govern-ment and the American states had been a source of disagreement since 1787 and this weakness led first to misunderstandings and then to rebellion. It was the clear intention of many of the founders of Canadian confedera-tion that one source of secessionism should be removed by way of a clear and supreme source of central authority.[8] Another fear was the continental ambitions of America itself. A strong, united Canada would be necessary to emphasize Canada's coherence as a state and to resist any American imperial strategy to include it within an expanding United States.

Others have viewed the centralising imperative from a more structural perspective. Interpreting Canadian confederation as emerging in the midst of the capitalist stage of historical development, the new union, it is argued, was one driven by the needs of modern capitalism, including the construction of an economy of scale.[9] Confederation served to supply Canada with a structure that would facilitate bourgeois nation-building, behind which lurked an economic dynamic.[10] There is ongoing disagreement about which of these factors was most influential, but in any case they all pointed in the same direction, towards the construction of a large state territory which would be subject to strong central government.

But each of these interpretations serves to take account of the perspective of only one set of actors at the time. If the influence of British or "English" Canada with its desire for strong central government was so overwhelming, then why opt for a federal (or confederal) model at all? The answer is in part the bicultural dimension of Canada but also the territorial particularities of the other territories which came together in 1867 as provinces, and which would be complemented by the other territories that would become provinces in due course. But it was French Canada whose influence in the move to a federal system was, of course, most salient. For the representatives of French Canada confederation would serve the key purpose of recognising its distinctive culture and offering it territorial protection. In light of this, confederation

---

[7]   "Although termed 'Confederation', the union of 1867 was intended to be anything but."
     T. O. Hueglin and A. Fenna, COMPARATIVE FEDERALISM: A SYSTEMATIC ENQUIRY
     (Peterborough, Ont., Broadview Press, 2006), 156.

[8]   Hueglin and Fenna, *supra* note 7, at 157.

[9]   P. J. Smith, *The Ideological Origins of Canadian Confederation.*

[10] A. Smith, *Toryism, Classical Liberalism, and Capitalism: The Politics of Taxation and the
     Struggle for Canadian Confederation*, THE CANADIAN HISTORICAL REVIEW 89, 1–25 (2008).

was a compromise. Referring to John A. Macdonald and Georges-Etienne Cartier as the two most powerful representatives of, respectively, the perspectives of English and French Canada, Hueglin and Fenna argue: "Macdonald preferred a unitary regime but had to settle for what he saw as a powerfully centralist federation. Cartier saw federalism as the best possible compromise guaranteeing the survival of the French language and culture in North America. In the end, both the modernizer and the traditionalist got what they bargained for – at least on paper."[11]

In constitutional theory there is now an extensive literature upon constitutional foundations, the constitutional moment, the relationship between constituent power and constitutional form, etc. What this has served to illustrate is how a constitution can take on a life of its own. Political imperatives may have led to a particular constitutional outcome, but the fact of constitutionalization sets the new regime on its own constitutional trajectory that may in time have unintended consequences for the founders, leading the state in an entirely different direction from that which was anticipated. This has very much been the story of Canadian federalism which, despite the strategy of key founders, has developed a generally decentralizing path over the past century and a half.

What is lacking in constitutional theory more broadly is a consideration of the nature of the federal constitution at its point of origin; in other words, of the features of federalism as a constitutional idea which set the coordinates for a particular constitutional course. It seems that if we develop a more sophisticated understanding of what the origin of a federation actually means, as a self-consciously constitutional act, then the story of how federations, including that of Canada, develop constitutionally over time can be better understood.

Since the seventeenth century the theoretical approach taken to the constitutional origins of the modern democratic polity has been characterized by contract theory. This in turn has been dominated by the liberal-legal focus upon the individual. Constitutional foundations have come to be envisaged in terms of the relationship between the emerging constitutional authority and the rights of individual citizens who are deemed to have come together in some real or fictional contract with one another, and/or with the government authority, to constitute the state. At the federal constituent moment, the normative matrix is both different and more complex than this simple binary relationship between state and individuals.

[11] Hueglin and Fenna, *supra* note 7, at 157.

What needs to be taken into account, as the Canadian founding moment illustrates, is that the distinguishing feature of the federal constitutional moment is the explicit or implicit recognition of *territorial diversity*. The federal polity in its point of origin does not ignore the emerging citizens' individual relationships to the state, but it also acknowledges the existence of territories, their significance to the citizens who comprise them, and, accordingly, their role in mediating the relationship between the individual and the state. The federal constituent moment is therefore the coming together not only of individuals but also of territorial communities in a more complex contractual pact.

It is surprising that this "federal contract" as an addition, or alternative, to the liberal social contract with which political theory is more familiar, has rarely featured in theoretical accounts of constituent power.[12] And while this neglect is hard to explain within political theory, it is simply unworkable in any serious approach to federalism grounded in constitutional theory. The federal constitution gives unequivocal constitutional recognition to territorial pluralism. The fact that territories matter is not simply a contestable theoretical claim, as it is within normative political theory. The constitution speaks for itself. In its very foundation it declares, in the act of constituent power, that the territorial nature of the state is of deep and foundational consequence. Not only that, the constitution in its act of promulgation proceeds to construct, and embed as second-order rules, a superstructure of rights and duties in relation to these territorial communities. What emerges in the end, therefore, is a constitutional contract that is an explicit union of communities.

As constitutionalists, therefore, we are less concerned with the political imperatives behind constitutional origins and more interested in the reality of the federal constitution that is created. What is needed is a full unpacking of the constitutional implications of foundational constitutional commitments that take territories seriously as constituent agents. In fact, the salience of territorial identities within states is something which has only recently been addressed within normative liberal theory, through the work of scholars addressing the resilience of nationalism, and in particular plurinationalism (the existence of more than one national society in a polity[13]), within states.

---

[12] This is notable even where the polity under discussion is in fact federal. S. M. Griffin, *Constituent Power and Constitutional Change in American Constitutionalism*, in M. Loughlin and N. Walker (eds.), *The Paradox of Constitutionalism* (Oxford, Oxford University Press, 2007 49–66).

[13] M. Keating, PLURINATIONAL DEMOCRACY: STATELESS NATIONS IN A POST-SOVEREIGNTY ERA (Oxford, Oxford University Press, 2001); M. Moore, *Normative Justifications for Liberal Nationalism: Justice, Democracy and National Identity*, NATIONS AND NATIONALISM 7, 71–20

This recent turn in political theory recognizes that most people in fact relate to their states through the "societal cultures" which shape these polities, and that these cultures provide "contexts of choice" through which people acquire their world views and develop their preferences and lifestyle choices.[14] The charge is that liberal theory has failed to appreciate, or indeed refused to accept,[15] the contextual salience of the territorial community to the individuals who comprise it. Although ground-breaking work has been done in the context of national pluralism, this is concerned with a limited sociological phenomenon – the presence of more than one national group within a limited number of states. Given the resilience and indeed the expansion of the federal model, it is the case that political and constitutional theory needs to take greater account of territorial pluralism more broadly.

Federalism at point of origin is therefore a foundational recognition not only of territorial difference within the polity, but of its deep and ongoing significance, a significance that results in foundational constitutional respect and protection. This serves further to make clear that federalism is more than a merely explanatory category, it is a normatively informed conceptual account which brings with it the potential for critical analysis: Whatever the particular territorial dynamics are in any emerging federal state, how well does the constitution live up to this territorial commitment?

This, I would submit, is the real starting point from which to understand Canadian confederation as an avowedly constitutional move, a move that puts territorial pluralism front and centre as the constitution's foundational commitment; this may seem like a truism but it is one that at times has been forgotten. It is also one that has often not been fully unpacked by asking: What was the specific nature of the territorial pact that characterized and thereby constituted the Canadian constitutional state?

Political motives and material conditions at the time can be picked over, but the fact of the constitutional pact as an explicitly federal agreement is of free-standing significance. Another consequence of an approach grounded in constitutional theory is that it also cuts through attempts to revive original intent. There has also been a further twist in the story of confederation in

---

(2001); F. Requejo, *Democratic Legitimacy and National Pluralism*, in F. Requejo (ed.), *Democracy and National Pluralism* (London, Routledge, 2001), 157–177; L. Orgod, THE CULTURAL DEFENCE OF NATIONS (Oxford, Oxford University Press, 2016).

[14] "Freedom involves making choices amongst various options, and our societal culture not only provides these options, but also makes them meaningful to us." W. Kymlicka, MULTICULTURAL CITIZENSHIP (Oxford, Oxford University Press, 1995).

[15] B. Barry, CULTURE & EQUALITY: AN EGALITARIAN CRITIQUE OF MULTICULTURALISM (Cambridge, Polity Press, 2001).

recent years, with some commentators arguing that ideology more than either pragmatics or a deeper structural materialism was the real inspiration for the confederal move. It is suggested that the fathers of confederation were driven by an overriding desire to protect individual liberty.[16] In such an approach, as with the others I have mentioned, there are at least two problems. One is that a focus that tries to elicit some form of original intent behind confederation will encounter the general difficulties that beset this type of analysis: a shortage of material, conflicting sources and a lack of relevance to evolving political contexts which it is supposed to inform. Indeed, one cannot help but think that this most recent turn which argues for a strongly individualist imperative behind confederation is subliminally informed by the contemporary world of "Charter Canada." A second and deeper problem is that these originalist approaches overlook that what matters in a constitutionalist reading of pact is not the political background but rather the constituent act and the commitments that in fact emerge in the constitution itself.

The task, then, is to explain what that territorial significance is, and of course this can vary from constitution to constitution. History does matter, but it matters in helping us to understand the constitution's commitment to territorial pluralism. Each federation is different and a historical perspective can illuminate the specificities of each. But it does so always by contextualizing the foundational territorial commitment. When history is deployed to suggest that territorial pluralism was not the key constitutional driver in an act of (con)federation it makes no sense. The very fact of constitutionalizing in a federal direction belies such an argument.

When we turn to the origins of the Canadian constitution therefore, history is indeed illuminating in helping to understand the motives of political actors and prevailing material conditions. But this explanatory work is not *constitutional* explanation. It does not serve in place of an understanding of the explicitly constitutional commitment that was made in that federal moment. Where history is of more consequence is in explaining what the territorial reality was that the federation served to accommodate. This, for the constitutionalist, is the crucial question. And it is here that I embark on the quest to articulate the complex territorial accommodation which did, in a constitutional sense, characterize 1867, itself the culminating event in a process dating back to 1791 and 1840 as vital constitutional staging posts.

---

[16] J. Ajzenstat, THE CANADIAN FOUNDING: JOHN LOCKE AND PARLIAMENT (Montreal, McGill-Queen's University Press, 2007); M. Ducharme and J.-F. Constant, LIBERALISM AND HEGEMONY: DEBATING THE CANADIAN LIBERAL REVOLUTION (Toronto, University of Toronto Press, 2009).

I have discussed elsewhere that we can characterize Canadian confederation as embodying a dual approach to territorial recognition.[17] On the one
hand there was recognition of the territorial prerogatives of all provinces
created in 1867, which would also set the constitutional groundwork for the
provinces which would later enter confederation. But on the other hand there
was also recognition of the French fact in Canada and its territorial concentration mainly in the province of Quebec, a territory the specificity of which
dated back to 1791. In Canada's modern foundation there was therefore a
double dimension to the federal constitutional contract that emerged from the
1867 constitutional moment: what has been called a "double compact."[18] The
constitution recognized the constituent power of its territories but it did so in
different ways for different territories for different reasons: the creation of
provinces in general served to recognize already incipient territorial differences as well as the practical importance of dividing sources of government
across such a vast state; at the same time, Quebec was recognized as a special
case for the way it embodied one of Canada's two founding cultures. This
territorial reality is complex both in political and in conceptual terms, but it is
what it is. Constitutional theory serves to help explain constitutional reality,
not to simplify that reality. Canada is united in conceptual terms with all
federal states in its foundational moment because that moment is the recognition and accommodation of the state's territorial diversity. But that territorial
diversity for Canada, as for all federal states, is unique. The task of the constitutional theorist is to explain not only the commonality of federal origins but
also their specificity. And the particularity of Canada's constitutional origins
were, and remain, in constitutional terms complex, challenging, ambiguous
and contested.

PURPOSES

The focus of political science has inevitably been upon the political motives
behind each instance of federal constitution-making, but it is important to
recognize that constitutionalism brings with it its own particular purposes,
creating legally conditioned path dependencies. Strategic political aims are of
course a relevant and important consideration in the framing of the constitution, but constitutionalism is by its nature about the *regulation* of political
power. On this basis not only may constitutional purposes take on a different

[17] S. Tierney, CONSTITUTIONAL LAW AND NATIONAL PLURALISM (Oxford, Oxford University
    Press, 2004).
[18] Discussed at "Dynamics" later in this chapter.

trajectory from the strategies of dominant political actors, the two may well exist in a state of tension.

There is of course an extensive literature within constitutional theory on constitutional purposes. This tends to frame the key purpose of the modern constitution as being the limitation, and thereby the legitimation, of political power. It is another trope that this legitimation rests upon consent at the point of origin and the ongoing assent of citizens exercised democratically. The notion of original consent is of course in most cases largely mythical,[19] but it serves the purpose of introducing a legitimizing narrative which is thereafter sustained by the reality of lived democracy. The focus therefore turns to how constitutional legitimacy can be calibrated, what democracy means in constitutional context, the interplay of majoritarianism vs. individual rights, the appropriate level of entrenchment of the constitution as a whole or particularly important provisions in particular, and the respective roles of constitutional institutions, with increasing attention focused upon the courts as constitutional adjudicators or "guardians."[20]

Again it is notable that within these debates there has been little consideration as to whether federalism brings with it a particular set of constitutional purposes which differ, at least in emphasis, from the broader purposes of liberal constitutionalism. This is also another significant gap which flows from the neglect of federalism in theoretical accounts of the state's moment of origin. Because thinking about federalism has been informed more by political theory than constitutional theory, some of the specifics of liberal constitutionalism have been grafted onto federal thought in a way that imposes upon federalism a liberal-individualist ideology that can fail to take account properly for, or which in fact runs counter to, the real purpose of the federal polity, namely the constitutional accommodation of territorial plurality.

This fundamental purpose of federalism leads to more specific purposes. Many of these are in fact analogous to those attributed to democratic constitutionalism more generally. And that is as it should be; federalism is an instance of democratic constitutionalism in its modern form. But it is also important to tailor these purposes to take account of the essentially territorial orientation of the federal state. In broader work I am undertaking I set out

---

[19] Many in fact reject the normative salience of constituent power altogether and focus instead upon the democratic legitimacy of the contemporary constitution and how it functions. E.g. D. Dyzenhaus, *The Politics of the Question of Constituent Power*, in M. Loughlin and N. Walker (eds.), *The Paradox of Constitutionalism*, 129–146 (Oxford: Oxford University Press, 2008).

[20] R. Hirschl, Towards Juristocracy the Origins and Consequences of the New Constitutionalism (Cambridge, MA, Harvard University Press, 2004).

what I take to be the core and common constitutional purposes that characterize federalism as an instance of modern constitutionalism:

- consent of the federation's constituent territories,
- democracy, taking account of the potential for the polity to contain
  multiple demoi,
- autonomy of the federation's territories,
- sharing by the constituent territories in the power of the state,
- horizontal and vertical reciprocity in relations, respectively, among the
  federal territories and between each of these and the state.

Each of these purposes can be used to assess the effectiveness of any federation
in fulfilling its core purpose of territorial recognition and accommodation. At
the same time they can each adapt to the specifics of each federation, and do
not presuppose the same institutional design across federations, a point I will
return to later in this chapter.

  Given the confines of space I will offer only one or two selected examples in
reference to the Canadian system. To begin, and taking legitimacy to be a
transferable benchmark within modern constitutionalism, we can say that
consent and *democracy* are fundamental purposes of a federal constitution as
they are of any legitimate constitution. But from here the logic of federalism
leads to more specific purposes which are not only distinguishable from,
but potentially contradictory to, the main normative thrust of liberal-unitary
constitutionalism. Democracy in the classical liberal tradition takes on a
strongly individualist strain which has elided with a monistic conception of
the demos. Within liberal constitutionalism, democracy and its *alter ego*
popular sovereignty have each served to legitimize and thereby underpin
unitary state construction through the idea of "we the [undifferentiated]
people." In turn, this unitary conception of the demos has elided with and
undergirded a unitary conception of the state to bolster centralizing constitutional projects. The turn in liberal theory towards "Liberalism II,"[21] which
questions liberalism's sociological assumptions about the nature of society,
proceeds to challenge liberalism's overwhelmingly individualistic conception
of democracy. For example, scholars of plurinationalism, by confronting the
implicitly unitary conception of the society of the state, assert that in a multinational state we cannot conceive of the founding moment (whether as real or
mythical point of origin) in exclusively individualist terms. The federal idea

---

[21] C. Taylor, *The Politics of Recognition*, in A. Gutmann (ed.), *Multiculturalism: Examining the
      Politics of Recognition* (Princeton, Princeton University Press, 1992) 25–74.

also makes this conceptual leap but it does so more broadly, calling for a reconceputalization of the federal social contract. By this construction, the consent that underpins the legitimacy of the federal polity is the consent of its constituent territories as well as that of the individual citizens of the state, and in the same way the operation of democracy as the ongoing reinforcement of that consent is also mediated by the empirical reality and normative valence of territorial union.

The political theory of liberalism has developed such a grip on modern constitutionalism that it is easy to overlook that political theory and constitutional theory are different phenomena, and that the purpose of constitutionalism is not simply to consolidate the liberal orthodoxy of methodological individualism through legal rules. Democracy is central to the functional normativity of modern constitutionalism, but constitutional theory must be capable of accommodating the different democratic variants that characterize lived constitutional practice. Federalism is such an alternative model of democracy, emerging as the real-life mediator between the interests of individuals, the interests of the territorial communities within the state to which individuals belong and from which they derive much of their political identity, and the interests of the state itself as both host and unifying polity.

The identification of the immanent constitutional purposes of federalism helps us to explain how so much dispute has taken place in Canada over the constitution. Let us take one example of how liberal thinking has come to be transplanted onto federal thinking, which has particular resonance in the Canadian system. Equality is a strong commitment of liberal constitutionalism. In terms of the principles of autonomy and representation, all individuals ought to be recognized equally by the constitution. There is of course much dispute about whether equality does in fact bear real meaning in social and economic terms, but as a principle of political representation it remains a firm totem of the liberal model of constitutionalism. This is all straightforward enough but a problem arises when the principle of equality is translated unreflectively onto federal theory. Whether and if so how the principle of equality applies, even as a principle of political representation, to a federation depends upon a combination of the societal conditions from which the federal constitution emerges, constitutional commitments made at this time, and subsequent constitutional developments. Federalism may bring together territories that are markedly different in terms of geographical or population size, history and the salience of the territory to its individual citizen, and in doing so it may accord to each asymmetrical constitutional recognition and protection. A sub-state nation for example can take on a significantly more important role in the lives of its individual citizens than a non-national territory that performs

48 *Stephen Tierney*

a more prosaic governmental and administrative role, and the constitution may well recognize that difference in the outcome of federalization.

Canada is a classic example, where the principle of provincial equality has become an idée fixe, but one that arguably reflects neither Canada's territorial reality nor its deeper constitutional commitments. This principle can be seen as in one sense an over-simplification of the purpose of Canadian federalism: taking seriously the issue of provincial recognition, but not taking full account of the second purpose which is Canada's biculturalism. It has also been argued that the valence of federalism in its entirety diminished in English Canada in the course of the twentieth century to be replaced with a more liberal vision which understands the constitution to be more about the protection of individual rights than territorial prerogatives. As Hueglin and Fenna put it: "Not unlike Americans, English Canadians tend to regard federalism as a structural device either promoting or inhibiting their individual aspirations."[22] Notably the same observe that liberalism is also strong in Quebec: "Individual liberalism among French Canadians may be as strong as anywhere else, but it is complemented by a much stronger commitment to collective cultural identity."[23] This latter comment is questionable, however, because it seems to conflate political identity and constitutional identity. It is not at all clear that French Canadians, or more specifically francophone Quebecers, have a stronger commitment to collective cultural identity as a matter of political ideology. What is clear is that within Quebec there is concern about the scope to maintain Quebec's cultural specificity. The stronger commitment is not to culture per se but rather to the constitutional protections for cultural identity which the federal system guarantees; this is of course less of an issue in English Canada, a culture which does not face the same existential challenges.

There is not scope here to explore in detail what explains the seeming decline in commitment to federalism in English Canada. But it is clear that the patriation process, which brought with it the Charter of Rights and Freedoms presenting a universalizing account of Canadian civic identity, has called into question the commitment to regional territorial attachments. The 1980–82 process can be read therefore as a move away, on the part of many, from the deep constitutional commitment which the union pact of 1867 involved, and a failure across Canada to agree upon (or even to articulate) what the specific territorial commitment the Canadian constitution in fact embodied – one of equal provinces or one that gives recognition also

[22] Hueglin and Fenna, *supra* note 7, at 67.   [23] *Id.*

to the asymmetry of territorial attachments which had been a social fact in Canada since at least the eighteenth century.

Although it is not a task that can be completed here, from this brief vignette it seems that Canadian federalism can and should also be reviewed against all of the constitutional purposes of federalism outlined above.

SUBJECTS

If the legitimation of political rule is the underlying purpose of contemporary constitutionalism, the key source of legitimacy for any polity is its subjects. In turn, the constitutional accommodation of territorial pluralism conditions how we must frame the relevant subjects of federal democracy within the federal idea. It is here that we see what is perhaps the most stark contrast between federal constitutional theory and that of unitary-liberal constitutionalism. The source of constituent power, and hence the exclusive bearers not only of the original source of legitimation but of the ongoing normative justification for the unitary-liberal polity, are individual citizens. But the methodological individualism which underpins this account renders it a highly partial approach to democratic government, and concomitantly to the key actors involved. Unitary-liberal constitutionalism reduces the relationship between state and subjects to a simple binary: the only significant actors in play are institutions of government (almost always framed conceptually in unitary terms) on the one hand, and individuals on the other.

Federalism is by definition the recognition of an additional, or indeed alternative, set of original subjects, and hence of an additional/alternative source of constituent power: the state's constituent territorial communities. The normative implications of broadening out the relevant list of subjects within the federal polity is a fundamental challenge to the universalistic assumptions which have underpinned liberal-unitary constitutionalism. But it is also a challenge for constitutional theory more broadly which remarkably has failed to address the implications of the collective constitutional subject for standard constitutional concepts such as constituent power, sovereignty and citizenship.

Again, the influence of liberal political theory is such that it has tended to elide with constitutionalism. The conflation of constitutional theory with liberal constitutional theory is apparent in the assumption that a social contract, configured in individual terms, offers a universalizable account of the legitimate constitution. And such an account, while perhaps applicable for states that seek self-consciously to constitute themselves as one undifferentiated territory of individuals, is not consistent with the federal idea. It fails to take account of the fact that sub-state territories, as well as individuals, are foundational subjects of the federal polity.

The Canadian adoption of the Charter of Rights and Freedoms as a key symbolic emblem of the patriation process brought the issue of subjecthood to a head. The original constituent power of the country – the provinces – were of course still central to the state in the 1982 Act, but their constitutive role was arguably undermined by patriation. The new Constitution Act, by constitutionally entrenching a national bill of rights, served to bolster the idea of one national civic identity that would increasingly transcend provincial borders.

Constitutional theory alerts us to the importance of major constitutional change for constitutional subjecthood itself. It is at significant moments of constitutional creation that a constitutional people is itself created or transformed, constitutional change taking on an important nation-building or nation-defining role. The 1980–82 period in Canada has certainly taken on such a significant symbolic function. The idea of Canada as a composite of provincial territories remained, but the move toward patriation came also to be seen in English Canada as the refoundational act of one constitutional people. The two are of course not incompatible. A federation is a state for one federated people. But the neglect of the second territorial dimension of Canadian federalism – the recognition that French Canada was a particular constitutional subject embodied increasingly in the province of Quebec – sat uneasily with a move to elevate a unitary-liberal conception of the constitutional subject (the individual citizen) in a vague relationship to the more complex matrix of territorial constituent power which had characterized the 1867 constitutional moment.

DESIGN

The origins and purposes of federalism, which enlighten how within constitutional theory we must understand federal subjecthood, also have inevitable implications for how the institutional structure of the state should be fashioned. But it is mistaken to try to lay out a highly detailed institutional template as the definitive representation of federal design. Empirical reality demonstrates that the institutionalization of federalism manifests itself very differently from state to state. And it is perfectly appropriate that it should do so, given that the primary purpose of federalism is to accommodate territorial pluralism which itself varies in form, often greatly, from place to place.

The task for the constitutional theorist therefore is to think about constitutional design by using the preceding conceptual building blocks. From here the goal is the identification of principles immanent within the federal idea,

TABLE 1. *Purposes and Principles of Federalism*

Purposes	Principles
consent/democracy	*territorial consensus*
autonomy	*subsidiarity*
shared rule	*representation* and *participation*
horizontal reciprocity	*social solidarity*
vertical reciprocity	*comity*

which can then be used to inform institutional design, tailored specifically to each situation based upon the specificities of origins and subjects within the polity and reflective of the particular manifestations of federalism's underpinning purposes as these apply in each state.

It seems clear that these principles will heavily overlap with the purposes of federalism considered above: *consent, democracy, autonomy, shared rule, and horizontal and vertical reciprocity.* The principles of institutional design will delve more deeply into these purposes by assessing how they have manifested themselves empirically from federal polity to federal polity, and in doing so drawing out more specific values that have become the generic ethics of the federal model. Each federation can be assessed by how well it fulfils the purposes of federalism, using these principles.

Of course federal principles need to be unpacked carefully and space forbids that, but Table 1 offers a precis.

The birth of Canadian federalism came with ambiguous intentions. The commitment to territorial accommodation was accompanied by provision for a strong central government, leading to the description of Canadian federalism as "executive federalism."[24] Institutional design has therefore been a source of ongoing tension. Canada was a very different model of federalism from that of the United States, largely because it retained a line of constitutional authority to the United Kingdom. In this way federalism was linked to the authority of the United Kingdom system of parliamentary government,

---

[24] D. V. Smiley, THE FEDERAL CONSTITUTION IN CANADA (Toronto, McGraw-Hill Ryerson, 1987), 83. But note D. Cameron and R. Simeon, *Intergovernmental Relations in Canada: The Emergence of Collaborative Federalism*, PUBLIUS: THE JOURNAL OF FEDERALISM 32 (2002), 49–71, where it was argued that by the early 2000s the Canadian system was better viewed in collaborative terms. The Supreme Court of Canada has described the more recent model as "co-operative federalism": *Attorney General (Canada) v. PHS Community Services Society* [2011] 3 SCR 134, para. 63, although this is called into question somewhat by *Attorney General (Quebec) v. Attorney General (Canada)* (2015) SCC 14.

and indeed a parliamentary system was also established for the new Canadian federal government itself. This meant that there were strong centralizing elements in the original design which contrasted with the American model. For example, the role of governor-general or vice-regal who acted as agent of the Crown. The governor-general even had power to disallow provincial legislation, which became in practice a power of the federal prime minister. Such powers seem to clash with federal principles of territorial consensus, representation and participation: in other words with the shared rule purpose of federalism. Shared rule was also not supported by strong bicameralism. In Canada the four regions have the same representation in the Senate but it is of course, in effect, a government-appointed body. Despite this, Canada demonstrates how over time a federal constitution can take on a path of its own in consequence of its original federal purposes.[25] In Canada we see such a trajectory in three main dynamics: other elements of the federal model compensating for the initial weakness in shared rule, the development of informal practices and conventions filling gaps in the constitutional text, and through judicial interpretation.

In terms of other elements compensating, Canada's adoption of the parliamentary system did not in fact have the centralizing effect that was intended. The constitution also gave the provinces considerable autonomy, for example in the specific allocation of powers between the provinces and the federal government. In many areas each level of government was accorded a complete set of powers, allowing it to form, legislate upon and administer its respective responsibilities. In a related way most powers were assigned exclusively to the respective level of government involved. These moves would in time bolster the self-rule dimension of Canadian federalism and in doing so gave the provinces significant push-back powers against a strong centre. The dynamic that developed therefore between a strong federal government and strong provinces was one of competition (even if that has modified considerably in recent times). Some suggest that the centralizing elements which were included within the 1867 Act, but which clashed with the federal idea, in fact helped foster a culture of resistance, providing "the Canadian provinces with a legitimate reason to pursue their own legislative options more aggressively."[26]

A second feature which helped embed the federal idea, despite design flaws, was the development of informal rules concerning the status of the provinces. One example is how conventions developed in relation to constitutional

[25] For example, coming to be described as "flexible federalism": *Canadian Western Bank v. Alberta* [2007] 2 SCR 3, para 42.
[26] Hueglin and Fenna, *supra* note 7, at 68.

amendment, an area to which I return in the Dynamics section of the chapter. The third factor, the judicial role, also played a significant role in bolstering the federal idea. For example, the property and civil rights clause came to be used to help protect the French fact in Canada. This clause dates back to 1791 and was in fact intended to offer guarantees to empire loyalists who were fleeing the United States and settling in the eastern part of Canada, to the effect that they would not have to adopt French civil law. It came in time, partly through the courts, to protect that very same civil law in Quebec, and in fact would be used to strengthen provincial prerogatives more widely.

The experience of the judicial role since the Supreme Court of Canada replaced the JCPC as the final court of constitutional arbitration has been considerably more mixed as we discuss later, but this took a dramatic turn in the Quebec Secession Reference[27] where the Court went so far as to move beyond the written constitution to identify unwritten principles in the constitution. One of the four principles was federalism, but the other three (democracy, constitutionalism and the rule of law, and minority rights) can also be read as bolstering the federal idea. At one stroke this opinion seemed to grasp the dual nature of Canada's federal structure: the territorial accommodation of provinces in general and the specific accommodation of the French fact of Canada, in particular the status of Quebec.

DYNAMICS

Constitutional theory is increasingly concerned with the issue of constitutional amendment.[28] A key question is how best to reach the appropriate balance between open democratic decision-making on the one hand and constitutional entrenchment on the other. The trajectory of unitary constitutionalism has been towards more and more elaborate constitutions and the attempt to embed certain political values by way of ever longer lists of rights, often in very rigid ways, including the use of so-called "eternity clauses,"[29] and the concept of unconstitutional constitutional amendments.[30] This trend is serving to remove important areas of decision-making from the hands of

[27] *Reference Re Secession of Quebec* [1998] 2 SCR 217.
[28] R. Albert, *Amending Constitutional Amendment Rules*, INTERNATIONAL 13 JOURNAL OF CONSTITUTIONAL LAW 655–685 (2015).
[29] S. Suteu, *Eternity and the Constitution: The Promise and Limits of Eternity Clauses*, PhD thesis, University of Edinburgh, 2016.
[30] Y. Roznai, UNCONSTITUTIONAL CONSTITUTIONAL AMENDMENTS: THE LIMITS OF AMENDMENT POWERS (Oxford, Oxford University Press, 2017).

citizens and politicians, leaving greater discretion over the meaning and application of these values in the hands of the courts.

One issue is whether federalism brings with it its own set of constitutional dynamics that make the trend towards more and more rigid constitutions particularly suitable or unsuitable for federal democracy. The relative neglect of federalism within constitutional theory means that no detailed consideration has ever been given to whether within the federal idea there is a different relationship between constitutional rigidity and open democracy than applies within liberal-unitary constitutionalism.

Beginning with the empirical question – how have federal constitutions regulated constitutional change? – we tend to find within federal constitutions that constitutional amendment requires special majorities, either within the central legislature, such as in Germany where the approval of two-thirds of both legislative chambers is required, or by a direct role for the states, as in the United States. This hints at the importance of legalism more generally within federal constitutions. In the federal constituent moment a careful balance is achieved between the prerogatives of the central government, the constituent territories and citizens. This can lead to a detailed demarcation of powers, rights and duties, establishing the contours of this complex set of relationships, which is reflected in concomitantly complex rules regarding constitutional change, hinting at an inherent rigidity within federal constitutionalism.

The issue of constitutional change has of course been a major irritant – possibly the major irritant – in Canadian constitutional disputes of the past fifty years. Two matters arose: one was how the constitution could be amended to bring about patriation of the constitution, the other was what new amending formula should be embedded in the newly patriated constitution. But two dimensions of Canadian constitutionalism combined problematically in these debates. One was the complex pattern of the original federal purpose – the creation of provinces, and the particular role of Quebec; the other was the informality of the constitution which had come to define this complexity in the absence of textual constitutional provision.

Both its federal, institutional setting as a province, and its specific historical experience, led Quebec to expect a central role in the general process of constitutional change within Canada; a role not only in changes affecting provincial autonomy, but in relation to constitutional amendment more broadly. But different understandings pertained as to how patriation could be brought about. One view was that the federal government could make a request unilaterally to Westminster without the need for provincial consent. Another view was based upon the so-called "compact theory" by which Canada was understood to be a compact of ten provinces each of which should have a power of veto over constitutional change.[31] A third understanding was that Canada was a country of two founding peoples – English-speaking and French-speaking – each of which had the right to veto constitutional change.[32]

In fact, given that Quebec was both a province, and "the particular inheritance of French Canada,"[33] an idea had developed in Quebec early in the twentieth century that the Canadian constitution preceding even Confederation was somehow a "double compact." This encompassed a "political" compact among the provinces and a "national" compact between the two founding peoples who had come together in 1791 to form the United Canadas. It was also understood that the two compacts were connected. The *national* compact united English and French Canada as two discrete founding cultures within the federation; and the *political* compact (or what we might think of as the *constitutional* compact), was the agreement by which French Canada's rights and prerogatives were recognized as attaching principally to the province of Quebec,[34] giving Quebec a unique provincial status.

And this is where we see the informal constitution becoming so important to this understanding. The British North America Act 1867 of course makes no direct reference to these compacts. Rather, it was widely believed within Quebec that the values and "spirit" of the constitution would protect these understandings. As Ramsay Cook put it, this vision was, "in the last analysis, a moral compact."[35] In the 1980–82 process the Supreme Court of Canada found that the written constitution did not expressly provide for such a compact; it was prepared to acknowledge the conventional role of the provinces in general but not that Quebec had a special position. And even the

---

[31] For the historical origins of the equality doctrine see K. McRoberts, MISCONCEIVING CANADA: THE STRUGGLE FOR NATIONAL UNITY (Toronto, Oxford University Press, 1997), 16–17.

[32] P. Oliver, *Canada, Quebec and Constitutional Amendment*, UNIVERSITY OF TORONTO LAW JOURNAL, 49 (1999), 519–610, p. 534 and p. 544, fns. 106–107.

[33] Cited by K. McRoberts, *Misconceiving Canada*, 20.

[34] P. Romney, *Provincial Equality, Special Status and the Compact Theory of Confederation*, 32 CANADIAN JOURNAL OF POLITICAL SCIENCE, 21–39 (1999).

[35] Cited by K. McRoberts, *Misconceiving Canada*, 21. See also D. M. Thomas, WHISTLING PAST THE GRAVEYARD: CONSTITUTIONAL ABEYANCES, QUEBEC AND THE FUTURE OF CANADA (Toronto, Oxford University Press, 1997), and P. Hogg, CONSTITUTIONAL LAW OF CANADA, 4th ed. (Toronto, Carswell, 1997) 62–3. Peter Oliver suggests that the "national" compact idea took on particular force within Quebec in the middle of the twentieth century. He suggests that the decline in the "political" compact in the rest of Canada led to a stronger assertion by Quebec of its roles as a founding province and the main territorial embodiment of French Canada. P. Oliver, "Canada, Quebec and Constitutional Amendment," 534. *See also* the Supreme Court of Canada in *Re Objection by Quebec to Resolution to Amend the Constitution* [1982] 2 SCR 793, para 59.

conventions which the Court did identify it could not enforce given the normative limitations of constitutional conventions. In short, the double compact could not or would not be articulated by way of judicial interpretation.

The federal government under PM Pierre Trudeau turned to Westminster with its request for patriation of the constitution. The issue that arose was whether the federal government by constitutional convention required the consent of any or all of the provinces in order to request the necessary constitutional amendments from Westminster. Eight provinces opposed the process but nonetheless the federal government proceeded with its unilateral request to the UK Parliament.[36] Three provinces (Quebec, Manitoba and Newfoundland) challenged the patriation process before the Supreme Court of Canada.[37] In their reference the three provinces asked two key questions: was there a constitutional convention whereby the consent of the provinces should be obtained before the federal government could request the UK Parliament to amend the constitution of Canada in a way that would affect the powers of the provinces? And secondly, was there a legal requirement that provincial consent should be obtained for such a process? On the second question, the Supreme Court held there was no legal requirement of provincial consent to the patriation process; but on the convention issue, a majority of judges found that there was a convention whereby the federal government should obtain a "substantial degree" or "substantial measure" of provincial consent before requesting the UK Parliament to pass the relevant legislation.[38]

In political terms a compromise was reached. The federal government arrived at a package of amendments with nine of the ten provinces on 5 November 1981. This agreement was then passed in a joint address to both Houses of the federal parliament[39] and sent to London for enactment as the Canada Act 1982. Quebec was the only province not to agree to the final deal. But in its submission to the Supreme Court in the *Patriation Reference* it had

---

[36] *See* E. McWhinney, CANADA AND THE CONSTITUTION 1979–1982 (Toronto, University of Toronto Press, 1982); K.G. Banting and R.E.B. Simeon (eds.), AND NO ONE CHEERED (Agincourt, Ontario, Methuen, 1983); B. Pelletier, LA MODIFICATION CONSTITUTIONNELLE AU CANADA (Toronto, Carswell, 1996).

[37] *Patriation Reference: Re Resolution to Amend the Constitution* [1981] 1 SCR 753.

[38] *Patriation Reference: Re Resolution to Amend the Constitution* at p. 905. Peter Hogg was generally critical of the *Patriation Reference* judgment. He took the view that Canada's constitutional history should have led to the Court to find either a convention of unanimity or no convention at all. P. Hogg, Comment, CANADIAN BAR REVIEW, 60 (1982), 307. Instead the result was that "the provinces had no legal protection from changes to the Constitution initiated unilaterally by the federal Parliament, a situation inconsistent with principles of federalism." P. Hogg, CONSTITUTIONAL LAW OF CANADA, at 64 fn. 16.

[39] By the House of Commons on 2 December 1981 and by the Senate on 8 December 1981.

not raised the issue of whether it, in particular, had a constitutional right to veto constitutional change. Following the November agreement Quebec brought a second reference which also reached the Supreme Court.[40] It argued that Quebec's constitutional position was unique, entitling it to a veto over the patriation process. The Court of Appeal rejected this claim and by the time it reached the Supreme Court, the Constitution Act had been passed. The Supreme Court did still address the issue but came to the view that Quebec's consent was not an essential component of the convention of "substantial degree" of provincial consent.[41]

Quebec also failed to secure any special role in the new amending procedures set out in the Constitution Act 1982.[42] There are certain matters in respect of which constitutional amendments require the unanimous assent of all of the provinces and the federal Parliament,[43] but in general, for those matters not otherwise expressly provided for,[44] a constitutional amendment will require the assent of both houses of the federal parliament and of two thirds of the provinces representing not less than 50 per cent of the population.[45] Quebec is accorded the same role in relation to constitutional amendment as any other province. Peter Hogg was very critical of this: "The new amending procedures denied a veto to Quebec, something that in the past had always been recognized in practice ... Thus the outcome of the constitutional changes of 1982 was a diminution of Quebec's powers and a profound sense of grievance in the province."[46]

In time this has been corrected to some extent. A "regional veto statute" for example has been passed.[47] But this was a compromise which did not distinguish between the two dynamics of Canadian federalism. However, although it did not lead to distinctive recognition for Quebec, it did strengthen the provincial control over the constitution more broadly. It did so by decentralising the constitutional amendment process in a radical way that could perhaps have been avoided. In this way the constitutional recognition of the

[40] *Quebec Veto Reference* [1982] 2 SCR 793.   [41] *Quebec Veto Reference* at 806.
[42] Part V of the Constitution Act 1982, ss. 38–49.   [43] Constitution Act 1982, s. 41.
[44] Constitution Act 1982, s. 42.   [45] Constitution Act 1982, s. 38, the so-called "7/50 formula."
[46] P. Hogg, CONSTITUTIONAL LAW OF CANADA, p. 67. See also K.G. Banting and R.E.B. Simeon (eds.), AND NO ONE CHEERED (Toronto: Methuen Publications, 1983).
[47] "An Act Respecting Constitutional Amendments," Statutes of Canada 1996, 1st session, 35th Parliament, Bill C-110. This restrains a minister of the Crown from proposing, in the federal Parliament, a motion for a resolution to authorize an amendment to the Constitution of Canada, if the amendment has not been consented to by five "regions," one of which is Quebec. This statute is of course not itself a constitutional amendment (which would require to be approved by way of the unanimity procedure contained within section 41(e) of the 1982 Act).

federal idea was reasserted. Provinces now have unprecedented control over constitutional change in Canada. Implicit if not explicit in this is a strong role for Quebec as one of the "regions." In this inelegant and largely unintentional way the original federal trajectory as one of dual compact has seemingly been consolidated.

CONCLUDING REMARKS

Federalism has both proliferated and diversified greatly in recent decades, and at the same time it has been the subject of renewed interest by scholars. These developments challenge many of the assumptions with which researchers have long worked, not least the notion that it is possible to understand federalism through institutional analysis alone. The emergence of innovative federal models, in response to ever more complex territorial situations, suggests that a more systematic theoretical intervention is needed. In taking Canada as a case study, I have argued that there is a federal idea which lies behind the practice of federalism, that this is at root a constitutional idea and that it is necessary to go back to first constitutional principles to try to explain the anatomy of this idea.

This task must be undertaken through the methodology of constitutional theory which allows us to draw out the conceptual and functional-normative components immanent within this idea. Constitutional theory offers an under-worked, enlightening and exciting new turn with which we can overcome the conceptual, classificatory and terminological essentialism that has gripped much of the political science and constitutional law scholarship in this area. It can also help explain much of the misunderstanding that has beset the constitutional history of particular states, Canada being a classic example. In this chapter I have sought to outline the essence of this methodology, applying it to sketch the skeleton of the federal idea in terms of origins, purposes, subjects, design and dynamics. These are the core elements of modern democratic constitutionalism. They have been deployed in many detailed studies of liberal unitary constitutionalism and therefore it remains surprising that such a conceptual constitutional study of federalism has not as yet been undertaken. Canadian constitutional history, which I have only been able to address briefly here, seems to offer an ideal project with which to take this forward.

3

Political Dynamics in Quebec
Charting Concepts and Imagining Political Avenues

ALAIN-G. GAGNON

This initiative is about measuring Canada's capacity to adapt to new circumstances in a world that has had its good and bad moments. My own task is to assess Quebec-Canada's evolving relations and situate these moments in a comparative interpretative framework. One way of doing this is to compare and contrast various models of governance under the vocabulary of competing narratives and conflicting/partial visions. These conflictual visions can also be introduced as evolving identities through the prisms of political communities and citizenship regimes rather than as a reading that would suggest the existence of a monist worldview.

Quebec has been a leader in advancing a politics of diversity for Canada. This has been particularly well documented by political scientists, historians, legal experts and other social sciences specialists. What comes immediately to mind is the 1864 Quebec Conference during which politicians from Canada East asked for recognition of both Catholics and Protestants as well as for English and French speakers.[1] A politics of diversity had already been imagined and a Quebec's school of diversity was being shaped.[2] The difficulty would be to make sure that institutions were erected and the political culture ready to take roots and could pursue the same objectives in the long haul and resist attempts by the central government to adopt (and at times impose) all encompassing policy stances (Conscription I and II, Charter of Rights and Freedoms, the Social Union Framework (Dis)Agreement).

Throughout the last 150 years, there has been a prevailing tension between the proponents of homogenization and those who wish to promote or

[1] LA CONFÉRENCE DE QUÉBEC DE 1864, 150 ANS PLUS TARD. COMPRENDRE L'ÉMERGENCE DE LA FÉDÉRATION CANADIENNE (Eugénie Brouillet, Alain-G. Gagnon & Guy Laforest eds., 2016).
[2] Alain-G. Gagnon, MINORITY NATIONS IN THE AGE OF UNCERTAINTY: NEW PATHS TO NATIONAL EMANCIPATION AND EMPOWERMENT (2014).

safeguard Canada's deep diversity. In French Canada and Quebec, we can document five prevailing faces. These represented five specific ways to advance political projects, namely French Canada as forming a political nationality, as constituting a sociological nation and Quebec either as being the political expression of a distinct society or a province state or else as being part of a multinational political setting. We will turn our attention to these five incarnations in a moment.

CHARTING POLITICAL SPACES THROUGH
THE USE OF CONCEPTS

The selection of concepts and narratives in the world of politics as well as in the real world is not a question of details but rather it is a way to adopt a worldview, to order priorities or, stated more simply, to advance a political posture. Similarly, it is not insignificant when politicians speak of levels of government rather than orders of government, utilize the notion of sub-national units to discuss bi-national and multi-national states or substitute the notion of region for the concept of founding member of a federation. Similarly, it matters when, in the Canadian context, our best scholars of federalism and veteran politicians use the notions of federal government, central government or the Government of Canada interchangeably.

My Canadian colleague, the late Richard Simeon, a foremost student of federalism, made a valid point when he stated forty years ago that the concept of "regions [and other concepts for this matter] are simply containers ... and how we draw the boundaries around them depends entirely on what our purposes are: it is an *a priori* question, determined by theoretical needs or political purposes."[3] Consequently, when discussing Quebec it is important to come to terms with the objectives being pursued by various individuals, groups and communities as well as by the judiciary, political parties, political institutions and political entrepreneurs in positions of influence and authority.

Various uses of key concepts such as *political nationality, nation, distinct society, province state* and *multinational federation* have a significant impact on the way one imagines political units. My intention in this presentation is to introduce the main images that have surfaced and resurfaced since the beginning of the Quiet Revolution in Quebec[4] and assess their impact on the mind-set of Canadians and Quebecers. I want to make clear though at the

---

[3]   Richard Simeon, Regionalism and Canadian Political Institutions, in Canadian Federalism: Myth or Reality 293 (Peter Meekison ed., 1977).

[4]   Alain-G. Gagnon & Mary Beth Montcalm, Quebec: Beyond the Quiet Revolution (1990).

very outset that I chose not to include the notion of *stateless nation* to depict Quebec since this political community has developed major state apparatuses active in education, culture, economy and intergovernmental matters that would make many existing countries very envious of its accomplishments.[5] I will not make use either of the concepts of *national minority* or the notion of *global society* to discuss the Quebec-Canada dynamics mainly because Quebecers conceives themselves as forming one of the two principal political communities in the country.

I intend to focus on five prevailing faces of Quebec, namely Quebec as forming part of an inclusive political nationality, as a co-founding nation, as a distinct society, as a province state and, finally, as a being a key partner in a multinational democracy.

Face 1: *Political Nationality*

Canada's beginning is characterized by a series of political events that have had a major impact on how Canadians see themselves. For instance, were French Canadians conquered by the British or did France simply cede its territory north of the 49th parallel to its arch rival? Was Confederation a compact between the French and the English cohabitating on Canadian soil? Or was it a political arrangement between the four original provinces and the imperial government? Who was the depository of sovereignty or, stated differently, who formed the constituent power(s)? Contradictory answers have been given to these questions based on people's vision of the original compact or else influenced by one's dominant identity.

George-Étienne Cartier remains a central figure throughout the last century and a half. Cartier wanted Canada to be built on the acceptance of political allegiance and loyalty to the country as a whole. This loyalty was not to be based on linguistic or cultural belonging although these ought to be cherished.

In other words, Cartier promoted a unity respectful of diversity. His understanding of the Canadian experiment, and to borrow from political scientist Donald Smiley, was a "noble vision"[6] that repudiated both parochialism, majority nationalism and imperialism and that did not seek to "impose a single way of life on its citizens"[7]:

---

[5] John MacInnes & David McCrone, *Stateless Nations in the 21st Century: Scotland, Catalonia and Quebec*, SCOTTISH AFFAIRS (2001).

[6] Donald V. Smiley, THE CANADIAN POLITICAL COMMUNITY 128 (1967).

[7] Samuel LaSelva, THE MORAL FOUNDATIONS OF CANADIAN FEDERALISM: PARADOXES, ACHIEVEMENTS, AND TRAGEDIES OF NATIONHOOD 24 (1996).

Confederation would be unacceptable if French and English had come together merely to war with each other; it would be equally unacceptable if it created an all-inclusive Canadian nationalism. If Confederation was to succeed, it had to create a new kind of nationality, which Cartier called a political nationality.[8]

It should be pointed out, however, that failing in Cartier's vision were arguably values and claims that ought to give a meaning to the fact of being Canadian while being respectful of territorialized and circumscribed identities.

Cartier made it clear that French Canadians would not renounce their culture and identity albeit they would form a national community respectful of different meaning systems with which "neither the national origin, nor religion of any individual would interfere."[9]

That being stated, the advent of a political community such as the one imagined by Cartier never gained the momentum he had hoped. The period preceding the Great Depression of the 1930s, World War II and the advent of the welfare state can be depicted as a tug of war between competing political projects that were revealing different intentions.[10] Meanwhile, the central government and the member states of the emerging federation were attempting to advance their respective worldviews and to stand up for their constituents. This is why authors such as Anthony Careless have depicted this condition as being the expression of "limited identities" and made clear that Canada was not based on a single identity under which all identities were to be subsumed.[11]

A point worth mentioning is the initial central role played by the Judicial Committee of the Privy Council (JCPC) between 1867 and 1949 when the JCPC was Canada's final court of appeal (the Supreme Court of Canada took on this role as of 1949). The JCPC was instrumental in defending the right of member states and contributed to protect their "limited identities." This has surely contributed to make Quebecers strong defenders of British parliamentary traditions and practices and to encourage them to invest gradually themselves in the Canadian federation.

[8] *Id.* at 25.
[9] PARLIAMENTARY DEBATES ON THE SUBJECT OF THE CONFEDERATION OF THE BRITISH NORTH AMERICAN PROVINCES 60 (1865) Québec, Hunter, Rose and Co.
[10] Alain-G. Gagnon & R. Iacovino, FEDERALISM, CITIZENSHIP AND QUEBEC: DEBATING MULTINATIONALISM (2007) Toronto, University of Toronto Press.
[11] J.M.S. Careless, *"Limited Identities" in Canada*, 50:1 CANADIAN HISTORICAL REVIEW 1, 1–10 (1969).

Another point worth mentioning before moving to the second narrative has been the capacity of the central government along with the anglophone provinces to repackage over the years the notion of political nationality as being the expression of Canada as an all-encompassing nation.[12]

Face 2: *The Two-Nations View*

George-Étienne Cartier is the political leader who best expressed the two-nations view without renouncing to the concept of political nationality. In 1867, at the moment that Quebec entered into Confederation, Cartier made a statement that was repeated with insistence throughout the following decades: "Such is ... the significance that we must attach to this constitution, which recognizes the French-Canadian nationality. As a distinct, separate national-ity, we form a State within a State with the full use of our rights and the formal recognition of our national independence."[13] For Quebec, what mattered most through this constitutional deal, as we will see shortly, was (1) that Quebec's civil law was recognized, (2) that provincial autonomy was affirmed and (3) that matters dealing with education, social policies and linguistic matters fell under the responsibility of Quebec. Those terms were central in the eyes of French Canadians in establishing a country in which the principle of equality between the two founding peoples was guaranteed.

The dualist character of Canada is surely an image that has been used mostly by French Canadians to depict Quebec-Canada dynamics. This image illustrates Canada as the constitutional expression of a compact that brought together two nations or, stated differently, two equal peoples with minority linguistic and religious guarantees secured throughout the country as a matter of right.[14]

Historian Ramsay Cook depicted this view in the following terms:

In the attempt to protect and extend the rights of the religious and linguistic minorities, the theory of Confederation as a compact between cultures, an Anglo-French entente, was developed. According to this theory, Confederation

---

[12] Alain-G. Gagnon, THE CASE FOR MULTINATIONAL FEDERALISM: BEYOND THE ALL-ENCOMPASSING NATION (2010) Oxon, Routledge.

[13] LA MINERVE, July 1st, 1867. Quoted in Gagnon and Iacovino, op. cit, pp. 78–79.

[14] For a discussion concerning the protection of Anglophones and Protestants living in Canada East (Quebec) at the times of Confederation, consult Guy Laforest & Félix Mathieu, *Le fiduciaire, le financier et le poète: Cartier, Galt et D'Arcy McGee, in* LA CONFÉRENCE DE QUÉBEC DE 1864, 150 ANS PLUS TARD. COMPRENDRE L'ÉMERGENCE DE LA FÉDÉRATION CANADIENNE 123 (Eugénie Brouillet, Alain-G. Gagnon & Guy Laforest eds., 2016).

was a partnership of equal cultures whose rights were guarantee mutually throughout the whole Confederation. It can be said that by 1921 the doctrine of provincial rights and its compact underpinnings had gained the ascendant among Canadian politicians, and was at least partly accepted by legal scholars.[15]

While the two-nation view gained some prominence from 1867 to the end of the 1920s, it remains that English-speaking historians (among which Michael Bliss and Jack Granatstein) have tended to refer to Canada as a single nation, showing a lack of sensitivity toward constitutive components of the Canadian federation.[16]

In contrast, the young Pierre Trudeau, in reference to Canada's early history remarked in 1962 that "British Canadians gave themselves the illusion of it [equating the Canadian state with the British Canadian nation] by walling in, as far as possible, the French fact in the Quebec ghetto – whose powers were often clipped by centralizing measures – and by fighting with astonishing ferocity against all symbols which could have destroyed this illusion outside Quebec."[17]

This two-nations interpretation gives credit to the view that "Canada" came into being in 1867, through the voluntary consent of two main political communities. However, there has been a fair amount of debate on this issue as federal government representatives have attempted at different moments to reinterpret such a key *formative moment*, and suggested that "Canada" predated the creation of the four original provinces (Lower Canada, Upper Canada, Nova Scotia and New Brunswick).[18]

It is worth underlining that, upon entering the Canadian federation, Quebec possessed its own political personality and maintained some of its original powers and institutions which had been formalized almost a century before in the Quebec Act of 1774, and which had been bestowed upon it by the British Crown.[19] In addition, Quebec consented to share some of its powers while relinquishing some others with the newly formed federal government that

[15] Ramsay Cook, *Provincial Autonomy, Minority Rights and the Compact Theory, 1867–1921*, in STUDIES OF THE ROYAL COMMISSION ON BILINGUALISM AND BICULTURALISM 65 (1969) Ottawa, Queen's Printer for Canada.
[16] Alain-G. Gagnon & Xavier Dionne, *Historiographie et fédéralisme au Canada*, 9 REVISTA D'ESTUDIS AUTONOMICS I FEDERALS 10 (2009).
[17] Pierre Elliott Trudeau, FEDERALISM AND THE FRENCH CANADIANS 164 (1968).
[18] Royal Commission on Aboriginal Peoples, PARTNERS IN CONFEDERATION : ABORIGINAL PEOPLES. SELF-GOVERNEMENT AND THE CONSTITUTION (1993) Ottawa, Canadian Government Publishing.
[19] Alain-G. Gagnon & Luc Turgeon, *Managing Diversity in the Eighteenth and Nineteenth Century Canada: Québec's Constitutional Development in Light of the Scottish Experience*, 4:1 COMMONWEALTH AND COMPARATIVE POLITICS 1 (2003).

brought together four member states and the central government. James Tully has argued approvingly in connection with this point that

> The acts of confederation did not discontinue the long-standing legal and political cultures of the former colonies and impose a uniform legal and political culture, but, rather, recognized and continued their constitutional cultures in a diverse federation in which the consent of each province was given.[20]

Tully's position has been profoundly influenced by the writing of members of a school of thought rooted in legal pluralism that was clearly influenced by legal experts such as Judge Thomas Loranger and Judge P.B. Mignault. Judge Loranger had summarized his interpretation in his famous 1883 Letters on the Constitution,[21] which were later developed by P.B. Mignault.

Here is what Mignault had to say on the notions of shared, divided and common sovereignties:

> We said that the contracting parties [federal and provincial governments] divide their sovereignty and create through common and reciprocal concessions a new power which contains them without absorbing them. We must draw one essential result from this. Each state or province maintains its own existence and the powers it has not yielded to the central government. The province is not subordinate to the central government nor is the latter subordinate to the province. There is absolute equality and a common sovereignty; each government is supreme within its own jurisdiction and within the scope of its power.[22]

Michael Burgess and I have actualized with a group of federalism scholars some of those well-anchored federal ideas in *Federal Democracies*,[23] and Burgess has pursued this task in recent and powerful book entitled *In Search of the Federal Spirit*.[24]

It should be noted that this take on legal pluralism has been frequently restated and actualized by Quebec representatives throughout the last century in various judgments and by various commissions. Examples of this are provided by the Tremblay Commission (1953–1956) and the Bélanger-Campeau

[20] James Tully, *The Crisis of Identification: The Case of Canada*, 42 POLITICAL STUDIES 77, 84–85 (1994).

[21] For a solid discussion of those Letters authored by Loranger, refer to Royal Commission on Aboriginal Peoples, *supra* note 18.

[22] Cited in Cook, *supra* note 15, at 66.

[23] Michael Burgess & Alain-G, Gagnon, FEDERAL DEMOCRACIES (2010) London, Routledge.

[24] Michael Burgess, IN SEARCH OF THE FEDERAL SPIRIT: NEW THEORETICAL AND EMPIRICAL PERSPECTIVES IN COMPARATIVE FEDERALISM (2012) Oxford, Oxford University Press.

Commission (1990–1992) as well as by various constitutional bouts going as far back as 1961.

Even during constitutional discussions leading to the Meech Lake Accord the then Quebec minister of Intergovernmental Affairs, Gil Rémillard, portrayed the British North America Act as a "constitutional treaty that would permit [French Canadians] to assert themselves as a distinct people on an equal footing with the anglophone majority."[25]

So the image of Canada as a compact between two founding peoples has continued to be used by representatives of the Quebec government. Over the years, though, and especially after the 1982 patriation of the Constitution Act from Britain, the two-nations view has lost much of its momentum. This is due in good part to the fact that the central government has sought to speak on behalf of all Canadians and to impose its political authority especially after the holding of Quebec's referendum on sovereignty-association in 1980. This loss of momentum in favour of a two-nations view is also due to the fact that there has been an important schism between francophone institutions evolving in minority context outside of Quebec and the Quebec government starting in the late 1960s.[26] This is a subject that political scientists, sociologists and historians alike should explore more fully.[27]

Over time, especially with the advent of the Quiet Revolution in the early 1960s, until the patriation of the Constitution Act in 1982, Canadians and Quebecers alike have usually used the notion of dualism to depict the Canadian experiment.[28] In proceeding to the patriation from Britain in 1982, Ottawa imposed its view that Quebec ought to be considered as a province like any of the others. This constituted a major setback for defenders of Canada as a bi-national political community and is part of the explanation why Quebec has already held two constitutional referendums.[29]

Let's turn our attention now to a third way of conceiving Quebec.

---

[25] Gil Rémillard, LE FÉDÉRALISME CANADIEN 112 (1980).

[26] Marcel Martel, Le débat de l'existence et de la disparition du Canada français: état des lieux, in ASPECTS DE LA NOUVELLE FRANCOPHONIE CANADIENNE 129 (Simon Langlois & Jocelyn Létourneau eds., 2003).

[27] RETOUR SUR LES ÉTATS GÉNÉRAUX DU CANADA FRANÇAIS: CONTINUITÉS ET RUPTURES D'UN PROJET NATIONAL (Joseph Yvon Thériault & Jean-François Laniel eds., 2016).

[28] Mason Wade & Jean-Charles Falardeau, LA DUALITÉ CANADIENNE: ESSAIS SUR LES RELATIONS ENTRE CANADIENS FRANÇAIS ET CANADIENS ANGLAIS/CANADIAN DUALISM: STUDIES OF FRENCH-ENGLISH RELATIONS (1960) Québec, Les Presses de l'Université Laval, University of Toronto Press.

[29] For an excellent comparative study on the conditions necessary for holding a constitutional referendum, consult Stephen Tierney, CONSTITUTIONAL REFERENDUMS: THE THEORY AND PRACTICE OF REPUBLICAN DELIBERATION (2014) Oxford, Oxford University Press.

Face 3: *Distinct Society*

By distinct society people have meant to convey the idea that Quebec possesses a specific culture in North America: a culture that has been shaped principally by its French language, its catholic heritage, its civil law tradition and its British parliamentary institutions. Over the years, the notion of distinct society has been transformed to mean a deeper commitment to public policies founded on a more pronounced solidarity in the areas of education, daycare, third-sector economy as well as regional development and fiscal policy.

Notions such as *special status* for Quebec or Quebec as forming a *distinct society* have often times been viewed with distrust by partners in the federation as they could constitute a slippery slope pointing towards Quebec's secession. Pierre Trudeau was very keen to oppose the concept of the distinct society during his tenure as Canada's Prime Minister as well as during the Meech Lake Accord debates as he chose to side with its opponents.

However, historian Ramsay Cook reminds us that the idea of Quebec as a distinct society has been present in Canada ever since the very beginning of Confederation, although we should stress that the use of the notion has been popularized only during the last half of the twentieth century. For example, Cook wrote that:

> Section 94 recognized the civil law of Quebec as distinct and, if the intent expressed in that provision had been fulfilled ("uniformity of all and any laws relative to Property and Civil Rights" in all provinces except Quebec), Quebec would have had a "special status" in that area. In addition the special character of Quebec was recognized in Section 133 which not only made French, for the first time, an official language of Canada, but also made Quebec alone among the original provinces, bilingual.[30]

The notion of distinct society entered political milieus in the late-1950s in the aftermath of the Tremblay Commission (1953–1956) as Quebec's provincial political parties were trying to identify the best ways to assert Quebec's place within the Canadian federation. Public intellectuals and politicians rallied together with the aim to make clear to other partners in the Canadian federation that Quebec needed empowering instruments to protect its institutions, values and culture, all of which made Quebec so unique in North America.

Over the years, the notion of distinct society has been interpreted by rival groups either as a dangerous concept that could lead to Canada's dismantlement (historians Michael Behiels, Michael Bliss, Jack Gratnastein) or else, by

[30] Cook, *supra* note 15, at 149–50.

Quebec independentists, as a political trick that could only bring about cosmetic constitutional changes that could in no way satisfy Quebec's political claims. In other words, the concept has been disqualified both by nationalist Canadians and nationalist Quebecers for opposite reasons contributing to discredit the notion amongst the two main language communities.[31]

Some efforts were made over the years to sensitize Canadians to the presence of Quebec as a distinct society. It is worth pointing at two of Ottawa's initiatives: the Special Joint Committee of the Senate and the House of Commons on the Constitution (especially through its 1972 minority report) and the Task Force on Canadian Unity known as the Pepin-Robarts Commission (1977–1979).

At the time that the Report of the Laurendeau-Dunton Commission was tabled, Ottawa decided to convene a federal-provincial conference in 1968 with a view to revamp the Constitution. Ottawa also struck a Special Joint Committee of the Senate and of the House of Commons on the Constitution to appraise potential changes. That committee tabled its report in March 1972. What matters here is not as much its main report but the Minority report that was signed by Martial Asselin and Pierre De Bané. Both opposed the main report since it did not mention that Quebec constitutes a distinct society in Canada. Here is what they wrote: "Nevertheless ... Quebec's society forms a distinct entity, and one in which is gradually realizing that it cannot achieve its fullest development without a freedom for action and the presence of certain psychological conditions which it lacks at the present time."[32] The two authors also heavily criticized the main report (and the Canadian Constitution) for the reason that "nowhere does it recognize the existence of a distinct Quebec society, a shortcoming which has real consequences."[33]

It is worth mentioning that this Minority report was received coldly in Ottawa and that indeed most MPs chose to ignore it. Nevertheless, with hindsight, we can say that Asselin and De Bané had clearly identified a fundamental shortcoming of the Canadian constitution.

Following the election of the Parti Québécois government in Quebec, in November 1976, the central government launched its Task Force on Canadian Unity that would bring to the fore the concepts of regionalism and dualism. Members of the Task force wrote extensively on the fact that Quebec

---

[31] James Bickerton, *Janus Faces, Rocks, and Hard Places: Majority Nationalism in Canada*, in Contemporary Majority Nationalism 144 (Alain-G. Gagnon, André Lecours & Geneviève Nootens eds., 2011).

[32] Pierre De Bané & Martial Asselin, Special Joint Committee of the Senate and of the House of Commons on the Constitution, A Minority Report 8 (1972).

[33] *Id.* at 10.

forms a distinct society, stressing that "Quebec is distinctive and should, within a viable Canada, have the powers necessary to protect and develop its distinctive character, any political solution short of this would lead to the rupture of Canada."[34] Language politics was specifically targeted by the task force that gave its endorsement to the Quebec government's language politics, namely Law 101, backing "efforts of the Quebec provincial government and the people of Quebec to ensure the predominance of the French language and culture in that province."[35] This position was in sharp opposition with the one adopted by the Liberal Party of Canada starting with the leadership of Pierre Trudeau in 1968.

Members of the Task Force were of the view that their report might be perceived as an encouragement for the development of asymmetrical federalism. To avoid this, they recommended to give all provinces the possibility to act within the same sphere of jurisdictions since, to do otherwise, would be resisted in other parts of Canada. They suggested granting "to all the provinces powers in the areas needed by Quebec to maintain its distinctive culture and heritage."[36] As a result, Quebec's status as a distinct society would be granted to all provinces if their recommendations were to be adopted.[37] It is worth noting that none of those powers were ever identified so as to give Ottawa significant leeway in its negotiation with the provinces. In brief, the Quebec's status as a distinct society was considered to be applicable to all provinces.

Face 4: *Province State*

For many decades, it has been acknowledged that Quebec is not a province like any other. That said, it remains clear that Quebec has been at the forefront of political battles to uphold provincial rights in the country since its very foundation. In fairness to other provinces, Quebec was never alone in doing so. It has been accompanied by various provincial partners at different historical junctures, though over the past several decades more often than not it has been Alberta and Newfoundland that have joined Quebec at the forefront in defending their provincial rights and political autonomy.

Keith Brownsey and Michael Howlett have introduced the notion of *province state* to depict provinces in Canada since "they qualify as states.

---

[34] Task Force on Canadian Unity, A FUTURE TOGETHER: OBSERVATIONS AND RECOMMENDATIONS 87 (1979).

[35] *Id.* at 51.   [36] *Id.* at 87.

[37] Alain-G. Gagnon, *La condition canadienne et les montées du nationalisme et du régionalisme, in* LE DÉBAT QUI N'A PAS EU LIEU. LA COMMISSION PEPIN-ROBARTS QUELQUE VINGT ANS APRÈS 105 (Jean-Pierre Wallot ed., 2002).

Not only are they constitutionally empowered to make binding decisions on their residents, they are shaped and defined by the very constitutional arrangements that give them their authority as much as they are by their internal class structures and external economic relations."[38] These authors made the valuable point that Canadian provinces and territories share significant institutional features that amount to state power. However, they fail to recognize the fact that Quebec is the only member of the federation that can fully be depicted as a *province state* since the principal focus of statehood is international; unlike other provinces, Quebec aspires to play a central role within the francophonie as well as being a leader, among minority nations, in the world seeking to obtain a larger political status.

There is an important stream of political science literature that insists on the central role of Quebec as a historic champion of provincial rights. While that story is generally well-known by English-speaking Canadians, it needs to be underlined here considering its influence in the defense of provincial autonomy and the non-subordination of government powers – two central features of federalism.

The Confederation of 1867 embodies a strong defense of provincial rights since the constitution confirmed that powers were to be shared between a central state and provincial states, all which were to be accountable for their own spheres of jurisdiction before their population. A convention developed that the British North America (BNA) Act provided both the central and provincial governments with exclusive jurisdictions in those domains that were essential to their particular interests. This interpretation emerges clearly from the Quebec resolutions (known also as the *Confederation proposals*). Quebecers cling to their own world-view on this interpretation of Confederation, and ever since then have asked that the spirit of 1867 be respected by its partners, translated into appropriate political institutions and reflected in power relations.

The most refined depiction of Canada as a compact of provinces was provided by Judge Loranger, one of Quebec's most influential jurists, who published a series of constitutional texts in 1883 that will have had a long-lasting effect on Canada's jurisprudence. The most recent echoes can be found in the 1993 and 1995 reports tabled by the Royal Commission on Aboriginal Peoples.[39] The basic premises of Loranger's account of provincial rights are threefold:

---

[38] Keith Brownsey & Michael Howlett, THE PROVINCIAL STATE IN CANADA: POLITICS IN THE PROVINCES AND TERRITORIES 14 (2009).

[39] Royal Commission on Aboriginal Peoples, *supra* note 18, at 22–23.

- The confederation made up of the British provinces was the result of a compact entered into by the provinces and the United Kingdom.
- The provinces entered into the federal union with their corporate identity, former constitutions and all their legislative powers intact. A portion of these powers was ceded to the federal Parliament, to exercise in the common interest of the provinces. The powers not ceded were retained by the provinces' legislatures, which continued to act within their own sphere according to their former constitutions, under certain modifications or form established by the federal compact.
- Far from having been conferred upon them by the federal government, the powers of the provinces are the residue of their former colonial powers. The federal government is the creation of the provinces, the result of their association and of their compact.

This interpretation laid the foundation for a school of thought supportive of provincial rights and provincial autonomy, exerting much influence within Quebec and some other provinces over the years. It is particularly noteworthy that Loranger's account has virtually gone unchallenged in Quebec. In contrast, many political leaders in ROC and centralizing federalists have usually rejected this view and argued instead that provinces are simply the creation of the central government and therefore subservient to it. At times, this fundamental disagreement created an uneasy relationship between certain provinces and the central government, as illustrated by intense conflicts between Ontario and Ottawa from the 1870s to the 1940s.

Before World War II, Liberal party leaders such as Wilfrid Laurier and Mackenzie King were inclined to support provincial rights as long as they did not weaken Ottawa's political leadership and authority. However, this defense of provincial rights at the federal level declined after World War II as a succession of Prime Ministers (mostly Liberal) sought to invest the central government in Ottawa with a domineering power position; this was especially the case under the leadership of Pierre Trudeau and Jean Chrétien.

The 1956 report of the Quebec Royal Commission of Inquiry on Constitutional Problems (the Tremblay Commission) was inspired by the Loranger doctrine. In that report, emphasis was given to the concepts of provincial autonomy and proper coordination between orders of government.[40] Both autonomy and coordination were to operate in tandem; otherwise the federal spirit would not be fully expressed. Based on this understanding, it was

---

[40] François Rocher, *The Quebec-Canada Dynamics or the Negation of the Ideal of Federalism*, *in* CONTEMPORARY CANADIAN FEDERALISM 81 (A.-G. Gagnon ed., 2009).

possible (and perhaps even a duty) for a member state of the federation to refuse central government assistance to fully exercise its responsibilities as agreed to in the original compact. Building on the principle of subsidiarity and influenced by the social doctrine of the Catholic Church, the Tremblay Report argued that higher levels of authority should not seek to exercise powers that can be employed more effectively at lower levels. The Report stated:

> Only federalism as a political system permits two cultures to live and develop side by side within a single state: that was the real reason for the Canadian state's federative form ... So, therefore, there can be no federalism without autonomy of the state's constituent parts, and no sovereignty of the various governments without fiscal and financial autonomy.[41]

The Tremblay Report provided additional philosophical support to Loranger's earlier arguments. It is this historical and philosophical grounding that has made Quebec's constitutional position so powerful and persistent, to the point that the First Nations have built their arguments upon it to advance their own claims for self-government, as have provinces such as Alberta and Newfoundland when seeking to defend provincial autonomy.

The Quiet Revolution pursued similar autonomist ambitions for Quebec and pushed them much further than at any time before.[42] This approach, known as the Gérin-Lajoie doctrine, argued for the extension of provincial jurisdictions beyond the borders of Canada: that is, any provincial competence could be exercised vis-à-vis other provinces or nation-states as long as Quebec (or any provincial state) was willing to assume its sovereign powers in areas of exclusive provincial jurisdiction.[43]

The Gérin-Lajoie doctrine attempted to shore up the role of Quebec as a province state by giving substance and meaning to Quebec's special status within Confederation. This doctrine was elaborated toward the end of the second Lesage government in the mid 1960s and has been revamped at different critical moments under successive Quebec governments, whether liberal in orientation under Premiers Robert Bourassa and Jean Charest or inclined toward social democracy under René Lévesque and Pauline Marois.

The Gérin-Lajoie doctrine remains to this day a constitutional position universally agreed to by key provincial actors in Quebec, and it confirms

---

[41] Cited in David Kwavnick, THE TREMBLAY REPORT: REPORT OF THE ROYAL COMMISSION OF INQUIRY ON CONSTITUTIONAL PROBLEMS, 209, 215 (1973).

[42] Gagnon and Montcalm, *supra* note 4.

[43] Stéphane Paquin, LES RELATIONS INTERNATIONALES DU QUÉBEC DEPUIS LA DOCTRINE GÉRIN-LAJOIE (1965–2005). LE PROLONGEMENT EXTERNE DES COMPÉTENCES INTERNES (2006) Québec, Presses de l'Université Laval.

Quebec's intention to play a central role in Confederation. Brian Mulroney's decision to grant Quebec the status of a participating government in the Francophonie starting in 1985 was inspired by the respect he had for the Gérin-Lajoie doctrine. One could make a similar remark with respect to Stephen Harper's decision to allow Quebec to play a significant role within the Canadian delegation at UNESCO starting in 2006.

Quebec has been (and continues to be) at the forefront of battles to defend provincial rights, to prevent Ottawa from intruding into provincial domains of competence and to roll back such intrusion where it has already occurred. The best example is provided by the leadership role played by Quebec in the establishment of the Council of the Federation in 2003, in large part due to the determination of Quebec's former minister of Intergovernmental Affairs, Benoît Pelletier. During his tenure, Pelletier continued to push for the notion of provincial autonomy and made it palatable to government leaders in many other provinces. He spoke at dozens of meetings across the country during the years that followed the election of the first Charest government in 2003, making an important statement at each:

> In its universal aspect, the federal formula implies the existence of two orders of government, each being sovereign in the exercise of their constitutional jurisdictions. However, certain conditions must be met in order for any federation to be able to function and evolve in a healthy manner:
>
> 1. There must be a balanced distribution of powers between the two orders of government.
> 2. Each order of government must have the capacity in terms of tax resources, to fully and adequately assume its responsibilities. No order of government should find itself in a position of financial dependence vis-à-vis the other.
> 3. The provinces must have the possibility to express their views on the governance of the federation and have a certain influence on the federal legislative process. As an example, this could be accomplished through a truly effective second house of the Federal Parliament, or other equivalent body, where the provinces could assert their points of view and, in so doing, have a real and positive influence on the future of our federation.
> 4. Effective mechanisms must be put in place to foster intergovernmental dialogue in sectors where convergence is required between a priori divergent interests.[44]

---

[44] Benoît Pelletier, *The State of Our Federation. A Québec Perspective*, Speech given during a luncheon organized by the Canada West Foundation (March 24, 2004).

Quebec has advanced the cause of provincial rights through different means since the end of World War II. Let's mention a few constitutional and political battles that have taken place since then: on the fiscal front, Quebec has fought to regain control over postwar tax-rental agreements and to expand its fiscal powers; on the constitutional front, Quebec has supported the idea of granting all provinces a right of veto over constitutional changes on different occasions (the 1966 Fulton/Favreau amending formula and again at the Patriation conference in November 1981); on the social union front, Quebec has insisted that each and every province could exercise its right to withdraw from pan-Canadian programs that fell within provincial jurisdiction, with full compensation.

Face 5: *Multinational Democracy*

To complete our sketch, let's examine the image of Quebec as a multinational democracy. At least four elements contribute to give shape to this emerging type of political association. And here I am particularly influenced and inspired by the pioneering work that Canadian philosopher James Tully has done.[45]

First, as a modern type of political association, a multinational democracy contains more than one nation. Minimally, members of these nations have the right to exercise internal self-determination and to engage in continuous deliberations and negotiations with a view to develop relations based on trust between partners. Representatives of these nations are free to seek recognition in international forums.

Comparativist Michael Keating makes a couple good points with respect to the view that self-determination does not necessarily lead to political secession. For Keating, there is "no logical reason why self-determination should be linked to statehood, apart from the entrenched dogmas of sovereignty discourse ... Another way of looking at self-determination is to see it as the right to negotiate one's position within the state and supranational order, without necessarily setting up a separate state."[46] We will come back to this second point shortly.

We are very far from the standard Westphalian model that conceives democracies as forming a *demos* with "internal, subnational 'minorities'

---

[45] In addition, one can also consult an important collection of essays edited by Michael C. van Walt van Praag & Onno Seroo, THE IMPLEMENTATION OF THE RIGHT TO SELF-DETERMINATION AS A CONTRIBUTION TO CONFLICT PREVENTION. Centre UNESCO de Catalunya (1999).

[46] Michael Keating, PLURINATIONAL DEMOCRACY: STATELESS NATIONS IN A POST-SOVEREIGNTY ERA 10 (2001).

seeking group rights within but societies of two or more, often overlapping nations that are more or less equal in status."[47]

Second, multinational democracies are also characterized by the fact that they form plural societies. Such is the case in Quebec. A concrete expression of this was given on 20 March 1985 when the Quebec National Assembly adopted a resolution recognizing the existence of the Abenaki, Algonquin, Attikamek, Cree, Huron, Micmac, Mohawk, Montagnais, Naskapi and Inuit nations.[48] An eleventh nation, the Malecites, was recognized in 1989. In connection with this interpretation of Quebec as constituting a plural society, Tully goes as far as saying that in such contexts "The jurisdictions, modes of participation and representation, and the national and multinational identities of citizens overlap and are subject to negotiation."[49]

Third, multinational democracies adopt the principles of constitutional democracy, which challenge the norm of a democratic setting founded on a single-nation. As such, this "multinational association rests on their adherence to the legal and political values, principles and rights of constitutional democracy and international law."[50]

Fourth, multinational democracies need to develop institutions that contribute to bring members and representative of the various nations in permanent contact while encouraging political exchanges. In the case of Quebec,[51] one can view the politics of interculturalism[52] as a clear expression of this desire to erect a polity founded on interconnectedness among societal partners and between citizens.

So far, Quebec's main political parties have been too slow in seeking to empower the Inuit and the ten Aboriginal nations. Arguably, Quebec's National Assembly has been a leader in identifying avenues for economic and social development of the North of Quebec, territory traditionally inhabited by many First Nations, but much more needs to be done to extirpate the colonial heritage which for too long dominated relations between Quebec and its original peoples. Denys Delâge aptly reminds us that "current Aboriginal leaders are

---

[47] James Tully, *Introduction, in* MULTINATIONAL DEMOCRACIES 1, 3 (A.-G. Gagnon and J. Tully, eds., 2001).

[48] For a solid discussion of Quebec's evolving policy in autochthonous matters, refer to Éric Gourdeau, *Quebec and the Aboriginal Question, in* QUEBEC: STATE AND SOCIETY 349 (A.-G. Gagnon ed., 2nd ed. 1993).

[49] Tully, *supra* note 47, at 3.   [50] *Id.*

[51] LES CONDITIONS DU DIALOGUE AU QUÉBEC: LAÏCITÉ, RÉCIPROCITÉ, PLURALISME (Alain-G. Gagnon & Jean-Charles St-Louis eds., 2016).

[52] Gérard Bouchard & Charles Taylor, BUILDING THE FUTURE: A TIME FOR RECONCILIATION (2008) Québec, Gouvernement du Québec.

more involved in fighting for their rights rather than in engaging in an overall questioning of the colonial system that constrains them ... The goal would be for aboriginal people to escape the colonial heritage of wardship and the denial of access to full citizenship."[53]

The pursuit of such objectives would contribute to bring Quebecers of all origins together with a purpose to building a better and a fairer world for all to share.

QUEBEC IN A COMPARATIVE CONTEXT

Nation-states and in particular multinational states are increasingly experiencing a pressing need for discourses that propose institutional accommodations with a view to maintain and, in some cases, even re-establish the bonds of trust between national communities. With respect to the Canadian case, I have argued elsewhere that the intrinsic legitimacy of the federation is founded on its multinational character.[54] Relying on the fact that Quebec constitutes a historical national community, such as Galicia and Catalonia in Spain, or Scotland and Wales in the United Kingdom, I have also asserted that asymmetrical federalism is a potential avenue to find a mid-way solution to accommodate Quebecers. Needless to say, a better equilibrium between autonomy (self-rule) and shared sovereignty is an essential condition for retaining Quebec in the Canadian federation with free will and enthusiasm.

Quebec is a host society in its own right, with its own historical and cultural development, its own sense of nationhood as well as with a distinct discourse with regard to the general orientations and choices of society. Constituting a distinct political community with a well-defined inclusive collective cultural project, Quebec needs to have the political instruments to integrate immigrants into its national fabric. Quebec, I would argue, requires specific powers in order to have the capacity to respond adequately to its own emerging challenges with respect to the integration of immigrants, to its place in the world economy, to its role within the *Francophonie* and, to name only a few, to the expansion of its social policies.

---

[53] Denis Delâge, *Quebec and Aboriginal People*, in VIVE QUEBEC: NEW THINKING AND NEW APPROACHES TO THE QUEBEC NATION 127, 135 (Michel Venne ed., 2001)

[54] Alain-G. Gagnon, *The Moral Foundations of Asymmetrical Federalism: A Normative Exploration of the Case of Quebec and Canada*, in MULTINATIONAL DEMOCRACIES 319 (Alain-G. Gagnon & James Tully eds., 2001); Alain-G. Gagnon & François Rocher, *Nationalisme libéral et construction multinationale de la nation dans la dynamique Québec-Canada*, 16 INTERNATIONAL JOURNAL OF CANADIAN STUDIES 51 (1997).

This is not an issue of narcissism as it was once referred to by Michael Ignatieff in *Blood and Belonging: Journeys into the New Nationalism of Small Nations.*[55] Quebecers have made serious efforts at informing their countrymen of their aspirations over the years. As André Laurendeau, co-chair the Canadian Royal Commission on Bilingualism and Biculturalism (1963–1968) stated, Quebecers who happen to be strong proponents of individual rights and freedoms felt that self-government over jurisdictions such as language, immigration, education and social policy, among others, was essential before they could live under the same conditions of existence as other Canadians.[56]

At stake are questions of recognition and rights, as has been so convincingly argued by James Tully in *Strange Multiplicity: Constitutionalism in an Age of Diversity.*[57] However, no one could have predicted that it was a question of time before Michael Ignatieff revised his position. In *The Rights Revolution*, as part of the CBC Massey Lecture Series inviting distinguished authorities to present their views, Ignatieff has significantly modified his take on the question, and now defends a position that is hardly distinguishable from the one supported by James Tully.

Indeed, Ignatieff argues, with reference to the Canadian case, that "At the moment, might lies with the majority and right with the minority. Mutual recognition must rebalance the relationship, with both power and legitimacy finding a new equilibrium. Then, and only then, will we be able to live together in peace in two countries at once, a community of rights-bearing equals and a community of self-governing nations."[58]

It is interesting to note that Ignatieff, whose views are generally taken as cosmopolitan, has now turned his attention to discourses which emphasize communities in proximity. Ignatieff goes on to make an important argument about reciprocity that Quebec autonomists and nationalists alike should take the time to appraise.

According to Ignatieff,

Quebec is entitled to recognition as a distinctive society and its language laws, immigration statutes, and education provisions should be different in order to protect what is different about the province...

[55] Michael Ignatieff, Blood and Belonging. Journeys into the New Nationalism (1993) Toronto, Penguin.
[56] Alain-G. Gagnon, *La pensée d'André Laurendeau: communauté, égalité et liberté*, 10 Cahiers d'histoire du Québec au XXᴱ siècle 31 (2000).
[57] James Tully, Strange Multiplicity. Constitutionalism in an Age of Diversity (1995) Cambridge, Cambridge University Press.
[58] Michael Ignatieff, The Rights Revolution 84 (2000).

Yet recognition of distinctiveness does not have to fragment the country.
What ought to balance these distinctive provisions is a politics of reciprocity.
If Quebec is granted certain rights in respect to its language and culture, the
rest of the country has a right to expect the province to protect the cultures,
languages, and religions of its minorities. Reciprocity rather than strict sym-
metry for all is the way to move beyond a politics of concession and threat
into a process of mutual recognition, in which each side acknowledges the
distinctiveness of the other.[59]

The latest work by Ignatieff leads me to believe that like the Westphalian
approach, the cosmopolitan approach is being called into question. It is thus
important to understand the evolving discourses to assess transformations
under way. I would contend that concepts such as the multination (United
Kingdom), historical regions (Spain) and the national space or even the
notion of province state (Quebec) represent discursive tools that allow us to
probe and appraise the challenges that these societies must address.

The advantage of encouraging Quebec to act as a proper deliberative
community within a multinational federal state is that it avoids the essential-
ist/primordialist trap while expanding democracy. Doing otherwise by encouraging a post-national or a post-sovereign world would be to allow Canadian
democracy to shrink through a strategy of estrangement. Providing Quebecers
means by which they can make decisions of their own choosing allow them to
be political actors rather than subjects within their own country. The national
form should not be abandoned since it is the primary basis on which democracies are established; it is a means by which citizens can be empowered most
efficiently, and finally it is a tool by which citizens can gather social cohesion.

Several challenges must still be discussed with regards to the establishment of this Quebec space, as it remains a project in construction. The
endurance of such challenges also reveals that important links between civil
society and political forces need to be renewed on a daily basis, and requires
an assurance that every Quebec citizen is included in the construction of the
national project.

The urgency of persisting with the affirmation of such a political space
becomes evident when we recognize that territory remains one of the rare
areas within liberal democracies where it is still possible to maintain representation and to force political actors to be accountable. Quebec as a province
state, short of being a nation-state, can serve at once as a hub of relations of
solidarity and as an expression for democratic practices. Nevertheless, it must

[59] *Id.* at 120.

be assured that the province state does not become a consuming project, and that defenders of diversity and difference remain at liberty to pursue their own ends.

I have attempted to illustrate that tensions between nations constitute an healthy expression of democratic practices since they contribute to forge identities. Challenges emerging from nations in nationalizing states are clear reminder of a new trend, and ought to be taken seriously and addressed positively rather than being viewed as threatening for the stability of political regimes. Philosopher Chantal Mouffe's comment to the effect that "the prime task of democratic politics is not to eliminate passions nor to relegate them to the private sphere in order to render rational consensus possible, but to mobilise those passions towards the promotion of democratic designs. Far from jeopardizing democracy, agonistic confrontation is in fact its very condition of existence."[60] In other words, political frictions and tensions between national identities are essential for the enlargement of democratic practices and more diverse systems of representation.

BY WAY OF CONCLUSION

In this presentation, I have analyzed what appear to me as the five prevailing faces used to depict Quebec, namely: Quebec as a political nationality, as a founding nation, as a distinct society, as a province state and, finally, as a multinational democracy. Each of these faces tends to propose and promote different characteristics and suggest a unique worldview with particular meaning systems. Viewing the world through one or the other of these prisms matters a great deal.

Also, these various portrayals of Quebec suggest different takes on the relations of power. The use of those images are not insignificant as we are reminded by E.E. Schattsscheider who argues that "the definition of alternatives [read faces] is the supreme instrument of power; the antagonists can rarely agree on what the issues are because power is involved in the definition. **He who determines what politics is about runs the country, because the definition of the alternatives is the choice of conflicts and the choice of conflicts allocates power.**"[61] So, he who determines the face of politics being used gives a special meaning to policy preferences and power arrangements.

---

[60] Chantal Mouffe, *Deliberative Democracy or Agonistic Pluralism*, 66:3 SOCIAL RESEARCH 745, 755–756 (1999).
[61] Elmer Eric Schnattsschneider, THE SEMISOVEREIGN PEOPLE: A REALIST'S VIEW OF DEMOCRACY IN AMERICA 66 (1983).

To conclude, and to return to the point made by Richard Simeon in my introduction, it is clear that defining concepts has consequences that go to the very core of a society and that can tilt the balance all of sudden as we have been reminded in 1982[62] at the time of the patriation and the establishment of a new constitutional order in Canada.

---

[62] For a critical account of the patriation of the Constitutional Act in 1982, consult LE NOUVEL ORDRE CONSTITUTIONNEL CANADIEN (François Rocher & Benoît Pelletier eds., 2013).

4

Indigenous Peoples and the Canadian State

The Prospects of a Postcolonial Constitutional Pluralism

PATRICK MACKLEM

Scholars refer to "legal pluralism" as a concept that denotes the existence of a plurality of legal orders existing within or across the territorial boundaries of a sovereign state.[1] Many institutional mechanisms give formal expression to the presence of a plurality of legal orders. A federal system constitutionally vests lawmaking authority in two levels of government, each relatively autonomous from the other in the production of legal norms. A state can also devolve power to regional and local levels of government, enabling the exercise of delegated lawmaking authority to a subsection of its population. Forms of minority protection may also promote legal pluralism, to the extent that they contemplate a minority community having a measure of lawmaking authority relatively shielded from the legislative power of the broader political community in which it is located.

Canada manifests strong commitments, in theory[2] and in practice, to legal pluralism. The most obvious example lies in the federal nature of its constitutional

---

This paper draws from Patrick Macklem, "Indigenous Peoples and the Ethos of Legal Pluralism in Canada," in P. Macklem and Douglas Sanderson (eds), FROM RECOGNITION TO RECONCILIATION: ESSAYS ON THE CONSTITUTIONAL ENTRENCHMENT OF ABORIGINAL & TREATY RIGHTS (Toronto: University of Toronto Press, 2016) 17–34.

[1] See Bruce Duthu, SHADOW NATIONS: TRIBAL SOVEREIGNTY AND THE LIMITS OF LEGAL PLURALISM (New York: Oxford University Press, 2013) 11–12 ("the legal pluralist is intensely interested in identifying the forms of normative ordering, including legal systems, that have meaning to the socially plural societies occupying the same social field and examining the operation of those normative ordering systems in relation to the power of the state"). For more discussion of legal pluralism, see Paul Schiff Berman, GLOBAL LEGAL PLURALISM: A JURISPRUDENCE OF LAW BEYOND BORDERS (Cambridge: Cambridge University Press, 2012); Boaventura de Sousa Santos, TOWARD A NEW LEGAL COMMON SENSE: LAW, GLOBALIZATION AND EMANCIPATION (2002); Carol Weisbrod, EMBLEMS OF PLURALISM: CULTURAL DIFFERENCES AND THE LAW (2002); William Connolly, THE ETHOS OF PLURALIZATION (Minneapolis: University of Minnesota Press, 1995).

[2] See Roderick A. MacDonald, *Metaphors of Multiplicity: Civil Society, Regimes and Legal Pluralism*, 15 ARIZ. J. INT'L & COMP. L. 69 (1998); Tim Schouls, SHIFTING BOUNDARIES:

order, which divides legislative, executive and judicial power between two levels of government each sovereign within their spheres of authority, protecting the distinctive cultural and linguistic identity of Quebeçois people by making them a majority in the province in which they reside. Many point to the federal nature of the Canadian state as a contributing factor to the rise of a secessionist movement in Québec by hardening cultural and linguistic differences into legal entitlements, and by empowering political actors to capitalize on national, ethnic, religious and linguistic differences to gain political power. But Canadian federalism as an instrument that fosters "exit" is supplemented by a set of countervailing constitutional arrangements designed to foster "voice" in national institutions, including a commitment to bilingualism, guaranteed seats on the Supreme Court of Canada for judges from Quebec, and extensive representation of Quebec in the House of Commons and Senate.

A less familiar commitment to legal pluralism lies in the constitutional relationship between Indigenous peoples and the Canadian state. But the legal pluralism relevant in this context is one where the sources of legal validity themselves are plural in nature. In the above examples, norms produced by legal actors other than the central government appear to possess legal validity by a plurality of sources. A provincial law is legally valid because it was enacted by a legislature possessing jurisdiction to enact it. A municipal bylaw is legally valid because it was enacted in accordance with relevant enabling legislation. A law promulgated by a minority community possesses legal validity because the community has a legal right to promulgate it. But ultimately the legal validity of each of these norms is derived from a singular source, the constitution of the state itself. In contrast, the legal pluralism that captures salient properties of Indigenous-settler relations is one of constitutional pluralism, to use Jean Cohen's phrase, where there exists a plurality of constitutional orders within and, conceivably, across state boundaries. In such an environment, there are multiple legal norms of different content, multiple sites of legal norm production, multiple legal sources for these sites and multiple forms of norm enforcement. As a result, "legal reality," according to John Griffiths, is "an unsystematic collage of inconsistent and overlapping parts, lending itself to no easy legal interpretation."[3]

ABORIGINAL IDENTITY, PLURALIST THEORY, AND THE POLITICS OF SELF-GOVERNMENT (Vancouver: University of Vancouver Press, 2003).

[3] John Griffiths, *What Is Legal Pluralism?*, 24 J. LEG. PLURALISM 1, 4 (1986). Legal scholars, myself included, often cite this article as a classic articulation of legal pluralism. David Schneiderman's work on the British legal and political pluralists, including F.W. Maitland, Harold Laski and John Neville Figgis, of the early twentieth century reveals Griffiths to have

At the time of initial contact between Indigenous peoples and Imperial powers and their colonial representatives, "legal reality" appeared receptive to an ethos of constitutional pluralism. Manifold Indigenous legal orders exercised lawmaking authority over territories and peoples in the Americas. The legal norms that constituted these legal orders specified and regulated the economic, social and political practices of individuals and groups belonging to distinct Indigenous nations as well as relations between and among Indigenous nations. The legal validity of these norms lay in the nature of the legal orders from which they emanated. European settlement imported colonial legal norms whose validity ultimately depended on the legal systems of France and the United Kingdom. Colonial settlement also marked the genesis of a series of intersocietal encounters, some friendly, others hostile, with mistrust, trust, suspicion and expectation alike participating in the formation of a pluralist ethos characteristic of their relations. In the words of Jeremy Webber, "the distinctive norms of each society furnished the point of departure, determining the spirit of interaction, colouring the first interpretations of the other's customs, and shaping the beginning of a common normative language."[4]

Contact thus set the stage for constitutionally plural relationships between Indigenous peoples and colonial powers. Treaties negotiated early in the history of European expansion formalized efforts to achieve peaceful coexistence between Indigenous nations and newcomers to the continent. A 1665 peace treaty between the French Crown and four Indigenous nations belonging to the Iroquois Confederacy, for example, confirmed a cessation of conflict and a state of peace between the parties. The text of the treaty indirectly acknowledged the First Nations' continuing title to their territories and certain territorial rights of the French Crown in the settlements of Montréal, Trois-Rivières and Québec City.[5]

It would be a stretch, I think, to construe the 1665 treaty and others like it as formal evidence of a strong ethos of constitutional pluralism animating

---

been a relative latecomer to the field. *See* David Schneiderman, *Harold Laski, Viscount Haldane, and the Law of the Canadian Constitution in the Early Twentieth Century*, 48 U.T.L.J. 521 (1998); David Schneiderman, *Haldane Unrevealed*, 57 McGILL L.J. 593 (2012).

4   Jeremy Webber, *Relations of Force and Relations of Justice: The Emergence of Normative Community between Colonists and Aboriginal Peoples*, 33 OSGOODE HALL L.J. 623, 627(1995).

5   *Treaty of Peace between the Iroquois and Governor de Tracy*, New York Papers 111 A28. The text of the treaty can be found in Clive Parry, ed., THE CONSOLIDATED TREATY SERIES (Dobbs Ferry: Oceana. 1969–1986), vol. IX, at 363; and E.B. O'Callaghan, ed., DOCUMENTS RELATIVE TO THE COLONIAL HISTORY OF THE STATE OF NEW YORK (Albany: Weed, Parsons, 1856–61), vol. III, at 21. For more discussion of the treaty, *see* Royal Commission on Aboriginal Peoples, TREATY MAKING IN THE SPIRIT OF CO-EXISTENCE: AN ALTERNATIVE TO EXTINGUISHMENT (Ottawa: Minister of Supply and Services Canada, 1995), at 18–20.

relations between Indigenous and colonial legal orders. "Legal reality" likely becomes constitutionally plural gradually, as repeated interactions deepen inter-societal commitments to plural legal orders. But the early treaties do suggest a nascent constitutional pluralism at play among the parties. Premised on mutual recognition, they stand as formal markers of early encounters and interactions that had the potential – if deepened and multiplied – to evolve into a durable form of constitutional pluralism structuring Indigenous-settler relations on the continent.

Fast forward to today. There exist more than five hundred treaties between Indigenous peoples and the Crown in Canada from the shores of the Atlantic Ocean to the Yukon in the western Canadian Arctic. Where territories have not yet been subject to treaty, in most of British Columbia, First Nations are negotiating new treaties to structure their relationships with federal and provincial authorities. The enactment of s. 35(1) of the *Constitution Act, 1982*, which recognizes and affirms "the existing aboriginal and treaty rights of the aboriginal peoples of Canada," has ushered in significant changes to the constitutional relationship between Indigenous peoples and the Canadian state.

The promise of a "common normative language" informing this relationship, however, remains unfulfilled. There are many complex reasons for its absence – reasons that span many domains, including epistemology, economics, politics and law. But one account merits attention, even though it glosses over the complexity of what it seeks to explain. The ethos of constitutional pluralism immanent in early encounters between Indigenous and colonial peoples failed to take root and was replaced by its antithesis: a monistic account of constitutional order, with decidedly non-Indigenous sources of legal authority initially grounded in British law and subsequently grounded in the Constitution of Canada.

The question, of course, is why did constitutional pluralism fail to take root? Although the Crown initially entered into treaties with Indigenous people to secure their precarious legal and factual footing on Indigenous territories by acts of mutual recognition, the Crown began to negotiate treaties for different reasons. International law had come to stabilize claims of sovereignty by imperial powers over Indigenous territory. Constitutional law assumed a singular, hierarchical conception of sovereignty incapable of comprehending multiple sovereign actors on a given territory. As a result, the Crown no longer regarded a treaty as necessarily linked to its sovereignty over Indigenous territory.[6]

---

[6] *Compare* P.G. McHugh, ABORIGINAL SOCIETIES AND THE COMMON LAW: A HISTORY OF SOVEREIGNTY, STATUS, AND SELF-DETERMINATION (New York: Oxford University Press, 2004) ("constitutional lawyers and courts intellectually to the unitary common law model of

During the nineteenth century, perhaps as a result of the dramatic shift in demography and in the balance of military and economic power between Indigenous nations and the Crown, the treaty process from the Crown's perspective instead became a means of facilitating the relocation and assimilation of Indigenous people. The Crown increasingly saw the treaty process as a means of formally dispossessing Indigenous peoples of ancestral territory in return for reserve land and certain benefits to be provided by state authorities, rendering remote the possibility of constitutional pluralism becoming "legal reality."

Moreover, although in the early treaties signalled a nation-to-nation relationship of mutual respect, the parties did not initially regard them as creating legal rights enforceable in a court of law. Instead, the treaty served as evidence of an ongoing relationship; rights and obligations flowed not from the document itself but from the relationship formalized by the treaty.[7] This early process of generating norms of conduct and recognition operated against the backdrop of a colonial legal imagination that had yet to experience a radical separation of law and politics, in which certain issues are regarded as legal and others as political.

When law gradually emerged as a relatively autonomous sphere of social life, the judiciary began to address the legal consequences of the treaty process. Judicial interpretation of treaties only started to occur in Canada in the late 1800s, when courts held treaties to be political agreements unenforceable in a court of law. International law provides that an agreement between two "independent powers" constitutes a treaty binding on the parties to the agreement.[8] But because courts regarded Indigenous nations as uncivilized and thus not independent, they refused to view Crown promises as legally enforceable obligations under international or domestic law. This view gradually was replaced by more accommodating approach that regarded a treaty as

---

sovereignty – itself . . . largely a nineteenth-century model – were unable to recognize a shared or multiple version").

[7]   *Compare* William Blackstone, 1 COMMENTARIES ON THE LAWS OF ENGLAND (Oxford 1765–9), 428 (vision of a contract as dependent on the existence of a social relation and pre-existing rights and obligations). *See also* Patrick Atiyah, THE RISE AND FALL OF FREEDOM OF CONTRACT (Oxford: Clarendon Press, 1979), at note 40, 143 (eighteenth century legal consciousness invoked the notion of promise "to support an independently existing duty"); Owen Kahn-Freund, *Blackstone's Neglected Child: The Contract of Employment*, 93 LQR 508, 512 ("the contract is only an *accidentale*, not an *essentiale* of the relation").

[8]   *See, e.g.,* Brownlie, PRINCIPLES OF PUBLIC INTERNATIONAL LAW, *supra* note 52, at 58–70. It should be noted that, even if treaties between the Crown and First Nations constituted treaties in international law, this fact alone would not render them enforceable in domestic courts; implementing legislation would be required: *see AG Canada v. AG Ontario (Labour Conventions)*, [1937] A.C. 326 (P.C.).

a form of contract.[9] Indigenous people were imagined as possessing legal personality similar to that possessed by non-Indigenous people in Canada and were therefore capable of entering into domestically binding agreements with the Crown.

But because treaties assumed the legal form of contract, their terms were subject to the exercise of unilateral legislative authority. Prior to 1982, this had the effect of permitting legislatures to unilaterally regulate or extinguish existing treaty rights. Moreover, when courts viewed treaties as contractual agreements, they initially interpreted their substance in a manner that was blind to Indigenous expectations of the treaty process. Treaty rights were interpreted solely by reference to non-Indigenous legal norms and values. In the words of Dale Turner, treaties were "textualized in the language of the dominant European culture."[10]

Despite its nascent presence in early treaties, constitutional pluralism thus did not take root in Canada in part because the Crown, protected by a robust, monist conception of sovereign authority, began to negotiate treaties for reasons antithetical to pluralism's promise. And when treaties assumed legal form in Canadian law, Canadian legal institutions did not comprehend them as instruments of mutual recognition, where each party acknowledged a measure of legitimacy of the legal order of the other and accordingly made arrangements for the co-existence and interaction of legal norms emanating from the two or more legal communities they represented. Their legal form as contracts rendered them unintelligible as instruments of mutual recognition. As contracts, they assumed a hierarchical legal relation between the Crown and Indigenous parties, given that the Crown in its legislative capacity had the authority to unilaterally override their terms. Their substance, too, rendered them unintelligible to constitutional pluralism as Indigenous legal norms played no role in clarifying their terms.

Another set of factors contributing to the failure of constitutional pluralism relates to how Canadian law comprehended the legality of Indigenous

9   See, e.g., *Pawis v. The Queen* (1979), 102 DLR (3d) 602 (F.C.T.D.), at 610 ("[t]he right acquired by the Indians in those treaties was ... necessarily subject to restriction through acts of the legislature, just as the person who acquires from the Crown a grant of land is subject in its enjoyment to ... legislative restrictions").

10 Dale Turner, *From Valladolid to Ottawa: The Illusion of Listening to Aboriginal People*, in Jill Oakes et al., eds., Sacred Lands: Aboriginal World Views, Claims, and Conflicts (Edmonton: Canadian Circumpolar Institute, 1998), 53–68, at 64. For a good example of this phenomenon, see *Pawis v. The Queen, ibid.*, at 609–10 (interpreting a treaty provision establishing a "full and free privilege to hunt and fish" to mean that "no consideration is to be extracted from those entitled to hunt and fish").

interests in their territories. With British sovereignty came underlying Crown title, with a particularly brutal twist. The fiction of underlying Crown title was developed in feudal times to legitimate the then-existing kaleidoscopic pattern of landholdings in England by treating the Crown as the original occupant and actual landholders as holding title by way of (mostly fictional) grants from the Crown. Its transplantation to the colonial context was not accompanied by the complementary fiction that the actual Indigenous landholders held title by way of a grant from the Crown. The fiction of underlying Crown title became a legal technology of Indigenous dispossession, radically disrupting the actual pattern of Indigenous landholding in British North America.

In the late 1800s, Canadian law, with its belated acceptance of a tepid form of common law Aboriginal title, did acknowledge that Indigenous peoples lived on and occupied the continent prior to European contact and, as a result, possess certain interests worthy of legal protection. This body of law prescribed ways of handling disputes between Indigenous and non-Indigenous peoples, especially disputes over land. It recognized, in common-law terms, Indigenous occupation and use of ancestral lands,[11] described rights associated with Aboriginal title in collective terms vesting in Indigenous communities,[12] and purported to restrict settlement on Indigenous territories until these territories had been surrendered to the Crown.[13] It prohibited sales of Indigenous land to non-Indigenous people without the approval of and participation by Crown authorities.[14] And it prescribed safeguards for the manner in which such surrenders can occur and imposed fiduciary obligations on government in its dealings with Indigenous lands and resources.[15]

The common law of Aboriginal title, however, historically failed to protect Indigenous territories from settlement and exploitation. Law's inability to protect Indigenous territories was in part a function of broader social and historical realities associated with colonial expansion. Governments and settlers either

---

[11] *See, for example, Hamlet of Baker Lake v. Minister of Indian Affairs and Northern Development*, [1980] 1 F.C. 518 (F.C.T.D.).

[12] *See, for example, Amodu Tijani v. Secretary, Southern Nigeria*, [1921] 2 A.C. 399 (P.C.).

[13] *See, for example, Guerin v. The Queen*, [1984] 2 SCR 335, at 383 ("[t]he purpose of this surrender requirement is clearly to interpose the Crown between the Indians and prospective purchasers or lessees of their land, so as to prevent the Indians from being exploited").

[14] *See, for example, Canadian Pacific Ltd. v. Paul*, [1988] 2 SCR 654, at 677 (Aboriginal title cannot be transferred, sold or surrendered to anyone other than the Crown).

[15] *See, for example, R. v. Guerin*, [1984] 2 SCR 335, at 382 (Aboriginal title "gives rise upon surrender to a distinctive fiduciary obligation on the part of the Crown to deal with the land for the benefit of the surrendering Indians"); *see also R. v. Sparrow*, [1990] 1 SCR 1075, at 1108 ("the Government has the responsibility to act in a fiduciary capacity with respect to Aboriginal peoples").

misunderstood or ignored the law of Aboriginal title. Crown respect for the law of Aboriginal title was eroded by the decline of the fur trade and the waning of Indigenous and non-Indigenous economic interdependence. Increased demands on Indigenous territories occasioned by population growth and westward expansion, followed by a period of paternalistic administration marked by involuntary relocations, only exacerbated the erosion of respect.

In addition to these external factors, law's failure to protect Indigenous territories can also be internally traced to legal choices of the judiciary. On more than one occasion, the judiciary suggested that Indigenous territorial claims might not possess any independent legal significance at all.[16] The possibility that Indigenous territories might not generate legal recognition by the Canadian legal order served as a legal backdrop for almost a century of relations between the Crown and Indigenous peoples, shaping legal expectations of governments, corporations, citizens and other legal actors. It contributed to a perception that governments and third parties were relatively free to engage in a range of activity on ancestral lands – a perception which, in turn, legitimated unparalleled levels of government and third party development and exploitation of Indigenous territories, which continue relatively unabated today.

Moreover, until recently, the legal significance that the judiciary attached to Indigenous territorial interests was minimal. Courts resisted characterizing Aboriginal title in proprietary terms, preferring instead to characterize it as a right of occupancy or a personal or usufructuary right,[17] or, more recently, as a *sui generis* interest.[18] Constructing Aboriginal title as a non-proprietary interest enabled its regulation and indeed its extinguishment by appropriate executive action,[19] disabled Indigenous titleholders from obtaining interim relief[20] and

---

[16] See, for example, St. Catherines Milling v. The Queen (1888), 14 A.C. 46 (P.C.) (Aboriginal rights with respect to land and resources did not predate but were created by the Royal Proclamation and, as such, are "dependent on the good will of the Sovereign").

[17] St. Catherines's Milling v. The Queen), ibid, at 54; see also Smith v. The Queen, [1983] 1 SCR 554.

[18] Canadian Pacific Ltd. v. Paul, [1988] 2 SCR 654, at 658 (Aboriginal title refers to an "Indian interest in land [that] is truly *sui generis*"); see also R. v. Sparrow, [1990] 1 SCR 1075, at 1112 ("[c]ourts must be careful ... to avoid the application of traditional common law concepts of property as they develop their understanding of ... the *sui generis* nature of Aboriginal rights").

[19] See, for example, Ontario (A.G.) v. Bear Island Foundation, [1991] 2 SCR 570, at 575 ("whatever may have been the situation upon signing of the Robinson-Huron Treaty, that right was in any event surrendered by arrangements subsequent to that treaty by which the Indians adhered to the treaty in exchange for treaty annuities and a reserve").

[20] A number of cases held that Aboriginal title does not constitute an interest in land sufficient to support the registration of a caveat or certificate of *lis pendens*, which would temporarily

frustrated access to the common law presumption of compensation in the event of expropriation.[21] Courts also indicated a willingness to view Aboriginal title as a set of rights to engage only in traditional practices on Indigenous territory, that is, those practices that Indigenous people engaged in at the time the Crown acquired territorial sovereignty.[22] Each of these legal choices had a profound effect on the ability of Indigenous peoples to rely on Canadian law to protect ancestral territories from non-Indigenous incursion. Each also represented another nail in constitutional pluralism's coffin.

Notwithstanding this history, and to return to the questions posed at the outset, how receptive is the Canadian constitutional environment to conceiving of Indigenous-Canadian relations in accordance with the ethos of constitutional pluralism that animated their origins? Are there institutional and doctrinal openings for such a reconstruction to take root? What forms of structural and political resistance might act as impediments? There are three developments that could form a foundation for the recovery of constitutional pluralism. Two are occurring inside Canadian law, looking out to Indigenous legal norms. The third is occurring beyond Canadian law, and is not necessarily looking in to Canadian legal norms.

With the enactment of s. 35(1) of the *Constitution Act, 1982*, treaty rights now assume the form of constitutional rights. No longer enforceable merely in the face of Crown inaction, treaties now constrain the exercise of legislative authority. To illustrate, in *R. v. Badger*,[23] at issue was whether the right to hunt contained in Treaty 8 provided a defence to a charge under Alberta's *Wildlife Act* which prohibited hunting out-of-season and hunting without a licence. The Supreme Court of Canada held that Treaty 8 protected hunting for food on private property that was not put to a "visible, incompatible use," and that the right to hunt was a treaty right within the meaning of s. 35(1) of the

---

prevent activity on ancestral territory pending final resolution of a dispute. *See, for example, Uukw v. AGBC* (1987), 16 BCLR (2d) 145 (BCCA); *Lac La Ronge Indian Band v. Beckman,* [1990] 4 W.W.R. 211 (Sask. C.A.); *James Smith Indian Band v. Saskatchewan (Master of Titles),* [1994] 2 C.N.L.R. 72 (Sask. Q.B.); *but see Ontario (A.G.) v. Bear Island Foundation,* [1991] 2 SCR 570.

[21] *See, for example, British Columbia v. Tener,* [1985] 1 SCR 533, at 559, quoting *Attorney-General v. De Keyser's Royal Hotel Ltd.,* [1920] A.C. 508, at 542, per Lord Atkinson ("a statute is not to be construed so as to take away the property of a subject without compensation").

[22] *See, for example, Baker Lake v. Minister of Indian Affairs,* [1980] 1 F.C. 518, at 559 ("the common law ... can give effect only to those incidents of that enjoyment that were ... given effect by the [Aboriginal] regime that prevailed before"); *AG Ont. v. Bear Island Foundation,* [1985] 1 C.N.L.R. 1, at 3 (Ont. S.C.) ("the essence of Aboriginal rights is the right of Indians to live on the lands as their forefathers lived").

[23] *R. v. Badger* [1996] 1 SCR 771.

Constitution Act. The Court stated that "a treaty represents an exchange of solemn promises ... [and] an agreement whose nature is sacred." It reiterated that treaties should be interpreted in "a manner which maintains the integrity of the Crown" and that ambiguities or doubtful expressions in the wording of the treaty should be resolved in favour of Indigenous people. *Badger* marks a significant transformation in the judicial understanding of a treaty's form and substance. No longer mere political agreements or contractual agreements, treaties now possess formal constitutional status. Their substance ought to be determined in a manner consistent with Indigenous understandings, flexible to evolving practices, inclusive of reasonably incidental practices and in a way that best reconciles the competing interests of the parties.

Badger's requirement that treaties be interpreted in a manner consistent with Indigenous understandings implicitly rests on an ethos of constitutional pluralism. Though each treaty is unique in its terms and scope of application, Indigenous understandings of treaties are relatively uniform. Indigenous people entered into treaties with the Crown to formalize a relationship of continental co-existence. They initially sought military alliances before and during the war between Britain and France and also sought to maximize benefits associated with economic interdependence. As the nineteenth century progressed, Indigenous peoples sought to maintain their autonomous legal orders and traditional ways of life in the face of railway construction, surveying activity, non-Indigenous settlement of Indigenous territory, and an unprecedented rise in hunting, fishing and trapping by non-Indigenous people. They sought to retain traditional authority over their territories and to govern their communities in the face of colonial expansion. In James Youngblood Henderson's words, "Aboriginal nations entered into the treaties as the keepers of a certain place."[24] Indigenous people regarded the treaty process as enabling the sharing of land and authority with non-Indigenous people while at the same time protecting their territories, economies and forms of government from non-Indigenous incursion.

The new constitutional status of treaties also recovers the promise of constitutional pluralism. Understanding treaties as constitutional instruments opens the pluralist legal door to comprehending treaties as constitutional accords. As constitutional accords, they articulate basic terms and conditions of social co-existence and making possible the exercise of constitutional authority. Unlike legal contracts between the Crown and private citizens, which distribute power delegated by the state to private parties in the form of legally

---

[24] James [Sákéj] Henderson, *Interpreting Sui Generis Treaties*, 36 ALTA. L. REV. 46, 64 (1997).

enforceable rights and obligations, treaties establish the constitutional parameters of state power itself.[25] Accordingly, treaties do not distribute delegated
state power, they distribute constitutional authority. Treaties are therefore as
much a part of the constitutional history of Canada as the *Constitution Act,
1867,* which distributes legislative power between the federal and provincial
governments. Treaty rights are constitutional rights that flow to Indigenous
people in exchange for allowing European nations to exercise a measure of
sovereign authority in North America.

The judiciary has begun to conceive of treaties in similar terms. In *Haida
Nation v. British Columbia,* the Supreme Court of Canada concluded that
British Columbia has a legal duty to consult with the Haida people about the
harvest of timber from lands subject to a claim by them of Aboriginal title.[26]
More generally, the Court held that where treaties remain to be concluded,
the Crown is required to participate in negotiations "leading to a just settlement of Aboriginal claims." According to the Court, "[t]reaties serve to reconcile pre-existing Aboriginal sovereignty with assumed Crown sovereignty."[27]

As constitutional accords, treaties operate as instruments of mutual recognition. Negotiations occur against a backdrop of competing claims of constitutional authority. The Crown enters negotiations under the assumption that
it possesses jurisdiction and rights with respect to the territory in question; a
First Nation enters negotiations on the assumption that it possesses jurisdiction
and rights with respect to the same territory. The treaty process is a means by
which competing claims of authority and right can be reconciled with each
other by each party agreeing to recognize a measure of the authority of the
other.[28] Recognition can occur geographically, as with a number of contemporary land claims agreements that distribute jurisdiction between the
parties based on different geographical categories of land within the territory

[25] *Compare* Robert A. Williams, Jr., Linking Arms Together: American Indian Treaty
    Visions of Law & Peace, 1600–1800 (New York: Oxford University Press, 1997), at 105 ("[I]n
    American Indian visions of law and peace, a treaty connected different peoples through
    constitutional bonds of multicultural unity").

[26] *Haida Nation v. British Columbia (Minister of Forests),* [2004] 3 SCR 511.

[27] *Haida Nation v. British Columbia (Minister of Forests),* [2004] 3 SCR 511, at para. 20. *See
    also Taku River Tlingit First Nation v. British Columbia (project Assessment Director),* [2004] 3
    SCR 550, at para. 42. According to Felix Hoehn, these statements represent a paradigm shift in
    Canadian jurisprudence on Aboriginal rights to "a new sovereignty paradigm." Felix Hoehn,
    Reconciling Sovereignties: Aboriginal Nations and Canada (Saskatoon: Native Law
    Centre, University of Saskatchewan, 2012).

[28] *See generally* Royal Commission on Aboriginal Peoples, Treaty Making in the Spirit of
    Co-Existence: An Alternative to Extinguishment (Ottawa: Minister of Supply and
    Services Canada, 1995).

in question. Recognition can also occur by subject, whereby the parties distribute jurisdiction between themselves based on various subject matters suitable for legislation. As an instrument of mutual recognition, a treaty is an ongoing process, structured but not determined by the text of the original agreement, by which parties commit to resolving disputes that might arise in the future through a process of dialogue and mutual respect.

Viewing treaties as constitutional accords is consonant with recent scholarly attempts to construct alternative legal histories of Indigenous-Crown relations. Legal histories typically trace the legal position of Indigenous people under Canadian law over time to demonstrate the redemptive potential, or lack thereof, of Canadian law for protecting Indigenous peoples from assimilation. What such histories lack, and what recent scholarship attempts to provide, is an appreciation of how Indigenous people actively participated in the production and reproduction of legal norms that structured their relations with non-Indigenous people on the continent. This scholarship, I believe, is consistent with "critical legal pluralism," an approach introduced by Kleinhaus and MacDonald that "focuses the spotlight on the citizen-subject and views them as sources of normativity in the sense that they are *law inventing*, not merely *law abiding*, forces within a society."[29]

James Tully, for example, has interpreted the treaty process as a form of "treaty constitutionalism" whereby Indigenous people participate in the creation of constitutional norms governing Aboriginal-Crown relations.[30] Robert Williams has written of the "long-neglected fact that . . . Indians tried to create a new type of society with Europeans on the multicultural frontiers of colonial North America."[31] James sakej Henderson has interpreted the treaty process as producing "treaty federalism" – a constitutional order grounded in the consent of Indigenous and non-Indigenous people on the continent and established well before Confederation.[32] In Henderson's words, treaty federalism "represents a belief in autonomous zones of power, freedom, and liberties in consensual and dynamic order, rather than the unexamined essence of divine sovereignty and its imposed hierarchies or parliamentary sovereignty."[33] What such scholarship shares is an appreciation of the active participation by Indigenous people in the production of basic legal norms governing the distribution

---

[29] *Shadow Nations, supra,* at 77, drawing from Martha-Marie Kleinhaus and Roderick A. MacDonald, *What Is a Critical Legal Pluralism?,* 12 Can. J. L. & Soc. 25 (1997).

[30] James Tully, Strange Multiplicity: Constitutionalism in an Age of Diversity (Cambridge: Cambridge University Press, 1995), at 117.

[31] Robert A. Williams Jr., *Linking Arms Together, supra,* at 9.

[32] Henderson, *Empowering Treaty Federalism,* 58 Sask. L. Rev. 241 (1997).

[33] Henderson, Sui Generis and Treaty Citizenship, 6 Citizensh. Stud. 415, at 422 (2002).

of constitutional authority in North America.[34] Viewed through the prism of constitutional pluralism, the treaty process is a formal manifestation of such participation through its active production of constitutional accords that distribute constitutional authority on the continent.

The second development relates to the form and substance of Aboriginal title and rights. With the enactment of s. 35(1) of the *Constitution Act, 1982*, and confirmed by the Supreme Court of Canada in *Delgamuukw v. British Columbia*,[35] Aboriginal title shed its common law status and assumed the form of a constitutional right. Although the Court extensively described the nature and scope of Aboriginal title and the circumstances under which it can be justifiably interfered with by the Crown, it offered little insight into why Aboriginal title merits constitutional protection, holding simply that a "plain meaning" of the Constitution and precedent were conclusive of the issue.[36]

But a deeper account of the constitutional status of Aboriginal title rests on an ethos of constitutional pluralism. On this account, Aboriginal title is a constitutional – as opposed to a common law or statutory – norm because it is an entitlement that is not conditional on the exercise of judicial and legislative authority. Instead, it is logically and historically antecedent to the exercise of judicial and legislative authority and owes its origins to facts and norms that predate the establishment of the Canadian state. Indigenous peoples possessed title to their territories according to their own laws prior to the establishment of a sovereign entity that assumed the legislative power to redistribute title to its citizens. In the words of Swepson and Plant, "rights of ownership already accrue to Indigenous populations, and are not ceded to them through the actions of nation-states."[37] Canada became a nation-state against the backdrop of a pre-existing distribution of territory among Indigenous nations. By recognizing and affirming Aboriginal title, s. 35(1) extends constitutional validity to Indigenous legal norms that inform and make sense of this pre-existing distribution of Indigenous territory. It ensures that state power will be exercised in

---

[34] See generally Jeremy Webber, *Relations of Force and Relations of Justice: The Emergence of Normative Community between Colonists and Aboriginal Peoples, supra; see also* Sidney L. Harring, WHITE MAN'S LAW: NATIVE PEOPLE IN NINETEENTH CENTURY CANADIAN JURISPRUDENCE (Toronto: Osgoode Society for Canadian Legal History, 1998).

[35] [1997] 3 SCR 1010.

[36] The Court held that the text of s. 35(1) and *R. v. Van der Peet*, [1996] 2 SCR 507 both suggest that s. 35(1) provides constitutional status to those rights that were "existing" prior to 1982 and, given that Aboriginal title was a common law right existing in 1982, s. 35(1) accords it constitutional status.

[37] L. Swepson & R. Plant, *International Standards and the Protection of the Land Rights of Indigenous and Tribal Populations*, 124 INTERNATIONAL LAB. REV. 91, 97 (1985).

a manner that respects these Indigenous legal norms and the Indigenous legal orders to which they owe their existence.

Also relevant to a recovery of legal pluralism's promise is a shift in how the judiciary assesses the validity of a claim of Aboriginal title. Indigenous legal norms can participate in establishing the requisite exclusive occupation on which Aboriginal title rests. In the words of Lamer C.J. in *Delgamuukw*:

> [I]f, at the time of sovereignty, an aboriginal society had laws in relation to land, those laws would be relevant to establishing the occupation of laws which are the subject of a claim of Aboriginal title. Relevant laws might include, but are not limited to, a land tenure system or laws governing land use.[38]

Elsewhere in his reasons, Lamer C.J. stated that Indigenous laws governing trespass and conditional land use by other Indigenous nations, as well as treaties between and among Indigenous nations also might assist in establishing the occupation necessary to prove Aboriginal title.[39]

These passages were instrumental to the Court's recent decision in *Tsilhqot'in Nation v. British Columbia* to grant a declaration of Aboriginal title to the Tsilhqot'in people, a collectivity of six communities sharing a common culture and history, who live in a remote valley bounded by rivers and mountains in central British Columbia.[40] The Court held that the Tsilhqot'in manifested sufficient and exclusive occupation and exclusive control of the land in question required for a declaration of Aboriginal title. Sufficiency of occupation was established by evidence at trial of a strong presence on or over the land claimed, manifesting itself in acts of occupation that could reasonably be interpreted as demonstrating that the land in question belonged to, was controlled by, or was under the exclusive stewardship of the Tsilhqot'in. Exclusivity of occupation was established by evidence that Tsilhqot'in laws excluded others from the land, except when they were allowed access to the land with the permission of the Tsilhqot'in. The presence of Indigenous laws emanating from an Indigenous legal order, in other words, translate into Aboriginal rights in the Canadian legal order.

Constitutional recognition of Indigenous legal norms is not restricted to the proof of Aboriginal title. Elsewhere the Court has spoken of the suggested that Indigenous laws compatible with the assertion of Crown sovereignty survived its assertion, were "absorbed into the common law as rights," and, if not surrendered or extinguished, received constitutional recognition as Aboriginal

---

[38] *Supra*, at para. 148.   [39] *Id.*, at para. 157.
[40] *Tsilhqot'in Nation v. British Columbia*, [2014] 2 SCR 257.

rights by s. 35(1).[41] This suggests that at least part of the reason something is an Aboriginal right in Canadian law is because it was an Indigenous legal norm at the time of the assertion of Crown sovereignty. Understanding Aboriginal rights as Indigenous legal norms renders s. 35(1) a provision performative of constitutional pluralism by formally acknowledging the constitutional significance of Indigenous legal orders.

A third development relevant to a resurgence of an ethos of constitutional pluralism lies outside the confines of constitutional recognition and affirmation of Aboriginal and treaty rights. Indigenous legal scholars have begun ambitious tasks of recovering and modernizing Indigenous legal norms or traditions that historically contributed to the social ordering of different Indigenous societies. This is no easy task, given the relative inaccessibility of oral traditions and Indigenous languages as well as the need to recover Indigenous patterns of being and ways of life ravaged by the history of colonialism.[42] One must then seek to identify the ideas and beliefs that underpin such legal norms – in order to make sense of them and understand their normative significance. And then they need to be placed alongside non-Indigenous norms for comparison and contrast to determine ways in which they might assist in structuring Indigenous and non-Indigenous legal and political relations.

John Borrows, for example, in *Canada's Indigenous Constitution*, details legal norms from the Mi'kmaq, Haudenosaunee, Anishnabek, Cree, Métis, Canarrier, Nisga'a and Inuit legal traditions.[43] Val Napoleon and Hadley Friedland focus on the *wetiko* in particular, a concept in Cree and Anishnabek societies that describes a person who is harmful to others in prohibited ways and the traditions, processes and principles developed to address people who fell within this legal category.[44] A number of law schools in Canada have institutionalized this development by offering courses on Indigenous legal traditions. The University of Victoria on Vancouver Island has taken this one step further, by working to offer a joint common law and Indigenous law degree.

Judicial decisions occasionally hint at an ethos of constitutional pluralism informing their characterizations of relations between Indigenous peoples and

---

[41] *Mitchell v. MNR*, 1 SCR 911, at para. 10 per McLachlin C.J.

[42] For thoughtful reflections on the challenges this work faces given the ongoing effects of colonialism on Indigenous identity formation, *see* Gordon Christie, *Culture, Self-Determination and Colonialism: Issues around the Revitalization of Indigenous Legal Traditions*, 6 Osgoode Hall L.J. 13(2007).

[43] John Borrows, Canada's Indigenous Constitution (Toronto: University of Torornto Press, 2010), at 59–106.

[44] Val Napoleon and Hadley Friedland, "Indigenous Legal Traditions: Roots to Renaissance," (2013) (on file with author).

the Canadian state. Chief Justice McLachlin, in *Haida Nation* and *Taku River*, wrote of treaties as instruments that "reconcile pre-existing Aboriginal sovereignty with assumed Crown sovereignty" or "*de facto* Crown sovereignty."[45] The Court regularly refers to "the pre-existing societies of aboriginal peoples,"[46] Indigenous "legal systems,"[47] "pre-existing systems of aboriginal law"[48] and "aboriginal peoples occupying and using most of this vast expanse of land in organized, distinctive societies with their own social and political structures."[49] And, in the following passage, Chief Justice McLachlin, in her dissent in *Van der Peet*, clearly summoned the spirit of legal pluralism:

> The history of the interface of Europeans and the common law with aboriginal peoples is a long one. As might be expected of such a long history, the principles by which the interface has been governed have not always been consistently applied. Yet running through this history, from its earliest beginnings to the present time is a golden thread – the recognition by the common law of the ancestral laws and customs of the aboriginal peoples who occupied the land prior to European settlement.[50]

Indeed, this passage seems to suggest that constitutional pluralism has always characterized the "the interface of Europeans and the common law with aboriginal peoples." But history tells us otherwise. Canadian courts describing relations between Indigenous peoples and Canada as constitutionally plural, as important as this development is, does not make them so. For an ethos of constitutional pluralism to restart animating relations between Indigenous peoples and Canada, constitutional recognition of Indigenous governments sovereign within their spheres of authority, capable of exercising exclusive and concurrent lawmaking powers formally equivalent to their federal and provincial counterparts, would need to occur, coupled with a deepening of the recent developments traced in this paper.

Nor is constitutional pluralism a one-way street. When Indigenous legal orders themselves pay homage to its premises, then constitutional pluralism will truly begin to become "legal reality." The capacity of Indigenous legal

---

[45] *Haida Nation v. British Columbia (Minister of Forests)*, [2004] 3 SCR 511, at para. 20; *Taku River Tlingit First Nation v. British Columbia Project Assessment Director)*, [2004] 3 SCR 550. For an extended reflection of this approach, *see* Felix Hoehn, RECONCILING SOVEREIGNTIES: ABORIGINAL NATIONS AND CANADA (Saskatoon: Native Law Centre, University of Saskatchewan, 2012).
[46] *R. v. Van der Peet*, [1996] 2 SCR 507, at para. 39, per Lamer C.J.
[47] *R. v. Sappier; R. v. Gray*, [2006] 2 SCR 686, at para.45, per Bastarache J.
[48] *Delgamuukw, supra*, at para. 145, per Lamer C.J.
[49] *Mitchell v. MNR*, [2001] 1 SCR 911, at para. 9, per McLachlin C.J.
[50] *Van der Peet, supra*, at para. 263.

orders to do so turns on, first, their capacity to resurrect Indigenous legal norms that can carry this message, and second, the willingness of the Canadian constitutional order to recognize, and affirm, its constitutional significance.

Were the ethos of constitutional pluralism to resurface in the Canadian constitutional order, this would render Canada a tri-federal state, with legislative, executive and possibly judicial power divided among three levels of government: federal, provincial and Indigenous. But the countervailing measures that promote "voice" for Quebec people in federal institutions would be absent in the constitutional relationship between Canada and Indigenous peoples. In future work, I plan to explore the potential consequences of this absence, what such countervailing measures might look like and what role they might play in reshaping the structure of the Canadian constitutional order.

5

Legality, Legitimacy and Constitutional Amendment in Canada

JAMIE CAMERON

INTRODUCTION

Amendment rules are a requisite feature of constitutional text. In that regard, the *British North America Act*, or *Canada Act*, 1867, stands almost alone among constitutions of the world in not prescribing rules for its amendment.[1] It was not so jarring an omission when four colonies joined in federal union under a constitution enacted by the British Parliament, and were first in the British Empire to earn Dominion status.[2] Over time, the text was modified twenty-one times by UK legislation before amending rules empowering Canada to change its own Constitution were added.[3]

Patriating the Constitution, entrenching an amending formula, and enacting a *Charter of Rights and Freedoms* in 1982 were transformative acts of constitutional renewal. Since then, the *Charter* has been presented to the world as a model that demonstrates how constitutional rights can be balanced

My thanks to Mr. John Wilson (JD 2016) and Mr. Tanner Stanley (JD 2018) for their valuable assistance in the preparation of this draft. I also thank Richard Albert and David Cameron for inviting me to participate in this conference.

[1] *See* Francesco Giavannoni, "Amendment Rules in Constitutions," *Public Choice*, 115 (2003), 37–61 (stating in 2003 that only 4 per cent of the world's constitutions lack a formal amending process).

[2] British North America Act 1867, 30–31 Vict., c. 3 (UK) (re-named the *Canada Act, 1867* and referred to in this chapter, for historical purposes, as the "*BNA Act*"). The 1867 Constitution was a hybrid of written and unwritten constitutionalism. While unwritten constitutions change informally, through a process of evolution, written constitutions prescribe amendment rules. This article is concerned with questions of amendment arising from Canada's written Constitution and its failure to prescribe rules for amendment of the text, and not with its unwritten Constitution, which is defined in the main but not exclusively by the Westminster tradition of parliamentary government.

[3] Canada Act 1982 (UK), 1982, c. 11, Sched. B ("*Canada Act, 1982*"); Patrick J. Monahan and Byron Shaw, CONSTITUTIONAL LAW, 4th edition. (Toronto: Irwin Law Inc., 2013),165.

against the legislature's democratic authority.[4] The transformation was messy, though, and left Canada in constitutional despair when profound divisions on renewal remained a flashpoint for years after patriation.

Amendment has been a preoccupation throughout Canada's constitutional history. Before the cauldron years prior to and after patriation, the search for an amending formula had been futile and demoralizing. Against that back-drop, the importance of entrenching a formula and "bringing the Constitution home" cannot easily be overstated.[5] Patriation and its successor initiatives – the Meech Lake and Charlottetown Accords – therefore represent a legal, political, and symbolic break between defining periods of amendment history: before and after textual rules.[6] Patriation marks the moment when a tradition of quiescent deadlock on constitutional change was replaced by a noisy contest to define Canada's constitutional core and even to break Confederation apart. The high-stakes drama of 1982, threat of Quebec separation and denouement of the post-patriation Accords were events of singular urgency. By dominating the literature, these events consigned the longer history of amendment to the background.[7]

---

[4]   *See generally* Stephen Gardbaum, *Reassessing the New Commonwealth Model of Constitutionalism*, INT'L. J. CONST. L., 8:2 (2010), 167–210; *see also* David S. Law and Mila Versteeg, *The Declining Influence of the United States Constitution*, N.Y.U.L.Rev. 87:3 (2012), 762–858 at 801–23 (asking, "Is Canada a Constitutional Superpower" and discussing Canada's status as a "constitutional trendsetter" among common law or Commonwealth countries).

[5]   Adding amendment rules "patriated" the Constitution by providing the legal framework for a domestic process of constitutional change. The term was reportedly used for the first time by Prime Minister Lester Pearson, who stated in 1966 that "[w]e intend to do everything we can to have the constitution of Canada patriated, or re-patriated." *Hansard*, HC vol. 373, col. 2, 28 January 1966.

[6]   Both Accords addressed the perceived deficits and unfinished business of 1982's patriation reforms. While the Meech Lake Accord (the "MLA") addressed Quebec's exclusion from patriation and was seen as the "Quebec Round," the Charlottetown Accord proposed comprehensive reform and is known as the "Canada Round." Canada's first ministers negotiated and reached agreement on the MLA on 30 April 1987, and ultimately it failed on 23 June 1990, at the end of a three-year ratification period. After agreement was reached on 28 August 1992, the Charolttetown Accord was voted down in a nationwide referendum held on 26 October 1992. The Accords are discussed later in the article.

[7]   *See, e.g.*, Keith Banning and Richard Simeon (eds.), AND NO ONE CHEERED: FEDERALISM, DEMOCRACY AND THE CONSTITUTION ACT (Toronto: Methuen Publications, 1983); Roy Romanow, John Whyte and Howard Leeson, CANADA … NOTWITHSTANDING- THE MAKING OF THE CONSTITUTION 1976–1982 (Canada: Carswell/Methuen, 1982) [*Notwithstanding*]; Robert Sheppard and Michael Valpy, THE NATIONAL DEAL: THE FIGHT FOR A CANADIAN CONSTITUTION (Toronto: Books, 1982) [*The National Deal*]; Edward McWhinney, CANADA AND THE CONSTITUTION, 1979–1982: PATRIATION AND THE CHARTER OF RIGHTS (Toronto: University of Toronto Press, 1982) [*Canada and the Constitution*]; Ron Graham, THE LAST ACT: PIERRE TRUDEAU, THE GANG OF EIGHT, AND THE FIGHT FOR CANADA (Canada: Penguin Canada, 2012) [*The Last Act*]; Patrick Monahan, MEECH LAKE: THE INSIDE STORY (Toronto:

Now that the crisis years have receded, fresh insight is emerging through a process of generational renewal in the scholarship.[8] This article joins the movement, exploring Canada's two uneven periods of constitutional change – before and after textual amendment rules. In drawing that longer history back into the discussion, it theorizes that rich insights into the riddles of Canada's amendment experience are found in the interface between the legality or formality of constitutional change, and its legitimacy or acceptance.

While much of the scholarship focuses on textual rules and design variables – or the legalities of amendment – this article takes a different path which draws the dynamics of legitimacy into discussion. Before turning to the rhythms of Canada's amendment experience it offers a primer on the foundational concepts of legality and legitimacy, and their alignment in the constitutional setting. The analysis then addresses how those concepts have interacted over Canada's amendment history, before and after textual rules. The discussion takes its cue from the 1867 Constitution, which was incomplete as constitutional text because it failed to include amendment rules. In default of rules, the Constitution was changed through a process of UK statutory legality which served, through most of Canada's history, as a proxy for constitutional legality, or textual amending rules. The legitimacy of amendment by this process was accepted, though more as a stopgap and with increasing discomfort after Canada's independence in 1931.[9]

University of Toronto Press, 1991) [*Inside Story*]; Andrew Cohen, A DEAL UNDONE: THE MAKING AND BREAKING OF THE MEECH LAKE ACCORD (Vancouver: Douglas & McIntyre, 1990) [*Meech Lake Accord*]; Kenneth McRoberts and Patrick Monahan (eds.), THE CHARLOTTETOWN ACCORD, THE REFERENDUM AND THE FUTURE OF CANADA (Toronto: University of Toronto Press, 1993) [*The Charlottetown Accord*]; Peter H. Russell, CONSTITUTIONAL ODYSSEY: CAN CANADIANS BECOME A SOVEREIGN PEOPLE?, 2nd edition (Toronto: University of Toronto Press, 1993) [*Odyssey*]; and Jeremy Webber, REIMAGINING CANADA: LANGUAGE, CULTURE, COMMUNITY, AND THE CANADIAN CONSTITUTION (Canada: McGill-Queens University Press, 1994) [*Reimagining Canada*].

8   *See, e.g.*, Lois Harder and Steven Patten (eds.), PATRIATION AND ITS CONSEQUENCES: CONSTITUTION MAKING IN CANADA (Canada: UBC Press, 2015); Richard Albert, *The Difficulty of Constitutional Amendment in Canada*, ALTA. L. REV., 53, 85–114 (2015); Richard Albert, *Constitutional Amendment by Stealth*, McGILL L.J., 60:4, 673–736; (2015) Richard Albert, *The Conventions of Constitutional Amendment in Canada*, O.H.L.J., 53:4, 399–442 (2016) (addressing aspects of Canadian amendment constitutionalism); Kate Glover, *Structure, Substance & Spirit: Lessons in Constitutional Architecture from the Senate Reform Reference*, S.C.L.R., 67, 221–255 (2nd edition) (2014); and Kate Glover, *Complexity and the Amending Formula*, CONSTITUTIONAL FORUM, 24:2, 9–16 (2015) (exploring the relationship between constitutional interpretation and constitutional amendment).

9   *See* W.R. Lederman, *The Process of Constitutional Amendment for Canada*, McGILL L.J., 12:4, 371–384 at 378 (1966–67) (stating that "[i]t is embarrassing for the British and humiliating for Canadians to maintain any longer these obsolete and incongruous formal steps of asking the

The absence of rules had profound implications for Canadian constitutionalism and how the Constitution was perceived. Throughout this period, Canada lacked amendment sovereignty because the Constitution could not amend itself.[10] Over time, the gap in constitutional legality presented acute legitimacy issues in a federal system of divided sovereignty between federal and provincial levels of government. In formal terms, the protracted search for amendment rules was about legality and filling a textual gap, but more fundamentally it required Canadian constitutionalism – as a matter of federalism as well as wider democratic governance – to define the terms and conditions of legitimate change.

As noted, patriation was transformative because that is when Canada acquired the authority to amend the Constitution domestically.[11] If the entrenchment of textual rules could be expected to bring the legality and legitimacy of amendment into alignment, that is not what happened. Despite ameliorating the omission of 1867, patriation could not close gaps in legitimacy that spread from their roots in the rivalries of federalism to a fresh dynamic of rising democratic expectations. The urgency of those gaps led, in short years, to the two Accords, both which represent flagship moments of defeat in Canada's constitutional history. More poignant than the failure of legality in each instance was the virtual collapse of legitimacy, or democratic confidence in constitutional renewal.[12] Despite a regime of constitutional legality which has been in place since 1982, that confidence has not been restored. As Canada approaches its sesquicentennial anniversary in 2017, what is required to align the legitimacy of constitutional change with the current scheme of amendment legality remains uncertain, if not unknown.

British Parliament to act for us"); Jamie Cameron, *To Amend the Process of Amendment*, in Gerald Beaudoin et al (eds.), *Federalism for the Future: Essential Reforms* (Montreal: Wilson & Lafleur Ltée, 1998), 319 (stating, years later, that it is questionable whether Canada was ever well served by a document that "robbed this country, from the outset, of the basic power to control its constitutional destiny").

[10] Again, the legal means for amending the text existed through the mechanism of statutory legality, which served that function. Moreover, statutory legality was a form of constitutional legality, because it governed the process of constitutional amendment. Yet the Constitution did not provide rules for its *constitutional* amendment, or amendment according to the terms of the text (such as the division of powers between federal and provincial levels of government).

[11] *Canada Act, 1982, supra* note 3, ss. 38–49 (prescribing the rules for amendment which are referred to, collectively, as the amending formula). Note that some changes and amendments could be undertaken domestically prior to 1982; *infra* note 31.

[12] The Accords failed on compound grounds of legality and legitimacy; the obstacles of legality might have been overcome had either or both Accords been able to muster sufficient legitimacy in the political community. *See infra* notes 75–78, 81 and 83 (citing scholarly analyses of the reasons the Accords failed).

The article's primary objective of theorizing legality and legitimacy in Canada's amendment history leaves little space for broader reflections on amendment and comparative constitutionalism. At a minimum, its symmetrical attention to these concepts – and treatment of legitimacy – is distinctive in a literature that focuses primarily on textual legality and how design variables affect amendment rigidity.[13] Others have pointed out that by privileging the legality of amendment, textual singularity necessarily discounts the role of ambient political and constitutional culture as an agent of change.[14] In providing an experiential analysis of Canada's amendment history, this chapter exposes the limits of legality, engages legitimacy as a critical variable in constitutional change, and piques interest in the dynamics of alignment between the two.

LEGALITY, LEGITIMACY AND CONSTITUTIONALISM

Law's authority derives from its legality and legitimacy, two concepts which can be but are not necessarily in harmony. Legality describes law's qualities by reference to the rules or requirements set out in formal or positive instruments, documents and enactments. Their terms may be complex, opaque or contested, but laws nonetheless prescribe the conditions of and prerequisites to the exercise of authority. Of the two, legitimacy may be more elusive because it describes a law's quality or quotient of authoritative value. Though defined in variable terms, legitimacy is concerned with the status of a law or rule and whether its claim to regulate, constrain, permit or prohibit is accepted by members of the community as a governing and binding obligation. Legitimacy generally attaches to the fact of legality because, in Weber's words, "the most common form of legitimacy is the

---

[13] Donald Lutz took the initiative in using quantitative models to study patterns of rigidity in constitutional amendment. *See* Donald Lutz, Toward a Theory of Constitutional Amendment, AM. POL. SCI. REV., 88, 355–370 (1994); Donald Lutz, PRINCIPLES OF CONSTITUTIONAL DESIGN (New York: Cambridge University Press, 2006) [*Principles*]; *see also* Astrid Lorenz, *How to Measure Constitutional Rigidity: Four Concepts and Two Alternatives*, J. THEORETICAL POLITICS, 17:3, 339–361 (2005).

[14] *See, e.g.*, Xenophon Contiades, "Constitutional Change Engineering," in Xenophon Contiades (ed.), ENGINEERING CONSTITUTIONAL CHANGE: A COMPARATIVE PERSPECTIVE ON EUROPE, CANADA AND THE USA (Oxfordshire and New York: Routledge, 2013), 1 (explaining that "[a]mending procedures dictate how constitutional change is supposed to take place [but] the reality of change is determined through the impact of other factors as well, such as the structure of the political system, the effect of civil or common law tradition, the system of judicial review and constitutional ethos").

belief in legality."[15] Whether these concepts are aligned – what that means, how it is determined and what happens in instances of mis- or non-alignment – are major themes in legal and philosophical discourse.

The concern here is less with that discourse and more with how framework concepts apply to the making and amendment of constitutions. In principle, a written constitution expresses a conception of virtue in a framework for government that is intended to endure. The text articulates the legality of that conception, reflecting and incorporating fundamental beliefs and expectations about the powers and structures of government, and its relationship to a political community. As such, it embeds a conception of constitutional sovereignty, wrapping it in legitimacy and a hope or expectation of immortality.[16]

Weber's observation translates to the constitutional setting because a duly ratified text which proclaims its status as the supreme law of the land will carry presumptive authority. Alignment questions can arise because legitimacy deficits may be present or may surface in a constitution's lifetime when there are gaps between a text's legal force and its moral, social, or democratic authority. To endure, a constitution fundamentally must "make sense to those who are under its dictates" and represent a constitutional bargain that members of the community are invested in supporting.[17] Legitimacy deficits are manifest in sham or camouflage constitutions, whose inauthentic texts purport to entrench rights or values that are a charade, disconnected from political reality.[18] Likewise, constitutions may exhibit congenital defects that undermine their legitimacy – or durability – and place them at risk of constitutional mortality.[19] As well, a text may lack or lose authority where its prescriptions violate social, political or moral norms, or lack acceptance in segments of the community.[20]

[15] Max Weber, ECONOMY AND SOCIETY: AN INTERPRETIVE SOCIOLOGY, Guenther Roth and Claus Wittich (ed.), Ephraim Fischoff, Hans Gerth, A.M. Henderson, Ferdinand Kolegar, C. Wright Mills, Talcott Parsons, Max Rheinstein, Guenther Roth, Edward Shils and Claus Wittich (trans.), 2 vols. (Berkeley. University of California Press, 1978), 37.

[16] Lutz, *Principles, supra* note at 13, 26–27 (stating that constitutionalism and the design of constitutions ultimately rest on the idea of sovereignty and that constitutionalism is one way of "organizing sovereignty").

[17] Zachary Elkins, Tom Ginsburg and James Melton, THE ENDURANCE OF NATIONAL CONSTITUTIONS (New York: Cambridge University Press, 2009), 7 [*Endurance*].

[18] Richard Albert, *The Expressive Function of Constitutional Amendment Rules*, McGILL L.J., 59, 257–64 (2013) ["Expressive Function'].

[19] Elkins, Ginsburg and Melton, *Endurance, supra* note 17 (examining constitutional endurability and including case studies of congenital defects and constitutional mortality).

[20] This points to a defect of inclusion, which is an important element of endurance – or legitimacy – both at the moment of constitution-making and over the life of a constitution. *Id.*, 78–81.

The dynamics can work in the other direction, though it is less problematic when a text presents a defect of legality but is accepted as legitimate, despite the flaw.[21]

Change is a vital part of durability, and how the text provides for amendment speaks, fundamentally, to what a constitution is.[22] The terms and conditions of change must be prescribed with care because the legitimacy that attaches to constitution-making is a requisite of change. Those rules negotiate difficult terrain, calibrating the balance between stability and change, securing the moment of constitution making but providing for its durability by enabling it to evolve through processes of formal amendment. The variables are almost limitless, with some constitutions inviting formal change and others discouraging it to forestall the risk of impulsive, improvident and ill-advised spurts of reform.[23] Whatever the design choice may be, amendment rules are an essential, foundational and indispensable part of constitutional text.[24] Those rules represent a form of legality which, in this article, is described as constitutional, amendment or textual legality.[25]

Tension between a constitution's legality and legitimacy can arise when the text is out of step with shifts in legal, political and social culture. Pinpointing the moment of critical divergence between the two is challenging because legitimacy is perceptive in nature and operates at the level of belief. It is an organic part of constitutional culture that is fluid, lacking in concreteness and at least difficult, if not impossible, to measure. In conceptual terms, legitimacy

---

[21] Richard H. Fallon Jr., *Legitimacy and the Constitution*, HARV. L. REV., 118:6, 1787–1853 at 1807 (2005) ["Legitimacy"] (citing the US Constitution as a case in point, and noting that although the prescribed ratification process was not legally legitimate, the Constitution's acceptance meant that it was sociologically legitimate).

[22] Albert, *Expressive Function*, *supra* note 18, at 225–82 (explaining how and why amendment rules importantly express and protect a constitution's values). *See also* Richard Albert, *The Structure of Constitutional Amendment Rules*, WAKE. FOREST. L. REV., 49, 913–76 (2014) ["The Structure of Rules"], (providing a structural framework for understanding formal amendment rules and their effectiveness in balancing stability and flexibility).

[23] *See* Albert, *The Structure of Rules*, *id.* (analyzing those variables and how they facilitate or constrain the amendment of constitutional text).

[24] Richard Albert, *Amending Constitutional Amendment Rules*, INT. J. CON. LAW, 13, 655–85 (2015) (declaring, at 655, that "[n]o part of a constitution is more important than the rules that govern its amendment" and adding that "[a]mendment rules are fundamental to constitutionalism").

[25] Amendment by informal or extra-textual means is also an important agent of constitutional change. *See generally*, Brannon P. Denning, *Means to Amend: Theories of Constitutional Change*, TENN. L. REV., 65, 155–244 (1997); David A. Strauss, *The Irrelevance of Constitutional Amendments*, HARV. L. REV., 114, 1457–1505 (2002); Brannon P. Denning and John Vile, *The Relevance of Constitutional Amendments: A Response to David Strauss*, TUL. L. REV., 77, 247–82 (2002).

is divisible and can be analyzed from perspectives that include the legal, sociological and moral.[26] Whatever the perspective, amendments must satisfy a standard of legitimacy, and that enterprise can be tricky when the status quo is under review and a democratic community has been asked to re-imagine a constitution's foundational structures and promises.[27]

Where amendment is concerned, legality and legitimacy are aligned, generally, when the text prescribes rules that enable change within a framework of durability that sufficiently represents and respects the values and choices of a constitutional community. It is difficult, then, to imagine how legality and legitimacy can be aligned in the anomalous circumstances of a written constitution without textual amendment rules. In other words, amending a written text is surely problematic when there is no basis in legality to inform the legitimacy of change. Putting it in Weber's terms, a text without rules would require belief in a legality that does not exist.

In Canada's case, the *BNA Act*'s silence did not preclude textual change, as amendments were achieved through a process of statutory legality. Despite its workability, a sub-constitutional process that could not be equated with constitutional legality led to shortfalls in the legitimacy of constitutional amendment over time.[28] Amendment is a core function of constitutionalism, and Canada's lack of amendment sovereignty had serious implications for the capacity and legitimacy of reform, especially after independence in 1931. Specifically, the Constitution established a federal union, but the text's failure to provide rules formally excluded the provinces from the process of amendment. Without legality in the domain of federalism, it was predictable that the legitimacy of amendments affecting provincial sovereignty would be open to serious question over time.[29] In point of fact, the lack of constitutional legality

---

[26] Fallon, *Legitimacy, supra* note 21, at 1790 (categorizing and analyzing three conceptions – the legal, sociological and moral – of a constitution's legitimacy and describing their relationship as "complexly interrelated").

[27] The American constitutional tradition attests that some of the most profound controversies about the legitimacy of change are provoked by judicial review and constitutional interpretation. *See, e.g., Brown* v. *Board of Education*, 347 US 483 (1954) (overruling separate but equal in public schools); *Roe* v. *Wade*, 410 US 113 (1973) (constitutionalizing a woman's right to seek an abortion).

[28] Although amendment by UK statutory legality was consistent with principles of Westminster and imperial constitutionalism, it was sub-constitutional in the meaning of this article because amendments were achieved by ordinary legislation rather than by the rules of a constitutional text.

[29] As Premier Allan Blakeney declared, "in a federal state, the procedure for amending the constitution is the most important part of the fundamental law; that I think is self-evident really." Quoted in Peter Oliver, *Canada, Quebec, and Constitutional Amendment*, U.T.L.J., 49, 519–60, 520 (1999) ["Canada, Quebec"].

became progressively more incapacitating until the process of amendment halted prior to 1982, pending the adoption of rules.

The challenge deepened when a fresh legitimacy variable surfaced during negotiations on patriation. Though not a vital factor before 1982, the federal government's proposal for a referendum explicitly provided for democratic participation, or popular sovereignty, as an alternative pathway to transformative change. Not surprisingly, popular legitimacy served as a check on both post-patriation Accords which failed, in large part, because of a profound lack of confidence in constitutional renewal at multiple levels – from the process and substance of reform, to complex synergies of federalism, regionalism and democratic participation.

According to Fallon, the foundations of contemporary constitutional legitimacy "necessarily lie in current states of affairs" and are "more uncertain and contingent" than may typically be assumed.[30] While his conception examines its legal, sociological and moral varieties, the key variables at play in Canada's history of amendment legitimacy concern elements of sovereignty: the sovereignty or authority to amend the Constitution, or amendment sovereignty; the sovereignty principles of federalism, including provincial sovereignty; and the latent role of popular sovereignty. Separately, in combination, and over time, these are the cornerstone concepts of sovereignty at stake in Canada's amendment history. From Confederation to the present, defining and aligning the legality and legitimacy of these sovereignties has been the primary burden of Canadian constitutionalism.

STATUTORY LEGALITY: 1867 TO 1982

Aligning the legality and legitimacy of amendment is by definition a challenge under a constitutional text that does not in terms authorize change. For Canada, the starting point is 1867 and a constitution that failed to provide rules for its amendment.[31] Whether it was a blunder or more an oversight at the time, the omission was costly and difficult to remedy.[32] Statutory legality

---

[30] Fallon, *Legitimacy, supra* note 21, at 1852.
[31] Certain changes and amendments could be undertaken domestically prior to 1982 (*i.e.*, altering "housekeeping" operations of the House of Commons and Senate, ss. 52, 40, 51, 35 and 18, and amending the constitutions of the provinces, s. 92(1), the 1867 Constitution, *supra* note 2; admitting new provinces to the federation, The Constitution Act, 1871, 34–35 Vict., c. 28 (UK); and amending the Constitution of Canada, s. 91(1), The British North America (No. 2) Act, 13 Geo. VI, c. 81 (UK); Monahan and Shaw, *Constitutional Law, supra* note 3, at 168–73.
[32] McWhinney describes it as a "major blunder" which "undoubtedly stemmed from the ignorance of British constitutional lawyers with the problems of written constitutions and the

offered a workaround that bridged the textual gap and enabled constitutional change to proceed between 1867 and 1931. Even so, there were diminishing returns to the legitimacy of statutory amendment after independence, and by the 1960s the mechanism was functionally illegitimate; after 1964 the Constitution was not amended again until 1982. The dilemma throughout was this: while statutory legality was sub-constitutional, the lack of textual rules created a vacuum which complicated the task of developing a scheme of amendment legality that could be accepted as legitimate.

Confederation was an initiative of four colonies that expressed their "Desire to be federally united into One Dominion" under British authority, with a Constitution "Similar in Principle to that of the United Kingdom."[33] UK legislation constituting Canada under those terms was legitimate because the colonies drafted the document and Britain gave it legal force by enacting the *BNA Act*.[34] The legalities at the time were two-fold: Dominion status described and determined the relationship between Canada and the United Kingdom, and the Constitution established the terms of federal union between the partners to Confederation.[35] As a Dominion, Canada was self-governing but was subject to forms of imperial oversight, including Britain's power to disallow federal legislation, and judicial review of domestic legislation by the Judicial Committee of the Privy Council.[36] Amending the 1867 Constitution was another area in which Canada lacked sovereign authority, because the *Colonial Laws Validity Act* prohibited domestic legislation that was in conflict with applicable imperial legislation.[37] The *BNA Act* was such a statute and could only be amended by the UK legislature.

In origin, amending the constitution by statutory legality was a function of imperial hierarchy and parliamentary sovereignty, having little on its face to do with constitutional legality or legitimacy. Yet in practice, Dominion status meant that the British Parliament would respect Canada's autonomy on

---

practical necessity of having amendment formulae built in"; *Canada and the Constitution*, *supra* note 7, at 65. Oliver, by contrast, suggests that it was "not likely to have been an oversight." *Canada, Quebec, supra* note 29, at 526–27.

[33] *BNA Act, supra* note 2, preamble.

[34] The four confederating colonies were Upper and Lower Canada – present day Ontario and Quebec – along with Nova Scotia and New Brunswick.

[35] *BNA Act, supra* note 2, ss. 91, 92 (defining the primary division of powers between the federal and provincial governments).

[36] *BNA Act, id.*, s. 56. The Judicial Committee of the Privy Council ("JCPC") served as Canada's final court of appeal until 1949, when the Supreme Court of Canada was empowered by federal legislation to assume that role; *Act to Amend the Supreme Court Act*, S.C. 1949 (2nd sess.), c. 37.

[37] 28–29 Vict. c. 63 (1865) (UK) ("CLVA").

matters of domestic governance. The United Kingdom never exercised its legal power of disallowance or amended the Constitution without Canada's consent, and soon after Confederation the United Kingdom agreed, as a matter of routine, to grant the federal government's requests for amendments to the *BNA Act*.[38] In this way, Britain fettered its legal power through a convention accepting Canada's authority to determine when and how the *BNA Act* would be amended.[39]

Because it was concerned with the relationship between imperial authority and a self-governing Dominion, the UK convention treated the federal government as the legitimate source of authority on amendment. The convention was political rather than legal in nature, and did not contemplate substantive review to ensure that proposed amendments complied with the terms of the *BNA Act*.[40] In structural terms, Canada's constitutionalism was based on hierarchical chains of legality, in the first instance between the United Kingdom and the federal government, and then domestically, between the federal government and the provinces. The significance of this hierarchy is that just as the federal government could not prevent the United Kingdom from amending the Constitution, the lack of rules in the *BNA Act* meant that the provinces had no legal authority to prevent it making a unilateral request for amendment by the federal government. While the UK amendment convention accepted that Britain could not exercise its legal powers without undercutting Canada's constitutional autonomy, there was no parallel recognition that unilateral federal amendment could undermine the sovereignty of the provinces and might be unconstitutional for that reason.

Amendments effected through a binary process between the United Kingdom and federal government could work in a unitary state or federal system that subordinated the provincial level of government, but that was decidedly not the way Canadian federalism evolved. The prevalent view that Canada's federal union was hierarchical in conception was offset, from the outset, by a

---

[38] The convention began to crystallize before or at the time of Confederation. Monahan and Shaw, *supra* note 3, at 174.

[39] The UK convention was complemented by a local convention requiring a resolution of the Canadian Parliament to activate the process of constitutional amendment. This convention simply complied with the norms of parliamentary government, including the principles of responsible government. *Id*, at 175–76.

[40] P. Gérin-Lajoie, CONSTITUTIONAL AMENDMENT IN CANADA (Toronto: University of Toronto Press, 1951), 217 (stating that the "most common view today [*i.e.*, 1951] is ... that British action would be automatic upon a request from the Canadian Houses of Parliament"). Note that it was unclear in 1981 whether the UK Parliament would grant the federal government's request for unilateral amendment and patriation of the Constitution. *Infra* note 66.

strong counter vision.[41] In the years after 1867, a robust tradition of judicial review developed to protect the constitutional division of powers. Shaping Canadian federalism by enhancing and entrenching provincial autonomy is one of the hallmarks of the Privy Council's constitutional jurisprudence, which granted the provinces co-equal status in their areas of exclusive constitutional jurisdiction under s. 92.[42] Outside the constitutional domain, the dynamics of federalism shifted as Confederation expanded and the provinces matured, gaining economic and political power.

As text, the *BNA Act* left the provinces powerless and without a voice on constitutional reform. Though amendments were infrequent in the early years of Confederation, the provinces began to resist the assumption that the federal government was in control of the amendment function.[43] Even so, a domestic convention to validate their role and constrain the federal government from acting unilaterally was slow to evolve. When Canada became independent in 1931, there was no established practice of consulting with provinces or obtaining their consent to proposed amendments, much less a crystallized convention binding the federal government to do so.[44] The legitimacy of that claim was acknowledged, importantly and for the first time, by the *Statute of Westminster*.

1931 was a transformative year for the British Dominions that gained independence under the *Statute of Westminster* and also for the United Kingdom, which had to reconcile a surrender of power with parliamentary and imperial sovereignty.[45] The *Statute* was unprecedented in the history of the Empire because it provided for its self-governing Dominions to attain independence and released them from the terms of the *Colonial Laws Validity Act*, including

---

[41] *BNA Act, supra* note 2; For textual indices of the federal government's dominant role *see, e.g.,* s. 90 (granting the federal government the power to disallow provincial legislation); ss. 91–92 (textualizing federal paramountcy); and ss. 55–57 and 58 (providing that the federal government would appoint the lieutenant governors of the provinces and could instruct them to withhold consent to provincial bills or to reserve them for the federal government's consideration).

[42] *See, e.g., Hodge v. The Queen* (1883) 9 App. Cas. 117 at 132; Dom. Sess. Pap. 1884, Vol. 17, No. 30 (pronouncing that within the scope of s. 92, the provinces are "supreme" and have "authority as plenary and ample" as the Imperial Parliament or the Parliament of the Dominion).

[43] Monahan and Shaw, *supra* note 3, at 176. Provincial opposition to a proposed constitutional amendment was registered for the first time in 1907, with British Columbia's objection to a new scheme for financial subsidies under s. 118 of the *BNA Act*. The amendment went ahead with the support of eight of nine provinces.

[44] At the time of independence there was little or no evidence of such a convention, which remained unclear up to patriation, and was grounded in four amendments in 1940, 1951, 1960, and 1964. *Infra* note 57.

[45] 1931, 22–23 Geo. 5, c. 4, s. 7 (UK).

its principle of repugnance.[46] Section 4 of the *Statute* stated that British law would no longer apply to the Dominions, except at their request and with their consent.[47] Force of circumstance led Canada to make an exceptional request.

For Canada, independence would bring UK statutory legality to an end and create a new void on amendment that would potentially enable either level of domestic government to alter the Constitution by ordinary legislation.[48] As a result, the Constitution could be more at risk of unilateral and unconstitutional amendment after independence than under the imperial regime of UK statutory legality. Even though the United Kingdom was bound by convention to grant the federal government's requests, the convention was perceived as protective, because the British Parliament retained the legal authority not to enact amendments that were repugnant to the *BNA Act*.[49]

In anticipation of independence, the federal government and provinces attempted to agree on amendment rules in 1927 and again in 1931.[50] Their lack of success created a predicament which presented Canada with an unsavoury choice between postponing independence until rules could be drawn, and accepting independence but preserving British authority over the Constitution. If neither was desirable, an exception to independence was more attractive than deferring a landmark moment in Canadian history. In response to the provinces' concerns, the federal government asked the *BNA Act* to be exempted from the *Statute of Westminster*, and Canada's independence was accompanied by a statutory asterisk preserving its dependence on the United Kingdom for amendments to the Constitution.[51]

---

[46] *Id.*, s. 1 (defining "Dominions" to include the Dominion of Canada, Commonwealth of Australia, Dominion of New Zealand, Union of South Africa, Irish Free State, and Newfoundland) and s. 2(2) (negating the principle of repugnance).

[47] *Id.*, s. 4 (stating: "No Act of Parliament of the United Kingdom passed after the commencement of this Act shall extend, or be deemed to extend, to a Dominion as part of the law of that Dominion, unless it is expressly declared in that Act that that Dominion has requested, and consented to, the enactment thereof").

[48] Peter Hogg, *A Comment on the Canadian Constitutional Crisis*, YALE STUDIES IN WORLD PUBLIC ORDER, 6, 285–296 at 286, 289 (1980) ["Constitutional Crisis"], (citing this risk).

[49] *See* Oliver, *Canada, Quebec, supra* note 29 at 526–27 (discussing the historical purpose of amendment by the United Kingdom and stating, in note 35, that "the Imperial Parliament could be at once a means of remedying any defect in the new Constitution and a force of stability and reason"); *see also infra* note 66.

[50] James Ross Hurley, AMENDING CANADA'S CONSTITUTION: HISTORY, PROCESSES, PROBLEMS AND PROSPECTS (Canada: Minister of Supply and Services Canada, 1996), 25–7 [*Amending Canada's Constitution*].

[51] *Supra* note 45. Section 7(1) states: "Nothing in this Act [*i.e.*, granting independence] shall be deemed to apply to the repeal, amendment or alteration of the British North America Acts, 1867 to 1930, or any order, rule or regulation made thereunder."

By outsourcing this function to a foreign sovereign after independence, Canada accepted a stunning and unusual limit on its authority. Importantly, the *Statute of Westminster's* exceptionalism for the BNA *Act* was formally and in functional terms an amending formula.[52] As a formula it was admittedly dysfunctional, because it continued the status quo of statutory legality and retained the trappings of colonial subservience. Despite the irregularity, the *Westminster* amending formula had at least transitional legitimacy because it created a form of legality that prevented self-interested parties to Canada's federal union from undercutting constitutional promises through ordinary statutory actions.[53] More to the point, s. 7's BNA *Act* exception codified the principle that constitutional legality was necessary to legitimize amendments to the Constitution.[54] In requesting that arrangement, the federal government and provinces recorded their agreement that the imperial monitor should remain in place to protect the integrity of Canadian federalism, pending textual rules. In this way, the status quo served as a placeholder that recognized the stake of the provinces, in the era of Canadian independence, in the process and substance of constitutional amendment. Whatever might be said of placing faith in an amendment protocol that had excluded the provinces for more than sixty years, the development was symbolically important and marked a significant evolution in the dynamics of federal-provincial relations.

In the circumstances, preserving British oversight of a vital constitutional function should have provided incentive for Canada's two levels of government to negotiate an amending formula. Instead, it signalled deepening distrust between the parties to federalism and foreshadowed years of stalemate. Prolonged dependence on UK statutory legality may have seemed innocuous but had the effect, over the next five decades, of incapacitating and disabling the amendment function.

Over the course of fourteen high-level meetings between 1931 and 1982, the process of executive federalism failed to produce agreement on an amending

---

[52] *See* Oliver, *Canada, Quebec, supra* note 29, at 573 (observing that Canada chose to retain the legislature of another country as its "ultimate amendment procedure" and that the Westminster Parliament was "simply an amending formula").

[53] *See* Fallon, *Legitimacy, supra* note 21, at 1809 (describing "minimal" legitimacy and suggesting that officials and citizens might accept a duty to support "even flawed legal regimes" in the absence of a better alternative).

[54] Russell, *Odyssey, supra* note 7, at 55 (commenting, in relation to the 1927 meeting that, "[t]he fact that the federal government would not act on ... Canada's constitutional sovereignty without full consultation with the provinces shows that the Government of Canada did not feel it had full authority to speak for ... Canadians" and that the provincial governments were "accepted as essential constituent elements of the 'autonomous community'").

formula.[55] The challenge was complicated by the dual nature of the task: as a matter of legality, the parties not only had to accept proposed amendment, but also had to decide *inter se* what level of agreement was necessary to legitimize and represent agreement to those rules. The federal government and provinces were able to agree on rules in 1964 and again in 1971, though both amending formulas stalled when unanimity faltered after the fact.[56] It could plausibly be argued that there was sufficient agreement to proceed with either the Fulton-Favreau formula or Victoria Charter. In the absence of any standard or measure of legality, it was instead assumed that amendment rules would not be legitimate without the agreement – depending on perspective – of Quebec or of all parties.

Meantime, the *Westminster* amending formula remained in place and the Constitution was amended nine times between 1931 and 1982. Provincial consent was sought and obtained for three amendments that directly affected s. 92 interests, but not when the federal government claimed that their interests were not at stake.[57] Though the status of a convention requiring provincial consent remained uncertain, the legitimacy of unilateral federal amendment diminished.[58] The longstanding negotiations made the claim of a formal role for provinces compelling, if not legally or politically binding on

---

[55] Hurley, *Amending Canada's Constitution, supra* note 50, at 22–63 (documenting this history).

[56] Monahan and Shaw, *supra* note 3, at 179–80. Whereas the 1964 Fulton-Favreau formula required unanimous consent for all amendments affecting the division of powers, the 1971 *Victoria Charter* was based on agreement by the federal government, Ontario, Quebec, and a majority of the western and Atlantic provinces. Quebec alone withdrew its support from the Fulton-Favreau proposal, and Saskatchewan and Alberta joined Quebec in withdrawing from the *Victoria Charter* after provincial elections, because Ontario and Quebec were the only provinces to receive a veto.

[57] *Id.*, at 170–73, 176–79. Four amendments were preceded by unanimous provincial consent (*i.e.,* unemployment insurance, 1940; old-age pensions, 1951; judicial tenure of office, 1960; and old-age benefits, 1964). Others proceeded without provincial consent or over provincial objection (*i.e.,* postponing the redistribution of House of Commons seats, 1943; adjusting the formula for House of Commons representation, 1946; enabling the federal government to amend the Constitution and admitting Newfoundland to Confederation, 1949). The 1949 amendment authorizing the federal government to amend the Constitution was particularly contentious; while the federal government insisted on the exclusive authority to make certain amendments to the Constitution, Quebec and six provinces demanded that the amendment be repealed. Oliver, *Canada Quebec, supra* note 29, at 535.

[58] The influential Favreau White Paper on constitutional amendment hedged the question of provincial consent, stating that "[t]he nature and degree of provincial participation in the amending process ... have not lent themselves to easy definition." G. Favreau, THE AMENDMENT OF THE CONSTITUTION OF CANADA (Ottawa: Queen's Printer, 1965), 15; *see also* Hogg, *Constitutional Crisis, supra* note 48, at 286 (discussing the status of such a convention and concluding, in 1980, that "[w]hether a convention requiring provincial consents to altering the distribution of powers has become established practice is not entirely clear").

the federal government. The federal government unilaterally amended the Constitution for the last time in 1949, and no amendments were advanced between 1964 and 1982.

Desperately unsuccessful negotiations took Canada to the brink in 1981. Events had demonstrated that the legality and legitimacy of constitutional amendment could not be aligned. As a matter of formal legality, Canada's Constitution could be amended by a foreign sovereign, acting at the request of a federal government that chose to disregard the terms of the Constitution and interests of the provinces. Amendments undertaken through that process would heighten misalignment between the two, satisfying the requirements of legality but manifestly lacking in the demands of legitimacy.

CONSTITUTIONAL LEGALITY: PATRIATION AND THE ACCORDS

Short of unanimity, a scheme of amendment legality that would satisfy the provinces could not be found. In due course, fault for the amendment impasse was attributed to the politicians who, "despite intermittent efforts since 1927 and very intensive efforts since 1968," were unwilling to set aside jealousies and differences to work together on domestic amendment rules.[59] By the 1970s, a self-reinforcing history of failed negotiations was aggravated by the rise of militance among the provinces.[60] The collapse of negotiations yet again, shortly after Quebec's May 1980 referendum on sovereignty-association, enabled Prime Minister Trudeau to claim the "political high ground" with his plan for the unilateral patriation of the Constitution.[61] This plan was designed to unblock constitutional reform by challenging the provinces and the tyranny of unanimity.[62]

---

[59] Hogg, *Constitutional Crisis, id.*, at 286. Frustration is also evident in remarks by Pierre Trudeau, who commented on "what enormous amounts of bile and wasted time constitutional conferences had produced ... only to discover how impossible it was to get [the first ministers] to agree on a constitutional amending formula"; quoted in Graham, *The Last Act, supra* note 7, at 15.

[60] McWhinney, *Canada and the Constitution, supra* note 7, at 4 (describing a "pan-Canadian confrontation in which all the provinces seemed to be joining together to make a common war against the federal government").

[61] Graham, *The Last Act, supra* note 7, at 68. The key elements of the plan were an amending formula, which would serve to patriate the Constitution, and a charter of rights. Also note for clarity that all references in this article are to Prime Minister Pierre Elliot Trudeau and not to the current Prime Minister, his son Justin Trudeau.

[62] As Prime Minister Trudeau complained, "we took the idea of unanimity and made it a tyrant ... We were led by the dictates of unanimity to bargain freedom against fish, fundamental rights against oil, the independence of our country against long-distance telephone rates." *Id*, at 68.

The prime minister's act of constitutional derring-do willed a breakthrough on patriation in a proposal that joined the federal government's authority to request amendments with a legitimizing referendum on the amending formula.[63] The referendum option gave the federal government leverage over the provinces and deflected their claims of sovereignty by highlighting alternative sources of legitimacy: its unquestioned mandate to act on its political authority, as duly elected representative of the Canadian people; and the democratic authority of an inclusive, nationwide referendum. Though patriation was achieved in 1982 without a referendum, the appeal to direct democracy and the "people's constitution or people's package" as the proposal – with its charter of constitutional rights – was styled, fundamentally altered the dynamics of constitutional reform. From that point on, popular legitimacy played an increasingly important role in shaping and determining the success or failure of constitutional reform.

Eight of the ten provinces opposed patriation by taking the federal government to court, and once it confusingly decreed that unilateral patriation was legal but unconventional, the Supreme Court of Canada's role in the amendment process could not be circumvented.[64] By endorsing its legality but rejecting the legitimacy of the federal proposal, a splintered Court wittingly or unwittingly played a vital role in brokering the ultimate patriation deal.[65] The *Patriation Reference*'s judicial draw between unilateral patriation's legal and constitutional status forced another round of negotiations, in particular because the federal government could not predict how the United Kingdom might respond to a fiercely resisted package of amendments.[66] In the fall of

---

[63] According to the proposal, the federal government and provinces would have two years to achieve unanimity on an amending formula, in default of which the provinces could propose an amending formula. That formula, along with the Victoria Charter, would be submitted in a referendum to the electorate within four years of patriation. Should the provinces fail to advance a formula, then the Victoria rules would come into effect within two years of patriation, without a referendum. McWhinney, *Canada and the Constitution, supra* note 7, at 53–54.

[64] *Re Resolution to Amend the Constitution* [1981] 1 S.C.R 753, 11 Man R (2d) 1 [the *"Patriation Reference"*]. Seven of nine judges agreed that the federal government had the legal power to proceed unilaterally, with two dissenting strongly to defend the integrity of Canadian federalism. A differently constituted majority of six judges then found that the patriation plan was unconstitutional because it violated a domestic constitutional convention that required an indeterminate but "substantial" level of provincial agreement. Three judges dissented strongly on the ground that such a constraint was unprecedented and unrecognized in constitutional law.

[65] For a recent comment, *see* Philip Girard, "Law, Politics, and the *Patriation Reference* of 1981," in Harder and Patten, *Patriation and Its Consequences, supra* note 8, at 115–36.

[66] A key question throughout was whether the UK Parliament would act on the federal government's request for unilateral constitutional amendments. By then, the United Kingdom

1981, Prime Minister Trudeau again pressed a referendum option to under-mine and outmaneuver the sovereignty claims of the provinces.[67] Not surpris-ingly, but with one critical exception, the provinces were uniformly opposed to a proposal that would deflect and diminish their importance in the process of amendment.[68] Agreement on patriation without democratic participation was reached when the federal government abandoned a referendum in exchange for consent to the patriation package from all provinces but Quebec.[69] As a matter of political calculation, the rest-of-Canada's leadership concluded that the 5 November patriation package was legitimate enough to satisfy constitutional standards, because the Supreme Court had refused to endorse a requirement of unanimity.[70] Despite satisfying a jurisprudential rule of substantial provincial support, the patriation plan provoked resistance, not only in Quebec but from powerful rights-seeking members of Canada's democratic community.[71]

had been lobbied in an attempt to persuade Parliament that convention did not require it to accede to the Canadian government's requests in all cases, and especially where the patriation package fundamentally lacked domestic legitimacy. Whether the United Kingdom might depart from the established protocol of statutory legality in response to such a serious legitimacy shortfall was part of the intrigue that compelled the federal government to resolve its differences with the provinces. See Romanow, Whyte and Leeson, *Notwithstanding, supra* note 7, chapter 5, "The Battle of Britain," 134–54; McWhinney, *Canada and the Constitution, supra* note 7, chapter 7, "Cutting the Gordian Knot," 65–71.

[67] Over the course of negotiations from 2–5 November 1981, the proposal for a referendum took many forms and was broadened to include a vote on patriation and the *Charter of Rights and Freedoms*, as well as the rules for amendment. For an account, *see* Romanow, Whyte and Leeson, *Notwithstanding, supra* note 7, chapter 7, "The Week That Was," 188–215.

[68] All provinces, except Quebec – in a moment of unguarded weakness – were opposed because a referendum would fundamentally re-focus the source of legitimacy for change on the democratic community, through a process managed by the federal government.

[69] Quebec's exclusion from the Kitchen Accord, in the so-called "night of the long knives," is a legendary part of the patriation saga and the catalyst for the Meech Lake Accord. *See generally* Graham, *The Last Act, supra* note 7, chapter 14 ("The Kitchen Accord"), 190–98, and chapter 15 ("The Night of the Long Knives"), 201–11.

[70] On the question of constitutionality, the Court held that a substantial degree of provincial consent was required and stated also that "[n]othing more should be said about this." *Patriation Reference, supra* note 64 at 905. The important element there was that the Court had stated that the rule of unanimity "under which past constitutional conferences labored and ultimately failed" was not a conventional – or constitutional – requirement. Romanow, Whyte and Leeson, *Notwithstanding, supra* note 7, at 188.

[71] After the re-negotiated plan was announced, the "unexpected" occurred with the genuine involvement of the general public in a "seemingly quite spontaneous and at first quite unco-ordinated public reaction, which was communicated directly and pressingly to the premiers and their supporters"; McWhinney, *Canada and the Constitution, supra* note 7, at 102. *See also* Sheppard and Valpy, *The National Deal, supra* note 7, at 307 (stating that in the face of intense pressure, especially on women's and aboriginal rights, the provincial governments "folded like omelettes").

Patriation came in 1982 at high cost: Quebec was dealt an unforgivable insult that largely robbed patriation of legitimacy in that province and radically escalated the danger of separation.[72] Quebec's exclusion and the gaping legitimacy deficit it caused set off a chain reaction that further imperiled the fragile status of constitutional reform and threatened Canada's durability as a nation. On its face, the Meech Lake Accord (MLA) was a well-intentioned reform initiative aimed at completing patriation by healing the wounds of 1982 through a "Quebec Round" which would redress the province's grievances.[73] Unanimous agreement at the level of executive federalism anchored the Accord's legitimacy, gestured in humility toward amend-making with Quebec, and initially augured well for the MLA's acceptance.

By courting Quebec's agenda, entertaining asymmetric arrangements, and privileging Quebec as a distinct society, the MLA ignored pent-up demands and expectations for movement on women's and aboriginal rights, as well as on Senate reform.[74] Over the MLA's three-year ratification period from 1987 to 1990, the legitimacy of prioritizing Quebec and sidelining other issues steadily declined.[75] Process deficits were a further, critical aggravation: the MLA process was closed, lacking in transparency and non-inclusive; it shut out newly empowered voices that had the resources, political will and visibility to confront the bygone legitimacy of executive federalism. Three years after its announcement was celebrated, the Accord failed for want of ratification

---

[72] Even before formal enactment on 17 April 1982 Quebec contested the constitutionality of patriation, claiming a veto over constitutional amendment, which was rejected by the Supreme Court of Canada; *Re: Objection by Quebec to a Resolution to Amend the Constitution*, [1982] 2 SCR 793, 140 DLR (3d) 385; The province also enacted legislation overriding the *Charter* across the spectrum of provincial statute law; *An Act respecting the Constitution Act, 1982*, S.Q. 1982, c. 21.

[73] The MLA proposed amendments that recognized Quebec as a distinct society; required the federal government to grant provinces a greater role in immigration and to select Supreme Court of Canada judges from lists of names from the provinces; entrenched Quebec's right to three judges on the Court; and allowed the provinces to opt out of share cost programs, under certain conditions; and granted all provinces a veto on s. 42 amendments. *See* Monahan, *Inside Story, supra* note 7, at 297–305 (Appendix 3, text of the MLA), pp. 306–14 (Appendix 4, 1990 Constitutional Agreement).

[74] Romanow, Whyte and Leeson, *Notwithstanding, supra* note 7, at 276–78 (stating that "the need for constitutional reform has not been lessened by the limited success of 1982" and pointing to unresolved constitutional dilemmas like Quebec, aboriginal peoples, the Senate, the Supreme Court of Canada and economic union).

[75] *See* Monahan, *Inside Story, supra* note 7 (analyzing the full history of the MLA and explaining Premier Bourassa's crucial decision to invoke the override to protect Quebec's language legislation from *Charter* review as a turning point in the saga, because it alienated Canadians outside Quebec and raised deep concerns about the constitutionalization of a "distinct society" clause for Quebec).

on 23 June 1990. The text of the Accord required unanimity and, as the deadline neared, the Manitoba and Newfoundland legislatures refused to ratify the MLA.

Accounts of the Accord's failure abound, and include attention to the obstacles arising from the legalities of amendment, which set a three-year time period and required all provincial legislatures and the federal government to ratify the agreement.[76] More telling than the obstacles of legality were the MLA's legitimacy defects and political miscalculations.[77] As one observer commented, "the Constitution [was] no longer an affair of governments" and not only had federalism "lost status in the Constitution as an organizing principle," there was outrage at the "illegitimacy of governments perceived as playing fast and loose with a Constitution which they had forgotten was no longer theirs alone."[78]

In a climate of escalating anxiety over Canada's future, Meech Lake's defeat made the next initiative inevitable. Quebec did not hesitate in issuing an ultimatum that brought urgency to the task of accommodating its minimum demands for constitutional amendment, without repeating the mistakes of the MLA.[79] The "Canada Round" was the result of an expedited but nationally inclusive process of democratic renewal, which proposed constitutional reforms across a range of institutional and substantive issues.[80] Addressing

---

[76] *See, e.g.*, Monahan, *id.*; Cohen, *Meech Lake Accord, supra* note 7 (pointing to the fundamental disconnect in the process between the political leadership and the electorate); Katherine Swinton, *Amending the Canadian Constitution: Lessons from Meech Lake*, U.T.L.J., 42, 139–169 at 144 (1992) ["Lessons from Meech Lake"] (pointing to changes in political will and provincial elections in New Brunswick, Manitoba and Newfoundland, which affected the MLA).

[77] Webber, *Reimagining Canada, supra* note 7, at 134–62 (explaining that "there was no coherent description of the whole, no explanation why Meech Lake made sense in terms of Canada" and it was "inevitably seen as a crass trade-off, extracted by threats from Quebec, contrary to constitutional principle"; *id.*, 162).

[78] Alan C. Cairns, "The Limited Vision Constitutional Vision of Meech Lake," in K.E. Swinton and C.J. Rogerson, (eds.), COMPETING CONSTITUTIONAL VISIONS. THE MEECH LAKE ACCORD (Canada: Carswell Co. Ltd., 1988), 259, 261 and 256.

[79] Quebec announced that with or without a constitutional overture from the rest of Canada there would be a referendum on separation no later than 26 October 1992.

[80] After reports, negotiations and a nationwide Renewal of Canada campaign, the federal government and provinces unanimously agreed, once again, to transformative constitutional change. *See, e.g., The Process for Amending the Constitution: The Report of the Special Joint Committee of the Senate and the House of Commons* (Canada: Queen's Printer, 1991) (the "Beaudoin-Edwards Report"); *The Citizen's Forum on National Unity* (the "Spicer Report") (Canada: Queen's Printer, 1991); and *Report of the Special Joint Committee on a Renewed Canada* (Canada: Queen's Printer, 1992) (the Beaudoin-Dobbie Report"). *See also* Monahan and McRoberts, *The Charlottetown Accord, supra* note 7, at 278–309 (Appendix 1, "Consensus Report on the Constitution," Final Text, 28 August 1992).

the substantive and procedural deficits of the MLA backfired, however, because the Charlottetown Accord's unwieldy reforms did not register as authentic in the democratic domain. Proposals which were inevitably and unavoidably dilute sounded in political expedience and inspired more antagonism than generosity in Canada's watchful and empowered democratic community.[81] Following an intense campaign the Accord was defeated in a national referendum held on 26 October 1992, which conclusively rejected the proposal.[82] Paradoxically, while the MLA failed because its agenda was perceived as grossly under-inclusive, the Charlottetown Accord was almost the precise opposite – cumbersome, bloated and over-inclusive, in terms, to a fault.[83]

Each of the post-patriation textual initiatives set a high threshold for the legality of constitutional reform. But in each instance, the proposals for change were misaligned with pre-existing and developing expectations of what legitimizes constitutional change. The lesson and legacy of the Accords is that constitutional reform cannot be attempted again, with any realistic prospect of success, until that threshold misalignment is addressed. In response to the failure of reform – and in search of that elusive alignment – a variety of statutory legalities, both federal and provincial, have been embossed on Part V's rules of amendment legality. In part, these requirements revolve around Quebec and its status in Confederation, but also respond to the dynamics of legitimacy in the rest of Canada.[84]

[81] See Webber, *Reimagining Canada*, *supra* note 7, at 174–75 (reflecting on the reasons for the Accord's failure and remarking on "a continued inability to resolve the basic tensions left over from Meech" and describing Charlottetown as "a set of largely ad hoc trade-offs, unsupported by a vision of the country as a whole." *Id.*, at 175).

[82] The Accord passed muster in four of ten provinces, and was defeated, as a matter of popular vote, by a margin of 54.3 per cent against and 45.7 per cent in favour; Monahan and McRoberts, *The Charlottetown Accord*, *supra* note 7, Appendix 3, "Official Voting Results, by Province."

[83] See, *e.g.*, Monahan and McRoberts, *id.* (presenting articles by a number of leaders discussing what was wrong, in process and substance, with the Charlottetown Accord); *see also* Matthew Mendelsohn, *Public Brokerage: Constitutional Reform and the Accommodation of Mass Politics*, CAN. J. POLI. SCI., 33:2, 245–272 (2000) ["Constitutional Reform"] (explaining that the 1992 Accord failed because compromises were forged at the elite level but ratification was sought and required at the mass level).

[84] See, *e.g.*, *An Act representing constitutional amendments*, S.C. 1996, c. 1 [*Regional Veto Act*] (prohibiting constitutional amendments from being proposed unless certain provinces have consented, namely Ontario; Quebec; British Columbia; at least two Atlantic provinces representing at least 50 per cent of the population; and at least two of the three prairie provinces having at least 50 per cent of the population). At the provincial level, Alberta and British Columbia require a binding referendum before their legislatures can approve constitutional amendments; *see Constitutional Referendum Act*, R.S.A. 2000, c. C-25; *Constitutional*

It is clear, from the nature and scale of these supplements, that Part V's amendment legality is not sufficient to legitimize constitutional change. Not only is the coexistence and overlap of constitutional and extra-textual regimes of legality confusing, it raises perplexing questions about the authority of the text.[85] The most critical of these asks why Part V's framework of constitutional legality, achieved in 1982 after such an ordeal and at great expense, is not enough. Moreover, instead of clarifying amendment legality, these extra- or super-textual requirements reveal ongoing angst about the source of legitimacy for change. It remains uncertain, in a bewildering array of rules, whether the legitimacy of constitutional change depends, fundamentally, on sovereignty principles of federalism, on a concept of regional or territorial sovereignty; on the popular sovereignty of Canada's democratic community; on the sovereignty interests of certain peoples, like aboriginal communities; or on some elixir mix of all elements. Though all are represented in the current mélange, their relationships, and the alignment of statutory and constitutional requirements, are muddled.

In the aftermath of failed reform, the amendment process was described as "deeply dysfunctional," because managing concurring and competing legitimacies spun out of control, creating a "widespread sense of powerlessness" and perception that constitutional change had been rendered impossible.[86] Time has not substantially altered that assessment, and though it is open to doubt that adding layers of legality will boost the legitimacy of constitutional reform, the issue may be academic. Canada's Constitution has become

Amendment Approval Act, R.S.B.C. 1996, c. 67. Saskatchewan also has referendum legislation but does not require or contemplate a referendum as an imperative; *Referendum and Plebiscite Act*, ss. 1990–91, c. R-8.01. It is now widely believed that legitimacy demands a national referendum to validate Part V amendments to the Constitution. *See also* Supreme Court of Canada decisions: the *Reference Re Secession of Quebec*, [1998] 2 SCR 217, [1998] SCJ No 61 (and the *Clarity* Act, S.C. 2000, c. 26); *Reference Re Supreme Court Act, ss. 5 and 6*, 2014 SCC 21, [2014] 1 SCR 433 and *Reference Re Senate Reform 2014 SCC 32*, [2014] 1 SCR 704 (placing judge-made caveats and qualifications on the substance and process of constitutional amendment).

[85]   Extra-textual constraints aimed at enhancing the legitimacy of amendment complicate and obscure the process, and delegitimize the textual rules for change. *See* Albert, *The Difficulty of Constitutional Amendment in Canada*, *supra* note 8 (explaining that in making the Constitution impossible to amend, extra-textual restrictions weaken democracy and undermine the purpose of "writtenness"). Possible solutions include treating Part V as a code for constitutional change, which may not be realistic, or amending Part V to formalize a referendum process in the legality of amendment. Such a requirement would not make reform more likely to succeed, but would address a perceived legitimacy gap and create textual certainty around what is required for constitutional renewal.

[86]   Mendelsohn, *Constitutional Reform*, *supra* note 83, at 272.

among the most rigid and most difficult to amend in the world.[87] There is
little doubt that reform cannot realistically be initiated again until the legality
and legitimacy of constitutional amendment are better aligned.

LEGALITY, LEGITIMACY AND AMENDMENT RIGIDITY

If not entirely anomalous in the time and place of Confederation, the
BNA Act's failure to provide amendment rules was incapacitating over time.
Negotiating a textual formula after independence was essentially an exercise
in defining the nation's sovereignty, because constitutional rules are "the
most basic expression of the legal nature of the country."[88] By the time of
the patriation crisis, the protracted lack of consensus on that core question
of constitutional sovereignty showed, contrary to perception, that Canada's
independence after 1931 may have been "illusory" after all, and that the roots
of our legal existence were "virtually untraceable."[89] Release from statutory
legality – the final yoke of dependence – would and could not occur until
conflict and confrontation forced a resolution that was costly for constitutional
legitimacy.

The impasse on amendment was an impasse on legality, on legitimacy, and,
more fundamentally, on how Canadian constitutional sovereignty would be
defined. In circumstances of deeply divergent conceptions of constitutionalism, perhaps that impasse could only be broken by a frontal challenge to
entrenched but contested assumptions about the role of the provinces in the
amendment process.[90] If so, patriation happened, in blunt terms, because a
willful prime minister was able in effect to impose it on the provinces. In such
circumstances, the legitimacy fallout from patriation could have been averted
or managed more effectively had the proposed referendum been more a
matter of conviction than a bargaining ploy. It is not difficult to imagine
how the legitimizing influence of popular ratification might have altered the
patriation narrative and the Constitution's evolution after 1982.[91] And, far from

---

[87] Richard Albert, *The Difficulty of Constitutional Amendment in Canada, supra* note 8 (arguing
that in combination Canada's formal and extra-textual requirements makes the constitution
"exceedingly rigid" and perhaps more rigid than the US Constitution).

[88] Romanow, Whyte and Leeson, *Notwithstanding, supra* note 7, at 163.   [89] *Id*, at 164.

[90] As then Prime Minister Trudeau shrugged, "My answer is there had been a hell of a lot of nice
guys since 1926 ... and the constitution was never patriated. Maybe it took a nasty guy."
Graham, *The Last Act, supra* note 7, at 41.

[91] *See generally* Russell, *Odyssey, supra* note 7 (sub-titled, *Can Canadians Become a Sovereign
People?*); *see also* Bruce Ackerman and Robert Charney, *Canada at the Crossroads*, U.T.L.J.,
34:2 (1984), 117–135 (stating that, "although aware of the legitimating power of a national
referendum" (129), the referendum proposal was "compromised away" and "rather than appeal

being ameliorated, the Constitution's legitimacy sorrows only deepened after 1982, when the political leadership attempted heroics, with the MLA, to reconcile Quebec to the Constitution and, in doing so, profoundly misread the mood of the country. Had missteps been avoided, the spectacle of Charlottetown's defeat in a national referendum might have been spared. If history could be rewritten, the legitimacy deficits that haunt the process today might have been attenuated, if not all but eliminated.

Patriation and the Accords were high-stakes initiatives, and each gambled in its own way on the legitimacy of constitutional reform. Legitimacy deficits that were unquestionably situational found strong voice in the fractures, expectations, demands, and emotions in play at a time when Canada's survival was in peril. Those dynamics spiraled during the patriation crisis and could not be contained when the follow-up Accords were proposed. Though the "current states of affairs" and factual rigidities of this narrative are compelling, the particulars of Canada's extended patriation crisis were forged in the longer history of amendment and a text that never provided for the legality – or legitimacy – of change.[92] It is the central purpose of this article to show that Canada's experience of amendment in and after 1982 is vitally connected to the primal challenge since Confederation in 1867, and that has been to define the terms of Canada's amendment sovereignty. That could and can only be done by bringing the legality and legitimacy of change into alignment. A project that has been a key preoccupation throughout is, today, still the unfinished work of Canada's 150-year-old Constitution.

As noted, a flourishing literature on amendment theory analyzes textual variables to determine, by quantitative and comparative measures, how amendment rules predict or determine the rigidity of constitutional change.[93] It is instructive that Part V's amendment rules place Canada at the extreme end of spectrum of textual rigidity, but perhaps more telling that a textual measure dramatically understates the obstacles to constitutional change. In principle, textual singularity is incomplete as a measure of amendment rigidity because it fails to validate a host of non-quantitative elements – including situational or factual rigidities – which play a determinative role in enabling and disabling constitutional change.[94] Significantly, it also fails to account for amendment rigidities which are grounded in legitimacy deficits that compromise

to the People ... Trudeau merely appealed to his fellow parliamentary sovereigns");
McWhinney, *Canada and the Constitution, supra* note 7 (describing the "'people's' route, via a referendum ... as one of the great 'might-have-beens'" of the patriation conflict).
[92] Fallon, *Legitimacy, supra* note 21. *See also* Contiades and Fotiadou, *supra* note 14, at 460 (referring to these as "factual rigidities").
[93] *Supra* note 13.   [94] *Supra* note 14.

or subvert the process of change. As shown in this chapter, these points have particular salience for Canada's amendment history.

In Canada's case, amendment rigidity springs from an intriguing interaction of textual and non-textual dynamics. Part V's rules may set Canada's scheme of constitutional legality at the rigid end of the spectrum, but a different kind of rigidity characterized and defined the history of change under the pre-textual regime of statutory legality. That rigidity was negative rather than positive in nature because it arose, not from the constraints of rules, but from their very absence. The negative rigidity arising from a lack of rules played a striking role in generating and embedding serious legitimacy gaps and obstacles to change. The inability to articulate and agree on a framework of legality exposed and reinforced legitimacy gaps which could not be overcome, and culminated in conditions of extreme rigidity. That cycle of dysfunction could and would not be broken without the conflicts of patriation and the two Accords though, ironically, that cycle deepened even as it was broken in 1982. In addition to the textual rigidities of Canada's complex requirements of constitutional and statutory legality, the rigidities associated with unresolved legitimacy deficits remain in place today.

This, then, is the object lesson for Canada, and for theories of amendment and amendment rigidity more generally. Just as a regime of legality is necessary to legitimize amendments to a constitutional text, legality has limits and is not sufficient where extra-textual legitimacy deficits undermine the authority and acceptability of constitutional change.

6

Constituting Citizens

Oaths, Gender, Religious Attire

AYELET SHACHAR

The issue which consumed the final few weeks of the 2015 Canadian Federal Election began innocuously enough. Zunera Ishaq, a permanent resident in Canada and citizen of Pakistan, had completed all of the other prerequisites for naturalization and been scheduled to attend a citizenship ceremony on January 2014.[1] There was only one hitch – she intended to recite the oath while wearing her *niqab*.[2] The government banned such a practice. Alas, only *after* taking the oath do the participants become full-fledged members of the new home country to which they have sworn allegiance.[3] Without it, the naturalization process remains incomplete. Citizenship is not conferred.[4] Ishaq's religious practice thus appeared to bar her from acquiring full and equal membership in her new home country.

An earlier version was presented at Yale Law School. I'm grateful for the lively discussion this paper provoked at Yale and would like to extend my gratitude to Richard Albert and David Cameron for the invitation to participate in this project. Special thanks are due to Owen Fiss and Ran Hirschl for their insightful comments and suggestions. Matthew Milne and Marinka Yossiffon provided invaluable research assistance.

[1] These requirements include: lawful residency, physical presence in the country, language proficiency in English or French as well as demonstration of adequate knowledge of the country's history, institutions, symbols, and core constitutional values.

[2] The *niqab* is a face veil worn by some Muslim women, leaving only the eyes revealed.

[3] At the end of the ceremony, each participant receives his or her citizenship certificate, which offers legal proof of their newly acquired full membership status. *See* www.cic.gc.ca/english/resources/tools/cit/ceremony/oath.asp.

[4] Citizenship Act, s. 24, RSC 1985, c. C-29. Taking the oath is a mandatory legal requirement of naturalization that applicants must meet to be granted citizenship. The minister may grant a waiver to this otherwise binding obligation to take the oath on compassionate grounds. These apply to minors under 14 years of age, persons incapable of forming intent or understanding the significance of taking the oath of citizenship by reason of mental disability, as well as discretionary "special cases." Citizenship Act, s. 3(3), 3(4), 3(6). An exemption may also apply in the case of citizenship granted on grounds of stateless as defined in s. 5(5) of the Act.

Citizenship tests and ceremonies have burst to the forefront of public and scholarly attention as countries across the world, primarily in Europe but also in traditionally immigrant-receiving societies such as Australia, Canada, the United Kingdom, and the United States. This contribution offers a comparative exploration of the culminating, performative act of *becoming* a citizen, without which the naturalization process remains incomplete: the citizenship oath. Why do states place a binding legal requirement on newcomers to take such an oath? What requirements may the admitting society impose on the transformative process of immigrant to citizen? Is it legitimate to impose a face-covering ban during the citizenship oath? What are the consequences of such a ban on the values of diversity and equality in a multicultural society? Proponents of such a ban argue that the oath is a public declaration that must be taken freely and openly; they construct face-veiled citizenship-candidates as distrustful, "hiding their identity" on the cusp of membership. This we might call the "distrusting" position. Opponents contend that the ban discriminates against minority women and restricts their religious freedom. They further ask what function or utility a citizenship oath may add to an already lengthy and tightly regulated process of naturalization. This I label the "trivializing" position. I will argue that both the distrusting and the trivializing positions overreach their claims and ultimately fail to persuade. Instead, I develop a perspective that emphasizes the links between control over women's bodies and religious attire in shaping identity-centered debates about continuity and change in sculpting the borders and boundaries of membership in the community. In rejecting the twin horns of the trivializing and distrusting positions, I wish to explore whether Canada's jurisprudence on questions of religious freedom, multiculturalism, and equality, while far from impeccable, nevertheless offers us resources to defend a position that seeks to neither erase diversity nor sacrifice equality.[5]

CITIZENSHIP-BY-NATURALIZATION

Naturalization, the mystical process by which the once-stranger is transformed into a constituent member, with all the rights and privileges pertaining to this legal status, has been variably described as "the most densely regulated and most politicized aspect of citizenship laws";[6] a filtering process that allows the recipient state to designate whom, among those *not* born as citizens,

[5] See Chapter 1 in this volume.
[6] Rainer Bauböck, Rainer and Sara Wallace Goodman, *Naturalisation*, EUDO Citizenship Policy Brief No. 2, at 1.

"we regard as our own – those to whom we owe a special obligation because they are fully-fledged members of our society";[7] "the central process of becoming part of a new country" by fostering a shared sense of commitment;[8] or, more critically, a "spectacle."[9] These various interpretations capture a range of meanings from the formal-legal to the relational-identitarian and expressive dimensions of citizenship and belonging.[10]

As the US Supreme Court memorably pronounced in *Wong Kim Ark*, there are "two sources of citizenship, and only two: birth and naturalization." The latter represents the *only* legal avenue for the acquisition of political membership after birth. Interestingly, the very term naturalization reflects an iconography of lineage, as well as its etymological roots. The word derives from *naturalis* (Latin), which means "confirmed by birth, according to nature"; the term naturalization implies that the post-birth admission to citizenship is a symbolic *rebirth* into the new membership community. As such, it is perceived as constituting a "rite of passage."[11] In the past, this act also simultaneously required renouncing or "erasing" previous allegiances to other political entities. Echoes of this history are still present today in the American naturalization oath of allegiance:

> I hereby declare, on oath (or, and solemnly affirm), that I absolutely and entirely renounce and abjure all allegiance and fidelity to any foreign prince, potentate, state, or sovereignty, of whom or which I have heretofore been a subject or citizen; that I will support and defend the Constitution and laws of the United States of America against all enemies, foreign and domestic; that I will bear true faith and allegiance to the same; ... and that I take this obligation freely, without any mental reservation or purpose of evasion; (so help me God).[12]

---

7   Stephen H. Legomsky, *Why Citizenship?*, 35 VA. J. INT'L L. 279, 291 (1994).

8   Noah Pickus, *Laissez-Faire and Its Discontents: US Naturalization and Integration Policy in Comparative Perspective*, 18 CITIZENSH. STUD. 160, 167 (2014) (referring to the view of naturalization expressed by American social reformers such as Jane Addams).

9   Geoffrey Brahm Levey, *Liberal Nationalism and the Australian Citizenship Tests*, 18 CITIZENSH. STUD. 175, 186 (2014).

10 Several scholars have referred to citizenship as capturing these various dimensions: status, rights, and identity. *See e.g.* Christian Joppke, *Transformation of Citizenship: Status, Rights, Identity*, 11 CITIZENSH. STUD. 37 (2007). For other categorizations, *see* Will Kymlicka and Wayne Norman, *Return of the Citizen: A Survey of Recent Work on Citizenship Theory*, 104 ETHICS 352 (1994).

11 Tomas Hammar, DEMOCRACY AND THE NATION-STATE (Aldershot: Averbury, 1990).

12 *See* 8 CFR 337.1(b). The oath also includes clauses referring to bearing arms on behalf of the United States and to performing noncombatant service in the US armed forces when required by law; a modification can be granted based on religious training and belief, or conscientious objection arising from a deeply held moral or ethical code. See INA 337(a)(5)(A) and INA 337(a)(5)(B).

In Canada, which will soon celebrate its sesquicentennial anniversary, entering the "Canadian family," as the citizenship oath is frequently described, still involves, to the surprise of many, swearing allegiance to the Queen of the Once-Dominion:

> I swear (or affirm) that I will be faithful and bear true allegiance to Her Majesty Queen Elizabeth the Second, Queen of Canada, Her Heirs and Successors, and that I will faithfully observe the laws of Canada and fulfil my duties as a Canadian citizen.

The content of the oath has been subject to a recent legal challenge by three permanent residents from Toronto who claimed that, as holders of anti-monarchist views, obliging them to swear to "be faithful and bear true allegiance to Queen Elizabeth the Second, Queen of Canada, her Heirs and Successors" during the Canadian citizenship ceremony breaches their freedom of expression and freedom of conscience guaranteed by the *Charter of Rights and Freedoms*. Their case was heard by the Superior Court of Justice of Ontario and then by a three-judge panel at the Ontario Court of Appeal.[13] A major bone of contention between the parties was how to interpret the oath: whether to follow the plain meaning method of interpretation (the appellants' position) or to rely on the purposive approach (the government's submission).[14] The court followed the latter to the exclusion of the former. The judges reasoned that swearing allegiance to the Queen was not a "literal" act of submission to a foreign-seated head of state, but an oath affirming "our form of government, as symbolized by the Queen as the apex of our Canadian parliamentary system of constitutional monarchy."[15] Moreover, in contrast to the application judge's prima facie conclusion that s.2(b) of the Charter was infringed (saved by s.1), the appeal court decision held that would-be citizens' freedom of expression is not violated as they may criticize, or even recant, what they characterize as the objectionable elements of the oath after having taken it.[16] This argument did not bode well for the claimants, the reciprocal conditions of membership in the community require that they are obliged to first take an oath that contradicts sincerely held beliefs, in order to reserve the opportunity to later "disavow" that very same oath that formalized their rebirth

---

[13] *McAteer v. Canada (Attorney General)*, 2013 ONSC 5895 (Ontario Superior Court of Justice). The applicants appealed this decision and sought the remedy of making the reference to the Queen optional rather than compulsory. The Attorney General of Canada cross-appealed and challenged the finding that the oath violates the appellants right to freedom of expression.

[14] *McAteer v. Canada (Attorney General)*, 2014 ONCA 578 (Ontario Court of Appeal).

[15] *McAteer v. Canada (Attorney General)*, 2014 ONCA 578 (Ontario Court of Appeal).

[16] *McAteer v. Canada (Ontario Court of Appeal)*, para. 79.

into and acceptance by the new political community. This incongruous rationale runs the risk of trivializing "compulsory declarations of attachment," as Cass Sunstein once called pledges of allegiance administrated by modern governments; prime among them is the citizenship oath.[17] Such a sentiment was expressed by one of the claimants, a Princeton-educated University of Toronto math professor, who, after learning that the Supreme Court of Canada denied leave to appeal to hear the case, stated: "I misunderstood the law in Canada. I thought vows had meaning."[18]

In contrast with the *trivializing the oath* position, the government expressed a diametrically opposed stance in the controversy that surrounded the face-covering ban during the swearing-in citizenship ceremony. Here, the oath is taken seriously and sternly, reflecting a "matter of deep principle that goes to the heart of our identity and our values."[19] The government introduced the said ban in 2011, through internal guidelines formalized in the operational bulletin. This particular bulletin stipulated that participants in a citizenship ceremony, the final step of the naturalization process, would not be permitted to take the oath while wearing face covering.[20] In explaining the objective of the new rules, the minister of citizenship and immigration reasoned that: "The oath of citizenship and the citizenship ceremony is a solemn and essentially public time when the individual expresses his or her loyalty to Canada in front of fellow citizens ... That is why I clarified yesterday that citizenship applicants will now be required to recite the oath in an open and transparent manner and to do so without being obscured by a face covering. This decision underscores the essentially public nature of the oath."[21] The minister further emphasized that the oath is *a* "public declaration that you are joining the Canadian family and it must be taken freely and openly."[22] In another public statement, Canada's citizenship and immigration minister

[17] Cass R. Sunstein, *Unity and Plurality: The Case of Compulsory Oaths*, 2 YALE J.L. & HUMAN. 101, 101 (1990).

[18] Jeff Gray, *Supreme Court Won't Hear Citizenship Oath to Queen Challenge*, THE GLOBE AND MAIL, February 26, 2015 (citing Dror Bar-Natan, one of the three claimants that brought the legal challenge before the court).

[19] Joanna Smith, *Muslim Women Must Show Face to Become Canadian Citizens*, THE TORONTO STAR, Dec. 12, 2011 (citing Jason Kenney, citizenship and immigration minister [as he was then]).

[20] Operational Bulletin 359, Dec. 2011, available at www.cic.gc.ca/ english/resources/manuals/ bulletins/2011/ob359.asp. The new policy states that "[c]andidates wearing face coverings are required to remove their face coverings for the oath taking portion of the ceremony."

[21] Jason Kenney, *Minister of Citizenship and Immigration*, Openparliament.ca (Dec. 13, 2011), https://openparliament.ca/debates/2011/12/13/jason-kenney-1/only/.

[22] Smith, "Muslim Women Must Show Face," *supra* note 19 (citing Kenney).

made an even stronger claim against face-veiled citizenship-candidates, as "hiding their identity."[23] This we might label the *distrusting of minorities* position.

Both the *distrusting* and the *trivializing* positions ultimately fail to persuade; they sidestep the core legal and philosophical questions at stake. What is the appropriate balance of religious accommodation or exemption that a new-comer on the cusp of membership can legitimately expect from their new country? What requirements may the admitting society impose on the trans-formative process of immigrant to citizen? These questions are anything but theoretical or abstract. The answers given to them bear immediate and concrete consequences in terms of defining burdens and opportunities. And the derivatives of these unanswered questions spiral out endlessly. Who must yield what, and according to what principles, to allow individuals to peacefully and openly interact in public spaces in a society which is officially committed to the values of diversity and equality? What are the background conditions and underlying values informing such compromises or trade-offs? Which responses are available through law and politics to situations whereby the language of social cohesion and coexistence is co-opted to promote ends and goals that are ultimately exclusionary?

Unlike the claimants who challenged the *content* of the oath due to the obligation to pledge allegiance to the Queen, Ishaq agreed with the content of the oath but objected to the *manner* by which she was compelled to take it, namely, with her face uncovered in public. As a devout Muslim woman, she sought exemption based on her religious belief from the government's policy that required her to reveal her face for the oath-taking portion of the cere-mony.[24] Her request was denied by the government. She challenged the face-covering ban in court, claiming that it will deny her citizenship unless she betrays her conviction. A legal saga quickly followed. As it coincided with a heated national election campaign, Ishaq's legal battle trigged an acrimonious debate in the public sphere.[25] Polls showed that a majority of those surveyed

---

[23] Government of Canada, *Speaking Notes for The Honorable Jason Kenney, Minister of Citizenship, Immigration and Multiculturalism, On the Value of Canadian Citizenship* (Dec. 12, 2011), available at: www.cic.gc.ca/english/department/media/speeches/2011/ 2011-12-12.asp.

[24] She expressed a willingness to unveil her face if absolutely necessary to do so for identification or security reasons, but even then only privately in front of women. *Ishaq v. Canada (Citizenship and Immigration)* 2015 FC 156 (Federal Court).

[25] Polls showed that a majority of those surveyed supported the government's position. Michael Friscolanti, *The Niqab: Trivial Politics, or Election Difference Maker?*, MacLean's Magazine, September 28, 2015 (citing pollster Darrell Bricker).

supported the government's position of demanding that one's face cover be removed for the oath portion of the citizenship ceremony.[26]

In court, government lawyer Negar Hashemi stated that "the case is about finding the 'right balance' between respecting differences and maintaining Canadian core democratic values." The *niqab* ban, she said, is part of a larger democratic scheme to ensure, via visual confirmation, that everyone vows loyalty to Canada, and that "there is no hidden agenda in this case."[27] The mention of a hidden agenda and the emphasis placed by the admitting society on vowing loyalty reveal core elements of the distrusting position. Those who favoured Ishaq's quest to take the oath without removing her face veil fell into the opposite trap. By claiming that the government's position was a political show and ideological imposition, they ignored altogether the value-laden disagreement that this policy evoked. The legal team representing Ishaq emphasized that there were fewer than 100 cases a year across Canada where someone wears a *niqab* to the ceremony, as if the value of constitutional and human rights is measured by the strength of their number rather than the principles they uphold. Another line of argument proclaimed that after having completed the lengthy and tightly regulated process of naturalization, it is unclear what function or utility the citizenship oath may add, again reflecting the trivializing position.

Ishaq's legal challenge was ultimately vindicated by the Federal Court and the Federal Court of Appeal. However, neither decision dealt with the constitutional issues at the heart of this controversy, namely, the ban's disproportionate effect on Muslim women who adhere to face-covering practices and their *Charter* rights to religious freedom and gender equality. Instead, both rulings relied on technical grounds, declining to answer the *Charter* questions posed by the case.[28] The government's leave to appeal to the Supreme Court of Canada was declined and we therefore have no judicial pronouncement by the country's highest court on these matters of vital importance in early twenty-first century law and politics.

This saga, despite its anti-climatic legal ending, provides an opportune occasion to explore the relations and tensions between conditioning access to citizenship on the removal of religious attire (worm primarily by women) and the broader Canadian multicultural promise – or "odyssey" – of promoting

---

[26] Michael Friscolanti, *The Niqab: Trivial Politics, or Election Difference Maker?*, MacLean's Magazine, September 28, 2015 (citing pollster Darrell Bricker).

[27] Nicholas Keung, *Ex-Immigration Minister Jason Kenney 'Dictated' Niqab Ban at Citizenship Ceremony*, court told The Toronto Star, Oct. 17, 2014 (citing *Negar Hashemi*).

[28] *Ishaq v. Canada (Federal Court)*, *supra* note 24; *Ishaq v. Canada (Minister of Citizenship and Immigration)*, 2015 FCA 194 *(Federal Court of Appeal)*.

both diversity and equality.[29] The *Canadian Charter of Rights and Freedoms* is globally unique in that it includes explicit commitments to the values of multiculturalism and gender equality.[30] Section 27 provides that: "This Charter shall be interpreted in a manner consistent with the preservation and enhancement of the multicultural heritage of Canadians," whereas section 28 states that: "Notwithstanding anything in this Charter, the rights and freedoms referred to in it are guaranteed equally to male and female persons."[31] The Canadian social and constitutional experiment offers us a rare, living laboratory in which a thriving constitutional system searches for legal and institutional pathways to addressing the seemingly intractable demands, obligations, rights, and protections endowed by sections 27 and 28. The Canadian experiment is fascinating to explore because it attempts to give meaning to the entrenchment of *both* values. No other country has officially enshrined both multiculturalism (section 27) and gender equality (section 28) as interpretive provisions that reflect the "broad directions" and "aims" of its constitutional order.[32] The *niqab*-ban in citizenship ceremonies will serve as a test case to evaluate the promises and pitfalls of the "Canadian multicultural-ism paradise." But we first need to step back and take in a broader comparative perspective.

CONSTITUTING CITIZENS THROUGH "WORDS THAT BIND":
A BRIEF COMPARATIVE JOURNEY

Citizenship tests and ceremonies have attracted significant attention in recent years as a growing number of countries have introduced or revisited formal citizenship ceremonies for prospective citizens, or revamped linguistic and other naturalization requirements. In the United Kingdom, for example, the status of "citizen of the United Kingdom and Colonies" was established through the adoption of its Nationality Act of 1948. The current Nationality Act for British citizenship was adopted in 1981. However, only since 2004 have

[29] For elaboration of the Canadian odyssey theme, *see* the Introduction and Chapter 1 in this volume.
[30] The Charter also includes specific rights provisions dealing with religious freedom and equality in sections 2(a) and 15(1) respectively.
[31] While not entrenching particular rights, these interpretative provisions express core values of Canadian society and its constitutional order; they are to be taken into account in interpreting the meaning of a right or freedom guaranteed by the Charter, or in assessing the justifications of limits under section 1 of the Charter.
[32] *See* Walter S. Tarnopolsky, "The Equality Rights (ss. 15, 27 and 28)" in Walter S. Tarnopolsky and Gérald-A Beaudoin, THE CANADIAN CHARTER OF RIGHTS AND FREEDOMS: COMMENTARY, 1st ed. (Toronto: Carswell, 1982), 441.

applicants for naturalization been required to take an oath of allegiance to the Queen as head of state and make a pledge to the United Kingdom:

> I will give my loyalty to the United Kingdom and respect its rights and freedoms. I will uphold its democratic values. I will observe its laws faithfully and fulfil my duties and obligations as a British citizen.

In the United States and Canada, by contrast, citizenship oaths have a longer historical record. In the United States, the oath requirement dates back to the Naturalization Act of 1790. It has gone through several changes since, most importantly the removal of racial and gender exclusions that long barred access to full and equal citizenship for women and racialized minorities.[33] However, the individual pledge of allegiance required of those seeking membership in the American political community has remained consistent throughout.[34] In Canada, the oath was formalized in 1947, with the adoption of the Citizenship Act. At the time, the Act was considered vanguard legislation across the commonwealth, since it broke with past notions of empire and imperialism by establishing independent citizenship in Canada before such status was salient in the United Kingdom.

Recounting his own oath-taking experience as involving "great solemnity" and "intensification of my feeling about American citizenship," Felix Frankfurter, a naturalized citizen and justice of the US Supreme Court, reminded his fellow justices that "[i]t is well known that the convert is more zealous than one born to the faith." He went on to describe naturalization as an act of "entering a fellowship which binds people together by devotion to certain . . . ideas and ideals summarized as a requirement that they be attached to the principles of the Constitution."[35] Taking this commitment seriously, and applying it to his judicial role, he held in a dissenting opinion in the *Schneiderman* case that a naturalized American could be deprived of his

---

[33] Of the vast body of literature exploring this history, *see e.g.* Ian Haney Lopez, WHITE BY LAW: THE LEGAL CONSTRUCTION OF RACE (New York: NYU Press, 1996); Nancy F. Cott, *Marriage and Women's Citizenship in the United States*, AM. HIST. REV. 103: 1440–1474 (1998).

[34] A standardized version of the oath only came into force in 1929. It has since been slightly amended; the basic structure holds, however, various commissions and a wide range of stakeholders that have called for updating the oath. US Citizenship and Immigration Services, Naturalization Oath of Allegiance to United States of America, available at www.uscis.gov/us-citizenship/naturalization-test/naturalization-oath-allegiance-united-states-america (last visited March 25, 2016). *See also* Pickus, *Laissez-Faire and Its Discontents, supra* note 7, at 162–163.

[35] From the Diaries of Felix Frankfurter 211–212 (J. Lash ed. 1975), cited in Levinson, *supra* note 30, at 1440–1441.

citizenship on the basis of adherence to certain political-ideological views (in this particular case: Marxism-Leninism), reflecting the same distrusting approach that we find reemerging half a century later in the Canadian debate.[36] In another landmark case, *Barnett*, involving a child who, as a member of the Jehovah's Witnesses, refused to take the pledge of allegiance at school, the majority reversed the child's suspension from school. Frankfurter, again in a minority opinion, held that the state could legitimately inculcate patriotism through the pledge of allegiance.[37] More contemporary reflections on Frankfurter's views challenge them as representing an over-muscular "new patriotism" that may coercively restrict individual freedoms as well as the rights of minorities or dissenters in the name of national (or majoritarian) interpretations that define the collective "we."[38]

Another manifestation of the competing views surrounding citizenship oaths is revealed by scholarship exploring the historical origins and ritual symbolism of swearing-in ceremonies. Critics have argued that such events are designed to artificially emphasize unity and conformity that conceals, counters or attempts to quell the reality of social heterogeneity.[39] Digging into the roots of naturalization oaths, Dora Kostakopoulou reminds us of the inequalities inherent in their medieval origins – "fealty" and the pledge of fidelity by the vassal to the feudal lord was publicly marked through the ceremony of homage, creating a mutual and indivisible bond between them.[40] In the history of the common law, the earliest and most influential theoretical articulation of the definition of access to membership – or, rather, at the time, "ligeance" under a fixed and hierarchical system of authority – is found in the landmark *Calvin's Case* (1608), where Lord Cook memorably stated that: "as the literatures or strings do knit together the joints of all parts of the body, so doth ligeance join together the sovereign and all his subjects."[41]

---

[36] *Schneiderman v. United States*, 320 US 118 (1943) (Frankfurter J., dissenting opinion).

[37] *West Virginia State Board of Education v. Barnette*, 319 US 624 (1943).

[38] This influential articulation is found in Levinson, *Words that Bind, supra* note 30, at 1447. *See also* Sanford Levinson, *Pledging Faith in the Civil Religion: Or, Would You Sign the Constitution?*, 19 Wм. & Mary L. Rev. 113 (1987). As one commentator eloquently observes, a recurring theme in Levinson's work is a "certain distaste for, even wariness of, any form of blind allegiance or thoughtless conformity." *See* Sherman J. Clark, *Promise, Prayer, and Identity*, 38 Tulsa L. Rev. 579, 579 (2002).

[39] Cass R. Sunstein, *Unity and Plurality: The Case of Compulsory Oaths*, 2 Yale J.L. & Human. 101 (1990). The focus on the conditionality of conformity is drawn from Bryan S. Turner, "National Identities and Cosmopolitan Virtues: Citizenship in a Global Age," in *Beyond Nationalism? Sovereignty and Citizenship* (Lanham: Lexington Books, 2001), 199–200.

[40] Dora Kostakopoulou, The Future Governance of Citizenship (Cambridge: Cambridge University Press, 2008), 89.

[41] *Calvin's Case*, 77 Eng. Rep. 377 (K.B. 1608).

With the rise of the modern state, notions of citizenship as a relation of equality gradually replaced that of subjecthood, but to their detractors, naturalization oaths are still charged with this ideologically encumbered past. In contemporary societies, the manifestation of such vestige is arguably found in the search for "'bonds of mutual understanding' [that] depend on the conformity of newcomers to the terms of integration articulated by the majority community."[42]

Those who view naturalization regimes in a more sympathetic light stress the symbolic value of the inductions and ceremonies that immigrants undergo at the very moment that they legally transition into citizenship. Capturing the "rite of passage" quality of the process, this more affirmative sentiment is captured by the recognition that joining a new political community is a constitutive moment for *both* the newcomers *and* the society they join. As one scholar put it:

> Moving to a new society with a view to full membership is a significant transition in anyone's life. It is also a significant moment for the host society. Human beings down the ages have marked such transitions with inductions and ceremony. Becoming a citizen of a new political community would seem to warrant at least as much fuss.[43]

In Australia, for example, not only immigrants partake in oath- and pledge-taking during the final stage of the naturalization process. Individual born Australian may also participate in affirmation ceremonies (as they are known), if they so wish, to "publicly affirm their loyalty and commitment to Australia and its people."[44] These ceremonies bear no legal standing, but were introduced by the federal government in response to popular demand by those who do not require such official "induction" into the political community due to their fortuitous circumstances of birth.[45] Manifesting explicitly an emphasis on affirming affiliation to "the polity, its political institutions and norms, and its people," Australia revoked the oath of allegiance to the Queen and replaced it with a citizenship pledge of commitment, which reads as follows:

> From this time forward, (under God,) I pledge my loyalty to Australia and its people, whose democratic beliefs I share, whose rights and liberties I respect, and whose laws I will uphold and obey.

---

[42] Kostakopoulou, *The Future Governance of Citizenship, supra* note 40, at 99.
[43] Levey, *Liberal Nationalism and the Australian Citizenship Tests, supra* note 9, at 185.
[44] Government of Australia, Citizenship Affirmation Ceremonies.
[45] Levey, *Liberal Nationalism and the Australian Citizenship Tests, supra* note 9, at 186.

But unique to Australia's oath is the view that citizenship pledges are relevant to *both* newcomers *and* settled populations as they are joined through public rites of passage and words that bind. Even here, however, inequality persists: participation in citizenship ceremonies is binding and compulsory for those not born as citizens while it remains purely volitional for those who gained such status by virtue of the birthright lottery.[46]

Questions surrounding access to citizenship have become ever more pressing in recent years as new and more demanding citizenship integration requirements have proliferated across Europe, requiring newcomers to explicitly pronounce their acceptance of the "values, culture, and practices of the host society."[47] Some of these new tests extended beyond civic knowledge acquisition; they probe into the "inner disposition" of applicants with regard to sensitive topics such as gender, religion, culture, marriage, same-sex relations, etc., leading scholars and critics to dub them as objectionable manifestations of "illiberal liberalism."[48]

Even if we accept that intrusive moral inquisition by state officials has no place in the naturalization process (as I believe is the case), citizens-in-the-making are routinely expected to demonstrate civic knowledge of the new country's political system, history, and governing institutions. Still, we might ask: is it fair that those not born as members are subject to what has been labeled a "probationary period" for many years before they can become full members, whereas those born into the political community are automatically granted the coveted prize of citizenship? Without fully resolving this dilemma, some have proposed that naturalization should be activated automatically if a person is "inhabiting a place," or residing in the country for a fixed number of years, without subjecting them to an additional demanding process of providing proof of language proficiency, civic integration, and successful passage of citizenship testing.[49]

Returning briefly to Ishaq's case, the idea of automatic naturalization would have entailed that as an aspiring citizen she would have had to do nothing

[46] For further discussion, *see* Ayelet Shachar, THE BIRTHRIGHT LOTTERY: CITIZENSHIP AND GLOBAL INEQUALITY (Cambridge, MA: Harvard University Press, 2009). *See also* Ayelet Shachar, "Citizenship" in Andres Sajo & Michel Rosenfeld, eds., *Oxford Handbook of Comparative Constitutional Law* (Oxford: Oxford University Press, 2012), 1002–1019.

[47] Pickus, *Laissez-Faire and Its Discontents, supra* note 7, at 161

[48] *See* Liav Orgad, THE CULTURAL DEFENSE OF NATIONS: A LIBERAL THEORY OF MAJORITY RIGHTS (Oxford: Oxford University Press, 2015). For comparative data, *see* Sara Wallace Goodman, IMMIGRATION AND MEMBERSHIP POLITICS IN WESTERN EUROPE (Cambridge: Cambridge University Press, 2014).

[49] Ruth Rubio-Marin on automatic naturalization; Dora Kostakopoulou on civic registration model. For critical accounts, *see, e.g.,* Rainer Baubock.

other than stare at the clock and wait for the passage of time (say, five years of lawful residence) before she would, mechanically, become a citizen at the stroke of midnight. This model waives linguistic competence requirements, abandons any requirement of public expression of familiarity with and willingness to adhere to the new home country's laws and constitutional norms. Some fear that such a vision of inclusion would in fact discourage integration into the fabric of society because it deserts the aspiration of creating some social glue or "shared values," however difficult it remains to pin down these shared values.

In practice, no country adheres to the model of automatic naturalization, although many polities provide expedited citizenship to "co-ethnic" returnees on account of presumed shared identity that transcends space and time. In Canada, however, all newcomers, whether they have arrived as family members, economic migrants, or humanitarian causes, must pass the standard naturalization process. Hence, we are still left with the nagging question: is it legitimate to demand that at the very moment they are committing to join the "Canadian family," as government officials repeatedly stated in the political storm that surrounded the face-covering citizenship-ban legal challenge, a female member of a minority community be forced to shed religious attire that expresses her sincere religious belief? Which perspectives should prevail: the sensitivities of the majority or minority communities' "claims of culture"?[50] These are the unanswered queries that the Ishaq saga has left open. Given that different countries adhere to different citizenship models (liberal, republican, multicultural, ethnonational, among others), they may choose to resolve this question differently, but our focus here is not on providing a universal answer. Rather, my inquiry is more narrowly and modestly tailored to identify the parameters that would define a made-in-Canada solution. Using this test case, I seek to explore whether the Canadian experiment can succeed in creating the alchemy of accommodating diversity with equality. It is useful to step back in time, roughly half a century ago, to acquaint ourselves

---

[50] This term is drawn from the title of an influential book: Seyla Benhabib, THE CLAIMS OF CULTURE: DIVERSITY AND EQUALITY IN THE GLOBAL ERA (Princeton: Princeton University Press, 2002). These claims are understood here as socially constructed, complex and multidimensional. In the legal context, they are typically referred to as intersectional claims for recognition that cannot be easily disaggregated or reduced to one axes only, such as religion, gender, tradition or intra- and inter-group demands for social change, as they intersect and interlace in complex ways. For a classic elaboration of intersectionality (in a different context), see Kimberly Crenshaw, *Demarginalizing the Intersection of Race and Sex: A Black Feminist Critique of Antidiscrimination Doctrine*, Feminist Theory and Antiracist Politics, 140 U. CHI. LEGAL F. 139 (1989).

with the genesis of the invention of Canadian multiculturalism as an official government policy – the first in the world.[51]

CANADA'S MULTICULTURALISM

The "multi" in Canadian multiculturalism represents an explicit rejection of the once unquestioned approach of privileging the dominant majority culture(s) while relegating minority communities to a marginalized, second-class position.[52] In Canada, the government policy of multiculturalism, articulated in 1971 and predating the *Charter*, rested on a combination of empirical and normative justifications for rejecting mono- or bi-culturalism: "In the face of this [country's] cultural plurality there can be no official Canadian culture or cultures," resoundingly stated a special joint parliamentary committee charged with the task of developing Canada's new constitutional bill of rights, the Canadian Charter of Rights and Freedoms.[53] As part of this effort, a new vision was crafted of a "pluralistic mosaic," promoting "equal respect for the *many* origins, creeds and cultures" that form Canadian society.[54]

In the post-Charter era, the earliest judicial pronouncement on religious freedom is found in the landmark decision of *R. v. Big M Drug Mart Ltd.*, in which the Supreme Court of Canada struck down the *Lord's Day Act*, a federal "Sunday closing law" prohibiting businesses from opening on Sunday, effectively protecting the sanctity the Christian Sabbath.[55] In an oft-cited paragraph of that decision, the Court stated that: "What may appear good and true to a majoritarian religious group, or to the state acting at their behest, may not ... be imposed upon citizens who take a contrary view. The Charter safeguards religious minorities from the threat of the 'tyranny of the majority.'"[56] This last point is crucial. The majority of Canadians may accept Sunday as the Lord's Day, but this does not represent the perspective of religious minorities in Canada, be they members of the Jewish faith,

---

[51] Government of Canada, *Canadian Multiculturalism: An Inclusive Citizenship*, available at www.cic.gc.ca/english/multiculturalism/citizenship.asp.

[52] This section draws upon the argument developed in Ayelet Shachar, *Squaring the Circle of Multiculturalism? Religious Freedom and Gender Equality in Canada*, 10 LAW AND ETHICS OF HUMAN RIGHTS 31 (2016).

[53] *Special Joint Committee of the Senate and House of Commons on the Constitution of Canada* (1972). The governmental policy was initially framed as "multiculturalism within a bilingual framework."

[54] *An Act Amending the Constitution*, Bill C-60, s. 4 "[emphasis added]."

[55] RSC 1970, c. L-13; *R. v. Big M Drug Mart Ltd.*, [1985] SCJ No. 17, [1985] 1 SCR 295 (SCC).

[56] *Id.*, at paras. 94–96.

Sabbatarians, Muslim Canadians, agnostics, or those with no theistic belief. As Dickson J. (as he then was) said, speaking for the Court: "To the extent that it binds all to a sectarian Christian ideal, the Lord's Day Act works a form of coercion inimical to the spirit of the Charter and the dignity of all non-Christians."[57] The Lord's Day Act, continues the Court, "takes religious values rooted in Christian morality and, using the force of the state, translates them into a positive law binding on believers and non-believers alike."[58] It is at this stage of the analysis that section 27 is brought into the discussion: "to accept that Parliament retains the right to compel universal observance of the day of rest preferred by one religion [the dominant majority religion] is not consistent with the preservation and enhancement of the multicultural heritage of Canadians."[59]

The *Big M* pronouncement forbidding direct compulsion is now deeply entrenched in Canadian law.[60] The Supreme Court of Canada recently referred to cases involving religious compulsion as "straightforward"; they fail the test of constitutionality without even triggering a balancing or proportionality analysis.[61] It is worth noting, however, that what is considered straightforward in Canada does not necessarily translate to other jurisdictions. Unlike the Supreme Court of Canada, other distinguished courts (whether national or supranational) have been reluctant to declare practices and policies enforcing majoritarian values as a "form of coercion inimical to the Charter [or other human rights instruments] and the dignity of all non-Christians."[62] Consider, for instance, the much-discussed *Lautsi* decision handed down by the Grand Chamber of the European Court of Human Rights ("ECtHR"), the apex judicial body in the European human rights system, entrusted with interpreting the provisions of the European Convention on Human Rights.[63] In *Lautsi*, the Grand Chamber of the ECtHR overturned an earlier unanimous decision by the Chamber. In it the Grand Chamber ruled that given the wide

---

57 *Id.*, at para. 97   58 *Id.*, at para. 98.

59 *Id.*, at para. 99. The emphasis on removing majoritarian religious indoctrination (*e.g.*, the "Lord's Prayer") is also found in constitutional challenges raised in the public school context.

60 This case has received not only favorable, but also unfavorable appraisal by legal commentators. *See, e.g.*, Benjamin L. Berger, *Law's Religion: Rendering Culture*, 45 OSGOODE HALL L.J. 227 (2007).

61 *Alberta v. Hutterian Brethren of Wilson County*, [2009] SCJ No. 37, [2009] 2 SCR 567, at para. 93 (SCC) [hereinafter "*Hutterian Brethren*"]; *R. v. Oakes*, [1986] SCJ No. 7, 1986] 1 SCR 103 (SCC).

62 *Big M, supra* note 57, at para. 97.

63 *Lautsi v. Italy*, No. 30814/06 (Eur. Ct. H.R. March 18, 2011) (European Court of Human Rights, Grand Chamber) [hereinafter "*Lautsi* (Grand Chamber)"]; *Lautsi v. Italy*, No. 30814/06 (Eur. Ct. H.R. Nov. 3, 2009) (European Court of Human Rights, Chamber).

variety of approaches adopted by European states regarding the place of religion in public schools, the Italian regulations requiring the prominent display of the crucifix in every classroom in state-run schools fall within the margin-of-appreciation owed to domestic authorities to "perpetuate a tradition," here, the tradition of the *majority* religion (Catholicism) in Italy. In effect, this decision means that children from different faiths, backgrounds and ways of life, including non-Christians and those professing no religion, will continue to be educated under the cross – literally – in Italian public schools.

The *Lautsi* decision has been criticized as taking a pro-majority stance in the "cultural wars currently raging in Europe [in which] the relationship between the majority and minorities in society, the extent of their respective claims to shape the social, cultural, and intellectual environment, and the role of the state in their tug-of-war is the source of recurring tensions."[64] Under the non-coercion variant of the fair inclusion framework informing the Canadian multiculturalism experiment, a decision like *Lautsi* would be objectionable in that it upholds, rather than dismantles, the "compulsory display of a symbol of a particular [majority] faith in the exercise of public authority," thus breaching the duty of neutrality and fair inclusion as non-coercion.[65] Recall that s.27 instructs that "[t]his Charter shall be interpreted in a manner consistent with the preservation and enhancement of the multicultural heritage of *Canadians*," not the preservation and enhancement of the heritage of a *majority* tradition or community in Canada. By contrast, the *Lautsi* decision reflects the continued privileging of the majority tradition and the use of the force of the law to inculcate certain values to a "captive audience" in and through a quintessential public institution: the public school.[66] In lieu of multiculturalism, it endorses *mono*culturalism by granting permission to display a "primarily religious symbol" (as the Strasbourg Court put it) – the crucifix – in every state-run classroom where attendance is compulsory regardless of religious convictions or lack thereof.

---

[64] Dimitrios Kyritsis & Stavros Tsakyrakis, *Neutrality in the Classroom*, 11 INT'L J. CONST. L. 200, 200 (2103).

[65] Importantly, the earlier unanimous decision in *Lautsi* (Chamber), which sided with the applicant against Italy's position, fully acknowledged the concern with compulsion and coercion, especially in the realm of education, holding that: "The Court cannot see how the display in state-school classrooms of a symbol that it is reasonable to associate with Catholicism (the majority religion in Italy) could serve the educational pluralism which is essential for the preservation of 'democratic society' within the Convention meaning of that term." *See Lausti* (Chamber), paras. 56–57.

[66] As the Chambers' ultimately-overturned *Lautsi* decision stated: "The State is forbidden to pursue an aim of indoctrination that might be considered as not respecting parents' religious and philosophical convictions." *Id.*, at para 47.

As comparative constitutional scholars have rightly observed, legal disputes such as *Lautsi* have come to the fore because the ECtHR itself has become a core arena where "some of the most challenging debates around European legal pluralism [now] take place, and its case law has centrally contributed to shaping the terms of such controversies,"[67] turning courts into the arenas in which core societal values are contested.[68] Moreover, it is increasingly recognized that the legal arena has become a strategic space for, not only exploring the "nature of religious communities, their relationship to state institutions, and the place of minority religious communities in society," but also for re-examining "the place, role and rights of the 'Christian majority'" in Europe.[69] These are highly charged issues (which have become intertwined with a deepening "cultural anxiety" about national identities and shared values perceived to be under threat and in danger of being "overwhelmed" by the members of minority religious communities, thus feeding into a dangerous narrative of *"nous" et les "autres"*) create a binary, zero-sum dynamic of "us" versus "them."[70] Canada is not immune to these pressures. However, these trends have been slower to take hold in Canada than elsewhere, arguably in part due to the fact that plurality and heterogeneity of peoples has always been part of that country's history. Since its introduction, a core goal of Canada's official multiculturalism policy has been the dismantling of majoritarian dominance and its replacement with a commitment to equal citizenship as safeguarding diversity-in-unity.[71]

The legal commitment to non-coercion can therefore be thought of as a concrete articulation of a broader normative principle and policy of fair inclusion: the removal of negative background conditions, statutes or regulations that may appear or purport to be neutral but in fact are "implicitly tilted towards the needs, interests, and identities of the majority group."[72] Beyond it lies a vast range of positive, concrete and often case-by-case exemptions and

[67] Effie Fokas, *Directions in Religious Pluralism in Europe: Mobilizations in the Shadow of European Court of Human Rights Religious Freedom Jurisprudence*, OXFORD J. L. & RELIGION (advance access), at 2 (2015). More generally, *see* Ran Hirschl, CONSTITUTIONAL THEOCRACY (Cambridge, MA: Harvard University Press, 2010).

[68] For extensive discussion, *see* Ran Hirschl, *The Judicialization of Mega-Politics and the Rise of Political Courts*, 11 AM. POLIT. SCI. REV 93 (2008).

[69] Fokas, *supra* note 69.   [70] Ralph Grillio, "Reasons to Ban"; Benhabib, *supra* note 52, 24–26.

[71] The term diversity in unity appears in *Discover Canada*, the official study guide issued by the government for citizenship applicants who seek to naturalize, a carefully regulated process that culminates with a public citizenship test. On the concept of the social imaginary, *see* Charles Taylor, MODERN SOCIAL IMAGINARIES (Durham, NC: Duke University Press, 2007).

[72] Will Kymlicka & Wayne Norman, "Citizenship in Culturally Diverse Societies: Issues, Contexts, Concepts" in Will Kymlicka & Wayne Norman, eds., CITIZENSHIP IN DIVERSE SOCIETIES (Oxford: Oxford University Press, 2000), 4.

accommodations from otherwise generally applicable laws, rules, regulations and other binding governmental policies. As we have just seen, refraining from coercively using state power to privilege the tradition(s) of the majority is anything but trivial.

The citizenship oath presents a more complex challenge, however, as it touches on the foundational question of defining "who belongs," or ought to belong, and according to what criteria. Does this requirement impose the traditions of the majority (however difficult they remain to define) in ways that make it objectionable as a coercive use of state power to promote what is (essentially) a partial position not fitting in a diverse and multicultural society, or is it a legitimate *civic* requirement that state officials may pursue to generate the "social glue" that holds us together beyond our acknowledged or self-professed differences? The jurisprudence on religious freedom under the *Charter* provides some useful guidance, although not a clear-cut answer. Writing for the majority in *NS* (a case examining whether a witness in a criminal trial may testify while donning a *niqab*), Chief Justice Beverley McLachlin reiterated that when faced with conflicts between freedom of religion and other values the Canadian tradition has been to respect the individual's religious belief and to accommodate it if at all possible.[73] In light of this framing of the analysis, the Court held that a total ban on the *niqab* is an intrusion by the state that is inconsistent with the *Charter*.

The debate about the relevance of the interpretative commitment to multi-culturalism to the analysis is most evident in the concurring opinion by LeBel J., which endorsed stability and continuity in responding to today's winds of multicultural change (reminiscent, in this sense, of recent European trends), insisting that the "openness of the trial process" requires a *categorical* ban on *niqabs* in the courtroom. In contrast, the dissenting opinion reached a dia-metrically opposed conclusion: while "conced[ing] without reservation that seeing more of a witness' facial expression is better than seeing less," Abella J. held that the assessment of demeanour can be reasonably achieved without seeing the bare (or "naked") face.[74] While the debate among the justices focuses on the technical difficulties of assessing demeanour, the case reveals a far deeper disagreement: it turns the veil into a test case for determining how

---

[73] *R. v. NS*, [2012] 3 SCR 726 (SCC). at para. 54. *See also* para. 51: rejecting the view that the *niqab*-wearing practice should be banned because it breaches "neutrality," the Chief Justice powerfully stated that such an approach is "inconsistent with Canadian jurisprudence, courtroom practice, our tradition of requiring state institutions and actors to accommodate sincerely held religious beliefs insofar as possible."

[74] The "naked face" imagery is somewhat provocatively evoked in this context, as a rhetorical tool to emphasize the harm that a woman may be exposed to.

far the principle of religious freedom will go when it fiercely conflicts with other protected *Charter* rights (in this case, the right to a fair trial), how to conceptualize the balance between stability and change in an increasingly diverse society, and how to navigate the competing interests of religious freedom, the right to a fair trial and access to justice for minorities-within-minorities, here, *niqab*-wearing Muslim women.

As a minority woman and a sexual assault complainant, NS's religious freedom claim also encapsulates a powerful plea for fair inclusion and equal access to justice for all women, including minority women who profess a non-dominant religious belief or practice. In this way the judgment also might be seen as relevant to section 28 (although that provision was not discussed in the decision). The value of fairness to the complainant and the broader societal interest of not discouraging *niqab*-wearing women from reporting offences and participating in the justice system is vital to the analysis; indeed these considerations are now part of the public record, expressed powerfully by the dissenting opinion and echoed in the majority's reasoning.[75] The Supreme Court of Canada ultimately adopted a contextual, case-by-case approach, resisting the idea that users of the justice system must "park their religion at the courtroom door," just as it rejected the response that says that "a witness can always testify with her face covered."

This contextual balancing approach allows courts in Canada to *avoid* grandiloquent value judgments of the face-covering practice. As Abella J. noted in her dissenting opinion, controversies surrounding the *niqab* are prevalent both within and outside the Muslim community. These controversies include questions such as "whether the *niqab* is mandatory for Muslim women or whether it marginalizes the women who wear it; whether it enhances multi-culturalism or whether it demeans it."[76] Justice Abella further states:

> These are complex issues about which reasonable people can and do strenuously disagree. But we are not required to try to resolve any of these or related conceptual issues in this case, we are required to try to transcend them in order to answer only one question: Where identity is not an issue, should a witness' sincerely held religious belief that a niqab must be worn in a courtroom, yield to an accused's ability to see her face.[77]

This lucid analytical approach, with its steadfast resistance of armchair social theory, allows Canadian courts to avoid the trap of *abstractly* stipulating

---

[75] Access to the courts by sexually assaulted women, an issue central to the dissenting opinion of Abella J., has been identified by the Chief Justice of the Supreme Court as "most pressing."

[76] *Id.*, at para. 80.   [77] *Id.*

inconsistencies between diversity and equality. Perhaps the most important conceptual lesson to be drawn from NS is that the adoption of a contextual, *"in concreto"* case-by-case approach that remains grounded in the law and facts of each particular dispute, even if it does not offer a perfect solution, is preferable when considered against the tendency towards the *abstract* declaration of irreconcilable value conflicts demonstrated by European courts as we shall explore below.

CONTEXT AND MEMBERSHIP MATTERS

Consider the contrast between the Canadian approach of side-stepping the debate about the symbolic meaning of the veil (and whether it is mandatory for Muslim women at all) and the framework of analysis emerging from Europe's highest human rights court, as reflected in the ECtHR's engagement with respect-for-differences claims brought by women who wish to practice a less extensive form of veiling, namely, donning the *hijab* (a head cover worn by some Muslim women, in which the face remains visible). Much like the decision in *N. (S.)*, the European Court of Human Rights decisions in the *hijab* cases of *Dahlab* and *Sahin* engage in proportionality analysis and balancing of competing interests.[78] The difference lies in the level of abstraction. Whereas in NS the Supreme Court of Canada endorses a contextual approach, reserving the ultimate balancing decision for the closest-to-the-ground judicial authority (the presiding judge), in *Dahlab* and *Sahin* the "'balancing' that takes place is a balancing of abstract stipulated inconsistencies (secularism and democracy vs. the religious symbolism of the veil; women's equality and tolerance vs. Islamic religious obligation) rather than evidentially demonstrated *in concreto* conflicts of rights with other rights, or of rights with important public interests."[79]

Similar concerns about the Strasbourg court "sacrific[ing] concrete individual rights guaranteed by the Convention to abstract principles" were even expressed by the two dissenting judges in the recent SAS decision, in which the majority of the ECtHR ultimately upheld the French legal ban that prohibits the wearing of face-veils in public.[80] In that decision, denounced by critics as reinforcing the ostracization of Islam as a minority faith, the Court

---

[78] *Dahlab v. Switzerland*, No. 42393/98, [2001] V ECHR 447; *Leyla Sahin v. Turkey*, No. 44794/98, [2005] XI ECHR.

[79] Nehal Bhuta, *Two Concepts of Religious Freedom in the European Court of Human Rights*, 113 SOUTH ATLANTIC QUARTERLY 9 (2014).

[80] *SAS v. France*, No. 43835/11, [2014] (joint dissenting opinion of judges Nussberger and Jadelblom, at para 2).

relied on the French government's argument that promoting "living together" (*le 'vivre ensemble'*) is a legitimate ground for restriction of fundamental rights protected by the Convention. To understand this last point, some background regarding the challenged legislation is required. In 2010, France became the first country in the world to criminalize the wearing of face veils, such as the *niqab*, anywhere in public – with the exception of houses of worship.[81] The draft of the 2010 Law included an explanatory memorandum that stated that "[e]ven though the phenomenon, at present, remains marginal, the wearing of the full veil is the sectarian manifestation of a rejection of the values of the Republic." The law was passed by the National Assembly by an overwhelming majority (335 votes in favor, one vote against, and three abstentions). The Senate also followed suit with 246 votes in favour and one abstention. In drafting the legislation, as part of its fact-finding mission a parliamentary committee concluded that "the wearing of the full-face veil on national territory" was a recent phenomenon in France, and by the end of 2009, was only practiced by about 1,900 women out of France's 4.7-million-strong Muslim population. This is a ratio of less than 1 in 2500 so there must have been something deeper reasons that motivated this legislative policy.

In the context of heightened political and legal tensions surrounding an "ostentatious" expression of a minority identity that is increasingly perceived as threatening and "foreign" in Europe, it is hard not to be reminded of William Blackstone's observation that whereas civil injuries are "an infringement . . . of the civil rights which belong to individuals . . . public wrongs, or crimes . . . are a breach and violation of the public rights and duties, due to the whole community."[82] The act of defining an expression of particular, more conservative, variants of the Islamic faith as a public wrong bears not only a punitive function, but also an *expressivist* meaning: the outrage of the majority community against what it perceives as an offensive repudiation of *laïcité* and other foundational values of the republic. From that vantage point, the person who breaches the criminal code's prohibition against face-veiling acts in violation of the whole community and its "common culture." In this way, the criminal code – and the state machinery that enacts and enforces it – expresses moral condemnation of the *actor*, not just the prohibited act. The face-veil banning legislation advances a particular vision of the public sphere that sheathes popular anxieties about the majoritarian discomfort of living side by side with veiled Muslim women who are *de jure* included in the polity, but are *de facto* ostracized as the "Other." Tremendous political capital is invested in such

---

[81] In France, the terminology of face veils confusingly conflates *niqab* and *burka*.
[82] Blackstone 1765–69 [1825], Book IV, Ch. 1, p. 5, para. 1.

laws as symbolic manifestations of an idealized "France [which] is never as much itself, faithful to its history, its destiny, its image, than when united around the values of the Republic: liberty, equality, fraternity," as the 2010 Law explanatory memorandum reads.

From the official French statist perspective, however, prohibiting such expression of religious minority identity, or "sectarianism," is not a failure of fair inclusion but merely a manifestation of the constitutionally entrenched *laïcité* principle, dating back to 1905, which resists *any* expression of religiosity as a breach of neutrality and secularism; it also a necessary measure for promoting social cohesion. However, this framework fails to take context into account – in which using the full force of the power of the state to legally prohibit a member of a minority community from expressing certain aspects of her religious identity holds additional dimensions of marginalization and exclusion. Equality among citizens is affected by defining her "veiled" presence in public spaces as harmful to others. These other dimensions are camouflaged when the statist discourse simply claims to be evenhandedly applying facially-neutral laws, practices and policies – a point that advocates of fair inclusion as non-coercion and accommodation have long emphasized in Canadian debates.[83] To put this last point differently, absent from the official narrative is an account of the power relations and context in which the encounter between the ("sectarian") individual and the ("universal") state occurs. The ECtHR, alas, sided with the latter over the former. It cited the French parliamentary report that described the practice of face-veiling as "at odds with the values of the Republic," implicitly reinforcing, in direct contrast to Canada's *Big M* approach, the power of a dominant majority to impose *its* (in this case, secularist) worldview by means of national, purportedly neutral, legislation that in effect imposes concrete and predictable burdens and restrictions on the protected rights of members belonging to already marginalized religious minority communities. Yet as we have seen earlier in the discussion, in the resounding words of *Big M*: "What may appear good and true to a majoritarian ... group, or to the state acting at their behest, may not ... be imposed upon citizens who take a contrary view."

Unlike the French approach, the Supreme Court in *NS* had no interest in ascribing meaning to the wearing of the *niqab* or making a judgment regarding whether that meaning accorded with Canadian values. This contextual approach helps avoid the dangerously charged terrain of assumed

---

[83] This point has been elaborated by many a political theorist, *see, e.g.,* Kymlicka and Norman, *supra* note 72; in legal terminology, we would refer here to the prohibition against both direct and indirect discrimination.

(rather than proven) tensions and inconsistencies. As Canadian courts have repeatedly stated, even if a given law and regulatory scheme promotes an important social goal, the burden is on the government to explain why a significantly less intrusive and equally effective measure was not chosen and to demonstrate that the chosen measure only minimally impairs the protected rights and interests at stake.[84] This is especially true given the profound significance of citizenship, which has been described as "nothing less than the right to have rights" by the US Supreme Court (echoing the famous words of philosopher Hannah Arendt); any restrictions must be narrowly tailored and operate as a last resort only, for at stake is the vital membership and dignity interest of the individual.[85]

TROUBLES IN PARADISE: WHEN DIVERSITY AND EQUALITY COLLIDE

Even in multicultural Canada, tensions have arisen in recent years surrounding questions of membership and belonging. As in other countries, the laws and regulations governing citizenship reveal much about the society that constructed them, telling us "who the state considers a full member, how that membership is transmitted inter-generationally, and how it can be lost, gained, and reclaimed."[86] The history of access to citizenship in Canada still bears the scars of past exclusion on the basis of considerations such as race, gender, national origin, religion and indigenous status.[87] While Canada now rightly takes pride in being an open, multicultural society that welcomes immigrants from the four corners of the globe, any restrictions on the basic right to have rights appearing to target a particular group of settled immigrants or new-comers as "too different" may taint this reputation and confirm a sense of injustice felt by those affected.

As mentioned earlier, in 2011, a ban was introduced that instructed government officials to ensure that participants in a citizenship ceremony, the final

---

[84] *See* the classic *R. v. Oakes* [1986] SCR 103 (establishing the "Oakes test").

[85] *Perez v. Brownell*, 356 US 44, 64 (1958) (Warren C.J., dissenting opinion). Hannah Arendt, THE ORIGINS OF TOTALITARIANISM (New York: Harcourt, Brace and Jovanovich, 1968 edition)177: "We became aware of the existence of a right to have rights ... and a right to belong to some kind of organized community, only when millions of people emerged who had lost and could not regain these rights." *See also* Shachar, "Citizenship," *supra* note 46.

[86] Kim Barry, *Home and Away: The Construction of Citizenship in an Emigration Context*, 81 NYU. L. REV. 11 (2006), at 20.

[87] For a concise historical overview of such exclusionary measures, *see* Ninette Kelley and Michael Trebilcock, THE MAKING OF THE MOSAIC: A HISTORY OF CANADIAN IMMIGRATION POLICY (Toronto: University of Toronto Press, 1998) 132–163.

step of the naturalization process, will not be permitted to take the oath of citizenship while wearing a face covering. On judicial review, this policy was described as "superfluous," in that neither the regulations nor the Citizenship Act required visual confirmation of the oath being recited.[88] The government, however, held its ground. A spokesperson for the immigration minister responded to the Federal Court ruling by stating that: "[n]ew citizens are obliged to confirm their identity when taking the Oath of Citizenship ... it is simply common sense to require removal of facial coverings or other items that hide new citizens' mouths from view. The oath, knowledge and language tests ... are among the basic requirements for joining the family of Canadian citizens."[89] The prime minister used even sharper language as he announced, symbolically in Quebec – the stronghold in Canada of a more "European" perception of state-religion relations – that the government intended to appeal, remarking:

> I believe, and I think most Canadians believe that it is offensive that someone would hide their identity at the very moment they are committing to join the Canadian family.[90]

The characterization of veiled oath taking as "offensive" by top government officials is arguably a manifestation of a majority-infused statist vision of "living together," echoing the positions we have already seen in the French face-veil ban and the *SAS* decision, despite the fact that Canada's constitutional tradition has never adhered to the *laïcité* principle. This belligerent rhetoric may, however, run amok and lead us to the (misguided) conclusion that, in order achieve fair inclusion and equal footing with other members of the shared political community, some members, but not others, will have to relinquish a sincerely held belief or be asked to denounce certain elements of minority identity that they view as constitutive of who they are and how they perceive themselves.

---

[88] *Ishaq v Canada (Federal Court)*, *supra* note 25.

[89] Nicholas Keung, *Niqab Ban at Citizenship Ceremony Struck Down by Court*, THE TORONTO STAR, Feb. 6, 2015, available at www.thestar.com/news/immigration/2015/02/06/niqab-ban-at-citizenship-ceremony-struck-down-by-court.html (citing the spokesperson for then Minister of Citizenship and Immigration, Chris Alexander).

[90] The "offensive" terminology was used by Canada's Prime Minister during a public meeting in Quebec and received significant coverage in the media. It was also later repeated in a Conservative party email signed by Chris Alexander, Minister of Citizenship and Immigration, soliciting signatures by those who "agree with our prime minister." *See, e.g.*, Morgan Lowrie, *Harper Says Ottawa Will Appeal Ruling Allowing Veil during Citizenship Oath*, THE GLOBE AND MAIL, Feb. 12, 2015, available at www.theglobeandmail.com/news/national/harper-says-ottawa-will-appeal-ruling-allowing-veil-during-citizenship-oath/article22979142/.

This rising "paradigm of suspicion," as one scholar has put it, is embedded in a larger narrative dating back to the early decades of the 2000s.[91] The Canadian Government had launched a campaign to "reinforce the value of Canadian citizenship," generating a spate of legislative and executive initiatives. Preventing women wearing the face-cover from accessing the citizenship ceremony is merely symptomatic competing currents between the "trivializing" and distrusting" positions.[92] Such heightened emphasis on expressing and demonstrating "loyalty" by erasing certain markers of religious or other identity-based minority affiliation is, alas, foreign to the letter and spirit of the concept of Canadian multiculturalism and fair inclusion as developed through jurisprudence. As the majority enunciated in *NS* when considering whether a witness may wear the *niqab* in court, "to remove religion from the courtroom is *not* the Canadian tradition. Canadians have, since the country's inception, taken oaths based on holy books – be they the Bible, the Koran, or some other sacred text."[93] The same considerations should, by analogy and with equal force, be applied in the context of taking the oath in a citizenship ceremony, where religious and cultural identities are to be celebrated according to Canada's multicultural tradition rather than forcibly removed from the public sphere.[94]

The face-veiling ban in citizenship ceremonies also stands in tension with the official version of multiculturalism that Citizenship and Immigration Canada itself publically endorses:

---

[91] Ronen Shamir, *Without Borders? Notes on Globalization as a Mobility Regime*, 23 SOCIOLOGICAL THEORY 197 (2005).

[92] *Strengthening Canadian Citizenship Act*, S.C. 2014, c. 22; Citizenship and Immigration Canada, "Backgrounder - Strengthening the Value of Canadian Citizenship: Amending the *Citizenship Act* to Protect the Integrity of Canadian Citizenship," available at www.cic.gc .ca/english/department/media/backgrounders/2010/2010-06-10.asp. The government also tabled the *Zero Tolerance of Barbaric Cultural Practices Act* (turning polygamy into an inadmissibility ground), which, given its provocative title, has led commentators to suggest that by using the term "barbaric" the government is "targeting particular [racialized immigrant] communities and the does not see the problem of polygamy and early and forced marriage as a 'Canadian issue,'" thus "sending a political message with this legislation." *See* Kim Mackrael, *Experts Question Need for Polygamy Bill*, THE GLOBE AND MAIL, A4, Nov. 6, 2014. The implied contrast between "civic/civilized" and "barbaric" that informs this legislation contributes to the construction of a dangerous "us"–"them" dichotomy, as discussed earlier.

[93] *N. (S.)*, *supra*, note 79, at para. 53 [emphasis added].

[94] Canada's Citizenship Regulations, SOR/93-246 requires in s. 17(1)(b) that citizenship judges "administer the oath of citizenship with dignity and solemnity, allowing the greatest possible freedom in the religious solemnization or the solemn affirmation thereof."

In 1971, Canada was the first country in the world to adopt multiculturalism as an official policy. By so doing, Canada affirmed the value and dignity
of all Canadian citizens regardless of their racial or ethnic origins, their
language, or their religious affiliation ... Multiculturalism ensures that all
[Canadians] can keep their identities, can take pride in their ancestry and
have a sense of belonging. Acceptance gives Canadians a feeling of security and self-confidence, making them more open to, and accepting of,
diverse cultures ... Multiculturalism has led to higher rates of naturalization
than ever before. With no pressure to assimilate and give up their culture,
immigrants freely choose their new citizenship because they want to be
Canadians.[95]

Recent legislative changes have made this rite of passage more difficult
to secure, however.[96] It is within this context that the face-veiling ban in
citizenship ceremonies, accentuated by the accompanying public declarations by government officials, was seen as part of a subtle yet persistent
attempt to distinguish between inclusion for the majority of newcomers who
willingly and "successfully demonstrate that they have internalized prevailing
'values' ... [and exclusion for those immigrants who are] judged to have
rejected liberal-democratic norms, through their deeds and/or speech."[97]

The Federal Court heard from the claimant that she conceived the "governmental policy regarding veils at citizenship oath ceremonies [a]s a personal
attack on me, my identity as a Muslim woman and my religious beliefs."[98] In a
well-publicized decision, the presiding judge accepted her claim and struck

---

[95] Citizenship and Immigration Canada, "Canadian Multiculturalism: An Inclusive Citizenship"
       (2012), available at www.cic.gc.ca/english/multiculturalism/citizenship.asp.
[96] In Canada, the transition from immigrant-to-citizen now incorporates tougher naturalization
       requirements, ranging from fulfilling a longer physical residency period prior to gaining
       eligibility to naturalize, to demonstrating an "intent to reside in Canada," to expanding the
       grounds on which dual citizenship can be revoked. See *Strengthening Canadian Citizenship
       Act, supra* note 94. Some of these legislative changes were later revoked.
[97] *See* Triadafilos Triadafilopoulos, *Illiberal Means to Liberal Ends? Understanding Recent
       Immigrant Integration Policies in Europe*, 37 J. ETHN. MIGR. STUD. 861 (2010), at 862. As Jason
       Kenney, former Minister of Citizenship and Immigration, put it: "Canadian citizenship is
       predicated on loyalty to this country." *See* Stewart Bell, *Jason Kenney Suggests New Legislation
       Is Need to Strip Citizenship of Dual Nationals Involved in Terrorism*, NATIONAL POST,
       Feb. 6, 2013.
[98] Douglas Quan, *Woman Asks to Be Sworn as Citizen as soon as Possible after Overturn of Policy
       Requiring Her to Remove Niqab*, NATIONAL POST, Feb. 11, 2015 (citing the claimant, Zunera
       Ishaq, a 29 year old Toronto resident who immigrated to Canada from Pakistan). The issue of
       expression of individual choice and "identity" has gained tremendous impact not only in
       scholarly circles, but also in recent judicial opinions. *See, e.g., Obergefell v. Hodges*, 576
       US (2015).

down the ban: "To the extent that the policy interferes with a citizenship judge's duty to allow candidates for citizenship the greatest possible freedom in the religious solemnization or the solemn affirmation of the oath," wrote the Federal Court, "it is unlawful."[99] Although the case was determined on regulatory rather than constitutional grounds, the decision also took account of the gendered and exclusionary message such a ban carries with it: "The policy in this case could dissuade women who wear the *niqab* from even applying for citizenship. In such circumstances, a direct challenge to the policy is appropriate," read the decision.[100] This last point is important. The court rejected the government's argument that the applicant was not obligated to pursue Canadian citizenship; she could simply remain a permanent resident (or what scholars have termed a "denizen" who lacks political rights) ignoring the *in*equality that such a "solution" perpetuates when compared to gaining full membership – and its accompanying rights and protections – including political rights to participate in the democratic act of authoring the laws that collectively govern our public life.[101]

The Federal Court's decision was swiftly appealed by the government. At this moment, in the middle of an election year, the citizenship-oath *niqab* saga gained attention well beyond the courtroom, receiving ample domestic and international media coverage.[102] In a much-anticipated decision, the Federal Court of Appeal, like the Federal Court before it, ruled against the new policy on technical grounds; again, the decision did not engage the *Charter* rights at issue. As in response to the previous court ruling, various government officials continued to tout the value of the new (and by then, struck down) policy. The minister responsible for citizenship and immigration expressed the view that: "new citizens should recite the oath proudly, loudly and for everyone to see and hear." He also implied that the policy might be extended to *hijabs*.[103] The Prime Minister was quoted as saying: "when someone joins the Canadian family, there are times in our open, tolerant,

---

[99] *Ishaq v. Canada*, 2015 FC 156, para. 68.   [100] *Id.*, para. 42.

[101] On the concept of denizen, *see* Thomas Hammar, DEMOCRACY AND THE NATION STATE: ALIENS, DENIZENS AND CITIZENS IN A WORLD OF INTERNATIONAL MIGRATION (Avebury: Aldershot, 1990).

[102] Douglas Quan, *'It's Classic Wedge Politics': Tories Continue to Tout Niqab Ban as Battle Heats Up in Court of Appeals*, NATIONAL POST, July 14, 2015, available at http://news.nationalpost .com/news/canada/its-classic-wedge-politics-tories-continue-to-tout-niqab-ban-as-battle-heats-up-in-court-of-appeals; John Barber, *Veil Debate Becomes Big Issue in Canada Election, Putting Conservatives into Lead*, THE GUARDIAN, Oct. 1, 2015, available at www.theguardian.com/ world/2015/oct/01/zunera-ishaq-veil-canada-election-conservatives.

[103] Quan, *supra* note 106.

pluralistic society that as part of our interactions with each other we reveal our identity through revealing our face."[104]

This articulation of the rationale for the ban represents the majority as generous and inclusive (hence the rhetorical power of the analogy between joining a family and one's new home society), while implicitly placing the "fault" for eroding such openness on those who are not willing to reveal their identity and their faces at the constitutive moment of *becoming* Canadian. This framing of the issue helps explain why analysts dubbed it a "wedge issue"; opinion polls showed ample popular support for the ban, while its detractors emphasized that "Canada defends the rights of minorities, we respect people's rights." A final twist in Ishaq's story was the government's request that the Federal Court of Appeal stay its ruling pending appeal, a legal move that would have had the immediate effect of barring Ishaq, the woman who challenged the face-covering ban, from obtaining citizenship and the franchise in time for the upcoming federal election.

WOMEN, CITIZENSHIP, AND THE FRANCHISE

Denying women access to the direct and reciprocal relationship of citizenship offends justice and democracy. It is particularly punishing for female members of minority communities who have historically been denied both membership and the franchise.[105] Threatening them with modern-day exclusion as they stand on the cusp of membership belittles their agency and makes them pawns in renewed state-religion struggles for power and recognition. Whatever the merits of such realignments, it is unfair to ask that they be borne disproportionately by those already marginalized and stigmatized. In Canada, it took a *niqab*-wearing immigrant, Zunera Ishaq, to challenge the government's ban, and to win her case. She was awarded the remedy she sought, namely, the opportunity to acquire citizenship by completing the naturalization process without having to compromise her religious practice. On the day of swearing-in, media crews arrived at the nondescript office building in which Ishaq's saga was about to reach its conclusion: members of her legal team and journalists from around the world video recorded her careful yet heartfelt recitation of the oath, with her face-veil on, in both official languages. A few

[104] Les Whittington, *Ottawa Wants Postponement of Ruling that Quashes Niqab Ban*, THE TORONTO STAR, Sept. 18, 2015, available at www.thestar.com/news/canada/2015/09/18/ottawa-determined-to-continue-niqab-ban-at-citizenship-ceremonies.html.
[105] Juan de villa, Veils, Oaths, and Canadian Citizenship: Ishaq v. Canada, *The Court*, March 2, 2015.

tears were shed; hugs were exchanged. As a newly minted citizen, she even got to exercise her right to vote in the election in which her own case became a *cause célèbre*.

What is the broader message that can we draw from Ishaq's story? Everybody in the Canadian legal community knew, or should have known, that the ministerial ban stood on shaky ground in light of the long list of constitutional cases providing hefty protection to religious freedom in Canada. Yet, in the court of public opinion, one of the government's strongest points was the appeal to gender equality; forcefully claiming that allowing a veiled woman (perceived as a sign of submission) to take the citizenship oath, without openly interacting with her future fellow co-citizens, flew in the face of cherished Canadian values of gender equality.

In closing, it is important, then, to address majoritarian and emotionally-charged argument head-on. Recall that in *NS*, Justice Abella already established that it is not necessary to determine in the abstract "whether the niqab is mandatory for Muslim women or whether it marginalizes the women who wear it; whether it enhances multiculturalism or whether it demeans it ... These are complex issues about which reasonable people can and do strenuously disagree." At stake in the *Ishaq* controversy was the concretization of these abstract questions – returning to our introductory remarks, manner of fulfillment is raised to the same level as content: in a free and democratic society committed to multiculturalism, can a minority woman who has fulfilled all the requirements of naturalization (except the oath) be deprived of citizenship on account of the government's refusal to accommodate her religious belief which did not harm or restrict other people's ability to take the oath or acquire citizenship?

Recall, also, that the oath is performative and constitutive, giving vitality for both newcomers and the society that accepts them to the words that bind them together as co-members of a shared political community. The "trivialists" are thus mistaken in taking the oath lightly or wishing it away. At the same time, those adhering to the "distrusting" position are equally misguided, for they seek to predetermine who is an insider and who an outsider, and do so based of majoritarian fears and perceptions that betray the unique Canadian experiment of unity-in-diversity. What is more, if we truly care about women's empowerment and their ability to stand on their own feet, we *cannot* coherently uphold a governmental policy that, while purporting to assist minority women, actually leaves them without access to citizenship because of the (controversial or not) religious attire they wear in expression of sincere religious belief. This flies in the face of equality and relegates them to a state of dependence rather than the liberty and independence that should come with acquiring full membership as equal citizens; these women are left, instead, in a twilight zone, without any direct link to the state, but only an attenuated relationship to it acquired through their spouses or other sponsoring family members. Canada's commitment to diversity and equality here must lead in tandem to a unified result: promoting, rather than inhibiting, women's access to the acquisition of full (formal, if not always substantive) membership, as equal citizens, with voting rights, with voice, with the potential and the ability to pursue change, whether legal or political, in their new home country as well as their own communities of faith. There are times when, instead of merely standing on the sidelines, it is imperative to take action. In taking the government to court, Ishaq openly and publically demonstrated her participation in and commitment to her adopted Canadian homeland and the quintessential values – diversity and equality – enshrined at its core.

PART II

The Court in Canadian Constitutionalism

7

The Judicial Constitutionalization of Politics in Canada and Other Contemporary Democracies

Comparing the Canadian Secession Case to South Africa's Death Penalty Case and Israel's Landmark Migdal Constitutional Case

MICHEL ROSENFELD

INTRODUCTION

There has been a vigorous debate about the "judicialization" of politics and criticisms of the expansion of the judicial role resulting in a seemingly ever more encompassing settling of policy issues by unelected judges.[1] Moreover, the use of legal interpretation practices by judges for purposes of securing a dominant role in the conduct of politics seems all the more objectionable where it appears that judges invoke the constitution in furtherance of the pursuit of their own political agenda. Indeed, whereas judicial overreaches in ordinary legislative settings may be overridden by ordinary majoritarian political means, judicial excursions into the realm of politics cloaked in the mantle of the constitution typically depend in a vast number of constitutional democracies[2] on cumbersome super-majoritarian processes in order to be nullified. Furthermore, the resolution of a great majority of the most important political questions confronting a polity by courts may not simply stem from judicial

---

[1] See Ran Hirschl, *Towards Juristocracy: The Origins and Consequences of the New Constitutionalism* (2004); Jeremy Waldron, *The Core of the Case against Judicial Review*, 115 YALE L.J. 1346, 1349–1353 (2006).

[2] Significantly, Canada stands as a notorious exception in this respect as its constitution allows for parliamentary override of specific provisions of the Charter of Rights and Freedoms and, by extension, of judicial interpretations of those provisions. *See* Canada Constitution Act, 1982, Sec 33. According to this override provision, the federal Parliament or a provincial legislature may declare by a simple majority that legislation that runs counter to a judicial interpretation of a right protected by the Constitution is valid, notwithstanding the conflict. The override involved cannot be extended to those rights that are essential to the democratic process itself, and it expires automatically after five years, though it can be extended by new legislation at that time. Although the override provision has been sometimes used by the Quebec legislature, it has had little impact in the rest of Canada.

self-aggrandizement, but also from the design of political and economic elites bent on insulating "substantive policy making from the vicissitudes of democratic politics."[3]

The constitutionalization of politics, particularly in the hand of judges who for all practical purposes have the last word, is certainly worrisome. Before issuing any wholesale condemnation of constitutional review by unelected judges, however, it is necessary to consider whether there may be extrinsic or intrinsic benefits in leaving authoritative constitutional review in the hands of judges. From an extrinsic standpoint, judicial review may not necessarily be more anti-majoritarian than the work product of a legislature beholden to lobbyists and special interests or an executive branch effectively dependent on a handful of business and social elites.[4] From an intrinsic perspective, on the other hand, a distinction must be drawn between judicial politics, framed by judges committing to choices among competing judicial philosophies, and ordinary politics, as customarily pursued through the electoral process and through the typical functioning of the legislative and the executive/administrative branches of government. Moreover, judicial politics seems closely linked to the constitutionalization of politics which, in turn, seems bound to culminate in the politicization of the constitution. To `get a more systematic handle on the potential limitation of the judicial constitutionalization of politics in contemporary political democracies, the first section below briefly explores the contrast between judicial and ordinary politics and the connection between the constitutionalization of politics and the politicization of the constitution. The second section focuses on the constitutionalization of politics as it emerges in particular cases drawn respectively from Canada, South Africa and Israel. The Canadian case regarding secession deals squarely with a subject that is ultimately quintessentially political – in an ordinary politics sense; the South African case concerning the constitutionality of the death penalty, on the other hand, is squarely about what typically ranks as a constitutional right – in the sense that it seems right to treat the question of whether to prohibit or allow the death penalty as a basic constitutional one; and, the

---

[3] Ran Hirschl, *The Judicialization of Mega-Politics and the Rise of Political Courts*, 11 ANN. REV. POLIT. SCI. 93, 108 (2008).

[4] *Compare* Nicholas Confessore, Sarah Cohen and Karen Yourish, *Just 158 families have provided nearly half of the early money for efforts to capture the White House*, NY TIMES, October 15, 2015
(reporting that a very small number of mainly white US families are having a decisive influence on the selection of candidates (both Democrat and Republican) for US presidential election) *with* Barry Friedman, *The Will of the People: How Public Opinion Has Influenced the Supreme Court and Shaped the Meaning of the Constitution* (2009) (indicating that US Supreme Court is often more attuned to public opinion within the country than the other two branches of the US federal government).

Israeli case questioning whether a "Basic Law" adopted by the Israeli parliament, the Knesset, should be treated as a constitutional norm rather than a statutory one in the context of that country's lack of a written constitution, appears above all to involve a constitution-making matter. Finally, the third section examines how the theoretical insights and case studies may be harmonized to provide a critical assessment of the potential and limitations of the constitutionalization of politics to the extent that the latter is entrusted to judges engaging in constitutional adjudication.

LAW AS A LANGUAGE GAME, JUDICIAL VERSUS ORDINARY
POLITICS AND THE DIALECTIC BETWEEN THE
CONSTITUTIONALIZATION OF POLITICS AND THE
POLITICIZATION OF THE CONSTITUTION

Law, in general, and constitutional law, in particular, are not ultimately reducible to any other practice, such as politics or philosophy.[5] Moreover, law carves out a domain for itself, not necessarily because of the material it incorporates, but because of the way it deals with such material. Thus, for example, law and philosophy may deal with some of same concepts, such as justice and equality, but discussion of these in a philosophy seminar is bound to differ from the same in a court of law. The legal advocate and the judge cannot merely engage in a philosophical debate. Indeed, to the extent that legal practitioners can make pertinent reference to the latter, they must do so in light of existing legal doctrine, the relevant constitutional provisions and authoritative judicial precedent (at least in common law jurisdictions). In other words, those operating within the practice of law must "translate" material they wish to draw from other practices into the language of law.[6] Thus, whereas a philosophical debate on the relationship between affirmative action and equality need not be constrained by national boundaries, the Canadian constitutional equality provision specifically recognizes the legitimacy of affirmative action while its US counterpart is silent on the matter.[7] In short, judges and legal practitioners must operate within the internal

---

[5] The discussion that follows is mainly drawn from Michel Rosenfeld, *Just Interpretations: Law between Ethics and Politics*, 42–45 (1998).

[6] For an argument that philosophical and constitutional equality cannot be mutually reducible although some concepts of philosophical equality may be translated for incorporation into the language of constitutional equality and constitutional equality doctrine may be critically assessed from the standpoint of philosophical conceptions of equality, *see* Michel Rosenfeld, *Affirmative Action and Justice: A Philosophical and Constitutional Inquiry*, 136–144 (1991).

[7] *Compare* Section 15(2) of the 1982 Canadian Charter of Rights *to* the Equal Protection Clause of the Fourteenth Amendment to the US Constitution.

perspective circumscribed by (constitutional) law as a practice with its own "language game", to borrow Wittgenstein's terminology.[8]

One need not embrace conceptions of law which cast law in key respects as completely "untranslatable" – such as Luhmann's autopoietic one which regards law as a self-contained system that is normatively closed,[9] or Kelsen's "pure theory of law"[10] – to maintain that the barrier between law and other practices is thick enough to generate significant obstacles to, and gaps in, translation. A particular telling example, in this connection, is the transformation undergone by Richard Posner, the leading US proponent of "law and economics", based on his experience after he left the academy for a US federal appellate judgeship.[11] Based on the assumption that human beings behave rationally,[12] as Posner envisages it, economics – in its two dimensions as a positive science that purports to explain the behaviour of instrumentally rational self-interested human actors and as a prescriptive science oriented toward wealth maximization – furnishes objective (in the sense of scientifically testable) criteria for the evaluation and interpretation of laws. Although Posner never abandons this ideal,[13] it is particularly telling that his practice as a judge leads him to conclude that some legal problems, such as whether constitutional privacy rights should be interpreted to cover a woman's right to an abortion, cannot be conceived cogently in terms of wealth maximization.[14] Moreover, even if in the most optimistic law and economic vein, one assumed that all intersubjective dealings were reducible to uninhibited fully competitive free market transactions, it would still seem impossible for law as a practice to completely give way to positive and normative economics.[15]

---

[8] See Ludwig Wittgenstein, *Philosophical Investigations* # 2, 7 (G.E.M. Anscombe, transl., 1968).

[9] See Niklas Luhmann, *Essays on Self-Reference* 3 (1990) and "Closure and Openness: On Reality in the World of Law" in Guenther Teubner, ed., *Autopoietic Law: A New Approach to Law and Society*, 335–348 (1987).

[10] In Kelsen's words, "The Pure Theory of Law undertakes to delimit the cognition of law against [psychology, sociology, ethics and political theory], not because it ignores or denies the connection, but because it wishes to avoid the ... mixture of methodologically different disciplines ... which obscures the essence of the science of law and obliterates the limits imposed upon it by the nature of its subject matter." Hans Kelsen, *The Pure Theory of Law* 1 (2d ed., M. Knight, trans. 1967).

[11] After becoming a practicing judge Posner has acknowledged the limits of law and economics and subsumed it under his pragmatism in contrast to his earlier position which boiled down to the prescription that law, in general, and judicial interpretation of law, in particular, ought to aim at wealth maximization. *Compare* his *Economic Analysis of Law* (1977) to his *Problems of Jurisprudence* (1990) and *Overcoming Law* (1995).

[12] See Richard Posner, *Problems of Jurisprudence*, at 367.   [13] See id., at 382.

[14] See Richard Posner, *Overcoming Law*, at 22.

[15] This last point is drawn from my discussion of Posner's economic analysis of law and pragmatism in my *Just Interpretations*, supra note 6, at 166.

Indeed, even the freest of all market societies could not function without a legal regime – albeit a limited one confined to the protection of property and contract rights. And that would mean, for example, that even a wealth maximizing theft by an entrepreneurial thief from an economically inactive wealthy victim, would have to be subjected to the strictures of property law. Accordingly, in such an instance legal practice would militate against wealth maximization, or at least proceed independently from it.[16]

If law is at least somewhat impermeable even in the context of a reductionist, such as Posner, who ideally, whenever possible, would prefer to dissolve it into economics, then, a fortiori, for anyone who believes that law ought not to be merely reducible to another practice, law must circumscribe some internal space for itself within which it can deploy its own language game. It also follows from this that law as a practice within its own space cannot be fully translatable into another practice or language game.

Pursuit of the polity's common good, policy making, managing clashes of interests within the polity, and making law or a constitution involve ordinary politics, whether it be highly principled and inclusive or purely strategic and bent on vindicating some narrow interests to the exclusion of others. Once a law or a constitution is enacted, however, its interpretation and application triggers a different kind of politics – one that clearly emerges as distinct in the context of judicial interpretation and can thus be designated as judicial politics. For example, it is a matter of ordinary politics whether a legislature ought to enact a law making industry liable for damages it causes due to the environmental pollution it generates. After such law is enacted though, and judges are charged to interpret it, the ordinary politics delimited by its proponents and opponents prior to enactment has become to a significant degree frozen, giving way to handling by judges within the practice and language game of law. One could envisage the interpretive role as purely technical and hence as involving no politics whatsoever, but that option seems out of place in the context of constitutional interpretation in which divisions among originalists, textualists, intentionalists and "living tree" proponents remain sharp and enduring. Thus, judges who differ along the forgoing divisions are engaged in politics regarding the judicial role and judicial interpretation of laws and the constitution or, in other words, in judicial politics. To be sure,

---

[16] Drawing on an analogy to the contrast between act-utilitarianism and rule-utilitarianism, one could argue that in the long run a legal prohibition of theft is likely to enhance rather than constrain wealth maximization. Be that as it may, a judge in a theft case would have to follow the law consistently regardless of whether it proved wealth maximizing or not, for otherwise she would run afoul requirements of consistency, integrity, and predictability imposed by law as a practice.

judicial politics can have ordinary politics consequences just as recognition of
a constitutional right to abortion can have economic implications. But also
just as abortion rights are impervious to economic rationalization or reduction, so too judicial politics emerge as not reducible to ordinary politics.[17]

It is true that judges, in general, and constitutional judges, in particular, can
foray into ordinary politics as will be briefly discussed below. Nevertheless,
most judicial decisions on politically divisive issues can clearly remain within
the boundaries of judicial politics. That is the case with numerous decisions
on abortion, assisted suicide, or same-sex marriage which genuinely remain
within the bounds of judicial politics even though they have ordinary politics
consequences much like a judicial decision interpreting an anti-monopoly
law is bound to have economic consequences.

That said, it seems appropriate in some contexts to reach beyond the
language game of law so long as relevant materials found in other language
game are properly adapted and reprocessed so as to "fit" within the language
game of law. To stick to the nexus between economics and law, in the case of
judicial interpretation of an anti-monopoly law, it would make obvious sense
to combine an economic and a legal analysis. Thus, if an economic inquiry
into the consequences of actual judicial interpretations of a given anti-
monopoly law has led to greater economic concentration contrary to the
purported intent of the legislator, that would be most helpful and would
facilitate a change in judicial interpretation – assuming that were feasible
with the constraints inherent within the language game of law – or a legislative
amendment or repeal of the law in question. In contrast, whereas a study of
the economic consequences of enforcement of a constitutional right to
abortion might well be a valuable addition to the economic literature, it
would be difficult to imagine it having any significant effect on constitutional
scholarship relating to fundamental rights.

The line between judicial philosophy and ordinary politics may often be
difficult to draw, but seems conceptually sound. A judge may be an originalist
or devoted to a restrictive interpretation of fundamental rights, or else one who
believes in the "living tree" approach to constitutional interpretation, thus
engaging with the morals and the mores of the present generation and taking
an adaptive and expansive approach to fundamental rights and yet adjudicate
without dwelling upon political consequences or impact of her decision.[18]

[17] *See* David M. Beatty, *The Ultimate Rule of Law*, ch. 1 (Oxford, Oxford University Press, 2004).
[18] *See, e.g.*, the Canadian Supreme Court decision in *Reference Re Same Sex Marriage* [2004] 3
    SCR 698, Para. 22: "Canada is a pluralistic society ... The 'frozen concepts' reasoning runs
    contrary to one of the most fundamental principles of Canadian constitutional interpretation:
    that our Constitution is a living tree."

For example, a judge may have a restrictive view of fundamental rights and of federal as opposed to state powers, but that would commit her to constitutionally upholding politically conservative policies, such as bans on abortion as well as politically progressive ones, such as the legalization of assisted suicide.

Although all legal determinations resulting from judicial review–and particularly those within the ambit of constitutional law where broad open ended standards predominate as against narrowly tailored rules–have political consequences, judicial politics remains distinct from ordinary politics. Moreover, even if certain particular brands of judicial politics seem better aligned with particular positions and ideologies within the ambit of ordinary politics, as already noted, a constitutional judge who adheres to her own judicial politics with integrity will undoubtedly have to rule on some occasions against her ordinary politics convictions and predilections. In short, the constitutional judge cannot be completely isolated from ordinary politics both because she cannot shed all her ordinary politics vestiges as she enters the language game of law and because it is, for the most part, impossible for judicial decisions not to have consequences that impact the realm of ordinary politics. That said, however, so long as the constitutional judge remains consistently within the strictures of the language game of law, presumably she will be able to purge her constitutional interpretations from the hold of ordinary politics or to reprocess ordinary politics materials so as to make them amenable to absorption within the bounds of judicial politics.

The constitutionalization of politics goes hand in hand, by and large, with transferring the resolution of political issues from the realm of ordinary politics to that of judicial politics. Take, for instance, the question of free public education which is quintessentially a political issue. If this issue becomes constitutionalized by being directly addressed in the constitution, then its resolution becomes a matter of judicial politics; and, otherwise, if it were a matter of ordinary politics, then it would be left to the majoritarian processes used to settle infra-constitutional political issues. Furthermore, in determining which matters should be left to the constitution and judicial politics, and which to ordinary politics, two important questions arise. First, is the matter in question better settled in a majoritarian or an anti-majoritarian institutional setting? And, second, are certain matters inherently better handled through the judicial politics process rather than through its ordinary politics counterpart?

Leaving aside that, as mentioned above, in some cases the judiciary may be more responsive to public opinion than the political branches of government, there are certain matters that seem inherently better suited for anti-majoritarian as opposed to majoritarian handling. Chief among the matters in question are minority rights as well as other fundamental rights, such as free speech, privacy or freedom of religion. Indeed, in a democracy, it is most likely that unpopular speech, non-mainstream aspects of privacy and religions that drift far apart from their widely accepted mainstream counterparts will require protection from majoritarian hostility or oppression. On the other hand, there are several matters that seem inherently well suited for ordinary politics and ill-suited for judge led constitutionalization. Obviously among these, are economic and social policy as well as diplomatic or military strategy. Finally, though the correlation need not be strict, fundamental rights best protected through anti-majoritarian means often seem optimally subjected to judicial rather than ordinary politics. Thus, free speech doctrine and jurisprudence seem best left in the hands of judges than in those of legislators or administrators.

The constitutionalization of politics, understood as involving a shift from ordinary to judicial politics, can have beneficial stabilizing effects so long as it is not too extensive. Thus, so long as there is a broad consensus, such as, for example, over the need for constitutional protection for unpopular political views, deference to constitutional judges may hold in spite of vigorous disagreements over judicial philosophies. On the other hand, in the context of extensive constitutionalization of politics, such as in the case of broad protection of social and economic rights or pervasive intervention into private transactions as exemplified by the doctrine of *Drittwirkung* under German constitutional law,[19] there is a great danger of (over) politicization of the constitution.[20] Indeed, if a large number of matters of social policy over which the polity is sharply divided are entrusted to constitutional judges, they will increasingly give the impression of usurping the realm of ordinary politics while seeking to obscure this overreach by articulating their decisions in the language of judicial politics.

THE CONSTITUTIONALIZATION OF POLITICS THROUGH CASE LAW: CANADIAN SECESSION, SOUTH AFRICAN DEATH PENALTY AND ISRAELI BASIC LAWS

As already noted, the three cases selected for comparison in terms of constitutionalization of politics are remarkable. This is not only because these cases are issued respectively from three prominent courts in diverse constitutional

[19] *See* Donald P. Kommers and Russell A. Miller, *The Constitutional Jurisprudence of the Federal Republic of Germany* (3d ed. 2012), 432.
[20] *See* Michel Rosenfeld, *The Rule of Law and the Legitimacy of Constitutional Democracy*, 74 S. CAL. L. REV. 1307, 1329 (2001).

systems, but also because they deal with what appear to be three very different subjects from the standpoint of the constitutionalization of politics. The Canadian case on secession is about a quintessentially political subject in the context of a constitution that has no explicit provision upon which the constitutional adjudicator can draw upon. The South African case, in contrast, is on a traditional constitutional issue, the death penalty, but it arises in an unusual setting as the makers of the post-Apartheid South African Constitution enlist the constitutional adjudicator to craft what amounts to a constitutional provision allowing or banning capital punishment. Finally, the Israeli case on the constitutional status of Basic Laws on "freedom of occupation" and on "human dignity and freedom" in the context of a country without a written constitution looms as an exercise of constitution-making, albeit one relating to subject-matters that are routinely cast as constitutional ones.

The Canadian Case: Reference Re Secession of Quebec[21]

After Quebec's refusal to accept the 1982 Canadian Constitution,[22] and the failure of the Meech Lake and Charlottetown constitutional accords designed fully to integrate Quebec within the new Canadian constitutional order,[23] Quebec held a referendum on October 30, 1995 on whether the Province should proclaim sovereignty from Canada and become an independent country. The Quebecois voters rejected secession by a 50.5 to 49.5 per cent vote and various political controversies ensued.[24] This led the Canadian federal government to refer the issue of the constitutionality of Quebec's secession to the Canadian Supreme Court for an advisory decision on the question: "Under the Constitution of Canada, Can the National Assembly, legislature or Government of Quebec effect the secession of Quebec from Canada unilaterally?"[25]

The Court recognized that whether or not Quebec secedes from Canada is ultimately a political matter, but emphasized that to be legitimate any political decision on the subject would have to be taken within "the legal framework" circumscribed by the country's constitution.[26] In other words, any decision on

---

[21] [1998] 2 SCR 217 (Supreme Court of Canada).
[22] *See Re: Objection to a Resolution to Amend the Constitution*, [1982] 2 S.C.R 793 (Supreme Court of Canada).
[23] *See* Andrew Cohen, *A Deal Undone: The Making and Breaking of the Meech Lake Accord* (1990); McRoberts & Monahan (eds.), *The Charlottetown Accord, the Referendum and the Future of Canada* (1993).
[24] *See* Mario Cardinal, *Breaking Point: Quebec, Canada, The 1995 Referendum* 405 (2005).
[25] *Reference Re Secession*, at Para. 2.   [26] *Id.*, at Para. 153.

secession must be left to ordinary politics, but the process leading to that decision must be framed by judicial politics based on interpretation of constitutional texts and jurisprudence that contain no explicit reference to the subject of secession.[27] Given these circumstances, the key question, from the standpoint of the present undertaking, is whether the Court's recourse to judicial politics is genuine, warranted and legitimate, or whether it amounts to an artifice allowing the Court to dissimulate its intervention into the arena of ordinary politics through invocation of the logic and vocabulary prevalent in the language game of (constitutional) law.

From a purely formal perspective, all ordinary politics within a constitutional democracy may well be dependent on a process framed by judicial politics. The latter, however, may often merely touch on procedural matters – e.g., whether the parliament lacked the requisite quorum to enact a contested piece of legislation – thus engaging the divide between judicial and ordinary politics in a rather trivial way. In contrast, the process at stake in the case under consideration emerged as heavily dependent on substantive constraints. As the Court insisted, to be legitimate any Quebec path to secession would have to conform to "four fundamental and organizing principles" of the Canadian Constitution: "federalism; democracy; constitutionalism and the rule of law; and respect for minorities."[28] Moreover, by weaving together a set of legal/ constitutional requirements stemming from the above mentioned four principles, the Court fashioned a hefty process-based judicial politics set of prerequisites to the ordinary politics resolution of any Quebec secession initiative. Couching these prerequisites in the language of judicial politics, however, does not in and of itself suffice to determine whether the Court's intervention should ultimately be deemed in substance to have been that of an actor in the realm of ordinary politics or to have circumscribed the latter within the strictures delimited by judicial politics. Indeed, even when judges do not deliberately conceal a conscious ordinary politics design by casting it in the language of judicial politics as they appear to have done in *Bush v. Gore* discussed below,[29] some kinds of adjudication seem better suited to maintaining a neat cleavage between judicial and ordinary politics than others. At one end of the spectrum is simple rule-like adjudication in a particular fact setting, such as a decision under the US Constitution that a proven thirty-three year old cannot serve as US President;[30] at the other end, a pure common law adjudication in an area completely bereft of any judicial precedent – e.g.,

---

[27] *Id.*, at Para. 32.   [28] *Id.*   [29] 531 US 98 (2000).
[30] *See* US CONST. art. 2, § 1 (No person shall be eligible to the office of President "who shall not have attained to the age of thirty five years").

whether an upstream river owner is liable to his downstream neighbour for damage resulting from material dropped into the river by the former – where the judicial decision figures at once as adjudication and lawmaking (retrospective for the parties before the judge and prospective for those who will come under the sway of the decision in question as binding precedent), thus conflating judicial and ordinary politics.

Where to place the Court's decision in the above sketched spectrum is not readily apparent for a variety of reasons. First, as noted, the Canadian Constitution is silent on secession. Second, although Canada has a current written constitution dating back to 1982, that constitution is by no means exclusive as is the current 1787 US Constitution which superseded that country's 1781 Articles of Confederation. And third, some of the four organizing principles of the Canadian Constitution factored into the process-based requirements imposed by the Court, namely federalism and democracy, at least in terms of their functioning as opposed to their particular design, seem for the most part to inhere within the realm of ordinary politics rather than in that of judicial politics.

Secession is ultimately a matter of ordinary politics, but customarily it also has a constitutional and international law dimension.[31] Moreover, the Canadian Constitution's silence on the matter is hardly dispositive given the nature of Canadian constitutionalism. As the Court emphasized in the decision under consideration, the 1982 constitutional text is not "exhaustive" as the Canadian Constitution also embraces "unwritten as well as written rules," constitutional conventions, the workings of parliament and judicial precedents. All of this is meant to contribute to the construction of "an exhaustive legal framework for [the country's] system of government."[32] The Canadian Constitution is the product of an evolution that has lasted around a century and a half,[33] and that links the Constitution Act of 1867 to that of 1982.[34] Finally, Canadian constitutionalism, unlike that of the US which came on the heels of a war of independence, readily incorporates the many of the mainstays of its UK counterpart going all the way back to the 1215 Magna Carta.[35]

Adding up all the features listed above, Canadian constitutionalism falls somewhere in between British immanent constitutionalism that emerges gradually by means of a process of accretion and US constitutionalism which is based on a written constitution that transcends the legal order in which it is

---

[31] *See* Susanna Mancini, "Secession and Self-Determination" in *The Oxford Handbook of Comparative Constitutional Law* 481 (Michel Rosenfeld & Andras Sajo, eds., 2012).
[32] *Reference Re Secession*, at Para. 32.   [33] *Id.*, at Para. 49.   [34] *Id.*, at Para. 52.
[35] *Id.*, at Para. 63.

deployed, but that has turned into an evolving living constitution propelled by over two centuries of judicial elaboration.[36] Also, all three constitutional traditions involved are steeped in a system of common law adjudication which is broad based, contextual, incremental and comprehensive in scope as opposed to the much more narrowly focused, largely deductive civil law model of adjudication. Accordingly, if the somewhat less expansive constitutionalism prevalent in the US could cogently incorporate within its judicial politics unenumerated constitutional rights, such as that to privacy enshrined in *Griswold v. Connecticut*[37] and its progeny, its more expansive Canadian counterpart could certainly plausibly (in part) constitutionalize secession.

Secession like federalism and democracy may be constitutionalized and yet all three may only leave room for a thin and shallow layer of judicial politics. For example, in all three cases, the relevant constitutional prescriptions and proscriptions may only require satisfaction of straightforward formal procedural steps that may for the most part fairly mechanically judicially supervised. The smaller the legitimate domain of judicial politics is, the more likely it will be that clear and uncontroversial boundaries could be drawn between judicial and ordinary politics. Conversely, the greater the domain of judicial politics, the more likely it would become that significant overlaps and boundary disputes between judicial and ordinary politics would abound.

The Canadian constitutionalization of secession, federalism and democracy is extensive and in significant part substantive. Moreover, when this constitutionalization is added to that of constitutionalism and the rule of law as well as that of the protection of minorities, it becomes manifest that the judicial politics that inform the Court's decision in the case at hand are thick and far reaching. To be able to determine whether the extensive judicial politics in question are genuine and legitimate, it is first necessary to briefly examine the Court's account of the constitutional prerequisites to a political settling of any eventual project of secession by a Canadian province.

As the Court emphasizes, Canadian federalism is not only meant to achieve an apportionment of sovereignty, but also to facilitate "the pursuit of collective goals by cultural and linguistic minorities which form the majority within a particular province."[38] For its part, the constitutional conception of democracy far exceeds majority rule alone[39] and encompasses substantive commitments to human dignity, social justice and respect for cultural identity.[40]

---

[36] See Michel Rosenfeld, *The Identity of the Constitutional Subject: Selfhood, Citizenship, Culture and Community* (2010), 164–168.
[37] 381 US 479 (1965).   [38] *Reference Re Secession*, at Para. 59.   [39] *Id.*, at Para. 67.
[40] *Id.*, at Para. 64.

In addition, democracy requires constitutional promotion of a deliberative process that fosters continuous discussion, including the right to initiate and promote constitutional change and the obligation to address the concerns of dissenters and of those who seek to secede from the Canadian Confederation.[41] Constitutionalism requires conformity with the Constitution, including the safeguarding of fundamental human rights[42] and the rule of law mandates compliance with all law.[43]

Based on its assessment of the requirements imposed by the four constitutional principles at play in the context of secession, the Court concluded that secession would signify a major change in the Canadian constitutional order and that it would therefore have to be preceded by a constitutional amendment.[44] Consistent with this, it would be unconstitutional for Quebec to decide unilaterally to secede from Canada.[45] To launch the quest for the constitutional amendment that must precede secession, Quebec could initiate the process based on the results of a referendum of those within the Province, provided that a clear proposal for independence were approved by a clear majority of the voters.[46] Thereafter, as the initiative regarding amendments to the Canadian Constitution is the responsibility of the elected representatives of the federal government and of those of all provinces,[47] all the governments involved would be obligated to enter into good faith negotiations.

The negotiations themselves would undoubtedly be political and, once set in process, it would be for the political actors, not the courts, to decide questions regarding conformity with the Constitution.[48] Also, whether good faith negotiations consistent with all constitutional constraints would lead to a consensus on secession would be a purely contingent matter. In short, a constitutional path to secession would require a confluence of judicial and ordinary politics. The boundaries between the two would seem fairly clear and the deployment of judicial politics relative to the four constitutional principles invoked by the Court amenable to being genuine and legitimate. That leaves open whether such deployment is ultimately desirable, a question that will be addressed in the next section.

The South African Death Penalty Case[49]

This case concerned two men sentenced to death prior to the end of the Apartheid regime in South Africa and awaiting execution after the end of

---

[41] *Id.*, at Paras. 68 and 69.   [42] *Id.*, at Para. 74.   [43] *Id.*, at Para. 73.   [44] *Id.*, at Para. 84.
[45] *Id.*, at Para. 87.   [46] *Id.*, at Para. 153.   [47] *Id.*, at Para. 88.   [48] *Id.*
[49] *S. v. Makwanyane*, 1995 (3) SALR 391 (Constitutional Court of South Africa).

Apartheid and while South Africa was operating under an interim constitution pending approval of its permanent post-Apartheid constitution by the country's Constitutional Court.[50] The interim constitution in question was silent about the death penalty and as emphasized by the Constitutional Court, it would "have been better if the framers of the Constitution had stated specifically, either that the death sentence is not a competent penalty, or that it is permissible in [certain] circumstances."[51] Instead of that, however, the framers left it up to the Constitutional Court to determine the constitutionality of the death penalty.[52] The reason for this delegation of constitution-making to the Constitutional Court stemmed from the South African post-Apartheid Constitution being a pacted one involving members of the outgoing Apartheid regime and liberation movements, principally Nelson Mandela's African National Congress (ANC).[53] An impasse was reached on the death penalty, with members of the outgoing regime wishing to preserve it for a limited number of cases but others involved in the constitutional negotiations opposed it outright. To avoid paralysis, a "Solomon solution" was adopted and the matter referred to the Constitutional Court for resolution.[54]

The lack of a specific constitutional provision prohibiting or authorizing imposition of the death penalty is not an impediment to a principled and legitimate consideration of the issue within the ambit of judicial politics. As the Court made clear, what it had to decide above all was whether "the death penalty is cruel, inhuman, or degrading,"[55] a question that is frequently and with scant objection entrusted to constitutional adjudication.[56] In contrast, what seems most remarkable about the *Makwanyane* case is that the Constitutional Court was explicitly cast as a constitution-maker; that the Court's constitutional interpretation drew on international legal instruments, such as the UN International Covenant on Civil and Political Rights and the European Convention on Human Rights, and foreign constitutional case law; as well as that the Court drew on the principle of proportionality that has emerged worldwide as the common currency embraced by a vast majority of constitutional adjudicators.[57]

---

[50] See *Certification of the Constitution of the Republic of South Africa*, 1996 (4) SALR 7440 (Constitutional Court of South Africa).
[51] *Makwanyane*, at Para. 5   [52] *Id.*   [53] *Certification*, at Para. 11.
[54] *Makwanyane*, at Para. 25.   [55] *Id.*, at Para. 78.
[56] See, e.g., *Gregg v. Georgia*, 428 US 153 (1976) (US Supreme Court majority and dissenting justices disagreeing over whether the death penalty amounts to "cruel and unusual" punishment).
[57] See David Beatty, *The Ultimate Rule of Law* (2004), 115–117.

The above circumstances raise two principal questions from the standpoint of drawing the legitimate bounds of judicial politics in the context of constitutional adjudication. First, should constitution-making be out of bounds for an adjudicatory body even in the case of the death penalty which is so well suited for handling within the realm of judicial politics – particularly in view of the fact that, as the Court acknowledged, a majority of the South African people was in favour of the death penalty for certain gruesome murders?[58] And second, whereas reference to international law, foreign case law and appropriation of a much utilized judicial tool throughout a very large number of jurisdictions falls well within the core of judicial politics, should these be avoided or limited in the context of constitutional adjudication?

There is a short answer to these two questions if one takes into account South Africa's unique constitutional predicament at the time of the *Makwanyane* decision. The judicial constitution-making at stake was directly delegated by the framers of South Africa's new constitution; and the references to international law were mandated by the Constitution which also provided that references to foreign case law were permissible.[59] From a broader perspective consistent with the aims of the present undertaking, however, the two questions under consideration raise larger genuine issues of legitimacy and desirability regarding the proper limits of judicial politics within the ambit of constitutional adjudication.

Leaving aside the Court's constitution-making mandate, the legitimacy of the judicial determination of the constitutionality of the death penalty is bolstered in the South African case by a combination of two crucial factors. First, like in the case of Canada, the South African Constitution is meant to be comprehensive[60] and its interpretation "generous" and "purposive" so as to give "expression to [its] underlying values."[61] And second, the South African Constitution specifically guarantees the rights to dignity,[62] life[63] and against cruel, degrading and inhuman treatment.[64] Consistent with this, it falls squarely within the canons of judicial politics, in general, and of constitutional interpretation, in particular, for judges to decide whether the three above mentioned rights proscribe or permit imposition of the death penalty. Accordingly, absent the mandate, the Court's decision on the death penalty would predominantly emerge as an ordinary and wholly legitimate instance of constitutional interpretation, with an incidental impact on constitution-making. The mandate imposed on the Court scarcely affects legitimacy, but as will be discussed below, it may have an impact on desirability.

---

[58] *Makwanyane*, at Para. 87.   [59] *Id.*, at Para. 34.   [60] *Id.*, at Paras. 9 and 10.
[61] *Id.*, at Para. 9.   [62] *Id.*, at Para. 58.   [63] *Id.*, at Para. 95.   [64] *Id.*, at Para. 78.

The Court's reference to international law and to foreign constitutional case law is well within the bounds of judicial politics, but raises another concern from the standpoint of legitimacy and desirability. Generally, within the language game of law, and more particularly within that of constitutional law, it is very important to distinguish between authoritative and relevant legal material on the one hand and inapposite and irrelevant material, on the other. Obviously, it is imperative to rely on the former and not on the latter, and arguably international and foreign materials should not be drawn upon unless somehow incorporated – as is the case in South Africa – within the domestic constitutional framework. To some extent, the relevance of international and foreign matters is a matter of judicial philosophy and hence legitimately within the scope of judicial politics.[65] At least in some cases, however, judicial reference to foreign material may be intended to dress up intervention into ordinary politics in the garb of judicial politics. One such example is provided by Justice Kennedy's reference to the fact that only the US and Somalia had not ratified an international convention prohibiting capital punishment for crimes committed by juveniles in *Roper v. Simmons*.[66] Arguably, from a purely legal/constitutional US standpoint, Justice Kennedy's linking his country to Somalia was irrelevant. But, at the same time, linking the two countries the way he does casts the US in an embarrassing political light and places his judicial arguments in favour of holding the juvenile death penalty unconstitutional in a broader moral and political context.

The South African Constitutional Court in *Makwanyane* took a restrained position on reference to foreign materials in deciding the constitutionality of the death penalty, thus avoiding crossing into ordinary politics as Justice Kennedy had in *Roper*. The Court stressed that reference to foreign "bill of rights" jurisprudence was useful particularly as there was no domestic equivalent in the early stages of post-Apartheid South Africa.[67] Nevertheless, the Court also expressed caution warning that foreign authorities may not afford an adequate guide to the interpretation of domestic constitutional law and that therefore considering foreign sources should not imply that the Court would follow them.[68] Consistent with this, the Court critically examined the constitutional jurisprudence legitimating the death penalty in India and the US, and

[65] *Compare* Richard Posner, *Forward: A Political Court*, 119 HARV. L. REV. 32, 84–89 (2005) (advising against reliance on foreign authorities based on high risk of unwarranted selectivity and culturally biased misreading) *to* Jeremy Waldron, *Foreign Law and the Modern Ius Gentium*, 119 Harv. L. Rev. 129, 143–146 (2005) (arguing that there is a body of law representing a worldwide consensus that ought to be relied upon much like an analogous consensus on public health would).

[66] 543 US 551 (2005).   [67] *Makwanyane*, at Para. 37.   [68] *Id.*

based on differences between its constitution and those of the latter two countries and on contrasts in the respective predicaments in the three polities involved, it concluded that the death penalty should be adjudged unconstitutional in South Africa. In view of this, the Court stayed well within the bounds of judicial politics raising no credible question of legitimacy.

The Israeli Basic Laws Case[69]

On its face, the Israeli Supreme Court decision in the *Migdal* case is by far the one, among the three examined, that strays the farthest from conventional conceptions of the proper bounds of judicial politics. Unlike Canada or South Africa, Israel does not have a written constitution. The country's parliament, the Knesset, was empowered to enact a constitution since the country's declaration of independence in 1948,[70] but has thus far failed to do so. The Knesset, however, has enacted Basic Laws – two of which, respectively on "Freedom of Occupation" and on "Human Dignity and Freedom" were at issue in *Migdal* – which require an absolute majority vote for passage as opposed to the simple majority vote required, provided there is a quorum, for passage of ordinary laws. In *Migdal*, the Court decided that Basic Laws enjoy a "constitutional superlegislative status"[71] and that therefore a subsequent ordinary law cannot supersede a prior Basic Law.[72] Furthermore, the Court also decided, albeit in the absence of any pronouncement or acknowledgement by the Knesset, that constitutional determination of the status of Basic Laws and resolution of conflicts between basic and ordinary laws were properly within the province of the courts.[73] In short, the Court in *Migdal* appropriates for itself two major tasks reserved to the constituent power: the constitutionalization of rights and the apportionment of powers among distinct branches of government. Both of these tasks are well within the domain of ordinary politics even if they pertain to constitutional as distinguished from infra-constitutional ordinary politics.

Upon further reflection, there is another way to understand what the Court sought to accomplish in *Migdal*, by placing the case in the unique context in which it arose. A full examination of Chief Justice Barak's opinion suggests that Israel views itself as a constitutional democracy that has yet to settle on a full-fledged written constitution. In the meantime, the Knesset has acted in a piecemeal fashion to secure some of the most basic fundamental rights customarily protected by democratic constitutions, such as those in the

---

[69] *United Mizrahi Bank Ltd. V. Migdal Village*, CA 6821/93, 49 (4) P.D. 221 (1995) (Supreme Court of Israel).

[70] *Id.*, at Para. 35.   [71] *Id.*, at Para. 36.   [72] *Id.*, at Para. 35.   [73] *Id.*, at Para. 77.

two Basic Laws at stake in *Migdal*. Moreover, as it is the practice in the overwhelming majority of contemporary constitutional democracies, courts handle conflicts between parliamentary laws and constitutionally protected fundamental rights, thus making it logical for Israeli courts to assume this role in the context of challenges to Basic Laws. In other words, the subject matter at play in *Migdal* fits logically within the ambit of judicial politics, and all the Court aimed to accomplish was to fill certain major judicial politics lacunae stemming from the lingering gap between Israel's putative constitutional aims and the constitutional means actually at its disposal. In light of this alternative perspective, *Migdal* embodies a dynamic tension between the ordinary politics linked to constituent powers and the judicial politics associated with constitutional protection through adjudication. This dynamic tension is also present in the Canadian case to the extent that constitutional preconditions intertwine with political secession negotiations; and in the South African case as a consequence of the Constitutional Court being enlisted as a constitution-maker respecting the death penalty. The main difference between the Israeli case and its two counterparts is that the dynamic tension is much more central, radical and intense in the former than in the latter.

Focusing on *Migdal* from the perspective of judicial politics, the Court invoked two principal sources for purposes of legitimating the constitutionalization of Basic Laws and entrusting constitutional review to itself. The first of these sources is a broad based consensus relating to constitutional essentials among post World War Two democracies, both with respect to the constitutional protection of certain basic fundamental rights and to reliance on constitutional adjudication to interpret such rights and to dispose of conflicts between parliamentary laws and constitutional rights.[74] The second source, in turn, which the Court invoked to justify declaring a law supported by the country's majority to be unconstitutional, was "the values of society as they are understood by the culture and tradition of the people as they move forward through history."[75] Chief Justice Barak specified, moreover, that the judge must not approach the values at stake subjectively, but instead objectively so as to reflect these as they inhere within the State of Israel "as a Jewish and democratic state."[76]

The first of the above mentioned two sources is grounded on the contemporary phenomenon described as the "internationalization of constitutional law."[77] Broadly speaking, there is a convergence among constitutional

---

[74] *Id.*, at Para. 58.   [75] *Id.*, at Para. 81.   [76] *Id.*
[77] *See* Wen-Chen Chang and Jiunn-Rong Yeh, "Internationalization of Constitutional Law" in *The Oxford Handbook of Comparative Constitutional Law* (Michel Rosenfeld & Andras Sajo, eds., 2012), 1165.

democracies that consists, in relevant part, in the protection of a bundle of core constitutional rights and in entrusting judges with specifying the proper bounds of these rights and adjudicating disputes regarding the latter. Consistent with this and with the near worldwide adoption of the standard of proportionality referred to above, judicial politics has arguably gone global to a significant degree.[78] Because of this, filling domestic gaps with widespread foreign imports may well pertain much more to judicial rather than to ordinary politics. Moreover, if the international convergence in question is deemed legitimate and sustainable, then there is only one seemingly irreducible instance of ordinary politics in the context of the Israeli incorporation of internationally predominant constitutional precepts. That instance consists in choosing the course of a constitutional democracy as contrasted to that of a democracy that has not yet embraced a particular concrete constitutional path.

In sharp contrast to the first source of legitimation of the constitutional status of Israel's Basic Laws, the second source referred to by the Court appears to reverse the ratio between ordinary and judicial politics. Chief Justice Barak alludes to the need for the constitutional judge to engage objectively with the societal values underlying the Basic Laws for purposes of achieving a proper judicial interpretation of the latter. If there were a national consensus on the values at stake, then the judge's task would be eminently manageable and the values relied upon could presumably be seamlessly woven into the requisite ongoing judicial politics process. If, however, the polity were profoundly split over the values that the constitutional judge is supposed to rely on objectively in order to legitimate the constitutionalization of basic rights and setting the Court as the constitutional adjudicator, then ordinary politics would be bound to vastly predominate over judicial politics. As many have observed, Israel is sharply divided on fundamental values and those divisions may have had more than their fair share of the responsibility for Israel's failure to date to have adopted a full-fledged constitution – e.g., divisions among orthodox and secular Jews have led to an impasse on the proper constitutional handling of the relationship between the state and religion.[79] To the extent that a profound clash of values and a heretofore unbridgeable cultural gap has thus far prevented Israel from achieving a constitutional consensus, judicial invocation of common values and a shared culture may well be perceived as a judicial usurpation of ordinary politics or as an ordinary politics fiat disguised

[78] *See generally*, Anne-Marie Slaughter, *A New World Order* (2004).
[79] *See* Gila Stopler, "National Identity, Religion-State Relations: Israel in Comparative Perspective" in *Israeli Constitutional law in the Making* 503, 510 (Gideon Sapir, Daphne Barak-Erez and Aharon Barak, eds. 2013) ("While some consider that the definition of Israel as a Jewish state constitutes an establishment of the Jewish religion in the state ... others argue that the term 'Jewish state'... merely designat[es] ... Israel as the home of the Jewish people ... ").

as a legitimate instance of judicial politics, albeit one that derives from one among several plausible but contestable judicial philosophies. Unsurprisingly, the *Migdal* decision has proved politically controversial and has given rise to a number of initiatives bent on depriving the Court of the power to engage in constitutional adjudication.[80]

All three cases examined above involve a mix between judicial and ordinary politics and raise questions regarding the legitimate and desirable bounds of judicial politics. Also, all three cases concern issues that are, by their very nature, politically highly controversial and potentially among the most divisive within the polity. None of the three cases can be uncontroversially fully encompassed within the confines of judicial politics, yet all three of them fit at least to some significant extent within the domain of constitutional adjudication. The analysis above has revealed certain similarities and contrasts among the three cases and these raise several questions about the proper and desirable place for judicial politics in the pursuit of an optimal constitutionalization of politics.

JUDICIAL POLITICS AND THE LEGITIMATE BOUNDS OF THE CONSTITUTIONALIZATION OF POLITICS

There is a popular general understanding of the constitution and of narrowly circumscribed judicial interpretation of the latter as not involving politics, and in fact as standing apart from all politics. In this understanding, constitution-making is political and so is amending the constitution, but the constitution itself and its proper narrow judicial interpretation are not. Accordingly, freedom of speech and freedom of religion would not be political and economic and social and economic policy would be. Similarly, a constitutional judge who interpreted free speech as equally protecting critiques of government coming from all ideological positions within the political spectrum would properly be viewed as remaining above politics. Within this basically essentialist perspective, which is squarely at odds with the one adopted in this chapter, the constitutionalization of politics would be an oxymoron or a pathology.

[80] *See* Tova Tzimuki, *[Minister of Justice] Friedman Seeks to Limit High Court's Authority*, Israel News, March 9, 2008, *Available at* www.ynetnews.com/articles/0,7340,L-3591427,00.html (last visited June 8, 2015) and Mark Hetfield, *Will Netanyahu Ever See Asylum Seekers as Human Beings with Human Rights?*, Haaretz Opinion, October 5, 2014 (opposing Prime Minister Netanyahu's proposal to eliminate the Supreme Court's power to invalidate legislation that tramples on fundamental rights after Court decision on asylum seekers) available at www.haaretz.com/opinion/.premium-1.619389 (last visited June 8, 2015).

The invocation of the above understanding seems useful, however, as a marker in the evaluation of the proper bounds of the constitutionalization of politics, both in terms of legitimacy and of desirability from the standpoint of the divide between judicial and ordinary politics. The divide in question presupposes that the constitution and constitutionalization are political all the way up and all the way down. Consistent with this, what distinguishes the constitution and constitutionalization from all else that belongs to the realm of (democratic) politics boils down to the following: First, that which is structurally and functionally constitutive or that which amounts to secondary rules as opposed to primary rules, to borrow H.L.A. Hart's distinction;[81] second, what is entrusted to anti-majoritarian as opposed to majoritarian politics within the ambit of a democratic polity; and third, what is amenable to judicial politics as distinguished to ordinary politics as a matter of substance as opposed to as a matter of pure form.[82]

Consistent with the examination of the three cases discussed above, the proper allocation of responsibilities between judicial and ordinary politics as well as an adequate setting the limits of the constitutionalization of politics with an eye to avoiding undue of politicization of the constitution depend on both content-based or structural factors and on contextual ones. Thus, even if one disagrees with the Canadian Supreme Court's fairly extensive constitutionalization of secession in the *Reference Re Secession of Quebec* case discussed earlier in this chapter, one would have to agree, consistent with the perspective adopted in the present chapter, that pressing concerns of minorities whose fundamental rights might be compromised by secession would be better entrusted to judicial rather than to ordinary politics. Indeed, the concerns of aboriginal groups living in Quebec would clearly seem better handled, because of their very minority status, by Canadian judges than by majorities in the Province of Quebec or, in case secession were successful, in an independent Quebec. On the other hand, *Migdal*'s judicial embrace of constitutional essentials and entrusting of fundamental rights protection to judicial politics may have been amply justified from the standpoint of principle and yet ill advised for contextual reasons, namely Israel's deep divide on the proper relationship between religion and the state, which has played a key role in that country's inability to give itself a full-fledged constitution.

---

[81] *See* H.L.A. Hart, *The Concept of Law* 71 (1961).

[82] Justice Kennedy coupling of the US and Somalia in the *Roper* case mentioned above as well as the US Supreme Court's decision in *Bush v. Gore*, also mentioned above and further discussed below, provide examples of judicial pronouncements within the formal bounds of the language game of law, but not within the latter's substantive confines.

To better grasp how content-based and contextual factors ought to be harmonized to generate an optimal division of labour between judicial and ordinary politics, it seems useful to start by considering two separate scenarios, each of which stands at the opposite end of spectrum extending from the most restrictive to the most expansive acceptance of judicial politics as presumptively legitimate. At the minimalist end of the spectrum is the basically essentialist conception that enjoys broad popular support and that has been briefly mentioned above. As translated into the language of the perspective advanced here, a constitution that appears to rise above politics amounts to one that commands a consensus within the realm of ordinary politics. Such a consensus, moreover, is likely to be based in part on ideological grounds and in part on contextual adherence to particular ordinary politics convictions. For example, in a classical liberal ideological setting, a constitution with formal negative constitutional rights and bereft of extensive social, cultural and economic rights is much more likely to garner widespread acceptance than a constitution that emphasizes positive and collective rights. Also, depending on the particular context involved, there may be significant variations even in the presence of a shared commitment to the same broad ideological ideals. For instance, constitutional democracies that are essentially secular in nature can differ on the particulars concerning the relationship between the state and religion. Thus, separationist countries, such as France and the US differ on particulars, including the permissibility of state subsidy of religious education, while non-separationist secular democracies, like Italy and Germany allow for certain preferences, including religious education in state schools, accorded to majority religions.[83] Furthermore, what the minimalists consider as being within the proper scope of authority of constitutional judges also translates into that which commands consensus within the realm of ordinary politics and also combines an ideological and a contextual component. In the narrowest version of this, the ordinary politics consensus must go all the way and accordingly legitimate judicial politics would be confined to the narrow spectrum of judicial decisions that would command a consensus throughout the polity. Thus, if there were a consensus on textualist interpretations of purely formal negative rights, then use of any other judicial technique or philosophy would be presumably illegitimate. In contrast, in the broadest version of this same position, the ordinary politics consensus is limited to drawing the line between what is fit to be entrusted to judicial politics, and

---

[83] See Susanna Mancini and Michel Rosenfeld, "Introduction" in *Constitutional Secularism in an Age of Religious Revival* (Susanna Mancini and Michel Rosenfeld, eds. 2014), xv, xxiii–xiv.

what not. Thus, for example, so long as constitutional judges are limited to deciding formal structural and process issues and negative rights controversies, differences relating to judicial philosophy over which the citizenry might be divided would not affect the legitimacy of the judicial politics generated outcomes actually produced.

At the other end of the spectrum is the situation in which a judicial decision is merely formally within the ambit of the language game of judicial politics, but substantively, for all practical purposes, altogether within the precincts of ordinary politics. Perhaps the best example of this is the US Supreme Court 5–4 decision that settled that country's 2000 presidential election in the *Bush v. Gore* case already alluded to above. That decision practically handed the highly contested 2000 US presidential election to George W. Bush, with all the justices in the majority having been nominated by Republican presidents.[84] What is the most remarkable about this case, for our purposes, is that the five justices who handed the presidency to Bush departed from their restrictive judicial philosophy which had hitherto led them to strike down an unusually high number of immensely popular federal laws – including the prohibition of possession of guns in schools[85] and the law tackling violence against women on a nationwide basis[86] – in order to deviate from one of the firmest and longest standing pillars of US federalism honoured consistently by restrictive and expansive judicial interpreters alike. Indeed, it is a mainstay of American federalism that the highest state court is the authoritative interpreter of that state's law and that federal judges are bound to conform to such highest state court's interpretation when considering the (federal) constitutionality of any such law. Despite this, however, the five justices involved in fact handed the election to Bush by ordering an end to the recount of Florida voting ballots which had been imposed by the Florida Supreme Court based on its interpretation of Florida's election law. In order to reach the result they did, these justices had to substitute their own interpretation of the relevant Florida law for that of that state's highest court. And this is precisely what they did. Also, significantly in cases following *Bush v. Gore*, these same justices almost immediately returned to their customary brand of conservative judicial politics

---

[84] For an extended account and critique of the US Supreme Court's *Bush v. Gore* decision, see Michel Rosenfeld, "*Bush v. Gore: Three Strikes for the Constitution, the Court and Democracy, But There Is Always Next Season*" in Arthur Jacobson and Michel Rosenfeld, eds., *The Longest Night: Polemics and Perspectives on Election 2000* (*University of California Press* 2002), 111. The discussion that follows is largely based on the account provided in the just cited work.

[85] *See United States v. Lopez*, 514 US 549 (1995).

[86] *See United States v. Morrison*, 529 US 598 (2000).

whereby they largely weighed in on the side of the states to invalidate a high number of national laws challenged on federalism grounds.[87] Furthermore, there was yet another glaring anomaly in the US Supreme Court decision which may not have been ultimately outcome determinative[88], but which figures as strong evidence of ordinary politics taking over standard judicial practice. Indeed, the Court majority held that the disparity in the means of recounting votes accepted by the Florida Supreme Court violated the Equal Protection rights of Florida voters, but specified that its decision on this issue should not be construed as a judicial precedent in the context of future elections. Arguably, for a responsible judge, serious consideration that present decisions will serve as future precedents provides a significant buffer against fashioning judicial results solely geared to the ordinary politics of the moment. If the Equal Protection holding in *Bush v. Gore* had become a precedent for future presidential elections, it would have required a complete overhaul of the way in which Americans vote. In 2000, in Florida alone, there were sixty-seven electoral districts with a variety of different ways of recording and counting votes leading to citizens in different districts having measurably different probabilities that their vote would be properly counted.

None of the three cases examined earlier fall at either end of the spectrum identified above. As already noted, each of these cases comprises unusual and problematic characteristics in terms of the dynamic between judicial and ordinary politics. The Canadian and South African cases can be solidly defended as legitimate exercises of judicial politics based on a combination of structural, substantive and contextual factors. Both these cases promote a significant degree of constitutionalization of politics: the Canadian case by imposing constitutional preconditions not explicitly found in the country's written constitution to the (ordinary) political process of secession; the South African case, by judicially opting for a constitutional provision against the death penalty notwithstanding that a majority of the country's citizens favoured capital punishment for certain crimes. Paradoxically, the Israeli case

---

[87] *See, e.g., Solid Waste Agency of Cook County v. US Army Corp., of Engineers*, 531 US 159 (2201) (decided within one month of *Bush v. Gore*) (5–4 decision striking down federal power to regulate local ponds that form habitat of migratory birds); *Board of Trustees of the University of Alabama v. Garrett*, 531 US 356 (2001) (5–4 decision invalidating federal disability protection provisions in the name of states' rights).

[88] Even if the methods of vote recount accepted by the Florida Supreme Court were unconstitutional, the US Supreme Court could have prescribed federally acceptable standards which would have allowed Florida to restart the recount from scratch and still meet all the pertinent deadlines for formally submitting the results of the recount to the US Congress which has the constitutional task of providing final certification of the outcome of presidential elections. *See* US CONST., amend. XII.

may on its face strike one as being of unquestionable legitimacy from the standpoint of judicial politics in as much as it lays out some basic fundamental rights protections that are well within the mainstream in relation to the central precepts associated with the internationalization of constitutional law. Viewed more closely, however, primarily because of contextual factors – namely the country's actual historical failure to settle on a a full-fledged constitution because of profound internal divisions and because of a lack of consensus on the societal values underlying the Basic Laws subject to constitutionaliza-tion – the *Migdal* decision emerges as one of questionable legitimacy.

The main danger stemming from taking the constitutionalization of politics too far is the unleashing of an excessive politicization of the constitution that tends to blur the proper boundary between ordinary and judicial politics. In other words, a matter may be well within the legitimate bounds of judicial politics structurally and substantively and yet prove so divisive on an ordinary politics plane – either because of the subject matter involved or because of a widely perceived undue extension of judicial power – that the polity at large regards an actual judicial decision on the matter in question as amounting to an abuse of power. A particular salient example of this is provided by the open defiance against the German Constitutional Court's decision that the display of the crucifix in state school classrooms in Bavaria was unconstitutional.[89] In Germany, the constitutionalization of politics has been quite extensive, due in significant part to the high regard to which constitutional judges had been held in comparison to the ordinary political branches which had been signifi-cantly diminished as a consequence of their reprehensible moral and political failures during the Third Reich.[90] In spite of this high regard for German constitutional judges and of the fact that their decision was on a question quintessentially within the realm of judicial politics relating to the freedom of religion rights of religious minorities and of the non-religious in Bavaria, the Bavarian polity reacted to the Court's decision as if it had been an illegitimate exercise of judicial power.

The precise boundaries between legitimate constitutionalization of politics and illegitimate politicization of the constitution are undoubtedly hard to draw and are in most cases likely to be genuinely contestable. Furthermore, a case such as that concerning the crucifix in Bavaria can equally plausibly be interpreted as involving an unacceptably poor exercise of judicial politics or as

---

[89] *See Classroom Crucifix II*, 93 BverFGE 1 (1995) (German Constitutional Court) and Michel Rosenfeld, *Constitutional Adjudication in Europe and the United States: Paradoxes and Contrasts*, 2 *Int'l. J. of Con. L.* (*I.CON*) 633, 668 (2004).

[90] *See id.*, at 665.

comprising an abusive intrusion by judges into the realm of ordinary politics. In the former alternative, the judges would be accused of having grossly misinterpreted the freedom of religion protections afforded by the German Basic Law; in the latter alternative, the judges would be charged with having usurped the right of the people of Bavaria to decide by majority vote whether or not to require the presence of crucifixes in public school classrooms by wrongly converting an (ordinary) political question into a constitutional one.

Taking into account the substantive and context-based considerations discussed above, there is a strong argument that the Canadian and South African decisions discussed in earlier in this chapter were ultimately desirable as well as legitimate. Indeed, in the case of Canada, placing the quintessentially political process of secession through constitutional filters may well enhance deliberation, comity and the protection of vulnerable fundamental interests traditionally entrusted the protection of judges. Moreover, the desirability in question is enhanced by Canada's traditional broad tradition of constitutionalism and extensive toleration of a broad conception of the constitutionalization of politics. The only apparent drawback from the standpoint of desirability would arise in the eventuality of a unilateral secession that would be carried out in open disregard of the constitutional prerequisites now in place. That drawback should be deemed as relatively minor, however, as such a unilateral secession would most likely be in any event politically divisive on a nationwide basis regardless of particular rule of law or constitutional considerations. Turning to the South African case, delegation of constitution-making regarding the death penalty to the Constitutional Court emerges as highly desirable for both substantive and contextual reasons. As already noted, the constitutionality of the death penalty is a subject that falls squarely within the ambit of judicial politics. In addition, the South African Constitutional Court, a highly trusted institution, in the context of South Africa's pacted post-Apartheid constitution-making involving both actors within the country's last Apartheid government and Nelson Mandela's ANC was entrusted with a unique role that place it at the centre of the entire constitution-making enterprise. Indeed, consistent with the country's interim constitution, South Africa's permanent constitution required prior approval by the Constitutional Court which was charged with determining the conformity of a pacted constitution with a set of previously agreed to constitutional principles.[91]

In the Israeli case, in contrast, there is a strong argument that the decision was undesirable in addition to being of questionable legitimacy. That argument

---

[91] *See Certification of the Constitution of the Republic of South Africa*, 1996 (4) SALR 744 (CC) (Constitutional Court of South Africa) (Paras. 11–13).

seems bolstered by the above noted subsequent efforts within the Israeli polity to formally deprive the Supreme Court of any power to engage in constitutional adjudication. Upon further thought, however, one may wish to be more cautious regarding the question of desirability without changing one's conclusion regarding legitimacy. Even if in the relative short term, the *Migdal* decision may well have been undesirable, it may still prove to have been retrospectively desirable in the long term. Israel's constitution-making fate is still very much in question, and if one day the profound differences that currently hamper it could somehow be bridged over and a an actual constitution agreed upon, then the desirability of *Migdal* might well be cast in an entirely different light.

CONCLUSION

Based on the preceding analysis and on focus on the salient implications deriving from the contrast between judicial and ordinary politics, it becomes clear that the much criticized "judicialization" or constitutionalization of politics is not in and of itself either good or bad. Although from the standpoint of the overall good of society as a whole all intersubjective dealings have (ordinary) political dimensions, as we have seen a combination of content-based and contextual considerations justify entrusting certain key decisions to judges while leaving others to those who operate within the realm of ordinary politics. The three cases discussed earlier were remarkable and offered a fertile testing ground for the thesis advanced here precisely because they all involved issues that are conceptually and contextually anchored in the domain of ordinary politics: secession in Canada; and constitution-making in both South Africa and Israel. Through the filter provided by the divide between judicial and ordinary politics, the Canadian and South African decisions emerged as both legitimate and desirable whereas the Israeli one did as being questionable both in terms of legitimacy and of desirability – at least in the short and perhaps even the medium term.

More generally, some constitutionalization of politics seems inevitable and desirable for any constitutional democracy. How much, however, depends on contextual factors. For example, in the early 1990s following the fall of the Soviet Union, constitutional courts in East/Central Europe, and most notably in Hungary, played a key and extensive role in the transition from communism to liberal democracy.[92] In the last few years, however, this trend has been

---

[92] *See* Wojciech Sadurski, *Rights before Courts: A Study of Constitutional Courts in Post-Communist States of Central and Eastern Europe* (2d ed., 2014), 13.

dramatically reversed, the Hungarian Constitutional Court stripped of most of
its powers, and that country as well as others stirred in a populist and illiberal
direction.[93] On the one hand, the new political ethos prevalent in those
countries has shown little patience toward the constitutionalization of politics.
On the other hand, because fundamental rights and minorities seem particularly threatened as illiberal populist democracy takes hold, there is a strong
argument that judicial politics and the constitutionalization of politics ought
to be preserved or expanded rather than dramatically limited. In short, the
contrast between judicial and ordinary politics provides us with a valuable
analytical and critical tool in the assessment of the optimal role that constitutional judges ought to play consistent with the pursuit or preservation of
liberal constitutionalism in various historical, political and cultural contexts.

---

[93] *Id.*, at 10–13.

8

Originalism in Australia and Canada
Why the Divergence?

JEFFREY GOLDSWORTHY AND HON. GRANT HUSCROFT

INTRODUCTION

This chapter examines the role of originalism in the interpretation of the
Canadian and Australian Constitutions. We show that a moderate version of
originalism was inherent in British principles of statutory interpretation used to
interpret those Constitutions for many decades following their enactment. We
then describe the divergent paths taken more recently: in Australia, an increased
interest in recovering the original meanings of constitutional provisions, despite
occasional doubts and wobbles; whereas in Canada, a seeming shift from
original meaning to a "progressive" approach based on conceiving of the Constitution as a "living tree," albeit with reliance on original meaning in many cases.

Any discussion of originalism is likely to provoke controversy. The concept
is often as vehemently rejected as it is misunderstood. It is said to have "never
enjoyed significant support in Canada, either in the courts or the academy."[1]
But many who purport to reject originalism in fact reject only an extreme
variant, associated with American political conservatism.[2] This holds that a
constitution should be interpreted in accordance with the expectations of
its founders – how they expected its provisions would be applied. But that
approach is rejected by the most popular modern version of originalism,
which regards only the constitution's original public meaning as binding.[3]

---

[1] P. Hogg, CONSTITUTIONAL LAW OF CANADA (5th ed, Thomson/Carswell, Canada, 2007
supplemented), vol I, 15–49; also vol II, 60–7.

[2] E.g., Justice Ian Binnie explicitly acknowledges this in *Constitutional Interpretation and
Original Intent*, in G. Huscroft and I. Brodie, eds, CONSTITUTIONALISM IN THE CHARTER ERA
(LexisNexis-Butterworths, Canada, 2004), 345, 370 and 380–81. He also expresses support for
"the traditional Anglo-Canadian" principles of interpretation described in this article (ibid,
360 and 369–70), which we maintain are plainly originalist.

[3] *See also infra* notes 78, 86–89, 142–43 and 169. American originalists in the 1970s, such as
Raoul Berger, were associated with expectations originalism. Justice Antonin Scalia professed

We suggest that there are fewer differences between public meaning originalism and living tree interpretation than is usually supposed. Properly understood, they necessarily co-exist in theory and practice, playing complementary roles.[4] Both approaches address important aspects of constitutional interpretation and each would be improved by acknowledging and accommodating the strengths of the other.

CONSTITUTIONAL INTERPRETATION UNTIL THE 1980S

Inherited British Principles of Statutory Interpretation

The foundational Canadian and Australian Constitutions were drafted and endorsed by colonial lawyers and politicians, before being formally enacted by statutes of the United Kingdom Parliament: the *British North America Act* 1867 (UK) (*BNA Act*) and the *Commonwealth of Australia Constitution Act* 1900 (UK).[5] When courts started to interpret these statutes, they were naturally guided by traditional British principles of statutory interpretation that would now be called originalist. Those principles remained orthodox for over a century in Canada, and are still accepted in Australia, albeit accommodating disagreement between judges of a textualist bent and those who prefer a more purposive approach.

British courts were firmly wedded to the core thesis of originalism: that until they are formally amended, statutory provisions continue to mean what they meant when they were enacted.[6] That principle had been endorsed in Coke's *Institutes* in the early Seventeenth Century.[7] In 1883, Maxwell stated that "the language of a statute, as of every other writing, is to be construed in the sense

public meaning originalism, but was frequently criticized for deciding cases inconsistently with its basic principles: see, e.g., Eric Segall, *Will the Real Justice Scalia Please Stand Up?* in http://wakeforestlawreview.com/2015/09/will-the-real-justice-scalia-please-stand-up/;Erwin Chemerinsky, *"The Jurisprudence of Justice Scalia": A Critical Appraisal* (2000) 22 U. HAWAI'I L. REV. 385; T B Colby and P J Smith, *Living Originalism* (2009) 59 DUKE L. J. 239, 293–97. We take no position on that criticism.

4   See the "Some Consequences of Canada's Rejection of Originalism" and "Conclusion" sections in this chapter. *See also* L. Sirota and B. Oliphant, *Originalist Reasoning in Canadian Constitutional Jurisprudence* (2017) 50 UBC L. REV. 505, and *Has the Supreme Court of Canada Rejected "Originalism"?* (2016) 42 QUEEN'S L. J. 107.

5   The Australian Constitution was also approved by voters in referenda prior to its enactment.

6   *See generally* D.J. Hurst, *The Problem of the Elderly Statute*, LEGAL STUDIES 21 (1983).

7   "[T]hose ancient acts and graunts must be construed and taken as the Law was holding at that time when they were made": 2 Co Inst 2.

which it bore at the period when it was passed."[8] This was presumably because otherwise, Parliament's statutes would be, in effect, vulnerable to amendment by extra-parliamentary means.[9] Lord Esher stated the principle categorically in 1888: "the words of a statute must be construed as they would have been the day after the statute was passed."[10]

A second thesis embraced by most versions of originalism is that the meaning of a law depends partly on the intentions of those who made it. For centuries, the common law had recognized that the object of all interpretation "is to determine what intention is conveyed either expressly or by implication by the language used," or in other words, "to give effect to the intention of the [law-maker] as that intention is to be gathered from the language employed having regard to the context in connection with which it is employed."[11] Tindall C.J. said in 1844 that this was "the *only rule*" for the construction of statutes.[12] Many early authorities consistently attested to the crucial role of legislative intention in statutory interpretation.[13]

Occasionally, textualist judges insisted that "we are not . . . concerned with what Parliament intended, but simply with what it has said in the statute."[14] That was one reason why British courts traditionally refused to consult legislative history.[15] But it would be wrong to infer that they did not take seriously the principle that interpreters should seek the law-making intentions that statutes convey, expressly or by implication.[16] They distinguished between whatever intentions individual legislators may have expressed, and the intention manifested by the words of the statute given readily available contextual knowledge of its purpose.[17] As Lord Blackburn explained:

---

[8]   P.B. Maxwell, ON THE INTERPRETATION OF STATUTES (2nd ed, Maxwell & Son, London, 1883), 75; also 366.

[9]   Condemned at *id*, 6–7.   [10] *Sharpe v. Wakefield*, 22 Q.B.D. 239, 242 (1888).

[11] P.B. Maxwell, ON THE INTERPRETATION OF STATUTES (London, 1875), 1; *Attorney-General v. Carlton Bank*, 2 Q.B. 158, 164 (1899) (Lord Russell).

[12] *Sussex Peerage Case*, 8 E.R. 1034, 1057 (1844) (Tindall C.J.).

[13] *See* J. Goldsworthy, *Originalism in Constitutional Interpretation*, 25 FEDERAL L. REV. 1, 9 (1997).

[14] *R v. Hertford College*, 3 Q.B.D. 693, 707; 47 L.J.Q.B. 649, 658 (1878).

[15] There were additional reasons, including the need for the meanings of laws to be reasonably open to the public, or at least their legal advisers, the unreliability of extrinsic evidence, and the costs in terms of time and money of investigating it.

[16] This mistaken inference badly mars the arguments made in H. Jefferson Powell, *The Original Understanding of Original Intent*, 98 HARV. L. REV. 885–90 at 895–6, 903–6, and 948 (1985).

[17] For analysis of the "objective" nature of such a "manifested intention," *see* R Ekins and J Goldsworthy, *The Reality and Indispensability of Legislative Intention*, 36 SYDNEY L. REV. 39, 46–51 (2014).

In all cases the object is to see what is the intention expressed by the words used. But, from the imperfection of language, it is impossible to know what that intention is without inquiring further, and seeing what the circumstances were with reference to which the words were used, and what was the object, appearing from those circumstances, which the person using them had in view, for the meaning of words varies according to the circumstances with respect to which they were used.[18]

The courts therefore took into account the legal and social circumstances when the law was made, and what it was intended to achieve, when these were, at least when the law was made, commonly known.[19] Some insisted that this was confined to cases in which "the words of an enactment are ambiguous and capable of two meanings,"[20] but ambiguity was in the eye of the beholder.

These principles can be found in Maxwell's 1875 treatise on statutory interpretation.[21] In 1904 they were accurately summarized by O'Connor J of the Australian High Court:

> [O]ur duty in interpreting a Statute is to declare and administer the law according to the intention expressed in the Statute itself. In this respect the Constitution differs in no way from any Statute ... The intention of the enactment is to be gathered from its words. If the words are plain, effect must be given to them; if they are doubtful, the intention of the legislature is to be gathered from the other provisions of the Statute aided by a consideration of surrounding circumstances. In all cases in order to discover the intention you may have recourse to contemporaneous circumstances - to the history of the law ... [and] historical facts surrounding the bringing [of] the law into existence.[22]

Application of These Principles in Canada

Professor Saywell has shown that Canadian courts frequently applied these principles after federation.[23] They accepted that the intended meaning and purpose of the BNA Act could be illuminated by the historical context in which it was made, including the meanings of terms used in earlier Canadian

---

[18] *River Wear Commissioners v. Adamson*, 2 A.C. 743, 763(1877); *see also* his remarks in *Edinburgh Street Tramways v. Torbain*, 3 A.C. 58, 68 (1877).

[19] *See, e.g.*, Maxwell (1875), *supra* note 11, at 20–1.

[20] *R. v. Bishop of London*, 24 Q.B.D. 213, 224–25 (1889).

[21] Maxwell (1875), *supra* note 11, at 1, 5–6, 18–23 and 49.

[22] *Tasmania v. Commonwealth*, 1 CLR 329, 358–60 (1904).

[23] J.T. Saywell, THE LAWMAKERS; JUDICIAL POWER AND THE SHAPING OF CANADIAN FEDERALISM (University of Toronto Press, 2002).

legislation and the political circumstances that led to federation.[24] In *Severn v. The Queen*, the first important constitutional case decided by the Supreme Court of Canada, Chief Justice Sir William Richards said:

> I think we may, without violating any of the rules for construing Statutes, look to the legislation which prevailed in any or all of the Provinces, in order to enable us to be put in the position of those who framed the Laws and give assistance in interpreting the words used and the object to which they were directed.[25]

Both the majority and dissenting judges claimed fidelity to the founders' intentions.[26] As Supreme Court Justice (subsequently Chief Justice) Sir Samuel Strong later observed, the rules of statutory interpretation required "recourse to external aids derived from the surrounding circumstances and the history of the subject-matter dealt with . . . so to put ourselves as far as possible in the position of the legislature whose language we have to expound;" otherwise, "the task of interpretation would degenerate into mere speculation and guess work."[27] Reference to the intended meaning of constitutional provisions was common.[28]

The Privy Council, on the other hand, adopted an ostensibly more textualist approach.[29] According to Saywell, the Privy Council "was not prepared to hear argument based on policy or history, pre-Confederation practice, or the Canadian use of language . . . as a clue to the intentions of the framers."[30] Lord Selbourne opined that "We know nothing about the mind of the legislature, and in point of fact, no legislature has any mind, except that which is expressed in the words which it has used."[31] But as Saywell points out, the Privy Council was inconsistent:[32]

> [W]hile denying the admissibility of empirical historical evidence, members of the Judicial Committee also felt free to impose their own assumptions about the context, meaning, and intentions of the 1867 constitution."[33]

Much anger was provoked in Canada because the Privy Council's blinkered, ahistorical approach was perceived to be distorting the intended nature of

---

[24] *Id.*, at 20–21, 26, 35.   [25] *Severn v. The Queen* (1878) 2 SCR 70, 93.

[26] Binnie, *supra* note 2, at 347 and 353–55.

[27] *St Catherine's Milling and Lumber Co v. The Queen*, 13 SCR 577, 606–7 (1887), quoted in Saywell, *supra* note 23, 36.

[28] E.g., *id.*, 38–9, 45, 49 n 66 and 54–5 n97.   [29] *Id.*, at 72.

[30] *Id.*, at 73–4; *see also* Binnie, *supra* note 2, at 356–58

[31] *The St Catherine's Milling and Lumber Co v The Queen: Arguments of Mr Blake Counsel for Ontario* (Toronto, 1888), 39, quoted in Saywell, *supra* note 23, 75.

[32] Saywell, *supra* note 23, 74–75.   [33] *Id.*, at 76–77.

Canadian federalism.[34] Some advocated a broader, more purposive approach believed to have been taken by the US Supreme Court.[35] The Privy Council backed down when its refusal to consider the well-known historical context of a provincial constitutional provision led to a decision blasted by Canadian Chief Justice Taschereau as "unreasonable, unjust, inconsistent and contrary to the intentions of the lawgiver."[36] Lord Herschell acknowledged that

> While ... it is necessary to resist any temptation to deviate from sound rules of construction in the hope of more completely satisfying the intention of the Legislature, it is quite legitimate where more than one construction of a statute is possible, to select that one which will best carry out what appears from the general scope of the legislation and the surrounding circumstances to have been its intentions.[37]

The prior existence and subsequent application of these traditional interpretive principles casts doubt on Professor Hogg's suggestion that the founders of the *BNA Act* probably did not intend that its interpretation would be governed by their intentions.[38]

Orthodox interpretive principles continued to be applied by the Supreme Court of Canada until the late 1970s, and to some extent thereafter. In the *Persons Case* (1928), the Court reaffirmed that "the various provisions of the BNA Act ... bear today the same construction which courts would ... have given to them when they were first enacted,"[39] and that

> we have to construe not merely the words of the Act of Parliament but the intent of the Legislature as collected, from the cause and necessity of the Act being made, from a comparison of its several parts and from foreign [extraneous] circumstances so far as they can be justly considered to throw light upon the subject.[40]

But the Supreme Court arguably misapplied these interpretive principles, in deciding that women could not be appointed to the Senate because they were not "qualified persons" as required by s 24 of the Act. The Court gave decisive weight not to the original meaning of the term "persons," but to

---

[34] *Id.*, at 74, 75, 86, 112; D.M Brown, *Tradition and Change in Constitutional Interpretation: Do Living Trees Have Roots?*, 19 NAT'L J. CONST. L. 33, 55 and 66 (2005/2006); Binnie, *supra* note 2, at 358–58

[35] Saywell, *supra* note 23, at 22, 73 and 196; D.M Brown, *supra* note 34, at 63–64.

[36] Saywell, *supra* note 23, at 75.

[37] *Brophy v. AG Manitoba*, AC 202, 215 (1894) quoted in *id*, at 76.

[38] Hogg, *supra* note 1, vol II, 60–10; Hogg, *The Charter of Rights and American Theories of Interpretation*, 25 OSGOODE HALL L. J. 87, 96 (1987).

[39] *Edwards v. Canada (A.G.)*, SCR 276, 288 (1928).   [40] *Id.*, 282.

how the founders would have applied it – the discredited variant of originalism we referred to earlier.[41]

Historical context was taken to bear on the founders' intentions in diverse
cases, for example, dealing with the meaning of "Indians" in s. 91(24),[42] the power
to implement international treaties,[43] and the jurisdiction of lower provincial
courts.[44] Even avowed non-originalist Justice Binnie has conceded "the existence
of many such examples."[45] He dismisses references to historical context and
legislative intention as "for the most part . . . little more than rhetorical flourishes
paraded to confirm a view reached by other means."[46] But this is debatable,[47] and
also overlooks an important negative function of originalist principles. Even if
historical evidence is often too slim or conjectural to provide much positive
guidance to interpreters, the requirement that any interpretation must be historically plausible is an important constraint on interpretive discretion.

In the 1980s, this orthodoxy came to be overshadowed by the Privy Council's
famous dictum in the *Persons Case* that the BNA Act had planted a "living tree
capable of growth and expansion within its natural limits."[48] The Privy Council
overturned the Supreme Court's decision, criticizing its "narrow and technical"
methodology.[49] But as Bradley Miller has shown, the "living tree" metaphor
played no part in the interpretive reasoning that followed, which after considering historical evidence of intention but rejecting its utility, carefully parsed the
use of the word "person" throughout the text of the BNA Act.[50]

---

[41] F. Vaughan, VISCOUNT HALDANE, THE WICKED STEPFATHER OF THE CANADIAN
CONSTITUTION (University of Toronto Press, 2010), 214–15; B.W. Miller, *Origin Myth: The
Persons Case, the Living Tree and the New Originalism*, in G. Huscroft and B. W. Miller, eds,
THE CHALLENGE OF ORIGINALISM, THEORIES OF CONSTITUTIONAL INTERPRETATION
(Cambridge University Press, New York, 2011), 125–28. For discussion of the distinction, *see* text
to *infra* notes 86–89.

[42] *Reference Re Eskimo* [1939] SCR 104.

[43] *Reference Re Labour Conventions* [1936] SCR 461, discussed in Binnie, *supra* note 2, at
360–61.

[44] *Reference Re Adoption Act (Ontario)* [1938] SCR 398, especially the judgment of Duff J.

[45] Binnie, *supra* note 2, at 352; also *id*, at 375.   [46] Binnie, *supra* note 2, at 375.

[47] B. Miller, *Beguiled by Metaphors: The "Living Tree" and Originalist Interpretation in Canada*,
22 CANADIAN J. L. JURISPRUD. 331, 345–48 (2009).

[48] John Finnis argues that the living tree metaphor referred to the Dominion itself, not the
Constitution that established it: *Judicial Law-Making and the "Living" Instrumentalisation of
the ECHR*, in N. Barber, R. Ekins, and P. Yowell. eds, LORD SUMPTION AND THE LIMITS OF
THE LAW (Hart Publishing, Oxford, 2016), 73, text to n. 32. For an alternative revisionary view,
see Miller, *Origin Myth*, *supra* note 41, 132.

[49] [1930] A.C. 124, 136 (PC).

[50] Miller, supra note 41, 133–36; D.M. Brown, *supra* note 34, 58–59 and 65; L.A. Walton, *Making
Sense of Canadian Constitutional Interpretation* 12 NAT'L CONST. L. 315, 336 (2000–2001).

Many have attributed to the Privy Council the modern nostrum that the meanings of constitutional terms evolve in response to changing community values. But the Privy Council never suggested that the meaning of "persons" had changed since 1867; indeed, it seems to have accepted that the meaning of statutory terms could only be changed by amendment.[51] As W. Ivor Jennings concluded in 1937, after discussing the decision:

> It may therefore be said that the Judicial Committee has never seriously wavered from the principle that it was their function to interpret the 'intention of Parliament' as laid down in the Act and not to fit the Constitution to the changing conditions of social life.[52]

Application of These Principles in Australia

Canadian criticisms of the Privy Council's interpretation of the BNA Act reverberated throughout the Empire, and reached the ears of Australian lawyers. In *The American Commonwealth* (1889), once called the "bible" of the Australian founders, James Bryce applauded the creative development of the American Constitution by the American Supreme Court.[53] This provoked disagreement among Australian lawyers about the relative merits of that Court's supposed broader, purposive methodology and the Privy Council's narrower textualism.[54]

This disagreement split the Australian High Court for two decades, in cases concerning the legitimacy of implied intergovernmental immunities, which its first three judges – influenced by American case-law – discerned within the Constitution. When the Privy Council criticized the High Court's approach as an "expansion" of orthodox interpretive principles,[55] it received a scathing rejoinder criticizing the quality of its interpretation of Canada's Constitution.[56]

---

[51] Miller, *supra* note 41, esp 129–31 and 136–38. He argues that the "living tree" metaphor was misunderstood when taken out of its context in the 1980s in order to validate the proposed "progressive" approach to interpreting the *Charter: ibid.*, 138. *See also* Vaughan, *supra* note 41, 214, and Brown, *supra* note 34, 68 and 95.

[52] W. Ivor Jennings, *Constitutional Interpretation: The Experience of Canada* 51 HARV. L. REV. 1, 35 (1937–1938). We thank Ben Oliphant for this reference.

[53] (2nd edn, Macmillan, London, 1889), esp 267–68, 363–68, 373–75. For "bible," see J.A. La Nauze *The Name of the Commonwealth of Australia* (1971) 15 HISTORICAL STUDIES 59.

[54] G. Craven, *Heresy as Orthodoxy: Were the Founders Progressivists?* (2003) 31 FEDERAL LAW REV. 87, esp 104, 107–8, 116–121, 108–9, 113–15 and 117–18.

[55] *Webb v. Outtrim* (1906) 4 CLR 356 (PC), 359–61.

[56] *Commissioners of Taxation (NSW) v. Baxter* (1907) 4 CLR 1087, 1110; *see also* 1111.

But in 1920, the Privy Council's approach prevailed when a majority of the High Court overruled the doctrine of implied intergovernmental immunities, and strongly affirmed British rather than American interpretive principles. The majority judgment laid down a more textualist or legalist approach that has dominated constitutional interpretation in Australia ever since.[57]

Yet even the Court's first three judges had insisted that ordinary principles of statutory interpretation, which they expounded with copious citations of British precedents, were applicable.[58] One of them, O'Connor J., accurately summarized those principles in the passage previously cited.[59] They had insisted that these principles required the special nature of a constitutional statute to be taken into account.[60] It was special in two main respects. First, it was not a detailed code, like a Tax Act, so some powers and rights were conferred by implication rather than expressly.[61] Secondly, it was intended to establish an abiding system of government able to cope with unpredictable future developments, so legislative powers should be construed broadly.[62] But neither consideration was thought to warrant a departure from more fundamental interpretive principles.

Those principles were often acknowledged to require that, until a statute is amended, its words continue to mean what they meant when they were first enacted.[63] As Barton J explained, "[t]o attempt to give [the words] a larger meaning is to attempt to alter the Constitution," which could be legitimately achieved only by referendum.[64] Orthodoxy also held the Constitution's meaning to depend on the context in which it was drafted and enacted, including pre-existing laws and general historical facts. The judges often referred to the intention of the legislature, but also to what was in "the minds of the framers" and of "the people" who had approved the Constitution before its enactment.[65] They studied earlier drafts of the Constitution to infer reasons for its

---

[57] J Goldsworthy, *Australia: Commitment to Legalism*, in J Goldsworthy, Interpreting Constitutions, a Comparative Study (Oxford University Press, 2006) 106, 119–20.

[58] *Tasmania v. Commonwealth* (1904) 1 CLR 329, 338–39 (Griffith CJ).

[59] *Id.*, 359 per O'Connor J, *cited supra* note 22.

[60] E.g. *Attorney-General (NSW) v. Brewery Employees Union of NSW* (1908) 6 CLR 469, 612.

[61] *Tasmania v. Commonwealth* (1904) 1 CLR 329, 338 (Griffith CJ).

[62] *Jumbunna Coal Mine, No Liability v. Victorian Coal Miners' Association* (1908) 6 CLR 309, 343, 356.

[63] *Attorney-General (NSW) v. Brewery Employees Union of NSW* (1908) 6 CLR 469, 501, 521; *see also R v. Barger* (1908) 6 CLR 41, 68, 116.

[64] *Brewery Employees Union, supra* note 63, 521.

[65] *Tasmania v. Commonwealth*, supra note 61, 343–44 (Griffith CJ), 348 and 351–52 (Barton J), 360 (O'Connor J). *See also Deakin v. Webb* (1904) 1 CLR 585, 630–31 (O'Connor J).

final wording.[66] They also examined the meanings of words in prior colonial legislation, on the ground that they would have been "in the minds of" the framers.[67]

Although the Court held that the original meaning of a provision was fixed, it accepted that a provision could apply to novel objects not envisaged by the founders.[68] The Court borrowed, from John Stuart Mill, the terms "connotation" and "denotation" to designate, respectively, the meaning of a word, and the objects to which it refers. The distinction helps explain many of its decisions. For example, in 1900 people born in Britain were not subject to Parliament's power with respect to "aliens," but due to Australia's later transition to independence, their status changed. The meaning of "aliens" did not change, but its application necessarily changed when the facts changed.[69]

The role of historical considerations after 1920 should not be exaggerated. In many cases they played little role. Until 1988, the Court was willing to infer the founders' intentions and purposes only from a very limited range of material. It often preferred not to gloss the ordinary or natural meaning of the text, especially when interpreting Commonwealth powers.[70] Sometimes the attribution of a purpose to a provision was little more than dogmatic assumption.[71] Nevertheless, as Professor Lane observed in 1979, "the High Court has frequently grubbed around the historical roots of a constitutional term in order to unearth its content."[72]

DEVELOPMENTS FROM THE 1980S

Canada: The Advent of the Canadian Charter of Rights and Freedoms

Supreme Court Justice Iacobucci claimed in 1993 that "this Court has never adopted the practice more prevalent in the United States of basing constitutional interpretation on the original intentions of the framers of the

---

[66] *Tasmania v. Commonwealth, supra* note 61, at 333.
[67] *Brewery Employees Union, supra* note 63, at 522 (Barton J).
[68] Stated clearly in Sir G. Barwick, Foreword to P.H. Lane, LANE'S COMMENTARY ON THE AUSTRALIAN CONSTITUTION (Law Book Co, Sydney, 1986), vii.
[69] See J Goldsworthy, *Original Meanings and Contemporary Understandings in Constitutional Interpretation,* in H.P. Lee and P. Gerangelos, eds, CONSTITUTIONAL ADVANCEMENT IN A FROZEN CONTINENT (The Federation Press, Sydney, 2009) 245, esp 250, 255–62 and 265–66.
[70] P.H. Lane, THE AUSTRALIAN FEDERAL SYSTEM (2nd ed, The Law Book Co ltd, Sydney, 1979), 1113–14.
[71] L. Zines THE HIGH COURT AND THE CONSTITUTION (4th ed, Butterworths, Sydney 1997), 450–51.
[72] Lane, *supra* note 70, 1110.

Constitution."[73] Given the foregoing, this seems to reflect ignorance of prior judicial practice.[74] But it may accurately express the Court's preferred approach since the *Charter* was enacted.[75] Originalism appears to have been roundly rejected by Canadian judges and legal scholars. For this there are both legal-theoretical reasons and social-political causes.

One suggested reason is, ironically, originalist: that the founders of the *Charter* did not intend originalist principles to apply to its interpretation.[76] This is dubious,[77] although they probably would have rejected the expected applications approach, rather than the original public meaning approach that characterizes modern originalism.[78] In any event, the Supreme Court has not relied on this reason for shifting to a "living tree" approach.[79] Other reasons include the mistaken belief that legislative intentions are either non-existent or unknowable, which would make nonsense of how statutes have been inter-preted for centuries,[80] and doubts about the capacity of general terms to apply to unforeseen future developments.

For example, Professor Hogg, has suggested that originalism cannot accom-modate the application of constitutional terms to anything that was unknown and unanticipated when the constitution was enacted:[81]

> If general language is apt to apply to a set of modern-day facts, then the doctrine [of progressive interpretation] stipulates that the language should be so applied, regardless of whether the founders contemplated its application to those facts.[82]

But all modern versions of originalism accept that, while the meaning of the text cannot change as facts change, its application often must. The Australian High Court has long held that an unchanging meaning can apply to new technological and social developments that the founders could not have envisaged.[83] Hogg then confuses his own point by adding: "Under the

---

[73] *Ontario Hydro v. Ontario (Labour Relation Board)* 3 SCR (1993)327, 409.
[74] *See* "Application of These Principles in Canada" in this chapter; *see also* quote at *infra* note 106.
[75] Miller, *supra* note 41, at 120.
[76] Binnie, *supra* note 2, at 347–48, 377–78 and 380; Hogg, *supra* note 1, vol II, 36–27 and 60–10; Miller, *Beguiled*, *supra* note 47, at 348.
[77] See text to *supra* note 38.   [78] *See* text to *supra* notes 2–3, and text to *infra* 86–89.
[79] Miller, *Beguiled*, *supra* note 47, at 348.
[80] *See* R. Ekins and J. Goldsworthy, *supra* note 17; Richard Ekins, THE NATURE OF LEGISLATIVE INTENT (Oxford University Press, 2012).
[81] Hogg, *supra* note 1, vol I, 15–47-15.51, vol II, 36–26; *see also* his "The Charter of Rights," *supra* note 38, at 96, 98–9, 101 and 113.
[82] *Id.*, 101.   [83] *See* text to *supra* notes 68–69.

doctrine of progressive interpretation the words of the text are given a meaning
that seems natural to contemporary eyes, not a meaning that has been distilled
from historic records extrinsic to the actual text."[84] But a contemporary meaning is different from a contemporary application of an original meaning, and
raises different issues.

The capacity of general terms to apply to new, unanticipated developments
is expanded if they are interpreted broadly. A presumption in favour of broad
interpretations, especially of legislative powers, has been adopted in Australia
precisely for that reason.[85] But this does not entail that the meanings of the
terms conferring those powers need to change. To the contrary, broad interpretations of provisions are preferred precisely so they will not need to be
changed.

Another common reason for rejecting originalism concerns the application of constitutional rights that embody broad moral principles (which
not all of them do[86]). Modern judges are rightly unwilling to apply such
principles in accordance with moral beliefs of the founders that are now
regarded as unacceptable or even reprehensible. But that is not a good
reason to reject originalism, because it does not require judges to defer to
the founders' moral beliefs.

Originalism requires fidelity to whatever textual and admissible contextual
evidence suggests the founders intended a constitutional provision to mean.
But how they hoped or expected the provision to be applied in a particular
instance is not directly relevant, let alone determinative, of its meaning.[87]
Their hopes and expectations are not part of the constitution and have no legal
status. The separation of powers entails that while lawmakers enact the law,
judges must apply it according to their best understanding of its true meaning,
regardless of the lawmakers' opinions or preferences concerning its application. Moreover, those opinions and preferences may be erroneous, because
(like the rest of us) lawmakers are prone to confuse what they intend to
communicate with what they succeed in communicating.

When a provision expressly incorporates a moral principle, as so many
Charter provisions do, judges must decide what the principle requires, not
what the founders – perhaps erroneously – believed it requires. Hence, the
American Supreme Court's decision in *Brown v. Board of Education*,[88] that

---

[84] Hogg, *The Charter of Rights, supra* note 38, 101–102.   [85] *See text to supra* note 62.
[86] Consider the "right to keep and bear arms" in the Second Amendment of the US
Constitution.
[87] It is at best indirectly relevant, insofar as it might illuminate what the founders intended the
provisions to mean.
[88] 347 US 483 (1954).

racially segregated education violated the equal protection clause, was correct even if it is inconsistent with how the authors of the clause expected it to be applied. Many originalists agree that it was correct, because the original intended meaning of the clause included a general moral principle of equality.[89]

Turning to socio-political causes, it is surely pertinent that at the very time Canadian judges began to interpret the *Charter*, originalism was becoming a lightning rod for political controversy in the United States. The appointment of US Supreme Court Justices became increasingly politicized during the 1970s, when President Nixon promised to nominate "strict constructionists" as a corrective to the Warren Court's supposed liberal activism.[90] By the 1980s, "originalism"[91] was promoted as a means of curbing judicial power, and President Reagan nominated two originalists to the Court for this purpose. The Court's most famous proponent of originalism, Antonin Scalia, was unanimously approved in the Senate,[92] but Robert Bork's nomination one year later ended in spectacular defeat, not only in the Senate, but more importantly in the arena of public opinion.

Bork was well qualified for appointment by traditional measures,[93] but his socially conservative positions on constitutional rights, tied to his conception of originalism, came under sustained attack. His constitutional approach became the stuff of parody, alternately mocked as ridiculous – why should anyone care about what the slave-owning white men who drafted the Constitution intended it to mean? – or condemned as dangerous, threatening to return America to the time of back alley abortions, segregated lunch counters and rogue police.[94] Rejection of Bork's appointment became synonymous with rejection of originalism in general.

---

[89] E.g., M. McConnell, *Originalism and the Segregation Decisions*, 81 VA. L. REV. 947 (1985); M. Perry, WE THE PEOPLE: THE FOURTEENTH AMENDMENT AND THE SUPREME COURT (Oxford University Press, New York, 2002); A. Scalia and B. A. Garner, READING LAW: THE INTERPRETATION OF LEGAL TEXTS (Thomson/West, St Paul Minn., 2012), 87–88. *Cf.* Hogg, who asserts that *Brown* cannot be defended on originalist grounds: *supra* note 1, at ch.60.1(c).

[90] See e.g., John W. Dean, THE REHNQUIST CHOICE: THE UNTOLD STORY OF THE NIXON APPOINTMENT THAT REDEFINED THE SUPREME COURT (Free Press, New York, 2002)

[91] The term "originalism" was coined by a critic, Paul Brest, in 1980: L. Solum, *What Is Originalism? The Evolution of Contemporary Originalist Theory*, in THE CHALLENGE OF ORIGINALISM, *supra* note 41, at 12, 13.

[92] The Senate had often deferred to judicial nominations; opposition usually focused on allegations of incompetence or unethical behavior, and in many ways the political stars aligned to smooth Scalia's path: Dennis J Goldford, THE AMERICAN CONSTITUTION AND THE DEBATE OVER ORIGINALISM (Cambridge University Press, New York, 2005), 170–173.

[93] Bork had previously been a Law Professor at Yale, Solicitor General, and unanimously confirmed to the Federal Court of Appeals. Goldford, *supra* note 92, at 170.

[94] Senator Ted Kennedy, quoted in www.nytimes.com/1987/07/05/opinion/washington-kennedy-and-bork.html.

It is hardly surprising that the Canadian Supreme Court wanted nothing to do with anything that smacked of originalism, now depicted as a political strategy designed to deliver conservative outcomes rather than a neutral method of constitutional interpretation. Under the leadership of Chief Justice Dickson, the Court wanted not only to strike its own constitutional course, but also to ensure that the *Charter* did not suffer the ignominious fate of its precursor, the *Canadian Bill of Rights*.[95] Interpretation of the *Bill of Rights* had been based partly on the so-called "frozen concepts" principle of interpretation, which was therefore tainted by association.[96]

Chief Justice Dickson signalled at the outset that the Court would not be bound by the history of the *Charter*. In *Hunter v. Southam*, he explained why:

> The task of expounding a constitution is crucially different from that of construing a statute. A statute defines present rights and obligations. It is easily enacted and as easily repealed. A constitution, by contrast, is drafted with an eye to the future. Its function is to provide a continuing framework for the legitimate exercise of governmental power and, when joined by a *Bill* or a *Charter of Rights*, for the unremitting protection of individual rights and liberties. Once enacted, its provisions cannot easily be repealed or amended. It must, therefore, be capable of growth and development over time to meet new social, political and historical realities often unimagined by its founders.[97]

Of course, the Chief Justice did not assert judicial authority to change the *Charter*; instead, he spoke of "growth and development" through interpretation. But the difference can be obscure.[98]

Justice Lamer's majority opinion in the *BC Motor Vehicle Reference*[99] is often cited as a rejection of originalism, but in fact he merely disapproved of legislative history being given "anything but minimal weight" in interpreting

---

95 R. J. Sharpe and K. Roach, BRIAN DICKSON: A JUDGES JOURNEY (University of Toronto Press, 2003), ch. 15.

96 B. Hovius, *The Legacy of the Supreme Court of Canada's Approach to the Canadian Bill of Rights: Prospects for the Charter*, 28 REVUE DE DROIT DE McGILL 31, 40–42 and 50–51 (1982); J.B. Kelly, GOVERNING WITH THE CHARTER; LEGISLATIVE AND JUDICIAL ACTIVISM AND FRAMERS' INTENT (University of British Columbia Press, 2005), 83.

97 *sub nom. Canada (Director of Investigation & Research, Combines Investigation Branch) v. Southam Inc.*, [1984] 2 SCR 145, 155.

98 Larry Alexander has argued that such arguments for "living tree" interpretation reflect opposition to the very idea of constitutionalism, which usually involves deliberate entrenchment against change. L. Alexander and E. Sherwin, DEMYSTIFYING LEGAL REASONING (Cambridge University Press, New York, 2008), 225–226.

99 *Re: B.C. Motor Vehicle Act*, 2 SCR 486 (1985).

the *Charter*.[100] He justified this partly on the basis of the inherent unreliability of such history. So many people at both federal and provincial levels helped negotiate, draft, and adopt the *Charter* that it would almost certainly be misleading to accord "any significant weight" to what particular individuals may have said.[101] Justice Lamer went on to reiterate Chief Justice Dickson's argument from *Southam*: the rights in the *Charter* should be allowed to develop and adjust to unanticipated social developments, rather than become frozen in time. "[C]are must be taken to ensure that historical materials . . . do not stunt its growth."[102]

But note that even justified skepticism about the relevance of legislative history does not dispose of originalism, because other more persuasive evidence of original meanings may be available.[103] Moreover, as we have seen, originalism does not maintain that the proper application of constitutional rights is fixed by the founders' moral beliefs or expectations.

Despite the widespread assumption that it has been rejected in Canada, originalist analysis continues to hide in plain sight in Supreme Court reasoning. Relevant cases span everything from federalism to education and language rights, aboriginal rights and the composition and nature of the Supreme Court itself.[104] Originalist analysis can even be found in many *Charter* cases.[105] As the Court put it in 1985, "[t]he jurisprudence of the Court evidences a willingness to supplement textual analysis with historical, contextual and purposive interpretation in order to ascertain the intent of the makers of our Constitution."[106] Consider two recent decisions.

---

[100] *Id.*, at para 52. Note that even Peter Hogg argues that in this case "the legislative history ought to have been respected. Not only was the legislative history unanimous, but it went to the fundamental question of why s. 7 had been included in the Charter in the first place." Hogg, *supra* note 1, vol II, 60.2(a).

[101] *Re: B.C. Motor Vehicle Act*, 2 SCR 486, (1985) para 52.

[102] *Re: B.C. Motor Vehicle Act*, 2 SCR 486, (1985) para 53.   [103] *See* text to *supra* notes 18–22.

[104] The founders' intentions or understandings are referred to in numerous cases including *Attorney General of Quebec v. Quebec Association of Protestant School Boards et al.*, 2 SCR 66 (1984); *R. v. Cornell*, 1 SCR 461 (1988); *Committee for the Commonwealth of Canada v. Canada*, 1 SCR 139 (1991); *Reference re Prov. Electoral Boundaries (Sask.)*, 2 SCR 158 (1991); *B. (R.) v. Children's Aid Society of Metropolitan Toronto*, 1 SCR 315 (1995); *Weber v. Ontario Hydro*, 2 SCR 929 (1995); *Ontario Home Builders' Association v. York Region Board of Education*, 2 SCR 929 (1996); *R. v. MacDougall*, 3 SCR 45 (1998); *Canadian Egg Marketing Agency v. Richardson*, 3 SCR 157 (1998); *Solski (Tutor of) v. Quebec (Attorney General)*, 1 SCR 201(2005), 2005 SCC 14; *R. v. Ferguson*, 1 SCR 96, 2008 SCC 6 (2008); *Nguyen v. Quebec (Education, Recreation and Sports)*, SCC 47, 3 SCR 208 (2009). *See also* articles by Sirota and Oliphant, *supra* note 4.

[105] See Sirota and Oliphant, *Originalist Reasoning in Canadian Constitutional Jurisprudence*, *supra* note 4, and Walton, *supra* note 50, 316–32.

[106] *Reference Re Language Rights Under s 23 of Manitoba Act, 1870 & s 133 of Constitution Act* [1985] 1 SCR 721, 751. *Cf*, quotation of Iacabucci J, *supra* note 73.

The majority's decision in the *Supreme Court Reference*,[107] that Federal Court judges appointed from Quebec are ineligible for appointment to the seats reserved for Quebec judges on the Canadian Supreme Court, depend heavily on textual and historical analysis. The majority quote Nineteenth Century legislative debates to support its interpretation of the *Supreme Court Act*, which it says best gave effect to the historic compromise that led to the creation of the Supreme Court.[108]

Subsequently, in *Caron v. Alberta*, the Court split 6–3 in concluding that Alberta was not constitutionally required to print laws in French as well as English.[109] As other commentators have pointed out,[110] both the majority and minority decisions are originalist, although based on different versions of originalism. Both focus on the history of the term "legal rights" in an assurance given by Parliament that was incorporated in the Constitution. But while the majority seeks the most likely original understanding of the term, the dissent focuses on the drafters' original intention. Both decisions rely on a variety of historical evidence, from parliamentary debates to correspondence. Although the majority reiterates "the primacy of the written text of the Constitution," it emphasizes the need to anchor analysis in historical context:

> Thus, we must assess the appellants' arguments by looking at the ordinary meaning of the language used in each document, the historical context, and the philosophy or objectives lying behind the words and guarantees. We cannot simply resort to the historical evidence of the desires and demands of those negotiating the entry of the territories, and presume that those demands were fully granted. It is obvious that they were not. The Court must generously interpret constitutional linguistic rights, not create them.[111]

Although the term "originalism" is not mentioned in either case, the importance of originalist analysis to these and many other decisions is undeniable.[112] Invoking the intentions of the founders to interpret the structural features of the *Constitution*, to give effect to the "bargain" (or political compromise) that led to confederation, or even to protect minority language and education rights,[113] does not raise the sorts of morally and politically charged issues that interpretation of *Charter* rights does.

---

[107] *Reference Re: Supreme Court Act*, SCC 21 (2014) paras. 48–62, ss. 5 and 6.

[108] *Id*, paras. 47–62. Although it also refers to more contemporary constitutional debates, the Court expressly prefers the former to the latter.

[109] [2015] SCC 56.

[110] L. Sirota and B. Oliphant, *Originalist Reasoning in Canadian Constitutional Jurisprudence*, *supra* note 4.

[111] SCC 56, (2015) para. 38.   [112] *See supra* note 104.

[113] *See e.g., Reference re: Bill 30, An Act to Amend the Education Act (Ontario)*, 1 SCR 1148 (1987).

Originalism is also resorted to in Canada when it is useful in precluding evolutionary interpretations regarded as undesirable. For example, the argument against property rights is thoroughly originalist. Peter Hogg makes the argument in categorical terms: "The framers ... deliberately omitted any reference to property in s. 7,"[114] and this "striking and deliberate departure from the constitutional texts that provided the models for s. 7 ... greatly reduces its scope."[115] Hence, the *Charter* provides no protection against the taking of property. For greater certainty, Hogg adds that this requires the terms "liberty" and "security of the person" in s. 7 to be interpreted "as excluding economic liberty and economic security; otherwise, property, having been shut out of the front door, would enter by the back."[116] This is straightforward originalism, invoked not simply as a relevant consideration but as determining the constitutional question.

But originalist analysis has also proven useful in supporting an argument to *expand* the scope of protected *Charter* rights. The Court invoked the intentions of the founders to justify overruling the *Labour Trilogy*, which had held that collective bargaining was not protected by the freedom of association. In *Health Services and Support – Facilities Subsector Bargaining Assn. v. British Columbia* the Court reasoned that:[117]

> Association for purposes of collective bargaining has long been recognized as a fundamental Canadian right which predated the *Charter*. This suggests that the framers of the *Charter* intended to include it in the protection of freedom of association found in s. 2(d) of the *Charter*.

The Court's analysis seemed to blend originalist and living tree reasoning. It took into account an interpretation of the *Declaration on Fundamental Principles and Rights at Work*, 6 IHRR 285 (1999) that was settled only in 1998, partly because the *Charter* was a "living document," and partly because the Declaration was based on interpretations of prior international instruments, "many of which were adopted by the ILO prior to the advent of the *Charter* and were within the contemplation of the founders of the *Charter*."[118]

These decisions suggest that the core theses of originalism — that original meanings are fixed, and depend partly on admissible evidence of original intentions – still have purchase in Canada despite the Court's reputed rejection of originalism. Justice Ian Binnie has called this "a home-grown version of originalism that [the Court] selectively applies."[119] He also described the

---

[114] Hogg, *supra* note 1, vol II, 47.7(b).　　[115] *Id.*, 47.9.　　[116] *Id.*
[117] 2 SCR 391(2007), 2007 SCC 27, paras. 40–41.　　[118] *Id.*, para 78.
[119] *See* S. Fine, *Retired Canadian Jurists Respectfully Dissent from Scalia's Approach*, Globe and Mail, February 16 2016, available at www.theglobeandmail.com/report-on-business/industry-news/the-law-page/retired-canadian-jurists-respectfully-dissent-from-scalias-approach-style/article28762762/.

search for original intent as inevitable: "The issue, then, is not whether the intent of the originating body should be taken into account because no one who expects to be taken seriously would argue that it should not be."[120]

Australian Developments

Until 1988, the High Court adhered to the interpretive principles it had endorsed in the first two decades of its existence, including the prohibition on the use of most legislative history in interpreting the Constitution. But that prohibition led to some interpretive errors with unfortunate consequences. For example, unwilling to admit historical evidence of the intended meaning of s 92's elliptical guarantee of "absolute" freedom of interstate trade and commerce, the Court "embarked on an abstract exercise of giving an almost context-free meaning to the words of the section."[121] This turned s 92 into a partial guarantee of laissez-faire, rather than the more limited prohibition of state protectionism intended by the founders. Consequently, it became the most litigated provision of the Constitution, an obstacle to the democratic regulation of business by all political parties, a source of bitter political controversy, and the subject of continual judicial disagreement, instability and uncertainty.

In 1988 the Court in *Cole v. Whitfield* restored the section's historically intended meaning.[122] To do so, it reversed its long-standing refusal to consult the published Convention Debates and other historical evidence. But it also insisted that such material could not be used "for the purpose of substituting for the meaning of the words used the scope and effect – if such could be established – which the founding fathers subjectively intended the section to have." It could only be used to identify "the contemporary meaning of language used, the subject to which that language was directed and the nature and objectives of the movement toward federation from which the compact of the Constitution finally emerged."[123] This is tantamount to the adoption of an "original public meaning," as opposed to an "original intentions," version of originalism.[124]

[120] Binnie, *supra* note 2, at 380.
[121] M. Coper *Interstate Trade and Commerce, Freedom of* in T. Blackshield, M. Coper and G. Williams, eds, THE OXFORD COMPANION TO THE HIGH COURT OF AUSTRALIA (Oxford University Press, 2001),356.
[122] *Cole v. Whitfield* 165 CLR 360 (1988).   [123] *Id.* at 385.
[124] Accord, H. Irving, *Constitutional Interpretation, the High Court, and the Discipline of History* 41 FEDERAL L. REV. 95, 109 (2013); L K Weis, *What Comparativism Tells Us about Originalism*, 11 INT'L J. CONST. L. 843 (2013).

This decision led to a substantial increase in judicial enquiries into the original meanings of constitutional provisions.[125] These are easier to make in Australia than in Canada which, at least in relation to the *BNA Act*, lacks the same quantity and quality of historical records of the founders' deliberations.[126] Overall, the High Court has been more rather than less originalist since 1988, although this has provoked dissent.

In 1994, Deane and Toohey JJ began to refer to the Constitution as a "living instrument" or "living force" that should not be constrained by the dead hands of the founders.[127] From his appointment to the Court two years later, Kirby J mounted a sustained campaign against the principle that the contemporary meaning of the Constitution is the same as its original meaning.[128] Instead, "the *Constitution* is to be read according to contemporary understandings of its meaning, to meet, so far as the text allows, the governmental needs of the Australian people."[129] But a majority of the Court rejected Kirby J's arguments. Gleeson C.J. said:

> It is in the nature of law that rules laid down in the past, whether the past be recent or distant, bind conduct in the future. It is in the nature of a written, federal Constitution that a division of governmental power ... agreed upon in the past, binds future governments... [T]he role of a court is to understand and apply the meaning of the terms, not to alter the agreement.[130]

McHugh J insisted that the function of the judiciary was not to "amend or modernise the *Constitution*," but

> to give effect to the intention of the makers of the Constitution as evinced by the terms in which they expressed that intention. That necessarily means that decisions, taken almost a century ago by people long dead, bind the people of Australia today even in cases where most people agree that those decisions are out of touch with the present needs of Australian society.[131]

It was often observed that the proper method for keeping Constitution up-to-date was amendment by referendum.[132]

---

[125] For data, *see* Irving, *supra* note 124 at 113–14.

[126] This is one of Justice Binnie's main objections to originalism in Canada. Binnie, *supra* note 2, at 370–74.

[127] Goldsworthy, *Australia: Commitment to Legalism*, *supra* note 57, at 150–52.

[128] *Id. See also* The Hon Justice M Kirby, *Constitutional Interpretation and Original Intent: A Form of Ancestor Worship?*, 24 MELBOURNE U. L. REV. 1 (2000).

[129] *Eastman v. R.*, 203 CLR 1, 80 (2000) [242].

[130] *Singh v. Commonwealth*, 222 CLR 322, 330 (2004) [6]; *see also id.*, [295] (Callinan J).

[131] *Re Wakim, e parte McNally* (1999) 198 CLR 511, 549–50 [35]-[39].

[132] E.g., *SGH Ltd v. Federal Commissioner of Taxation*, 210 CLR 51 (2002), 75 (Gummow J).

Although the High Court seems committed to a version of public meaning originalism, it is wary of theories and, in a unanimous judgment, emphatically eschewed any "single all-embracing theory of constitutional interpretation."[133] It added that:

> Debates cast in terms like "originalism" or "original intent" (evidently intended to stand in opposition to "contemporary meaning") with their echoes of very different debates in other jurisdictions are not to the point and serve only to obscure much more than they illuminate.[134]

In an earlier case, Gummow J observed that constitutional issues "are too complex and diverse" to be resolved by any one theory, and "are not determined simply by linguistic considerations which pertained a century ago."[135] We suspect that there are various reasons for this caution.

One reason involves difficulties in applying the established principle that while the meaning of the Constitution's words cannot change, their application can.[136] Many words cannot be precisely defined by a list of criteria that are necessary and sufficient for their correct application.[137] Moreover, unexpected developments can reveal that previous beliefs about essential criteria were mistaken (as when the discovery of black swans showed that swans need not be white). Therefore, when a word enacted in 1900 must be applied to later developments unanticipated by the founders, it may be impossible to know what criteria they themselves – had they envisaged those developments – would have regarded as essential to the word's correct application.[138] The solution must lie in their apparent purpose in using the word. Thus, in deciding whether or not modern reforms to jury trials are consistent with the constitutional requirement of "trial . . . by jury," the Court recognized that although the requirement "is referable to that institution as understood at common law at the time of federation," its "essential features are to be discerned with regard to the purpose which [it] was intended to serve."[139]

Another reason for caution concerns the right to vote – unsurprisingly, given that judges required to protect rights are especially reluctant to be governed by the moral beliefs of past generations.[140] Australian judges have struggled to reconcile orthodox interpretive principles with their strong intuitive sense that if Parliament were to abolish the right of women to vote, it would violate the constitutional requirement that members of Parliament be

---

[133] *Commonwealth v. ACT*, 250 CLR 441, 455 (2013) [14]. [134] *Id.*
[135] *SGH Ltd v Federal Commissioner of Taxation* 210 CLR 51, 75 (2002) [42].
[136] Text to *supra* note 68–69. [137] Goldsworthy, *supra* note 69, at 257–62. [138] *Id.* at 259–60.
[139] *Ng v. R.*, 217 CLR 521, 526 (2003); *see also Brownlee v. R* 207 CLR 278, 298 (2001).
[140] *See* text to *supra* note 86–89.

"directly chosen by the people."[141] The question is not determined by the biological meaning of the word "people": after all, children are also people in that sense, but cannot vote. The difficulty is that, in 1900, the founders deliberately left it to Parliament to decide whether or not women would be permitted to vote (it decided in 1902 that they could). They must have believed that the term "the people" had a non-biological meaning that permitted a choice either way. But if it did, how in the absence of amendment could it no longer do so today?

Various solutions have been proposed, including the "evolving meaning" gambit.[142] But the best solution does not require rejecting originalism. When legislation gave women the right to vote in 1902, they became part of "the people" understood as those members of the community who are civically engaged and participate in public decision-making.[143] The original meaning of "the people," thus understood, did not change, but its application did.[144] Moreover, legislation to reverse that development would now be inconsistent with these crucial social facts of membership and participation, which determine the current application of "the people."

The different approaches of the High Court and the Canadian Supreme Court can be seen in the way they resolved the question of legislative power to authorize same-sex marriage. In both countries, the national Parliament has power to make laws with respect to "marriage," but in Nineteenth Century ordinary usage that word surely meant a union of a man and a woman. If so, it might seem that originalists would have to interpret the word today as excluding national power to authorize same-sex marriages.

To avoid that conclusion Canada's Supreme Court, citing Lord Sankey in the *Persons Case*, reaffirmed that "our constitution is a living tree which, by way of progressive interpretation, accommodates and addresses the realities of modern life."[145] By contrast, Australia's High Court identified a more abstract original meaning: the constitutional term "marriage," even in 1900, was a "topic of juristic classification" that included "laws of a kind 'generally considered, for comparative law and private international law, as being the

---

[141] *Commonwealth of Australia Constitution*, ss 7 and 24.

[142] *Roach v. Electoral Commissioner* (2007) 233 CLR 162, 180 and 186 (Gummow, Kirby and Crennan JJ).

[143] P. Emerton, *Political Freedoms and Entitlements in the Australian Constitution – An Example of Referential Intentions Yielding Unintended Legal Consequences*, 38 FEDERAL L. REV. 169, 195–202 (2010).

[144] See The meaning of "aliens," discussed at *supra* note 69.

[145] *Reference re Same-Sex Marriage*, 3 SCR 698, 2004 SCC 79, (2004) para 22.

subjects of a country's marriage laws.'"[146] It was, in effect, a legal term of art that included legal relationships foreign to British common law, such as polygamy. This enabled Parliament to recognize such foreign relationships as marriages,[147] and to amend Australian law in accordance with changing mores – which is, after all, a principal purpose of conferring legislative power.[148] The results in the two cases are the same, but the approaches are significantly different.

It might be objected that the High Court's attempt to show that its conclusion was consistent with original meaning was strained, barely concealing a desire to update the Constitution to accord with modern values. There are certainly other recent decisions at which that criticism could fairly be aimed.[149] But in this case, the Court's conclusion can be supported by an alternative form of originalist reasoning. If the Court was wrong about the original meaning of "marriage," then the consequence of developments in social mores unanticipated by the founders would be to frustrate their purpose in enacting the power. The purpose of granting power over "marriage" to the national Parliament was not to forbid same-sex marriages, and it could not have that effect on any interpretation. If the constitutional term "marriage" were confined to heterosexual marriage, same-sex marriages could be authorized by State legislation.

But that would defeat the founders' purpose of enabling uniform national regulation of a vitally important legal relationship underpinning family life, child rearing and social stability throughout the nation. A new legal relationship of the same kind as heterosexual marriage, and its dissolution, would have to be governed by disparate State rather than uniform national laws. That consequence would be prevented by a version of originalism that permits a word's original meaning to be incrementally extended to give effect to its original purpose. But that form of originalism would admittedly be open to abuse by pitching original purposes at a very high level of abstraction; it would therefore be difficult to confine, and is therefore controversial among originalists. It is no doubt due to such complications that the High Court has been wary of endorsing *any* particular theory of constitutional interpretation.

---

[146] *Commonwealth v. ACT*, 250 CLR 441, 455 (2013), [14] and 458–59 [20] and [22], quoting Windeyer J in *Attorney-General (Vic) v. The Commonwealth (Marriage Act Case)* 107 CLR 529, 578 (1962).

[147] *Commonwealth v. ACT, supra* note 146, 461–62 [32], [33] and [35].

[148] *Id.* at 456–59 [16]–[21].

[149] See J Goldsworthy, *Kable, Kirk and Judicial Statesmanship*, 40 MONASH U. L. REV. 75 (2014).

SOME CONSEQUENCES OF CANADA'S
REJECTION OF ORIGINALISM

Originalism has largely been ignored as a viable approach to constitutional interpretation in Canada, while debates about originalism elsewhere have generated increasingly deep and sophisticated theories on both sides.

For example, there has been a flourishing of Australian scholarly literature debating originalism and related issues.[150] This work is not linked to the politically conservative agenda of the 1980s version of American originalism rejected in Canada, which even in the US has been superseded by politically non-partisan and even "progressive" versions of originalism that focus on the Constitution's original public meaning.[151]

In the perceived absence of strong competition in Canada, "living tree" constitutionalism has remained under-theorized.[152] It is difficult to explain what it is, other than that – supposedly – it is *not* originalism. The very idea of a "living constitution" is also philosophically problematic. No less an avowed critic of originalism than Ronald Dworkin once repudiated the notion that constitutional provisions "are chameleons which change their meaning to conform to the needs and spirit of new times" as "hardly even intelligible."[153]

The rationale for living tree interpretation – the need to accommodate growth and development in response to new circumstances – does not differentiate it from contemporary public meaning originalism, which allows constitutional law to evolve for various reasons. One is that unchanging meanings can apply to technological and social developments that the founders did not anticipate.[154] A second reason is that the application of broad moral

---

[150] Space does not permit a detailed list of this literature, but contributors include Jeffrey Goldsworthy, Jeremy Kirk, Helen Irving, Natalie Stoljar, Leslie Zines, Nicholas Aroney, Greg Craven, John Williams, Michael Stokes, Lael Weis and Patrick Emerton.

[151] E. g., K. E. Whittington, Constitutional Interpretation: Textual Meaning, Original Intent, and Judicial Review (University Press of Kansas, 1999); R. E. Barnett, Restoring the Lost Constitution, The Presumption of Liberty (rev'd ed, Princeton University Press, 2014); and J. Balkin, Living Originalism (Belknap Press, Harvard, 2011); see also *Symposium, Originalism and Living Constitutionalism*, 92 B.U. L. Rev. 129 (2012). Lawrence Solum discusses the evolution of the theory in *What Is Originalism? The Evolution of Contemporary Originalist Theory* in The Challenge of Originalism, *supra* note 41, 12. See also Steven D. Smith, *That Old-Time Originalism*, in *id.*, 223.

[152] An exception is W. J. Waluchow, A Common Law Theory of Judicial Review (Cambridge University Press, 2007).

[153] R. Dworkin, *Comment*, in A. Scalia, A Matter of Interpretation, Federal Courts and the Law (Princeton University Press, 1997), 122; see also L Tribe, *Comment*, in *id.*, 73.

[154] *See* text to *supra* notes 68–69 and 80–84.

principles, including most rights, requires judges to make moral judgments independently of the founders' moral beliefs, and subject to *stare decisis* – which is less significant in constitutional rights adjudication – those judgments may change over time.[155] A third reason is that when the original meaning of a constitution is insufficiently determinate to resolve a legal dispute, creative judicial "construction" is required to add flesh – in the form of constitutional doctrine – to the bare bones of the text.[156] That doctrine may also change over time. But while the original meaning of the constitution is thereby supplemented, it is not changed.[157] A possible fourth reason would go further, and allow the original meaning of a provision to be adjusted incrementally if, due to changed circumstances, it no longer fulfills the provision's original purpose.[158] This, however, is controversial among originalists and raises difficulties requiring further examination.

For these reasons, originalism is – up to a point – perfectly consistent with living constitutionalism. Indeed, it offers the best interpretation of the Privy Council's metaphor in the *Persons Case*, that the *BNA Act* planted "a living tree capable of growth and expansion within its natural limits."[159] Originalism can explain both the "natural limits" and the "growth and expansion," whereas living constitutionalism addresses only the latter. This then enables originalism to explain the necessary limits to the recognition of "unwritten principles," and to the discovery of new rights in the context of express *Charter* rights.

The Supreme Court has not taken a consistent approach to the discovery of new rights, such as in *BC Motor Vehicle Reference*.[160] Some judges have condemned as improper, and even "dangerous,"[161] the purported discovery of rights that were deliberately omitted by the founders or are "foreign to the original purpose of the provision."[162] Yet in *Gosselin v. Quebec (Procureur general)*,[163] two dissenting judges held that s 7 of the *Charter* should be given a novel interpretation, imposing positive obligations on governments to provide

---

[155] See text to *supra* notes 86–89.
[156] L. Solum, *The Interpretation-Construction Distinction*, 27 CONST. COMMENT. 95 (2010).
[157] "The vague terms in the Constitution empower legislatures and judges to put flesh on the bones of the text, provided they don't break any of the bones": R. Barnett, *The Gravitational Force of Originalism*, 82 FORDHAM L. REV. 411, 420 (2013).
[158] See text following *supra* note 149.
[159] [1930] A.C. 124, 136 (PC), discussed at *supra* notes 48–52.
[160] *Re: B.C. Motor Vehicle Act*, 2 SCR 486 (1985), discussed at *supra* notes 99–102.
[161] *R v. Prosper*, 3 SCR 236, (1994), para 70 (L'Heureux-Dube J, dissenting).
[162] *R v. Blais*, 2 SCR 236 (2003), para 40.   [163] 4 SCR 429 (2002).

economic benefits, while the majority said that this interpretation might be adopted at some future, more opportune moment.[164]

The living tree metaphor is too vague to resolve such issues. In the absence of rigorous analysis, potentially illuminating distinctions have not been drawn. They include the differences between: (a) original public meaning, (b) original intended meaning, (c) original purpose, and (d) original expected applications. They also include the difference between "interpretation," concerned with revealing original meanings, and creative "construction," concerned mainly with developing doctrine to supplement those meanings when they are insufficiently determinate to resolve disputes.[165]

CONCLUSION

We have shown that courts applied traditional, originalist interpretive principles for many decades after the Canadian and Australian constitutions were enacted: the original meaning of those constitutions was held to be both fixed, and partly revealed by admissible evidence of the founders' intentions. But from the 1980s, while the Australian High Court continued to apply those principles, and expanded the kinds of evidence of original meaning that were admissible, the Canadian Supreme Court shifted to a form of "progressive" interpretation based on a metaphor of the constitution as a "living tree."[166]

The title of our paper asks "Why the Divergence?" The answer is clear: the Supreme Court shifted to the "living tree" metaphor in the 1980s, both to signal a break from the past and to ensure that the newly enacted *Charter* would be given a broad, progressive interpretation, rather than the narrow interpretation that the *Canadian Bill of Rights* had received. Coincidentally, across the border, originalism had become tainted by association with a conservative political agenda from which Canadian judges sought to distance themselves. Originalism had also been subjected to sustained scholarly criticism in the US, which persuaded many lawyers that it was no longer theoretically respectable.

Originalist theory, however, has evolved considerably since then, becoming more sophisticated, less vulnerable to theoretical objections, and free of

---

[164] *Id.*, paras. 317 (Arbour J.) and 82 (McLachlin C.J.C.), discussed in G. Huscroft, *Vagueness, Finiteness, and the Limits of Interpretation and Construction,* in THE CHALLENGE OF ORIGINALISM, *supra* note 41, 203, 218–22.

[165] *See* text to *supra* notes 156–157.

[166] These are the general trends; neither Court has been entirely consistent.

political bias.[167] The currently dominant "public meaning" version of originalism is consistent with both the traditional interpretive principles applied in Canada and Australia before the 1980s, and their subsequent development by the Australian High Court.

It might be doubted that the Supreme Court of Canada ever intended to repudiate those principles. As we have shown, it has continued to apply them in many cases even since the advent of the *Charter*. Moreover, the most thoughtful Canadian critics of originalism, such as Justice Binnie and Professor Hogg, clearly had in mind the 1980s American version of that doctrine. For his part, Justice Binnie seems favourably disposed to traditional interpretive principles, while Professor Hogg's critique of originalism is based on a misunderstanding of it.[168]

Moreover, the Court did not need to shift from traditional principles to the vague "living tree" metaphor. Those principles are perfectly consistent with *Charter* rights being interpreted progressively. Public meaning originalists accept that when constitutions embody moral principles, judges are not only permitted but required to make moral judgments in order to apply them, rather than counter-factual judgments about how the founders would probably have applied them.[169]

For these and other reasons, public meaning originalism is consistent with progressive interpretation, and with the metaphor of the constitution as a "living tree" whose trunk and roots are fixed.[170] The Privy Council's rightful acknowledgement that there must be "natural limits" to "growth and expansion" - that *something* must be fixed – entails the truth of some version of originalism. The alternative view, that nothing is fixed and everything is potentially open to judicial development, is hard to reconcile with any plausible rationale for a written constitution that prohibits its own future amendment except by a formal, democratic law-making procedure. See, e.g., *supra* note 98.

---

[167] In practice, originalism can have either conservative or progressive political consequences. See Y. Tew, *Originalism at Home and Abroad*, 52 COLUM. J. TRANSNAT'L L. 780 (2014).

[168] See *supra* note 2 and text to *supra* notes 81–84.   [169] See text to *supra* notes 86–89.

[170] See J Goldsworthy, *The Case for Originalism*, in THE CHALLENGE OF ORIGINALISM, *supra* n. 41, 42, 64–5.

9

Rights Inflation in Canada and the United States

MARK TUSHNET

INTRODUCTION

Proportionality review is generally acknowledged to lead to "rights inflation," whereby an individual's assertion that legislation adversely affects one of his or her interests almost always triggers substantial judicial inquiry into the question of whether the adverse effect amounts to a violation of the person's constitutional rights.[1] The term "rights inflation" seems to have a pejorative tone, but the reasons for thinking that rights inflation is a problem are a bit obscure.[2] This Chapter sketches a more analytic approach to rights inflation, in the hope that doing so will help us understand why or when the term is pejorative. By examining some aspects of relevant doctrine in the United States and Canada, we may be able to develop what I call a "cultural" account of the valence of "rights inflation" in political-legal discourse.

Rights inflation occurs, it appears, because it typically has only modest legal consequences. Consider cases involving a not-very-important interest adversely affected by legislation, or a reasonably important one on which the adverse effect is small (though not insubstantial).[3] In such cases the courts find

---

I thank Ricki-Lee Gerbrandt for very helpful research assistance.

[1] In the context of freedom of expression, see Adrienne Stone, "Canadian Constitutional Law of Freedom of Expression," text accompanying notes 9–10 [this collection].

[2] Sometimes the objection is phrased as a concern about rights *inflation* when it is actually a concern that the *substantive* rights newly protected should not actually be treated as rights. I believe that this phenomenon occurred during the development of the substantive concept of gender equality recounted in Catharine A. MacKinnon, "Substantive Equality Past and Future: The Canadian Charter Experience" [this collection].

[3] The reason for the parenthetical qualification lies in some Canadian jurisprudence to the effect that an insubstantial adverse effect on an interest does not trigger Section 1 scrutiny. See text at notes 39–41.

it easy to reject the constitutional claims on the merits, as they work through the stages of proportionality analysis. And, it is said, rights inflation is beneficial in those – perhaps rare – cases where legislation adversely affects a relatively minor interest for no particularly good reason, that is, is disproportionate even with respect to a relatively minor interest, or in cases, perhaps more frequent, where legislation has a small but discernable adverse impact on quite important interests.

This chapter contrasts rights inflation in Canadian constitutional law, where the dominant doctrine is proportionality, with the US approach to questions about constitutional limits on the regulation of relatively minor interests, or of relatively minor adverse effects on important interests, through the Due Process Clause. The Canadian and US approaches are somewhat different. Under US doctrine, that approach has, for present purposes, two stages. The first stage is a threshold inquiry: Does the legislation adversely affect a *fundamental* interest? If so, the legislation is constitutionally permissible only if it advances a compelling governmental interest and does so in a narrowly tailored way. If the legislation adversely affects an interest that is not fundamental, it is constitutionally permissible if it satisfies a weak test of minimal rationality. In contrast, the more nuanced proportionality inquiry might lead to finding a constitutional violation even with respect to relatively minor interests. Still, Canadian cases occasionally treat the question of whether a right is engaged as a threshold inquiry. Yet, where the overarching approach is proportionality, the difference between finding a right not implicated at the threshold stage and finding that a rights infringement is justified is small, certainly smaller than the difference made in US doctrine by treating the engagement (or coverage) question as a threshold question. As with much in comparative constitutional law, one can find both similarities and differences between the doctrinal approaches taken in different systems. I suggest that differences between the US and Canadian constitutional cultures may account for what differences there are.

Two themes emerge from the discussion. (1) As a doctrinal matter rights inflation (and rejecting it) may not have many consequences. Pretty much every outcome that results when rights are inflated can be reached when they are not, although reaching the same outcomes may require modest doctrinal innovation. And pretty much every outcome that is reached when rights are *not* inflated can be reached when they are, and rather little doctrinal tweaking is required to do that. (2) Concerns about rights inflation are more about constitutional, legal and political cultures than they are about doctrine or results. In consequence, they may be well-taken in some polities but not in others.

TWO TYPES OF RIGHTS INFLATION

Identifying precisely what is at stake in the discourse of rights inflation is surprisingly tricky. I think it useful to distinguish between rights inflation in connection with two types of constitutional provisions, which I imperfectly label *general* and *specific*. Examples of general provisions are the Due Process Clause of the US Constitution, the protections of human dignity and the right to free development of one's personality in the German Basic Law, and the right to life in the Indian Constitution. In many legal cultures lawyers will find it relatively easy to generate professionally acceptable arguments to the effect that these clauses should be given quite a broad range of application.[4]

Rights inflation might occur in connection with these general clauses as lawyers generate, and courts accept, arguments that a large number of specific activities fall within the provisions' coverage. Yet, it is not clear why rights inflation with respect to general clauses should be regarded with suspicion. The phenomenon is not "inflation" at all, but the simple application of the provision pursuant to its terms.

Consider, for example, the proposition that people living in a liberal democracy have a right to do whatever they want unless their actions are prohibited by a constitutionally valid law. Call this a world in which people have a general right to liberty. In such a world every statute that purports to limit one's ability to do *anything* infringes the general right to liberty, which means – only? – that someone prevented from doing what she wants can go to court to obtain a determination of the statute's constitutionality. So, for example, legislation that makes it more difficult for someone to pursue her hobby of bird watching or riding horses can be brought into question in court. In this world rights have been inflated to the greatest possible extent, and yet I find it difficult to see why one would object in principle to the recognition of a general right to liberty.[5] Here rights inflation occurs in some sense, yet hardly seems problematic. I believe that the term "rights inflation" is invoked in these contexts not because of concern for the *rights* but rather out of concern over what will count as sufficient justification for the

---

[4] Although I refer here to constitutional texts, sometimes legal cultures will acknowledge that there are nontextual rights as well. Almost necessarily such rights are general in the sense I am using.

[5] The bird watching and horse riding examples are frequent objects of derision in the literature on rights inflation, but only because the right said to be implicated – a right to pursue one's hobbies – is described at a low level of generality. If we see pursuing one's hobbies as an exercise of a general right to liberty, as I think we should, the sting of "rights inflation" would be taken away.

infringement – or, put differently, concern that courts will inappropriately require strong justifications for the infringements.

The second form of rights inflation occurs in connection with (relatively) specific constitutional provisions, particularly in constitutional systems that do not recognize a general right to liberty but only specific constitutional rights. Where a constitution contains only specific rights, those whose interests are adversely affected by legislation have an incentive to characterize what they want to do as covered by one of the enumerated rights. So, for example, a company that wants to mine data whose collection is mandated by the government for commercial purposes has an incentive to characterize limitations on its ability to gain access to that data as an infringement of its right to freedom of speech.[6] But, the thought is, the word "speech" must have *some* limits, often described as internal to the term, such that some things simply cannot be characterized as speech.[7] Consider the quite detailed provisions in the South African constitution about the conditions for pretrial detention. These provisions *must* have internal limits: It cannot be that someone could invoke those provisions as the basis for finding a statute restricting the distribution of sexually explicit materials unconstitutional.

Rights inflation in general then is inconsistent with the proposition that all specific constitutional rights have internal limits whose cumulative effect is to exclude some interests from the domain of *any* enumerated right.[8] A related concern is that litigants *faut de mieux* will do their best to fit their claims into the terms used in some specific constitutional right, and that the claim fits badly with those terms. The right to free speech, for example, is "inflated" by the litigant so that it covers data mining.

That some rights have internal limits seems reasonably clear.[9] Other terms commonly used to describe the fact of internal limits are: "Covered," as in "This activity is covered by the right"; "engaged," as in "The right is engaged here"; and "within the ambit" or "within the sphere" of the right. Yet, the question of what exactly a provision covers is often a difficult one. The US

---

[6] *Sorrell v. IMS Health*, 564 US 552 (2011).

[7] See *Baier v. Alberta*, 2 R.C.S. 673, 709 (2007) (reasons of LeBel, J.) ("Charter rights ... are usually broad and often overlapping. Nevertheless, they are not formless and boundless.")

[8] The image here is one of a series of circles of constitutional coverage, which cumulatively do not cover the entire range of human activities. Note that the general right to liberty *does* cover that entire range.

[9] One example from the Canadian literature involves constitutional protection against – in terms – unreasonable searches. One can challenge a particular search as unreasonable, but cannot claim that a search that is concededly reasonable violates this constitutional provision (though it might violate some other provision).

Constitution guarantees freedom of "speech." The US Supreme Court has struggled with cases involving what it calls expressive conduct, but it has not struggled with perhaps more obvious linguistic difficulties about treating abstract art and instrumental music as "speech," assuming that such activities are covered by a provision referring only to speech.[10] Similarly, are modern forms of remote surveillance "searches"?

WHY BE CONCERNED ABOUT RIGHTS INFLATION? A POLITICO-CULTURAL ACCOUNT

Rights inflation occurs when the terms used in specific constitutional provisions are stretched to cover things not plausibly covered by those terms. Here the word "plausibly" does a great deal of work. Critics of rights inflation seem to assume that they can readily identify when a claim about a term's coverage is implausible. I suggest, though, that the criterion of plausibility is not a linguistic one but rather one arising within particular political-legal cultures, and that plausibility can vary over time. So, for example, a claim that is implausible at one time – for example, that commercial solicitations are covered by guarantees of freedom of speech, or that remote surveillance is a search – can become plausible, and even obviously true, at some later time. Further, litigants' claims about a specific provision's coverage can have an effect on the political-legal culture – can contribute to making previously implausible claims plausible. Seen in this way the concern about rights inflation is an intervention in ongoing efforts to transform or preserve an existing political-legal culture.

Critics of rights inflation sometimes offer an account along the following lines to support their intervention. They acknowledge, as they must, that rights inflation involves claims about a specific provision's coverage and not about the protection it affords. To say that advocacy of violence is covered by a guarantee of free speech is not thereby to say that the guarantee actually protects those who advocate violence, that is, that they have a constitutionally based defence against a prosecution for advocating violence.[11] Yet, critics suggest, the distinction between coverage and protection is difficult to sustain in ordinary (even ordinary legal) discourse. One finds judges saying that some

---

[10] For discussion, *see* Mark Tushnet, Joseph Blocher, and Alan Chen, FREE SPEECH BEYOND WORDS (2017).

[11] They might have such a defense, as they would in the United States, but that is a question to be resolved on the merits, not by saying that the words they uttered were not covered by the First Amendment.

activity is not covered by a specific provision when they mean that it is not protected by that provision, for example. In proportionality doctrine, the distinction between coverage and protection is mirrored by a distinction between an infringement on a right and a violation of that right. But, it is said, the distinction between infringements and violations is "not well understood by non-jurists"[12] or even, sometimes, by jurists.[13] Rather than saying that a right is infringed and asking whether the infringement is unjustified so that the right is violated, for example, judges sometimes say that the right is violated and then ask whether the violation is justified,

The overall picture, then, would be something like this: Rights inflation requires the development of a distinction between coverage and protection or between infringement and violation, but such distinctions are difficult to communicate to both non-jurists and jurists. In the political-legal culture, the idea of rights violations will take hold, and people will come to believe that the inflated claims of rights are claims about rights violations (not infringements). At this point two competing – and inconsistent – accounts of the political effects of the language of rights inflation are offered.

The first is this: Often enough, people will think that, though a right is infringed, in the circumstances it is a mistake to see a rights violation, as when a statute seems to place reasonable limits on the exercise of a relatively minor "right." This will lead to "a cheapening of rights," which is particularly troubling if it is extended to what might be thought to be the core of rights such as political expression.[14] A related concern is that rights inflation means that we no longer have a distinct category of rights. Expansion of specific rights via inflation, or the acknowledgement of a general right to liberty, means that almost any adverse impact on any interest counts as an infringement of rights. Again, infringements are not always violations, but rights inflation means that we can no longer distinguish between interests and rights – and, it is said, such a distinction is an important one even at a threshold stage prior to analysis of whether an infringement is a violation.

[12] Bradley W. Miller, "Justification and Rights Limitations," in Expounding the Constitution: Essays in Constitutional Theory (Grant Huscroft ed. 2008), 93, 96. See also Kai Möller, "Proportionality and Rights Inflation," in Proportionality and the Rule of Law: Rights, Justification, Reasoning (Grant Huscroft et al. eds 2014), 155, 171 ("ordinary citizens without legal training could occasionally get confused about rights").
[13] Guy Régimbald & Dwight Newman, The Law of the Canadian Constitution 521 (2013) ("The term 'violated' is sometimes used at this step of the analysis, but can be deceptive because a 'violation' at this stage is not the end of the matter and does not imply a constitutional 'violation'. It is less pejorative to speak of an 'infringement' of the right.").
[14] Dwight Newman, *Canadian Proportionality Analysis: 5 ½ Myths*, Supreme Court Law Review (forthcoming 2016), manuscript p. 8.

The competing account treats the rhetoric of rights inflation as validating rather than cheapening rights. The distinction between rights and interests is said to be important because of how claims of rights-violation function in political-legal cultures. As Miller puts it in connection with claims about discrimination, "the declaration [that a right to nondiscriminatory treatment has been infringed] is a powerful tool in the campaign for social recognition."[15] And, the argument goes, that remains true even if the infringement is ultimately found to be justified – that is, even if the right to nondiscriminatory treatment has not been violated.

It is worth noting that the arguments canvassed to this point are mostly about how rights-claims function in public or political or legal discourse, and are fundamentally empirical. It would be useful to have evidence about whether in fact jurists and non-jurists are confused about the distinction between infringements and violations, and about whether the acknowledgement that a right has been infringed but not violated is actually a powerful tool. I am skeptical about these empirical claims, though they may be accurate in some contexts, inaccurate in others.[16] That skepticism, or determination of the accuracy of the accounts, can be validated only through a kind of cultural inquiry that, I believe, might be quite revealing.

RIGHTS INFLATION: A DOCTRINAL ACCOUNT

A different set of concerns about rights inflation deals with the legal *effects* of subsuming all interests into the category of rights. Here Canadian law and US law diverge. Finding that a statute infringes a right – or that an activity is covered by a right – triggers an inquiry into whether the infringement is justified. As noted in the Introduction, in the United States, such a finding triggers a relatively stringent test for justification, while in Canada it triggers proportionality review. But, often statutes cannot pass the stringent test of compelling interest and narrow tailoring, and yet seem either justified, or within the permissible bounds of legislative choice, or such minor infringements as not to warrant the use of the heavy artillery of constitutional invalidation.

Where rights infringements trigger a stringent test, the obvious solution is to distinguish between interests whose infringements trigger the stringent

---

[15] Miller, *supra* note 13, at 97.
[16] I acknowledge that judges sometimes incautiously refer to infringements as violations – but then go on to determine whether the thing they are talking about, however described, is justified. What such confusions communicate to the political-legal culture is unclear to me.

standard – and call them and only them rights, or call them fundamental rights – and interests whose infringement can be justified by some less stringent test. But, as Canadian law shows, there is no need to draw such a distinction if the test triggered by a finding of an infringement is not necessarily stringent. Proportionality review is precisely that – not stringent when stringency is not appropriate, as when the interest adversely affected is a relatively minor one, and stringent when stringency is appropriate. Rather than using the importance or fundamentality to trigger different standards of review, proportionality review is a unitary test that incorporates importance at the stage of determining whether the infringement is justified.

The comparison with the United States is this: Suppose someone says that a specific interest is not fundamental as a matter of US constitutional law (and therefore infringements trigger only rational basis review). That assertion will be backed up by reasons explaining why the interest is not fundamental. But, in proportionality analysis, those reasons, whatever they are, are relevant to determining whether the infringement is justified. In short, proportionality analysis addresses concerns about finding rights violated "too often" by building the reasons for justified infringements into the analysis on the merits. We can describe the difference between the US and Canadian approaches in terms of thresholds. In the United States, determining whether a right is engaged or not is a threshold inquiry, with one form of analysis – rationality review – appropriate before the threshold is crossed and another, stringent review, after. In Canada there is in general no threshold, and only the single analytic mode, proportionality, for every rights claim.

Before examining US and Canadian law in more detail, I note one advantage the latter has over the former. Sometimes, for reasons to be discussed, legislatures enact statutes that adversely affect relatively minor interests – infringe on rights that are not fundamental in the US sense – but that are really not well-justified as a matter of public policy.[17] A proportionality test allows courts to invalidate some of these statutes by finding, to put it informally, that the amount of social good the statute does is smaller than the adverse effect on the admittedly not all that important private interest. As structured today, US law lacks the resources to reach similar cases, at least without substantial analytic work.[18]

---

[17] Occupational licensing laws are a good example.

[18] There is a small-ish literature urging revision of the current standard – rational basis review – for addressing infringements of non-fundamental rights. For an advocate's version, *see* Clark Neily, TERMS OF ENGAGEMENT: HOW OUR COURTS SHOULD ENFORCE THE CONSTITUTION'S PROMISE OF LIMITED GOVERNMENT (2013).

THE UNITED STATES: RIGHTS-CHARACTERIZATION
AS A THRESHOLD QUESTION

Why have US constitutional lawyers and judges resisted the adoption of an analytic structure that leads to rights inflation? Note that the term is "resisted," not "avoided." Rights inflation of a sort has occurred in connection with some specific constitutional rights, as my prior allusions to the law of free speech and of searches suggest. It is true, of course, that constitutional scholars today retain the sense that there are some activities than cannot plausibly be described as expressive, and similarly with other internally limited constitutional rights.[19] In my view, though, this is a historically contingent matter, not one tied to constitutional texts as such, and so the sources of resistance in the United States must be identified through a historical or sociological inquiry. Here I speculate about what that inquiry might reveal.

For the United States, the general constitutional provision that might be inflated is of course the Due Process Clause, and the primary source of resistance to its inflation seems to me reasonably clear.[20] The shorthand is "*Lochner* and *Roe*." Both progressives and conservatives can identify occasions on which the Due Process Clause was, in their view, inappropriately inflated. Yet, the historical or cultural account of resistance has to grapple with the flip side of that observation: Both progressives and conservatives can identify occasions on which the clause was quite appropriately inflated. My speculation is that the US legal culture is committed enough to a certain type of proceduralized discourse – and is somewhat uncomfortable with a directly substantive discourse – with the effect that conservatives are uncomfortable about making the argument that rights should be inflated in a rightward direction and progressives are similarly uncomfortable about making the argument that they should be inflated leftward. The result is pushback against rights inflation on the ground that it is rights inflation (rather than that it is rights inflation in an undesirable direction), imputations of bad faith to advocates of right inflation in only one direction, and – I think – a sense among such advocates that the imputations are not entirely misplaced.

---

[19] I regularly use the example of someone who seeks to open a locavore grocery store in an area zoned for residential use only, believing that operating locavore grocery stores communicates important messages against the evils of factory farming. I have no doubt that the zoning rule would be found not to violate the First Amendment, but most people, I believe, think that the claim should not even trigger First Amendment scrutiny.

[20] One could substitute other doctrines for the textual Due Process Clause: a somewhat nontextual right to privacy, for example, or a nontextual right to personal autonomy.

Contemporary free speech doctrine in the United States is often described in terms resonant of the rights-inflation claim. Matters historically left outside the First Amendment's coverage, notably commercial speech, are now not only within its scope, but regulation of commercial speech often seems subject in practice to a stringent standard of review, precisely what one would expect from the US threshold approach to constitutional rights. So, for example, the argument that requiring that sellers of food products identify the nations of origin of those products violates the First Amendment is plausible,[21] and the argument that compelling sellers of tobacco products to display vivid messages bringing home the health consequences of smoking violates the First Amendment was accepted by a prominent appeals court.[22]

Free speech and abortion rights are "big" political issues, and perhaps it is not surprising to discover resistance to rights inflation if the effect is juridification of such issues. As the Introduction suggests, I find resistance at the low end, so to speak, more interesting. Here the relevant cases involve occupational licensing. Some such regulations are widely regarded as unsound public policy.[23] Constitutional doctrine in the United States treats the right to pursue one's chosen profession or occupation as a non-fundamental right or as a mere interest, subject only to weak rational basis review. And, from the point of view of those who would uphold such regulations, that is a good thing. Some of the regulations could not survive any more intense review because they do not serve compelling interests or do so in a narrowly tailored way.

Licensing regimes are among those most often criticized as mere market-protecting devices, and licensing of cosmetologists, which appears to be rather widespread, and of flower arrangers, which is not, are prime candidates for that criticism. And, indeed, it is sometimes difficult to defend specific occupational licensing requirements on the ground that they serve some general public interest. More often, the requirements result from ordinary interest group lobbying, where interest groups assure politicians of the groups' support in the next election if the politicians give the interest groups the protections they want.

---

[21] *American Meat Institute v. US Dep't of Agriculture*, 760 F.3d 18 (D.C. Cir. 2014) (upholding the requirement over two dissents).
[22] *R.J. Reynolds Tobacco Co. v. FDA*, 696 F.3d 1205 (D.C. Cir. 2012).
[23] That the concern with occupational licensing is not a concern only for conservatives is indicated by a report from the (Obama) White House, "Occupational Licensing: A Framework for Policymakers," available at www.whitehouse.gov/sites/default/files/docs/licensing_report_final_nonembargo.pdf.

The fact that a licensing regime is special-interest legislation should not alone be a ground for finding that the regulation violates the Constitution because there may be plausible public interest purposes for the licensing scheme. Cosmetologists sometimes use chemicals that are dangerous to them and their customers, and the dangers are not always apparent. One public interest purpose for licensing cosmetologists might then be to ensure that practitioners are aware of the dangers and know how to use the materials safely. For present purposes I will treat this as a reasonably plausible public interest purpose for requiring that cosmetologists obtain licences. The case for licensing flower arrangers is less clear, but here is one candidate for a public interest purpose: Sometimes flowers and the soil in which they might be potted are infested with insects that are dangerous to humans or that might spread disease to other plants and trees. A licensing system might be used to ensure that flower arrangers know how to identify insect infestations and know what to do with them. For myself, I would treat this as "barely plausible," but above some minimal threshold, although for present purposes it would not matter if we were to treat the justification as not plausible at all. So, as a matter of US constitutional doctrine, these licensing regimes might well be constitutionally permissible.

Critics of these aspects of occupational licensing respond that they actually are not justified in public policy terms, and should be invalidated. The difficulty here is doctrinal and political. On the level of doctrine, the problem is that some aspects of occupational licensing might be justified while others are not, and the two tests available in US constitutional doctrine do not readily allow for the kind of differentiation that would let courts separate the justified regulations from the unjustified ones.[24] One obvious response, of course, would be to adopt a doctrine that allows for such differentiation – as proportionality does. Alternatively, one might end up thinking that there are enough justified licensing regulations (or at least enough as to which the public policy arguments in favour are strong enough to leave regulation to legislative choice) that courts would mess up the overall system if they tried – and inevitably failed to some extent – to differentiate among regulations.[25]

---

[24] Perhaps one could fit the challenges into the traditional framework by saying that, even with respect to non-fundamental rights legislation must satisfy a test of rationality, and that it is irrational to require, for example, more than a demonstration that cosmetologists know the characteristic dangers associated with the products they use – a test of knowledge rather than a requirement that cosmetologists pursue an extensive training course.

[25] I should note that I am attracted to these second-order institutional arguments, but that many others find them insensitive to the real unfairness that they perpetuate.

The political dimension to resistance to rights inflation may be more important than the doctrinal one. As a matter of simple empirical fact, there are people who engage in political action to advance what they understand to be a general public interest, and others who engage in such action to advance what they understand to be their own special interests. This creates some difficulties for the analysis of specific items of legislation taken in isolation from a larger legislative program.

It is easy to describe the general problem. In a polity where interest groups play a large role in the political process – a "pluralist" polity – tradeoffs occur. The lobbying arm for cosmetologists says, "We will support this obviously important public policy – building roads, national defense, whatever – but only if you support our special-interest licensing rules." Judicial invalidation of some of the licensing rules would disrupt the pluralist bargaining process, as special interest groups learned that the deals they reached in the legislature would be undone by the courts – and so they would not make the deals in the first place, thereby impeding the adoption of good policies.[26]

To summarize, first with respect to occupational licensing, which might be thought a promising domain for rights inflation, and then more generally: Occupational licensing would seem to be a good candidate for abandoning or loosening the US approach to rights violations, because some occupational licensing requirements have a substantial adverse impact on people's ability to pursue their chosen occupation, and yet accomplish relatively little public good. Yet, doing so might well destabilize the interest group bargaining, pluralist policy-making process characteristic of the United States. Resisting rights inflation might then be one form that the desire to preserve such a process takes.

More generally, the US policy-making process is pluralist one in which interest group bargaining plays an important role across a wide range of policies, not confined to "special interest" legislation of concern to particular interest groups. Rights inflation would increase the amount and intensity of judicial consideration of enacted statutes. And, to the extent that rights infla-tion was accompanied by more judicial invalidation of statutes, that would alter the pluralist policy-making process, pushing it in a more deliberative direction. Such an alteration might be desirable, but the US constitutional culture is one in which it is thought that such changes ought to emanate from "ordinary" politics rather than from the courts.

---

[26] One further dynamic effect should be noted: Were courts regularly to undo interest group deals, interest groups might not participate in the political process. Or, put differently, judicial invalidation of interest group deals might in the long run transform a pluralist polity into a different type.

To end this section on a comparative note: One might find more resistance to rights inflation in the United States than in Canada (and elsewhere) because the US policy-making process is more pluralist, as I have described it, than the policy-making process in Canada and other nations. Imposing a requirement of something close to deliberative rationality would be more disruptive of ordinary politics in the United States than it would be in Canada, where – so the speculation would go – the policy-making process is already substantially deliberative, with only occasional intrusions of pluralist bargaining. This is of course entirely speculative.

CANADA: RIGHTS INFLATION AND PROPORTIONALITY

Committed to proportionality review, Canada's Supreme Court is a prime candidate for rights inflation, and it is my impression – difficult though it is to confirm – that rights inflation has in fact occurred there. An example is *Saskatchewan Federation of Labour v. Saskatchewan*, where the Supreme Court held that the Charter's guarantee of freedom of association protected the right of public employees to strike.[27]

In some ways, then, the more interesting cases are those in which the Court found, or noted in dicta or individual justices found, a Charter right not infringed, not engaged, or otherwise below some threshold (and so did not move on to the step of determining whether the legislation at issue was justified as proportional). The canonical language is from *Irwin Toy*: "The first step asks whether the activity is within the protected sphere of free expression."[28] The cases of interest here are those that are stopped at this first step. An example is *R. v. Khawaja*, an antiterrorism case.[29] Prior cases had held that actual violence – presumably even in the service of a political goal – was not covered by the Charter's guarantee of freedom of expression. Chief Justice McLachlin wrote in *Khawaja* that "the exclusion of violence from the s. 2(b) guarantee of free expression extends to threats of violence," because such threats, "like violence, undermine the rule of law ... the very values and social conditions that are necessary for the continued existence of freedom of expression." So, "Threats of violence fall outside the s. 2(b) guarantee of free expression."[30] This is the language of internal limits, of absence of coverage rather than of lack of protection.[31]

---

[27] 2015 SCC 4, 1 SCR 245 (2015).　　[28] 1 SCR 927 (1989).　　[29] 3 SCR 555 (2012).
[30] *Id.* at 585–86.
[31] Illustrating the point made by critics of rights inflation about the difficulty of maintaining consistent usage, the Chief Justice did write, as well, that "Neither [violence nor threats of violence] are worthy of *protection*," and that "counselling ... [unlawful violent action] can find no *protection* under s. 2(b)." *Id.* at 585, 587 (emphasis added).

Exactly why the Chief Justice pursued this course rather than finding that restrictions on threats of violence are typically justified by the proportionality test is unclear. That is particularly so because, as my discussion of rights inflation as a general phenomenon suggests, the reasons she gives for finding threats of violence outside the scope of freedom of expression are perfectly good reasons for finding that punishment of threats of violence is generally justified – and her approach has the disadvantage of ruling out the possibility that one might occasionally find a threat of violence uttered in circumstances where it does not in fact undermine the values and conditions necessary for maintaining a system of free expression.

Perhaps the fact that *Khwaja* was a case involving unquestionable terrorism distorted the Court's articulation of doctrine. A comparison with US doctrine dealing with true threats is instructive. Under US law, threats of violence are covered by the First Amendment, but they are not protected when they are true threats rather than, for example, hyperbolic metaphoric statements.[32] In Chief Justice McLachlin's terms, true threats do undermine the values she identifies. I assume that Chief Justice McLachlin would, in an appropriate case, confine the exclusion of threats of violence to real threats or some similarly narrowly defined category.[33] If so, it is unclear what the exclusion accomplishes. The things one would take into account in determining whether a restriction on threats of violence was justified after crossing the threshold are merely transferred to the definitional determination, done before crossing the threshold, of whether the threats were true threats (or whatever the definitional exclusion requires). As I have suggested, the doctrinal consequences of avoiding rights inflation seem relatively small, and probably not beneficial.

That conclusion is supported as well by *Baier v. Alberta*, which upheld the exclusion of school teachers from eligibility to sit on school boards anywhere in the province, not just – as had been the case – on the school boards for the jurisdictions where they were employed.[34] Noting that "governments should not be required to justify every exclusion or regulation of expression under s. 1," Justice Rothstein referred to a series of cases that the Court had characterized as involving claims for "a positive right to be provided with a specific means of expression."[35] Those cases resulted in an approach

---

[32] See especially *Watts v. United States*, 394 US 705 (1969) (finding no true threat in the statement, "If they ever make me carry a rifle the first man I want to get in my sights is L.B.J.").

[33] See *Khajawa*, at 586–87 ("The particular nature of the enumerated conduct justifies treating counselling . . . to that conduct as being *intimately connected* to violence") (emphasis added).

[34] 2 SCR 673 (2007).   [35] *Id.*, at 685–86.

crystallized in *Dunmore v. Ontario.*[36] For present purposes, the important component of the *Dunmore* test – which, again, operates as a threshold that must be satisfied before the challenger puts the state to the task of justification – is that the challenger must "demonstrate[e] that exclusion from a statutory regime permits a substantial interference" with protected activity, or that "the purpose of the exclusion was to infringe such activity."[37] When juxtaposed to the analysis that would occur were the state required to justify an infringement, this component seems a bit peculiar. For example, proportionality analysis requires the court to ask whether the statute advances a permissible purpose, and I would think that the purpose of infringing expressive activity, standing alone, would never be permissible.[38] And, the "substantial interference" requirement is almost transparently the importation of concerns expressly taken into account in proportionality analysis into a threshold inquiry about coverage and infringement.

Baier exemplifies another form of resistance to rights inflation – the development of a highly elaborated doctrinal structure. One can find cases in which judges write that a Charter right is "engaged" or the regulated activity is "within the ambit" of the Charter right, but then hold that the right is not even infringed.[39] In one such case, the judge offered five reasons for that conclusion, including that "the appellants have the ability to freely express their dissenting views."[40] Here too such an observation would easily fit into proportionality analysis.

One can fairly wonder whether anything useful is accomplished by all this. Why not say that the Charter right is indeed infringed, but that the infringement is quite easily justified because the impact on the Charter right is insubstantial? Two possibilities suggest themselves. The first is that, at least in concept, a proportionality analysis might lead to invalidation even if the

---

[36] 3 SCR 1016 (2001). *Dunmore* itself deals with whether an exclusion from a statutory scheme is governmental action subject to constitutional evaluation, but the Supreme Court has used *Dunmore* in formulating its approach to determining when the Charter requires that the government provide a speaker with a platform for speech.

[37] *Baier*, at 690.

[38] One complication should be noted: Suppose that the only purpose revealed by ordinary methods of determining legislative purpose is an impermissible one. Could the courts nonetheless ask whether some permissible purpose, not present in the legislative mind (or whatever metaphor one chooses to describe ordinary inquiries into legislative purpose) can be imputed to the legislation. The case *for* imputing permissible[purposes is that, once the legislature knows that its legislation will survive constitutional review if only it has the imputed purpose, it will insert the imputed purpose into the statute even though the purpose is not at all a motivation for the statute's enactment.

[39] See *McAteer v. Canada*, 2014 ONCA 578 (2014).   [40] *Id.*, ¶86.

rights infringement is quite small, if the degree to which the government's permissible interests are advanced is even less substantial. And, one might think, that could describe *Baier* itself. One can fairly easily see why the public interest in developing good education policy is advanced by excluding the very teachers who would be affected by the policy – that is, the original arrangement in Alberta. It is more difficult to see how that interest is advanced by excluding someone who teaches in Drumheller from sitting on the school board in Calgary. Still, one might then fairly wonder why the statute should *not* be invalidated.[41]

The second possibility emerges from the language in *Dunmore, Baier* and related cases. The Court characterizes those cases as ones in which the claimant is seeking a positive right – of access to what the Court calls a "statutory platform," a platform the creation of which is optional with the government. The Court may be interested in developing some sort of threshold inquiry in such cases for several reasons. Governments engage in a large number of positive programs that have some expressive dimension.[42] Without a threshold test the courts would have to evaluate a perhaps large number of claims of expressive access to such programs on the merits.[43] And, even though many might be dismissed rather easily using proportionality analysis, some might require complex analyses – only to yield the conclusion that the rights infringements occasioned by the programs are indeed justified. It might be better to cut the inquiry short by using a threshold test even if, as might be true in *Baier*, a proportionality anlaysis would lead to finding a particular infringement unjustified.

In addition, it is easy to characterize rights infringements associated with the construction of statutory platforms as conditions on the definition of the platforms themselves. Doing so then leads one to ask whether the condition is

---

[41] The government argued that the exclusion from eligibility "was avoidance of conflict of interest," *Baier*, at 700, but it is not at all obvious that conflicts of interest will arise when teachers who live in Drumheller sit on the Calgary school board any more frequently than conflicts of interest arise in connection with Calgary school board members who are building contractors, owners of stationery stores, and the like.

[42] I note the well-known difficulties associated with drawing the line between negative and positive rights. In *Baier*, Justice Rothstein described a statute prohibiting school board members "from criticizing government underfunding of schools" as implicating a "typically negative right." *Baier*, at 696. Suppose, though, that the statute provided that only those who supported the present levels of funding, or lower ones, were eligible to run for the school board. Would someone challenging that statute be claiming a positive right of access to a statutory platform?

[43] See *Baier*, at 703 ("The platform approach strikes an appropriate balance by maintaining this Court's traditional broad approach to freedom of expression, without constitutionalizing a positive obligation on governments to provide platforms of expression except in unusual circumstances."). Note again how easy it would be to incorporate that line into a s. 1 proportionality analysis.

an unconstitutional one. Experience in the United States with the doctrine of unconstitutional conditions is not a happy one, and a threshold test keeps the courts from even attempting to develop such a doctrine.

Finally, and Somewhat related to the concern about unconstitutional conditions, these programs are optional with the government. Were the government required to eliminate a rights violation by expanding the program – for example, by allowing those who teach in Drumheller to run for the Calgary school board – it might not create the program in the first place.[44] That might be a loss to good public policy, for example in limiting the scope of democratic governance in connection with education. Better, it might be thought, to have many people eligible to run for school board positions, even if teachers may not, than to eliminate school board elections entirely.[45] A threshold inquiry accomplishes that result.

Finally, and with implications beyond the context of free expression, the requirement that there be a statutory platform before one asks whether a right is infringed may rest upon an ideological rooted opposition to the proposition that the government is ever under a constitutional duty to create such platforms. If so, the requirement has a political valence to the extent that "left" leaning programs involve new statutory platforms whereas "right" leaning ones seek to expand the domain of market institutions and so rarely require new statutory platforms. Rights inflation is then constrained toward the left but not toward the right.[46]

CONCLUSION

Rights inflation has occurred in Canada, with its characteristic proportionality doctrine, and in the United States, where constitutional analysis distinguishes between tiers of review. And, in Canada question of whether a right is engaged

---

[44] *See Haig v. Canada*, 2 SCR 995 (1993) (holding that the Charter did not require that the right to vote in a referendum be extended to all possible voters); *Baier*, at 684 ("To hold otherwise would mean that once a government had created a statutory platform, it could never change or repeal it without infringing s. 2(b) and justifying such changes under s. 1."). I note that I do not know whether provinces are under some presumably constitutional obligation to run schools through elected school boards. If they are, the particular example would not work, but the general point would remain valid with respect to programs whose creation is truly optional.

[45] Here too constitutional culture might matter. Responding to invalidation by eliminating the program seems rather similar to "reading down" a statute to eliminate discrimination. And (again speculatively), it seems to me that Canadian constitutional culture seems more receptive to "reading up" than to reading down, whereas reading down seems relatively more acceptable in US constitutional culture. For a recent example of reading down, see *Sessions v. Morales-Santana*, No. 15-1191, Oct. Term, 2016, United States Supreme Court, Jun. 12, 2017.

[46] Patrick Macklem suggested this possibility in a comment on an earlier version of this Chapter.

sometimes operates as a threshold question, as the question of coverage always does in the United States. Does this mean that the structure of constitutional doctrine in both nations is the same? No, because doctrinal structures can "overlap" and resemble each other without being the same. The threshold inquiry is more common, and more important, in the United States than in Canada, and when it occurs in Canada it is manifestly less important to outcomes than in the United States.

I have suggested that some aspects of constitutional culture, such as the degree to which each nation is committed to the idea that public policy results from self-interested bargaining rather than deliberation over the public good, may account for these differences. Of course constitutional cultures are not sharply distinguishable in a world with substantial legal and cultural interchange, such as occurs between the United States and Canada. We should not expect to discover dramatic consequences from differences in constitutional culture. Perhaps, though, inquiring into rights inflation in Canada and the United States can suggest some modest conclusions about constitutional culture in each nation.

10

Substantive Equality Past and Future

The Canadian Charter Experience

CATHARINE A. MACKINNON

"Equality is a protean word."

John H. Schaar[1]

Andrews v. The Law Society of British Columbia,[2] in 1989, the first equality decision under Canada's new Charter of Rights and Freedoms, marks the first time the Aristotelian formal equality approach, revolving around sameness and difference, was explicitly rejected in law.[3] Substantive equality – predicated on but not limited to the situation of women – was expressly argued and embraced as the preferable paradigm, its substantive content turning on change in the lived inequalities of historically disadvantaged groups defined by concrete grounds. To this end, equality claims under section 15 of the Charter were subjected to "the purposive approach," meaning assessed "bearing in mind that the purpose ... to promote the equality of those who have been disadvantaged"[4] – in other words, concretely, generous in relief, change-oriented and asymmetrically.[5] The factual inquiry into substantive

Jessica Eisen and Daniel Del Gobbo provided extremely helpful comments on an earlier draft. Nayoung Kim assisted with technical aspects. The University of Michigan Law Library makes my work possible.

[1] John Schaar, EQUALITY OF OPPORTUNITY AND BEYOND, IN NOMOS IX: EQUALITY (J. Roland Pennock & John W. Chapman, eds., Atherton Press, 1967), 228.

[2] *Andrews v. Law Society of British Columbia*, 1 SCR 143 (1989).

[3] *Id.* at 166 (rejecting "the similarly situated test [which] is a restatement of the Aristotelian principle of formal equality" as "seriously deficient" in that it would justify "the Nuremberg laws of Adolf Hitler" or "the formalistic separate but equal doctrine.")

[4] *Id.* ¶ 33.

[5] An asymmetrical equality approach, so termed, is expressly argued to my knowledge for the first time to a court of law in Women's Legal Education and Action Fund, *Andrews v. The Law Society of British Columbia and the Attorney General of British Columbia*, in Equality And The Charter: Ten Years Of Feminist Advocacy Before The Supreme Court Of Canada 3 (Emond Montgomery Publications Ltd., 1996) ("*Andrews* factum") ¶ 36.

inequality, as proposed by the factum whose main features were embraced by the Court in *Andrews*,[6] was to be guided by the relation of the claim to an enumerated ground, the institutionalization of the ground or practice throughout society "so as to affect, in a systematic and cumulative way, dignity, respect, access to resources, physical security, credibility, membership in community, or power," and whether the group making the claim has "a social history of disempowerment, exploitation, and subordination to and by dominant interests."[7]

Despite its firm rejection of formal equality, Mr. Justice McIntyre's *Andrews* opinion, with the majority agreeing in his articulation of the equality principle, thought equality "an elusive concept [that] lacks precise definition."[8] In the subsequent defining *Law* case ten years later, the Court majority still thought that section 15 "is perhaps the Charter's most conceptually difficult provision."[9] That the Supreme Court of Canada discerns the distinction between substantive and formal equality has been made clear recently, for example, in its *Withler* admonition of 2011: "care [is] needed to avoid converting inquiry into substantive equality into formalistic and arbitrary" analysis.[10] Yet many judges and legal scholars have found substantive equality's central "single principle" to continue to "resist capture" after almost thirty years.[11]

Hierarchy is that central principle, defining the substance of inequality. Hierarchy is what is unequal about inequality in substance. Social hierarchy encompasses categories of humanity that rank above over below, more above less, higher above lower, dominant over subordinate, advantaged over disadvantaged, supreme or superior above inferior, visible over invisible, valued

---

6   See, e.g., *Andrews* factum, ¶¶ 23, 24, 28, 64 & 68. *See also* Catharine A. MacKinnon, SEXUAL
    HARASSMENT OF WORKING WOMEN: A CASE OF SEX DISCRIMINATION 106–141 (Yale, 1979);
    Catharine A. MacKinnon, *Difference and Dominance: On Sex Discrimination, in,* Feminism
    Unmodified: Discourses on Life and Law 32 (Harvard, 1987) ("Difference and Dominance");
    Catharine A. MacKinnon, National Meeting of Equality-Seeking Groups in Ottawa, Canada
    18 (Jan. 13–16, 1989) ("the alternate view that could change things is best pursued ... through a
    substantive analysis of each particular inequality") (unpublished manuscript) (on file with
    author); Sheila McIntyre, *Timely Interventions: MacKinnon's Contribution to Canadian
    Equality Jurisprudence,* 46 TULSA L. REV. 81 (2010).
7   *Andrews* factum at ¶ 50.   8   *Andrews*, at 164.
9   *Law v. Canada (Minister of Employment and Immigration)*, 1 SCR 497, 507 (1999); Ontario *v.*
    M. & H., 171 DLR (4th) 577 (1999).
10 *Withler v. Canada (Attorney General)*, 1 SCR 396, 401, 413 (2011) (referring to abstraction in
    search of "proper" comparator group) (emphasis added).
11 Sandra Fredman, *Substantive Equality Revisited,* 14:3 Int'l J. Con. L. (I.Con) 712 (2016). For fuller
    discussion, *see* Catharine A. MacKinnon, "*Substantive Equality Revisited: A Reply to Sandra
    Fredman,*" 14:3 I.Con 739 (2016); Sandra Fredman, "*Substantive Equality Revisited: A Rejoinder
    to Catharine MacKinnon,*" 14:3 I.Con 747 (2016); Catharine A. MacKinnon, "*Substantive
    Equality Revisited: A Rejoinder to Sandra Fredman,* 15:4 I.Con (forthcoming December 2017).

over devalued, worthy over unworthy, silenced over listened to, credible over
disbelieved, empowered over disempowered, powerful over comparatively
powerless.[12] The advantaged are those in whose inexplicit tacit interest substantive law and procedure has been written, often at the expense of the
disadvantaged, since law began. Gender hierarchy is a false fact, men not
being inherently superior to women, merely so placed in discriminatory social
orderings. Aristotle's image of inequality as a level line unequally divided[13] is
supplanted in the substantive equality approach by a ladder or layers of strata
in vertical orderings.

Opposition to hierarchy can be seen as having been a tacit guiding light in
much Canadian equality jurisprudence all along, if not consistently, in
section 15's development. Its explicit embrace as the core substantive inequality concept would thus clarify and fortify the existing Canadian constitutional
approach rather than overhaul it, although some outcomes, especially in close
cases, may naturally be altered with its express recognition and consistent
application.[14] If overtly embraced, hierarchy would be no more abstractly or
universally prohibited than all grounds have been as bases for discrimination.
The Charter's enumerated and analogous grounds would necessarily continue
to identify the concrete bases of the hierarchies that are rejected by Canadian
constitutional law, although some grounds may be recognized as analogous
that previously had not been. Actually, hierarchy may not have been recognized as the animating equality principle to date precisely because it is not
an abstraction. It refers to the concrete social content specific to each "pre-
existing disadvantage"[15] in social reality. Hierarchy is intrinsically comparative,[16] a grounded strength of substantive equality as a principle, making it
impossible for antihierarchical equality standards to be ahistorical or acultural.
Substantive equality walks on the ground rather than floating suspended from

---

[12] For further discussion, *see* Catharine A. MacKinnon, *Substantive Equality: A Perspective*, 96
    MINN. L. REV. 1, 12 (2011) ("Substantive Equality"). For a sustained and detailed tracing of
    substantive equality developments in Canada, with parallels and contrasts including South
    African and US constitutional law, *see* Catharine A. MacKinnon, *Sex Equality* (St. Paul:
    Foundation Press, 2001, 2007, and 2016).
[13] 3 Aristotle, *The Nicomachean Ethics*, 1131a–1131b, 112–17 (J.L. Ackrill & J.O. Urmson, eds.,
    David Ross trans., (1980) (1925).
[14] *See, e.g.*, text accompanying notes infra 62–73 and 87–93.
[15] *Auton (Guardian ad litem of) v. British Columbia*, 3 SCR 657, 670 (2004) (analyzing here the
    point of section 1 equality inquiry) (emphasis added). *See also R. v. Turpin*, 1 SCR 1296,
    1330–34 (1989).
[16] *Andrews* at 164 (holding equality "is a comparative concept, the condition of which may only
    be attained or discerned by comparison with the condition of others in the social and political
    setting in which the question arises.").

a skyhook. "Disadvantage," the Canadian Charter term,[17] intrinsically identifies a hierarchy relative to the comparatively advantaged. As admirably encapsulated by Margot Young, "Social divisions structure and form the axes of social power, and actual, concrete people are caught up along these axes. The resulting hierarchies of differential access to a range of resources constitute the stuff of equality analyses."[18] The conceptual question is how legal equality analysis is to recognize and rectify the social inequality stuff.

Two ways of looking at stereotyping, as just one form discrimination recognizeably takes, briefly illustrate the distinction between substantive equality, with its flexible grounded grasp of social maldistributions and social injustices, and abstract formal equality's rigidity and emptiness, beginning with its "similarly situated" requirement. If a factor can be flipped, its dimensions as readily filled by dominant as by subordinate groups, it is neutral as between equality and inequality, meaning a substantive equality approach is not being taken. One can be equally stereotyped as a white man or as a Black woman, for example; the stereotyping per se can be equal. Formal inequality equates the two, as if the core of the inequality injury is being seen as a member of a group of which one is a member. The substantive inequality approach identifies the substance of the stereotypes as far from equal, promoting substantive hierarchies of male dominance or white supremacy or both together in social reality. Stereotyping as a concept, when it means simply overgeneralization from group characteristics, accurate or inaccurate, will thus not necessarily guide an equality determination, the formal equality approach to the contrary notwithstanding. By contrast, sensitivity to stereotyping as an authentic engine of hierarchical domination turns on the substantive content of the stereotypes. This is not to say that substantive equality always supplants formal equality, or that individual members of dominant groups cannot be found discriminated against through arbitrary categorization, as genuinely unusual as that is. Rather, it does not equate dominance and its results with subordination and its consequences and recognizes injuries of inequality that formal equality is incapable of grasping and routinely misses.

Distinguishing these two approaches clarifies much that has vexed the doctrine of equality law around the world, if less in Canada. Proceeding along the formal equality route, the many doctrinal guises of sameness/difference analysis in equality law struggle, usually ineffectively, toward outcomes that a substantive equality theory would readily require (if the cases even had to be

---

[17] Canadian Charter of Rights and Freedoms § 15(2), Part I of the Constitution Act, 1982.
[18] Margot Young, *Social Justice and the Charter: Comparison & Choice*, 50 OSGOODE HALL L. J. 669, at 675 (2013).

brought at all). The fraught place of the standard doctrines of the existing equality canon is typically due to knowing where they want to go, but not the way in which getting there is antithetical to what the mainstream theory contemplates or, in the hands of many courts, allows. Indeed, the tension between formal and substantive equality has largely been missed. Adverse effects/indirect discrimination or disparate impact theory is a particularly valiant attempt to remedy the consequences of hierarchy in reality that can otherwise be reinforced rather than challenged by conventional equality theory. But substantive equality is not just a form of disparate impact. If hierarchy is not recognized as the concept core to inequality against which an equality guarantee is set, disparate impact/discrimination-in-effect doctrine is vulnerable to repeated failure. This is because unless a court already knows that a challenged disparity is the impact or effect of a pre-existing substantive hierarchy, and is permitted to be guided by that understanding – in other words, can pursue what formal equality theory terms its political perceptions rather than what the Aristotelian approach sees as a principle – addressing those effects can be, and repeatedly is, precluded or evaded.

Reasonable accommodation, similarly, is a "difference" theory: an attempt to accommodate the perceived incoherent or undesirable implications of imposing sameness. This attempt, which also serves to save the sameness approach, is fraught as well, given that differences can as well justify reinscribing disadvantages by law. It can also be symbolically stigmatic even when a desirable material outcome is achieved. Apparently substantive equality's rejection of *both sides* of the Aristotelian formula – both "sameness" and "difference," each of which takes its measure by reference to a dominant standard being obscured as such[19] – has not been widely understood.[20] Along the same lines, affirmative action, by (as it is expressed) taking race or sex into account, continually founders on the rock of "special treatment" and is endlessly open to the charge of being a form of discrimination itself within the formal paradigm because it directly addresses a ground of inequality.[21] Where this confusion prevails (as in the US, not in Canada, due to the Charter language at section 15(2)), this conundrum endangers the existence of such programs (a relative of positive discrimination in some systems), as

---

[19] This is explained in Difference & Dominance.
[20] The *Andrews* confusion on this point has not helped, where not disadvantaging the disadvantaged was at points referred to as recognition of "differences." *Andrews* at 165, 169, 175, 193.
[21] *See, e.g., Regents of the Univ. of Cal. v. Bakke,* 438 US 265 (1978); *Grutter v. Bollinger,* 539 US 306 (2003); *Fisher v. University of Texas at Austin,* 133 S. Ct. 2411 (2013) in the United States.

well as stigmatizes its beneficiaries by failing to criticize as biased the hierarchical standard by which its recipients are disadvantaged, against which
affirmative action, demeaned under formal equality as "preferential treatment,"[22] attempts equalization. Opposition to systemic discrimination, for its
part, is definitely integral to substantive equality, but is frequently not recognized as a legal claim or doctrine.[23] "Unfair" discrimination, a constitutional
term in South Africa,[24] is clearly a reaction to the traps of formal equality,
specifically to its sidelining of substance. Had equality been understood
substantively there, i.e. anti-hierarchically, fairness would not be needed as
a modifier.

To illustrate further on the systemic rather than doctrinal level of equality
reasoning, the reason Peter Westen could think that equality and rights are
redundant is because he missed the way Aristotelian equality has become a
systemic norm, absorbed into the rule of law itself, guiding its approach to
analogy (sameness) and distinction (difference) in precedential systems in
particular. As LEAF lucidly explained in its *Andrews* factum, "[t]he 'similarly
situated' notion is already embodied in the rule of law. The rule of law is
satisfied if officials enforce rules impartially against all those to whom they
apply ... To say that likes should be treated alike in the formal sense of
equality is to say only that laws should be laws ... [T]his formal approach does
not assist in deriving the underlying meaning of equality in the context of a
claim to substantive equality."[25] Westen saw that equality could be a right in
itself, at least in a racial context,[26] but he did not see the need to develop its
substance.[27] Equality became an "empty idea" because it was all formal and
no context or content.

In the Canadian setting, lacking explicit grip on hierarchy of status and
privilege under compulsory heterosexuality, namely in homophobia, made it
possible to argue, tracking formal equality methodology, that being excluded
from the definition of "spouse" because both in a couple are of the same sex
was not an equality violation.[28] And even when that discrimination was

---

[22] Justice Scalia of the US Supreme Court was particularly fond of this formulation. *See, e.g.*,
   Romer v. Evans, 517 US 620, 638–639 (1996). Instances proliferate in the United States.
[23] *Action Travail des Femmes v. Canadian National Railway Co.*, 1 SCR 1114 (1987) is a stunning
   exception.
[24] S. Afr. Const., ch. 2 § 9(4).   [25] *Andrews* factum, ¶ 65.
[26] See the bare mention of "racial injury" at Peter Westen, *The Empty Idea of Equality*, 95 HARV.
   L. REV. 537, 568 (1982).
[27] The US Supreme Court's identification in so many words of its own blind spot on this score is
   analyzed in MacKinnon, *Sex Equality* at 1241–1244 (3rd ed. 2016).
[28] *M. v. H.*, 2 SCR 3 (1999). Mr. Justice Gonthier's dissent does this at ¶¶ 261–263.

understood, as the majority did, without embracing hierarchy as the main-spring of substantive inequality – a test of historical subordination that lesbians and gay men amply satisfy beyond any shadow of doubt – the search was on for a doctrinal way to express the inequality involved in excluding them from the definition of spouse, hence the process of dissolution of spousal relationships in Ontario. "Dignity," announced as equality's central principle two months earlier,[29] was seized upon as providing that substance. The placement of dignity at the core of the substantive legal equality canon dug the Court into years of abstraction and detour, as the *Kapp* Court eventually acknowledged had occurred.[30] Indignity, encompassing differentials of status, has always been integral to any robust understanding of inequality,[31] despite the resist-ance of the formal equality approach to its legal recognition. It is almost always an effect or incident of discrimination, part of its damage, although seldom its preceding or defining cause or the discrimination itself. Thankfully, the problems of making indignity the *sine qua non* of discrimination[32] are now relatively well-recognized in Canada, although latecomers to Canada's clarity have yet to catch up.[33]

Going down this road after *Law* in *M. v. H.*, producing the interregnum of years of wandering in the Canadian wilderness followed by reinstatement of the original principle, was a symptom of Canada's failure to grasp hierarchy explicitly as the substance of substantive inequality, despite it being arguably already the tacit centre of its approach. That is, excluding gays and lesbians from the definition of "spouse" in the mandatory scheme for the dissolution of long-term relationships in Ontario would only not readily fit into the Court's conception of "disadvantage" because it had overlooked the place of hierarchy doctrinally, there and commonly, as the substance of substantive inequality, as the Court had already effectively recognized it in much of its equality juris-prudence, including in the gay and lesbian rights area.[34] When discrimination is defined as a distinction based on grounds that have "the effect of imposing

---

[29] *Law v. Canada*, 1 SCR 497, (1999) ¶ 53. *Law* was handed down March 25, 1999, *M. v. H.* May 20, 1999.

[30] *R. v. Kapp*, 2 SCR 483 (2008) ¶¶ 21–22.

[31] *See, e.g.*, Harlan's *Plessy* dissent as well as the more substantive of rulings in the US courts, *Loving v. Virginia*, 388 US 1 (1967); *Brown v. Board of Educ.*, 347 US 483 (1954); *Palmore v. Sidoti*, 466 US 429 (1984).

[32] For one discussion, see Substantive Equality at 11–12.

[33] In the United States, "equal dignity" folds the concepts more helpfully together. *United States v. Windsor*, 133 S. Ct. 2675, 2681, 2693, 2708 (2013); *Obergefell v. Hodges*, 135 S. Ct. 2584, 2595, 2603, 2608 (2015).

[34] The best articulation of this understanding can be found in the opinion of Mr. Justice Cory, dissenting, but not on this ground, in *Egan v. Canada*, 2 SCR 513, (1995) ¶¶ 173–175.

burdens, obligations, or disadvantages on [an] individual or group not imposed upon others, or which withholds or limits access to opportunities, benefits, and advantages available to other members of society,"[35] a hierarchy between the former and latter groups or individuals is precisely delineated. When this must legally occur in a social setting of the "proper linguistic, philosophic and historical contexts,"[36] a context that on the ground points unquestionably to the elevation of some groups *over* others, all the elements are there for the conclusion that social hierarchy is the *sine qua non* of substantive inequality. All that is lacking is the label.

The substantive inequality of gay men and lesbians, recognized in the undeniable fact of the social hierarchy of straight over gay, would have readily encompassed deprivation of dignity and worth as one expression of it. "Dignity" would not have been needed to be discovered as the core equality concept, because that place would already have been adequately filled by hierarchy, encompassing indignity or lower status as one measure or indicator of it. The same point can be made in a different posture by reconsidering *Brown v. Board of Education* in the United States, where racial segregation of schools by law was recognized as damaging Black children because it "generates a feeling of inferiority as to their status in the community that may affect their hearts and minds in a way unlikely ever to be undone"[37] – a form of indignity by any other name. If "dignity" had needed to be singled out in or by the equality canon, if it did any work a (there somewhat substantive) understanding of equality did not already do, surely this would have been the place. It was not needed because "a sense of inferiority,"[38] in the context of the tacit realization of the elevation of white over Black in social reality that *Plessy* had previously (under a paradigmatic application of the formal equality approach) considered equality,[39] was clearly grasped as an inequality injury.

To further illustrate the distinction, US constitutional equality jurisprudence would have been far more substantive had it proceeded from Justice Harlan's explicit rejection of substantive social hierarchy in his dissent in the Civil Rights Cases – "[T]here cannot be, in this republic, any class of human beings in practical subjection to another class, with power in the latter to dole out to the former just such privileges as they may choose to grant."[40] – rather

---

[35] *Andrews* at 174, quoting Mr. Chief Justice Dickson in *Action Travail* quoting The Abella Report, written by (as she then was) Judge Rosalie Abella.

[36] *Andrews* at 169 (quoting Mr. Chief Justice Dickson in *Hunter v. Southam*).

[37] *Brown v. Board of Education*, 347 US 483, 494 (1954).   [38] *Id.* at 494.

[39] *Plessy v. Ferguson*, 163 US 537 (1896); for discussion, *see* MacKinnon, *Sex Equality* at 66–78 (3rd ed. 2016).

[40] *US v. Stanley (Civil Rights Cases)*, 109 US 3, 62 (1883) (Harlan, J., dissenting).

than from the "colorblind"-ness of his *Plessy* dissent.[41] His *Plessy* dissent also repudiated a role for law in social equality, given his apparently essentialist belief in natural hierarchy, which is why he thought that equality could not be done if differences (here of color) were seen. The grounding of US equality law in presumptive natural hierarchy, "differences" impervious to law, was laid.

The Supreme Court of Canada, by contrast, has often understood well the meaning of hierarchy, how it works as a dynamic, and its invidious consequences in its equality jurisprudence. As a relatively superficial matter of constitutional structure, the Court has rejected hierarchy in favour of equality among sections of the Charter[42] and among prohibited grounds because they all matter.[43] In *Dagenais*, it opposed an approach to rights that "places some over others;"[44] in *Lavoie*, it rejected a "ranking" of analogous grounds.[45] In *Kapp*, prioritizing some rights meant that others "give way," some predominate over others, an approach rejected in favour a "flexible, non-hierarchical approach to Charter rights."[46] Similarly in *Gosselin*, the Court opined that "all parts of the Constitution must be read together" as exemplifying non-hierarchy among constitutional rights.[47] This is not to say that the rejection of hierarchy among abstractions or in some constitutional structural matters supports an equality approach grounded in social hierarchy, or that a Court that rejects hierarchy in analytical frameworks is prepared to reject hierarchy among people. It is only to say that this Court, in other settings, knows a hierarchy when it sees one and identifies its wrongs as resounding in inequality.

To the substantive point, the Court has clearly perceived hierarchy in the facts of some of its equality cases. In *Janzen*, for instance, it described a low place in an employment hierarchy, adopting an expert's words, as an "inferior ascribed status."[48] The Court criticized hierarchy in social institutions formerly maintained by force in a case on the corporal punishment of children when it described rejected practices as "rooted in an era where deploying 'reasonable' violence was an accepted technique in the maintenance of

---

[41] Harlan, J., dissenting in *Plessy* at 559. Of course his repudiation of caste there, *id.*, cut the other way.

[42] *Dagenais v. Canadian Broadcasting Corp.*, 3 SCR 835, 877 (1994).

[43] *Eaton v. Brant County Board of Education*, 1 SCR 241 (1997) at ¶ 36, opposing hierarchy of prohibited grounds within section 15, which would elevate distinctions based on some to a more suspect category than others.

[44] *Dagenais* at 877.　　[45] *Lavoie v. Canada*, 1 SCR 769 (2002) at ¶ 51.

[46] *R. v. Kapp*, 2 SCR 483 (2008) at ¶ 89.　　[47] *Gosselin v. Quebec*, [2005] 1 SCR 238 at ¶ 2.

[48] *Janzen v. Platy Enterprises Ltd.*, 1 SCR 1252 (1989) at ¶ 19 of V.

hierarchies in the family and in society."[49] In opposing a "hierarchy of beliefs" inherent in a state adherence to a religion, the Court noted that such a position "cast[s] doubt on the value of those it does not share … denying … equal worth,"[50] which "marginalizes" the unofficial religions.[51] One member of the Supreme Court of Canada recently observed the role of hierarchy in inequality through quoting Dean Nathalie des Rosiers in a case involving access of common law spouses to state family breakdown mechanisms, stating "In a democratic society, hierarchies between forms of relationships based on a status wholly unrelated to their needs are not appropriate."[52]

Revisiting a closely related question from Quebec in 2013, the Court saw that laws can devalue individuals, including unintentionally, by conveying a "negative social image," "favour[ing] certain individuals at the expense of others" because of enumerated or analogous characteristics.[53] "Such laws would perpetrate prejudice against certain individuals by establishing a hierarchy of worth based on prohibited grounds of discrimination, such as sex or sexual orientation."[54] This analysis, it is observed, requires contextual inquiry and account of disadvantages suffered by groups,[55] both key substantive considerations in an anti-hierarchical approach. While excluding common law spouses (gay and straight alike) from the state-mandated marital property regime was considered as possibly imposing a "hierarchy of conjugality,"[56] it was found not to impose a "hierarchy of worth,"[57] a concept that conveys a "negative social image," "favors certain individuals at the expense of others," and "express[es] or perpetuate[s] prejudice."[58] Whatever one's view of its application in this setting, the meaning of hierarchy as a concept could not have been better expressed.

---

[49] *Canadian Federation for Children v. Canada (Attorney General)*, 1 SCR 76 (2004), re section 43, at ¶ 173.

[50] *Mouvement laique quebecois v. Saguenay (City)*, 2015 SCC 16, 2 SCR 3 (2015) at ¶ 73.

[51] *Id.* ¶ 73.

[52] *Nova Scotia v. Walsh*, 4 SCR 325, (2002) ¶ 132 (2002) (quoting Des Rosiers in Madam Justice L'Heureux-Dube's dissent at ¶ 132) (ruling exclusion of common law couples from definition of "spouse" under division of property act not discriminatory).

[53] *Quebec (Attorney General) v. A.*,1 SCR 61, (2013) ¶ 197 (finding de facto spouses' exclusion from family property system on dissolution does not violate section 15).

[54] *Id.* ¶ 197.   [55] *Id.* ¶ 251.   [56] *Id.* ¶ 255.

[57] *Id.*¶ 266. The "reasons for judgment" quoted here were accepted by four justices; Madam Chief Justice McLachlin's section 1 opinion provided the fifth vote for the result, upholding the exclusion. Madam Justice Abella's dissent, finding the exclusion discriminatory under section 15, was endorsed by a majority of the Court in a disadvantage analysis attentive to hierarchy, see, e.g., ¶ 323, although that language is not used.

[58] *Id* . at ¶ 197.

It remains for the Court to embrace hierarchy doctrinally as inequality's central animating principle, impliedly there all along under section 15 but in need of express recognition, articulation and development. Its absence has had consequences, despite the Court having produced a good many results consistent with a hierarchical inequality analysis. Express equality rulings on hate propaganda in *Keegstra*, on pornography in *Butler* and *Little Sisters*, as well as the very substantive ruling on expert testimony in domestic violence cases without mentioning equality in *Lavallée*, are striking instances.[59] For sex, as these cases grasp, part of the substance of gender hierarchy is sexual and physical violation, together with (often consequent) deprivation of reproductive control.[60] Litigation on these issues, argued by LEAF in many cases as equality questions under section 15, have frequently (not always) been won in the result if not on the equality grounds argued. In the reproductive setting, *Borowski*, *Daigle*, and *Sullivan & Lemay*[61] illustrate a result argued on equality terms prevailing, without the Court applying an equality analysis in so many words.

Decisions that may have gone the other way under an express anti-hierarchical standard prominently include *Gosselin*, where cutting social assistance to adults under thirty to a below-subsistence rate was found, on "insufficient evidence," not to violate section 15.[62] Despite promising recognitions that discrimination can exist without stereotypes,[63] the Court's analysis of the axis of age in this case ignored the extreme specific intersectional hierarchies in which poor young women can be caught. The Court's finding that reduced welfare benefits for the young woman complainant did not infringe her dignity exposes the hazard that dignitary standards sideline material hierarchy, here ignoring the evidence that the benefit levels were so low that many women had to resort to prostitution and other unwanted sexual

---

[59] *R. v. Keegstra*, 3 SCR 697 (1990); *Butler v. R.*,1 SCR 452 (1991); *Little Sisters Book & Art Emporium v. Canada*, SCC 69 (2000), where LEAF's factum opposing a harm test for same-sex pornography was rejected in favor of embracing the sex equality argument made by Equality Now, recognizing the harm of gay pornography when it is sex-based; *R. v. Lavallée*, 1 SCR 852 (1990).

[60] Catharine A. MacKinnon, TOWARD A FEMINIST THEORY OF THE STATE 3–4, 126–154, 172–178 (Cambridge, MA, London, England, Harvard University Press, 1989).

[61] *Borowski v. Attorney-General of Canada*, [1989] 1 SCR 342; *Daigle v. Tremblay*, 2 SCR 530 (1989); *R. v. Sullivan & Lemay*, 1 SCR 489 (1991).

[62] *Gosselin v. Quebec*, 1 SCR 238 (2005).

[63] An early example can be found in *Vriend v. Alberta*, 1 SCR 493, 538 (1998) (Cory & Iacobucci, JJ, quoting Sopinka, J. in *Eaton v. Brant County Board of Education*, 1 SCR 241 (1997) ("It has subsequently been explained ... that it is not only the 'stereotypical application of presumed group personal characteristics' that discrimination can occur, although this may be common to many instances of discrimination.")

relationships in exchange for housing,[64] which circumstances actually violate their dignity as well.[65] The pervasiveness of such circumstances on myriad grounds make it unlikely that, under a hierarchical recognition, the last successful section 15 claim would have been brought as far back as 2007.[66]

The doctrinal vacuum remains. Sometimes cases were lost,[67] arguably a result of the failure of the Court to see hierarchical sex inequality as such in the facts at issue, despite having later squarely recognized the gender inequality issues in the same factual area.[68] *Osolin*, for example, recognized that "[s]exual assault is in the vast majority of cases gender based" and took sections 15 and 28 into account in reasonably limiting cross-examination of a rape victim, even as it found equality considerations "not determinative."[69] In *Mills*, the Court applied equality thinking in upholding Parliament's limits on access to counselling records of survivors of sexual assault, explicitly stating that equality concerns must inform contextual determinations of full answer and defence in sexual assault cases.[70] However, equality was seen to be an issue on both sides and gender hierarchy was not mentioned. The trio of cases on consent in 2011 provided what might have been a context for considering the effect of the power differentials involved in gender hierarchy in the sexual assault context.[71] The opportunity not having been taken, we remain less unenlightened as to the Court's view of substantive sex equality standards for sexual assault law.[72]

---

[64] See Gwen Brodsky & Shelagh Day, *Denial of the Means of Subsistence as an Equality Violation*, ACTA JURIDICA 149, 156 (2005).

[65] Although economic status could be added to the Charter by interpretation, and is definitely hierarchical, a hierarchical recognition as core to equality would not necessarily add it as an enumerated ground, although it would help. Other cases that might have been litigated differently might include *Dunmore v. Ontario*, 3 SCR 1016 (2001), where the exclusion of agricultural workers from the labour relations regime might have been brought under section 15 as well as 2(d) (under which it was won). So, too, *Ontario v. Fraser*, 2 SCR 3 (2011).

[66] See *Canada v. Hislop*, 1 SCR 429 (2007) (finding that exclusion of same-sex pension survivors from before 1998 discriminated based on sexual orientation).

[67] See, e.g., *Canadian Newspaper Co. v. Canada*, 2 SCR 122 (1988); *R. v. Seaboyer*, 2 SCR 577 (1991) (invalidating rape-shield provision of Criminal Code).

[68] *R. v. Osolin*, 4 SCR 595, 669 (1993) (Cory, J.) ("The eradication of discriminatory beliefs and practices in the conduct of [sexual assault] trials will enhance rather than detract from the fairness of such trials. Conversely, sexual assault trials that are fair will promote the equality of women and children, who are most often the victims."); *R. v. O'Connor*, 4 SCR 411, (1995) ¶ 129.

[69] *R. v. Osolin*, 4 SCR 595, 669 (1993).   [70] *R. v. Mills*, 3 SCR 668, (1999) ¶ 90.

[71] For a productive analysis, see Emma Cunliffe, *Sexual Assault Cases in the Supreme Court of Canada: Losing Sight of Substantive Equality?*, 57 S.C.L.R. (2d) 295, 301–315 (2012).

[72] Some of my views on the topic can be found in Catharine A. MacKinnon, *Rape Redefined*, 10 HARVARD L. & POL'Y REV. 431 (2016), where aspects of Canadian sexual assault law are also discussed.

The Court's jurisprudence on sexual assault arguably amounts to much, if not all, that a substantive equality analysis would require.[73] Yet section 15 has never been the basis for a sexual assault ruling. Had rape been expressly identified as a substantive issue of hierarchy based on sex in legal doctrine, rather than being considered a sex equality question only socially or as a matter of policy or in terms of a constitutional value to take into account sometimes, the connections with other issues to which rape is integral, such as prostitution and pornography, would have been illuminated, as would Charter equality standards on these issues. In its absence, the failure to identify the substance of substantive equality has led the Court down some blind alleys and restricted its development of an equality doctrine that continues to harbour immense unrealized promise. Some indications of substantive equality's potential beginning to be realized can be found in jurisdictions where Canada's approach has been influential, taken root and flourished. The equality analysis of sexual abuse is one example. Indeed, around the world, it is principally in the law of sexual abuse that the substantive sex equality action can be found. There, the hierarchy of sex is being exposed in substantive social practice, and the substantive equality approach is escaping legal silos and leaping jurisdictional boundaries to address it.

Although the US Supreme Court, a comparative backwater on these questions, explicitly said in *Lawrence v. Texas* that equal protection has no substantive component,[74] the US Supreme Court was the first to recognize that sexual harassment states a sex inequality claim.[75] Under the European Convention on Human Rights, a new sex equality jurisprudence can be seen to be developing in application to rape[76] and, most stunningly, to domestic violence.[77] In international criminal law, substantive sex equality concepts are

---

[73] *See, e.g., R. v. Ewanchuk*, 1 SCR 330 (1999); Janine Benedet, *Marital Rape, Polygamy and Prostitution: Trading Sex Equality for Agency & Choice?*, 18 REV. CONST. STUD. 161, 164 (2013); Janine Benedet, *Sexual Assault Cases at the Alberta Court of Appeal: The Roots of Ewanchuk and the Unfinished Revolution*, 52 ALTA. L. REV. 127, 144 (2014). The *R. v. J.A.*, 2 SCR 440 (2011), majority is another example, hewing closely to Parliament's guidance in defining consent to sex in concluding that consent cannot be adequately given or withdrawn while a person is unconscious.

[74] *Lawrence v. Texas*, 539 US 558, 574–75 (2003).

[75] *Meritor Savings Bank v. Vinson*, 477 US 57 (1986), extended to men sexually abused by men in *Oncale v. Sundowner Offshore Services, Inc.*, 523 US 75 (1998). The same theory is applied under Equal Protection by US courts below.

[76] *M.C. v. Bulgaria*, App. No. 39272/98, Eur. Ct. H.R. (2003). *See also Vertido v. The Philippines*, Communication No.18/2008, Views under art. 7, para. 3, of the Optional Protocol, CEDAW/C/46/D/18/2008 (Sept. 1, 2010).

[77] *Opuz v. Turkey*, App. No. 33401/02 Eur. Ct. H.R. ¶ 153 (2009). *See also Gonzales v. United States*, Case 12.626, Inter-Am. Comm'n H.R., Report No. 80/11 (2011)

being fielded in prosecutions for gender crime, including in the ad hoc tribunals for genocidal rape[78] and in the International Criminal Court in its statute for crimes against humanity and war crimes,[79] as well as in its first case for recruitment and use of child soldiers,[80] bringing together substantive equality principles from human rights with international criminal law. The UN Secretary General's Report of 2006 recognized sexual violence explicitly as a form of gender-based inequality,[81] as did the dual resolutions issued on the same day in 2013, one from CEDAW,[82] the other by the Security Council,[83] converging human rights with humanitarian law, both recognizing gender-based violence as a substantive form of sex inequality, exposing the hierarchy involved and casting it as a threat to international security and peace. Yet no country has technically applied sex equality law to its criminal cases for sexual assault, and only Canada has approached sex equality principles in this area.

Laws on prostitution and sex trafficking represent one of the fastest-moving and most promising areas of law moving toward substantive equality around the globe. Sweden's criminalization of sex purchasers and pimps and decriminalization of prostituted people, now legislatively followed both in Canada

---

[78] The legal recognition of rape in a genocide originated in *Kadic v. Karadzic*, 70 F.3d 232 (2d Cir. 1995) and was first applied by an international authority in *Prosecutor v. Akayesu*, Case No. ICTR 96 4 T ¶¶ 731–734 (1998).

[79] *See* Rome Statute of the International Criminal Court, art. 7, ¶ 1(g), July 17, 1998, 2187 UNTS 3 (defining "crime against humanity" to include "[r]ape, sexual slavery, enforced prostitution, forced pregnancy, enforced sterilization, or any other form of sexual violence of comparable gravity"); *id.* art. 7, ¶ 1(h) (recognizing persecution based on gender as a "crime against humanity"); *id.* art. 8, ¶ 2(b)(xxii) (defining "war crimes" perpetrated during international armed conflicts to include "rape, sexual slavery, enforced prostitution, forced pregnancy, as defined in article 7, paragraph 2(f), enforced sterilization, or any other form of sexual violence also constituting a grave breach of the Geneva Conventions"); *id.* art. 8, ¶ 2(e) (vi) (extending definition to encompass non-international armed conflicts); *id.* art. 6(b) (defining "genocide" to include "[c]ausing serious bodily or mental harm to members of [a] group," which has been interpreted to apply to sexual atrocities including rape in genocides).

[80] Almost all the first cases prosecuted at the ICC include gender crimes in some form. A particularly useful example can be found in the prosecutor's opening argument in *Lubanga*, gendering the claim for violation of the prohibition on child soldiers, *Prosecutor v. Thomas Lubanga Dyilo*, ICC-01/04-01/06, Prosecutor's Opening Statement, at 8–9 (Jan. 26, 2009), available at www.icc-cpi.int/NR/rdonlyres/89E8515B-DD8F-4251-AB08-6B60CB76017F/279630/ICCOTPSTLMO20090126ENG2.pdf.

[81] *See generally* UN Secretary-General, *In-Depth Study on All Forms of Violence Against Women, Delivered to the General Assembly*, UN Doc. A/61/122/Add. 1 (Jul. 6, 2006).

[82] *Committee on the Convention on the Elimination of All Forms of Discrimination against Women, General Recommendation* 30, UN Doc. CEDAW/C/GC/30 (Oct. 18, 2013).

[83] SCR 2122 (Oct. 18, 2013).

and France, is, in effect and in legislative history, a substantive sex equality law.[84] Perhaps the most striking illustration of the contrast between formal and substantive equality analysis in the constitutional canon can be found in South Africa's decision in *Jordan v. State*, considering the law's criminalization of prostituted people and not sex buyers,[85] where the dissent virtually maps a substantive anti-hierarchical sex equality approach to prostitution law.[86] Contrast this with the disappointing Canadian decision in *Bedford*,[87] not so much because the Criminal Code provisions regulating prostitution were struck down, but because the Court, in the absence of applying a substantive sex equality approach, could be misled into thinking that prostitution's criminalized forms, rather than prostitution itself, were responsible for its harms. A substantive equality understanding, supported by creditable empirical data produced through reliable methodologies,[88] would have exposed the gendered hierarchies in the practices involved and supported such a recognition of reality. The systemic links within gender-based inequality between prostitution, often termed "serial rape" or "paid rape" by its survivors,[89] and rape outside prostitution would have been highlighted equality principles had been applied to the law of sexual assault generally.

---

[84] On Sweden, *see* Brottsbalken [BrB] (Criminal Code) 6:1 (Swed.); *see* Max Waltman, *The Politics of Legal Challenges to Pornography: Canada, Sweden, and the United States*, PhD. Diss., University of Stockholm 277–286, 294–298 (2014) (recounting sex equality dimensions of passage of Swedish law against prostitution). Canada passed a version of the Nordic model on prostitution in December 2014. Protection of Communities and Exploited Persons Act, S.C. 2014, c.25, available at www.canlii.org/en/ca/laws/astat/sc-2014-c-25/latest/sc-201425.html?resultIndex=1. France passed it in April 2016. Loi visant à renforcer la lutte contre le système prostitutionnel et à accompagner les personnes prostituées, Loi n° 2016-444 du 13 avril 2016 parue au JO n° 0088 du 14 avril 2016 (Legislation to strengthen the fight against the system of prostitution and to support prostituted persons, Legislation No. 2016-444 of April 13, 2016, appearing in Journal No. 0088 of April 14, 2016), available at www.senat.fr/dossier-legislatif/ppl13-207.html. Both Northern Ireland and the Republic of Ireland have passed it as well.

[85] *Jordan v. State*, 2002 (6) SA 642 (CC) at ¶ 69 (S. Afr.)

[86] *Id.* at ¶ 63–69 (O'Regan and Sachs, dissenting).

[87] *See* prior to the new legislation noted above, *Canada v. Bedford*, 3 SCR 1101 (2013).

[88] For an excellent analysis of the empirically deeply flawed decision on this point in the Ontario Court of Appeals in this case, *see* Max Waltman, *Assessing Evidence, Arguments, and Inequality in Bedford v. Canada*, 37 Harv. J. L. & Gender 459 (2014).

[89] Many survivors have said this to me. For some documentation, see, e.g., Evelina Giobbe, *Prostitution: Buying the Right to Rape*, in Rape & Sexual Assault III 144 (Ann Wolbert Burgess ed., 1991) (quoting interview with MD: "Prostitution is like rape … it felt like rape. It was rape to me"); Melissa Farley, *Prostitution Is Sexual Violence*, PSYCHIATRIC TIMES (Oct. 1, 2004), available at www.psychiatrictimes.com/sexualoffenses/prostitutionsexual violence (referring to prostitution as "'paid rape,' as one survivor described it"). *See also* Warren Kinsella, *Prostitution isn't sex, it's bought rape*, QMI Agency (Jan. 11, 2014), available at

Another arm of the sex industry, pornography, was successfully litigated against on sex equality terms in *Butler*.[90] The facts that the actual pornography in *Butler* remains on the street all over Canada, and that since 2000, only two reported Canadian cases appear to have been brought against producers or online distributors for pornography of adults, call for further analysis of the adequacy of the constitutional tools available. Soon after *Butler*, the Court of Appeal for Ontario ruled that so-called nonviolent materials did not meet the harm test because the court saw women taking "the lead in inducing the sexual activity with the men … they at last are asserting their equality."[91] A hierarchical understanding of gender-based abuse – the substantive inequality in and of pornography – would not be capable of being flipped in this fashion.[92] Similarly, in *Price*, one of the two cases brought, the producer/distributor of material containing acts to which the judge observed the woman in them was "obviously" not consenting, videos from which a risk of harm was inferred, was acquitted based on community standards of tolerance for violence against women on evidence of widespread violent pornography.[93] The clearer recognition that sexual aggression against women is a form of sex inequality that recognition of the hierarchy principle would support might have provided guidance to the contrary. Community tolerance of sexual abuse, including in prostitution and pornography, describes a rape culture.

Similarly, after ten years of litigation, the defendant in *Smith* was convicted of snuff-themed verbal and visual pornography sexualizing the torture and murder of women, a conviction upheld on an appeal that did not discuss community standards.[94] Whether sexual abuse in pornography short of murder would be seen as obscene under the Canadian definition, far less successfully reach the "degrading and dehumanizing" treatment *Butler* recognized as

www.lfpress.com/2014/01/10/prostitution-isnt-sex-its-bought-rape ("so say former prostitutes themselves"); Sigma Huda, UN Commission on Human Rights, Report of the Special Rapporteur on the Human Rights Aspects of the Victims of Trafficking in Persons, Especially Women and Children, E/CN.4/2006/62, at 12 (Feb. 20, 2006) ("By engaging in the act of commercial sex, the prostitute-user is thereby directly inflicting an additional and substantial harm upon the trafficking victim, tantamount to rape"); Coalition Against Trafficking in Women Australia, Frequently Asked Questions (2007), available at http://catwa.org.au/?q=faq ("Prostitution cannot eliminate rape when it is itself bought rape.").

90 *Butler v. R.*, 1 SCR 452 (1992).
91 *R. v. Hawkins* [1992] CarswellOnt 1940 ¶ 14 (Ct. J. Gen. Div.) (involving materials described as presenting men ejaculating onto women's faces and into their mouths and women presented as sexually insatiable and looking for sex with strangers).
92 *See R. v. Hawkins*, 15 O.R. (3d) 549 (1992), 565–68, 573 (C.A.) (*sub nom R. v. Ronish*).
93 *R. v. Price*, 2004 B.C.P.C. 103, ¶¶ 83, 99–100 (Prov. Ct.).
94 *R. v. Smith*, [2002] CarswellOnt 6125 (Super. Ct. J.), aff'd in part, retrial ordered in part (2005), 76 O.R. (3d) 435 (C.A.), aff'd with modifications, 2012 ONCA 892, [2012] CarswellOnt 15792 (C.A.).

unequal on the basis of sex, remains unclear.[95] Since two store owners selling and renting nonviolent pornography that the defendants conceded were degrading and dehumanizing were acquitted in 1994, no published Canadian obscenity case has prosecuted for nonviolent adult pornography. The principle of substantive hierarchy as core to the inequality prohibition – degradation and dehumanization being clear hierarchy measures – could give constitutional spine to community standards and clarify the Court's view of equality's meaning in this setting, one badly in need of further direction.[96]

As highlighted by the role of extreme destitution in the typical realities of those caught in the sex trade, one distinct advantage of the substantive hierarchical approach to equality lies in its grip on material reality. Addressing economic disadvantage as such has to date been precluded in US equality law,[97] is not yet an enumerated or analogous ground in Canada,[98] as well as so far is not targeted as such for remedy by equality law in the UK or South

[95] To further illustrate a legal equality approach in this area, consider *Jorgenson*, in which a pornography store owner was acquitted by the Court because he said he knew the materials he sold contained sex but not, as the statute requires, that they were obscene. *See R. v. Jorgenson* [1995] 4 SCR 55, 104–07, 121–22. This scienter defense, a sort of intent requirement, conflicts with Canadian equality standards; reframed, Jorgenson claimed he may have engaged in objectively discriminatory behavior but he did not intentionally discriminate. Intent expressly does not define discrimination in Canada, *see Andrews* at 174–175 ("whether intentional or not"); *see also R. v. Big M Drug Mart Ltd.*, [1985] 1 SCR 295 (speaking of equality, per Wilson, J., the Charter is "first and foremost an effects-oriented document" at ¶ 158); *Quebec v. A.*, 2013 SCC 5, although this rule has not been considered in a criminal law setting. Somewhat further afield but within the ambit of the Court's developing standards in this general area, in *R. v. Labaye*, [2005] 3 SCR 728, the Court invalidated a conviction for "indecency" in a prosecution of a private swinger's club for group sex. Had a Charter gender hierarchy standard been applied to the provision, in addition to the objectively proven harm the Court sought, it might have asked for, and the Crown might have developed, evidence of whether gender hierarchy, as one form of harm, was imposed and practiced in this club. Was this a sexual venue for gender (and other) equality or for inequality? Were women (or anyone) exploited or violated there? Did they truly want to be there or were they coerced?
[96] *R. v. Erotica Video Exchange Ltd.* (1994) 163 A.R. 181, 184 (Alta. Prov. Ct.).
[97] *See San Antonio Indep. Sch. Dist. v. Rodriguez*, 411 US 1 (1973).
[98] "Canadian courts ... have exhibited increasing resistance to the possibility that claims of discrimination on the basis of grounds related to economic disadvantage might be found valid discrimination claims under section 15." Jessica Eisen, *On Shaky Grounds: Poverty and Analagous Grounds under the Charter*, 2 CANADIAN J. POVERTY L. 1 (2013). Arguing that it should be so found, *see* Martha Jackman, *Constitutional Contact with the Disparities of the World: Poverty as a Prohibited Ground of Discrimination under the Canadian Charter and Human Rights Law*, 2 REV. CONST. STUD. 76 (1994). Justice Deschamps, now retired, has alone stated that while employment status "at least at this time" is not regarded as an analogous "to redress economic inequality ... would be more faithful to the design of the Charter ... "but "would constitute a sea change" in its interpretation. *Ontario v. Fraser*, 2 SCR 3 (2011), ¶¶ 315, 317.

Africa either. Although recognition of substantive inequality on other grounds cannot satisfactorily resolve this problem, because the recognized historic grounds for disadvantage so often map onto and are fused with relative poverty, recognition of substantive equality in law makes addressing some grinding realities of economic class more possible and likely. Indeed, what makes inequalities hierarchical is often the material factor of economic inequality, making class an intersectional feature of most social hierarchies through which inequalities, with all their disadvantages, operate. Consider, for instance, the relative wealth and poverty, respectively, of so-called white people above anyone but, men over women, adults over children. Material disadvantage measured in lack of wealth tends to track enumerated and analogous grounds that define subordinated groups. So, if discrimination against those recognized grounds was actually ended, how much economic disadvantage would be left?

Amid this call for express recognition of equality rights as such in their substantive forms, it is worth noting that often equality has been most substantively advanced, its hierarchical content most clearly foregrounded, the less it is identified as equality. The Palermo Protocol to the Transnational Organized Crime Convention, defining sex trafficking to include sexual exploitation through "abuse of power or position of vulnerability,"[99] as well as through force, fraud and coercion, is *de facto* a strong substantive equality anti-hierarchy law. Apparently equality is more easily embraced by some institutions of power as a good idea than as a legal right. Its often gingerly treatment under the Charter suggests that equality of the sexes is regarded more as a positive moral value than as a fact denied realization in social and legal orderings. Is there some reason, after thirty years, that sex equality cannot be spoken aloud in certain contexts even while being tacitly advanced, or can be named and weighed as a constitutional value but cannot be recognized as a constitutional right? It speaks to the comparative world context that even that much is a major step forward over the lack of substantive equality recognition at all that tends to prevail in most states. Taking the further step of rendering hierarchy based on concrete grounds the explicit doctrinal handle for unconstitutional inequality would provide clarity, effectiveness and direction to Canadian equality law and reaffirm Canada's place at the forefront of world constitutional leadership.

---

[99] GA Res. 55/25, UN Doc. A/55/383, Protocol to Prevent, Suppress and Punish Trafficking in Persons, Especially Women and Children, Supplementing the United Nations Convention against Transnational Organized Crime, art. 3 (a) (15 November 2000).

11

Canadian Constitutional Law of
Freedom of Expression

ADRIENNE STONE

The Canadian law of freedom of expression represents a distinctive and important contribution to global constitutionalism. In this paper, I will reflect upon it with three aims. First, I will examine Canadian free speech law to identify the fundamental commitments on which it depends: equality, multiculturalism and a conception of the state as a positive agent in the protection of rights, the last of which I think is sometimes underemphasized in comparative debate. Second, I will argue that these distinctive substantive commitments – most especially the conception of the state – are also evident in the methodology of Canadian constitutional law of freedom of expression.

The first two of these points are very revealing of the fundamental commitments of Canadian constitutional law, especially when considered in comparison with the United States. My third aim in this chapter is to consider what Canadian constitutional law, viewed in comparative perspective, tells us about freedom of expression. This comparative study provides a precise illustration of how rights like freedom of expression are inevitably realized in quite different ways in different constitutional systems. In part, these differences reflect deep and ineradicable moral disagreement of the kind that philosophers of rights have identified as a general feature of rights. In addition, I suggest, these differences are likely to reflect judgments that are constructed by the broader constitutional culture. In particular, the law of freedom of expression may reflect cumulative and historically driven judgments about the extent to which a state is likely to abuse or mishandle the power to regulate expression.

Before proceeding further, I should note that the principle comparator jurisdiction for the purpose of my analysis is the United States, though towards the end of the paper I do offer a wider comparative lens. Approaching comparative analysis of freedom of expression by reference to the First Amendment has obvious dangers given the exceptional nature of First Amendment law.

245

Overemphasis therefore gives undue prominence to the First Amendment and risks treating aspects of First Amendment law – which may well be contingent and particular to that tradition – as necessary elements of a concept of freedom of expression. Yet it is appropriate in this context because First Amendment law was an important foil for the Canadian courts.[1] That is, the Supreme Court of Canada deliberately sought a distinctive Canadian approach and in doing so rejected core elements of First Amendment law. A full understanding of the Canadian constitutional law of freedom of expression requires attention to that body of law which the Supreme Court of Canada sought to reject.

FREEDOM OF EXPRESSION VALUES

I will begin by tracing two notable features of the Canadian constitutional law of freedom of expression, each of which reveal a distinctively Canadian set of values. As a preliminary matter, however, I will make a few obvious points for the sake of completeness.

Preliminaries

First, the *Canadian Charter of Rights and Freedoms* guarantees that "everyone has … freedom of thought, belief, opinion and expression, including freedom of the press and other media of communication." In its textual form, then, the *Charter* resembles other constitutional rights (such as s 15 of the *South African Bill of Rights* and art 10 of the *European Convention on Human Rights* [ECHR]) that consist of a positive conferral of a right on individuals rather than the more unusual form of the First Amendment, which is expressed as a limitation on government. It also has a general limitation clause (in s 1). In this respect it is different both from freedom of expression guarantees that contain limitations internal to the provision itself (like art 10 of the ECHR or art 5 of the German Basic Law) and the ostensibly unqualified right conferred by the First Amendment.

Second, the Canadian Supreme Court has been explicit about the values underlying s 2(b) of the *Charter*, describing them in the following terms:

> (1) seeking and attaining the truth is an inherently good activity; (2) participation in social and political decision-making is to be fostered and encouraged; and (3) the diversity in forms of individual self-fulfillment and human flourishing ought to be cultivated in an essentially tolerant, indeed

[1] *R v. Keegstra*, 3 SCR 697 (1990), 741–744; *R v. Butler*, 1 SCR (1991) 452, 503–504. For a comparison of Canadian and US constitutional law in the contexts of remedial legislation and equality jurisprudence, see Chapter 12 in this volume; Chapter 10 in this volume.

welcoming, environment not only for the sake of those who convey a meaning, but also for the sake of those to whom it is conveyed.[2]

Thus the Canadian Supreme Court essentially adopts mainstream positions found in liberal political theory of freedom of expression though, as we shall see, these are developed with a distinctively Canadian flavour.

Finally, I will note some features of the basic structure of Canadian law of freedom of expression. To recite a few well-known facts: the right to freedom of expression is found in s 2(b) of the *Charter* while s 1 governs the permissible limits on freedom of expression and other *Charter* rights. The coverage of s 2 (b) is very broad. Almost any act that "conveys or attempts to convey meaning," with the exception only of "violence as a form of expression"[3] qualifies for protection, making it unnecessary to engage in complex decisions about what counts as "expression" or to identify categories of high and low value expression.[4] Because of the breadth of s 2(b), s 1 – as elaborated in *R v. Oakes* and the subsequent case law[5] – dominates most freedom of expression controversies. Unlike the rule-based categories arising in First Amendment law,[6] the *Oakes* test is designed to provide a flexible, context-sensitive framework for the assessment of a *Charter* claim.[7]

The Canadian Concept of Expression

Turning to the substantive aspects of the protection of freedom of expression, the Canadian contribution starts with the foundational concept of "expression," which determines the scope or "coverage" of the right.

[2] *Irwin Toy v. Quebec* (Attorney-General), 1 SCR 927, 976 (1989).

[3] *Irwin Toy v. Quebec* (Attorney-General), 1 SCR 927, 970 (1989). By contrast, communication in the course of criminal activity is generally thought to be excluded from First Amendment conception of speech. *See* Greenawalt, Fighting Words: Individuals, Communities and Liberties of Speech at 17–21 (1995).

[4] When it comes to determining whether "expression" falls within the coverage of the *Charter*, then, rationales for the protection of freedom of expression are usually irrelevant. An exception arises when the government's purpose was not to control or restrict attempts to convey a meaning, in which case, s 2(b) is only violated if the law restricts expression relating to the underlying values. *See Irwin Toy v. Quebec* (Attorney-General), [1989] 1 SCR 927, 976.

[5] 1 SCR 103 (1986). A law violating a *Charter* right must serve a "pressing and substantial objective" and use means that are "reasonably and demonstrably justified." The second requirement in turn requires that the law be "rationally connected" to that objective; "minimally impair" the protected right; and that there is "a proportionality" between the restrictions imposed and the objective pursued: *R v. Oakes*, 1 SCR 103, 138–39 (1986).

[6] *See* Jamie Cameron, *The Past, Present, and Future of Expressive Freedom under the Charter*, 35 OSGOODE HALL L. J. 1, 7–22 (1997).

[7] *Edmonton Journal v. Alberta*, [1989] 2 SCR 1326, 1355–56; *R v. Keegstra*, 3 SCR 697, 737 (1990); *Thompson Newspapers v. Canada*, 1 SCR 887, 939 (1987).

All systems of freedom of expression face conceptual difficulties in determining the activity to which the right applies. The Canadian framing of the right as a freedom of *expression* – which in global terms is common – overcomes some of the most basic questions that arise in relation to freedom of *speech*, but many questions remain. What about expression that forms an element of a criminal offence (like the words used to commit a criminal conspiracy)? How do we understand cases where expression is "mixed" with non-expressive activity such as picketing, protesting or draft card burning? What about activity (like making a political donation) that facilitates expression?

The notable feature of the Canadian approach to this question is that very little of the conceptual "work" is done by the concept of "expression." It has meant, for instance, that soliciting for the purposes of prostitution was held to constitute "expression" for the purposes of s 2(b) (though a prohibition on solicitation was then upheld under s 1).[8] As the *Prostitution Reference* case shows, the breadth of the concept means that almost all freedom of expression cases will turn on the application of s 1. The breadth of this concept has been the subject of some scholarly criticism. Kent Greenawalt, for instance, has suggested that this approach puts excessive pressure on analysis under s 1[9] and that it would be better to define the concept taking account of the values on which freedom of expression depends, a line of criticism to which I will later return. For the moment it is necessary only to note that this approach to the concept of expression[10] is to make the second stage of the *Charter* analysis – that mandated by s 1 – exceptionally important and I turn to this analysis.

Limits on Freedom of Expression: The Hate Speech and Pornography Cases

It is in the application of s 1 that the most important and distinctive aspects of Canadian law of freedom of expression are found. To illustrate these elements I will undertake a detailed analysis of the Canadian Supreme Court's case law on hate speech and pornography. Both bodies of law are particularly distinctive and revealing of the central commitments of Canadian law of freedom of expression.

[8] *Reference re ss. 193 and 195.1(1)(c) of the Criminal Code* (Man.), [1990] 1 SCR 1123. Though note that the Supreme Court's decision in *Bedford v Canada (AG)* 2013 SCC 72, [2013] 3 S.C.R 1101, finding a cognate provision to be invalid on s 7 grounds.
[9] Greenawalt, *supra* note 3, at 19–20 (1995).
[10] However, see Chapter 9 in this volume for discussion of cases which have failed at the first stage, such as *Khawaja*.

The leading Canadian authorities are *R v. Keegstra*[11] and *R v. Butler*.[12] An important element of the s 1 analysis in these cases was the acceptance of claims pioneered by critical race and feminist theorists that these forms of speech cause harm to their victims that goes beyond hurt feelings or offended sensibilities.[13] In *Keegstra*, it was accepted that racist hate speech undermines the "sense of human dignity and belonging to the community at large"[14] of its victim, undermines their social equality and increases discrimination and violence against them.[15] The *Butler* Court made a similar finding about some sexually explicit expression. Depictions of explicit sex that is violent or that subjects participants to treatment that is degrading or dehumanizing harms its victims: it "reinforce[s] male-female stereotypes to the detriment of both sexes. It attempts to make degradation, humiliation, victimization and violence in human relationships appear normal and acceptable."[16] The Canadian Supreme Court has maintained this position despite a strong challenge, at least as it relates to the harm caused by sexually explicit expression.[17]

Equality

The Canadian approach in these cases is usually explained as revealing fundamental and distinctive Canadian constitutional values of "equality" and "multiculturalism."

The central insight on which the argument from equality depends – that hate speech and pornography harm the equality interests of their victims – was first developed in critiques of the First Amendment.[18] When translating the argument into the Canadian constitutional context, the starting point is s 15 of the *Charter*. The guarantee of equality in that section is said to provide content to the "free and democratic society" referred to in s 1 of the *Charter* and in turn to the s 1 requirement of a "pressing and substantial objective."[19]

---

[11] 3 SCR 697 (1990).   [12] 1 SCR 452 (1992).

[13] The Canadian Supreme Court does not deal directly with the claim that these forms of speech also "silence" their victims.

[14] 3 SCR 697, 746 (1990).   [15] 3 SCR 697, 747 (1990).

[16] *R v. Butler*, 1 SCR 452, 493–94 (1992).

[17] *See* Richard Moon, *R. v. Butler: The Limits of the Supreme Court's Feminist Re-Interpretation of Section*, 163 25 OTTAWA L. REV. 361 (1993); Leslie Green, *Pornographies*, 8 J. POLIT. PHILOS. 27 (2000). For an examination of the aftermath of Butler, see Chapter 2 in this volume, which argues that the Court's failure to embrace hierarchy as the "animating principle" of inequality has led to the misapplication of Butler in later cases.

[18] For prominent accounts, *see* Charles R. Lawrence III, *If He Hollers Let Him Go: Regulating Racist Speech on Campus* (1990) DUKE L. J. 431, 462–66; MacKinnon, *Feminism Unmodified* (1987), 146–62.

[19] 3 SCR 697, 743 (1990). Section 1 subjects *Charter* rights to "such reasonable limits prescribed by law as can be demonstrably justified in a free and democratic society."

As a result, laws that pursue the equality of persons have a strong claim to be a justifiable limit on freedom of expression.

The claim that hate speech and pornography harm the equality of their victims depends in part on the idea that these forms of speech promote discrimination and violence. In *Keegstra*, Cory J writing for the majority concluded:

> The message of the expressive activity covered by [the challenged hate speech law] is that the members of identifiable groups are not to be given equal standing in society, and are not human beings equally deserving of concern, respect and consideration. The harms caused by this message run directly counter to the values central to a free and democratic society and in restricting the promotion of hatred Parliament is therefore seeking to bolster the notion of mutual respect necessary in a nation, which venerates the equality of all persons.[20]

In addition, these forms of speech undermine equal democratic participation.[21] In *Keegstra*, the Supreme Court therefore concluded:

> [E]xpression can work to undermine our commitment to democracy where employed to propagate ideas anathemic to democratic values. Hate propaganda works in just such a way, arguing as it does for a society in which the democratic process is subverted and individuals are denied respect and dignity simply because of racial or religious characteristics ... Indeed one may quite plausibly contend that it is through rejecting hate propaganda that the state can best encourage the protection of values central to freedom of expression.[22]

Perhaps the strongest form of this argument is that hate speech and pornography actually "silence" their victims and thus interfere with their equal participation in public debate.[23]

---

[20] 3 SCR 697, 756–57 (1990). *See* David Dyzenhaus, "Obscenity and the Charter: Autonomy and Equality," (1991) 1 *Criminal Reports* (4th) 367, 376; Kathleen Mahoney, *R v. Keegstra: A Rationale for Regulating Pornography*, 37 McGill LJ 242, 257.

[21] Frederick Schauer, *Free Speech: A Philosophical Enquiry* (1982) 40–41. *See also* Lorraine Eisenstat Weinrib, *Hate Promotion in a Free and Democratic Society: R v. Keegstra*, 36 McGill L.J. 1416, 1429–30 (1991); Vicki C. Jackson, *Holistic Interpretation, Comparative Constitutionalism and Fiss-ian Freedoms* 58 U. Miami L. Rev. 265, 284–88 (2003); J. Skelly Wright, *Money and the Pollution of Politics: Is the First Amendment an Obstacle to Political Equality?* 82 Colum. L. Rev. 609, 625–6 (1982).

[22] 3 SCR 697, 764 (1990).

[23] For an important defence of this idea, see Rae Langton, *Speech Acts and Unspeakable Acts*, 22 Philosophy and Public Affairs 305 (1993).

Multiculturalism

These arguments are buttressed by reference to the value of encouraging cultural diversity, which looms particularly large in the context of racist hate speech. Like equality, multiculturalism receives express protection in the *Charter* (s 27), which in turn provides content to the concept of a "free and democratic society" in s 1. As the Court in *Keegstra* put it, ss 15 and 27 "inextricably infuse each constitutional guarantee with values supporting equal social participation and the security and dignity of all persons."[24] Reference is also made to the protection of ethnic and indigenous minorities in the Canadian Constitution through language and education rights.[25]

The protection of language and education rights – rights held by groups – lays the foundation for a distinctively Canadian version of multiculturalism in which cultural groups retain their identity and form the Canadian "ethnic mosaic."[26] Canada has faced especially acute challenges of multiculturalism – in particular the rather stark challenges posed by its bilingualism.[27] It is not surprising, therefore, that the Canadian experience has been a leading influence in the development of political theory sensitive to the importance of community and the recognition of group rights.[28] Drawing on this body of thought – and its emphasis on the importance of "community" in the lives of individuals[29] – the *Charter* conception of rights is therefore open to the possibility that individual freedoms can be limited in order to protect groups' identities and communal practices.[30] Canadian law of freedom of expression

[24] 3 SCR 697, 733 (1990).
[25] For a more detailed discussion of the constitutional history of religious, language and education rights of minorities in Manitoba, see Chapter 12 in this volume.
[26] Will Kymlicka, Multicultural Citizenship (1995) 14. *See also* Leighton McDonald, *Can Collective and Individual Rights Coexist?* 22 Melb. U. L. Rev. 310 (1998).
[27] *See* Jeremy Webber, *Reimagining Canada* (1994) for an analysis of the failure of the Meech Lake and Charlottetown Accords (recognizing Quebec as a "distinct society").
[28] *See especially* Charles Taylor, Multiculturalism and The Politics of Recognition (1992). For a defence of group rights within the liberal tradition, see Kymlicka *supra* note 26.
[29] For a more detailed discussion of the many ideas found in communitarian political theory, see Will Kymlicka, *Community*, in Robert E. Goodin and Phillip Pettit (ed.), A Companion to Contemporary Political Philosophy 366 (1995).
[30] For a sustained analysis, see Greenawalt, *supra* note 3. Not all analysts of the *Charter* make this claim. Richard Moon, in his extensive work on freedom of expression under the *Charter*, has argued that the *Charter* framework for the protection of expression is insufficiently responsive to the "relational" nature of freedom of expression and neglects to attend to its dependence upon community resources and social practices. See Richard Moon, The Constitutional Protection of Religious Freedom (2000); Richard Moon, *Justified Limits on Expression: The Collapse of the General Approach to Limits on Charter Rights*, 40 Osgoode Hall L. J. 335 (2002). I set this more radical critique aside because I am interested in positive claims that Canadian approaches to freedom of expression are responsive to communitarian concerns.

in turn is especially sensitive to the individual's need to take part in the communal life of cultural groups to which they belong.[31]

A Qualification and an Additional Point

Before proceeding, I should acknowledge that all the arguments just made could also be wielded to quite different ends. That is, arguments from equality and multiculturalism could support arguments in favour of a strong principle of freedom of expression that does *not* permit the regulation of hate speech and pornography in the Canadian manner.

That is, on some accounts, equality and multicultural diversity are values advanced as justifications for *protecting* speech and in particular for protecting hate speech and pornography. Not coincidentally, all of these arguments can be found in the law and literature on protection of freedom of speech under the First Amendment.

It is perhaps not surprising that an equality argument is wielded in support of First Amendment approaches to freedom of expression, given the Fourteenth Amendment's guarantee of equal protection. In general terms, the argument is that equality requires strong limitations on governmental powers of censorship to protect those least likely to dominate majoritarian processes.[32] A power to regulate hate speech and pornography would inevitably be disproportionately invoked against the least powerful. Thus it is said that speech by and on behalf of minority groups and women, the very groups whom these laws aim to protect, is most likely to be suppressed.[33] So Akhil Amar turns to history to support the case. He argues that dissenters – principally women and African Americans – benefited from the enactment of the Fourteenth Amendment's guarantee of equality and used their new found status to challenge prevailing social ideas. So, he argues, in a neat mirror of the Canadian position, that the Fourteenth Amendment's guarantee of equality is integral to freedom of speech under the First Amendment and bolsters, rather than weakens, the case for protecting racist hate speech.[34]

The same is said of the idea of equal participation as a democratic value. It is claimed that equal participation is best pursued through a strong free speech

---

[31] See Greenawalt, *supra* note 3, at 149, 255; Roy Leeper, *Keegstra and R.A.V.: A Comparative Analysis of the Canadian and U.S. Approaches to Hate Speech Legislation*, 5 COMMUNICATION LAW AND POLICY 295 (2000).

[32] Nadine Strossen, *Hate Speech and Pornography: Do We Have to Choose between Freedom of Speech and Equality?* 46 CASE W. RES. L. REV. 449 (1996).

[33] *Id.* at 459.

[34] Akhil Amar, *The Case of the Missing Amendments: RAV v City of St Paul*, 106 HARV. L. REV. 124 (1992).

principle not qualified by a concern about the capacity of speech to undermine participation. On the contrary, it is argued that a strong free speech
principle protects the most unpopular speakers and ideas from exclusion from
the democratic process.[35]

And, to repeat the point a third time, the value of multiculturalism or
cultural diversity is claimed to cut both ways: in support of freedom of
expression as well as in support of certain limits on expression. Like other
liberal rights, freedom of speech can be understood as directed toward freedom of individual choice. Diversity, including some degree of cultural diversity, is a perhaps inevitable and valued result of such liberty. When individuals
are free to pursue their own styles of life, we can expect that they will
sometimes do so by taking part in communal life, forming and preserving
groups that share the kinds of things that qualify them as a culture. Freedom of
speech contributes to cultural diversity by allowing individuals with diverse
ideas and desires to communicate and thus to form distinctive group identities. If claims like these are accepted, the American commitment to a strong
free speech principle can be seen as a means of ensuring vibrant communal
life in a multicultural society.[36]

All these points have been thoroughly ventilated in a comparative debate
that has occurred across North American borders and let me be perfectly
clear that I have no intention of entering that debate. Rather, my point is
to show that *viewed comparatively*, the Canadian constitutional law of freedom
of expression reveals that values on which freedom of expression apparently
depends can be wielded either in its favour or in favour of restricting the right.

Given its "double-sided" nature, the precise meaning of freedom of expression must therefore turn on something more than a commitment to values like
equality, multiculturalism (or diversity) or analogous ideas. At the very least it
is necessary to develop a more precise conception of these values. So for
instance, the Canadian conception of equality is often characterized as "substantive" and the American ideal (at least as revealed in First Amendment law)
as "formal."[37] However, for reasons I have discussed elsewhere,[38] claims of this

---

[35] Schauer, *supra* note 21, at 43–44.
[36] This idea is most fully developed in the work of Robert Post. *See especially* Robert C. Post,
Cultural Heterogeneity and the Law: Pornography, Blasphemy, and the First Amendment, 76
CALIF. L. REV. 297 (1988); *Community and the First Amendment* 29 ARIZ. STATE L. J. 473,
482 (1997).
[37] *See* MacKinnon, above n 2, at [n 3].
[38] Adrienne Stone, *How to Think about the Problem of Hate Speech*, in Katharine Gelber and
Adrienne Stone (eds.), FREEDOM OF SPEECH AND HATE SPEECH IN AUSTRALIA, Federation
Press 2007.

kind often fall prey to the same problem seen when these values are conceived at a higher level of generality. Even if we identify our conception of equality or of multicultural diversity more precisely, it is likely that both sides of this divide can lay claim to a commitment to that conception. Put simply, even once we agree on a substantive or positive conception of equality, there is disagreement as to how that state of equality is to be achieved and, specifically, as to how expressive freedom contributes to its achievement. Even these more precise conceptions of equality therefore do not yield a clear answer to free speech questions.

A full account of the Canadian constitutional law of freedom of expression therefore needs to take account of the attitudes toward state power that it reveals. This line of inquiry seems to direct us to a very old free speech idea: mistrust in government.[39] At the core of this ideal is belief that officials will, almost inevitably, abuse their power by acting illegally, dishonestly, self-servingly or in violation of some widely shared public morality.[40] In addition, it encompasses skepticism that government can make reliable judgments about speech, even when government is acting in good faith. Misjudgment is partially a function of the human fallibility emphasized by John Stuart Mill[41] but it is compounded by the majoritarian nature of democratic governments and the natural human tendency towards intolerance, which are likely to lead government to censor ideas because they are unconventional or unpopular.[42] That mistrust is compounded by fears arising from the large and complex nature of modern government. The possibility of bias and prejudice seem especially prevalent when laws are enforced by a bureaucracy that might apply laws in a manner not contemplated by the lawmakers.[43]

By contrast to the well-known American mistrust of government reflected in First Amendment law, in Canada the spectre of governmental abuse of power and misjudgment does not loom so large. The explicit acknowledgement in s 1 – the "central organizing principle" of the *Charter* – that rights

---

[39] The relevance of mistrust should perhaps be obvious. It is an important element of any free-speech principle and it finds especially clear expression in First Amendment law. Schauer, *supra* note 21, at 96.

[40] Vincent Blasi, *The Checking Value in First Amendment Theory*, AM. B. FOUND. RES. J. 521 (1977).

[41] J.S. Mill, ON LIBERTY (Elizabeth Rapaport ed 1978) (1st ed 1859), 15–52.

[42] *Abrams v. United States*, 250 US 616, 630 (1919): "Persecution for the expression of opinions seems to me perfectly logical. If you have no doubt of your premises or your power and want a certain result with all your heart you naturally express your wishes in law and sweep away all opposition." John Hart Ely, DEMOCRACY AND DISTRUST (1981), 103.

[43] Blasi, *supra* note 40, at 543.

are subject to limitation seems to signal that the Canadian Court should be sympathetic towards arguments for limitation on speech and defer more readily to legislative judgment.[44]

Particularly revealing of the Canadian understanding of the state is a distinction, drawn in *Irwin Toy v. Quebec*, between two kinds of *Charter* cases: those in which the government acts as the "singular antagonist" of the individual and those where the state is "mediating between the claims of competing groups."[45] In the latter class of cases, "vulnerable groups . . . claim the need for protection by the government" and thus the Court should be deferential to the legislature and mindful of its representative function. Neatly inverting the American idea that certain minorities require special protection from the state,[46] vulnerability of citizens or groups is a reason to strengthen the state's role in their protection rather than a reason to strengthen limitations on the state.

The cases examined here demonstrate the Canadian Supreme Court's confidence in government in several ways. First, it is evident in the Supreme Court's assessment of the harm caused by these forms of speech. In each case, there is some doubt about the causal link between the targeted speech (hate speech and pornography) and the harm that is said to result. Nonetheless, in each case, the Canadian Supreme Court responded by deferring to legislative judgment, according the government a margin of appreciation in the assessment of harm.[47] Second, it is seen in the response of the Canadian Supreme Court in *Little Sisters Book and Art Emporium v. Canada*[48] to a strong challenge to the *Butler* test.

Little Sisters revealed that customs officials had used their power to seize obscene material in a manner that disproportionately affected gay and lesbian erotica. Critics of *Butler* argue that this problem is inherent in the *Butler* standard. The reliance on "the community standards of tolerance" test imposed majoritarian standards that excluded minority representations of

---

[44] On the relevance of the text, 251–2; Jamie Cameron, *The Original Conception of Section 1 and its Demise*, (1989) 35 McGILL L.J. 254, 261. *See also R. v. Edwards Books*, 2 SCR 713 (1986). The Court is wary of the substantive due process jurisprudence of the Lochner Era, during which the United States Supreme Court invalidated much progressive economic regulation. *See also R. v. Wholesale Travel Group Inc.*, 3 SCR 154 (1991); Sujit Choudhry, *The Lochner Era and Comparative Constitutionalism*, (2004) 2 I. CON 1.

[45] [1989] 1 SCR 927, 993.

[46] *United States v. Carolene Products*, 304 US 144, 152 n. 4, elaborated in Ely, *supra* note 42.

[47] *Butler* [1992] 1 SCR 452, 503, *Keegstra*, 3 SCR 697, 776 (1990). In each case, the Court cites *Irwin Toy v. Quebec* [1989] 1 SCR 927, 994.

[48] 2 SCR 1120 (2000).

sex and sexuality, allow for the imposition of homophobic prejudice and, in effect, reinstate a test based on community standards of morality.[49] For this reason, it is said, biased application of the censorship scheme in a manner that oppressed minority sexual identities was inevitable. The Supreme Court recognized the danger of discrimination but nonetheless adhered to the *Butler* standard confident that, under a slightly altered scheme, the state could make appropriate judgments in this area.[50]

Third, the Canadian Supreme Court has proved receptive to the idea that restrictions on freedom of speech sometimes actually help promote the goals of freedom of speech.[51] Its vision of freedom of speech acknowledges that limits on speech may operate to ensure a richer, fairer, more respectful public debate in which all have an opportunity to participate. The Court in *Keegstra* accepted that hate speech can undermine the pursuit of truth[52] and the achievement of democratic government, concluding "one may quite plausibly contend that it is through rejecting hate propaganda that the state can best encourage the protection of values central to freedom of expression."[53] Accepting that view requires, of course, some confidence that the state can be relied upon to regulate speech fairly and competently.

Before concluding let me acknowledge that the idea that Canadian constitutional law exhibits a measure of "trust" in government should neither be overemphasized nor oversimplified. Obviously, Canadian law does not entirely abandon the insight that the individual requires protection from state intrusion in the realm of expressive freedom. Moreover, taking into account the institutional context in which the protection of freedom of expression occurs, one way to understand its law is as acknowledging *judicial* fallibility with respect to freedom of expression (and other rights). Peter Russell summarized the point in this way: "[b]y providing a legislative counter-weight to judicial power the Canadian *Charter* establishes a prudent system of checks and balances which recognizes *the fallibility of both courts and legislatures* and gives closure to the decisions of neither."[54]

---

[49] Brenda Cossman, *Disciplining the Unruly: Sexual Outlaw, Little Sisters* and the Legacy of *Butler*, U. B. C. L. Rev. 77 (2003). Brenda Cossman et al., *Bad Attitudes on Trial: Pornography, Feminism and the Butler Decision* (Toronto, Toronto University Press, 1997).

[50] Though it reversed the onus of proof: 2 SCR 1120, 1181 (1990).

[51] This idea is powerfully expounded in the work of Owen Fiss and Cass Sunstein. *See* Owen M. Fiss, *The Irony of Free Speech* (Cambridge, MA, Harvard University Press, 1996); Cass R. Sunstein, *Democracy and the Problem of Free Speech* (New York, NY, Free Press, 1993).

[52] 3 SCR 697, (1990) 762–3.   [53] 3 SCR 697, 764 (1990) (emphasis added).

[54] Peter Russell, *Standing Up for Notwithstanding*, 29 Alta L. Rev. 293, 301 (1991).

THE METHODOLOGY OF THE CANADIAN CONSTITUTIONAL
LAW OF FREEDOM OF EXPRESSION

The final feature of Canadian constitutional law that is worth dwelling on in this context is methodology. Through s 1, the courts apply a proportionality test, the well-known form of means-ends analysis coupled with an element of balancing. In this respect, Canadian approaches are mainstream in world terms,[55] however, in the context of the law of freedom of expression, the interesting feature of proportionality analysis is its marked contrast with the United States Supreme Court's development of more tightly confined, highly specific rules for particular categories of speech.

To understand the distinctive qualities of proportionality in the context of the comparative constitutional law of freedom of expression, it is necessary then to focus on its "standard-like" features, that is its capacity for flexibility and context sensitivity. These features allow judges to take into account the circumstances of a particular case and respond to fine-grained differences between cases as well as unforeseen developments.

Two explanations for the Canadian preference for proportionality immediately reveal themselves. The first is constitutional text. It might be said that the reference in s 1 to "such reasonable limits prescribed by law as can be demonstrably justified in a free and democratic society" calls for a judgment, it might be said, as to whether any law is a proportionate restriction of the protected rights.[56]

Finally, the adoption of proportionality analysis could be taken simply to reflect the relatively short history of the *Charter*. Frederick Schauer has predicted that these methodological preferences between the United States and Canada (and other countries) may become less marked over time as rule-like approaches become more flexible and proportionality approaches generate more and more concrete and specific categories. This dynamic is a general feature of the enforcement of rules through law at least within the common law tradition.[57] Schauer identifies a set of techniques, commonly employed in common law adjudication, to avoid rules[58] and practical and psychological

---

[55] Though of course there are some differences among forms of proportionality. See David Law, *Generic Constitutional Law*, 89 MINN. L. REV. 652, 698 (2005).

[56] Nor does it have the invitation to positive lawmaking for the protection of rights (see ss 6(4), 15(2), 16(3), 16.1(2), but cf section 5 of the XIVth amendment) or the explicit recognition of a multicultural society (see additionally s 27).

[57] Frederick Schauer, *The Convergence of Rules and Standards*, NEW ZEALAND L. REV. 303 (2003).

[58] Rules can be avoided by creating exceptions at the point of application (often to accommodate situations that are not anticipated by the rule); treating rules as subject to an implicit

reasons that decision-makers might wish to concretize standards[59] and mechanisms by which this might occur.[60] The Canadian preference for proportionality may over time dissipate and as the courts sift and sort through cases, a more specific and concrete body of doctrine may emerge.

However, while these features are likely to be part of the story, there is a link between method and substance that links these methodological preferences to deeper values and makes them more likely to be permanent. Schauer himself has identified the connection between the rigidity of First Amendment doctrine and the "culture of extreme distrust" that underlies it:[61] "balancing categorically and not in individual cases is far less likely to result in an erosion of free speech principles."[62] The American preference for rules is further reinforced by institutional factors. Case-specific balancing (particularly balancing that engages with the empirical and policy issues that motivate and justify governmental action) excites more concern in America about the legitimacy of judicial review than rule-based constitutional adjudication.[63] It is also more compatible with the guidance function that the Supreme Court must perform, a function that is particularly salient given the minuscule fraction of the cases presented to it that it can give substantive attention.[64]

Canadian constitutional law provides the other side of this argument, revealing a different set of substantive underpinnings. The first of these is a relatively open attitude toward foreign influence in law. Proportionality tests have made their way into common law systems via European law, perhaps most directly the law of the ECHR, though the origins of the doctrine are, of course, German. The comparative openness of the Canadian Supreme Court to influence of foreign law explains why it is proportionality rather than some other form of doctrinal flexibility that has prevailed in the Canadian courts.

In addition, it is likely influenced by the structure of judicial review. A constitutional order like Canada's, committed to facilitating inter-institutional

---

requirement of reasonableness and as subject to override "in exigent circumstances"; and allowing "departure from the specificity of a rule in order to rely on its less specific purpose": *Id.* at 312–315.

[59] "As a consequence of the numerous reasons of time, energy, efficiency, comparative advantage, and psychological makeup that would lead nominally unconstrained decision-makers to constrain themselves more than others would wish to constrain them, it is thus possible that rule-enforcers, rule-interpreters, and rule-appliers, even if they in theory enjoy the considerable discretion granted to them, will supplement the standards with more specific "guidelines" or "rules of thumb" that in practice have all of the characteristics of rules": *Id.* 316.

[60] Including the adoption of such guidelines; incorporating other rules; and when decisions under standards are taken as having precedential status: *Id.* at 317–318.

[61] *Id.* at 64.   [62] *Id.*   [63] *Id.* at 65.   [64] *Id.* at 66.

interaction,[65] may well be more receptive than others to proportionality-based review as opposed to more rulified forms of constitutional doctrine. First, where a law fails a proportionality test on the means-ends element of the proportionality analysis, it is open to the parliament to respond with a law that more effectively pursues its objective or does so in a manner more narrowly tailored towards that objective. Similarly, if a law fails the balancing element of the test, it is open for the legislature to attempt to "reset" the balance by reducing the impact of the impugned law on the protected right or drafting the law in a manner that identifies and pursues a "weightier" objective.

Finally, the Canadian preference for proportionality reinforces the analysis I have advanced in Part I: proportionality is a better fit in the context of a social democratic (rather than libertarian) state.[66] The very flexibility and fact-specificity of the proportionality test arguably facilitates greater institutional dialogue thus giving greater room for the state to pursue its objectives than is likely under a more rulified system. Freedom of expression provides a very clear illustration of the point, as the rigidity of First Amendment doctrine is celebrated precisely for its propensity to protect speech from state intrusion[67].

In conclusion, then, methodology of freedom of expression under the Canadian *Charter* is as illustrative of deep constitutional commitments as

---

[65] Peter W. Hogg and Allison A. Bushell, *The Charter Dialogue between Courts and Legislatures (Or Perhaps The Charter Of Rights Isn't Such A Bad Thing After All)*, 35 Osgoode Hall L. J. 75 (1997). The other features are the s 33 legislative override power; the "qualified rights" (ss 7, 8, 9 and 12) "which allow for action that satisfies standards of fairness and reasonableness"; and the s 15(1) equality rights "which can be satisfied through a variety of remedial measures" (at 82). The dialogue metaphor introduced by Hogg and Bushell has been subjected to withering critique, on empirical and normative grounds (eg Christopher P. Manfredi & James B. Kelly, *Six Degrees of Dialogue: A Response to Hogg and Bushell*, 37 Osgoode Hall L. J. 513 (1999); Christoper P. Manfredi and James B. Kelly, *Dialogue, Deference and Restraint: Judicial Independence and Trial Procedures*, Saskatchewan L. Rev. 64 (2000); Ted Morton and Rainer Knopff, *The Charter Revolution and the Court Party* (2000); F. L. Morton, *Dialogue or Monologue?*, Policy Options (April 1999) 23), and equally spirited defence (Peter W. Hogg and Allison A. Thornton, *Reply to Six Degrees Of Dialogue*, 37 Osgoode Hall L. J. 529 (1999)). But it remains, however, a central element of the Supreme Court's conception of Canadian constitutionalism. *See generally*, Rosalind Dixon, *A New Theory of Charter Dialogue: The Supreme Court of Canada, Charter Dialogue and Deference*, 47 Osgoode Hall L. J. 235 (2009).

[66] Richard Mullender, *Theorizing the Third Way: Qualified Consequentialism, the Proportionality Principle, and the New Social Democracy*, (2000) 27 J. Law Soc. 493, 503: "proportionality is a mediating principle": "[i]t provides guidance on the question as to how we should seek to accommodate both the public interest in the pursuit of generally beneficial outcomes and the countervailing interests of individuals and collectivities."

[67] *See* Chapter 9 in this volume for discussion of first amendment's wide scope and "stringent standard of review."

the more obviously substantive areas of Canadian law. The overall picture it presents is of a constitutional commitment to freedom of expression that is developed in the context of strong constitutional commitments to equality and multicultural diversity and with a social democratic attitude toward state power.

INSIGHTS INTO FREEDOM OF EXPRESSION?

I have so far presented the Canadian constitutional law of freedom of expression as a means for understanding the central commitments of the Canadian constitutional order, especially contrasted with the United States.

It is not especially surprising that different constitutional systems reach different conclusions on questions about freedom of expression. It is a widely noted feature of rights generally that they command a high level of agreement when expressed at a high level of generality but that this fractures when it comes to determining their precise meaning.[68] Freedom of expression provides a very powerful illustration of the point. Agreement upon its place in the canon of liberal rights is exceptionally high as its inclusion, in one way or another, by every democratic constitution bears witness.[69] And yet, this widespread commitment to freedom of expression quickly disappears when it comes to determining its meaning in specific circumstances, as this comparative study shows.[70]

A broader comparative study would further complicate the picture revealing even more diverse concepts of freedom of expression and, in turn, something about the fundamental values of the constitutional system in which they sit. For instance, the German law of freedom of expression shares some features with Canadian law. On the question of methodology in particular, German law, in the development of proportionality analysis, is clearly the progenitor of the approach that has come to dominate in Canada.[71] On questions of levels of trust in government, the German approach perhaps even exceeds the

---

[68] Jeremy Waldron, LAW AND DISAGREEMENT (2000).

[69] In a few cases where constitutions do not provide explicit protection – Australia and Israel – the courts have stepped into the breach developing rights of freedom of expression derived from other constitutional features. *See* Adrienne Stone, "The Comparative Constitutional Law of Freedom of Expression," RESEARCH HANDBOOK ON COMPARATIVE CONSTITUTIONAL LAW, Rosalind Dixon, Tom Ginsburg, eds., (2011).

[70] For further comparative study *see* Stone, supra note 69; Adrienne Stone et al., *The Constitutional Law of Freedom of Expression in Asia*, Rosalind Dixon and Tom Ginsburg (eds.), COMPARATIVE CONSTITUTIONAL LAW IN ASIA (2013).

[71] Moshe Cohen-Eliya and Iddo Porat, *American Balancing and German Proportionality: The Historical Origins*, 8 I.CON 263 (2010).

Canadian. Article 5 of the *German Basic Law* has a positive aspect, imposing a duty on the state to ensure that broadcasters maintain "balance, objectivity and reciprocal respect" in programming.[72] Other aspects of the German approach to freedom of expression demonstrate the centrality of dignity to that constitutional system through a cultural commitment to demonstrating respect for dignity and equality through a conception of "honour." As James Whitman has memorably shown, German law (like French law) has pursued equality in the realm of insult and defamation law by "levelling up" and extending to all the honour once the preserve of the elite.[73]

The more we widen our comparative lens the more complex and varied this picture becomes. In Australia, for instance, it seems that the courts share the comparative levels of trust in government seen in Canada[74] (and like them do not go so far as to use constitutional rights to impose positive duties on government)[75]. At the same time, however, the Australian constitutional culture seems to share the "levelling down" impulse of First Amendment law: in freedom of expression generally, the Australian courts countenance regulation to allow for fairness and balance in public debate, such as regulation of election funding, but at the same time Australian constitutional law has celebrated the intemperate incivility of Australian public discourse and proved highly resistant to laws that promote "civility."[76] The Australian attitude is characterized, I suggest elsewhere, by a level of acceptance of the positive role for the state in securing various kinds of goods, leavened by an Australian "irreverence" for authority.[77]

This comparative picture of freedom of expression provides a fascinating insight into constitutional culture. In addition, I wish to consider what this picture tells us about *freedom of expression*. In particular, I want to consider whether the Canadian constitutional law of freedom of expression, viewed comparatively, has any significance for our understanding of disagreements

---

[72] *Television I Case* (1961) 12 BVerfGE 205.

[73] Whitman, James Q., *Enforcing Civility and Respect: Three Societies*, 109 YALE L. J. 1279 (2000)

[74] Australia and Canada, along with a number of other common law jurisdictions, have reached similar positions on the interaction of freedom of expression with the law of defamation extending the traditional common law to provide greater protection for political expression but not going so far as to adopt *New York Times v. Sullivan*. Adrienne Stone and George Williams, *Freedom of Speech and Defamation in the Common Law World*, (2000) 26 MONASH UNIVERSITY LAW REVIEW 362–378.

[75] *McClure v. Australian Electoral Commission* [1999] HCA 31, (1999) 163 ALR 734

[76] *Coleman v. Power* (2004) 220 CLR 1.

[77] Adrienne Stone, *"Insult and Emotion, Calumny and Invective": Twenty Years of Freedom of Political Communicatio,n* 30 UNI. QUEENSLAND LAW J. 79 (2011).

about freedom of expression.[78] I have already mentioned the widespread acceptance that disagreement is widely recognized to be an inevitable attendant of rights. The disagreement partly stems from the general terms in which rights are expressed in constitutional text. But it is also a consequence of the fact that disagreement is an inevitable and ineradicable part of moral discourse.[79] The comparison I have drawn between Canadian law of freedom of expression and First Amendment law provides a detailed demonstration of disagreement about the meaning of an undeniably moral idea like equality and the significance of multicultural diversity in a democracy.

To this picture of reasonable disagreement, I have sought to emphasize differences along another axis: different judgments about the extent to which the state is to be trusted. Differences on this score in part reflect a variant of reasonable moral disagreement evident in relation to other freedom of expression values. No doubt the libertarian infused First Amendment and the high level of distrust that is exhibited to state power is a reflection of the moral priority given to the individual over collective good while the more social democratic, communitarian commitments of Canadian law represent the reverse. However, these attitudes also represent something else: a historically derived judgment about how much government can actually be trusted. This kind of judgment is not a moral judgment as to the relative priority of the individual over the collective. Nor is it straightforward empirical judgment. (It is based on experience but it would seem to overstate the rationality of the process to describe it as an "empirically based" prediction as to how the state will act.) It might better be described as a "construction" of the constitutional culture. That is, it is an understanding derived in part from constitutional theory, reinforced by historical experience and which receives authoritative exposition in judicial decisions. The nature of such a construction and the process through which it is derived is underdeveloped in constitutional theory and worthy of future study. However, even in its embryonic form, the idea of freedom of expression as partly a "construction" lends a different perspective to cross-cultural disagreements. It raises the prospect that freedom of expression is in part an historically and culturally contingent value.

CONCLUSION

The law of freedom of expression provides a decisive demonstration of the distinctiveness of Canadian constitutional law. Substantively and methodologically,

[78] Much of this literature uses the terminology "freedom of speech." Though that that term is not precisely the equivalent of "freedom of expression" for my purposes I will treat them as such.
[79] Jeremy Waldron, LAW AND DISAGREEMENT (2000), 225–6.

the Canadian Supreme Court made a sharp break from the United States and developed an understanding of freedom of expression that is sensitive to Canadian conceptions of equality and multiculturalism. As I hope to have shown, moreover, the Canadian constitutional law of freedom of expression reveals something of general significance for freedom of expression. Viewed in comparative perspective, it illustrates a role in constitutional reasoning for ideas about the nature (and likely future exercise) of governmental power, which are best understood as the inherited "constructs" of a constitutional culture.

12

The Judicial, Legislative and Executive Roles in Enforcing the Constitution

Three Manitoba Stories

KENT ROACH

INTRODUCTION

The 150th anniversary of Canada's Constitution provides an excellent opportunity to reflect on the relation between the Constitution Act, 1867 and the 1982 additions to the Constitution. There has been a tendency to emphasize the differences between the two constitutions and to characterize the 1982 Charter of Rights and Freedoms as an innovation if not a revolution. Critics on both the right[1] and the left[2] have characterized the Charter as a radical innovation that by increasing the judicial role in enforcing rights present threats to Canadian democracy. In her chapter in this volume, Jamie Cameron also draws a stark contrast between pre-Charter eras based on "statutory legitimacy" and a post-Charter era based on "constitutional legitimacy."[3] Benjamin Berger has associated the Charter with a universal and liberal logic while recognizing that Canada is still influenced by a more particular and political logic that includes a tradition of Parliamentary supremacy including its use to assist the disadvantaged and the reciprocal protection of specific minorities.[4]

Arguments about the nature of judicial review that are not immersed in empirical detail, however, tend to cast more heat than light. Much of the debate about the role of the Charter in the Canadian Constitution has

I thank the Pierre Trudeau Foundation and the Centre for Transnational Legal Studies for their support during the writing of this chapter which forms part of a larger projects on remedies for violations of human rights.
[1]   *See* F.L. Morton and Rainer Knopff, THE CHARTER REVOLUTION AND THE COURT PARTY (Peterborogh: Broadview Press, 2000).
[2]   *See* Andrew Petter, THE POLITICS OF THE CHARTER (Toronto: University of Toronto Press, 2010).
[3]   Chapter 5 in this volume.
[4]   Benjamin Berger, *Children of Two Logics: A Way Into Canadian Constitutional Culture*, 11 I.CON. 319 (2013).

downplayed historical antecedents to "judicial activism" and how parts of the Charter addressed such concerns.[5] In addition, commentators have frequently ignored questions of remedies.[6] Remedies often involve courts in nuanced interaction with Parliament, the executive and civil society.

This chapter will focus on the roles and records of courts, legislatures and the executive in enforcing the Constitution both before and after the Charter. This can be done by examining a series of constitutional cases starting in the 1890s involving the enforcement of Manitoba Act, 1870[7] which created that province in response to the first Riel rebellion. Any case study is inevitably partial, but this one involves the fundamental Canadian cleavages of religion, language and relations with Indigenous peoples. It also deals with rights that are quite specifically spelled out in the constitution. This should avoid the problems of alleged "rights inflation"[8] and alleged departures from the text,[9] or intent of the framers[10] that are discussed in other chapters in this volume. The tensions and even conflicts between courts, legislature and the executive revealed in these cases suggest that even clearly defined minority rights will be controversial. They will not always be respected or enforced by legislatures, the executive and courts.

Examining the Manitoba remedial cases will also allow for some selective engagement with comparative constitutional law. Both s.22 of the Manitoba Act and s.93 of the Constitution Act, 1867 empower the federal Parliament to enact remedial legislation to enforce denominational school rights. The Civil

---

5   For my own attempt to integrate this often forgotten past including the Supreme Court's activism in the 1950's in protecting religious minorities in Quebec, *see* Kent Roach, THE SUPREME COURT ON TRIAL: JUDICIAL ACTIVISM OR DEMOCRATIC DIALOGUE, revised ed (Toronto: Irwin Law, 2016), chs. 3–4.

6   Daryl Levinson, *Rights Essentialism and Remedial Equilibration*, 99 COLUM.L.REV. 857 (1999).

7   S.C. 1870, c.3. This act is defined as part of the Constitution of Canada in schedule 2 of the Constitution Act, 1982.

8   Chapter 9 in this volume. The cases examined in this chapter do not involve proportionality analysis which Professor Tushnet suggests has been an engine of rights inflation in Canada.

9   Chapter 7 in this volume. The cases examined in this chapter deal with the rights of minorities in a province, an issue that Professor Rosenfeld suggests lie well within the legitimate constitutionalization of politics.

10 Jeffrey Goldsworthy and Grant Huscroft in "Originalism in Australia and Canada: Why the Divergence?" in chapter 8 of this volume cite the Privy Council's decision in *Brophy v. Attorney General of Manitoba* [1895] A.C. 202 that affirmed the remedial jurisdiction of Parliament as consistent with originalism. Perhaps an even stronger example would be the Supreme Court's decision in *Barrett v. City of Winnipeg* (1891) 19 SCR 374 at 384 holding that Manitoba's law abolishing publicly funded separate schools was unconstitutional, a decision subsequently overruled by the Privy Council which as they note has widely been criticized as departing from the intent of the original framers of the 1867 Constitution.

War amendments of the American constitution enacted around the same time similarly provided Congress with jurisdiction to enforce the rights of minorities. The American courts have, however, tended to interpret Congress's remedial jurisdiction in a restrictive manner whereas the Canadian approach has in law if not actual practice been more generous.[11] A continued Canadian deference to the role of legislatures in enacting remedial laws to benefit minorities is also seen in provisions in the 1982 Charter that specifically contemplate that legislatures can enact "affirmative action" programs designed to ameliorate the conditions of disadvantaged individuals and groups.[12]

The suspended declaration of invalidity was first created and used by the Supreme Court of Canada in the 1985 *Manitoba Language Reference*[13] as a creative means to deal with the constitutional crisis that would have resulted from the invalidation of almost of all of Manitoba's laws because they were enacted in English only. It gave the government time to translate old laws, but also responded to the failure of the Manitoba legislature in 1983 to approve a constitutional amendment that would have made much of the translation unnecessary while providing Franco-Manitobans with the modern remedy of the right to receive bilingual services from the Manitoba government. In any event, section 172 of the South African Constitution embraced the Canadian innovation of allow courts to suspend declarations of invalidity to allow legislatures to enact new and constitutional legislation.[14] Not without its critics, the suspended declaration of invalidity allows courts and legislatures to work in partnership in enforcing rights. It facilitates a concrete interaction or dialogue between courts and legislatures that draws on the strengths of courts in identifying rights violations and disproportionate limits on rights and the strengths of legislatures in placing such violations into a larger policy context where the legislature can clarify and expand its objectives and justify limits on rights.[15]

---

[11] For example, *compare Brophy v. Attorney General of Manitoba* [1895] A.C. 202 (P.C.), *with The Civil Rights Cases* 109 US 3 (1883).

[12] Canadian Charter of Rights and Freedoms ss.6(3) and (4), s.15(2). The Supreme Court of Canada has been quite deferential to governmental attempts to devise affirmative action or ameliorative programs and only require a rational basis for such programs. For a case upholding an ameliorative program for the Metis in Alberta *see Alberta (Aboriginal Affairs and Northern Development) v. Cunningham*, 2011 SCC 37, [2011] 2 SCR 670.

[13] [1985] 1 SCR 721.

[14] Heinz Klug's chapter in this collection examines other influences that the Canadian Charter had on the new South African constitution.

[15] For a critical discussion of dialogue between courts and legislatures in Canada *see* Alison Young "Exporting Dialogue: Critical Reflections on Canada's 'Commonwealth' Model of Rights Protection." For my own views on the existence and desirability of dialogue including remedial dialogues between courts and other branches of government on the basis that each institution plays distinct and complementary roles *see* Kent Roach, THE SUPREME COURT ON TRIAL: JUDICIAL ACTIVISM OR DEMOCRATIC DIALOGUE, revised ed (Toronto: Irwin Law, 2016).

It also involves civil society groups who must engage with the legislative process to maintain and solidify court-room victories.

The suspended declaration of invalidity also provides an important precedent for the courts retaining supervisory jurisdiction when necessary to ensure that the Constitution be enforced. Canadian courts, however, remain less comfortable with administering complex relief than their American counterparts. They also have been less willing to provide interim relief for those adversely affected by a suspended declaration of invalidity than their South African counterparts. Canadian courts tend to rely on declaratory relief as in the 2013 *Manitoba Métis Federation* litigation[16] another case that will be examined in this chapter. Declarations assume that governments will promptly and in good faith comply with constitutional requirements once they have been articulated by the courts. They also create space for civil society engagement in the enforcement of the Constitution.

Unfortunately the case studies examined in this chapter suggest that Canadian governments have not always promptly or in good faith responded to all declarations. Some early judicial decisions enforcing s.22 of the Manitoba Act and requiring bilingual laws were simply and regrettably ignored by the Manitoba government. After some initial delay in responding to the Supreme Court's 2013 declaration in *Manitoba Métis Federation* that the land grants required under the Manitoba Act to the Métis were not properly administered, a 2016 Memorandum of Understanding has been signed to facilitate land claims negotiations between the federal government and the Manitoba Métis Federation. In short, the Manitoba remedial cases provide an excellent context to assess the respective role of all three branches of government and civil society in enforcing the constitution and to compare the Canadian approach to constitutional remedies with those of other countries.

THE CONTEXT. THE MANITOBA ACT, 1870

Manitoba was a revolutionary constitutional order in a country known for its rejection of revolution. The Métis under Louis Riel's leadership seized power and formed a provisional government in an attempt to safeguard their interests against the expansion of Canada into the Red River territory. Attempts to impose individual grid-like land holdings on the river lots of the Métis, the product of European fur-traders and the Indigenous population, were a particular source of friction that provoked the successful 1870 rebellion.

[16] [2013] 1 SCR 623.

The Riel government seized power and after selecting even numbers of francophone and anglophone delegates made a series of demands on the federal government. The Riel government was not without fault. It even executed Thomas Scott, an Orangeman, for his resistance. Although he was on the losing side in the rebellion and was even imprisoned for a time by the government, Dr. Schultz would eventually become Lieutenant Governor of the rapidly expanding Prairie province. As will be seen, he would refuse to use his executive powers to block 1890 legislation that would repeal some of the most important concessions and guarantees that Riel obtained in 1870 for the French language and Catholic schools.

The Manitoba Act, 1870 was the product of successful negotiation between Riel's provisional government and Sir John A. Macdonald's federal government. The Supreme Court has recently explained:

> Settlers began pouring into the region, displacing the Métis' social and political control. This led to resistance and conflict. To resolve the conflict and assure peaceful annexation of the territory, the Canadian government entered into negotiations with representatives of the Métis-led provisional government of the territory. The result was the *Manitoba Act, 1870* . . . which made Manitoba a province of Canada.[17]

Macdonald was not happy about negotiating with the rebels and would later not save Riel from the gallows, but he was anxious to settle the Red River uprising in order to prevent possible American expansion into the Northwest and to build a transcontinental railway.

The Red River Rebellion was successful in obtaining a variety of constitutional guarantees in the Manitoba Act, 1870, but Riel fled the province. He was subsequently tried and hanged for treason in relation to the less successful Saskatchewan rebellion of 1885. According to one of the six jurors who had recommended mercy, Riel was really "hanged for the murder of Scott."[18]

Riel made a speech at his trial explaining that the 1870 Red River Rebellion was necessary because there was no prior "consultation" with the Métis and that the 1885 rebellion was "the continuation of the troubles of the Red River." He call the Manitoba Act, 1870 "a treaty", but complained that the Métis were forced to move west to Saskatchewan because they were not given the one seventh of Manitoba's lands promised to them in s.31 of the Manitoba Act. In an appeal to anti-majoritarian rights, Riel argued that the European majority

---

[17] *Manitoba Metis Federation, supra,* at para 4.
[18] George Stanley, Louis Riel: Patriot or Rebel? (Ottawa: Canadian Historical Society, 1979), 23.

"had no greater rights than the small because the right is the same for everyone" and that "the right of nations wanted that the treaty of Manitoba should be fulfilled towards the little community of Red River in the same condition that they were treated."[19] Today, Riel still remains Canada's most controversial figure. He is celebrated by a holiday in Manitoba, but efforts to pardon or exonerate him for his treason conviction has so far been unsuccessful.[20]

By the force of their seizure of power, the three overlapping groups of the Métis, Roman Catholics and Francophones had significant political strength when Manitoba was created in 1870. Indeed, they constituted the majority of the Red River settlement, but it was clear that they would become a minority with the opening up of the West and the construction of a transcontinental railway. The political strength of the soon to be overlapping minorities was manifested in three provisions in the Manitoba Act: sections 22, 23 and 31 of the Manitoba Act.[21]

Section 22(1) provided that while the new province could legislate with respect to education, none of its laws "shall prejudicially affect any right or privilege with respect to Denominational Schools which any class of persons have by Law *or practice* in the Province at the Union." This went beyond s.93 of the Constitution Act, 1867 which only protected denominational school rights enjoyed "at law" at the time of Confederation.

Section 22(2) and (3) provided that the Protestant or Roman Catholic minority could appeal to the federal Cabinet "any Act or decision" affecting its rights or privileges and that the federal Parliament retained the right to "make Remedial laws for the due execution of the provisions of this section or of any decision of the Governor in Council under this section" but only "as far as the circumstances of each case require."

Section 23 guaranteed language rights by providing that either English or French could be used in the Manitoba legislature and that "the acts of the Legislature shall be published and printed in both languages." It also provided for the use of either French or English in Manitoba's courts.

---

[19] Louis Riel "Address to the Court, Aug. 1, 1885" in Hans Hansen ed. *Riel's Defence* (Montreal: McGill Queens Press, 2015), 48–57. For a powerful contemporary reading of s.31 of the Manitoba Act as a treaty or land claims agreement between the Métis and the federal government *see* Darren O'Toole, *Section 31 of the Manitoba Act: A Lands Claim Agreement*, 38 MANITOBA L. J. 73 (2015).

[20] Jean Teillet, *Exoneration for Louis Riel: Mercy, Justice, or Political Expediency*, 67 SASKATCHEWAN L. REV. 359 (2004).

[21] 33 Vict ch. 3 (Canada).

Section 31 recognized Métis concerns and claims over land by providing that 1.4 million acres would be appropriated to the "children of the half-breed heads of families" residing in Manitoba at the time of the union in part because it was "expedient towards the extinguishment of the Indian title to the lands in the Province."

French speaking Métis were a slim majority of Manitoba's population under the 1871 Census, but by the 1891 Census Francophones constituted only 7 per cent of the province's growing population and Catholics only constituted 13 per cent.[22] The number of Métis had also decreased as many had moved westward in part because of delays in distributing land under s.31. Many Métis sold their land to new settlers who would "subsequently challenge the Métis language, values, and religion" with legislation being enacted to encourage this process.[23]

The year 1890 was a particularly bad one for the Catholic and francophone minority. The Manitoba legislature enacted the *Official Language Act*[24] that declared English the only official language of the Manitoba legislature and courts. It also created a non-denominational publicly funded school system and withdrew public funding to Catholic schools that had been provided since 1871.[25]

The minorities in Manitoba claimed their rights and sought redress in a variety of ways. They asked the federal executive to disallow both pieces of legislation. When the federal government refused to so, they went to court including two separate trips to the Judicial Committee of the Privy Council in England which was Canada's final court of appeal until 1949. They also obtained an 1892 court ruling that the *Official Language Act* was unconstitutional[26], a ruling that the Manitoba government ignored. All of these claims sounded in the language of rights.

All of this litigation suggests that it is wrong to portray the 1982 Charter as a radical innovation that injected an uncompromising language of rights and litigation into Canadian political culture.[27] Rights for minorities, including a

---

[22] Gordon Bale, *Law, Politics and the Manitoba School Question*, 63 CAN. BAR REV. 461 at 467–8 (1985).

[23] Raymond Hebert, MANITOBA'S FRENCH-LANGUAGE CRISIS (Montreal: McGill Queens Press, 2004), 10.

[24] S.M. 1890 c.14.   [25] Public Schools Act S.M. 1890 c.3.

[26] *Pellant v. Hebert* first published in *Le Manitoba* Mar. 9, 1892 reprinted (1981) 12 R.G.F. 242.

[27] For example, Nelson Wiseman has wrongly asserted that "the concept of fixed and permanent rights was alien" to Canada in the 1890's. Nelson Wiseman "The Questionable Relevance of the Constitution in Advancing Minority Cultural Rights in Manitoba" (1992) 25 C.J.P.S. 697 at 704. *See also* Morton and Knopff *The Charter Revolution and the Court Party* (2000) at 149 lamenting "the growth of court-room rights talk" under the Charter and Dennis Baker,

demand for reciprocal respect of the rights of Catholic and French minorities in Manitoba and Protestant and English minorities in Quebec and respect for Treaties that Indigenous groups signed with the Crown, were an important element of the Canadian constitution from the start. At least since the rejection of Lord Durham's report calling for a legislative union between what is now Quebec and Ontario, constitutional justice in Canada has never been a simple majoritarian matter of tallying up votes for and against.[28]

THE MANITOBA SCHOOLS CRISIS AND QUESTIONS
OF REMEDIAL CHOICE AND DIALOGUE

The 1890 *Public Schools Act* reflected the influence of D'Alton McCarthy's Equal Rights Association. It appealed to an English Canadian nationalism "still rooted in the idea of a homogenous language and culture."[29] The new law abolished publicly funded Protestant and Catholic school boards that had been in existence since 1871. It replaced publicly funded denominational school with a single public system that would be run on a "non-sectarian" basis. The only religious instruction allowed would be voluntary and at the end of the school day.

SIR JOHN A HIDES BEHIND THE COURTS

The Catholic minority appealed to the federal government to disallow the provincial law, but Prime Minister John A. Macdonald refused. He argued that the issue was better resolved before the courts. The phenomena of "politicians hiding behind the courts"[30]did not start with the Charter. A number of critics have bemoaned "the legalization of politics"[31] under the

NOT QUITE SUPREME (Montreal: McGill Queens Press, 2010) for a defence of legislatures acting on their own interpretation of the constitution that does not deal with Manitoba's defiance of the rule of law in refusing to follow the 1892 ruling or other problematic acts of coordinate construction such as 1980 Manitoba legislation that interpreted minority language rights as non-binding.

[28] *Cf* Jeremy Waldron, THE DIGNITY OF LEGISLATION (Cambridge: Cambridge University Press, 1999). For an argument that Canada is based on "incomplete conquests" of both Indigenous and French Canada *see* Peter H. Russell, CANADA'S ODYSSEY: A COUNTRY BASED ON INCOMPLETE CONQUESTS (Toronto: University of Toronto Press, 2017).

[29] Bale, *supra* note 22, at 472.

[30] Andrew Petter, "Legalise This: The Chartering of Canadian Politics" in Kelly and Manfredi eds. *Contested Constitutionalism* (Vancouver: University of British Columbia Press, 2009), 36.

[31] Michael Mandel, THE CHARTER OF RIGHTS AND THE LEGALIZATION OF POLITICS IN CANADA, revised ed (Toronto: Thompson, 1994); Andrew Petter, THE POLITICS OF THE CHARTER (Toronto: University of Toronto Press, 2010).

Charter but this discounts that the executive will often have an incentive
to avoid conflict based on rights claims. This is true even when there is a
significant support for the rights claims, as there was in the Manitoba Schools
case where the Catholic Church and many in Quebec (including Protestants
who had their own publicly funded denominational schools) would have
supported disallowance of the *Public Schools Act* even if others would have
seen it as federal interference in provincial affairs.

OFF TO COURT: ROUND ONE

Having been denied relief from the executive, the Catholic minority turned to
the courts. Both the trial judge and the majority of the Manitoba Court of
Appeal held, as the Privy Council would eventually, that no minority rights
were violated because in 1870 Catholics only enjoyed the negative liberty of
opening and paying for their own schools. The only dissenting Manitoba
judge was Joseph Dubuc, the only Catholic to sit on the case. He was also
Louis Riel's best friend at the College de Montreal. He stressed, as would the
Supreme Court of Canada when it heard the appeal, that the Catholic
minority was disadvantaged by having to pay for non-sectarian public schools
that they could not conscientiously send their children to attend.

As Professor Gordon Bale has argued, the Supreme Court's unanimous
decision to declare that Manitoba's 1890 *Public Schools Act* violated s.22(1) of
the Manitoba Act was admirable in several respects. It avoided the regrettable
religious splits among the judges that beset the Manitoba courts.[32] Chief
Justice Ritchie stressed that the Manitoba government's defence of the law
meant that "We are now practically asked to reject the words 'or practice' and
construe the statute as if they had not been used."[33] He was comfortable with
the idea of rights as restraints on otherwise sovereign Parliaments and concluded that the Manitoba legislature "was powerless to affect [the Catholic
minority] prejudicially in the manner of denominational schools."[34] Rights
that impose limits on Parliament were not invented in 1982.

Two other judges stressed the practicalities of the matter in a manner that
foreshadowed the Supreme Court's generous effects based approach to interpreting whether Charter rights were violated and its substantive approach to
equality.[35] Justice Taschereau emphasized that the Catholic minority had by
practice at Confederation not only the right to have schools but "de ne pas
contribuer a aucun autre systeme d'education" and that the new Act would

[32] Bale, *supra* note 22.   [33] *Barrett v. City of Winnipeg* (1891) 19 SCR 374 at 384.
[34] *Id.* at 388.   [35] For a discussion of substantive equality *see* Chapter 10 in this volume.

harm Catholic schools by leaving them "a la merci de contributions volun-taires."[36] Justice Patterson similarly stressed that "the value of the right depends upon the practical use that can be made of it."[37] Much more than the English judges who sat on the Privy Council, the Supreme Court in Ottawa was also aware of the need for reciprocity between the treatment of the Catholic minority in Manitoba and the Protestant minority in Quebec which enjoyed publicly funded schools.[38]

THE PRIVY COUNCIL'S FIRST DECISION

The government of Manitoba appealed the decision to London. The case for the minority was not well argued in London, in part because the Conservative federal government refused to pay for the services of the brilliant but Liberal lawyer, Edward Blake, who had won the case for the Catholics at the Supreme Court.[39] The case for publicly funded Catholic schools was also strategically paired with a weaker case for Anglican schools. Strategic litigation, battles over the funding of litigation[40] and concerns about the inflation of rights are not an invention of the Charter.

The Judicial Committee of the Privy Council overturned the Supreme Court's unanimous judgment. Lord MacNaughten, like the Manitoba courts, took a narrow and restrictive approach by holding that the only rights that religious minorities enjoyed by either law or practice at 1870 was the right to run and support their own schools. He dismissed concerns that Catholics would under the 1890 law be taxed to support non-sectarian schools while having also to pay for their own schools. He essentially blamed the Catholics for their belief that religion was a pervasive part of education by asserting "it is not the law is at fault" but rather the Catholics' "religious convictions" and "teachings of their Church."[41].

The Privy Council also demonstrated sympathy for the policy behind the 1890 act by expressing concerns that preserving public support for denomin-ational schools might frustrate Manitoba's ability "to provide for educational wants of the more sparsely inhabited districts"[42] of the Prairie province. Within

---

[36] *Barrett v. City of Winnipeg* (1891) 19 SCR 374 at 413, 416.   [37] *Id.* at 422.

[38] In this way, the Supreme Court decision could be defended as consistent with the intent of the framers including Louis Riel. For a discussion of originalism but interestingly not a defence of this 1892 decision where a court defended the rights of minorities *see* Chapter 8 in this volume.

[39] Bale, *supra* note 22, at 483.

[40] In 2006, the Harper government cut all funding to the Court Challenges program that had financed minority language and equality rights litigation.

[41] *City of Winnipeg v. Barrett; City of Winnipeg v. Logan* [1892] A.C. 445 at 458.   [42] *Id.* at 459.

the limits of funds, however, Manitoba might have continued to fund Catholic schools while also funding non-sectarian public schools, a state of affairs that continues in Ontario to this day.[43] The Privy Council was not sensitive to the need for reciprocal protection of Catholic minorities in Ontario and Manitoba and Protestant minorities in Quebec.[44]

BACK TO COURT: ROUND TWO

Despite their loss in Privy Council and the reelection of the Greenway Liberal government that had enacted the 1890 *Public Schools Act*, the Catholic minority persisted in their claims that their rights had been violated. Their rights had been violated and they wanted justice from whatever forum would provide it. Having lost in the courts, the Catholic minority now appealed to the federal Cabinet under s.22(2) of the Manitoba Act.

The Conservative federal government was caught in a bind. It could have enacted remedial legislation straight away, but that would have been unpopular with both those in Quebec sensitive to federal legislation that affected provincial jurisdiction over education as well as those who opposed publicly funded Catholic schools. The government again decided to delay by punting the issue to the courts. It referred the question of whether it had jurisdiction to enact remedial legislation to the Supreme Court of Canada. Again the habit of hiding political controversies behind the courts and of direct dialogue between governments and courts is hardly an invention of the 1982 Charter.

The Supreme Court ruled 3:2 that the federal Parliament did not have jurisdiction to enact remedial legislation to restore publicly funded schools in Manitoba. Chief Justice Strong held that in the absence of any legally

---

[43] The Supreme Court has rejected a number of Charter challenges to the Ontario scheme on the basis that Catholic school rights in Ontario were part of the Confederation bargain not subject to Charter challenge. *See* Reference re Bill 30 [1987] 1 SCR 1148; Adler v. Ontario [1996] 3 SCR 609. For an assessment of these cases as a clash between universalist and particularist logics in the Canadian Constitution, *see* Benjamin Berger, *Children of Two Logics: A Way Into Canadian Constitutional Culture*, 11 I.CON. 319 (2013).

[44] Outside Ontario, denominational school rights have now been eclipsed by protection of linguistic minorities. A 1997 constitutional amendment agreed to between the Quebec and federal government, replaced the Catholic and Protestant schools guaranteed by s.93 of the Constitution Act, 1867 with French and English schools. The notwithstanding clause to override freedom of religion and equality rights was used from 2000 to 2005 to allow French and English schools to offer voluntary Protestant and Catholic religious teaching *An Act to amend Education Regarding Confessional Matters* S.Q, 2000 c.24, s.44. The override was not renewed and Quebec public schools now offer spiritual and ethical teachings not limited to Christian denominations.

enforceable rights, Parliamentary supremacy meant that the Manitoba legislature was free to repeal the 1871 legislation establishing publicly funded Catholic schools.[45]

The Catholic minority appealed this decision to the Privy Council, this time making sure Edward Blake would argue its case. The Privy Council was made aware that some in Canada were very unhappy with its previous decision. The court papers included a petition by the Conservative League of Montreal who argued that Manitoba's 1890 *Public Schools Act* was "inspired by intolerance and fanaticism and is of a nature to inspire fear of the very existence of Confederation, if a remedy is not applied in good time."[46] In a precursor to the use of interveners in Charter litigation, this group sought both to appeal to the Conservative federal government and defend the rights of the English Protestant minority in Quebec who enjoyed publicly funded schools. Long before the Charter, civil society groups intervened to lobby courts as well as legislatures.

The Privy Council defensively noted its earlier decision "seems to have given rise to some misapprehension." It concluded that while the Catholics had no right to publicly funded schools in 1870, the 1890 law adversely affected them and the federal Parliament had jurisdiction to enact remedial legislation to restore public funding. Unlike in its earlier decision, the Privy Council took a modern effects based and substantive equality approach that focused on "the position of the Roman Catholics prior and subsequent to the Acts from which they appeal." Belatedly it now recognized that Catholics would be taxed for "schools which they regard as no more suitable for the education of Catholic children than if they were distinctively Protestant in their character"[47] without attempting to blame or dismiss the fact on the Catholics themselves.

The Privy Council interpreted the federal Parliament's remedial jurisdiction broadly to include more than the rights that the courts would enforce under s.22(1) of the Manitoba Act. The Privy Council relied on the textual distinctions between ss.22(1) and 22(2), but there was a hint of a living tree approach to constitutional interpretation in its recognition that the latter was intended to provide protections when Manitoba's demographics changed. Indeed, the Privy Council concluded that "it does not appear to their Lordships an extravagant notion that in creating a Legislature for the province with limited powers it should have been thought expedient, in case either

---

[45] *Re Certain Statutes of the Province of Manitoba Regarding Education* (1894) 22 SCR 577.
[46] Case on Appeal *Brophy v. Winnipeg* at p.31.
[47] *Brophy v. Attorney General of Manitoba* [1895] A.C. 202 at 226–7.

Catholics or Protestants became preponderant...to give the Dominion Parliament power to legislate upon matters of education so far as was necessary to protect the Protestant or Catholic minority as the case may be."[48] In the end, the Privy Council affirmed that the federal Parliament could act. At the same time, it stressed that "it is not for this tribunal to intimate the precise steps to be taken."[49] This contemplated a kind of partnership between courts and the federal Parliament in protecting the rights of the minority in Manitoba.

REMEDIAL LEGISLATION AND LEGISLATIVE BLOCKAGE

The Privy Council's decision dumped a political hot potato on the lap of a federal government that was in disarray in the aftermath of Macdonald's death. Some Catholic ministers resigned from Cabinet because the government was too slow in enacting remedial legislation while some Protestant ministers resigned because of the prospect of such legislation.

Even though it had no strict legal obligation to do so, the federal government introduced remedial legislation that would have restored publicly funded Catholic schools. The legislation was, however, left on the order paper because D'Alton McCarthy and other opponents of Catholic schools filibustered eventually causing the government to dissolve Parliament and go to the polls. A minority in Parliament was able to prevent the vote, again suggesting that romantic and abstract celebrations of "the dignity of legislation"[50] or of "constitutional counter-balancing"[51] do not always look as appealing when viewed in light of political practice as opposed to theory. As will be seen in the next section, this was not the last time that obstruction of a legislature by those opposed to minority rights would prevent the enactment of legislation to assist minorities in Manitoba. The courts were successful in placing the schools issue on Parliament's agenda but could not force remedial legislation through.

THE 1896 ELECTION AND THE "SUNNY WAYS" OF COMPROMISE

The 1896 election was one of Canada's strangest. Charles Tupper, the Protestant leader of the Conservatives, campaigned for remedial legislation with the active assistance of the Catholic Church. Wilfred Laurier, who became Canada's first French-Canadian Prime Minister, campaigned against remedial legislation as an infringement of provincial rights. He promised

[48] *Id.*   [49] *Id.*   [50] Waldron, *supra* note 28.   [51] *See* Chapter 14 in this volume.

"the sunny ways" of compromise. Laurier won the election with majorities in both Quebec and Ontario.

Shortly after the election, Prime Minister Laurier and Manitoba Premier Greenway agreed to a compromise that avoided the need for remedial legislation. The compromise was denounced in an 1897 Papal encyclical pronounced as "defective, imperfect, insufficient" with Catholics being urged to continue to lobby in all venues including the press for the restoration of publicly funded Catholic schools.[52] The Laurier-Greenway "sunny ways" compromise was largely consistent with a concession already made in Manitoba's 1890 *Public Schools Act*. It simply allowed voluntary religious and language instruction where numbers warranted at the end of the school day. This of course fell fall short of restoring publicly funded Catholic schools. It denied the central role that religion and in many cases the French language played in publicly supported Catholic schools in Manitoba from 1871 until 1890. It also gave no special status to French as opposed to other languages. By 1916, 13 different languages were being used in the rapidly expanding province causing this part of the compromise to be abolished.[53]

SUMMARY: COMPARING EXECUTIVE, LEGISLATIVE AND JUDICIAL PERFORMANCE

What does the Manitoba Schools question reveal about the respective role of courts, legislatures and the executive in enforcing constitutional rights designed to protect minorities?

The federal executive could have enforced Catholic school rights by disallowing the 1890 provincial legislation but was reluctant to do so given the support for the legislation in Manitoba and elsewhere. Prime Minister John A. Macdonald deferred the question on the basis that the minority might get redress from the courts. The Catholic minority obtained redress from the Supreme Court of Canada that recognized the adverse effects of repealing public funding, but this decision was reversed by the Privy Council in London. The Catholic minority then asked the federal government to enact remedial legislation to restore funding, but the federal government hid behind the courts by referring to the Supreme Court the question of whether it had jurisdiction to enact remedial legislation. It was only after the Privy Council

---

[52] *Encyclical Letter from Pope Leo XIII, Manitoba School Question,* (1898) 23 *** 189 at 193.

[53] Nelson Wiseman, *The Questionable Relevance of the Constitution in Advancing Minority Cultural Rights in Manitoba,* 25 C.J.P.S. 697, 713 (1992).

ruling in 1895 that affirmed its jurisdiction that the federal government was prepared to enact remedial legislation. This suggests that the constitutional rulings of courts forced issues concerning rights onto the legislative agenda well before the advent of the Charter.

Although the courts placed the issue of publicly funded Catholic schools on Parliament's agenda, a filibuster by vehement opponents of minority rights prevented the enactment of remedial legislation. Even in Canada's central-ized Parliamentary system, there are limits to the government's ability to enact legislation. The schools question was an important issue in the 1896 election illustrating that dialogue between courts, legislatures and the populace pre-dated the Charter and that courts could help frame such dialogues. Although the incumbent Conservatives promised to enact remedial legislation to restore funding to Catholic schools, it was Laurier's Liberals who won by promising the "sunny ways" of compromise. The subsequent compromise negotiated with the Manitoba government was not so "sunny" for the minority. It fell far short of restoring publicly funded Catholic schools, relegated religious instruc-tion to the last half hour of the school day and treated French on a par with any other language. The executive and the legislature failed the minority in the face of strong support for public schools and despite strong and organized demands for remedial legislation from the Catholic Church.

The Supreme Court of Canada would have enforced the rights of the Catholic minority in its unanimous decision in *Barrett*. This would have resulted in continued public funding for Catholic schools. This case provides a precedent for Pierre Trudeau's vision of a national court enforcing the rights of unpopular minorities in the provinces whether they be the Catholics of Manitoba in the 1890s or the Jehovah Witnesses in Quebec in the 1950s or Francophone or Anglophone minorities under the 1982 Charter. Alas, the Privy Council unanimously reversed the Supreme Court. It left the Catholic minority with the empty right of paying taxes for non-sectarian schools and then having to raise money to run private Catholic schools. The courts did not always enforce the rights of the Catholic minority and the Privy Council was insensitive to the text and history of s.22 of the *Manitoba Act*. At the same time, the executive refused to use disallowance to enforce minority rights and Parliament was unable to enact remedial legislation because of a filibuster.

CONTRASTING CANADIAN AND AMERICAN APPROACHES
TO REMEDIAL LEGISLATION

The Privy Council partially redeemed itself in the 1895 *Brophy* case by belatedly accepting that the Catholic minority had suffered grave prejudice with the enactment of the 1890 *Public Schools* Act. Its ruling that the federal

Parliament had a wide jurisdiction to enact remedial legislation stands in contrast to the more restrictive interpretation that the US Supreme Court has generally provided to Congress's ability to enact remedial legislation to enforce the Civil War amendments. In the *Civil Rights Cases*[54], the US Supreme Court held that Congress lacked the power to regulate private conduct as an incident of enforcing the 14th Amendment. More recently, the Court has struck down Congressional attempts to change restrictive judicial decisions with respect to freedom of religion in part of the basis of somewhat exaggerated fears that deferring to Congress would allow the legislature effectively to amend the constitution.[55] The Court has also held that Congress cannot use its remedial legislation jurisdiction to impose more exacting prohibitions on age discrimination[56] or to provide Federal causes of action to victims of gender violence.[57]

It is unlikely that Canadian courts would impose similar restrictions on the ability of legislatures to enact remedial legislation. In 1987, the Supreme Court affirmed that Ontario had a broad jurisdiction to restore full funding for the upper years of Catholic high school and that Ontario's exercise of this jurisdiction as part of the Confederation bargain was immune from Charter challenge.[58] The Supreme Court has interpreted s.15(2) of the Charter to shelter governmental affirmative action programs from reverse discrimination claims that might be accepted by American courts.[59] The restrictions imposed by the US Supreme Court on remedial legislation designed to enforce equality rights may help explain why many progressive commentators in the United States defend coordinate construction where legislatures can act on interpretations of the constitution that differ from those of the courts[60] while such views in Canada tend to be embraced by those who are skeptical or

---

[54] 101 US 3 (1883). [55] *City of Boerne v. Flores*, 521 US 507, 529 (1997).
[56] *Kimel v. Florida Board of Regents*, 528 US 62 (2000).
[57] *US v. Morrison*, 529 US 598 (2000).
[58] Reference re Bill 30 [1987] 1 SCR 1148. Estey J. in his concurrence stressed that the federal power to enact remedial legislation was a "a key provision in the delicate balance of interests found in s.s. 93, and it is a grant of federal power as vital as any found in s.91 of the Constitution Act 1867. Consequently it is difficult to understand how lack of exercise can operate as a repeal." Ibid at para 76.
[59] *Compare Alberta (Aboriginal Affairs and Northern Development) v. Cunningham*, 2011 SCC 37, [2011] 2 SCR 670, and *R. v. Kapp* [2008] 2 SCR 483 accepting race-based affirmative action on a rational grounds basis, *with Fisher v. University of Texas*, 133 S.Ct 2411 (2013) affirming strict scrutiny for race-based affirmative action.
[60] *See* Mark Tushnet, TAKING THE CONSTITUTION AWAY FROM THE COURTS (Princeton: Princeton University Press, 1999); Larry Kramer, THE PEOPLE THEMSELVES POPULAR CONSTITUTIONALISM AND JUDICIAL REVIEW (New York: Oxford University Press, 2005); Robert Post and Reva Siegel, *Protecting the Constitution from the People: Juricentric Restrictions on Section Five Powers*, 78 IND. L.J. 1 (2003).

hostile to the rights that Canadian courts have recognized.[61] It also explains why Canadian constitutional culture may view the state as a somewhat less hostile force than American constitutional culture.[62]

THE MANITOBA LANGUAGE CRISIS
AND REMEDIAL RESISTANCE

In 1890, the Manitoba legislation enacted the *Official Language Act*[63] providing that "any statute or law to the contrary notwithstanding" only English could be used in legislatures and courts in Manitoba and that Manitoba's laws "need only be printed and published in the English language."[64] This effectively was an override of s.22 of the Manitoba Act or what Richard Albert has termed a "stealth constitutional amendment."[65] Unlike under the override in s.33 of the Charter or the bi-lateral amendment process requiring federal and provincial agreement for parts of the Constitution that affect only one province, there were no special signals or requirements before the new law abolishing French language rights was enacted. Constitutional French language rights were abolished by ordinary legislation enacted by the majority of the Manitoba legislature.

APPEALS TO EXECUTIVE DISCRETION
TO RESERVE OR DISALLOW LAWS

One of the two legislative members who had spoken against the 1890 *Official Language Act* asked the Lieutenant Governor to reserve the bill on the basis that it was ultra vires s.23 of the Manitoba Act. Reservation was part of the imperial structure of the 1867 Constitution that allowed a Lieutenant Governor to reserve provincial legislation pending federal disallowance.

Lieutenant Governor John Schultz did not reserve the bill even though his predecessor Joseph Cauchon had reserved and refused to sign a similar bill

---

[61] There are defenders of coordinate construction in Canada, but they tend to focus on the use of coordinate construction to restrict judicial protections of rights rather than to expand legislative protections of rights. *See*, for example, Christopher Manfredi, JUDICIAL POWER AND THE CANADIAN CONSTITUTION 2ND ED (Toronto: Oxford University Press, 2001); Dennis Baker, *supra* note 27; Grant Huscroft, *Rationalizing Judicial Power: The Mischief of Dialogue Theory*, in Kelly and Manfredi *Contested Constitutionalism*.

[62] Mayo Moran, *Talking About Hate Speech*, WIS. L.REV. 1425 (1994); Berger, *supra* note 43.

[63] An Act to Provide that English shall be the Official Language S.M. 1890 c.14 s.2.   [64] *Id.* s.1.

[65] As Professor Albert has argued, stealth amendments by ignoring amendment procedures threaten rule of law values including intergenerational precommitments. *See* Richard Albert, *Constitutional Amendments by Stealth*, 60 McGILL L.J. 674, 733 (2015).

in 1878.[66] Schultz, who had fought against and been imprisoned by Riel during the Red River Rebellion, was supportive of the bill to make English the only official language in Manitoba whereas Cauchon from Quebec supported official bilingualism. Arguments that either Cauchon or Schultz were biased and had made up their minds would not have been tenable given the refusal of courts to review the exercise of the power of reservation or disallowance.[67]

THE EXECUTIVE HIDING BEHIND THE COURTS

The federal Minister of Justice John Thompson next refused to disallow the act on the basis that while the provincial power to repeal s.23 of the Manitoba Act "admits of great doubt" that the validity of the new law "may be very easily tested by legal proceedings on the part of any person in Manitoba" who wants to use French in court or the legislature. He noted that "a large section of the people of the province desire that English alone should be used in such matters" and concluded: "a judicial determination of that question will be more permanent and satisfactory than a decision of it by the power of disallowance."[68] As in the Manitoba Schools crisis, the government was more than happy to defer to the courts and effectively to hide behind them when it came to popular legislation that threatened the rights of minorities.

SUCCESSFUL BUT IGNORED COURT CHALLENGES

The prediction that the *Official Language Act* would soon be challenged in court proved correct. In 1892, Judge Prud'homme of the County Court of St. Boniface, the French part of Winnipeg, held that "section 23 of the *Manitoba Act* cannot be changed and even less repealed by the Legislature of that province."[69] This decision recognized the constitutional nature of the right, but it was not followed by the government of Manitoba and not even

---

[66] Wiseman, *supra* note 53, at 700.

[67] *Reference Re Power to Disallow Legislation* [1938] SCR 71. In some cases, the power of reservation and disallowance was exercised to protect rights but in other cases it was not. *See* Gerald La Forest, Disallowance and Reservation of Provincial Legislation (Ottawa: Department of Justice, 1955), Kent Roach, Constitutional Remedies in Canada 2nd ed (Toronto: Canada Law Book, 2013) at 2.70.

[68] Report of the Minister of Justice as quoted in Margaret Banks, *Defining 'Constitution of the Province'– The Crux of the Manitoba Language Controversy*, 31 McGill L.J. 466, 474–75 (1986).

[69] *Pellant v. Hebert*, first published in *Le Manitoba* (a French language newspaper), Mar. 9, 1892, reported in (1981), 12 R.G.D. 242.

published in the law reports. The government did not bother to appeal the judgment. It simply ignored it. This underlines how respect for the rule of law can be fragile and dependent on voluntary and good faith implementation by the government.[70]

The beleaguered minority prioritized the extensive litigation over public funding of Catholic schools and the issue was not raised in court again until 1909. The same judge again declared the *Official Language Act* to be ultra vires the Manitoba legislature, only again to be ignored by the Manitoba government. Nelson Wiseman has suggested that the minority may not have continued to litigate because French was unofficially tolerated. This may be so, but Professor Wiseman's parallel argument that "the concept of fixed and permanent rights was alien"[71] in the 1890s is inconsistent with both the language of the judgments or indeed the demands made to courts, legislature and the executive to restore both language and denominational school rights.

RIGHTS WITHOUT REMEDIES

Litigation over French language rights did not resurface until the 1970s when Georges Forest refused to pay his parking ticket because it was not issued in French. The case eventually made its way to the Supreme Court in 1979. The Court paired the Manitoba case with a case from Quebec that challenged a 1977 law enacted by the separatist Parti Quebecois that allowed laws to be enacted in the Quebec legislature in French only. This reflected the deep sense of the need for reciprocal treatment of the English minority in Quebec and French minorities outside of Quebec that had been ignored by the Privy Council in London in the Catholic schools cases.

In both cases, the Supreme Court declared the laws restricting the use of minority languages to be unconstitutional and null and void.[72] In *Forest*, the Court concluded that the language rights of s.23 of the Manitoba Act were as "entrenched"[73] as the denominational school rights in s.22. As such, neither should be subject to unilateral amendment by Manitoba. Alas the Court remained silent on the remedial implications of its holding either for Manitoba's unilingual statute book or for Catholic schools. Silence about

---

[70] For discussion of contemporary failures by the federal executive promptly to respond to a few declarations made by the Supreme Court under the Charter *see* Roach, *The Supreme Court on Trial, supra* note 15, at 403–4.

[71] Wiseman, *supra* note 53, at 704.

[72] *Blaikie v. Attorney General of Quebec* [1979] 2 SCR 1016; *Forest v. Attorney General of Manitoba*, 2 SCR 1032 (1979).

[73] *Id.* at 1038.

remedies or reliance on remedial discretion can be a means to submerge some of the most sensitive issues in judicial review.[74]

THE MANITOBA LEGISLATURE'S USE OF COORDINATE CONSTRUCTION TO DILUTE FRENCH LANGUAGE RIGHTS

Quebec was able quickly to reenact its unilingual legislation bilingually, but the matter was much more difficult for Manitoba which had a century of unilingual legislation. The Conservative government of Sterling Lyon responded to *Forest* with unilingual legislation that effectively interpreted s.23 as only requiring voluntary enactment of bilingual legislation. The law also deemed that the original English language versions of Manitoba's laws would prevail over any translated law. The law gutted the clear text of s.23 of the Manitoba Act of its constitutional force by asserting that laws would not be invalid because they had only been enacted in English.[75] This 1980 legislation can be seen as an act of coordinate construction of the type defended in Canada by Professors Manfredi, Baker and Huscroft.[76] Predictably, however, the legislative interpretation of constitutional rights minimized and essentially repealed the right of the minority by stating that the constitutional obligation to enact bilingual legislation was not mandatory. This law made the "great constitutional victory for the Francophone community" in *Forest* "virtually meaningless."[77]

The Lyon government's 1980 interpretation of s.23 of the Manitoba Act was arguably at odds with the Supreme Court's interpretation of s.23 in the 1979 *Forest* case. It was most certainly at odds with the Court's interpretation in 1985 when it held that the 1980 law was unconstitutional because it was enacted only in English and ignored established precedent that bilingual laws should be enacted in equally authoritative English and French versions.[78] Defenders of coordinate construction celebrate the ability of legislatures to interpret rights differently than courts, but do not always grapple with what this will mean for rights holders, especially minorities who are excluded from governing coalitions.

[74] Kent Roach "Charter Remedies" in Des Rosiers, Macklem and Oliver, *Oxford Handbook of the Canadian Constitution* (Toronto: Oxford University Press, 2018) Chapter 32.

[75] An Act in respecting the operation of Section 23 of the Manitoba Act S.M. 1980 c.3.

[76] Christopher Manfredi, JUDICIAL POWER AND THE CANADIAN CONSTITUTION 2ND ED (Toronto: Oxford University Press, 2001); Baker, *supra* note 27; Grant Huscroft, "Rationalizing Judicial Power: The Mischief of Dialogue Theory" in Kelly and Manfredi *Contested Constitutionalism* supra.

[77] Hebert, *supra* note 23, at 38.   [78] *Manitoba Language Reference*, *supra*, at paras 122, 130–141.

The 1980 law should also be viewed in the context of Premier Lyon's opposition to Pierre Trudeau's plan to add a Charter of Rights and Freedoms featuring protection of minority language rights to the Canadian Constitution. In introducing the 1980 legislation, Lyon asserted that he was committed to the rule of law and constitutional rights, thus suggesting that he was simply engaging in a reasonable disagreement with the Supreme Court about the meaning of s.23 of the Manitoba Act. The Conservatives who voted for the 1980 law had more votes behind them than the seven judges who signed on to the "by the Court" decision in *Forest*.[79] Opponents of judicial review such as Professor Waldron might also argue that it was simply a reasonable disagreement about rights especially given Premier Lyon's defence of the 1980 law as based on "a spirit of fair play and compromise which continues to motivate most Manitobans, rather than by legal decree."[80]

In my view, Manitoba's 1980 law represents nothing less than the tyranny of the anglophone majority over the francophone minority in Manitoba. It provides support for my concerns about legislatures engaging in coordinate construction that acts on constitutional interpretation that differ from those of the courts. As I have argued elsewhere[81] legislatures have incentives to ignore or trivialize the rights of unpopular minorities. To the extent that the Charter allows coordinate construction that runs contrary to judicial interpretation of Charter rights, such acts should be accompanied by the special signals and sober second thoughts of the s.33 override which must be renewed after five years. In any event, s.33 does not apply to minority language rights. As suggested above, a constitutional amendment was necessary if one wanted to change s.23 of the Manitoba Act in the way that Manitoba's 1980 law attempted to do so. It is unthinkable that federal governments of the day under either Prime Ministers Pierre Trudeau or Joe Clark would have agreed to a constitutional amendment endorsing Premier Lyon's interpretation of s.23 as not imposing mandatory bilingualism obligations on the Manitoba government.

A number of Francophone lawyers in the province disagreed with the Lyon's government's minimalistic legislative interpretation of s.23 and they

---

[79] For arguments that courts should defer to legislatures when they engage in reasonable disagreements about rights because the latter represent more people, *see* Jeremy Waldron, LAW AND DISAGREEMENT (Oxford: Oxford University Press, 1999), 306–307; Jeremy Waldron, POLITICAL POLITICAL THEORY (Cambridge: Harvard University, 2016), chs. 9 and 10.

[80] As quoted in Hebert, *supra* note 23, at 39.

[81] Roach, *The Supreme Court on Trial, supra* note 15, at 272–274. For my argument that Canadian defenders of coordinate construction have ignored concerns about how legislative interpretations of rights will trivialize the rights of unpopular minorities, *see id.* ch. 17.

engaged in litigation designed to flesh out the remedial implications of the Forest case. In a recurring pattern in these case studies, they lost in the Manitoba courts only to find more sympathy in the Supreme Court. A majority of the Manitoba Court of Appeal agreed in 1981 with the legislature's minimal interpretation of s.23 as directory but not mandatory largely because of concerns that the wholesale invalidation of all of Manitoba's largely unilingual laws would result in "chaos."[82] A concern about remedies inspired a minimalistic interpretation of rights that confirmed Premier Lyon's minimalist approach to language rights.

Justice Monnin strongly dissented on the basis that the majority and the 1980 legislation ignored the mandatory language in the reference to the printing of Manitoba's laws in English and French and undermined the very point of entrenching minority language rights in 1870.[83] As will be seen, the Supreme Court would eventually settle the matter and decide, consistent with Justice Monnin, that s.23 of the Manitoba Act imposed mandatory duties to enact equally authoritative English and French language versions of legislation.[84]

LEGISLATIVE BLOCKAGES AND THE FAILED CONSTITUTIONAL AMENDMENT

Sterling Lyon's minimalist interpretation of French language rights prevailed in the Manitoba Court of Appeal, but his Conservative government lost the 1981 Manitoba election. A new New Democratic Party (NDP) government was more committed to minority language rights and less confident that the Supreme Court would find s.23 only to be directory. It also found the process of attracting qualified translators to Manitoba difficult and recognized that the money spent on translating old laws into French could be better spent providing more French language services for the minority.

In May, 1983, the provincial government, the federal government and the Societie Franco-Manitoba agreed to a constitutional amendment that essentially forgave the translation of many older laws for the recognition of French as an official language of Manitoba and a guarantee that francophones could receive certain services from the Manitoba government in French. The amendment also provided a mechanism for resolving future disputes about French language

---

[82] *Bilodeau v. Attorney General (Manitoba)* (1981) 61 C.C.C.(2d) 217 at 225 (Man.C.A.) aff'd [1986] 1 SCR 449 on the more limited basis that unilingual summary conviction offence had been granted temporary force and s.23 did not require bilingual traffic summons.

[83] *Id.* at 229.   [84] *Manitoba Language Reference* [1985] 1 SCR 721 discussed infra note 92.

services that would entail government institutions submitting compliance plans for judicial approval, thus involving the courts working in partnership with the government in the remedial process.[85] The central involvement of the Societie Franco-Manitoban in the amendment is significant. It acknowledges that the flurry of (pre-Charter) French language litigation had roots in civil society constitutionalism[86] and that the agreement of advocacy groups enhanced the legitimacy of the proposed amendment.

Alas, the proposed amendment to give the minority more modern rights was unpopular. Municipal referenda in thirty cities including Winnipeg were held with about 75 per cent of voters opposing the proposed amendments. Some civil society groups including various churches, the Canadian Jewish Congress and groups representing Ontario's francophone and Quebec's anglophone minorities opposed the plebiscites on the basis that they were "not an appropriate means of determining minority rights ... What appears democratic is in fact deeply undemocratic."[87] One sign displayed in Winnipeg during the referendum reflects some of the tenor of the debate. It read "My Prayer, God Save the Queen and Damn the French."[88] There was also a regrettable act of political violence in the form of arson against the offices of Societe Franco-Manitoban in January, 1983.[89] Canada cannot afford to be smug or complacent about its commitment to the peaceful processes of the rule of law and constitutionalism.

Sterling Lyon fused his opposition to the proposed amendment with his opposition to the Charter. In a precursor to some right wing opposition to the Charter, he argued that constitutional rights protections were "alien importations of European or even, to some extent, United State concepts" that would be used "as a form of tyrannical weapon by minorities ... who have no concerns...for the social fabric of this province."[90]

Even though the elected government of Manitoba supported the amendment and held a majority in the legislature, the Manitoba legislature was never able to enact legislation necessary to trigger the amendment. The Conservative official opposition, led first by Sterling Lyon and then by Gary Filmon, obstructed the legislature by refusing to answer the division bells. Filmon attempted to justify his actions by arguing that "if you're expanding any minority rights at the expense of a majority, then you have to be

---

[85] Gordon Mackintosh, *Heading off Bilodeau: Attempting Constitutional Amendment*, 15 MAN. L.J. 271, 290–1 (1986).

[86] On the role of civil society constitutionalism *see* David Cole, ENGINES OF LIBERTY: THE POWER OF CITIZEN ACTIVIST TO MAKE CONSTITUTIONAL LAW (New York: Basic Books, 2016).

[87] As quoted in Hebert, *supra* note 23, at 133.   [88] *Id.* at 165.

[89] Wiseman, *supra* note 53, at 717.   [90] As quoted in Hebert, *supra* note 23, at 81–82.

concerned with the effects ... you have to look at the practicality ... and what does it accomplish."[91]

The story here is depressingly similar to the failed 1895 remedial legislation to restore public funding to Catholic schools. The ringing of the division bells meant that the government could not obtain a much needed supply bill. Eventually, it reluctantly abandoned its attempt to amend the constitution. All three parties in the federal Parliament were prepared to support the progressive amendment. Nevertheless without supporting legislation from Manitoba, s.23 of the Manitoba Act could not be amended to provide more modern protections for the province's official bilingualism.

BACK TO COURT AND THE VINDICATION
OF MINORITY LANGUAGE RIGHTS

The federal government then referred the remedial consequences of Manitoba's unilingual statutes directly to the Supreme Court. The use of the reference both in this case and in the earlier Catholic schools case illustrates a particular form of dialogue between Canadian governments and courts that would not be possible in the United States. For better or worse, Canadian governments have over the last 150 years called on the courts for constitutional guidance, most often not about the Charter.

An unanimous Supreme Court rejected Manitoba's arguments that s.23 was only directory or that all of its unilingual laws and regulations could be sustained by doctrines of necessity, res judicata, mistake of law or the de facto exercise of power. It reasoned that "It would do great violence to our Constitution to hold that a provision on its face mandatory, should be labelled directory on the ground that to hold otherwise would lead to inconvenience or even chaos."[92] This was a direct rejection of the Lyon's government's strained attempt to interpret s.23 as not imposing a mandatory constitutional requirement of bilingualism.

The Court not only assumed responsibility for interpreting the Constitution but in enforcing it. The Court concluded that s.23 "confers upon the judiciary the responsibility of protecting the correlative language rights of all Manitobans including the Franco-Manitoban minority. The judiciary is the institution charged with the duty of ensuring that the government complies with the Constitution. We must protect those whose constitutional rights have been violated, whomever they may be, and whatever the reasons for

[91] Mackintosh, *supra* note 85, at 280.
[92] *Manitoba Language Reference* [1985] 1 SCR 721 at para 39.

the violation.[93] Defenders of coordinate construction might argue that this appropriated a dangerous judicial monopoly on the interpretation of the Constitution, but they should also confront that the Manitoba legislature trivialized minority rights in the 1980 legislation.

THE INVENTION OF THE SUSPENDED
DECLARATION OF INVALIDITY

The Supreme Court formally declared all unilingual acts and regulations to be null and void but then immediately held that the unconstitutional laws should be given temporary effect to avoid the emergency that would be caused to the rule of law by the wholesale invalidation of all of Manitoba's laws. The Court employed the novel remedy of a suspended declaration of invalidity and held that the unconstitutional unilingual laws would have temporary validity for the minimal amount of time required for their translation, reenactment and publishing in both English and French.

The Court refused requests by some of the interveners that it give immediate effect to its wholesale declaration of invalidity as a way of unsticking the constitutional amendment process that had been abandoned in the face of Conservative obstruction of the Manitoba legislature. It reasoned that such an approach would "deprive Manitoba of its legal order and cause a transgression of the rule of law" and it would abdicate the court's "responsibility as protector and preserver of the Constitution" by making preservation of the rule of law dependent "on a future and uncertain event."[94] This approach ignored the illegitimacy of obstruction of Parliament by the opposition so that a vote could not be taken. It also probably underestimated the ability of quick bargaining in the shadow of the law to revive the constitutional amendment. It was unlikely that the province would have descended into chaos if the declaration of invalidity was suspended for a short period that would allow constitutional negotiations or even if no suspension had been entered. In any event, the Court suggested that its remedies should not depend on "future and uncertain events." Complex remedies, including the seven year translation process started by the Court's judgment, alas can depend on such events, but the case reflected the Court's unease with engaging in additional remedial experimentation.

The Court gave more compelling reasons for rejecting Manitoba's ironic suggestion that powers of executive reservation and disallowance could be relied upon. These powers had been tried, but failed in the 1890s. The Court did not advert to these failures, but reasoned that such an approach "would be

---

[93] Id. at para 47.   [94] Manitoba Language Reference [1985] 1 SCR 721 at para 68.

entirely inconsistent with the judiciary's duty to uphold the Constitution"[95] because it would delegate constitutional compliance to executive decisions that may be unreviewable. At a time when it was emboldened by its new responsibilities under the Charter, the Dickson Court affirmed that the courts, and not the legislature or the executive, had the ultimate responsibility for interpreting and enforcing the Constitution.

The novel remedy of a suspended declaration of invalidity did not abdicate the court's duty to enforce the constitution. First, the suspension was not indefinite and indeed the one used in the Manitoba case has so far been the Court's only open-ended one. Second, the Court affirmed its obligation to enforce the Constitution by indicating that "As concerns the future, the Constitution requires that, from the date of this judgment, all new Acts of the Manitoba Legislature be enacted, printed and published in both French and English. Any Acts of the Legislature that do not meet this requirement will be invalid and of no force or effect."[96] The Court backed this statement up by declaring parts of the 1980 law immediately invalid to the extent that it did not contemplate that laws would be enacted and be equally valid in both English and French.[97] As suggested above, this affirmed that the Lyon government had erred it its minimalist interpretation of s.23 of the Manitoba Act in the 1980 legislation. The Supreme Court vindicated Justice Monnin who in his earlier dissent had accused the 1980 legislation of doing "violence to the Constitution."[98]

In the *Manitoba Language Reference* the only constitutional option short of an amendment was the translation of many old laws. Some defenders of coordinate construction might argue that Manitoba should have continued to act on its government's argument to the Court that s.23 was only directory and not mandatory on the basis that there was a reasonable disagreement about the meaning of the Constitution and the judiciary should not have a monopoly on the interpretation of the Constitution. In my view, however, such an approach would have been unjustified defiance of the Court, the Constitution and the rule of law.

The Supreme Court retained jurisdiction and held subsequent hearings in 1986, 1990 and 1992 .[99] These hearings established a schedule for translation. The Court subsequently revised that schedule and elaborated on the extent of Manitoba's bilingual obligations as applied to legal instruments other than statutes. Compliance took time, but during this time the Court was guided by

---

[95] *Id.* at para 70.   [96] *Manitoba Language Reference*, at para 112.   [97] *Id.* at paras 139–140.
[98] *Bilodeau v. Attorney General (Manitoba)* (1981) 61 C.C.C.(2d) 217 at 229 (Man.C.A.) aff'd on other grounds [1986] 1 SCR 449.
[99] [1985] 2 SCR 347; [1990] 3 SCR 1417, [1992] 1 SCR 212.

the sound principle that temporary validity should only be granted for the minimum time necessary to allow for compliance.

THE GROWTH OF SUSPENDED DECLARATIONS OF INVALIDITY

The *Manitoba Language Reference* was the Court's first use of a suspended declaration of invalidity, an innovative remedy that has subsequently been used frequently and in cases that are not related to threats to the rule of law or public safety. Such remedies give legislatures an opportunity to select among a variety of constitutional options and to devise complex and multi-faceted remedies that the courts could not devise. They contemplate a partnership or dialogue between courts and legislatures. Suspended declarations of invalidity have played an important role in mitigating some of the effects of controversial Charter decisions over matters such as medicare, labor relations, prostitution and assisted suicide.[100]

One weakness of the suspended declaration of invalidity is that it provides no immediate remedy for successful litigants.[101] Canadian courts have so far been reluctant to provide exemptions from suspensions or devise interim guidelines to minimize risk to constitutional violations, but this may change in light of the recent *Carter*[102] decisions allowing individual litigants to be exempted from a prohibition of assisted suicide while Parliament devises a more comprehensive approach. Such an approach can combine judicial enforcement of rights with judicial deference to the legislature's ability to justify limits on rights.

THE EXPORT OF THE SUSPENDED DECLARATION OF INVALIDITY

The suspended declaration of invalidity has also been one of Canada's more interesting but often neglected constitutional exports. Section 172(1)(b) of the

---

[100] For discussion of this jurisprudence *see* Roach, CONSTITUTIONAL REMEDIES IN CANADA 2ND ED (Toronto: Canada Law Book, as updated), 14.153 off.
[101] Bruce Ryder, *Suspending the Charter.* 21 S.C.L.R.(2D) 267 (2003); Robert Leckey, COMMON LAW BILLS OF RIGHTS (Cambridge: Cambridge University Press, 2015), ch 8. For my own response to these criticisms and defence of an approach that allows courts to suspend declarations of invalidity while taking more responsibility for granting individual remedies and providing guidelines for governments during the period of suspension *see* Roach, "Remedies for Laws that Violate Human Rights" in John Bell et al. *Public Law Adjudication in Common Law Systems* (Oxford: Hart Publishing, 2016).
[102] 2016 SCC 4.

1996 South African Constitution provides not only that courts must declare laws invalid to the extent of their inconsistency with the constitution but also that the court

> may make any order that is just and equitable, including—

> (i) an order limiting the retrospective effect of the declaration of invalidity; and
> (ii) an order suspending the declaration of invalidity for any period and on any conditions, to allow the competent authority to correct the defect.

The suspended declaration of invalidity is well suited to the enforcement of constitutional rights that require positive government action to enforce including the various socio-economic rights entrenched in the South African constitution. The South African Constitutional Court has been bolder than Canadian courts in providing guidelines to govern the period of suspension.[103] Both courts have also affirmed the ability of courts to retain jurisdiction when necessary to ensure compliance with the constitution.[104] Hong Kong's Final Court of Appeal has also used suspended declarations of invalidity with reference to the Canadian experience. It has, however, drawn an interesting distinction between suspension and validity. It has preferred temporary suspensions because they leave open the possibility of the executive being held responsible for acts even while the legislature deliberates about its response to the judicial ruling.[105]

CONTINUED CANADIAN REMEDIAL ACTIVISM?

The *Manitoba Language Reference* remains one of the Court's most important remedial cases establishing precedents for suspended declarations of invalidity and retention of supervisory jurisdiction. The case, however, has been more influential with respect to the former than the latter remedy. A trial judge who retained jurisdiction in a complex minority language school case was harshly criticized by four dissenters in the Supreme Court[106] for acting in

---

[103] But *see* R. *v.* Swain [1991] 1 SCR 933 where the Court crafted guidelines to minimize the harm caused by the unconstitutional law during a 6 month suspension. On the more robust South African experience *see* Sandra Liebenberg, Socio-Economic Rights (Claremont: Juta, 2010), 389–397.

[104] Kent Roach and Geoff Budlender, *Mandatory Relief and Supervisory Jurisdiction*, 122 S.A.L.J. 325 (2005).

[105] *Koo Sze Yiu v. Chief Executive of the HKSAR* [2006] 3 HKLRD 455 at paras 33–35. For other uses of Canadian jurisprudence *see* Chapter 16 in this volume.

[106] *Doucet Boudreau v. Nova Scotia* [2003] 3 SCR 3. *See also Thibodeau v. Air Canada* [2014] 3 SCR 340 setting aside a structural order to ensure bilingualism on the basis of concerns about insufficient clarity and judicial resources.

an non- judicial manner. In my view, the trial judge's approach was praise-
worthy in its attempt to bring transparency and speed to the compliance
process while relying on public and fair hearings. The trial judge did not
try to micro-manage the construction of minority language schools required
under s.23 of the Charter but rather made a "best efforts" order that recognized
that the executive has expertise in the construction of schools that the judiciary does not have. That said, very few Canada trial judges have retained
jurisdiction and embarked on the challenging process of structural reform.
The efforts that have been made have focused on minority language rights
and have not extended to other institutions that may not comply with the
Constitution.[107]

<h2 style="text-align:center">SUMMARY: COMPARING EXECUTIVE, LEGISLATIVE
AND JUDICIAL PERFORMANCE</h2>

What does the Manitoba language crisis reveal about the respective role
of courts, legislatures and the executive in enforcing constitutional rights
designed to protect minorities?

As in the Schools cases and with the exception of Lieutenant Governor's
Cauchon's 1878 reservation of a predecessor of the *Official Language Act*, the
executive was reluctant to intervene and exercise powers to reserve or disallow
popular legislation that violated minority rights. Indeed, the Supreme Court
in the *Manitoba Language Reference* ruled that reliance on such powers
would abdicate the judicial duty to protect and enforce the Constitution.
This is a sound principle, but the seven years it took to translate Manitoba's
unilingual laws and the difficulties that Canadian courts have encountered
in other cases in exercising supervisory jurisdiction suggests that courts may
often rely on executive good will and expertise in enforcing the constitution.
This is especially the case when courts chose to rely on general declarations as
a remedy, a remedy often used by Canadian courts and as will be seen play a
central role in our next case study.

Like the executive, the legislature under-performed as a provider of remedies. The 1980 legislation enacted by the Lyon government claimed that s.23
was directory only and asserted that English language versions of Manitoba's
laws should prevail. This law trivialized minority rights and should be an

---

[107] Canadian courts may well be deterred by both the strong dissent in *Doucet-Boudreau* and
the majority's warning that trial judges should make clear and unenforceable orders that may
test judicial competence. *See* Kent Roach, *Polycentricity and Queue Jumping in Public Law
Remedies: A Two Track Response*, 62 *U.T.L.J.* 3 (2016).

embarrassment to Canadian defenders of coordinate construction who argue that legislatures should be free to act on their interpretations of rights even when they differ from those of the courts. The Supreme Court eventually found Manitoba's 1980 law to be unconstitutional in 1985 on the basis that it "did violence" to the clear words and intent of s.23 of the Manitoba Act mandating official bilingualism. This suggests that even clearly worded text protecting minority rights supported by evidence of the framers intent may not restrain legislatures and executives who are hostile to minority rights. The 1980 law enacted by the Lyon government was a foreshadowing of the resistance to minority language rights, if not outright prejudice and bigotry, that subsequently informed the municipal referenda and the 1983 obstruction of the Manitoba legislature by the opposition Conservative party to block a progressive constitutional amendment recognizing French as an official language in the province.

Without a doubt, the Francophone minority would have been better served had the Manitoba legislature been able to enact legislation that, combined with federal legislation, would have amended the Constitution to ensure that the minority would have modern rights to French language services from the Manitoba government but also that the government would not have to go to the expense of translating every dusty statute. As had occurred in 1895 when a filibuster in the federal Parliament blocked remedial legislation to restore public funding to Catholic schools, a determined minority in the legislature was able to obstruct the enactment of needed remedial legislation by methods that were illegitimate because they prevented a vote on the merits. In both cases, the minority in the legislature appealed to the unpopularity of minority rights including prejudice and bigotry. This case, combined with the school cases, goes a long way to confirming the need for robust anti-majoritarian judicial enforcement of minority rights.[108]

That said even a determined judiciary will have difficulties in enforcing minority rights in the face of executive, legislative and popular resistance. The County Court of St. Boniface correctly held that the 1890 *Official Language Act* was unconstitutional in both 1892 and 1909, but the government ignored these decisions without even appealing them. Canadians should not romanticize the history or willingness of governments to implement judicial judgments in good faith.

---

[108] As defended, for example, in John Hart Ely, DEMOCRACY AND DISTRUST (Cambridge: Harvard University Press, 1980) and Roach, *The Supreme Court on Trial, supra* note 15, at ch. 12.

In 1979, the Supreme Court affirmed the mandatory nature of Manitoba's constitutional commitments to bilingualism, but ducked the all-important question of remedies. In 1985, the Court invented the new remedy of a suspended declaration of invalidity to reconcile the mandatory nature of s.23 of the Manitoba Act with the need to preserve the rule of law. The unanimous Court retained jurisdiction and expended considerable resources and capital on the case, but it still took over seven years for Manitoba's laws to be translated into French. Alas in subsequent minority language cases, the Court has been much more divided and hesitant about retention of jurisdiction as a mechanism to ensure compliance with the Constitution. A conclusion that courts are the most reliable institution to enforce minority rights does not mean that they will always do so or do so effectively.

THE MANITOBA MÉTIS LAND GRANT LITIGATION

The third Manitoba case study involves prolonged litigation over the way that the Manitoba government discharged its obligation under s.31 of the Manitoba Act to the Métis. The purpose of s.31 was to allow 1.4 million acres quickly to be distributed to the children of the head of Métis families in order to make sure that they would not be swamped by immigration into Manitoba. Some opposed this provision as rewarding Riel and the Métis for the rebellion. They warned that "any attempt to limit a special tract of country to a special class of the people and religion — leading to land not being improved and occupied — is greatly to be deprecated in the general interests of the community..."[109] This again confirms one of the central lessons of this chapter: minority rights are controversial.

Nevertheless attempts to remove s.31 from the Manitoba Act, 1870 were defeated. Canada would never have succeeded as a country if it was run as a simple majoritarian democracy as proposed by democratic reformers from Lord Durham to Jeremy Waldron. At the same time, Canadians should not be overly romantic about either s.31 or the Treaties that the Crown signed with many Indigenous communities. Section 31 reflected a realistic concession that Riel's forces had just fought a successful rebellion and many of the Treaties reflected the settlers' need for peace and friendship with the First Nations.

Despite the clear intent to grant land to benefit the Métis, it took four separate allotments between 1871 and 1885 to distribute the land. Mistakes were made by the executive in determining who was eligible for the land

---

[109] *Manitoba Metis Federation v. Attorney General of Canada et al.*, 2007 MBQB 293 at para 150 quoting an Anglican bishop's letter to the Governor General.

grants and the land grants for the Métis were not a priority. By the time of the last allotment, there was no land left to give the Métis in the rapidly expanding province. Instead they received $240 instead of the planned 240 acres. One problem was that the 240 acres on the booming Prairie now cost almost $500. Another problem was that many of those waiting for their allotments had already sold them to land speculators. As the Supreme Court has noted "the Métis community began to unravel. Many Métis sold their promised interests in land and moved further west. Those left amounted to a small remnant of the original community."[110]

LITIGATION IN AID OF EXTRA-JUDICIAL SETTLEMENTS

There appears to have been no litigation by the Métis in the 19th century about their land grants. This may have reflected that many Métis left Manitoba in part because of the delays in land grants. In any event, there has been much Métis litigation in the modern era.

ROUND ONE

Litigation started in the early 1980s about the implementation of s.31 of the Manitoba Act. The government challenged it on the basis that the applicants lacked standing and raised non-justiciable political questions. The Manitoba Court of Appeal agreed concluding that the litigation "does not affect anyone's current rights" and only affected "statutory rights of individuals who are now deceased." It concluded that "It is a well-established principle that a declaration is not available as a cure for past ills."[111]

In 1990, the Supreme Court reversed with Justice Wilson stating for the Court that the allegations that legislation relating to s.31 was unconstitutional "is justiciable in the courts and that declaratory relief may be granted in the discretion of the court in aid of extra-judicial claims"[112] such as the land claims agreement sought by the Métis. Once again and consistent with Pierre Trudeau's vision of a Supreme Court enforcing the rights of local minorities, the Métis received a better reception in the Supreme Court than in the Manitoba Court of Appeal.

---

[110] *Manitoba Metis Foundation* [2013] 1 SCR 613 at para 39.
[111] *Dumont v. Canada (AG)* (1988) 52 DLR (4th) 25 at 35 (Man C.A.).
[112] *Dumont v. Canada (AG)* [1990] 1 SCR 729.

ROUND TWO

The Supreme Court's 1990 decision in favour of the Métis simply meant that a trial could go ahead. There was much delay and Manitoba courts continued not to be receptive. The trial judge held in 2007 that the Métis claim was precluded by limitation periods and the equitable doctrine of laches in part on the basis that the Manitoba school cases demonstrated that the minority were able to litigate those issues.[113] This, however, disregards the formidable support that the Catholic Church played in all aspects of the Manitoba schools question. It provided a "support structure"[114] for both litigation and lobbying that the less affluent Métis did not have until the 1980's. The Métis were not supported by the Catholic Church. Rather, many of them suffered in residential schools run by the Catholic Church that were designed to destroy their Indigenous identity.[115]

The trial judge also found no basis to declare that Manitoba's implementing legislation was unconstitutional or that Manitoba failed to fulfil its obligations under s.31. The Manitoba Act was in the trial judge's view not a treaty between the Crown and the Métis or even intended to protect minorities.[116] He also dismissed the argument that the federal government should have disallowed inequitable land grants to the Métis in part on the basis that federal discretion in such matters could not be subject to judicial review.[117] In the end, the trial judge concluded that the Métis case was "fundamentally flawed" because it "seeks relief that is in essence of a collective nature, but is underpinned by a factual reality that is individual."[118] This was also consistent with the 1988 Manitoba Court of Appeal case that concluded that the fact that individual Métis had received land was "totally inconsistent with a collective grant to a community of persons."[119] The Manitoba courts were reluctant to see Métis rights as Aboriginal rights.

[113] *Manitoba Metis Federation Inc. et al. v. Attorney General of Canada et al.*, 2007 MBQB 293.
[114] Charles Epp, THE RIGHTS REVOLUTION (Chicago: University of Chicago Press, 1998). On the indispensible role of the Manitoba Métis Federation founded in 1967 in the long and complex litigation *see* Thomas Berger, *The Manitoba Métis Decision and the Uses of History*, 38 MANITOBA L. J. 1, 24–25 (2015).
[115] Clifford Sifton, one of the architects of residential schools, argued that they were "not established for the purpose of carrying out a treaty or complying with any provision of the law, but were prosecuted in the public interest, so that there should not grow up on reserves and uneducated and barbarous class."as quoted in *Truth and Reconciliation Commission of Canada Canada's Residential Schools: The Métis Experience* (Vol 3 of the Final Report) (Montreal: McGill Queens Press, 2015), 16.
[116] *Manitoba Metis Federation Inc. et al. v. Attorney General of Canada et al.*, 2007 MBQB 293 at paras 510, 534.
[117] *Id.* at para 923.   [118] *Id.* at para 1197.
[119] *Dumont v. Canada (AG)* (1988) 52 DLR (4th) 25 at 35 (Man C.A.) rev'd [1990] 1 SCR 759.

As in the earlier round of litigation, the Métis enjoyed more success when they reached Ottawa. The Supreme Court ruled that neither limitation periods or laches should apply because the honour of the Crown in dealing with Aboriginal people was at stake in implementing s.31. This generous ruling was also premised on the fact that the plaintiffs were seeking declarations about unconstitutional state action as opposed to damages.[120] At the same time, it recognizes that out of time defences are in tension with the goal of reconciliation.

The Supreme Court concluded that the delay in making land grants from 1870 to 1885 and "persistent pattern of inattention"[121] towards the Métis land grants violated the Crown's duty to act honourably in discharging their constitutional obligations to the Métis. The implementation of s.31 was "ineffectual and inequitable. This was not a matter of occasional negligence, but of repeated mistakes and inaction that persisted for more than a decade. A government sincerely intent on fulfilling the duty that its honour demanded could and should have done better."[122].

The Métis did not win complete victory at the Supreme Court. The Court agreed with the trial judge that Manitoba's action did not violate any fiduciary duty in large part on the basis that there was no pre-existing communal Métis interest in the land. In other words, the Court upheld the trial judge's findings that the Métis owned land only as individuals and not in a collective manner as required to establish Aboriginal title. The Supreme Court also held that the decision to assign lands to the Métis on a random basis, to allow the land to be sold and to grant script rather than land did not violate any Aboriginal right, though it acknowledged that all of these governmental actions aggravated the prejudice from the delay. There has been some criticism of this aspect of the decision as rejecting the notion that the Métis had Aboriginal title to land and advancing the idea propounded by Professor Thomas Flanagan that the Métis and indeed all Aboriginal people would be better off if they could freely sell their land.[123] Jean Teillet has argued the case was not really about

---

[120] The Truth and Reconciliation Commission recommended that the Crown should not rely on limitation periods in legal actions about historical abuse of Aboriginal peoples. Truth and Reconciliation Commission of Canada Report Volume 5 *The Legacy of Residential Schools* (Montreal: McGill Queens Press, 2015) at 203.

[121] [2013] 1 SCR 613 at para 103.   [122] *Id.* at para 128.

[123] Darren O'Toole, *Manitoba Metis Federation v. Canada: Breathing New Life into the "Empty Box" Doctrine of Indian Title*, 52 ALBERTA L.REV. 669 (2014). Professor Flanagan concluded in his expert report that "The major finding of my research is that the federal government appears to have fulfilled or even overfulfilled its obligations under ss. 31 and 32 of the Manitoba Act" (at p. 4)." as quoted in *Manitoba Metis Federation v. Canada* 2010 MBCA 71 at para 163. This finding is at odds with the Supreme Court's findings of delay and breach of honour of

establishing title and that the only evidence heard at trial about the nature of Métis land ownership came from the Crown's expert witnesses including Professor Flanagan.[124]

ARE GENERAL DECLARATIONS SUFFICIENT?
THE UNFINISHED DECLARATORY REMEDY

The declaratory remedy provided by the Court in 2013 has not yet resulted in any concrete gains for the Manitoba Métis in litigation first started in 1981. The UN Special Rapporteur on Indigenous Rights criticized Canada in 2015 for not negotiating land claims with the Métis.[125] It took over 2 years from the March 2013 judgment for the Harper government to appoint a special representative to deal with the issue.[126] A memorandum of agreement was, however, signed by the Justin Trudeau government and the Manitoba Métis Federation in May, 2016 to negotiate a land claims and reconciliation settlement, with a subsequent framework agreement signed between the two parties in November, 2016.[127] The Supreme Court also held in 2016 that the Métis as Aboriginal persons are subject to federal jurisdiction under s.91(24) of the Constitution Act, 1867.[128] This important ruling may facilitate negotiations between the Métis and the federal government, but it may also delay them as the federal government adjusts to assuming new responsibilities. In any event, the implementation of land claims and self-government agreements will require provincial cooperation and be vulnerable to provincial resistance

the Crown. It also is at odds with John A Macdonald's 1885 admission in the wake of the Northwest Rebellion that: "The claims of the half-breeds in Manitoba were bought up by speculators. It was an unfortunate thing for those poor people; but it is true that this grant of scrip and land to those poor people was a curse and not a blessing. The scrip was bought up; the lands were bought up by white speculators, and the consequences are apparent.", as quoted [2013] 1 SCR 613 at para 158. *See generally* Thomas Flanagan, METIS LANDS IN MANITOBA (Calgary: University of Calgary Press, 1991), and Thomas Flanagan, FIRST NATIONS SECOND THOUGHTS 2ND ED (Montreal: McGill Queens, 2008).

[124] Jean Teillet, METIS LAW IN CANADA (Vancouver: Pape, Salter, Teillet, 2015), 3–10.

[125] *See* Jason Madden, *Metis have rights too*, WINNIPEG FREE PRESS, Oct. 7, 2015.

[126] Mia Rabson, *Special representative appointed to assist in Metis rights issues*, WINNIPEG FREE PRESS, June 5, 2015.

[127] *Canada and Manitoba Metis Federation sign MOU after Historic Supreme Court ruling*, CBC NEWS, May 27, 2016, available at http://www.cbc.ca/news/canada/manitoba/metis-federation-of-manitoba-signs-mou-1.3604370; *Métis Nation 'finding ourselves in Confederation' with land claims negotiation*, CBC NEWS, Nov. 16, 2016 available at http://www.cbc.ca/news/canada/manitoba/métis-confederation-land-claim-negotiations-mmf-1.3854022.

[128] *Daniels v. Canada* 2016 SCC 12. The Court only refused to declare that the federal government had fiduciary obligations and the duty to consult because it would simply be a restatement of existing and applicable law. Ibid at paras 53 and 56.

including from those who may be hostile to giving the Métis minority a land base and self-governance powers.

SUMMARY: COMPARING EXECUTIVE, LEGISLATIVE AND JUDICIAL PERFORMANCE

What does the controversy over Métis land grants under s.31 of the Manitoba Act tell us about the respective role of courts, legislatures and the executive in enforcing constitutional rights designed to protect minorities?

The legislative record was complex and mixed. Some legislation was enacted in an attempt to protect Métis from land speculators, but that legislation was relaxed later to ensure that speculators could purchase the land even though it was to be granted to benefit Métis children.[129] Although the Métis claimed that the federal government should have used disallowance to protect the Métis, no particular claim seems to have been made by the Métis to the federal executive. Even if one had been made, the record on the parallel schools and language controversies suggests that it was unlikely that the federal government would have intervened in this matter.

The courts again emerge as the most robust source of remedies even though the Métis are still awaiting a land claim agreement after close to four decades of litigation. As was the case in the Manitoba schools controversy, the courts in Manitoba refused to grant the minority relief in both the initial and later round of litigation about s.31. As it had with the schools issues, the Supreme Court reversed the Manitoba courts in both cases enabling the Métis claims to be heard on their merits.[130]

It is important, however, not to overstate the extent of the Métis victory in court. The Supreme Court affirmed that the Métis did not hold Aboriginal title even though s.31 on its own terms indicates an intent to extinguish such title. The Supreme Court described its declaration that the government had breached the honour of the Crown as a "limited" and a "narrow remedy" that was neither a "personal" or "coercive "but meant to achieve "reconciliation."[131] This declaratory remedy was much less robust than that used to ensure that Manitoba translate its unilingual statutes. Reconciliation is a frequently used

---

[129] An Act to Enable Certain Children of Half-Breed Heads of Families to Convey Their Lands S.M. 1878 41 Vict, c.30; An Act Respecting Half-Breed Lands and Quieting Certain Titles Thereto, S.M. 1881, 44 Vict, c.19.

[130] *Dumont v. Canada* [1990] 1 SCR 729; *Manitoba Metis Federation v. Canada* [2013] 1 SCR 613.

[131] *Manitoba Metis Federation v. Canada* [2013] 1 SCR 613 at para 143.

concept in the context of Indigenous rights, but one that often and especially in the absence of mutual agreements falls far short of its promise.

Even when courts are prepared to grant remedies to assist minorities, the optimal remedy will often depend on legislative and executive and even federal-provincial cooperation. In the Indigenous rights context, consensual agreements between governments and rights holders are especially important. They harken back to the role of Treaties as Canada's first constitutional documents.[132]

CONCLUSIONS

The three Manitoba case studies in this chapter should rebut any arguments that the 1982 Charter was novel in introducing rights claims to the Canadian constitution. The Manitoba minorities made their rights claims to the executive, the legislature and the courts. They asserted their rights to anyone who would listen. In the case of the Métis, they continue to make such claims to this day. Rights have always been part of Canadian Constitution. The Charter simply expanded the range of rights claims.

The minorities were well aware when their rights were compromised perhaps most dramatically in the so-called "sunny ways" Laurier-Greenway Compromise of 1897 which fell far short of restoring public funding to Catholic schools or French language rights. In addition, there is plenty of raw material in these Manitoba stories to suggest the need for courts to play a robust anti-majoritarian role in enforcing the rights of unpopular minorities. To be sure, Manitoba's francophone, Catholic and Métis minorities benefited from being organized into pre-existing organizations that strongly lobbied all branches of government.[133] Nevertheless their organization and even the support they received from the Catholic Church with respect to the extensive schools litigation largely failed to restore their minority rights. There is no public funding of Catholic schools in Manitoba to this day and the Métis are still awaiting a land claims agreement. Manitoba's old laws were only translated into French after the Supreme Court retained jurisdiction over the case. This record provides no grounds for Canadian self-congratulation.

The judicial record in providing relief for the three minorities while far from optimal is, however, superior to the executive and judicial record. This finding would be even more robust if the Supreme Court's defence of minority rights in the Catholic school case had not been overturned by the

---

[132] As discussed in Chapter 4 of this volume.
[133] Bruce Ackerman, *Beyond Carolene Products*, 98 HARV.L.REV. 713 (1985).

Judicial Committee of the Privy Council in London. Nevertheless the lesson that emerges from these stories is that we cannot simply rely on independent and even heroic judges to deliver effective remedies. Remedies are deeply dialogic in requiring good faith and prompt cooperation from the executive, the legislature and the larger society to be truly effective.

More meaningful remedies in these cases might have emerged not simply from independent judges staring down majority sentiment and prejudice and reminding people about various constitutional commitments made in 1870, but from a partnership or dialogue between courts and legislatures. The 1895 remedial bill that would have restored public funding to Catholic schools, the 1983 constitutional amendment that would have provided for modern French language government services and a land claims and self-government agreement between the Métis and the federal and provincial governments would have been the most effective remedies.

Civil society groups played an important even critical role in all three episodes. The Catholic Church played a role in the failed 1895 remedial legislation, the Societe Franco-Manitobans was a partner to the failed but progressive 1983 amendment to guarantee French language services and most recently, the Manitoba Métis Federation has agreed to a memorandum of understanding to negotiate with the federal government in light of the Supreme Court's 2013 decision in their case.

But remedies that involve legislation and partnerships can encounter many obstacles. In both 1895 and 1983, small minorities in the legislature strongly opposed to minority rights were able to obstruct the legislature and prevent a vote on the merits of remedial legislation or a constitutional amendment. It is possible to imagine that legislation implementing land claims and self-government agreements with the Métis could be obstructed especially in the Manitoba legislature including by those opposed to the very notion of Indigenous rights.

Nevertheless, it is clear that without successful litigation there would be very little chance for any remedies to enforce minority rights. The Privy Council's 1895 *Brophy* decision inspired the proposed remedial law restoring publicly funded Catholic schools and the 1983 constitutional amendment would not have been negotiated without the Supreme Court's 1979 ruling affirming Manitoba's bilingualism obligations and the threat of wholesale judicial invalidation of all of Manitoba's unilingual laws in the air. Similarly, court victories by the Métis in 1990, 2013 and again in 2016 have been necessary to the place the still unresolved issue of land redress for the Métis onto the political agenda.

The Canadian Constitution both in 1867 and today contemplates that all three branches of government have a role in respecting the constitution.

One of the reasons why new remedies such as the suspended declaration of invalidity first used by the Supreme Court in the 1985 *Manitoba Language Reference* and now specifically provided for in the 1996 South African Constitution are a promising means to enforce a range of rights (including socio-economic ones) is that they have a potential to harness both judicial and legislative capacities with respect to remedies.

The Privy Council in *Brophy* was less resistant to remedial legislation than American courts. A similar residual Canadian deference to the state can also be found in those parts of the Charter that protect state attempts to ameliorate the conditions of disadvantaged individuals and groups and the Canadian Supreme Court's more easy acceptance of affirmative action than American courts. In theory, the Canadian constitution may be more receptive to remedial legislation, but the sad fact remains that Manitoba's Catholic, francophone and Métis minorities have yet to benefit from remedial legislation. They all have had to go to court multiple times to achieve the limited and less than optimal remedies they have received for the way that majorities have violated and neglected the rights they fought for and gained under the *Manitoba Act, 1870*. This is unfortunate because the case studies in this chapter suggest that constitutional remedies will be more effective when all three branches of government cooperate and when they seek agreement with minorities about the optimal content of remedies.

PART III

The Global Impact of Canadian Constitutionalism

·

13

Going Global?

Canada as Importer and Exporter of Constitutional Thought

RAN HIRSCHL

In this chapter I assess the transformation of Canada's stature as "giver" and as "taker" of constitutional thought. The discussion advances in three main parts. I begin by addressing the status of constitutional innovation as one of Canada's main intellectual exports. A confluence of factors, chief among them are the 1982 constitutional transformation, the relative decline in the international influence of American constitutional tradition, and the growing quest world-wide for constitutional innovation concerning burning matters such as the tension between constitutionalism and democracy, cultural and religious diversity, and the management of internal strife through constitutional means, has brought an incredible rise in the global stature of and respect for the Canadian constitution and Canadian constitutional thought. In the second part of the chapter, I assess the status of constitutional importation in Canada, i.e., the Canadian approach toward engagement with constitutional concepts and materials drawn from other constitutional democracies. The rise of a confident, distinctly Canadian approach to constitutionalism and a corresponding maturation of the Supreme Court, all enriched by general appreciation of and selective engagements with comparative constitutional ideas, mainly in the area of constitutional rights, brought about a sharp decline in judicial reliance on British constitutional ideals and jurisprudence. In that respect, in addition to the formal one, the Canadian constitution has indeed been repatriated. These changes are closely linked to the 1982 constitutional makeover, but also to broader transformations in Canada's self-perception, sense of collective identity, and the re-conceptualization of its place in the

I thank Debbie Boswell for the helpful research assistance, as well as Ayelet Shachar, the editors of this volume, and the participants of the *Canada in the World: Comparative Perspectives on the Constitution of Canada* Conference (Yale Law School, Apr. 12, 2016) for their valuable suggestions and queries.

world. I conclude in the third part by suggesting that while the contemporary
Canadian constitutional sphere is engaging closely with constitutional jurisprudence and constitutional concepts in the area of rights and liberties, the
comparative turn has not, by and large, penetrated the discourse concerning
some of Canada's structural or organic constitutional failings. In that sense, the
promise of comparative constitutional inquiry has not fully materialized, and
has largely fallen short of making a meaningful contribution to the advancement of a sophisticated, well-informed discourse about constitutional renewal
in early twenty-first century Canada.

CANADA AS "EXPORTER" OF CONSTITUTIONAL THOUGHT

Arguably the most significant development in contemporary comparative constitutionalism is the global spread of constitutional courts, judicial review, and
bills of rights as the cynosures of the comparative constitutional universe.[1] No
single country's constitutional landscape exemplifies this transformation more
vividly than Canada, which offers a paradigmatic illustration of the focus and
preoccupations of contemporary comparative constitutionalism. Canada
entered the twentieth century embodying the deferential, British-style constitutional tradition and emerged out of it with a robust constitutional culture
featuring active judicial review, an acclaimed constitutional bill of rights – the
Canadian Charter of Rights and Freedoms[2] – pervasive rights discourse and one
of the most frequently cited high courts in the world.[3] As the Chief Justice of the
Supreme Court of Canada recently observed: "Canadian decisions are routinely
cited by courts in South Africa, New Zealand, Israel, the United Kingdom,
Australia and India, and by the European Court of Human Rights."[4] Likewise,
Aharon Barak, former Chief Justice of the Supreme Court of Israel and a
member of honour in the emerging global epistemic community of judges,
has praised the Supreme Court of Canada for being "particularly noteworthy for

---

[1] *See generally* Ran Hirschl, COMPARATIVE MATTERS: THE RENAISSANCE OF COMPARATIVE
     CONSTITUTIONAL LAW (Oxford University Press, 2014).
[2] Part I of the *Constitution Act, 1982*, being Schedule B to the *Canada Act 1982* (UK), 1982,
     c 11 [Charter].
[3] *See, e.g.,* James Allan, Grant Huscroft & Nessa Lynch, *The Citation of Overseas Authority in
     Rights Litigation in New Zealand: How Much Bark? How Much Bite?*, Otago Law Review 11
     433, 455 (2007) (showing that Canadian decisions in civil rights cases are far more cited in
     New Zealand than those of any other nation).
[4] The Honourable Beverley McLachlin, "The Canadian Charter of Rights and Freedoms'
     First 30 Years: A Good Beginning" in Errol Mendes & Stephane Beaulac, eds., *Canadian
     Charter of Rights and Freedoms/Charte canadienne des droits et libertés*, 5th ed. (LexisNexis,
     2013), 25, 41.

its frequent and fruitful use of comparative law. As such, Canadian law serves as a source of inspiration for many countries around the world."[5]

This is a stunning change considering that it was not until the late 1940s, when appeals to the Judicial Committee of the Privy Council were abolished, that the Supreme Court of Canada became the top court of the land. The first century of the Supreme Court of Canada's constitutional jurisprudence was not very relevant or inspiring to jurists, legal academics, and constitutional drafters overseas. But things changed almost overnight with the adoption of the *Constitution Act 1982*. A key feature of this change was Canadian constitutional ingenuity. As part of the 1982 constitutional revolution, innovations such as explicit constitutional commitment to bilingualism, multiculturalism, Aboriginal peoples' rights, proportionality (via section 1 of the *Charter* – the "limitations clause"), and potential political override of certain rights provisions (via section 33's "override clause") were introduced in Canada, and later analyzed and emulated abroad.[6] Because these mechanisms were designed to mitigate the tension between rigid constitutionalism and judicial activism on the one hand, and fundamental democratic governing principles on the other – a general challenge involving active judicial review – they were quick to attract the attention of constitutional reformers overseas.[7]

Supreme Court of Canada decisions concerning section 1's limitation clause – most notably *R v Oakes* – now feature in many comparative constitutional law textbooks,[8] and have served as the basis for the so-called proportionality analysis – the contemporary Esperanto-like *lingua franca* of constitutional interpretation throughout much of the liberal democratic world.[9] It is here where the exportability of Canada's "new constitutionalism" model has been evident; Canada's model of formal limitations on rights has

---

[5] Aharon Barak, THE JUDGE IN A DEMOCRACY (Princeton University Press, 2006), 203.

[6] Adam Dodek, "The Canadian Override: Constitutional Model or *Bete Noire* of Constitutional Politics?" *Israel Law Review* 49 (2016): 45–65.

[7] Thirty-five years after their introduction, it is fair to say that section 1's limitation clause has been a greater success than section 33's override clause. Whereas the idea former has become a cornerstone of rights jurisprudence in Canada and elsewhere, the latter lacks wide public legitimacy and has not been very popular beyond Canada either. To describe it as a political "dead-letter" would be an exaggeration. However, since 1982 there have only been a handful of significant instances in which governments have either invoked or seriously attempted to invoke this clause. Even the change of guards in Ottawa following the 2006 federal election and the ensuing nine years of Conservative government, have not changed that trend.

[8] *R v. Oakes*, [1986] 1 SCR 103.

[9] Marie Deschamps, Maxime St-Hilaire, and Pierre Gemson, THE CROSS-FERTILIZATION OF JURISPRUDENCE AND THE PRINCIPLE OF PROPORTIONALITY: PROCESS AND RESULT FROM A CANADIAN PERSPECTIVE (2010), available at: http://papers.ssrn.com/sol3/papers.cfm?abstract_id=2327537

served as point of reference to constitutional framers in other countries,[10] and is frequently cited in leading textbooks and journals in comparative constitutional law.[11] Subsequently, the so-called "dialogue" thesis, as well as "weak-form" and "commonwealth" models of judicial review were subsequently developed,[12] debated extensively and have been analyzed comparatively by scholars in Canada and abroad.[13]

Another main area wherein Canadian constitutional thought is referred to frequently overseas is the managing of secessionist impulses through constitutional means. Landmark Supreme Court of Canada rulings concerning the Quebec saga, chief among them is of course the *Reference re Secession of Quebec*, have been commonly invoked in comparative constitutional design discourse and in international legal conversation on secession and self-determination. As is well known to Canadian observers and to comparative constitutional scholars, the constitutional battle over Quebec has reached its zenith in 1998 with the *Quebec Secession Reference* – the first time a democratic country had ever preemptively tested the legal terms of its own dissolution.[14] The case was launched at the request of the federal government following the slim 50.6 per cent to 49.4 per cent loss by the Québécois secessionist movement in the 1995 referendum (a shift of approximately 50,000 votes would have pushed the pendulum in the separatist direction). In a widely publicized ruling in August 1998, the SCC unanimously held that unilateral secession would be an unconstitutional act under both domestic and international law, and that a majority vote in Quebec was not sufficient to allow Quebec to legally separate from the rest of Canada. However, the Court

---

[10] *See, e.g.*, Lorraine E. Weinrib, *The Canadian Charter of Rights and Freedoms as a Model for the New Israeli Basic Laws*, CONSTITUTIONAL FORUM 4, 85–87 (1993); Yash Ghai, *Sentinels of Liberty or Sheep in Wolf's Clothing? Judicial Politics and the Hong Kong Bill of Rights*, MODERN LAW REVIEW 60, 459–480 (1997).

[11] *See, e.g.*, Vicki Jackson and Mark Tushnet, *Comparative Constitutional Law* (University Casebook Series, 3rd Edition) (Foundation Press, 2014); Steven Calabresi et al., *The US Constitution and Comparative Constitutional Law: Texts, Cases, and Materials* (University Casebook Series, 1st Edition) (Foundation Press, 2016).

[12] *See, e.g.*, Peter W. Hogg & Allison A. Bushell, *The Charter Dialogue Between Courts and Legislatures (or Perhaps the Charter of Rights Isn't Such a Bad Thing After All*, OSGOODE HALL LAW JOURNAL 35, 75–124 (1997); Stephen Gardbaum, *The New Commonwealth Model of Constitutionalism*, AMERICAN JOURNAL OF COMPARATIVE LAW 49, 707–760 (2001); Mark Tushnet, *Weak-Form Judicial Review and 'Core' Civil Liberties*, HARVARD CIVIL RIGHTS-CIVIL LIBERTIES LAW REVIEW 41, 1–22 (2006); Stephen Gardbaum, *Reassessing the New Commonwealth Model of Constitutionalism*, INTERNATIONAL JOURNAL OF CONSTITUTIONAL LAW 8, 167–206 (2010).

[13] Stephen Gardbaum, THE NEW COMMONWEALTH MODEL OF CONSTITUTIONALISM: THEORY AND PRACTICE (Cambridge University Press, 2013).

[14] *Reference re Secession of Quebec*, [1998] 2 SCR 217.

also noted that if and when secession were approved by a clear majority of people in Quebec voting in a referendum on a clear question, the parties should then negotiate the terms of the subsequent breakup in good faith. As for the question of unilateral secession under Canadian law, the Court's answer provided both federalists and separatists with congenial answers.

In strictly legal terms, the Court ruled that the secession of Quebec would involve a major change to the constitution of Canada that would require amending the Constitution, which in turn would require negotiations among all parties involved. On the normative level, the Court stated that the Canadian Constitution is based on four equally significant underlying principles: (1) federalism, (2) democracy, (3) constitutionalism and the rule of law, and (4) the protection of minorities. None of these principles trump any of the others. Hence, even a majority vote (i.e., strict adherence to the fundamental democratic principle of majority rule) would not entitle Quebec to secede unilaterally. However, the Court stated that if a clear majority of Québécois were to vote "oui/yes" to an unambiguous question on Quebec separation, this would "confer legitimacy on the efforts of the government of Quebec to initiate the Constitution's amendment process in order to secede by constitutional means." Such "a clear majority on a clear question" would require the federal government to negotiate in good faith with Quebec in order to reach an agreement on the terms of separation. As for international law, the Court's answer was much shorter and less ambiguous; it found that the right of peoples to self-determination under international law did not apply to Quebec. While avoiding the contentious question of whether the Quebec population or part of it constituted a "people" as understood in international law, the Court held that the right to unilateral secession was not applicable here, and that the Québécois are neither denied their rightful ability to pursue their "political, economic, social and cultural development within the framework of an existing state," nor do they constitute a colonial or oppressed people.

Over the last few years alone, the *Quebec Secession Reference* ruling and the jurisprudential framework it provided for dealing with the constitutionality and legality of secession claims has been referred to frequently in polities facing secessionist challenges, ranging from Catalonia[15] and Scotland[16] to

[15] Hermann-Josef Blanke and Yasser Abdelrehim, *Catalonia and the Right to Self-Determination from the Perspective of International Law*, MAX PLANCK YEARBOOK OF UNITED NATIONS LAW 18, 532–564 (2014).

[16] Mark Walters, *Nationalism and the Pathology of Legal Systems: Considering the Quebec Secession Reference and Its Lessons for the United Kingdom*, MODERN LAW REVIEW 62, 371–396 (1999).

Chechnya,[17] Taiwan,[18] and the former Yugoslavia.[19] It has likewise become a main point of reference for general scholarly debate about the constitutional law and international law of secession.[20]

And then there is the extensive and sophisticated Canadian rights jurisprudence of the Charter era. Over the past few decades, the SCC has become one of the country's most important decision-making bodies. Beyond its traditionally significant role in adjudicating disputes involving federalism and the separation of powers, it has been called upon to decide on many fundamental rights and liberties issues: freedom of expression; religion and assembly; voting and citizenship rights; due process rights; the right to privacy and human dignity; equality rights in the context of gender, age and sexual preference; the rights of indigenous people; as well as language and minority language education rights. In some of these areas the SCC has developed innovative modes of reasoning and interpretation that are of significance to scholars and jurists worldwide.[21] In a stark contrast with the pre-Charter era, when the impact of Canadian rulings within the common law world was quite modest (and frankly negligible to non-existent beyond it),[22] from the 1980s onward, Canadian rights jurisprudence has become a brand name of sorts among relevant epistemic communities worldwide. American jurists, parochial as they sometimes are, seldom pay attention to foreign, including Canadian, jurisprudence. However, scholars, policy-makers, and jurists throughout the rest of the common law world and increasingly beyond it are now frequently inspired by, and sometimes emulate, Canadian constitutional rights jurisprudence.

In this respect, it is important to acknowledge the ever-accelerating trend towards inter-court borrowing and the establishment of a globalized, non-US-centred judicial discourse. Constitutional courts worldwide increasingly rely on comparative constitutional jurisprudence to both frame and articulate their

[17] Diana Draganova, *Chechnya's Right of Secession under Russian Constitutional Law*, CHINESE JOURNAL OF INTERNATIONAL LAW 3, 571–589 (2004).
[18] Jonathan Charney and J.R.V. Prescott, *Resolving Cross-Strait Relations between China and Taiwan*, AMERICAN JOURNAL OF INTERNATIONAL LAW 94, 453–477 (2000).
[19] Zoran Oklopcic, *The Migrating Spirit of the Secession Reference in Southeastern Europe*, CANADIAN JOURNAL OF LAW & JURISPRUDENCE 24, 347–376 (2011).
[20] See, e.g., Sanford Levinson, ed., NULLIFICATION AND SECESSION IN 21ST CENTURY CONSTITUTIONAL THOUGHT (University of Kansas Press, 2016); Don H. Doyle, ed., SECESSION AS AN INTERNATIONAL PHENOMENON (University of Georgia Press, 2010).
[21] See, e.g., Lorraine E. Weinrib, *The Supreme Court of Canada in the Age of Rights: Constitutional Democracy, the Rule of Law and Fundamental Rights under Canada's Constitution*, CANADIAN BAR REVIEW 80, 699–748 (2001).
[22] See, e.g., George Winterton, *Comparative Law Teaching*, AMERICAN JOURNAL OF COMPARATIVE LAW 23 (1975): 69–118, at 74.

own position on a given constitutional question. This phenomenon is particularly evident with respect to constitutional rights jurisprudence. As early as 1998, the MJ Claire L'Heureux-Dubé of the Supreme Court of Canada noted "how globalization is also occurring in the process of judging and lawyering, and how growing international links and influences are affecting and changing judicial decisions, particularly at the level of top appellate courts throughout the world. More and more courts, particularly within the common law world, are looking to the judgments of other jurisdictions."[23] Other observers concur: "constitution interpretation across the globe is taking on an increasingly cosmopolitan character, as comparative jurisprudence comes to assume a central place in constitutional adjudication";[24] "Courts are talking to one another all over the world."[25]

Canadian constitutional rights jurisprudence is among the more popular topics they talk about. Examples are many, from common reference to early Charter-based rulings on freedom of expression or gender equality to later decisions on same-sex marriage. In particular, landmark Supreme Court rulings concerning the constitutional accommodation of religious difference – from the early Charter rulings regarding Sunday closing to more recent ones such as *Amselem, Multani* and *Loyola High School v. Québec*[26] – have become cornerstones of comparative reference in jurisprudence concerning religious freedoms and claims of culture, and have served as a viable alternative to the rather idiosyncratic American jurisprudence in that area.[27] This trend has been given added impetus in recent years with the rise of dilemmas of citizenship, multiculturalism, diversity, and accommodation throughout much of the Western world. In that way,

---

[23] The Honorable Claire L'Heureux-Dubé, *The Importance of Dialogue: Globalization and the International Impact of the Rehnquist Court*, 34 TULSA LAW REVIEW 15–40, at 16 (1998).

[24] Sujit Choudhry, *Globalization in Search of Justification: Toward a Theory of Comparative Constitutional Interpretation*, INDIANA LAW JOURNAL 74, 820–892, 820 (1999).

[25] Anne-Marie Slaughter, *A Typology of Transjudicial Communities*, UNIVERSITY OF RICHMOND LAW REVIEW 29, 99–134 (1999).

[26] *Syndicat Northcrest v. Amselem*, [2004] 2 SCR 551; *Multani v Commission scolaire Marguerite-Bourgeoys*, [2006] 1 SCR 256; *Loyola High School v. Quebec (Attorney General)*, [2015] 1 SCR 613.

[27] *See* Ayelet Shachar, *Squaring the Circle of Multiculturalism? Religious Freedom and Gender Equality in Canada*, LAW AND ETHICS OF HUMAN RIGHTS 10, 31–70 (2016); Benjamin L. Berger, LAW'S RELIGION: RELIGIOUS DIFFERENCE AND HE CLAIMS OF CONSTITUTIONALISM (University of Toronto Press, 2015); Ran Hirschl and Ayelet Shachar, "The Constitutional Boundaries of Religious Accommodation," in Michel Rosenfeld and Susanna Mancini, eds., *Constitutional Secularism in an Age of Religious Revival* (Oxford University Press, 2014), 175–191.

Canadian-style constitutional rights jurisprudence has become an effective way for marketing Canadian values abroad.[28]

Meanwhile, the Charter revolution has served as a key case-study in comparative social science accounts of the political origins and consequences of constitutional transformation.[29] Even harsh criticisms from left and right, of the newly formed Canadian constitutional setting, have inspired similar-in-nature critical accounts elsewhere.[30] And in discordant constitutional settings facing internal tensions between religion- or ethnicity-based and universalist notions of collective identity (e.g., Israel, Pakistan or India), Canadian constitutional values are frequently invoked by proponents of cosmopolitanism, universalism and liberal ideals in their attempt to articulate in a public way who "we" are as a political community and what "our image" or "place" in the world are or should be.[31] These trends have been reinforced by the disproportionally large number of Canadian scholars (several of whom are among the contributors to this volume) at the forefront of comparative constitutional law discourse, as well as by the involvement of Canadian constitutional experts in attempt to mitigate ethnic tensions through constitutional design in troubled places such as Nepal, Sri Lanka, Somalia, and South Sudan.

[28] A notable and puzzling anomaly in this context is in the area of social and economic rights, where there is a considerable gap between Canada's long-standing commitment to a relatively generous version of the Keynesian welfare state model (certainly as compared to the United States) and the general exclusion of subsistence social rights from the purview of Charter provisions. See Ran Hirschl and Evan Rosevear, "Constitutional Law Meets Comparative Politics: Socio-Economic Rights and Political Realities," in Tom Campbell et al., eds., *The Legal Protection of Human Rights: Sceptical Essays* (Oxford University Press, 2011), 207–222.

[29] See e.g., Charles R. Epp, *Do Bills of Rights Matter? The Canadian Charter of Rights and Freedoms*, American Political Science Review 90 (1996): 765–779; Charles R. Epp, The Rights Revolution: Lawyers, Activists, and Supreme Courts in Comparative Perspective (University of Chicago Press, 1998); Ran Hirschl, Towards Juristocracy: The Origins and Consequences of the New Constitutionalism (Harvard University Press, 2004).

[30] See, e.g., Michael Mandel, The Charter of Rights and The Legalization of Politics in Canada (Thompson, 1989); F.L. Morton & Rainer Knopff, The Charter Revolution and the Court Party (Broadview Press, 2000).

[31] See Ran Hirschl, *In Search of an Identity: Voluntary Foreign Citations in Discordant Constitutional Settings*, 62 American Journal of Comparative Law, 547–584 (2014). As noted above (e.g., Barak, *supra* note 5), Aharon Barak, former Chief Justice of the Israeli Supreme Court, has been a long term proponent of Canadian rights jurisprudence and a frequent visitor to and lecturer at the University of Toronto Faculty of Law. Ajmal Mian, former Chief Justice of Pakistan and a pro-modernization voice in that country's constitutional scene, takes great pride in the fact that Justice Claire L'Heureux-Dubé of the Supreme Court of Canada – a major proponent of international constitutional cross-fertilization – visited the Supreme Court of Pakistan and expressed keen interest in its jurisprudence on constitutional matters. See Ajmal Mian, A Judge Speaks Out (Oxford University Press, 2004), at 135.

In summary, in a stark contrast with the first century plus of Canada's constitutional history, constitutional thought of every variety is now one of Canada's main intellectual exports.[32] Although it is seldom mentioned in the context of what Joseph Nye famously called "soft power" in international diplomacy (essentially, the ability to shape the preferences of others through appeal and attraction and the power of ideas, not through force, coercion and domination), constitutional innovation has become an important element in marketing the Canadian image among jurists, policy-makers, peace, makers and political reformers abroad.[33] Fortunately for the Canadian constitutional scene of the last thirty-five years, this trend has corresponded neatly with the relative decline in the international significance of American constitutional thought and the rise of alternative sources of constitutional diffusion, emulation and borrowing that in addition to Canada include Germany, the European Court of Human Rights, South Africa and to a lesser degree India, Australia, and occasionally several other smaller jurisdictions. The admiration of Canadian constitutional creed abroad has also coincided with broader global processes of democratization, advances in information technology and the increasing prevalence, perhaps even near-canonical status of what may be termed "liberal constitutionalism" throughout much of the developed world. The turn of Canadian constitutionalism into "hot commodity" overseas is therefore the by-product of a near perfect alignment of key supply and demand factors.

CANADA AS A CONSTITUTIONAL "TAKER"

When it comes to Canada as "taker" of constitutional thought, the picture is somewhat more complex. Unlike in its neighbour to the south, judicial reference to foreign materials has never been a contested practice in Canada. Whereas some would like to see even more engagement with comparative jurisprudence, or note that the practice has not really burgeoned as one might

---

[32] *See, e.g.,* Adam Dodek, *Canada as Constitutional Exporter: The Rise of the 'Canadian Model' of Constitutionalism,* 36 SUPREME COURT LAW REVIEW 309–336 (2007); Sujit Choudhry, *The Globalization of the Canadian Constitution,* 91 THE TRUDEAU FOUNDATION PAPERS 98–104 (2012); David S. Law & Mila Versteeg, *The Declining Influence of the United States Constitution,* 87 NEW YORK UNIVERSITY LAW REVIEW 762, 809–823 (2012); Mark Tushnet, *The Charter's Influence Around the World,* 50 OSGOODE HALL LAW JOURNAL 527 (2013).

[33] *See, generally,* Joseph Nye, SOFT POWER: THE MEANS TO SUCCESS IN WORLD POLITICS (Public Affairs, 2004). On the idea of counting a given nation's constitutional influence abroad as soft power, *see* Tushnet, *supra* note 32.

expect, the Supreme Court continues to take an open-minded approach to the matter – both in theory and in practice.[34] Traditionally, the Canadian constitutional scene relied heavily on English sources. Back in 1951, for example, the young Bora Laskin acknowledged the Supreme Court's "three-fourths century habit of obedience and uncritical deference to English decisions."[35] Canadian law students, lawyers and courts in the pre-1970s era studied the decisions of English courts and treated them as practically binding.

A new pattern was gradually establishing itself in the 1970s, when the Court's reference to its own rulings began to rise. Whereas reference to the Supreme Court's own rulings by Rinfert Court (1944–1954) stood at 21.7 per cent or all its references and at 28.7 per cent by the Kerwin Court (1954–1963), it rose to over 38 per cent by the Laskin Court (1973–1984), to nearly 56 per cent by the Lamer Court (1990–1999), and to 58.7 per cent by the McLachlin Court (during the 2000–2015 period).[36] In his comprehensive studies of the Supreme Court of Canada's citation practices from 2000 onward, Peter McCormick concludes that by 2009, "[t]he McLachlin Court has made just over 1,500 citations to non-Canadian judicial authority, this comprising roughly one-tenth of all judicial citations."[37] That percentage rose slightly to 11.2 per cent by 2015.[38] With respect to citations to the United States, McCormick observes that "we are seeing less of a sustained intellectual exploration of American ideas than an occasional selective raid."[39] Of the 13,602 total citations to judicial authority (including foreign and domestic) the SCC made between 2000 and 2008, a relatively small percentage (476 or

[34] Several studies of the practice are: Bijon Roy, *An Empirical Survey of Foreign Jurisprudence and International Instruments in Charter Litigation*, 62 UNIVERSITY OF TORONTO FACULTY OF LAW REVIEW 99 (2004); Adam Dodek, *Comparative Law at the Supreme Court of Canada in 2008: Limited Engagement and Missed Opportunities*, 47 SUPREME COURT LAW REVIEW 445 (2009); Peter McCormick, *Waiting for Globalization: An Empirical Study of the McLachlin Court's Foreign Judicial Citations*, 41 OTTAWA LAW REVIEW 209 (2010); C. L. Ostberg, Matthew E. Wetstein & Craig R. Ducat, *Attitudes, Precedents and Cultural Change: Explaining the Citation of Foreign Precedents by the Supreme Court of Canada*, 34 CANADIAN JOURNAL OF POLITICAL SCIENCE 377 (2001).

[35] Bora Laskin, *The Supreme Court of Canada: A Final Court of and for Canadians*, 29 THE CANADIAN BAR REVIEW 1038, 1075 (1951).

[36] Data is drawn from Peter McCormick, THE END OF THE CHARTER REVOLUTION: LOOKING BACK FROM THE NEW NORMAL (University of Toronto Press, 2015), 217.

[37] Peter McCormick, *Waiting for Globalization: An Empirical Study of the McLachlin Court's Foreign Judicial Citations*, 41 OTTAWA LAW REVIEW 209 (2009). See also Adam Dodek, *Comparative Law at the Supreme Court of Canada in 2008: Limited Engagement and Missed Opportunities*, 47 SUPREME COURT LAW REVIEW 445 (2009).

[38] McCormick, *supra* note 36, at 216.

[39] Peter McCormick, *American Citations and the McLachlin Court: An Empirical Study*, 47 OSGOODE HALL LAW JOURNAL 83 (2009).

3.5 per cent) were to American authorities. Whereas use of American authority rose sharply in the early Charter era, it "has now fallen back to its modest pre-Charter levels, [the Court's foreign] references failing to reflect more recent American jurisprudence." MJ Claire L'Heureux-Dubé observed that "an informal analysis of Canadian Supreme Court decisions since 1986 revealed that the Rehnquist court was cited in fewer than one-half as many cases as the Warren Court, and in just under one-third the number of Burger Court cases."[40]

A recent survey of the Supreme Court's foreign citation patterns in constitutional cases reports a total of 1,944 such citations from 1982 to 2013. Of this total, 1,183 (61 per cent) were American cases, 516 (27 per cent) were United Kingdom cases, and about 12 per cent were rulings from other jurisdictions such as Australia (87 citations), New Zealand (35 citations) and the European Court of Human Rights (69 citations).[41] The majority of references to American court rulings were made in the first fifteen years of the Charter, while the late 1990s saw a considerable decline in citation of American sources,[42] reflecting both the declining relevance of US jurisprudence as persuasive authority, and at the same time, the increasing confidence of the Supreme Court of Canada.[43]

The ostensive decline in direct reference to American constitutional jurisprudence, at least in Canada, Australia and other similarly situated countries, may thus also be the result of greater confidence by the borrower side rather than of a decline by the supplier side. We may call it the "jurisprudential maturation" factor: the more established a given constitutional court is or the more developed its jurisprudence, the lesser the likelihood it will refer to foreign precedents. As Aaron Aft argues, "the dip in US citations in [Canada in] the early twenty-first century is better explained by a maturing SCC jurisprudence, rather than an effect caused by US hostility to comparative exercise, or political disagreements."[44] He suggests that "when facing novel constitutional cases, a court might be more inclined to look abroad to more

---

[40] *Supra* note 23, at 29.

[41] See Gianluca Gentili, "Enhancing Constitutional Self-Understanding through Comparative Law – An Empirical Study of the Use of Foreign Case Law by the Supreme Court of Canada (1982–2013)," in Mads Andenas and Duncan Fairgrieve, eds., *Courts and Comparative Law* (Oxford University Press, 2015), 378–406.

[42] *Id.*

[43] *See* Adam Liptak, *US Court Is Now Guiding Fewer Nations*, NEW YORK TIMES (17 Sept., 2008), available at www.nytimes.com.

[44] Aaron B. Aft, *Respect My Authority: Analyzing Claims of Diminished US Supreme Court Influence Abroad*, 18 INDIANA JOURNAL OF GLOBAL LEGAL STUDIES. 421, 439 (2011).

experienced tribunals for guidance. One would anticipate an increase in
the citation to the US Supreme Court when addressing novel constitutional
instruments or issues, and that such citations would recede in favour of reliance on domestic precedent once it is established." A similar "court newness/
maturation" factor in affecting patterns of voluntary reference to comparative
sources is supported by findings in other new constitutionalism jurisdictions.[45]

The relative openness of the Supreme Court of Canada, and Canada's
constitutional domain more generally to insights from abroad is embedded in
the ideational and social context within which the Court and its interlocutors
operate. Many observers have acknowledged the link between America's
decades-long deep culture war and the fierce debate over the use of comparative legal materials in the US Supreme Court.[46] The continental divide, to
borrow Seymour Martin Lipset's metaphor, between the current controversy
in the United States over reference to the constitutional jurisprudence of other
countries, and the Canadian antidote – selective reception and meaningful
contribution to comparative constitutional inquiry – illustrates vividly the
significance of ideational and political factors, not merely constitutional
factors, in explaining a given polity's or a given apex court's attitudes towards
the constitutive laws of others. Pertinent arguments raised in the United States
against borrowing reflect a view of American constitutionalism as unique,
exceptional, and particular – a shining city upon a hill to draw on a familiar
image – whereas the main arguments for the practice are neatly aligned with a
universal and cosmopolitan view of constitutionalism and of human experience more generally.[47]

Republicans and other right-wingers tend to resent borrowing; Democrats,
liberals and progressives tend to support it. Much like other ostensibly principled interpretive debates in the United States and elsewhere, the debate over
reference to foreign law in the United States is portrayed as analytical but is
mainly political. It cannot be understood separately from the deep culture

---

[45] *Id.*, at 453. In his study of the influence of the Canadian Charter in Hong Kong's development
of human rights jurisprudence after returning to China in 1997, Simon Young finds support
for the "maturation" point. Simon N. M. Young, "The Canadian Charter of Rights and
Freedoms in Hong Kong Jurisprudence," paper presented at the University of Toronto, Faculty
of Law, Oct. 12, 2012; on file with author.

[46] Mark Tushnet, *Referring to Foreign Law in Constitutional Interpretation: An Episode in the
Culture Wars*, 35 University of Baltimore Law Review 299 (2006).

[47] As many authors have observed, the US Constitution is the nation's most revered text and has
evolved into a pillar of American "civil religion." *See, e.g.,* Sanford Levinson, CONSTITUTIONAL
FAITH (Princeton University Press, 1988); Jack Balkin, "Why Are Americans Originalist?"
in Richard Nobles and David Schiff, eds., *Law, Society and Community: Socio-Legal Essays
in Honour of Roger Cotterrell* (Ashgate Publishing, 2014), 309–326.

wars that have characterized the American polity for decades and are omnipresent in the American public sphere, from Yale Law School to Wyoming's ranches, from PBS to Fox News, and from the *New Yorker* to the *Christian Science Monitor*. The stark contrast with Canada's engagement with comparative constitutionalism further suggests that the variance across time and space in attitudes toward the constitutive laws of others is as much a sociopolitical phenomenon as it is a juridical or a constitutional one.

Chief Justice McLachlin is certainly correct in pointing to the different constitutional histories, founding documents and values between the United States and Canada in explaining the difference between American and Canadian attitudes towards reliance on foreign constitutional sources.[48] But broader societal and collective identity processes seem to be at play here too.

Although the astounding turn in Canadian constitutionalism can be traced to the adoption of the *Constitution Act, 1982* explaining the Charter's specific innovations requires a broader context. For example, an account of the weak-form judicial review mechanisms established in section 33 must consider Canada's Westminster parliamentary tradition and the concrete circumstances that catalyzed the 1982 constitutional overhaul. In this sense, a fuller understanding of how Canada has emerged from a humble former British colony into its current role as comparative constitutional powerhouse necessitates a broader look at the social and ideational transformation – specifically the profound multicultural and cosmopolitan shift in the national meta-narrative – that Canada has witnessed for more than half a century.

Students of Canadian politics are familiar with how the Quebec question has dominated modern-day Canadian politics. The "Quiet Revolution" and the emergence of cultural nationalism and secessionist sentiments in Quebec in the early 1960s triggered a series of attempts to amend the constitution in order to address Quebec's claims. As a result, over a period of twenty-five years, from the mid-1960s to the early 1990s, Canada experienced a continuous state of constitutional flux. During that period alone, five major constitutional overhauls were attempted; all but one – the "patriation round" of 1982 – failed. No other established democracy has ever been through so many grandiose attempts at constitutional reform within such a short period. The challenge of acknowledging difference, and recognizing linguistic, religious, and cultural diversity within a framework of national unity lay at the heart of all these attempts.

[48] *See*, The Honorable Beverley McLachlin, *The Use of Foreign Law – A Comparative View of Canada and the United States*, 104 Proceedings of the Annual Meeting (American Society of International Law) 491 (2010).

Concurrently, the dynamics of Canadian immigration changed in the second half of the twentieth century. Highly sought immigrants from the British Isles received preferential treatment until the 1960s, while others were "non-preferred," or excluded. In 1967, ethnicity and race ceased to be key determinants of admission under Canada's immigration policy as it became distinctly more universal through the introduction of criteria such as educational attainment, language competency and employment potential.[49] By 1977, immigrants from Asia, Latin America, and Africa made up over 50 per cent of annual flows.[50] As a result, the demographics of the Canadian body politic have transformed in an unprecedented way. When compared with other countries such as the United States, the United Kingdom, the Netherlands, Germany and Spain, Canada has the highest percentage of foreign-born residents in overall population – according to the 2011 national census, over 20 per cent of Canada's population is foreign born.[51] In Toronto – Canada's largest city and the fourth largest urban centre in North America – over 48 per cent of the population is foreign born.[52] Relative openness to the world therefore has become an essential part of public life.

In tandem with these immigration changes, an official policy of multiculturalism was introduced in the early 1970s: "In the face of this [country's] cultural plurality there can be no official Canadian culture or cultures," stated the 1972 Special Joint Committee of the Senate and House of Commons on the Constitution of Canada.[53] Instead, a new vision was crafted of a "pluralistic mosaic," promoting "equal respect for the many origins, creeds and cultures"

---

[49] *See* Triadafilos Triadafilopoulos, "Dismantling White Canada: Race, Rights, and the Origins of the Points System" in Triadafilos Triadafilopoulos, ed., *Wanted and Welcome? Policies for Highly Skilled Immigrants in Comparative Perspective* (Springer, 2013) 15–37, at 16.

[50] *See* Monica Boyd and Naomi Alboim, "Managing International Migration: The Canadian Case," in Dan Rodríguez-García, ed., *Managing Immigration and Diversity in Canada: A Transatlantic Dialogue in the New Age of Migration* (McGill-Queen's University Press, 2012), 123–150; more generally, Triadafilos Triadafilopoulos, BECOMING MULTICULTURAL: IMMIGRATION AND THE POLITICS OF MEMBERSHIP IN CANADA AND GERMANY (UBC Press, 2012).

[51] According to Statistics Canada 2011 National Household Survey (2011), 20.6 per cent of Canada's population was born outside the country (foreign born immigrants). According to OECD Migration Data 2013, (https://data.oecd.org/migration/foreign-born-population.htm #indicator-chart), comparable figures are 13.1 per cent in the United States; 12.3 per cent in the United Kingdom; 11.6 per cent in the Netherlands; 12.8 per cent in Germany; and 13.4 per cent in Spain.

[52] According to the Statistics Canada 2011 National Household Survey (NHS), as of 2011, 48.6 per cent of the population of Toronto was foreign-born.

[53] Parliament, *Special Joint Committee of the Senate and of the House of Commons on the Constitution of Canada Final Report*, at 2.

that comprise Canadian society.[54] This vision was given constitutional recognition in 1982 under section 27 of the Charter, according to which the Charter is to be "interpreted in a manner consistent with the preservation and enhancement of the multicultural heritage of Canadians." The adoption of the *Canadian Multiculturalism Act* further reflects a concerted focus by federal institutions to build awareness of multiculturalism and promote inclusiveness and accommodation of diversity.[55]

The scholarly response to these changes was immediate; Canadian political science underwent a considerable "comparative turn."[56] Charles Taylor, Will Kymlicka, James Tully and other Canadian philosophers are often considered among the most prominent theorists of multiculturalism, citizenship and the constitutional accommodation of difference. Unlike Canada's neighbour to the south, the practice of foreign citation by the Supreme Court is met with considerably less resistance and has seldom been seriously contested within Canada's legal academia, let alone in the popular media or the broader political sphere. And as I mentioned earlier, during the 1990s, Supreme Court of Canada Justice Claire L'Heureux-Dubé emerged as an international champion of inter-jurisdictional constitutional cross-fertilization and helped to entrench this trend within the Canadian judiciary. Canada has since become known to a younger generation of productive scholars as a setting conducive for the comparative study of constitutional law and courts. As well, a disproportionally large number of comparative constitutional law scholars work in Canada or have Canadian roots.

While cosmopolitanism does face some internal opposition, national pride in Canada's "cultural mosaic" (often contrasted with the American supposed "melting pot" approach) and the country's openness toward the foreign and different remains distinctive, especially when compared to the toxic debates in the United States. Beyond Canada's constitutional transformation *per se* (signalled, most notably, by the adoption of the *Charter* of Rights and Freedoms), Canada's endorsement of and considerable contributions to, comparative constitutionalism should be understood in relation to this profound shift in Canada's national meta-narrative and self-perception about its place and role in the world.

---

[54] *See* Ayelet Shachar, "Interpretation Sections (27 & 28) of the Canadian Charter," in Mendes & Beaulac, eds., *supra* note 4, at 147.

[55] RSC 1985, c 24 (4th Supp). *See* Howard Kislowicz, *Freedom of Religion and Canada's Commitments to Multiculturalism*, NATIONAL JOURNAL OF CONSTITUTIONAL LAW 31 (2012): 1–23.

[56] *See* Linda White et al., eds., THE COMPARATIVE TURN IN CANADIAN POLITICAL SCIENCE (UBC Press, 2008).

THE LIMITS OF SELECTIVE ENGAGEMENT

And yet, when we look more closely at the scope of the comparative turn in Canadian constitutional thought, its boundaries become vividly revealed. Despite the fact that Canada's stature as an exporter of comparative constitutional thought has unprecedentedly surged over the past few decades, expectations that this comparative turn might impact some of Canada's own burning constitutional shortcomings – through importation of, or consultation with comparative constitutional thought – have been disappointed.

The Court's openness to engagement with foreign rulings and constitutional concepts in the area of rights and liberties often masks the fact that the comparative turn has not, by and large, penetrated the judicial, academic or political discourse concerning some of Canada's organic constitutional failings. Tellingly, in its two recent landmark rulings on rights issues – the right to die with dignity (*Carter v Canada*) and the right to strike (*Saskatchewan Federation of Labour v Saskatchewan*) – the Supreme Court of Canada referred to 5 and 6 foreign rulings, respectively. In its two recent landmark rulings on structural matters – judicial appointments (*Reference re Supreme Court Act, ss 5 and 6*) and Senate reform (*Reference re Senate Reform*) – the Supreme Court did not cite a single foreign ruling and based its entire opinion on Canadian precedents.[57] Anecdotal as this observation may be, it supports the proposition that there are areas of constitutional jurisprudence – most notably the interpretation of rights – where cross-jurisdictional reference is more likely to occur than in other areas, such as the more aspirational or organic (e.g., federalism, separation of powers, amending procedures) features of the constitution, where national idiosyncrasies and contingencies are more prevalent.[58] Either way, when we turn our gaze to the structural features of the Canadian constitution, there is, as we often say in the academia, "some room for growth" as far as Canadian engagement with the constitutional experience overseas is concerned.

Some of the challenges have been widely acknowledged: loose constitutional definitions of Canada's executive branch; an appointed upper house (Senate) that is marred with considerable shortcomings with regard to both popular representation and institutional efficacy; a federal electoral system

---

[57] *Carter v. Canada (Attorney General)*, [2015] 1 SCR 331; *Saskatchewan Federation of Labour v Saskatchewan*, [2015] 1 SCR 245; *Reference re Supreme Court Act, ss 5 and 6*, [2014] 1 SCR 433 [Supreme Court Act Reference]; Reference re Senate Reform, [2014] 1 SCR 704.

[58] *See generally* Vicki Jackson, *Comparative Constitutional Federalism and Transnational Judicial Discourse*, 2 INTERNATIONAL JOURNAL OF CONSTITUTIONAL LAW 91 (2004).

that many see as perpetuating democracy deficits; and judicial appointment processes, in particular to the Supreme Court, that are largely controlled by the Prime Minister's Office. Other challenges are equally burning, if somewhat less frequently discussed, such as: the constitutional powerlessness of megacities – a modern phenomenon unanticipated by the framers of the *Constitution Act, 1867*; a rigid constitutional amending formula that makes formal constitutional change near impossible; the inexplicable gap between Canada's long-standing commitment to a relatively generous version of the Keynesian welfare state model and the outright exclusion of subsistence social rights from the purview of rights provisions; the apparent tension – or at least uneasy relationship – between Canada's constitutional commitment to English-French bilingualism and its commitments to multiculturalism and Aboriginal peoples' rights; or the plain demographic fact that Canada is one of the most significant immigrant-receiving polities in the world with an increasing number of citizens and residents whose first language is neither English nor French. In any and all of these challenges, a close look at the constitutional experiences of comparable jurisdictions overseas may enrich the constitutional discourse and provide ample guidance and food for thought.

Consider, for example, the constitutional powerlessness of megacities. One of the most burning yet under-explored challenges in Canadian constitutional law is the hindering effect of a dated or stagnant constitutional order on effective urban governance. The past half-century has seen extensive urbanization processes virtually everywhere. Approximately 80 percent of the industrial world's population now lives in cities. In most OECD countries, that percentage exceeds 90 per cent. Recent data suggest that 600 urban centres generate about 60 per cent of global gross domestic product (GDP), with the 100 largest cities generating approximately 40 per cent of global GDP.[59] But constitutional recognition is often lacking. Toronto, for example, is the fourth largest city in North America (after Mexico City, Los Angeles and New York) and is consistently ranked among the world's top financial centres. Metropolitan Toronto's population has passed 7 million with a growth rate of approximately 18 per cent over the last decade, nearly double that of Canada or Ontario. It is estimated that every second immigrant to Canada settles in the Greater Toronto Area. Yet from a constitutional standpoint, the city's powers are delineated by a constitutional order that dates back to 1867.

In constitutions conceived before the emergence of the mega-city, local governments' powers are often inhibited by the broad scope of federal and

---

[59] *World Cities Report 2016: Urbanization and Development-Emerging Futures* (UN Habitat, 2016).

state powers. Due to a lack of constitutional status, megacities such as Los Angeles, Chicago, or Toronto are required to provide a vast array of services to their residents while their independent taxation and legislative authority is limited. Moreover, because the metropolis is not recognized as an autonomous constitutional entity, it often lacks independent bargaining power with respect to shaping national policies on welfare, housing, health care and labour. Due to the "hard-wired" structural elements of old constitutions, the interests of major urban centres are often under-represented in national political bargaining. By contrast, newer constitutions recognize this problem and extend political voice and authority to local government. Several big cities in other countries enjoy the status of an independent federal district, are recognized as a separate region, or enjoy considerable planning autonomy. Both the Chinese and the Russian constitutions, for example, assign special status to megacities (e.g., Beijing, Shanghai, Tianjin and Chongqing in China; Moscow and St. Petersburg in Russia) that are viewed as engines of economic growth and entrust their authorities with considerably wider policy-making tools than those available to other cities. The Swiss constitution, to pick another example, guarantees cities' input in major zoning and public works issues, protects the power of citizens (most of whom live in big cities) to initiate constitutional amendments, and includes split cantons in regions where a disproportionally large percentage of a canton's population lives in a single big city within that canton. These and other innovative constitutional mechanisms developed by new constitutions in addressing the representation, taxation, and service-provision challenges faced by the modern metropolis remain beyond the purview of constitutional renewal discourse in Canada.

Several essays in a recently published and well-timed symposium issue of the *Queen's Law Journal* begins to address the potential contribution of comparative materials, primarily with respect to the key areas of constitutional amendments, reforms to judicial selection and appointment processes, and attempts to transform and revitalize political institutions such as the Senate.[60] In these and other related aspects of constitutional governance, the experience of comparable settings such as Australia, the UK, Germany, South Africa, Brazil or the emerging pan-European constitutional order may provide valuable insights. However, with few exceptions, the comparative constitutional renaissance, so prevalent in conversations about rights or judicial interpretive methods, is yet to feature prominently in public discourse concerning these more structural or organic deficiencies of Canada's constitutional order.

---

[60] *See, e.g.*, Richard Albert, *The Theory and Doctrine of Unconstitutional Constitutional Amendment in Canada*, 41 QUEEN'S LAW JOURNAL 143 (2016).

In summary, any examination of Canada's first 150 years of modern constitutionalism must acknowledge the stunning transformation of Canada from a humble follower of British constitutional tradition to one of the main innovators and contributors to global constitutional discourse. To put it bluntly, Canada has become a global powerhouse and a household name in comparative constitutional law. This is reflected, *inter alia*, in patterns of foreign reference to Canadian sources and by the extensive engagement with Canadian constitutional ideas by scholars and policy-makers overseas. To a lesser degree, the cosmopolitan trend is also reflected in patterns of engagement with comparative constitutional materials in Canada. While the Supreme Court, legal academia, constitutional commentators, and policy-makers are generally open to comparative constitutional engagements (undoubtedly more so than their American counterparts), the promise of comparative constitutional inquiry has not fully materialized and has largely fallen short of advancing sophisticated, well-informed discourse about constitutional renewal in Canada. Granted, a few Canadian authors aim at expanding the scope of engagement with comparative constitutional experiences beyond flashy rights issues to help address some hard-wired structural elements of the Canadian constitution.[61] But the general canon of comparative engagement is confined to rights issues. Perhaps the time has come to extend an invitation for Canadian constitutional scholars, jurists, and policy-makers – indeed to the Canadian citizenry at large – to engage more closely with the world of new constitutionalism, not merely as producers and exporters of innovative constitutional thought or as analyzers of fleshy rights issues, but also as curious observers who study the constitutional experiences of other polities to engender self-reflection through analogy, distinction, and contrast, as well as to identify creative ideas, "best practices", and effective solutions to some of Canada's unresolved constitutional shortcomings.

---

[61] *See, e.g.*, Kent Roach and Craig Forcese, FALSE SECURITY: THE RADICALIZATION OF CANADIAN ANTI-TERRORISM (Irwin Law, 2015); Richard Albert, *The Difficulty of Constitutional Amendment in Canada*, 53 ALBERTA LAW REVIEW 85 (2015).

14

Exporting Dialogue

Critical Reflections on Canada's "Commonwealth" Model of Human Rights Protections

ALISON L. YOUNG

It is easy to argue that the UK's Human Rights Act 1998 (HRA) was heavily influenced by the Canadian *Charter* of Rights and Freedoms (*Charter*). It was not long before academic commentators were drawing comparisons between the 1998 Act and the *Charter*. Moreover, the similarities between the *Charter*, the HRA and the New Zealand Bill of Rights Act 1990, the Australian Capital Territory's Human Rights Act 1984 and Victoria's Charter of Human Rights and Responsibilities Act 2006 led Stephen Gardbaum to designate these forms of human rights protection as being part of a distinct family – the commonwealth model of rights protections.[1] Gardbaum argues that the commonwealth model has four distinct features: a legalized, but not constitutional, charter of rights; mandatory rights review by political branches at the pre-legislative stage; a power of the courts to determine whether legislation is compatible with human rights, which goes beyond traditional powers of interpretation; and the formal power of the legislature to definitively determine the content of legislation, including the content of human rights.[2]

In addition to exporting a model of constitutional design, Canada also exported a justification for this model – dialogue. Hogg and Bushell (now Thornton)'s seminal article defined dialogue as occurring when there is the opportunity for the legislature to respond to judicial decisions through "legislative reversal, modification or avoidance."[3] As such, the *Charter* provides a

---

[1] S. Gardbaum, THE NEW COMMONWEALTH MODEL OF CONSTITUTIONALISM: THEORY AND PRACTICE (Cambridge University Press, 2012).

[2] *See* the contributions of Chapters 13 and 17 to this volume, explaining how Canada's approach to human rights protections extends beyond these countries that have specifically adopted a "commonwealth" model, particularly South Africa and its adoption of a similar general restrictions clause.

[3] P. Hogg and A. Bushell, *The Charter Dialogue between Courts and Legislatures (Or Perhaps the Charter of Rights Isn't Such a Bad Thing After All)*, 35 OSGOODE HALL LAW JOURNAL 75, 79

means of protecting human rights which is not as susceptible to the "demo-cratic deficit" criticism of strong constitutional protections of rights. When unelected/unaccountable members of the judiciary strike down legislation as unconstitutional, they harm democracy by overturning the will of a democrat-ically mandated and democratically accountable legislative body. To recog-nize that there are opportunities for the democratically elected legislature to respond to these judicial decisions lessens these criticisms. Hogg and Bushell's work merely described the way in which the legislature could respond, setting out an account of legislative responses to *Charter* decisions by the Canadian Supreme Court, in addition to explaining how the "notwithstanding" clause, the general restrictions clause, equality protections and specific non-absolute rights provides a means of facilitating legislative response. Canadian commen-tators, most notably Kent Roach and Janet Hiebert, have built on this analysis to provide a normative framework for and justification of dialogue.[4] Their work goes beyond description to evaluate how the judiciary and the legislature should use their powers under the *Charter*, both in first look and second look decisions by the Canadian Supreme Court.

Nor is Canada's contribution limited to the adoption of a model of rights protections and the justification for this novel method of protecting human rights. The Human Rights Act 1998 does not provide for a specific, "British" set of rights, instead incorporating the European Convention on Human Rights into UK law.[5] Moreover, section 2(1) of the Human Rights Act 1998 obliges the UK courts to take account of decisions of the European Court of Human Rights when interpreting Convention Rights. Nevertheless, as Garlicki explains, UK courts have also referred to decisions of the Canadian Supreme Court when interpreting human rights, particularly in the contro-versial areas of prisoner voting rights and the delicate issue of balancing the right to life and the right to self-determination when considering the

---

(1997). *See also* P. Hogg, A. Thornton and W. Wright, *Charter Dialogue Revisited: Or Much Ado about Metaphors*, 45 Osgoode Hall Law Journal 1 (2007).

4 K. Roach, The Supreme Court on Trial: Judicial Activism or Democratic Dialogue (Toronto: Irwin Press, 2001) and J. Hiebert, Charter Conflicts: What Is Parliament's Role? (McGill-Queen's University Press, 2002).

5 This has led, in part, to a manifesto pledge in 2015 of the Conservative Government to "scrap" the Human Rights Act and replace this with a British Bill of Rights. However, to date, no new Bill has appeared and it may be that this project is severely delayed in the light of the Referendum decision in favour of the UK leaving the European Union. See, for example, statements of the then Lord Chancellor/Justice Secretary, Liz Truss, before the Justice Committee of the House of Commons, available at http://data.parliament.uk/writtenevidence/committeeevidence.svc/evidencedocument/justice-committee/the-work-of-the-secretary-of-state/oral/37565.pdf.

Convention-compatibility of the criminalization of assisted suicide. In turn, as the European Court of Human Rights reviews decisions of domestic courts when determining Convention-compatibility, decisions of the Canadian Supreme Court have been referred to in decisions of the European Court of Human Rights, most notably as regards prisoner voting rights.[6]

It is easy to understand why the commonwealth model and accounts of dialogue were so attractive to the UK. The *Charter* appeared to offer the "holy grail" of rights protections, enabling the UK to both provide for a stronger protection of human rights and preserve their tradition of Diceyan parliamentary sovereignty. It promised to combine the strengths and minimize the weaknesses of strong constitutional and purely parliamentary protections of rights. However, in addition to exporting a constitutional model, a theory of rights protections and a series of influential decisions of the Canadian Supreme Court, Canada also appears to have exported the problems attached to both the model and the theory. Was there no "middle ground" for the account to occupy, meaning that it would inevitably collapse into either a strong legal, or a weak political protection of rights?[7] Is the commonwealth model sufficiently distinct from other forms of rights protections, particularly when evidence of "dialogue" can be found in systems with a strong, constitutional protection of rights?[8]

It is easy to "blame Canada" for the UK's problematic import of the commonwealth model and democratic dialogue. However, to do so is a mistake. As with most constitutional imports, problems arise through a misunderstanding of the history and context of any particular model or theory. Too much hope was placed in the model with its normative justification of dialogue, without realizing that the two are not synonymous. Merely adopting the model is not enough, more attention needs to be paid as to the way in

---

[6] See Chapter 15 in this volume.
[7] M. Tushnet, *New Forms of Judicial Review and the Persistence of Rights and Democracy-Based Worries*, 38 WAKE FOREST LAW REVIEW, 813 (2003).
[8] *See, for example*, L. Fisher, CONSTITUTIONAL DIALOGUES: INTERPRETATION AS A POLITICAL PROCESS (Princeton University Press, 1988), B. Friedman, *A Different Dialogue: The Supreme Court, Congress and Federal Jurisdiction*, 85 *Northwestern University Law Review* 1 (1990); B. Friedman, *Dialogue and Judicial Review*, 91 MICHIGAN LAW REVIEW, 577 (1993); C. Bateup, *The Dialogic Promise: Assessing the Normative Potential of Theories of Constitutional Dialogue*, 71 BROOKLYN LAW REVIEW, 1109 (2006); M. Cohn, "Sovereignty, Constitutional Dialogues and Political Networks: A Comparative and Conceptual Study" in R. Rawlings, P. Leyland and A.L. Young (eds) *Sovereignty and the Law: Domestic, European and International Perspectives* (Oxford University Press, 2013) in relation to the US. *See also* S. Fredman, *From Dialogue to Deliberation: Human Rights Adjudication and Prisoners' Right to Vote*, PUBLIC LAW 292 (2013), in relation to the South African Constitution and its approach to prisoner voting decisions.

which each institution ought to exercise its powers under the commonwealth model. Moreover, the UK focused too greatly on the provisions of the *Charter* without fully understanding the history of its adoption, paying little attention to the Canadian Bill of Rights 1960.

This chapter will argue that inter-institutional interactions serve two purposes, which I will refer to as constitutional collaboration and constitutional counter-balancing. This recognition will be used to re-evaluate both the HRA and the *Charter*, providing a different account of their relative strengths and weaknesses. Finally, an understanding of the evolution of the Canadian Bill of Rights 1960 to the *Charter* will be used to evaluate the direction of travel of the UK from the HRA towards a new British Bill of Rights.

BLAME CANADA?

Both the HRA and the *Charter* fit Gardbaum's description of the commonwealth model. The HRA is a legalized and codified protection of human rights, with the First Schedule to the HRA listing the provisions of the European Convention on Human Rights (ECHR) it incorporates into British law. There are no specific provisions in the HRA itself making it harder to overturn than other legislation, although the HRA has been classified as a "constitutional statute," which may mean that its provisions are not subject to the doctrine of implied repeal.[9] Its provisions can be repealed simply by further legislation which makes clear its intention to overturn the HRA. The *Charter* differs from the HRA in that it is contained in the Constitution Act 1982/ Canada Act 1982, legislation of Canada and the UK respectively. Its provisions can be amended by a majority decision of the Senate and the House of Commons and two-thirds of the legislative assemblies of the Province, provided that this represents at least 50 per cent of the population, with a greater majority being required for those amendments which erode legislative powers.[10] Although both are recognized as "constitutional," and thereby harder to overturn than non-constitutional legislation, neither appears to be best described as providing for a particularly difficult method of amendment, distinguishing both from more traditional forms of constitutional entrenchment and amendment.

Both provide for mandatory review of rights by the legislature. Under the HRA, section 19 requires a Minister in charge of a Bill to issue a statement

---

[9]   *Thoburn v. Sunderland City Council* [2002] EWHC 195 (Admin), [2003] QB 151 R *(HS2 Action Alliance) v. Secretary of State for Transport* [2014] UKSC 3, [2014] 1 WLR 324.

[10]   Constitution Act 1982, section 38.

either that the proposed legislation is believed to be compatible with Convention rights,[11] or that although the Minister is not able to state that the proposed
legislation is compatible, nevertheless the Government wishes to enact the
legislation.[12] In Canada, section 4(1) of the Department of Justice Act 1985
requires the Minister of Justice to assess the compatibility of primary legislation with the *Charter*, reporting any inconsistency to the House of Commons.[13] Moreover, both provide courts with the power to review legislation
which goes beyond the power to ensure that ambiguous legislation is interpreted in a manner which complies with human rights. Under the HRA, these
powers of the court are found in sections 3 and 4 of the Act. Section 3 requires
courts to read and give effect to legislation in a manner compatible with
Convention rights, so far as it is possible to do so. Under *Ghaidan v. Godin-
Mendoza*, courts can interpret legislation even when this is not ambiguous,
having the power to read words in to legislation, as well as reading words
down, to ensure its compatibility with Convention rights.[14] However, courts
are sensitive to linguistic restraints,[15] in addition to ensuring that interpretations do not contradict a fundamental feature of the legislation in question.[16]
When it is not possible to interpret legislation in a manner compatible with
Convention rights, courts of the level of the high court or above may issue a
declaration of incompatibility.[17] Declarations of incompatibility do not affect
the validity, force or effect of legislation.[18] In Canada, section 32 of the Constitution Act 1982 confirms that the *Charter* provisions apply to both Federal and
Provincial legislation. In addition, section 24(1) confirms that the courts have
responsibility for enforcing the *Charter*, including the ability to strike down
legislation which is incompatible with the *Charter*.

Fourth, both include mechanisms designed to ensure that the legislature
can provide the final authoritative determination of the meaning of legislation, including the scope of human rights. Under the HRA, this ability is
preserved through both sections 3 and 4 of the Act. Courts may use section 3 to
interpret legislation in a manner which appears to question the intention of
Parliament when enacting that legislation.[19] However, it is still possible for

[11] Human Rights Act 1998, section 19(1)(a).   [12] Human Rights Act 1998, section 19(1)(b).
[13] The procedure is regulated by the Canadian Charter of Rights and Freedoms Examination Regulations SOR 85/781.
[14] [2004] UKHL 30, [2004] 2 AC 557.
[15] For example, in *R (Wilkinson) v. Inland Revenue Commissioners* [2005] UKHL 30, [2005] 1 WLR 17818, courts were not able to interpret "widow" to include "widower."
[16] *Ghaidan v. Godin-Mendoza*, n 14 and *R (Secretary of State for the Home Department) ex parte Anderson* (2002) UKHL 46, [2003] 1 AC 837.
[17] Human Rights Act 1998, section 4.   [18] Human Rights Act 1998, section 4(2)(b).
[19] P. Sales and R. Ekins, *Rights-consistent Interpretation and the Human Rights Act 1998*, 127 LAW QUARTERLY REVIEW 217 (2011).

Parliament to respond to such judicial determinations by re-enacting legislation, making its distinct interpretation of rights a fundamental feature of the legislation.[20] Moreover, a section 19(1)(b) statement can be used to indicate that Parliament wishes to enact legislation, even though its provisions may contradict Convention rights.[21] Section 4 clearly reserves the final word to the legislature. As a declaration of incompatibility does not affect the validity, force or effect of legislation, the legislature needs to intervene if it is to change the legislation and ensure compatibility with human rights. In Canada, the final word is reserved to the legislature through section 33 of the Constitution Act 1982, the "notwithstanding clause" which empowers the Provincial and Federal legislatures to enact provisions notwithstanding *Charter* rights. Moreover, in a similar manner to section 3 of the Human Rights Act 1998, there is the possibility for the legislature to respond to determinations of the Canadian Supreme Court, particularly where the court applies section 1, or other non-absolute rights, or applies the equality provisions.

A NEW MODEL?

Nevertheless, there are difficulties regarding the distinct nature of the commonwealth model. First, if we are to count legislative response following an application of section 3 of the HRA or to a *Charter* determination by the Canadian Supreme Court as exemplifying that the legislature can have the final word on rights determinations, it can be difficult to distinguish the commonwealth model of rights protections from other models. For example, Sandra Fredman argues that the South African case law on prisoner disenfranchisement fosters dialogue between the courts and the legislature.[22] South Africa had no legislation prohibiting prisoners from voting. However, it also had no legislation which provided for the means through which prisoners would be able to exercise their right to vote. This was challenged in *August v. The Electoral Commission.*[23] The Supreme Court of South Africa

---

[20] T. Hickman, PUBLIC LAW AFTER THE HUMAN RIGHTS ACT (Oxford: Hart Publishing, 2010), chapter 3.

[21] *See, for example, R (Animal Defenders International)* v. *Secretary of State for Culture, Media and Sport* [2008] UKHL 15, [2008] 1 AC 1312 in which the House of Lords exercised deference in response to a section 19(1)(b) statement, scrutinising carefully the assessments of the Joint Committee on Human Rights in response to the section 19(1)(b) statement and concluding that the Strasbourg decision which appeared to contradict the legislation could be distinguished. This assessment was upheld, by a narrow majority decision, by the European Court of Human Rights, *Animal Defenders International* v. *UK* [2013] ECHR 48876/08.

[22] S. Fredman, *From Dialogue to Deliberation: Human Rights Adjudication and Prisoners' Right to Vote,* PUBLIC LAW 292 (2013).

[23] (CCT8/99) [1999] Z.A.C.C. 3 (South African Constitutional Court).

concluded that, as there was no legislation removing the right to vote from prisoners, it should be assumed that prisoners had the right to vote, breaching article 19 of the Constitution, protecting the right to vote. The decision effectively empowered the South African legislature to remove the power to vote from some, or all, prisoners should it wish to do so – i.e. the decision enabled the legislature to respond to the decision of the South African Supreme Court. Hirschl and Klug's analysis of South African law in this volume adds weight to this analysis, focusing in particular on the extent to which proportionality – and its specific iteration in *R* v. *Oakes*,[24] can be used to facilitate dialogue in a similar manner to dialogue found in commonwealth models of rights protections.

A similar argument can be applied to the US Constitution. In *Richardson* v. *Ramirez*, the US Supreme Court concluded that State laws forbidding convicted felons or prisoners from voting are not, in and of themselves, contrary to the Equal Protection clause found in the Fourteenth Amendment to the Constitution as there was express constitutional authority for States to enact laws removing the vote from those convicted of crimes.[25] The only exemption is for laws where there is an express intention to discriminate when enacting a prisoner disenfranchisement law.[26] This conclusion means that it is possible for each State legislature to respond to the decision of the US Supreme Court. Although both may appear to grant the opportunity for the legislature to respond to a decision of a constitutional court, neither is described as having a commonwealth model of rights protections.

Second, the difficulties in defining the criteria of the commonwealth model are exacerbated due to the interaction between the powers granted to institutions under any particular model and the manner in which institutions exercise their powers. A possible response to the finding that there can be legislative responses in both South Africa and the US is to recognize that, in both situations, the court could have had the final word through definitively declaring these legislative provisions as unconstitutional and delineating how future provisions could ensure that they complied with human rights. Moreover, both the South African Supreme Court and the US Supreme Court can determine the constitutionality of future legislative responses, seemingly leaving the final word to the courts.[27] However, we can describe

---

[24] [1986] 1 SCR 103 (Supreme Court of Canada).   [25] 418 US 24 (1974).
[26] *Hunter* v. *Underwood* 417 US 222 (1985).
[27] This occurred in South Africa, where the legislature's response was struck down by the Constitutional Court in *Minister for Home Affairs* v. *National Institute for Crime Prevention and the Re Integration of Offenders (NICRO)* (CCT 03/04) [2004] Z.A.C.C. 10.

the situation in Canada in a similar manner, not just generally but also specifically in relation to prisoner voting rights.

The Canada Elections Act 1985 originally removed the right to vote from all prisoners. This was challenged in the Supreme Court in *Sauvé* v. *Canada (Attorney General)* *(Sauvé I)* which concluded that the blanket ban on prisoner voting breached section 3 of the *Charter*.[28] The Canadian legislature responded by amending the legislation, enacting section 51(e) of Canada Elections Act RSC 1985, which removed the right to vote from prisoners serving a sentence of two years or more. This, in turn, was challenged before the Supreme Court in *Sauvé* v. *the Attorney General of Canada* *(Sauvé II)*, which held by a majority of one that the new legislation was contrary to section 3 of the *Charter* and could not be justified under section 1.[29] In both South Africa and Canada the Supreme Court took decisions to which the legislature was able to respond, with the courts then striking down the legislature's response, giving, in practice, the final word on prisoner voting to the courts.[30]

A STRONG, CONSTITUTIONAL PROTECTION OF RIGHTS IN ALL BUT NAME?

Canada has not just exported a model of rights protections, and a theory purporting to provide a better protection of rights occupying the middle ground between strong legal and weak political protections of rights. It has also exported the problems which accompany the commonwealth model and democratic dialogue. Manfredi classified dialogue as both empirically problematic and normatively flawed.[31] The experience of Canada and the UK would suggest that both of these assessments are correct. Both have arguably developed a midway protection of rights which is best described as a strong constitutional protection of rights in all but name, suggesting support for the claim that dialogue is empirically flawed. Moreover, the literature in both the UK and Canada suggests a plethora of interpretations of dialogue, providing support for the claim that dialogue is normatively flawed.

Three assessments of how the *Charter* and the HRA operate in practice can be used to support the assertion that both Canada and the UK are best

---

[28] [1993] 2 SCR 438.   [29] [2002] 3 SCR 519.

[30] For a more detailed analysis of the Canadian Supreme Court's decisions on prisoner voting, and an assessment of their influence beyond Canada, see Chapter 15 to this volume.

[31] C. Manfredi, *The Day the Dialogue Died: A Comment on Sauvé v. Canada*, 45 OSGOODE HALL LAW JOURNAL 106 (2007).

understood as illustrating how a commonwealth model of rights protections has collapsed into a strong constitutional protection of rights in all but name. First, both illustrate that the legislature has little ability in practice to respond to judicial determinations of rights. In Canada, the notwithstanding clause has been used so rarely, and with accompanying criticism of its pre-emptive use, that it has arguably lapsed into desuetude.[32] If we regard the notwithstanding clause as the main way through which the legislature is able to respond to judicial determinations, then its lack of use in practice, combined with the ability of the Canadian Supreme Court to strike down unconstitutional legislation, makes it hard to conclude that the *Charter* applies any differently from a strong protection of constitutional rights.

A similar story appears to be emerging in the UK. The declaration of incompatibility is regarded as the main means through which the legislature can respond to judicial determinations of rights. Although there have been more declarations of incompatibility than there have exercises of the not-withstanding clause, nevertheless a recent report of the Joint Committee on Human Rights reported a "significant downward trend" in their use.[33] Only three declarations of incompatibility were issued under the 2010–2015 coalition Government, of which one is under appeal.[34] Under the Conservative Government of 2015–2017, there were two declarations of incompatibility, one of which is currently under appeal.[35]

In addition, there is clear evidence that the UK Government normally responds to declarations of incompatibility, modifying legislation to ensure its compatibility with Convention rights as interpreted by the court. Of the current 31 declarations of incompatibility, of which 21 are final, the UK Parliament has resolved all but one – the declaration of incompatibility in relation to the blanket ban on prisoner voting rights.[36] The actions of the UK Parliament can be explained not just because of the potential political

---

[32] S. Gardbaum, *The New Commonwealth Model*, n 1, chapter 5; G. Huscroft, *Constitutionalism from the Top Down*, 45 Osgoode Hall Law Journal 91 (2007); A Vermeule, *The Atrophy of Constitutional Powers*, 32 Oxford Journal of Legal Studies 421 (2012).

[33] Joint Committee on Human Rights, "Human Rights Judgments" Seventh Report of Session 2014–2015 HL Paper 130 HC 1088, 11 March 2015, paragraph 4.2.

[34] *Reilly (2) v. Secretary of State for Work and Pensions* [2014] UKHC (Admin) 2182 and [2016] EWCA Civ 413, [2016] 3 WLR 1641. It is believed that the Government will appeal this decision.

[35] *R (Johnson) v. Secretary of State for the Home Department* [2016] UKSC 56, [2017] AC 365 and *R (Miranda) v. Secretary of State for the Home Department* [2016] EWCA Civ 6, [2016] 1 WLR 1505.

[36] Joint Committee on Human Rights, "Human Rights Judgments" Seventh Report of Session 2014–2015 HL Paper 130 HC 1088, 11 March 2015.

pressure to comply with human rights judgments, but also because of the role of the European Court of Human Rights. The role of the Strasbourg Court has been interpreted as combining with the Supreme Court so as to transform the UK Supreme Court into a constitutional court, its judgments having the same impact as if they had struck down legislation as unconstitutional.[37]

Second, there is a perception of judicial activism in both the Canadian and the British courts. The Canadian Supreme Court is regarded by some as taking a proactive approach to rights, providing a broad interpretation of rights, leading to the courts engaging more in balancing rights and balancing rights and responsibilities, rather than defining rights more narrowly and thus avoiding performing more delicate balancing tasks.[38] Criticism has been levelled in particular at "second look" cases, where the Canadian Supreme Court revisits an issue following a legislative enactment in response to an earlier decision.

The UK courts are also regarded as having provided a strong protection of rights, both in regard to their interpretation of rights and also as to the extent to which they are prepared to use section 3 to provide a Convention-compatible interpretation of legislation. Criticisms of the perceived activism of the UK courts are coupled with criticism of the European Court of Human Rights, most recently accused by the Conservative Government as being engaged in "mission creep," using the Convention as a living instrument in order to provide a stronger protection of rights beyond the original intentions of the authors of the Convention. Section 2(1) of the HRA requires the UK courts to take decisions of the Strasbourg Court into account when determining Convention rights.[39] The UK courts have moved on from the stringent interpretation of the "mirror principle" advocated by Lord Bingham in *Ullah*.[40] Nevertheless, it is clear that the UK courts will normally follow a clear and constant line of case law from the Strasbourg court, being prepared to not follow a decision of the Strasbourg court either where the decision made a legal error, or contradicted a fundamental constitutional principle.[41] The UK courts have also been prepared to go beyond Strasbourg decisions, providing a stronger protection of human rights, particularly when this is in the direction

---

[37] See Sales and Ekins "Rights-Consistent Interpretation" n 19, I. Leigh and R. Masterman, *Making Rights Real: The Human Rights Act in Its First Decade* (Oxford: Hart, 2008) and S. Gardbaum, *The New Commonwealth Model*, n 1, chapter 7.

[38] C. Manfredi, *Judicial Power and the Charter: Reflections on the Activism Debate*, 55 UNIVERSITY OF NEW BRUNSWICK LAW JOURNAL 185 (2004).

[39] Conservative policy document, manifesto.

[40] *R (Ullah)* v. *Special Adjudicator* [2004] UKHL 26, [2004] 2 AC 323.

[41] *Manchester City Council* v. *Pinnock* [201] UKSC 45, [201] 3 WLR 1441.

of travel of the Strasbourg court.[42] In addition, the UK Supreme Court has been prepared to protect rights through the common law when the Convention does not appear to provide sufficient protection of rights.[43]

The UK courts have also been prepared to read words in to legislation in a manner which may appear to stretch language to breaking point. Perhaps the clearest example of this is in *AF* regarding the creation of closed material proceedings.[44] The legislation provided that, where closed material proceedings applied, a special advocate would be appointed who would be able to receive and read classified information, but who was not allowed to pass on information to her client. However, following the decision in *A v. UK* that this process breached Article 6 ECHR unless the special advocate was able to provide the gist of the information to her client, the courts read into the general prohibition that the special advocate was able to pass on the gist of the information contained in the closed material to her client.[45] This interpretation was given despite the misgivings of some of their Lordships[46]

Moreover, the UK courts have recently expanded their protection of human rights, through the enforcement of the EU Charter of Fundamental Rights and Freedoms and the common law. The EU Charter can apply whenever the case before the court is in the scope of EU law.[47] In four recent cases, including one from the Supreme Court, court orders have been issued to suspend legislation which contravenes Convention rights.[48] This enables those whose situations are governed by EU law in some way to achieve a stronger protection of rights, particularly in terms of the remedies available. These developments have been interpreted as contributing to the juridification of English law – it remains to be seen whether this juridification will

---

[42] *Re P, In re G (Adoption: Unmarried Couple)* [2008] UKHL 38, [2009] AC 173; *Rabone v. Pennine Care NHS Foundation Trust* [2012] UKSC 2, [2012] 2 AC 72.
[43] *Osborn v. Parole Board* [2012] UKSC 61, [2014] AC 1115; *Kennedy v. Charity Commission* [2014] UKSC 20, [2015] AC 455.
[44] *Secretary of State for the Home Department v. AF* [2009] UKHL 28, [2010] 2 AC 269.
[45] [2009] ECHR 355/05, (2009) 26 BHRC 1.
[46] See, in particular, the judgments of Lord Hoffmann and Lord Brown.
[47] C-617/10 *Åklagaren v. Hans Åkerberg Fransson* [2013] 2 CMLR 1273.
[48] *Walker v. Innospec Ltd* [2017] UKSC 47. See also *Benkharbouche v. Embassy of the Republic of Sudan* [2015] EWCA Civ 33, [2016] QB 347, *Vidal Hall v. Google* [2015] EWCA Civ 311, [2015] 3 WLR 409 and. The High Court in *R (Davis) v. Secretary of State for the Home Department* [2015] EWHC 2092 (Admin), [2016] 1 CMLR 13, also issued a court order to disapply provisions in the Data Retention and Investigatory Powers Act 2014. However, on appeal the Court of Appeal were not convinced that the provisions of the Act breached EU law, and instead recommended a preliminary reference to the Court of Justice of the European Union, *R (Davis) v. Secretary of State for the Home Department* [2015] EWCA Civ 1185, [2017] 1 All ER 62.

continue, or be reduced, following the referendum decision in favour of the UK leaving the European Union.[49]

Third, there appears to be a lack of engagement of the legislature in rights scrutiny. Both Canadian and UK legislatures have been accused of using legal advice on rights-compatibility in a risk-avoidance manner. Given the relative strength of the executive in both legislatures, there is a greater concern as to how a Government can achieve its policy objectives, without the possibility of future challenge in the courts on human rights grounds, as opposed to seeing pre-legislative scrutiny as providing an opportunity for discussion of the scope of human rights.[50] The work of the UK's Joint Committee on Human Rights, in addition to the requirement of the Minister in the UK to make an announcement of compatibility for all legislation, rather than only announcing that legislation is not compatible with human rights, does mean that there is more evidence of engagement with rights issues in the UK legislature than in Canada, particularly as regards the House of Lords.[51] However, discussion is more effective when legislatures are focusing more on how to provide the means of protecting human rights, when the courts have determined the scope of the right, but have left the means through which the potential breach of a right can be remedied to the court, rather than when legislatures are determining the scope of a right.[52]

A PLETHORA OF THEORIES?

Dialogue has been criticized for failing to provide a stable theory.[53] Once more, it is easy to see the force in these criticisms. There would appear to be as

---

[49] P. Birkinshaw, *United Kingdom Judges and European Integration*, 25 RIVISTA ITALIANA DI DIRITTO PUBBLICO COMUNITARIO 363 (2015). *See also* M. Kuo, *Discovering Sovereignty in Dialogue: Is Judicial Dialogue the Answer to Constitutional Conflict in the Pluralistic Legal Landscape?*, 26 CANADIAN JOURNAL OF LAW AND JURISPRUDENCE 341 (2013); M. Kuo, *In the Shadow of Judicial Supremacy: Putting the Idea of Judicial Dialogue in Its Place*, RATIO JURIS 29, 83 (2016).

[50] *See* J. Hiebert, *Parliamentary Engagement with the Charter: Rethinking the Idea of Legislative Rights Review*, 58 SUPREME COURT LAW REVIEW (2d), 87 (2012); J. Hiebert and J. Kelly, PARLIAMENTARY BILLS OF RIGHTS: THE EXPERIENCE OF NEW ZEALAND AND THE UNITED KINGDOM (Cambridge University Press: 2015), chapters 7–9.

[51] D. Feldman, *Parliamentary Scrutiny of Legislation and Human Rights*, PUBLIC LAW 323 (2002); D. Nicol, *The Human Rights Act and the Politicians*, 24 LEGAL STUDIES 464 (2004); M. Hunt, H. Hooper and P. Yowell (eds), PARLIAMENT AND HUMAN RIGHTS: REDRESSING THE DEMOCRATIC DEFICIT (Oxford: Hart, 2015), chapters 5–8.

[52] A.L. Young, *Is Dialogue Working under the Human Rights Act?*, PUBLIC LAW 773 (2011).

[53] Huscroft, *Constitutionallism from the Top Down*, supra note 32; C Manfredi, *The Day the Dialogue Died: A Comment on Sauvé* v. *Canada*, 45 OSGOODE HALL LAW JOURNAL 105 (2007)

many accounts of dialogue as there are academics willing to produce one. Moreover, these accounts can be classified along a sliding scale, depending on the relative role each account gives to the legislature and the judiciary when protecting rights. This is definitely true of the theories which draw on dialogue in order to provide an account of how the legislature and the judiciary should exercise their relative powers under the HRA.

At one end of the scale are those theories which give a prominent role to the courts, for example, Tom Hickman's account of dialogue.[54] Hickman regards dialogue as occurring through both sections 3 and 4 of the Act, as well as providing an account of dialogue that includes an assessment of the further response of the judiciary to following the legislature's reaction to the court's initial judgment.[55] He prefers dialogue to occur through section 3 as opposed to section 4. Courts should be prepared to read legislation to provide as strong a protection of Convention rights as possible, with section 4 being reserved for extreme circumstances where this is not possible.[56] Danny Nicol's account is at the opposite end of the scale, preferring dialogue to occur through an application of section 4. He advocates that judicial output should be "reconceptualised as a contestable entity," where courts provide their honest and forthright account of the meaning of a human right, providing Parliament with the opportunity to respond to this account either by accepting the opinion of the judiciary, or substituting its own interpretation of a human right.[57]

In Canada, Kent Roach and Janet Hiebert provide accounts of dialogue which aim to provide a more equal role for the legislature and the judiciary.[58] Whereas Roach's work focuses on the relative institutional features of the legislature and the courts, Hiebert focuses more on the need for comity, with each institution respecting the determinations of the other. However, looking for a midway position between strong legal and weak political protections of rights can be just as unstable as aiming to find a specific account of rights. Theories that have been regarded as arguing against or in favour of a strong constitutional review of rights or a weak political protection of rights can be

---

and A. Kavanagh, *The Lure and the Limits of Dialogue,* 66 UNIVERSITY OF TORONTO LAW JOURNAL 83 (2016).

[54] T. Hickman, *Constitutional Dialogue, Constitutional Theories and the Human Rights Act 1998,* PUBLIC LAW 306 (1995); T Hickman, *The Courts and the Politicians after the Human Rights Act,* PUBLIC LAW 84 (2008); T. Hickman, *Public Law after the Human Rights Act n 20,* Chapter Three.

[55] Hickman, *Constitutional Dialogue* supra note 54, at 328–329.   [56] *Id.*

[57] D. Nicol, *Law and Politics after the Human Rights Act,* PUBLIC LAW 722, 743 (2006).

[58] K. Roach, THE SUPREME COURT ON TRIAL, supra note 3; Hiebert, *Charter Conflicts,* supra note 4, at chapter 3.

easily re-interpreted as ones which support democratic dialogue. Waldron, for example, provides one of the strongest arguments against constitutional review of rights.[59] However, Waldron accepts that his arguments could be compatible with the commonwealth model of rights protections. From the opposite perspective, Matthias Kumm provides a justification of judicial review which rests on the role of proportionality, constructing a Socratic dialogue between the legislature and the court.[60]

This potential cross-over is hardly surprising. It recognizes both that there is confusion between whether democratic dialogue can be best described as a distinctive account of constitutional design, or as an account of the way in which institutions should behave in order to provide for a better protection of human rights. It also recognizes that the same arguments which are used to justify providing either the legislature or the courts with a stronger role in the protection of human rights influence the justification for providing each institution with a greater role in the protection of rights under a legal system which has adopted the commonwealth model of rights protections. Rather than using these arguments to argue that, generally, rights are better protected by legislatures or the courts, dialogue aims to combine relative strengths and weaknesses. However, as accounts in favour of strong and weak roles for the judiciary and the legislature in the protection of rights rely on generalizations, these theories often advocate that institutions exercise their powers to a greater or lesser degree in certain circumstances. The UK appears to have imported a model without definition leaving the UK with a strong protection of rights in all but name, with ever greater juridification.

REDISCOVERING DIALOGUE

If we are to understand dialogue further, we need to recognize that its distinctive feature is not that it can provide for a middle ground between legal and political protections of rights. Rather, its distinctiveness stems from its focus on how institutions interact, examining those interactions which can facilitate and hinder a better protection of human rights. Once this is recognized, we can begin to understand that the Canadian experience teaches us that these interactions serve two distinct purposes; constitutional collaboration and constitutional counter-balancing. If we are to understand the

---

[59] J. Waldron, *The Core of the Case against Judicial Review*, 115 YALE LAW JOURNAL .1346 (2006).
[60] M. Kumm, *Institutionalising Socratic Contestation: The Rationalists Human Rights Paradigm, Legitimate Authority and the Point of Judicial Review*, 1 EUROPEAN JOURNAL OF LEGAL STUDIES 1 (2007).

commonwealth model and dialogue fully, we need to re-examine the Canadian and UK experience, distinguishing between these two purposes of dialogue.

CONSTITUTIONAL COLLABORATION AND
CONSTITUTIONAL COUNTER-BALANCING

Constitutional collaboration occurs when the legislature and the courts act together to protect rights. Each institution draws on its different institutional strengths when reasoning about rights. The relative strengths and weaknesses of judicial and legislative protections of rights are well-known, running through accounts of dialogue in both the UK and Canada. Courts are better able to reason about rights through orientating values. Courts draw on long-standing principles and can help to protect these principles from accidental erosion; they recognize when general legislative provisions may erode individual rights and are regarded as better able to protect the rights of minority and unpopular groups. Legislatures, on the other hand, are better able to co-ordinate wide ranging interests; can provide broader mechanisms through which to protect rights and provide a more legitimate means through which to balance rights and policies. The extent to which each of these advantages and disadvantages reflects reality depends on constitutional design and institutional composition. Constitutional collaboration requires an understanding of the separation of powers, where both theoretical and practical constraints may hinder the extent to which the legislature and the courts can work together to provide a better protection of rights. This form of dialogue is similar to co-operative dialogue between courts, as discussed by Garlicki. Constitutional collaboration may also occur in a less facilitative manner, similar to Garlicki's account of co-habitational or accommodational dialogue between courts.[61]

Constitutional counter-balancing performs a different function. To understand this we need to examine a further criticism of dialogue made by Luc Tremblay.[62] Tremblay argues that dialogue requires interaction between two or more persons, who are recognized as equal partners:

> [e]ach participant must be equally entitled to put forward theses, to make proposals, to defend particular options, and to take part in the final decision. No one should be excluded from the dialogue, no one should impose by fiat where the dialogue should lead, and no hierarchy must confer in advance on one or more of the participants the authority to settle the disagreements.[63]

---

[61] Chapter 15 in this volume.
[62] L.B. Tremblay, *The Legitimacy of Judicial Review: The Limits of Dialogue between Courts and Legislatures*, 3 INTERNATIONAL JOURNAL OF CONSTITUTIONAL LAW 617 (2005).
[63] Tremblay, *The Legitimacy of Judicial Review*, supra note 62, at 632.

Constitutional counter-balancing facilitates the achievement of dialogue. Dialogue does not require complete parity between the legislature and the courts. It is also compatible with each institution performing a different role. However, if constitutional collaboration is to take place, then there has to be a means of ensuring that no one institution is able to "impose by fiat where the dialogue should lead."

Constitutional counter-balancing helps to provide a means of ensuring that each institution has the ability of responding to the other when it transgresses its proper constitutional role, however, that is defined in a particular constitution. Without constitutional counter-balancing, the aim of constitutional collaboration, and the better protection of rights, will not be achieved. If the commonwealth model is to achieve a better protection of rights, there needs to be both an understanding of constitutional collaboration as well as constitutional counter-balancing. Constitutional collaboration should be the main purpose of inter-institutional interactions and, if they are to work effectively, they need to be applied in a manner which is sensitive to the separation of powers, both in terms of the division of powers between institutions of the constitution and, in addition, the way in which actors in each institution regard their relative roles which influences how they behave. Constitutional counter-balancing mechanisms are not as effective at providing a better protection of rights. In this regard they are similar to the co-habitational or confrontational forms of court-court dialogue discussed by Garlicki.[64] Nevertheless, they are needed to ensure sufficient parity between the legislature and the judiciary to ensure that no one institution will always prevail when institutions interact. They are a means of preserving constitutional roles and should be used when an institution believes that the other has transgressed its constitutional role.[65] They can also be used to prompt constitutional collaboration.

APPLICATION TO CANADA AND THE UK

The previous section argued that both Canada and the UK provided examples of a commonwealth model of rights protections that operated in practice in a manner little different from a system with a constitutional protection of rights. The argument was based, in part, on the dwindling use of the notwithstanding clause and declarations of incompatibility. However, this criticism can be

---

[64] *See* Chapter 15 in this volume.
[65] Nick Barber and I have referred to these in the past as constitutional self-defence mechanisms. *See* N. Barber and A.L. Young, *The Rise of Prospective Henry VIII Clauses and Their Implications for Sovereignty*, PUBLIC LAW 113 (2003).

questioned when we recognize that both of these mechanisms are better suited to facilitating constitutional counter-balancing than constitutional collaboration.

The notwithstanding clause operates more as a means through which legislation can be enacted despite its contradiction of *Charter* rights, as opposed to a means through which the legislature may reach a different conclusion as to the scope of a right.[66] There is also a high political cost of initiating the notwithstanding clause.[67] Both are understandable by recasting the clause as a means of achieving constitutional counter-balancing. As such, the notwithstanding clause should only be used in those situations where the legislature has good reason to believe that courts have transgressed the proper bounds of their constitutional authority. This may be particularly relevant, for example, in "second look" cases where there is good reason to believe that courts did not give appropriate weight to the legislative deliberations in response to a first constitutional review by the Canadian Supreme Court. This is not to argue that courts should always be deferential in these cases.[68] Rather, it is to recognize that when there are good reasons to argue that the legislature is better placed to balance interests, or to provide a broader resolution to a specific issue, and there is evidence that the legislature has deliberated carefully when weighing conflicting interests, that there are good reasons for the court to give weight to the resolution of the legislation. If courts are to strike down this legislative response in a second look case, it should be either because there is a manifest disregard for a right, or where there has been an error in the reasoning of the legislature which the court is in a better position to be able to remedy.

An understanding of constitutional counter-balancing can also explain the reduction in the use of declarations of incompatibility. It would be wrong to see declarations of incompatibility as only being used to achieve constitutional counter-balancing. They may also be used to facilitate constitutional collaboration, this collaboration being particularly effective when declarations are issued because the legislature is better able to provide a remedy for a breach of a Convention right. However, the more declarations of incompatibility are

---

[66] *See* R. Dixon, *The Supreme Court of Canada, Charter Dialogue and Deference*, 47 Osgoode Hall Law Journal 235 (2009); T. Kahana, *Understanding the Notwithstanding Mechanism*, 52 University of Toronto Law Journal 221 (2002).

[67] S. Gardbaum, *The Commonwealth Model*, supra note 1, at chapter 5; R Albert, *Advisory Review: The Reincarnation of the Notwithstanding Clause*, 45 Atlanta Law Review 1037 (2007–08).

[68] Similar to but not the same as the arguments of R. Albert, *Advisory Review*, supra note 67; R. Dixon, *Charter Dialogue and Deference*, supra note 66.

regarded as requiring that legislation is remedied to comply with judicial decisions, the more difficult it is for them to facilitate collaboration. Declarations may therefore become predominantly used as a means through which to achieve constitutional counter-balancing. This may explain the reduction in their use – declarations may be best used when section 3 interpretations would entail courts transgressing the proper constitutional limits of their power.[69]

An understanding of constitutional counter-balancing and constitutional collaboration may explain the perceived judicial activism in both Canada and the UK. In Canada, if we regard the notwithstanding clause as predominantly facilitating constitutional counter-balancing, then we need to additionally recognize that constitutional collaboration will occur predominantly through the other means in which the legislature can respond to court determinations of *Charter* rights – e.g. section 1, the equality provisions and non-absolute rights. For dialogue to work, judges need to be more willing to defer when there are good reasons for believing that legislatures are better placed to determine the scope of a particular right. This may not occur in Canada partly because of the history of the application of the Canadian Bill of Rights 1960, where the courts were less willing to provide strong determinations of human rights,[70] in addition to the perception that it is section 33 which provides the main means of facilitating dialogue, or because there is no need to exercise judicial minimalism as a means of facilitating dialogue when the constitution provides for a commonwealth model of rights protections which is designed to facilitate dialogue. If the commonwealth model is to facilitate constitutional collaboration, it will be through a recognition of the need for courts to use deference and minimalism to facilitate constitutional collaboration, not through merely relying on the *Charter* being an example of a commonwealth model of rights protections due to the existence of the notwithstanding clause.

The criticism of the UK courts has been two-fold – the courts use living instrument interpretations to interpret Convention rights beyond the intentions of the authors of the Convention and interpret legislation in a manner which thwarts parliamentary intention in order to comply with Convention rights. The first criticism focuses on the extent to which UK decisions mirror those of the Strasbourg court. However, this criticism fails to recognize how

---

[69] This may explain its use in the prisoner voting scenario.

[70] *See* W. Tarnopolsky, *The Historical and Constitutional Context of the Proposed Canadian Charter of Rights and Freedoms*, 44 LAW AND CONTEMPORARY PROBLEMS 169 (1981); B. Hovius, *The Legacy of the Supreme Court of Canada's Approach to the Canadian Bill of Rights: Prospects for Canada*, 28 McGILL LAW JOURNAL 31 (1982–3).

the relationship between the UK courts and the Strasbourg court facilitates constitutional counter-balancing and constitutional collaboration. UK courts will normally follow a clear and constant line of case law, but will not follow a decision of the Strasbourg court which misunderstands the law, or which undermines a fundamental aspect of the UK constitution. This can be used to facilitate constitutional counter-balancing.

For example, in *Vinter* v. *UK* the Grand Chamber concluded that, although life sentences *per se* were not incompatible with Article 3 ECHR, nevertheless for a mandatory life sentence to be compatible with Article 3 there must be the prospect of a release and a possibility of review.[71] Although recognizing that UK law did include review, the Grand Chamber concluded that the published policy allowing for release on compassionate grounds did not comply with the Convention. Although the policy may be exercised in a manner which did fulfill Convention rights, nevertheless the lack of clarity surrounding the application of the rules meant that there had been a breach of Article 3 ECHR. Following this decision, the Attorney General referred the matter to the Court of Appeal, which reviewed the decision in *Vinter* and disagreed with its conclusion that English law was insufficiently clear to provide a real hope and possibility of release.[72] Although the Lifer Manual referred to "compassionate grounds," which may be read as too narrow as to provide any real hope or possibility of release, it was important to recognize that the Secretary of State was not able to fetter her discretion and, therefore, was not bound to merely follow the criteria set out in the Manual. Rather, she had to hear the exceptional circumstances of any application for release, ensuring that her assessment of whether this gave rise to compassionate grounds for release was determined in line with the requirements of Convention rights. Any refusal of release would then be subject to judicial review, which would also take account of Convention-compatibility. When understood in this way, the Court of Appeal concluded that English law did provide a real hope and possibility of release that was sufficiently clear and certain, thus satisfying the requirements of Article 3 ECHR as established in *Vinter* v. *UK*.[73] The issue of the compatibility of life sentences with Article 3 ECHR then returned to the ECtHR in *Hutchinson* v. *UK*.[74] Here the attention of the ECtHR was drawn to the decision of the Court of Appeal in *R* v. *Newell*. The ECtHR followed

---

[71] [2013] ECHR 66069/09.
[72] *Attorney General's Reference (No 60 of 2013), R* v. *McLoughlin; R* v. *Newell* [2014] EWCA Crim 188; [2014] 3 All ER 73.
[73] *Attorney General's Reference (No 60 of 2013), R* v. *McLoughlin; R* v. *Newell* [2014] EWCA Crim 188; [2014] 3 All ER 73, [29]–[36].
[74] [2015] ECHR 57592/08.

the decision of the Court of Appeal, concluding that there had been no breach of Convention rights. The interaction between the two courts facilitated constitutional counter-balancing, empowering the UK courts to prevent Strasbourg courts from over-protecting rights through a misunderstanding of UK law.[75]

An understanding of inter-institutional interactions also casts doubt on our use of *AF* as an example of judicial activism. It is clear that the UK courts did apply their ability to read and give effect to legislation in a manner which could well be regarded as a linguistically strained interpretation. However, it is important to recognize that the Supreme Court did so in response to the Strasbourg decision in *A v. UK*, which was itself the final decision of the Grand Chamber of the Strasbourg Court in response to a series of decisions of the UK Supreme Court and the Strasbourg Court. These interactions may have produced an outcome which some of the Justices of the Supreme Court were reluctant to adopt. However, the fact that this outcome was the result of a series of inter-institutional interactions may explain why the UK courts were so willing to apply section 3 so strongly. Constitutional collaboration between the two courts led to a better definition of the right, providing the courts with a stronger justification when interpreted legislation so as to comply with this right.

An understanding of constitutional counter-balancing and constitutional collaboration may provide a better understanding of the relative experiences of the UK and Canada. However, it suggests a need to examine how powers are exercised as opposed to merely comparing models of protecting rights, recognizing that inter-institutional interactions may facilitate constitutional collaboration and constitutional counter-balancing. This recognition may go some way to minimize the criticism that both the UK and Canada exemplify commonwealth models of rights which have collapsed into systems with a strong constitutional protection of rights in all but name, However, if we are to fully understand the relative experiences of the application of the commonwealth model in Canada and the UK, we need to add in an analysis of the separation of powers. In particular, we need to recognize how the commonwealth model may require the legislature and the courts to act in a manner different from their expectations, or from the description of their roles according to an account of the separation of powers.

The former may explain why there is little evidence of legislative engagement with human rights scrutiny. If the legislature regards the courts as the

---

[75] *See* Chapter 15 in this volume for further discussion of this case law and an assessment of the influence of the Canadian Supreme Court.

main institution of determining rights, or believes that its main task is to facilitate the enactment of legislation in line with the policies of the Government, which dominates the legislature, then it is understandable that a model of democratic dialogue may not be enough in and of itself to facilitate constitutional collaboration. The latter interpretation may explain why the UK legislature finds it difficult to respond to declarations of incompatibility as anything other than a request to amend legislation to ensure it complies with Convention rights as determined by the courts. It may also explain why the Canadian courts in particular provide a stronger protection of rights and perhaps are less willing to engage in deference. The Constitution Act 1982 expressly gives courts the responsibility of enforcing the *Charter*, including over Federal and Provincial legislation. In these circumstances, it can be harder to exercise interpretation of rights in a deferential manner.

CONCLUSION

The experience of Canada and the UK appeared to suggest that the commonwealth model and dialogue might be best regarded as a failed constitutional export. Rather than providing a model which could balance democracy and the protection of rights, both appear to exemplify a commonwealth model of rights protections which has collapsed into a strong protection of rights in all but name. This chapter has argued that some of the weaknesses of the commonwealth model can be explained through a misunderstanding of the relationship between the commonwealth model and dialogue and a failure to recognize that inter-institutional interactions may serve two aims – constitutional collaboration and constitutional counter-balancing. Understanding these two inter-related aims of democratic dialogue can help to explain the lack of use of the notwithstanding clause, as well as suggesting that, if the commonwealth model is to facilitate dialogue between the legislature and the courts, then the judiciary need to be more willing to facilitate constitutional collaboration through exercising deference, allowing the legislature a greater ability to determine the content of rights. Moreover, this recognition of constitutional counter-balancing and constitutional collaboration questioned whether all of the criticisms levelled at the UK judiciary were valid, particularly when understood in the light of the way in which dialogue between the UK courts and the Strasbourg court may facilitate constitutional counter-balancing and constitutional collaboration. However, the recognition of the two aims of inter-institutional interactions does not provide the full picture. Difficulties still arise when the commonwealth model requires institutions to act in a manner differently from their expectations according to their understanding of the separation of powers, as iterated in their particular constitution arrangement.

The UK has learned much from the Canadian experience. The UK also has much to learn from Canada in the face of criticisms of the HRA and the current plan of the Conservative Government to replace it with a British Bill of Rights, albeit this has now been put on the back-burner in the face of the constitutional challenges posed by the UK's exit from the European Union. To understand the *Charter* fully, we need to understand how its provisions can be seen as a response to Canada's first attempt to devise a commonwealth model of rights protections in the Canadian Bill of Rights 1960. The Canadian Bill of Rights provides a clear example of a commonwealth model of rights protections which collapsed into a weak parliamentary protection of rights in practice. This can be explained both in terms of the definition of rights found in the Bill and in terms of the lack of remedy given to the courts. Section 1 of the 1960 Bill of Rights protected a specific set of rights which "have existed and shall continue to exist" leading to what Tarnopolsky refers to as the "frozen concepts" principle.[76] The Canadian courts were less willing to see the Bill of Rights as capable of being interpreted as a living instrument, instead seeing the rights it was protecting as those which were in existence during its enactment in 1960. In addition, courts were unwilling to see legislation as having breached rights, regarding legislation as an expression of the rights in existence. The Bill failed to provide the Canadian courts with a remedy when it was unable to read and give effect to legislative provisions. In the seminal *Drybones* decision, the Canadian Supreme Court devised the declaration of inoperability, enabling legislation which contravened the 1960 Bill to be disapplied.[77] However, due to the more radical nature of this remedy, coupled with the frozen concepts principle, it was only applied once. In the face of such a weak protection of rights, it is hardly surprising that the *Charter* provides for a much stronger protection of rights.

This contextual understanding of the evolution of the *Charter* may sound a note of warning for the current proposal to introduce a British Bill of Rights. There would appear to be seven main reform proposals which can be gleaned from the Conservative Party's original policy document,[78] the Conservative Party's manifesto[79] and accounts of Michael Gove MP, the former Minster

---

[76] Tarnopolsky, *The Historical and Constitutional Context*, supra note 70.

[77] *R v. Drybones* [1970] SCR 282.

[78] "Protecting Human Rights in the UK: The Conservatives' Proposals for Changing Britain's Human Rights Laws," available at www.conservatives.com/~/media/files/downloadable %20Files/human_rights.pdf.

[79] www.conservatives.com/manifesto.

for Justice.[80] There is a desire to disconnect from Strasbourg; to redress the balance between the legislature and the courts; to remove the obligation to adhere to Convention rights from the armed forces; to redress the balance between rights and responsibilities; to repatriate rights to ensure a more "British" interpretation of rights; to limit the application of human rights to the most serious of cases; and more recently, to provide a legislative framework for rights which can be used to operate as a constitutional brake against the application of the EU Charter of Rights and the ECHR[81] – although the former will no longer be needed given the clear statement in the recently published European Union (Withdrawal) Bill 2017–19 to ensure that "Brexit" means the Charter will no longer apply in UK law post "exit day."[82] The theme running through these reforms is to see the British Bill of Rights as a means of redressing a perceived tipping of power away from Parliament to the courts and from the UK towards Europe. Whereas the *Charter* is influenced by the weak protections found in the Canadian Bill of Rights 1960, the British Bill of Rights appears to express a desire to travel in the opposite direction.

Our analysis of the Canadian and UK experience may sound four warnings, concerning the necessity and the effect of the proposed reforms. Some of the calls for reform misunderstand the nature of the relationship between the Strasbourg and the UK courts. Inter-institutional interactions between these courts facilitate constitutional collaboration and constitutional counter-balancing. The UK courts may influence the development of rights in Strasbourg to a greater degree than is considered by those proposing reform. In addition, a misunderstanding of the relationship between the commonwealth model and dialogue may lead to a possible over-reaction, reducing the powers of the judiciary to a greater extent than is required. Our analysis would also suggest that, to the extent that difficulties in the relationship between the two exist, they may be better remedied through the encouragement of greater engagement in rights scrutiny by the legislature, or a re-examination of the relative power of the Government in the House of Commons and the House of Lords. Finally,

---

[80] *See*, in particular, the statements of Gove before the House of Commons' Justice Committee on 9 July 2015, available at www.parliament.uk/business/committees/committees-a-z/commons-select/justice-committee/one-off-sessions/parliament-2015/work-of-the-secretary-of-state-for-justice/ and before the House of Lords EU Committee: Justice Sub-Committee on 2 February 2016, available at http://data.parliament.uk/writtenevidence/committeeevidence.svc/evidencedocument/eu-justice-subcommittee/potential-impact-of-repealing-the-human-rights-act-on-eu-law/oral/28347.html.

[81] *See* in particular the statements of Gove MP before the Justice Sub-Committee of the House of Lords' EU Committee. *Id.*

[82] https://publications.parliament.uk/pa/bills/cbill/2017-2019/0005/18005.pdf, clause 5(4).

given the success of the commonwealth model depends more on how institutions exercise their powers than upon the powers the model grants to the legislature and the judiciary, it may well be that the proposed British Bill of Rights will make little difference. A reduction in the powers of the judiciary may well lead to the judiciary exercising these powers to a greater extent, as is perhaps already illustrated by their increased reference to common law rights and their use of the EU Charter to disapply national legislation. If the UK is to continue to learn from the Canadian commonwealth model, it would do well to focus more on how the legislature and judiciary interact than an analysis of the provisions of the *Charter*.

15

The European Court of Human Rights
and the Canadian Case Law

LECH GARLICKI

GLOBALIZATION AND HUMAN RIGHTS

While globalization constitutes a universal feature of the modern world, its intensity and importance has already taken a particularly developed dimension in the human rights field. At least in the perspective of Europe, there is a visible trend towards converging different human instruments, independently on their – international, supranational or domestic – origin.

In the substantive dimension, these instruments, due to their natural-law connotation, address the same bunch of human (individual, fundamental) rights. So, all the national (historical, cultural) singularities notwithstanding, the core rights and liberties are guaranteed everywhere and are drafted in a similar language.

In the institutional dimension, those rights and liberties are enforced (i.e., developed) by judicial or quasi-judicial bodies that enjoy a considerable degree of independence. There are numerous similarities between the ECtHR, the CJEU and the national constitutional/supreme courts and, what is even more important, they share a common will to act as judicial bodies and not as political agencies.

In the procedural dimension, the jurisdiction of all courts is based on the case-or-controversy concept and ensure some access for individuals.

Finally, in the operational dimension all courts not only apply similar intellectual concepts (like, human dignity, equality or proportionality) and similar decision-making techniques, but – in their daily practice, they refer to each other's case law and use it in their own decisions.

The latter seems to be of a particular importance. The mutual use of "other's case law" on human rights leads to different forms of "judicial borrowing" or "cross-fertilization."[1] In effect, a common body of legal concepts, rules and

---

[1] See, e.g., E. Benvenisti, G. W. Downs, *Court Cooperation, Executive Accountability and Global Governance*, 41 N.Y.U. J. INT'L L. & POL. 931 (2009); E. Voeten, *Borrowing and*

techniques has already emerged in Europe. Although, due to obvious reasons, the formalized procedures of such exchange remain quite limited, the practice of dialogue is ever-present in the practical operation of almost all highest courts in Europe. In the human rights field, it finds a strong encouragement in that the courts of all types and regions are dealing with similar texts and similar matters.

The above-mentioned process is often described as "constitutionalization" of international law,[2] and – at the same time – there is a parallel trend towards "internationalization" of constitutional law. Some authors talk about "the emergence of a transnational legal-pluralist order"[3] or about a "common law of fundamental rights" and "liberties."[4] From the domestic law perspective, this process is sometimes discussed in the perspective of "multi-centrism" of legal systems.

The question is whether those trends should be regarded as distinct developments which still remain placed within constitutional or international law seen as two distinct branches of law. Or, whether there are already some indications that "internationalization" of constitutionally protected individual rights and "constitutionalization" of internationally protected human rights has reached a new stage of development.

It cannot be excluded that a "melting stage" has been reached, in which constitutional, supranational and regional human rights instruments should

---

Non-Borrowing among International Courts, J. Legal Stud. 537ff (2010); A. M. Slaughter: *A Global Community of Courts*, 44 Harv. Int'l L. Rev. 194ff (2003); V. Perju, "Constitutional Transplants, Borrowing, and Migrations" in: *Oxford Handbook of Comparative Constitutional Law*, Oxford 2012.

2   What makes the system "constitutional" is the overarching normative structure: the code of rights that officials are under the legal duty to enforce, and a set of share techniques that judges, in particular, have developed to adjudicate rights. A. Stone Sweet, *A cosmopolitan legal order: Constitutional pluralism and rights adjudication in Europe*, Global Constitutionalism, *supra* note 1, at 62. On the process of "constitutionalization" of the Strasbourg Court, *see*, in particular, S. Greer, L. Wildhaber, *Revisiting the Debate about "Constitutionalising" the ECtHR*, Hum. R.s L. Rev. 4 (2013); W. Sadurski, *Partnering with Strasbourg: Constitutionalization of the ECtHR, the Accession of Central and East European States to the Council of Europe and the Idea of Pilot Judgments*, Hum Rts L Rev 3 (2009); A. Stone Sweet, *Sur la constitutionalisation de la Convention europeenne des droits de l'homme: la CEDH comme une Cour constitutionnelle*, Revue Trimestrielle des Droits de l'Homme 4 (2009).

3   P. Zumbansen, *Comparative, Global and Transitional Constitutionalism; The Emergence of a Transnational Legal-Pluralist Order*, Global Constitutionalism 1 (2012). *See also* D. Barak-Erez, *The International Law of Human Rights and Constitutional Law: A Case Study of an Expanding Dialogue*, Int'l J. Const. L. (I*CON) 4 (2004).

4   R. Arnold, *La multiciplication des garanties et de juge dans la protection des droits fondamentaux*, Allemagne, Annuaire International de Justice Constitutionnelle, vol. XXIX, 108 (2013).

be regarded as "a whole." In other words, there is an emerging amalgam which can be described as "the law on human (fundamental) rights." It is true that such conclusion may be disputed under the traditional objection against "fragmentation" of international law. But, whether we like it or not, such fragmentation has already taken place in regard to the international humanitarian law and the international criminal law. What is proposed here, is to take one step further.

The advantage of such approach is mostly practical. If it could be accepted that "the law on human (fundamental) rights" has already emerged as a specific branch which combines constitutional and international law, the logical conclusion is that this branch cannot belong to either of those traditional "laws." Therefore, the "law on human (fundamental) rights" could and should be regarded as a distinct category. In the perspective of constitutional law, it legitimizes the expansion of constitutional jurisdictions at the expense of the traditional understanding of sovereignty and separation of powers. In the perspective of international law, it assumes certain detachment from the traditional scheme focused on relations between sovereign states.

The "law on human (fundamental) rights" is, by its nature, constitutional and international at the same time. Like international law, it does not stop at the state borders in its quest for universal standards. Like constitutional law, it offers not only the recognition of rights and claims of individuals, but also it ensures a judicial protection in case of their violation and opens an access to a (national, supranational or international) judge.

HUMAN RIGHTS AND JUDICIAL DIALOGUE

Such homogeneity of human rights (and of the mechanisms of their protection) encourages a cross-national (or – even – cross-systemic) dialogue between courts and judges. All constitutional and supreme courts are participating in this dialogue albeit in different forms and with different effects. A particular role belongs to the "strong" courts which represent well-established constitutional systems. Thus, the Supreme Court of Canada makes a prominent partner for other jurisdictions dealing with human (fundamental) law cases.

There is no need here to enter into different theories and concepts of the judicial dialogue. Generally speaking, what we have in mind are situations where one court refers to what has already been said by another court and takes it into account in the process of its own decision-making and decision-drafting.

Judicial dialogue takes a particularly fascinating form where there is no direct and full link of subordination between the partnering courts, in other words, where none of the partners has a "right to the last word," i.e., the power to impose its solution on the other court. Thus, dialogue – in this "external" understanding, presupposes certain degree of mutual autonomy. This situation is different from the classic relation within the judiciary, where there is a higher court vested with a power of full review over decisions of a lower court, and this power is accepted and respected by the lower court. Such procedural arrangement leaves but a limited zone of autonomy for the lower court.

On the other hand, the absence of any direct and full link of subordination creates a separation of both partners. It finds its reflection in the separation of their territorial, or/and substantive jurisdiction as well in the absence of the direct power to annul or modify the decisions (legal positions) of the other court. The degree of that separation (autonomy) may vary. There are situations where both courts, albeit technically separated and independent, operate within the same system, but – due to the multi-centric nature of this system – both preserve a considerable degree of autonomy. Such is often the relation between the constitutional court and the Supreme Court on the domestic level as well as the relation between the ECtHR and the national constitutional courts of the Member States. Although their jurisdiction often overlaps, there still may not be clear whose decision prevails in case of a conflict. A constant dialogue and cooperation are here indispensable for the proper operation of the whole system.

Another type of dialogue develops between courts which belong to the entirely different structures and/or systems. In horizontal dimension, it may include two constitutional jurisdictions (like, e.g., the US Supreme Court and the German Constitutional Court), two European courts (the ECtHR and the CJEU) or two regional courts (like the ECtHR and the I-ACtHR). While it is clear that the decisions of one of such partners cannot be binding on the other one, it does not mean that they cannot matter in the decision-making process. Even if some courts and judges may remain hostile against open references to the foreign law, this law is usually known to them and, therefore, it cannot be intellectually ignored.[5] At the same time, many courts (like the Supreme Court of Canada, the South African Constitutional Court, the Supreme Court of Ireland, the Supreme Court of Israel, the High Court of Australia, as well as the I-ACtHR)[6] have no problem in admitting that foreign

---

[5] As recently observed by S. Breyer (*The Court and the World*, New York 2015, p. 245), "a great many recent cases – whether involving treaties, the foreign reach of American statutes, or questions of US jurisdiction over activity taking place abroad – made it unavoidable that the Court analyze foreign or international legal rules, statutes, or practices to arrive at a reasoned decision. In such cases, doing so was not simply helpful but essential."

[6] T. Groppi and M.-C. Ponthoreau, "Conclusion" in: *The Use of Foreign Precedents by Constitutional Judges*, ed. by T. Groppi and M.-C. Ponthoreau, *Hart Studies in Comparative Public Law*, vol. 1, Oxford and Portland 2014, p. 412.

decisions are taken into account on a regular basis. In brief, openness to information on (and – influences of) foreign law became a regular feature of most of the human (fundamental) rights jurisdictions around the world. And, once one court begins to refer to decisions of another court, it may trigger some reaction of that court. This moves their relation from a one-way process of borrowing/fertilization towards a two-way-street of genuine dialogue.

There are different forms of such dialogue:

- *a cooperative dialogue* takes place where one court refers to the case law of another court in order to elaborate common positions in as many matters as possible. This may be particularly useful when both courts, albeit formally separated and independent, act in the same legal space. Both courts may strive *to coordinate* their case law on similar matters[7] and, sometimes, to reinforce their positions in dialogue with other external partners.[8] In the latter situation, the quotations of foreign law may be seen as a *legitimization factor*: the referring court, when encountering a "sensitive" gap in its case law needs to rely on decisions already made elsewhere. Such "external legitimization" of own decisions is typical for younger or "weaker" jurisdictions which may need additional arguments to ensure the acceptance and compliance of their domestic and international partners.[9] Finally, if one court is not ready to follow the other partner's position, it may refer to it only *to explain* why the case under consideration can be distinguish from (allegedly similar) cases already decided by the other partner. The principal goal here is to preserve a good cooperation in the future, to avoid retaliatory measures and not to unnecessary alienate the other court. The highest courts act often like human beings and react emotionally if not respected and cherished by their partners.

[7] See, e.g., the so-called "blacklisting cases" decided by the Luxembourg courts (Kadi, 2005, 2008, 2010 and 2013 and by the ECtHR (*Nada v. Switzerland*, 2012; *Al-Dulimi v. Switzerland*, 2013).

[8] E.g., in cases concerning the European Arrest Warrant. The CJEU, in *Melloni v. Ministerio Fiscal* (C-399/11, 26 February 2013) suggested that the Spanish Constitutional Court should revise its constitutional interpretation and relied on the standard already elaborated by the ECtHR (*Sejdovic v. Italy*, 2006). The position of the CJEU was accepted by the Spanish Constitutional Court (judgment no. 24/2014 of 13 February 2014). However, the German Constitutional Court, in another case decided (judgment of 26 January 2016) that – as the German constitutional standard is more protective than the EU standard – the former must prevail.

[9] E.g., in the Death Penalty Case decided by the Constitutional Court of South Africa (*S. v. Makvanyane*, 6 July 1995) and the Lustration Case decided by the Polish Constitutional Court (judgment of 11 May 2007, K 2/07).

- an *accommodational (co-habitational) dialogue* constitutes a variation of cooperative dialogue. In such situations there may be less sympathy between the partners, but – as both courts have to cooperate on a permanent basis – references to the partner's case law serve to elaborate some patterns of common relations. A court may, for example, acknowledge the other partner's claim to decide or determine a particular case or particular matter, but – at the same time – it may delineate certain "sacred" boundaries for its exclusive area of authority, or establish certain "safety valves" for cases of conflict, and provide methods of communication and dialogue in complicated cases. Once such patterns have been established in the case law, a court may refuse to decide certain matters on the assumption that – under the "accommodation agreement" – they have to be left for the other partner.[10] The problems may, however, arise in situations where both courts differ in setting these boundaries and/or where a "safety valve" established by one court is not accepted by the other one. As quite often those boundaries and safety valves are first established in form of obiter dicta, it delays a prospect of an open conflict, but – at the same time – it leaves a grey zone of uncertainty.[11]
- a *confrontational dialogue* arises in situations where both courts – while addressing similar problems – are unable (or – unwilling) to elaborate a common ground. In effect, a solution earlier adopted by one court may not be followed by the other one; sometimes such refusal may be based on a jurisdictional claim to review the conformity of the other court's decision with some "higher" principles and rules. The very existence of such confrontation may remain hidden, as the courts are usually reluctant to admit it in an open manner.[12] The usual method is rather to accommodate the position of the other partner or, at least, to pretend that it has been duly taken into account.

---

[10] See, in particular, the so-called Bosphorus Case (*Bosphorus Hava Yollari Turizm v. Ireland*, judgment of 30 June 2005) in which the ECtHR declared its deference to the protection of fundamental rights ensured by the European Union.

[11] See, e.g., the Akerberg judgment of the CJEU (*Aklagaren v. Hans Akerberg Fransson*, C 617–10, 26 February 2013) and its criticism expressed by the German Constitutional Court (judgment of 24 April 2013 – Anti-Terror Database) or the controversies around the Gorgulu decision of the German Constitutional Court (order of 14 October 2004 – *see*, e.g., Ch. Tomuschat, *The Effects of Judgments of the ECtHR According to the German Constitutional Court*, 11 GERMAN L. J., 2010, p. 513 et seq.).

[12] However, already in 1960 a "war of courts" erupted in Italy (J. H. Merryman, V. Vigoriti, *When Courts Collide: Constitution and Cassation in Italy*, 15 A. J. COMP. LAW, 665 et seq. (1966–1967)), For other examples *see* L. Garlicki, *Constitutional courts v. Supreme Courts*, 5 I*CON 43 et seq (2007).

The judicial dialogue takes different forms and its richness often escapes precise definitions. There is no clear delimitation of cooperation, accommodation and confrontation, the dividing lines remain blurred and leave grey zones which allow to find escape paths and "face-saving" solutions. Contacts between highest court are not always easy as they involve an inevitable aspect of tension and rivalry. The very sense of a reasonable judicial dialogue is to reduce tensions, to establish certain level of mutual respect, and to avoid frontal collisions.

Finally, the *dialogue between courts does not develop in an abstract space*. In the reality, judicial decisions are addressed to different external partners, in particular to the legislative and executive bodies as well as to other courts and institutions. Their compliance is essential and, particularly in the sensitive matters, the highest courts may seek an additional legitimization of their decisions. It need not be reminded that, next to the dialogue between courts there is also a constant dialogue between the judiciary and the legislative branch.[13] While it takes different forms – from collaboration to open conflict, it is never easy to the courts to convince law-givers to their concepts and interpretations. That is why judicial cooperation and accommodation are more productive than collision and conflict.

Not all courts are equally open to such dialogue, but – as regards overlapping jurisdictions (like ECtHR and CJEU) – mutual referrals and reactions are simply unavoidable for the good administration of justice. More flexibility remains in deciding whether, and to what extent, to refer to judgments adopted by entirely "external" jurisdictions. Although the choices must not be taken arbitrarily, there is also no general obligation to look into all systems and their case law. Thus, if such "foreign" decisions are, nevertheless, referred to, it can, usually, be explained either by a particular authority of a particular court or by a particular similarity of the matters under consideration.

THE "FOREIGN LAW" IN THE EUROPEAN COURT OF HUMAN RIGHTS

The European Court of Human Rights has always been quite active in its use of decisions of the "foreign courts." Due to its nature of a court of international law, the ECtHR has no alternative but to maintain a constant dialogue with external jurisdictions. This dialogue takes different forms depending on its partners.

---

[13] *See* Chapter 14 in this volume.

First of all, the ECtHR deals with the courts of the "defendant State." Almost all Convention cases originate in individual applications directed against one of the Member States. Due to the requirement of exhaustion of the domestic remedies, most of the cases have to be first decided in the domestic courts. Thus, the ECtHR has to examine the "conventionality" of domestic decisions in individual case as well as the general legal background of this case, i.e., the state of the domestic legislation and the relevant case law of the constitutional and/or Supreme Court. This has to be a thorough and complete examination and is concluded by a judgment in which the ECtHR decide whether there has been a violation of the Convention and how this violation should be remedied by the defendant State. In the dimension of an individual case, the ECtHR judgment is of a final and binding nature. At the same time, such judgment often has a precedential authority, which should be respected and followed not only by the courts of the defendant State but also, whenever appropriate, by courts (and legislators) of other Member States. It is not always easy to secure full compliance and cooperation of other courts in this dimension and the ECtHR must sometimes remain very diplomatic not to provoke conflicts and not to offend some powerful constitutional or supreme courts.[14]

The second area extends to all Member States to the European Convention. Decisions of the ECtHR are very often based on the assessment of proportionality and – in the balancing process – the Court takes into account the width of the "margin of appreciation" left to the Member-State. The delineation of this margin is a complicated enterprise and depends, in the first place, on the nature of the infringed right and the intensity of the alleged interference. Another decisive factor is the existence of "a common approach" on the European level. The existence of such approach or, at least- the presence of a "European common trend" leaves less room for those States that are not ready to follow. On the other hand, where there is no consensus within the Member States, either to a relative importance of the interest at stake or as to the best means of protecting it, the margin of appreciation becomes wider.[15] Thus, the Strasbourg Court must examine the state of law

---

[14] *See*, the controversy between the ECtHR and the German Constitutional Court which resulted upon the judgment of 24 June 2004 (*von Hannover v. Germany* – see J. Hedigan, "The Princess, the Press and Privacy" in: *Liber Amicorum Luzius Wildhaber*, Kehl 2007, p. 193 et seq.) and was "peacefully" solved by the German Constitutional Court (order of 26 February 2008) and the ECtHR (judgment of 7 February 2012, *von Hannover v. Germany*, no. 2).

[15] The more a consensus matures on a certain issue involving a right protected under the Convention, the smaller the margin of appreciation of the domestic authorities to determine freely the purview" (Ch. Rozakis, *The European Judge as Comparatist*, 80 TUL. L. REV. 257, 273 (2005–2006) 22).

in all of the Member States and it means that all relevant decisions taken at the national level should be taken into account. In addition, the case law of the CJEU is regarded as a very important confirmation of the European consensus.

Finally, the Court is quite open to information on judicial decisions taken outside the Convention states. Although, a more systematic research is undertaken only in important cases,[16] foreign precedents are also quoted in the parties' and amicus curia briefs. The ECtHR always takes them into account, but usually only mentions those precedents in the informative part of the judgment and, rather exceptionally, refers to them in its legal reasoning. The reasons to consider foreign judgments are manifold. Sometimes, such quotation may serve a purely decorative purpose. Usually, however, the Court turn towards "the outer world" when it is difficult to find a solid answer within the case law of the Member States or when it appears useful in establishing the existence of a common approach or common trend. Finally, there are cases, in particularly – concerning extradition or deportation to a non-Convention state, in which the decision of the Court must be based on the assessment of the foreign law.[17] The bottom-line of most references is the legitimization argument: information on external precedents may be helpful in convincing other courts that the ECtHR has adopted a correct decision. That is why it is usually more attractive to borrow from a strong and well-established jurisdiction than from a new and week one.

THE CANADIAN CASE LAW: MORE THAN ONE OF THE FOREIGN LAWS?

It goes without words that Canada and its Supreme Court occupy a prominent place in the ranking of attractiveness. The input of the Canadian Court jurisprudence on human rights is impressive. On the substance, Canadian judgments on abortion, same-sex marriage, religious attire, as well as on other sensitive issues, may easily serve as guidance for courts and judges all over the world. In the methodological dimension, the dynamic approach to the constitutional interpretation (the "living tree" doctrine) encourages other constitutional jurisdictions to follow.[18]

---

[16] In all such cases, the comparative law data are prepared by the Research Division (situated within the Court's Registry) which ensures a very high quality of information.

[17] E.g., in Babar Ahmad (judgment of 10 April 2012, *Babar Ahmad and Others v. the UK*), the ECtHR, when decided on extradition to the US, had to assess whether the detention in a US super-max prison facility would be compatible with Article 3 of the Convention.

[18] As the Constitutional Court of Spain observed in the Same-Sex-Marriage Case (judgment no. 198/2012 of 6 November 2012, par. 9: "In order to move forward in our reasoning, we will take one more step in our interpretation of [Article 39 of the Constitution which defines

Quite obviously, the Canadian jurisprudence appears particularly attractive for other Commonwealth countries, the United Kingdom included. The UK courts refer to the Canadian case law on a regular basis and it seems that, at least in some "hard cases" involving human rights, Canadian citations are regarded as an additional legitimization of decisions adopted by the domestic courts.

Almost automatically, it brings the Canadian case law into the Strasbourg deliberations. In most of the UK cases, the ECtHR is confronted with a reasoned judgment of the UK Supreme Court (the House of Lords) or, at least, one of the appellate courts. The ECtHR considers these judgments in a very careful manner and only rarely has problems in sharing the approach of the UK highest courts.[19] And, if a UK judgment invokes a Canadian precedent, the latter enters, almost automatically, into the case and must be taken into account by the Strasbourg Court. That is why, most references to the Canadian jurisprudence appear in cases in which the United Kingdom act as the defendant state. This makes the Canadian case law less "foreign" than suggested by the geography and clearly more close than the case law of the United States.[20] Once reference to a Canadian case enters into the reasoning of a UK court (or – of a court of any other Convention State), it becomes absorbed into the Convention legal space and, therefore, its role and authority may surpass what is usually reserved for non-European precedents. That is why, in the Strasbourg case law, the Canadian cases (as well as cases from other Commonwealth countries) are present more often than the decisions of the US Supreme Court.

There is no single pattern in the ECtHR's references to the Canadian case law. But, at least on two occasions, decisions of the Supreme Court of Canada have influenced the Strasbourg approach in a serious and visible manner. Both cases can be regarded as examples of "a judicial borrowing," in which

---

marriage as a union of man and woman]. We will start off with an initial presumption, based on the idea that the Constitution is a 'living tree' ... recovered by the Supreme Court of Canada in its judgment of December 9th, 2004 on marriage between persons of the same sex – i.e., a progressive interpretation allowing the Constitution to be adjusted to the realities of modern life as means to guarantee its own relevance and authority."

[19] And, where there are problems, like in cases concerning hearsay evidence cases (judgment of the ECtHR of 20 January 2009, *Al-Khawaja and Tahery v. the UK*, practically rejected by the UK Supreme Court in *R. v. Horncastle and Others*, 9 December 2009, and, finally, modified by the Grand Chamber of the ECtHR in the judgment of 15 December 2011, *Al-Khawaja and Tahery v. the UK*), both partners are usually able to arrive to a common conclusion.

[20] This "jurisdictional link" seems to be more important, in the Strasbourg perspective, than the general decline in influence of the case-law of the US Supreme Court. While, as correctly observed by R. Hirschl in Chapter 13 of this volume, it may be quite relevant for the growing attractiveness of the Canadian jurisprudence in the worldwide perspective, the ECtHR has always been rather careful in referring to the US precedents.

the solution (and reasoning) of the Supreme Court was absorbed into the law of the European Convention.

THE ASSISTED SUICIDE CASES

In *Rodriguez*,[21] the Supreme Court confirmed the applicability of section 241(b) of the Criminal Code to assistance of terminally ill persons in suicide. The Court held (by a 5:4 majority) that the blanket ban on assisted suicide is not in conflict with the Charter. At the same time, however, it was recognized that the prohibition engages the appellant's security interest (considered in the context of the life and liberty interest). In other words, as there is a constitutional right involved, a restriction must meet a heighten scrutiny required by the Charter. Thus, *Rodriguez* was the first case in which a respected constitutional court recognized the constitutional dimension of assisted suicide.

Another approach was adopted by the US Supreme Court in *Washington v. Glucksberg*[22] (1997). In reversing the en banc decision of the Court of Appeals, the justices held (unanimously) that "the asserted 'right' to assistance in suicide is not a fundamental liberty interest protected by the Due Process Clause." Thus, the ban on assisted suicide must meet only "the rational relationship test" and there are several state interests which may justify the blanket nature of the prohibition. The majority opinion referred to the Dutch legislation on euthanasia, but did not mention the *Rodriguez* judgment.

This was the background for the *Pretty* case which, in 2001–2002, gave the European courts an opportunity to address the problem. In 2001, the House of Lords held[23] that the Suicide Act 1961 is, in particular, compatible with Articles 2 and 8 of the European Convention.[24] The House of Lords decided that "the right to life" (Article 2) cannot be interpreted as also including its antithesis, i.e., the right to die. Such interpretation would be inconsistent with principles "deeply embedded in English law." Assisted suicide must, therefore be distinguished from the – already recognized – right to refuse a medical treatment.[25] All, but one, justices accepted that "the applicant's rights under

---

[21] *Rodriguez v. Attorney General of Canada* (1994).   [22] 521 US 702 (1997).
[23] *Pretty v. Director of Public Prosecutions and Secretary of State for the Home Department* (29 November 2001).
[24] As it is well known, the 1998 Human Rights Act absorbed the Convention rights and liberties into the UK legal system, allowed the courts to review the "conventionality" of legislation, but limited their powers to so-called "declarations of incompatibility" and – in regard to the primary legislation – reserved the final decision for the Parliament.
[25] The latter right was confirmed, in particular, by the House of Lords in its judgment Airedale *NHS Trust v. Bland* (1993) where it was observed that a distinction must be made between

Article 8 are not engaged at all." However, in anticipation of a possible different conclusion of the Strasbourg Court, the Lords held that even "if this conclusion is wrong, and the [blanket] prohibition of assisted suicide infringes a Convention right under Article 8 ... such infringement is justifiable under the terms of Article 8 par. 2."

The House of Lords seemed to prefer the "no-right-approach" adopted by the US Supreme Court. Nevertheless, the *Rodriguez* case was duly taken into account. It was noted that "the most detailed and erudite discussion ... of the issues in the present appeal is to be found in the judgments of the Supreme Court of Canada ... It is evident that all save one of the judges of the Supreme Court were willing to recognize sec. 7 of the Canadian Charter as conferring a right to personal autonomy extending even to decisions on life and death ... [But] the judgments were directed to a provision with no close analogy in the European Convention" (par. 19 and 23). Although the House of Lords was not ready to follow the Canadian Supreme Court as to the principle, it took into account its reasoning concerning the justification of prohibition. In effect, several arguments raised in interpretation of Article 8 sec. 2 of the European Convention remained quite close to the language and logic of the *Rodriguez* case.

The ECtHR, in *Pretty* v. *the UK*,[26] confirmed (repeating most of the arguments submitted in the House of Lords judgment) that the ban on assisted suicide does not engage any rights which can be derived from Article 2 or 3 of the Convention. However, the ECtHR rejected the House of Lords' position on inapplicability of Article 8. The Court, at first, noted that "the very essence of the Convention is respect for human dignity and human freedom ... It is under Article 8 that notions of the quality of life taken on significance" (par. 65). Then, the Court, in an expressed reference to *Rodriguez*, observed that "although the Canadian court was considering a provision of the Canadian Charter framed in different terms from those of Article 8, comparable concerns arouse regarding the principle of personal autonomy" (par. 66). This led the ECtHR to the conclusion that as "the applicant is prevented by law from exercising her choice to avoid what she considers will be an undignified and distressing end of her life, [the Court] is not prepared to exclude that this constitutes an interference with her right ... guaranteed under Article 8 par. 1 of the Convention" (par. 67). Thus, the Court had to examine whether this

---

the cessation of life-saving or life-prolonging treatment on one hand and the taking of action lacking medical, therapeutic or palliative justification but intended solely to terminate life on the other.

[26] Judgment of 29 April 2002.

interference conformed with the requirements of Article 8 par. 2 and – ultimately – held that the blanket ban on assisted suicide may be justified as "necessary in a democratic society" (par. 78). The arguments raised by the ECtHR duplicated, to a considerable extent, the "alternative reasoning" of the House of Lords and, therefore, the Canadian Supreme Court. The ECtHR referred again to both judgments and indicated its "agreement" on the matter (par. 74).

For both *Pretty* judgments, *Rodriguez* can be seen as a "fertilization source." Although, the House of Lords was not ready to accept the very existence of a Convention right,[27] it did not affect the general lines of further reasoning. The House of Lords as well as the ECtHR examined at length whether the prohibition was justified (proportional) and, in this part, both courts relied quite closely on arguments elaborated by the Canadian Supreme Court. Thus, the latter's position could be regarded as an intellectual basis for the reasoning of both European courts.

This base, however, began to erode in the current decade. On the one hand, the ECtHR is more ready now, than in 2002, to confirm, in a clear language, that Article 8 encompasses the right (of a competent adult) to decide how and when to die, and in particular, the right to avoid a distressing and undignified end to life.[28] On the other hand, in the *Nicklinson Case* (2014)[29] the UK Supreme Court abandoned its acceptance for the blanket prohibition on assisted suicide. The Court abstained from declaring incompatibility, but – in the same time – it indicated that the present regulation falls short from the present standards[30]. Finally, in *Carter* (2015),[31] the Supreme Court of Canada has developed its own position and – de facto – overruled the holding of *Rodriguez*. This removed the "Canadian basis" from the global law on human rights, or – rather, replaced it with a new approach which confirms the right of

[27] However, in a perfect example of a cooperative dialogue, the House of Lords, in *R (Purdy) v. Director of Public prosecutions* (30 July 2009) revised its position and accepted that the prohibition constitutes an interference with rights guaranteed in Article 8 of the Convention.

[28] In particular judgments in: *Haas v. Switzerland* (20 January 2011), *Koch v. Germany* (19 July 2012), and *Gross v. Switzerland* (14 May 2013).

[29] *R (on the application of Nicklinson and another) v. Ministry of Justice* (25 June 2014).

[30] More traditional stance was adopted by the Irish Supreme Court. In *Fleming v. Ireland, Attorney General and the Director of Public Prosecutions* (29 April 2013), the Supreme Court rejected the earlier position of the High Court that the ban on assisted suicide involves a restriction on a constitutionally protected interest in personal autonomy. Instead, the Supreme Court held that no constitutional right was involved. This was closer to the Glucksberg approach. The Irish Supreme Court referred to both Rodriguez and Glucksberg. Also the Carter case was presented at length, but – as, in the material time, only the trial court decision was available, its persuasive authority was of only limited nature.

[31] *Carter v. Canada (Attorney General)*, 26 February 2015.

terminally ill persons to assistance in suicide. Thus, the process of fertilization of the European partners may be started again.

THE PRISONERS' VOTING RIGHTS CASES

In *Sauvé no. 1* (1993),[32] the Supreme Court constitutionalized voting rights of convicted prisoners and held that general exclusion from voting constitutes an unjustified denial of the right to vote. Subsequent legislative amendment limited the ban to prisoners serving sentences of two years or more. It was upheld by the Federal Court of Appeal, but struck down by the Supreme Court (*Sauvé no. 2*, 2002).[33]

In Europe, the controversy on prisoners' voting rights surfaced in the beginning of this Century. Although a majority of the European countries did not provide for a general exclusion, the United Kingdom (and several other states, including Russia) did. The UK legislation was challenged by three prisoners who had applied for registration as electors and been refused. In 2001, the Divisional Court rejected the claim that the exclusion was incompatible with the European Convention. The Court referred to *Sauvé* (1993) as well to the US decision in *Richardson v. Ramirez* (1974),[34] and observed that the Parliament was entitled to decide that disenfranchisement of prisoners served a legitimate purpose. The application for permission to appeal was refused.

The ECtHR, in the 2004 Chamber judgment,[35] held that the blanket exclusion of all convicted prisoners constitutes a breach of the Convention. The Court noted the provisions of the International Covenant on Civil and Political Rights (and one of the General Comments of the UN Human Rights Committee), the "soft law" of the Council of Europe, and – last but not least – the second Sauvé decision (2002). In the reasoned part of the judgment, the Court observed that the *Sauvé no. 2* judgment "provides a detailed and helpful examination of the purposes pursued by prisoner disenfranchisement … Taking due account of the difference in text and structure of the Canadian Charter, the Court nonetheless finds that substance of the reasoning may be regarded as apposite in the present case" (par. 43). It was further noted that "the majority in the Sauvé case also found no evidence to support the claim that disenfranchisement deterred crime and considered that the imposition of a blanket punishment on all prisoners … indicated no rational link between the punishment and the offender" (par. 45).

---

[32] *Sauve v. Canada (Attorney General)*, 27 May 1993.
[33] *Sauve v. Canada (Chief Electoral Officer)*, 31 October 2002.   [34] 418 US 24 (1974).
[35] *Hirst v. the UK* (no. 2), 20 March 2004

Hirst was reheard by the Grand Chamber which, in 2005,[36] confirmed (by a twelve to five majority) the finding of a violation. The Grand Chamber noted the *Sauvé* judgment (as well as the 1999 *August* judgment of the Constitutional Court of South Africa[37]). Although the Grand Chamber seemed less inclined to copy-paste the reasoning of the Canadian Supreme Court[38] and focused on the proportionality analysis,[39] it easily arrived to the conclusion that "such a general, automatic and indiscriminate restriction on a vitally important Convention right must be seen as falling outside any acceptable margin of appreciation, however wide that margin might be" (par. 82).

In the methodological dimension, both *Hirst* judgments were similar to the *Pretty* case in that the ECtHR not only mentioned the Canadian decisions, but also, to a considerable extent, rely on the argumentation of the Supreme Court. At the same time, however, there are two important differences. On the one hand, in *Pretty* (as well as in *Rodriguez*) the courts upheld the domestic legislative solution and such decision removed any potential for conflict with the defendant State. In contrast, *Hirst* (as well as both *Sauvé* judgments) found that the existing legislation was defective which raised the problems of compliance and implementation. On the other hand, while in *Pretty*, the ECtHR was confronted with a clear and well-reasoned judgment of the House of Lords, in *Hirst*, the only domestic decision had been taken on a relative low level of the judicial hierarchy. Thus, there was less risk that the ECtHR holding would provoke an immediate collision with the highest court of the United Kingdom.

The Grand Chamber judgment did not end the disenfranchisement controversy.

In the political dimension, *Hirst* is still awaiting implementation. Unfortunately, the UK authorities not only refused to modify the 1983 Representation of the People Act, but also launched ferocious political attacks at the Court

---

[36] *Hirst v. the UK* (no. 2), 6 October 2005.

[37] *August and Another v. Electoral Commission and Others*, 1999 (4) BCLR 363 (CC).

[38] In particular, it was observed that: "the Court accepts that [the UK legislation] may be regarded as pursuing the aims identified by the Government. It observes that, in its judgment, the Chamber expressed reservations as to the validity of the aims, citing the majority opinion in … Sauvé no. 2. However, whatever doubt there may be as to the efficacy of achieving these aims through the bar on voting, the Court finds no reason in the circumstances of this application to exclude these aims as untenable or incompatible per se with the right guaranteed under Article3 of Protocol No. 1" (par. 75).

[39] In a conciliatory gesture towards the 2001 Divisional Court judgment, the ECtHR observed that "it was evident from the judgment of the DC that the nature of restrictions … was generally seen as a matter for Parliament and not for the national courts. The DC did not, therefore, undertake any assessment of proportionality of the measure itself. It may also be noted that the DC found support in the decision of the Federal Court of Appeals in Sauvé (no. 2) which was later overturned by the Supreme Court" (par. 80).

and its judges. Although, this policy did not find support of the other Convention States, it did not assist the Court in its relations with those States in which observance of human rights presents more serious problems than in the United Kingdom.

In the jurisprudential dimension, the lack of proper implementation of *Hirst* led to several subsequent judicial decisions. The Scottish Registration Appeal Court adopted, in 2007, a declaration of incompatibility of the relevant provision of the 1983 Act in terms of the Human Rights Act.[40] Its position found support of some other courts in the United Kingdom,[41] but they found no need to repeat declarations of incompatibility.[42] Also the Strasbourg Court had no hesitations as to the validity of the *Hirst* judgment. In *Greens*[43] the Court reiterated its position and observed that the continued failure to amend the legislation imposing a blanket ban on voting constitutes a violation of the Convention. The Court decided to apply its "pilot judgment procedure"[44] to the case, it did not, however, prompt any legislative reaction in the United Kingdom. In *Greens*, the Court did not refer, expressly, to *Sauvé*, however, as its confirmed both, the holding and the reasoning of *Hirst*, it was also clear that the "Sauvé spirit" remains alive in Strasbourg.

The *Hirst* judgment was revisited by the Grand Chamber in the 2012 *Scoppola* case.[45] Although the problem was different in that the Italian legislation did not provide for a blanket disenfranchisement of all convicted prisoners, such ban was, nevertheless, applied to all persons convicted of certain offences and sentenced to at least three years of imprisonment. The main question in the case was, therefore, a compatibility of a "partial" ban with the Convention. At the same time, the UK Government, acting as *amicus curiae*, suggested a total overruling of the *Hirst* judgment. The ECtHR held that the Italian regulation remained within the national "margin of appreciation" as each State has a wide discretion as to how it regulates the ban, both as regards the types of offence that should result in the loss of the vote and as to whether disenfranchisement should always be ordered by a judge in an

---

[40] *Smith v. Scott* (2007 SC 345).
[41] See the references in the ECtHR judgment in *Greens and M.T. v. UK* (23 November 2010), par. 27–40.
[42] As the High Court observed in *Chester v. the Secretary of State for Justice* (2009), "I am content to say that there is no need for any declaration to be made by yet another court, as one has already been made which is binding on the UK Government".
[43] *Greens and M.T. v. the UK*, 23 November 2010.
[44] On "pilot judgments" see, L. Garlicki, "*Broniowski and after: On the Dueal Nature of the Pilot Judgments*" in: *Liber Amicorum*, op. cit., p. 177 et seq.; *Responding to Systemic Human Rights Violations*, by Ph. Leach and Others, Intersentia 2010; D. Haider, *The Pilot Judgment Procedure of the ECtHR*, Brill 2013.
[45] *Scoppola v. Italy* (no. 3), 22 May 2012.

individual case or should result from general application of a law.[46] At the same, the Court flatly rejected the UK criticism of *Hirst*[47] and reaffirmed that "when disenfranchisement affects a group of people generally, automatically and indiscriminately, based solely on the fact that they are serving a prison sentence, irrespective of the length of the sentence and irrespective of the nature or gravity of their offence and their individual circumstances, it is not compatible with Article 3 of Protocol No. 1" (par. 96). Therefore, the Court made it clear that while the *Hirst* principles stand, the United Kingdom enjoys a wide margin of appreciation in deciding how to replace its blanket exclusion.

This opening did not help and the United Kingdom is still refusing to implement the *Hirst* judgment. On the other side, the ECtHR is not ready to reconsider its interpretation of the Convention and not only, in several subsequent UK cases, it found a violation of Article 3 of Protocol No. 1[48] but also applied the Scoppola-Hirst approach to other Convention States.[49] The UK Supreme Court had to find its own place between these entrenched positions. It seems that the Justices opted for keeping some distance: while it was confirmed that the prisoners voting ban is incompatible with the Convention, it was also held that a declaration of incompatibility had already been made in *Smith v. Scott* and there is no point in making another one now.[50]

---

[46] In this, the Grand Chamber rejected the position taken in the Chamber judgment *Frodl v. Austria* (8 April 2010), in which it was held that decision on disenfranchisement has always to be made individually by the trial judge.

[47] The Court noted that "it does not appear, however, that anything has occurred or changed at the European and Convention levels since the *Hirst* (no. 2) judgment that might lend support to the suggestion that the principles set forth in that case should be re-examined. On the contrary, analysis of the relevant international and European documents and comparative-law information reveals the opposite trend, if anything – towards fewer restrictions on convicted prisoners' voting rights" (par. 95). The Court again referred to Sauvé (as well as to two other judgments from South Africa and one from Australia), but abstained from quoting this decision in the reasoned part of Scoppola judgment.

[48] *Firth and Others v. the UK* (12 August 2015); *McHugh and Others v. the UK* (10 February 2015 – this case concerned applications of 1015 prisoners).

[49] *Anchugov and Gladkov v. Russia* (4 July 2013); *Murat Vural v. Turkey* (21 October 2014).

[50] *R (Chester) v. Secretary of State for Justice; McGeoch v. The Lord President of the Council* – judgment of 16 October 2013, par. 39–42 (Lord Mance). While the Supreme Court demonstrated some restraint as concerns its own declaration of incompatibility, it rejected, in clear terms, Attorney General's suggestion that the Supreme Court should not followed the Strasbourg case-law on the matter. It was noted that "the Grand Chamber in Scoppola was prepared to give the Italian legislator a greater margin of maneuver than one would have expected from its previous decision in Hirst (No 2). But this was on the basis that the Italian law did not involve a blanket ban in respect of all or almost all convicted prisoners. [...]. Nothing in Scoppola therefore suggests that the Grand Chamber would revise its view in Hirst (No 2) to the point where it would accept the United Kingdom's present general ban. There is on this point no prospect of any further meaningful dialogue between United Kingdom Courts and Strasbourg" (par. 34).

The prisoners' voting cases can be regarded as another example of an extra-systemic absorption. In all important cases, the ECtHR expressly referred to *Sauvé* (no. 2) and "borrowed" several arguments elaborated earlier by the Canadian Supreme Court. Nevertheless, the *Sauvé's* fertilization effect had its limits. Although the ECtHR has always been clear that no blanket and general exclusion of prisoners cannot be accepted, it allowed the Italian solution of a partial ban provided for by the law. This followed *Sauvé* (no. 1), but was not fully in line with *Sauvé* (no. 2).

BEYOND *RODRIGUEZ* AND *SAUVÉ*: A FEW EXAMPLES

The Supreme Court judgments in *Rodriguez* and *Sauvé* were of primary relevance for the position of the Strasbourg Court. Both dealt with sensitive matters which has not yet been addressed in the ECtHR case law and, in sense, helped to fill the gap. The absorption of *Rodriguez* was less direct as it was, at first, re-taken by the House of Lords and only after followed, at least in part, by the ECtHR. By contrast, *Sauvé* was applied by the ECtHR in a more direct (but also more limited) fashion since the UK courts were, at first, not ready to follow the 1993 judgment and, later, were addressing primarily the *Hirst* and *Scoppola* judgments of the ECtHR. On both occasions, the dialogue between the ECtHR and the House of Lords (the UKSC) tended towards a cooperative direction.

The Canadian case law has also been referred to in several other cases, albeit in none of them its impact was of a decisive nature. Most of the cases arrived, not surprisingly, from the United Kingdom and several of them were connected to that national security issues.

In *Chahal* (1996),[51] the ECtHR dealt with the human rights aspects of a deportation of an alleged terrorist. While no Canadian cases have been mentioned, the Court noted (on the initiative of the Amnesty International) the techniques concerning the use of confidential material developed in Canada (par. 144). In A. *and Others* (2009) – indefinite detention of non-deportable aliens of allegedly terrorist attachments),[52] the Court – in reviewing and accepting the UK system of procedural safeguards[53] – referred to the 2007 *Charkaoui*[54] judgment. In 2012, in *Othman (Abu Qatada)*,[55] the Court held

---

[51] *Chahal v. the UK* (15 November 1996).   [52] A. *and Others v. the UK* (19 February 2009).
[53] At the same time, the ECtHR found that the very system of administrative detention was not compatible with the Convention quarantees. The Strasbourg relied on the position taken earlier by the House of Lords which adopted a declaration of incompatibility not followed by tke UK Parliament.
[54] *Charkaoui v. Canada* (Minister of Citizenship and Immigration), 23 February 2007.
[55] *Othman (Abu Qatada) v. the UK* (17 January 2012).

that no extradition could be allowed as long as there is a substantial possibility of the use of torture-extracted evidence at the subsequent trial. In more general consideration of the human rights limits to extraditions and deportations, the ECtHR referred to several Canadian cases, first of all to *Suresh* (2002).[56] In *Babar Ahmad and Others* (2012),[57] the ECtHR reiterated its case law on assurances and referred to *Burns* (2001) and *Ferras* (2006)[58] as well as – in consideration of grossly disproportionate sentences – to *Smith* (1987), *Luxton* (1990) and *Latimer* (2001).[59]

Finally, in both *Vinter* cases,[60] the ECtHR, when considering whether an irreducible life-sentences should be qualified as an inhuman and degrading punishment, recognized to numerous international and foreign authorities, including the Canadian judgments in *Smith*, *Luxton* and *Latimer*.[61]

Canadian judgments were also taken into consideration in other types of cases:

> In *Allan* (2002),[62] the ECtHR, while considering the use of informers to obtain incriminating statements from persons in police custody, quoted *Hebert* (1990), *Broyles* (1991) and *Liew* (1999),[63] as well as one of the

---

[56] *Suresh v. Canada* (Minister of Citizenship and Immigration), 11 January 2002. The Canadian case law was not only mentioned in the general presentation of foreign and international authorities (par. 139–140), but Suresh and Lai Sing were also referred to in the reasoned part of the judgment concerning the necessary level of assurances submitted by the receiving State (par. 189).

[57] *See* FN 16. The ECtHR held that the extradition of all, but one, alleged terrorists to the US would not violate their Convention rights. The Court took into account the assurances of the US authorities that the trial wouldnot take place before a military commission and that no capital punishment would be imposed. The Court held the mere prospect of detention in the super-max facility in Florence (CO) is not sufficient to exclude extradition. The Court mentioned several international and foreign law, due to the obvious grounds, its freferences were focused on the US cases.

[58] *United States v. Burns* (15 February 2001); *United States v. Ferras* (21 July 2006). The European Court observed, however, that "in interpreting Article 3, limited assistance can be derived from the approach taken by the Canadian Supreme Court in Burns and Ferras." Those cases were about the provision of the Canadian Charter on fundamental justice and not the Charter's prohibition on cruel or unusual treatment or punishment. Furthermore, the Charter system expressly provides for a balancing test in respect of both of those rights, which mirrors that found in Articles 8–11 of the Convention but not Article 3 (par. 174).

[59] *R. v. Smith* (25 June 1987); *R. v. Luxton* (13 September 1990); *R. v. Latimer* (18 January 2001).

[60] In the first Vinter judgment (*Vinter and Others v. the UK*, 17 January 2012), the Chamber (by a 4:3 majority) decided that the UK system was compatible with the Convention guarantees. One year later, the Grand Chamber overruled (*Vinter and Others v. the UK*, 9 July 2013) and held that there had been a violation. Although Vinter addressed only the domestic aspects of life-imprisonment-without-parole system, its reasoning was also applied to extradition cases.

[61] *See* FN 57. [62] *Allan v. the UK* (5 November 2002).

[63] *R. v. Hebert* (21 June 1990); *R. v. Broyles* (28 November 1991); *R. v. Liew* (19 March 1999).

Australian cases, and concluded that there had been a violation of Article 6 of the Convention.

In the *Appleby* case[64] (2003), the ECtHR dealt with freedom of expression within private shopping establishments (quasi-public forum). Although the UK Court of Appeal referred to a Canadian case decided in 1975,[65] the ECtHR focused, quite untypically, on the US case-law and only mentioned Justice McLaughlin's obiter in a 1991 case.[66] In *Appleby*, no violation has been found by the Strasbourg Court.[67]

In *S. and Marper*[68] (2008) – retention of fingerprints and DNA samples of persons who have not been eventually charged or convicted), the ECtHR referred to the 2005 *R. v. R.C.* judgment of the Supreme Court of Canada.[69] The ECtHR disagreed with the House of Lord's position[70] and found a violation of Article 8 of the Convention in this case.

Finally, in the *Eweida* case[71] (limitations of wearing a religious symbol in a workplace), the Court – while finding a violation in the case of one of the applicants, considered the Canadian case law on turbans and kirpans.[72]

---

[64] *Appleby and Others v. the UK* (6 May 2003).   [65] *Harrison v. Carswell* (26 June 1975)
[66] "Prior to the entry into force of the Canadian Charter of Rights and Freedoms, the Canadian Supreme Court had taken the view that the owner of a shopping centre could exclude protesters (*Harrison v. Carswell*, 62 DLR (Dominion Law Reports) 3d 68 (1975)). After the Charter entered into force, a lower court held that the right to free speech applied in privately owned shopping centres (*R. v. Layton*, 38 C.C.C. (Canadian Criminal Cases) 3d 550 (1986) (Provincial Court, Judicial District of York, Ontario)). However, an individual judge of the Canadian Supreme Court has since expressed the opposite view, stating obiter that the Charter does not confer a right to use private property as a forum of expression (McLachlin J, *Committee for Cth of Can. v. Canada* [1991] 1 SCR (Canada Supreme Court Reports) 139, 228)" (Appleby, par. 31).
[67] Appleby is interesting as it was one of the cases in which the Court had an opportunity to address the so-called "horizontal effect" of the European Convention (*see* L. Garlicki, "Relations between Private Actors and the ECHR" in: *The Constitution in Private Relations*, ed. by A. Sajo and R. Uitz, Eleven International Publishing 2005, pp. 138–139).
[68] *S. and Marper v. the UK* (4 December 2008).
[69] Gross disproportionality of the retention of a DNA sample of a first-time juvenile offender.
[70] *R. v. Chief Constable of South Yorkshire Police* (22 July 2004). The ECtHR partly concured with Baroness Hale opinion in this case (see S. and Marper, par.86).
[71] *Eweida and Others v. the UK* (15 January 2013).
[72] "41. Religious freedom is constitutionally protected under the Canadian Charter of Rights and Freedoms. Section 1 of the Charter provides the state with authority to infringe on freedom of religion in the least restrictive way possible for a "compelling government interest" (*see B(R) v. Children's Aid Society of Metropolitan Toronto* (1995) 1 SCR 315). Canadian employers, in general, are expected to adjust workplace regulations that have a disproportionate impact on certain religious minorities. The standard applied by the courts in this connection is that of "reasonable accommodation" (*see R v. Big M Drug Mart Limited* (1985) 1 SCR 295). Recent litigation on this point has centred on the rights of Sikh persons to wear a turban or kirpan at

In the non-UK cases, references to the Canadian case law are very rare. One of the most prominent examples was *Nada* v. *Switzerland*[73] (blacklisting of an alleged terrorism supporter). In finding a violation of the Convention (albeit on a very narrow ground), the ECtHR mentioned the Canadian case of *Abdelrazik*[74] as well as the UK Supreme Court judgment in *Ahmed*[75] and the UNHRC opinion in *Sayadi and Vinck*.[76] The primary point of reference, however, constituted the 2008 CJEU judgment in *Kadi*.[77] All the above-mentioned cases (and the second CJEU judgment in *Kadi*[78]) were also cited in the second "blacklisting case" decided by the ECtHR,[79] *Al-Dulimi* v. *Switzerland* (2013).[80]

In the *Hristozov* case[81] (refusal to allowing access to a non-licensed drug for a terminally ill patient), the ECtHR, while finding no violation, considered regulations adopted in Canada (the so-called "special access program" provided in the Food and Drug Regulations), the US and Australia, and also some judicial decision from those countries (including the 2006 *Delislie* judgment of the Federal Court).[82]

---

work. In *Bhinder v. Canadian National Railway Co.* (1985) 2 SCR 561, the Supreme Court determined that the claimant could not wear a turban at work because it interfered with his capacity to wear a hard helmet. This was found to represent a "bona fide occupational requirement". The Canadian courts, rather than purporting to define a religion or religious practice, are more interested in the sincerity of the belief in a practice that has a nexus with a religion (*see Syndicat Northcrest v. Amselem* (2004) 2 SCR 551). In *Multani v. Commission scolaire Marguerite-Bourgeoys* (2006) 1 SCR 256, in which the Supreme Court of Canada upheld a Sikh student's right to wear a kirpan to school, the court did not undertake a theological analysis of the centrality of kirpans to the Sikh faith. Instead, the court considered that the claimant "need[ed] only show that his personal and subjective belief in the religious significance of the kirpan [was] sincere".

[73] Judgment of 12 September 2012.

[74] *Abdelrazik v. the Minister of Foreign Affairs and the Attorney General of Canada*, 2009 FC 580 (4 September 2009).

[75] *Ahmed and Others v. the HM Treasury* (27 January 2010).

[76] *Sayadi and Vinck v. Belgium*, views of the UN Human Rights Committee of 22 October 2008 (Comm. 1472/2006).

[77] *Yasin Abdullah Kaadi and Barakaat International Foundation v. the Council of the EU and the Commission of the EC* (C 402/05 P and C-415/05 P) – 3 September 2008.

[78] *European Commission and Others v. Yasin Abdullah Kadi* (C 584/10 P; C 593/10 P; C 595/ 10 P) – 18 July 2013.

[79] *Al-Dulimi and Montana Management Inc. v. Switzerland* (26 November 2013).

[80] In Al-Dulimi, the ECtHR went much further than in Nada in that it, practically, applied its Bosphorus doctrine (see FN 10) to the UNSC resolutions.. No wonder that the case is now pending before the Grand Chamber.

[81] *Hristozov and Others v. Bulgaria* (13 November 2012).

[82] *Delisle v. Canada* (Attorney General), 2006 FC 933. The Hristozov case had a clear "Canadian connection" as the drug in question was an experimental anti-cancer product (MBVax Coley Fluid) which was being developed by a Canadian company, MBVax Bioscience Inc.

CONCLUSION

The ECtHR references to the Canadian case law are mostly focused on cases arriving from the United Kingdom. This is partly the reflection of references made by the UK courts at the earlier stages of the proceedings, but is also due to the impressive record of the Supreme Court of Canada in human rights cases.[83] That is why the ECtHR mentions Canadian cases also as an additional argument in its discussions with the UKSC (the House of Lords). In brief, a "joint effort" of the Strasbourg Court and the Supreme Court of Canada may influence the Supreme Court of the United Kingdom in its evolution towards constitutional court.[84]

Although the Canadian references are not very often made, it seems that the Supreme Court of Canada is quoted more regularly than any other foreign jurisdiction, including the US Supreme Court and the I-ACtHR.

The Canadian references are usually of mostly informative value, sometimes they play also a legitimization function. On two occasions, the judgments of the Supreme Court of Canada played a more prominent role and – to a considerable extent – "fertilized" the final decisions of the ECtHR.

This is not a right place to debate at length the opposite direction of the relations between Ottawa and Strasbourg and to consider the use made of the ECtHR case law by the Supreme Court of Canada. A recent empirical study[85] showed that, due to obvious reasons, the Supreme Court of Canada looks, in the first place, into other common-law jurisdictions, in the first place – the United States, and then – the United Kingdom, Australia and New Zealand.[86] The ECtHR judgments were referred to in sixty-seven cases which places the Strasbourg on the "fourth place" among foreign jurisdictions. It is neither possible nor necessary to enter into more detailed analysis of those statistical (and therefore – sometimes misleading) data.[87]

---

[83] And, perhaps, also to the dynamic approach of the Supreme Court to the constitutional interpretation. The – already mentioned – Canadian ""living tree" doctrine seems to be not very far from the ECtHR's ""living-instrument" approach.

[84] see Chapter 14 in this volume.

[85] G. Gentili, "Canada: Protecting Rights in a Worldwide Rights Culture: An Empirical Study of the Use of Foreign Precedents by the Supreme Court of Canada" (1982–2010) in: *The use of foreign precedents*, 39ff. *See also* Chapter 13 in this volume.

[86] Between 1982 and 2010, the Supreme Court of Canada cited (in constitutional cases) 1144 US decisions, 502 UK decisions, 81 Australian and 32 New Zealand cases – *see* G. Gentili, op. cit., p. 58.

[87] As observed by G. Gentili: "a clear pattern emerged: English or domestic cases are cited predominantly for federalism issues, while US, Australian, New Zealand and ECtHR precedents predominantly are cited for human rights cases" (id., at 56).

As far as the substance is concerned, it seems sufficient to mention Ran Hirschl's conclusion that "while the contemporary Canadian constitutional sphere is engaging closely with constitutional jurisprudence and constitutional concepts in the area of rights and liberties, the comparative turn has not, by and large, penetrated the discourse concerning some of Canada's structural or organic constitutional failings. In that sense, the promise of comparative constitutional inquiry has not fully materialized."[88]

It is, however, possible to conclude that the relations between the Canadian Supreme Court and the ECtHR are not limited to a one-way process of borrowing/fertilization in isolated cases. It seems that they are developing towards a regular dialogue in which both partners' input is visible, attractive and – at least on the Strasbourg end – influential.

---

[88] Chapter 13 in this volume.

16

Canadian Rights Discourse Travels to the East

Referencing to Canadian Charter Case Laws
by Hong Kong's Court of Final Appeal
and Taiwan's Constitutional Court

WEN-CHEN CHANG

INTRODUCTION

How ideas travel across boundaries has always been an intriguing issue. Colonialism was a dominant driving force for legal imposition or transplantation.[1] With the rise of globalization especially in recent decades, the development of comparative law or transnational judicial dialogue has been made visible in nearly all jurisdictions.[2] There is no exception to Asia. Hong Kong and Taiwan have both been deemed as embracing transnational judicial dialogue, if not already heavily engaging in it.[3] The exchanges of judicial dialogues have been usually made to the United Kingdom (UK) in case of Hong Kong,[4] and to Germany, United States (US) or Japan in case of Taiwan.[5]

Canada, a fairly distant country from Asia, has made a global acclaim for her rights discourse, especially after the enactment of the 1982 Charter of Rights and Freedoms. The Charter includes a bill of rights reflective of

---

The author would like to thank Ms. Shao-Man Lee for her superb research assistance.

[1] W.-C. Chang, L.-A. Thio, K. YL Tan & J.-R. Yeh, CONSTITUTIONALISM IN ASIA: CASES AND MATERIALS (Oxford: Hart Publishing, 2014), 17–18.

[2] T. Groppi & M.-C. Ponthoreau, "The use of foreign precedents by constitutional judges: A limited practice, an uncertain future" in T. Groppi and M.-C. Ponthoreau (eds.), *The Use of Foreign Precedents by Constitutional Judges* (Oxford: Hart Publishing, 2013), 412–31, 413; C. Saunders, "Judicial engagement with comparative law" in T. Ginsburg and R. Dixon (eds.), *Comparative Constitutional Law* (New York: Elgar, 2011), 574.

[3] S. N. M. Young, *Constitutional Rights in Hong Kong's Court of Final Appeal*, 27 CHINESE (TAIWAN) YEARBOOK OF INTERNATIONAL LAW AND AFFAIRS 67 (2011); D. S. Law & W.-C. Chang, *The Limits of Global Judicial Dialogue*, 86 WASHINGTON LAW REVIEW 523 (2010); W.-C. Chang & J.-R. Yeh, "Judges as discursive agent: The use of foreign precedents by the Constitutional Court of Taiwan" in Groppi and Ponthoreau (eds.), *The Use of Foreign Precedents by Constitutional Judges*, 373–392.

[4] Young, *Constitutional Rights*, supra note 3.

[5] Chang & Yeh, "Judges as discursive agent," supra note 3.

and receptive to international human rights, and has developed – by way of judicial articulation – a strong reliance on the principle of proportionality that strikes a delicate balance between competing rights or values.[6] Perhaps not so surprisingly, these features have become less Canadian but more global as they have been found influential to some of nascent constitutional jurisdictions, one example of which was the South African Constitutional Court.[7]

It is particularly intriguing to inquire if the above-featured Canadian rights discourse has found its way to Asia, and if so, what are the driving forces and what may be the impacts. In order to achieve such goals, this chapter is set forth to examine references made to Canadian Charter case laws by the Hong Kong's Court of Final Appeal (HKCFA), a common law court, and Taiwan's Constitutional Court (TCC), a civil law court. By carefully observing the ways by which referencing to Canadian Charter case laws was made in the HKCFA and TCC, this chapter is aimed at finding whether legal family or legal tradition is still a key factor on how law travels, and what other factors may be more determinative in directing the development and impacts of comparative constitutional studies or transnational judicial dialogues.

Aside from the introduction and conclusion, this chapter is divided into three main parts. Part I and Part II analyze the references to Canadian Charter case laws respectively by the HKCFA and TCC, followed by functional analyses in Part III. Special focuses are placed on the analyses of legal family or recognition of courts, the differences between judge-initiated or litigant-initiated references, open or reticent attitudes for references and last but not the least, functions of references in terms of protecting or restricting rights.

HONG KONG'S COURT OF FINAL APPEAL REFERENCING TO CANADIAN CHARTER CASE LAWS

The Basic Law of Hong Kong expressly permits the courts to refer to precedents of other common law jurisdictions.[8] Since the Basic Law became effective on 1 July 1997, Hong Kong courts have never been shy away from referencing to cases of other jurisdictions. According to a research conducted

---

[6] See, e.g., J. Webber, THE CONSTITUTION OF CANADA: A CONTEXTUAL ANALYSIS (Oxford: Hart Publishing, 2015), 186–89.

[7] Groppi & Ponthoreau, "The use of foreign precedents by constitutional judges," supra note 2, at 419.

[8] Article 84 of Hong Kong Basic Law states that the courts of the Hong Kong Special Administrative Region shall adjudicate cases in accordance with the laws applicable in the Region as prescribed in Article 18 of this Law and may refer to precedents of other common law jurisdictions.

by Simon Young, a professor at the University of Hong Kong Faculty of Law, most foreign references were still made to the UK, a clear influence from the colonial past plus the continued presence of eminent overseas judges sitting on the HKCFA.[9] Noticeably, Hong Kong courts have referred not only to common law courts, but also to other world-renowned courts, for example, the European Court of Human Rights (ECtHR).[10] Between 1999 and 2009, in all of majority, concurring and dissenting opinions, 48 per cent of these opinions made references to UK cases laws and 27 per cent of them made references to non-Hong Kong and non-UK authorities such as Canada and United States (9 per cent), international courts (8 per cent), Australia and New Zealand (7 per cent), among others.[11]

The following analyzes the references that the HKCFA has made to the case laws of the Canadian Charter of Rights and Freedoms (Canadian Charter). Having researched on both the database of the Legal Reference System of the Judiciary of the Hong Kong[12] and Westlaw, using "Canadian Charter" as the exact search phrase, I found only nine cases in which such references were made in the majority opinion of the HKCFA between 2001 and 2006. While references to Canadian Charter case laws continue to appear in lower courts,[13] no such reference has appeared in the HKCFA since 2006.

References by Judges

Among the nine cases with references to Canadian Charter case laws, five cases include references initiated by judges while four cases contain references initiated by litigant parties. In the following 5 cases, 4 cases concern criminal matters and only one case involve civil matters.

Secretary for Justice v. Lam Tat Ming & Another

The first case of HKCFA's referencing to Canadian Charter case laws was *Secretary for Justice v. Lam Tat Ming & Another* decided in 2000.[14] The respondents were police officers facing corruption charges. In an undercover operation, conversations during which the police officers incriminated

[9] Young, *Constitutional Rights*, supra note 3. [10] *Id.* at 82 [11] *Id.*
[12] Legal Reference System, available at http://legalref.judiciary.gov.hk/lrs/common/ju/judgment.jsp (last visited July 8, 2016).
[13] Using the same database, I found 24 cases referencing to Canadian Charter case laws in the Hong Kong Court of Appeal between 1987 and 2016, 57 cases in the Hong Kong Court of First Instance between 1991 and 2014 and 9 cases in the Hong Kong District Court between 1991 and 2015.
[14] *Secretary for Justice v. Lam Tat Ming & Another*, 3 HKCFAR 168 (2000).

themselves were tape-recorded. While the prosecution relied on those state-ments, the police officers sought to challenge their admissibility. The trial judge held that those self-incriminatory statements were involuntary and hence inadmissible. The attention of appeal was drawn to the trial judge's discretion to exclude the evidence and examining whether there was manifest unfairness upon the respondents by the undercover operation. The appeal court agreed with the exclusion of evidence and dismissed the prosecution's appeal.[15]

Interestingly however, the HKCFA reversed the judgement of acquittals and remitted the matter to the trial judge.[16] According to the HKCFA, con-fessions obtained by undercover operations are not necessarily exclusionary or compromising a fair trial. Whether a suspect's right to silence is infringed depends on the dynamics of undercover operations especially given their valuable use in ongoing criminal activities.[17] If what an undercover officer is merely to provide a speaking opportunity for the suspects, there is no persua-sive reason to exclude such confessions. If however what the officer does amounts to interrogation, the discretion to exclude the evidence must be exercised.[18] The HKCFA supported this line of reasoning by referring exten-sively to Hong Kong and English authorities, followed by in passing references to Australian and Canadian authorities. Without any substantial discussion, the HKCFA simply noted that "[i]n Canada, the matter has developed based on the right to silence held to be included in s.7 of the Canadian Charter of Rights and Freedoms. That section provides that: "Everyone has the right to life, liberty and security of the person and the right not to be deprived thereof except in accordance with the principles of fundamental justice." See R v. Broyles (1991) 9 CR (4th) 1; R v. Hebert (1990) 77 CR (3d) 145."[19]

Shum Kwok Sher v. HKSAR

Two years later, in 2002, the HKCFA made again a very brief reference to Canadian Charter case laws in Shum Kwok Sher v. HKSAR.[20] In this criminal case, the appellant was a civil servant convicted of four misconduct offences as he used his position to provide preferential treatments to an interested party for tenders. On appeal, the appellant argued that the common law offence of public misconduct as set out in an English precedent[21] was so vague, uncer-tain and ill-defined as to be unconstitutional. According to that English case, the offence must be of such a degree that the misconduct impugned was calculated to injure the public interest for condemnation and punishment.

[15] Id. at 175.   [16] Id. at 186.   [17] Id. at 180–81.   [18] Id. at 181.   [19] Id. at 185.
[20] Shum Kwok Sher v. Hksar, 5 Hkcfar 381 (2002).   [21] R v. Dytham [1979] Qb 722.

Yet, art.28 and art.39 of the Hong Kong Basic Law guarantee the freedom of the person from unlawful or arbitrary imprisonment, and do not permit the restrictions of a basic right unless prescribed by law. The same can be said to the Hong Kong Bill of Rights Ordinance (the Ordinance) providing for the incorporation of the International Covenant on Civil and Political Rights (ICCPR) as applied for Hong Kong.[22]

The HKCFA disagreed with the appellant. According to the HKCFA, in interpreting the provisions of the Basic Law and the Ordinance, it may take account of "the established principles of international jurisprudence as well as decisions of international and national courts or tribunals on like or substantially similar provisions in the ICCPR, other international instruments and national constitutions."[23] The HKCFA understood the requirement of "prescribed by law" in both the Basic Law and the Ordinance as mandating the principle of legal certainty, and consulted the decisions of ECtHR on the same requirement stipulated in the European Convention on Human Rights and Fundamental Freedoms (the European Convention). Following that, the HKCFA made a brief reference to Canadian Charter case laws,[24] along with the decisions of the Privy Council. The HKCFA clarified that the elements of the common law offence in this case included 1) a public official, 2) who in the course of or in relation to his public office, 3) willfully and intentionally, and 4) culpably misconducted himself in a serious way, and so understood, they were not at all imprecise or arbitrary against those international authorities referenced.[25]

HKSAR v. Lee Ming Tee & Securities and Futures Commission

The third time that the HKCFA initiated a reference to Canadian Charter case laws was in *HKSAR v. Lee Ming Tee & Securities and Futures Commission* decided in 2003.[26] Like the first time, s.7 of the Canadian Charter was made references to. In this case, the respondent was charged with conspiracy to defraud and publishing false statements of account. The trial of first instance was aborted after a forensic expert witness failed to disclose his connection with the company under investigation. The trial judge granted a permanent stay on the ground of intolerable abuses of process. The HKCFA

---

[22] *Shum Kwok Sher v. HKSAR*, 5 HKCFAR 381, 400. [23] *Id.* at 401–02.

[24] It states that "the Supreme Court of Canada has expressed the principle of legal certainty in like terms in the context of fundamental rights and freedoms guaranteed by the Canadian Charter of Rights and Freedoms (*R v. Nova Scotia Pharmaceutical Society* (1992) 74 CCC (3d) 289; *R v. Morales* (1992) 77 CCC (3d) 91)." *Id.* at 402.

[25] *Id.* at 410.

[26] *HKSAR v. Lee Ming Tee & Securities and Futures Commission*, 6 HKCFAR 336 (2003).

however allowed the prosecution's appeal and remitted the matter to the trial judge for the respondent to be tried. According to the HKCFA, that the prosecution bore a common law duty to disclose to the defence material or information in its possession in the interests of a fair trial was not disputed, but what was really disputed was the nature and scope of that duty.[27]

In searching for guiding principles, the HKCFA traced the development of the common law duty to disclosure, first extensively in England and then briefly in Canada. It was found that although the breach of the prosecution's duty of disclosure may result in the setting aside of a conviction, there may be exceptions or qualifications on the basis of a fair trial.[28] In referencing to Canada, the HKCFA noted that the general rule was that all relevant information must be disclosed, subject to the discretion to withhold information due to privilege consideration or to delay disclosure so as not to impede an investigation.[29] More importantly, while s.7 of the Canadian Charter has given a new rigour to the common law right of the accused to make full answer and defence as one of the principles of fundamental justice, the Canadian Supreme Court has made exceptions to that right where "evidence is beyond the control of prosecution, clearly irrelevant, privileged or subject to a right of privacy."[30] Eventually, the HKCFA decided that the failed disclosure of information by the expert witness in the case has not sufficed a stay when a fair trial may still be possible.

So Wai Lun v. HKSAR

In 2006, again in a criminal case, Canadian Charter provisions as well as case laws were made reference to. In *So Wai Lun v. HKSAR*, the appellant was convicted of unlawful sexual intercourse with a girl under the age of 16, contrary to s.124 of the Crimes Ordinance.[31] Yet, he challenged the constitutionality of that provision, arguing that it criminalized the conduct of the male to the exclusion of the female, and thus was arbitrary as violating art.28 of the Hong Kong Basic Law and deprived the male of equality before the law as guaranteed under art.25 of the same document. The HKCFA however found no such violations.

In considering whether the impugned criminal provision deprived the male of equal protection, the HKCFA referred to the cases of the United States Supreme Court, Canadian Supreme Court and the Supreme Court of Ireland.[32] All of these cases found similar criminal provisions in their

---

[27] *Id.* at 382.   [28] *Id.* at 382.   [29] *Id.* at 386.
[30] *R. v. O'Conner* (1996) 130 DLR (4th) 235, 238 G-H.
[31] *So Wai Lun v. HKSAR*, 9 HKCFAR 530 (2006).   [32] *Id.* at 539–40.

respective countries no violation of male equality. Intriguingly, the HKCFA discussed Canadian Charter provisions and case laws more extensively than the US or Ireland ones. The HKCFA specifically referred to *R v. Nguyen & Another*,[33] in which the Supreme Court of Canada reviewed the constitutionality of a similar provision that penalized a male person having sexual intercourse with a female person under the age of 14, noting that Canada's top court found no violations of four sections in the Charter including s.1 that permitted reasonable limits to Charter rights, s.7 on liberty of persons, s.15 of equal protection in general, and s.28 of sex equality.[34]

Town Planning Board v. Society for the Protection of the Harbour

All of the above-discussed cases where the HKCFA initiated references to Canadian Charter were in a criminal context. The only civil case of judge-initiated references was *Town Planning Board v. Society for the Protection of the Harbour*.[35]

In this case, the appellant, the Town Planning Board, decided to submit a plan that proposed reclaiming 26 hectares from Victoria Harbour to the Chief Executive-in-Council for approval. The respondent, an NGO who opposed to such an excessive reclamation in the Harbour, challenged that the Board misinterpreted the Protection of the Harbour Ordinance which should be read as having a presumption against reclamation by demanding the Harbour to be protected and preserved as a special public asset and a natural heritage of Hong Kong people.[36] The respondent was successful before the lower court finding that the Board indeed misinterpreted the Ordinance and confirmed an assumption against reclamation, to be rebutted only if 1) there was a compelling interest, overriding and present public need for reclamation, 2) there was no viable alternative to reclamation, and 3) the proposed reclamation involved minimum impairment to the Harbour.[37] The Board obtained a grant for direct appeal to the HKCFA.

The HKCFA, while agreeing that the Board misinterpreted the Ordinance, held that the lower court's test in overriding the assumption against the reclamation was too rigid and "going too far."[38] In arriving at a proper test for statutory interpretation, the HKCFA consulted the Supreme Court of Canada.[39] As the HKCFA noted, the Supreme Court of Canada held in *R v. Chaulk*[40]

---

[33] 59 CCC (3d) 161 (1990). [34] *So Wai Lun v. HKSAR*, 9 HKCFAR 530, 539–40 (2006).
[35] *Town Planning Board v. Society for the Protection of the Harbour*, 7 HKCFAR 1 (2004).
[36] *Id.* at 1–2. [37] *Id.* at 12–13. [38] *Id.* at 20. [39] *Id.* at 18–9.
[40] *R v. Chaulk*, (1990) 62 CCC (3d) 193.

that whether a statutory presumption of sanity was inconsistent with the constitutional assumption of innocence guaranteed by s.11 of the Charter[41] must be judged by the test developed in *R v. Oakes*.[42] According to the test, first, the objective of the impugned provision must be sufficiently important to warrant overriding a constitutionally protected right and such an objective must relate to concerns which are pressing and substantial in a free and democratic society, and secondly, the means chosen to achieve such an objective must pass a proportionality test as they must: a) be rationally connected to the objective and not be arbitrary, unfair or based on irrational considerations; b) impair the right or freedom in question as little as possible, and c) be such that their effects on the limitation of rights and freedoms are proportional to the objective.[43] Eventually the Supreme Court of Canada ruled that the statutory presumption of sanity satisfied the Oakes test and was justified in limiting constitutional presumption of innocence.[44]

Having acknowledged that the Oakes test was developed for constitutional interpretation while the issue at hand was concerned with statutory, the HKCFA nevertheless decided to adopt the Oakes test for the proper interpretation of the Ordinance. For the HKCFA, the test developed by the lower court demanded the presumption against reclamation to "be rebutted by a need which the community cannot do without, which "would be going too far"[45] but the Oakes test permitted such a presumption to be overridden if the objective would be sufficiently important and the means chosen to achieve such an objective reasonable and proportional.[46] Accordingly, the HKCFA dismissed the appeal but also remitted the case to the Board for reconsideration of the matter.[47]

References by Litigant Parties

In the following four cases where references were made by litigant parties, only one case involved civil matters as opposed to the other three criminal cases. It is also worth noting that all four cases in which litigant parties made references to Canadian Charter case laws concentrated between 2001 and 2002.

---

[41] S.11 of Canadian Charter guarantees that any person charged with an offence has the right to be presumed innocent until proven guilty according to law in a fair and public hearing by a independent and impartial tribunal.

[42] *R v. Oakes*, (1986) 24 CCC (3d) 321, 26 DLR (4th) 200.

[43] *Town Planning Board v. Society for the Protection of the Harbour*, 7 HKCFAR 1, 19 (2004).

[44] *Id.* at 19.   [45] *Id.* at 20.   [46] *Id.* at 20.   [47] *Id.* at 22.

HKSAR v. Lee Ming Tee & Another

The first case in which litigant parties made references to Canadian Charter case laws was *HKSAR v. Lee Ming Tee & Another*[48] decided in 2001, a year after the HKCFA initiated the first reference to Canadian Charter in *Secretary for Justice v. Lam Tat Ming & Another* in 2000.[49]

In *HKSAR v. Lee Ming Tee & Another*,[50] the issue was concerned with the right against self-incrimination. The respondents, directors in a group of companies, were under investigation pursuant to the Companies Ordinance, which authorized the inspector to examine company officers and compulsorily obtain information. The Ordinance further prescribed that individuals under such investigation could not be excused from answering questions on the ground that it might incriminate them, but assured that the answers could not used as evidence against them in criminal proceedings if the individuals claimed privilege before answering questions.[51] After the investigation, the appellees were charged with conspiracy to defraud and publishing false statement of account. The trial judge, however, ordered a permanent stay as the trial was the result of the inspector's power abuse and the violation of respondents' right against self-incrimination. The prosecutor appealed against the order of stay to the HKCFA.

To articulate both direct and derivative use immunities on the basis of the right against self-incrimination, the respondents suggested the HKCFA to follow the approach adopted by the Canadian decisions in the context of the Canadian Charter.[52] After a thorough discussion of relevant Canadian Charter provisions and case laws, however, the HKCFA held that "the Canadian jurisprudence does not provide any basis for deducing a derivative use immunity" in Hong Kong as "the Canadian case law developed in a highly specific context, responding to the peculiar statutory and constitutional needs and values of that jurisdiction."[53] The HKCFA stated that s.13 of the Canadian Charter guaranteed the right against self-incrimination, and due to the narrower scope of s.13, the Canadian Supreme Court "took steps to broaden the scope of protection by recognizing that the privilege against self-incrimination had the status of a principle of fundamental justice" under s.7 of the Charter,[54] and has "settled on the recognition of a direct use

[48] *HKSAR v. Lee Ming Tee & Another*, 4 HKCFAR 133 (2001).

[49] *Secretary for Justice v. Lam Tat Ming & Another*, 3 HKCFAR 168 (2000).

[50] *HKSAR v. Lee Ming Tee & Another*, 4 HKCFAR 133 (2001).   [51] *Id.* at 133.

[52] *Thomson Newspaper Ltd v. Canada* (1990) 67 DLR (4th) 161; *RJS v. The Queen* (1995) 121 DLR (4th) 589; and *British Columbia Securities Commission v. Branch* (1995) 123 DLR (4th) 462.

[53] *HKSAR v. Lee Ming Tee & Another*, 4 HKCFAR 133, 179 (2001).   [54] *Id.* at 178.

prohibition plus a "partial derivative use immunity" after initial doubts as to the nature and extent of alternative protections.[55]

The HKCFA stressed that given different constitutional and statutory contexts of Hong Kong and Canada, the issues facing the Canadian Supreme Court were not the same as those arising in the present case. Accordingly the HKCFA concluded that in the constitutional, legislative and common law context of Hong Kong, the impact of directly or derivatively using compulsorily obtained evidence on the fairness of a trial and on the presumption of innocence must be assessed, not in absolute terms, but by balancing the competing public interests.[56] Interestingly, perhaps for additional justification, the HKCFA specifically noted that its balancing approach would still be in line with a decision rendered by the Privy Council.[57] In the end, the HKCFA unanimously granted the appeal, set aside the order of permanent stay and remitted the matter to the Court of First Instance for the accused to be tried before a different judge.[58]

Ma Bik Yung v. Ko Chuen

The second case, *Ma Bik Yung v. Ko Chuen* decided in 2001, in which litigant parties referred to Canadian Charter case laws was concerned with an apology order against an unwilling respondent.[59] The appellant of this case, a paraplegic, was insulted by the respondent, a taxi driver, when he boarded the taxi. The appellant considered such an insult discriminatory under the Disability Discrimination Ordinance, and sued the respondent. The district court ordered the respondent to pay damages and make an apology to the appellant. The respondent appealed and succeeded in quashing the order of apology and reducing the compensation.[60] The appellant made an appeal to the HKCFA.

The respondent, the taxi driver who insulted the appellant, the paraplegic, referred to a number of Canadian decisions to argue that an order of apology would contravene the freedom to express one's opinions.[61] For example, in *National Bank of Canada v. Retail Clerks' International Union*,[62] the Canadian Supreme Court declared that a letter in specified terms be sent by the bank's president to all employees was totalitarian, and that the parliament could not have intended to confer such a power to impose it. In particular, the HKCFA's attention was drawn to two Canadian cases in the context of

---

[55] *Id.* at 178.   [56] *Id.* at 179.   [57] *Brown v. Stoot*, SLT 59 (2001).
[58] *HKSAR v. Lee Ming Tee & Another*, 4 HKCFAR 133, 195 (2001).
[59] *Ma Bik Yung v. Ko Chuen*, 9 HKCFAR 888 (2001).   [60] *Id.* at 888.   [61] *Id.* at 905–07.
[62] 1 SCR 269 (1984).

employment, in which the employers were demanded for issuing letters of recommendation or apologies. In *Slaight Communications Inc v. Davidson*,[63] the Supreme Court of Canada ruled the orders requiring employers to provide unjustly dismissed employees a letter of recommendation as infringing the freedom of thought, belief, opinion and expression, but those orders were nevertheless saved pursuant to s.1 of the Canadian Charter, which subjected fundamental rights and freedoms to "reasonable limits prescribed by law as can be demonstrably justified in a free and democratic society." In *Perera v. Canada*,[64] it was also ruled that an apology order by an employer who systematically discriminated employees could only be granted if the limits to the freedom of thought were justifiable under s.1 of the Canadian Charter.

Having carefully discussed these Canadian cases, the HKCFA concluded that whether an apology order could be issued was a question that could not be answered in the abstract without knowledge of all the circumstances of the case.[65] The circumstances to be considered in each case will include the defendant's circumstances and the reasons for his or her unwillingness to apologize. The HKCFA reasoned that before an order for an apology could be made against an unwilling defendant, it would be required that an apology be a reasonable act for the defendant to perform in the circumstance of the case in question. With an unwilling defendant, an apology – which would be an insincere one – would usually not be a reasonable act, but there may be exceptional cases where an apology – albeit insincere – would be reason-able.[66] However, the HKCFA eventually held that the circumstances of the present case did not fall into the exceptional cases, and as a result, dismissed the appeal and sustained the quashing of the apology order by the Court of Appeal.

Li Defan & Another v. HKSAR

The third case in which Canadian Charter case laws were referred to by litigant parties was *Li Defan & Another v. HKSAR* decided in 2002.[67] In this case, the defendant was charged with bribery, but the prosecution had no direct evidence as to why the money was paid. During the investigation, the defendant had provided explanations of why he paid the money, which the trial judge rejected. However, in the trial, the defendant refused to give any explanation on oath as to why the money was paid, which strengthened the

---

[63] 1 SCR 1038 (1989).   [64] 3 FC 381 (1998), 158 DLR (4th) 341 (1998).
[65] *Ma Bik Yung v. Ko Chuen*, 9 HKCFAR 888, 907 (2006).   [66] *Id.* at 908.
[67] *Li Defan & Another v. HKSAR*, 5 HKCFAR 320 (2002).

inference to be drawn for the prosecution and the defendant was convicted.[68] Arguing that his right against self-incrimination as well as a broader right of silence was infringed,[69] the defendant appealed to the HKCFA.

The lawyer for the defendant, now the appellant, had a powerful reliance on a judgment of the Canadian Supreme Court, *R v. Noble*,[70] which gave a right of silence construction to provisions in the Canadian Charter very similar to those in the Hong Kong Bill of Rights Ordinance.[71] The HKCFA, however, did not find the majority judgment in *R v. Noble* and its reasoning convincing.[72] For the HKCFA, the situation in the present case could not be said to "compel" the accused to give evidence. Drawing on the case laws of the Privy Council, the HKCFA reasoned that the absence of a denial or explanation by the accused might sometimes give the prosecution evidence greater probative force.[73] The HKCFA also disagreed with too broad a construction of the right of silence, as such a right was "a generic label for a number of rules having the common characteristic that an individual is in certain circumstances not to be compelled to give information," but "what those circumstances are and what would count as being compelled for the purpose of a particular rule cannot be deduced from the label."[74] Accordingly, the HKCFA unanimously dismissed the appeal.

Lau Cheong & Another v. HKSAR

The fourth, and the last, case where litigant parties made reference to Canadian Charter case laws was *Lau Cheong & Another v. HKSAR*, also decided in 2002.[75] The appellants were convicted of murder according to the grievous bodily harm rule, under which a killing accompanied by an intention to cause grievous bodily harm constituted murder, and imposed with mandatory life sentences pursuant to the Offences against the Persons Ordinance.[76] Having relied upon Canadian Charter case laws along with other English and European authorities, the appellants argued that the grievous bodily harm rule

---

[68] *Id.* at 320.   [69] *Id.* at 329–30.   [70] (1997) 114 CCC (3d) 385.
[71] *Li Defan & Another v. HKSAR*, 5 HKCFAR 320, 330 (2002). Art. 11(2)(g) of the Hong Kong Bill of Rights provides that in the determination of a criminal charge against him, everyone shall be entitled not to be compelled to testify against himself or to confess guilt. S.13 of the Canadian Charter proscribes that a witness who testifies in any proceedings has the right not to have any incriminating evidence so given used to incriminate that witness in any other proceedings, except in a prosecution for perjury or for the giving of contradictory evidence.
[72] *Li Defan & Another v. HKSAR*, 5 HKCFAR 320, 330 (2002).   [73] *Id.* at 330.
[74] *Id.* at 330–31.   [75] *Lau Cheong & Another v. HKSAR*, 5 HKCFAR 415 (2002).
[76] *Id.* at 415.

as well as the mandatory life sentence was arbitrary and disproportionate, thus violating their freedoms of person guaranteed in the Hong Kong Bill of Rights Ordinance and art.28 of the Basic Law.[77]

On the issue of the grievous bodily harm rule, the appellants made references to the two decisions of the Canadian Supreme Court, *R v. Vaillancourt*[78] and *R v. Martineau*,[79] to support their argument that a separate mens rea for murder should have been required. The HKCFA, having carefully discussed the two cases and related Canadian Charter provisions, however, decided not to accept the views expressed by the Canadian authority.[80] The HKCFA distinguished the present case from the two Canadian cases, stating that the requirement in Hong Kong law of an intention to cause grievous bodily harm is a subjective form of mens rea far-removed from the constructive liability created by the compared Canadian criminal law provision.[81] It was therefore incorrect to conclude that the grievous bodily harm rule offended any principles of fundamental justice.

On the more challenging issue of death penalty, the appellants put forward a line of foreign cases including Canadian ones, arguing that the mandatory life sentence for murder constituted a cruel, inhuman or degrading punishment because it would inevitably be disproportionate in some cases.[82] Before having any substantial discussions on these foreign authorities, the HKCFA made an intriguing remark on their comparability. In its view, because these foreign authorities were concerned with death penalty, their assessments of disproportionality in relation to mandatory death sentence cases may "proceed on a qualitatively different footing and provide no authority for the assessment" in the preset case.[83] Still, the HKCFA continued discussing on these cases, comparable or not.[84]

---

[77] Sec. 1, Art. 28 of the Hong Kong Basic Law guarantees that the freedom of the person of Hong Kong residents shall be inviolable. Sec. 2 of the same Article further states that no Hong Kong resident shall be subjected to arbitrary or unlawful arrest, detention or imprisonment. Arbitrary or unlawful search of the body of any resident or deprivation or restriction of the freedom of the person shall be prohibited. Torture of any resident or arbitrary or unlawful deprivation of the life of any resident shall be prohibited.

[78] (1987) 47 DLR (4th) 399.   [79] (1990) 58 CCC (3d) 353.

[80] *Lau Cheong & Another v. HKSAR*, 5 HKCFAR 415, 437–40 (2002).   [81] *Id.* at 439.

[82] *Id.* at 455.   [83] *Id.* at 456.

[84] The HKCFA indeed found a case by the Privy Council, *Reyes v. the Queen*, "no authority" for the present case. For, in *Reyes v. the Queen*, the effect of the Privy Council's order – striking down the mandatory death sentence – was to remit the case to the trial judge for re-sentencing where the judge's options were either to impose a death sentence afresh as a matter of discretion or in default of doing so. As no similar legal or institutional preconditions existed in the present case, *Reyes v. the Queen* was "therefore certainly no authority for the proposition

The council for the appellants referred to one Canadian case, *United States of America v. Burns and Rafay*,[85] in which the Supreme Court of Canada held that the extradition of defendants facing death penalty was a cruel and inhuman punishment. Interestingly however, the HKCFA referred two other decisions made by the Supreme Court of Canada, *R v. Luxton*[86] and *R v. Latimer*,[87] where the mandatory life sentence for murder was held not infringing relevant provisions of Canadian Charter.[88] In the former case, the Canadian Supreme Court held constitutional the mandatory life sentence with the mandatory minimum periods of ineligibility for parole, by demonstrating the proportionality between the moral turpitude of the offender and the malignity of the offence, in addition to other objectives of a system of sentencing so identified.[89] In the latter case, the mandatory life sentence for murder was held not "grossly disproportionate" or infringing relevant Charter provisions.[90] The HKCFA also referred to *R v. Smith*,[91] a case establishing that the threshold for such disproportionality as would suffice to make a punishment cruel or inhuman was either the same or higher than the threshold for arbitrariness.[92]

On the basis of these relevant authorities, the HKCFA concluded with an approach to assessing disproportionality of mandatory life sentence: considering individual culpability, factoring in other legitimate penological aims, and also giving due weight to the legislative choice of sentence. Having considered the gravity of the crime and gave the particular weight to the legislature's insistence on a statute-based regime for review by an independent board of all life sentences, the HKCFA eventually maintained the sentencing of this case and dismissed the appeal.

It is worth nothing here that in all of four cases where the Canadian Charter references were initiated by litigant parties, not a single reference was deemed relevant by the majority opinion. The HKCFA either found the Canadian Charter case laws unconvincing, distinguished them from Hong Kong case laws or found them not interfering with the present doctrine. The judicial attitude for litigant-initiated reference is clearly very different from that for judge-initiated reference.

that a mandatory life sentence is to be regarded as inhuman or degrading punishment."
Id. at 456.
[85] *United States of America v. Burns and Rafay* (2001) 151 CCC (3d) 97.
[86] (1990) 58 CCC (3d) 449. [87] (2001) 150 CCC (3d) 129.
[88] *Lau Cheong & Another v. HKSAR*, 5 HKCFAR 415, 456 (2002). [89] Id. at 457–58.
[90] Id. at 458–59. [91] *R v. Smith (Edward Dewey)* (1987) 34 CCC (3d) 97.
[92] *Lau Cheong & Another v. HKSAR*, 5 HKCFAR 415, 459 (2002).

TAIWAN'S CONSTITUTIONAL COURT REFERENCING
TO CANADIAN CHARTER CASE LAWS

TCC enjoys an exclusive power to review and invalidate unconstitutional statutes and all other subsidiary rules.[93] Through its own construction, it also exercises the power to review and invalidate unconstitutional constitutional amendment.[94] Established in 1948, the TCC did not function effectively until the democratization began in the late 1980s.[95] The number of decisions, published as "interpretations," was merely 200 by 1985, but has since risen sharply and reached to 739 as of July 2016.[96] The ratio of TCC's unconstitutional findings is also high in recent years: in 67 out of 150 interpretations (45 per cent) made between 2003 and 2013, the TCC held impugned rules unconstitutional.[97]

Standing as an assertive court, the TCC has been known for its extensive engagements in comparative constitutional analysis.[98] Unlike common law courts, the TCC has rarely made direct and explicit references to foreign or international laws in majority opinions.[99] However this does not mean that the TCC has not considered foreign or international laws in the course of decision-making. The TCC's extensive engagement in comparative analysis has been well documented,[100] and one of the indicators is frequent references to foreign or international laws in concurring or dissenting opinions issued by individual justices.[101] For example, from *JY Interpretation No 1* to *No 680*,

---

[93] Articles 78 & 79 of Taiwan's Constitution officially titled the Republic of China (ROC) Constitution. The ROC Constitution was promulgated on the Chinse mainland in 1946 but has since only applied to Taiwan after the ROC government was defeated by the Chinese Communist Party that subsequently established the People's Republic China on the Chinese mainland.

[94] In *JY Interpretation No 499* decided in 2000, the Constitutional Court reviewed and invalidated the constitutional revision of 1999 due to both procedural and substantive constitutional violations. More recently, the Constitutional Court also reviewed but sustained the constitutional revision of 2000 regarding the revision of parliamentary electoral rule.

[95] For discussions on Taiwan's constitutional development including that of the Constitutional Court, *see* J.-r. Yeh, THE CONSTITUTION OF TAIWAN: A CONTEXTUAL ANALYSIS (Oxford: Hart Publishing, 2016); T. Ginsburg, JUDICIAL REVIEW IN NEW DEMOCRACIES: CONSTITUTIONAL COURTS IN ASIAN CASES (Cambridge University Press, 2003), 106–57.

[96] The most recent judgment of the Constitutional Court, *JY Interpretation No 739*, was made on 29 July 2016. The Court's first decision, *JY Interpretation No 1*, was made on 6 January 1948.

[97] Yeh, THE CONSTITUTION OF TAIWAN, supra note 95, at 170.

[98] Law & Chang, *The Limits of Global Judicial Dialogue*, supra note 3.

[99] *Id.* at 557–58. *See also* Chang & Yeh, "Judges as discursive agent," supra note 3.

[100] Law & Chang, *The Limits of Global Judicial Dialogue*, supra note 3, at 558–62; Chang & Yeh, "Judges as discursive agent," supra note 3, at 379–80.

[101] Law & Chang, *The Limits of Global Judicial Dialogue*, supra note 3, at 557–58; Chang & Yeh, "Judges as discursive agent," supra note 3, at 382–83.

altogether 685 opinions – including majority, concurring and dissenting – were issued, and among them, 108 separate opinions (15.8 per cent) referred to foreign case laws. In all of these majority and separate opinions, the foreign judicial decisions – explicitly referred to – were mostly from Germany (291 citations), the United States (120 citations), Japan (52 citations), the European Court of Justice and the European Court of Human Rights (23 citations).[102]

The following analyses the references that the TCC has made to the Canadian Charter case laws. Having researched on the TCC's website,[103] I found only two interpretations with references to Canadian Charter case laws: one – *JY Interpretation No 617* – by a judge in his dissenting opinion and the other – *JY Interpretation No 577* – by litigant parties in their petitions. Additionally, there are another two interpretations – *JY Interpretation Nos 689 and 708* – where Canadian Charter rights or constitutional practices were briefly mentioned by individual justices in their separate opinions. Similar to Hong Kong, slightly more references were made by judges than by litigant parties. All of these references were made in the recent years, and the first in *JY Interpretation No 577* was in 2004.

References by Judges

The explicit reference to Canadian Charter case laws appeared in the dissenting-in-part opinion by Justice Tzu-Yi Lin in *JY Interpretation No. 617* decided in 2006.[104] In this interpretation, the TCC considered the constitutionality of art.235 of the Criminal Code penalizing a person who distributed or sold, among other means, obscene or sexually explicit materials or objects. The petitioners, owners of bookstores including one well-known gay bookstore, were convicted and sought to challenge the constitutionality of that criminal provision on the ground of free speech.

Having acknowledged that the circulation of sexually explicit material should fall into constitutional protection of the freedoms of speech and publication, the TCC nevertheless sustained the impugned criminal provision.[105] Notably, however, the TCC held that the impugned criminal provision must be construed narrowly, limiting only to those obscene or sexually explicit

---

[102] Chang & Yeh, "Judges as discursive agent," supra note 3, at 382.

[103] The official website (in Chinese) provides all of the interpretations (from No 1 to No 739) with the majority, concurring and dissenting opinions as well as the petitions by applicants, available at www.judicial.gov.tw/constitutionalcourt/P03.asp.

[104] *JY Interpretation No 617* (English translation), available at www.judicial.gov.tw/constitutional court/EN/p03_01.asp?expno=617.

[105] *Id.*

materials "whose content includes violence, sexual abuse or bestiality but is lacking in artistic, medical or educational value"[106] and "is manufactured or possessed with the intent to disseminate same, or where, with the intent not to adopt adequate protective and isolating measures before disseminating to the general public any other obscene material or object that is so sexually stimulating or gratifying by objective standards that the average person will either find it not publicly presentable or find it so intolerable as to be repulsive, such material or object is manufactured or possessed."[107]

Justice Tzu-Yi Lin, a law professor specializing in free speech prior to his judicial appointment, referred to the Canadian Supreme Court twice in his dissenting-in-part opinion.[108] The first mentioning of the Canadian Supreme Court was made in passing,[109] to support a crucial point made by the majority opinion, confirming that "the expression of sexually explicit language and the circulation of sexually explicit material should also be subject to constitutional protection of the freedom of speech and publication"[110] Citing Eric Barendt's book entitled *Freedom of Speech*,[111] Justice Lin explained that in the United States, whether to deem obscene speech as a protected speech was debated, but an alternative approach was adopted by the Canadian Supreme Court, German Constitutional Court and European Court of Human Rights, under which obscene speech would be deemed as a protected speech and examined with the reasonableness or necessity of its restriction. Justice Lin, who obtained LLM and SJD degrees from Cornell Law School, nevertheless preferred the non-American approach.[112]

Having deemed obscene speech as a protected speech, Justice Lin examined whether art.235 of the Criminal Code was a reasonable restriction. This was where he disagreed with the majority opinion and discussed in detail a decision of the Canadian Supreme Court, *R. v. Butler*,[113] to support his view. For him, because obscene speech was a protected speech, the legislative purpose for its restriction must be important or even compelling, and much beyond a general respect of public morals. According to Justice Lin, the Canadian Supreme Court in *R. v. Butler* sustained the restriction of obscene speech, the purpose of which was to prevent women from being treated as sex object and to ensure sex equality and sexual autonomy, and such purpose

---

[106] *Id.* Holding, para.3.   [107] *Id.* Holding, para.3.

[108] *JY Interpretation No 617*, Dissenting-in-part, Justice Tzu-Yi Lin, available at www.judicial.gov .tw/constitutionalcourt/p03_01.asp?expno=617 (in Chinese).

[109] *Id.* at 2.   [110] *JY Interpretation No 617*, Holding, para.1.

[111] E. Barendt, Freedom of Speech, 2nd ed (Oxford University Press, 2005), 362, 365, 369.

[112] *JY Interpretation No 617*, Dissenting-in-part, Justice Tzu-Yi Lin, at 3–4.

[113] *R. v. Butler*, [1992] 1 SCR 452.

along with a very few of others, for example prevention of child sexual abuse, would be sufficiently important to sustain the restriction.[114] Because the majority opinion in *JY Interpretation No 617* sustained the speech restriction on the ground of public morals without heightened scrutiny, Justice Lin thus issued a dissenting-in-part opinion.

In another opinion, Justice Lin also mentioned – albeit in passing – Canadian rights jurisprudence. In *JY Interpretation No 689*, the majority sustained a provision of the Social Order Maintenance Act that authorized the police to impose fines on those who stalked or followed others without legitimate reason and would not stop after being urged to do so.[115] The context of this case involved news media trying to chase a business tycoon and his newly-wed wife, previously a popular star, for reporting their private life. Justice Lin issued a concurring-in-part and dissenting-in-part opinion, joined by another justice, agreeing with the majority that the right of privacy was not absolute and must be balanced with freedom of media while disagreeing that the police would enjoy the power to fine.[116] In articulating the protected scope of privacy, Justice Lin made detailed references to the reasonable expectation of privacy test in American jurisprudence and mentioned in passing that a similar test was also adopted by European Court of Human Rights, UK, New Zealand and Canada, citing a scholarly authority.[117]

So far, the last and most recent reference to Canadian constitutional practice by judges appeared in a concurring opinion of *JY Interpretation No 708*.[118] In this decision, the majority held unconstitutional a provision of the Immigration Act that authorized the immigration agency to temporarily detain a foreigner without prior judicial review. Justice Su Yeong-Chin, also a German-trained law professor prior to his judicial appointment, issued a concurring opinion stating that the majority's decision requiring both prior and post judicial review of foreigner detentions would provide a much better protection to foreigners than that of many other jurisdictions such as the United States, Canada, France, Japan, Korea or Singapore, among others.[119]

[114] *JY Interpretation No 617*, Dissenting-in-part, Justice Tzu-Yi Lin, at 16.
[115] *JY Interpretation No 689* (English translation), available at www.judicial.gov.tw/constitutional court/EN/p03_01.asp?expno=689.
[116] *JY Interpretation No 689*, Concurring-in-part and Dissenting-in-part, Justice Tzu-Yi Lin, joined by Justice Pi-Hu Hsu, at 18–20.
[117] D. J. Solove, UNDERSTANDING PRIVACY (Cambridge, MA: Harvard University Press, 2008), 71–72. In *JY Interpretation No 689*, Concurring-in-part and Dissenting-in-part, Justice Tzu-Yi Lin, joined by Justice Pi-Hu Hsu, at 11.
[118] *JY Interpretation No 708* (English translation), available at www.judicial.gov.tw/constitutional court/EN/p03_01.asp?expno=708.
[119] *JY Interpretation No 708*, Concurring Opinion, Justice Su Yeong-Chin, at 2–3.

References by Litigant Parties

The only reference to Canadian Charter case laws by litigant parties appeared in *JY Interpretation No 577*.[120] This interpretation made in 2004 was involved with the protected scope of commercial speech. A cigarette manufacturer challenged the constitutionality of the Tobacco Product Labelling Act requiring that the amount of nicotine and tar contained in a tobacco product be labelled on the package and stipulating administrative penalty in case of noncompliance.

Prepared by two attorneys, Nigel N. T. Li[121] and Joyce C. Fan,[122] both of whom obtained a LL.M. degree from the US, the petition referred to both American and Canadian jurisprudences in arguing that the impugned provision should be held unconstitutional. They referred to specifically *RJR-MacDonald Inc v. Canada*,[123] a case also concerning the constitutionality of Canada's Tobacco Products Control Act banning all advertisement and promotion of tobacco products and their sale unless the package included health warnings and lists of toxic constituents. The petition argued that the test by which the Canadian Supreme Court determined whether a limitation to free speech was demonstrably justified in a free and democratic society pursuant to s.1 of Canadian Charter should be of relevance to the present interpretation. The test involved the examinations of both the objective and the measures chosen to achieve the objective, and the latter must be proportional to the former in that 1) the measures chosen must be rationally connected to the objective; 2) they must impair the guaranteed right or freedom as little as possible; and 3) there must be proportionality between the deleterious effects of the measures and their salutary effects.[124]

Notwithstanding the detailed references by the petitioner, the majority opinion in *JY Interpretation No 577* did not respond to these American or Canadian jurisprudences. Although the impugned provision was eventually sustained, the majority opinion did provide a relatively more detailed discussion on the test it applied to examine the constitutionality. According to the majority, the impugned provision was "to serve significant public interests in safeguarding the health of the people and providing necessary trade information to consumers," and "the restrictive means adopted by the

---

[120] *JY Interpretation No 577* (English translation), available at www.judicial.gov.tw/constitutional court/EN/p03_01.asp?expno=577.
[121] www.leeandli.com.tw/TW/Professions/2/116.htm.
[122] www.leeandli.com.tw/TW/Professions/3/63.htm.   [123] [1995] 3 SCR 199.
[124] [1995] 3 SCR 199, 268.

government to serve the ends was "reasonably necessary" and "in proportion to the public interests served."[125]

ANALYSES OF HKCFA'S AND TCC'S REFERENCING TO CANADIAN CHARTER CASE LAWS

Based upon the above discussions, the following analyzes the driving forces, comparative relevance and functions of HKCFA's and TCC's references to Canadian Charter case laws and makes comparisons between them. Special focuses are placed on the analyses of legal family or recognition of courts, the differences between judge-initiated or litigant-initiated references, open or reticent attitudes for references and last but not the least, functions of references in terms of protecting or restricting rights.

Legal Family v. Recognition of the Court

The influence of legal tradition or legal family has been identified as one key factor to determine transnational judicial dialogue or comparative judicial practices.[126] Common law courts – with the exception of the US courts – are found more likely to make comparative law references especially to other common law courts. In contrast, civil law courts usually do not make direct or explicit comparative law references.[127] However, the referencing practices of HKCFA and TCC to Canadian Charter case laws have not squarely reflected upon such an influence of legal family or legal tradition.

As previously discussed, the number of cases referencing to Canadian Charter case laws by the HKCFA is nine, higher than that of TCC, four. This might indicate an influence of legal family since Hong Kong and Canada are both common law jurisdictions. Yet, given its vast number of references to other jurisdictions, the HKCFA's references to Canadian Charter case laws are not at all significant. According to the research by Simon Young, the number of references to international courts was more than that of references to Australia and New Zealand, and the number of references to Australia and New Zealand was almost equal to that of references to the US and Canada combined.[128] In a similar vein, while there are only four interpretations of TCC referencing to Canadian Charter cases laws, this

---

[125] *JY Interpretation No 577*, Reasoning, para. 3.
[126] Groppi & Ponthoreau, "The use of foreign precedents by constitutional judges," supra note 2, at 413; Saunders, "Judicial engagement with comparative law," supra note 2.
[127] Groppi & Ponthoreau, "The use of foreign precedents by constitutional judges," supra note 2, at 412–13.
[128] Young, *Constitutional Rights*, supra note 3, at 82.

number is not entirely insignificant given the TCC's very few foreign law references. More noteworthy is the supplementary nature of both HKCFA's and TCC's referencing to Canadian Charter case laws. As shown in the previous sections, the HKCFA's and TCC's references to Canadian Charter case laws have seldom appeared alone, but always with references to other jurisdictions such as UK, US or the European Court of Human Rights, among others.

Indeed, judicial comparativism has been influenced by more than legal family or legal tradition. Factors including institutional designs such as having foreign judges or foreign law clerks,[129] the strengths or strategies of the courts,[130] an open legal culture that does not necessarily coincide with legal tradition or legal family,[131] or the learning backgrounds of judges,[132] among others, have influenced the development of transnational judicial dialogues. Albeit not substantial, the HKCFA's and TCC's references to Canadian Charter case laws have shown certain recognition – if not acclaim – of the Canadian Charter jurisprudence developed by the Canadian Supreme Court in recent decades. Particularly noteworthy was the reference to the globally acclaimed Oakes test, or the Canadian principle of proportionality, by both the HKCFA and TCC.[133] Other researchers have found that the Supreme Court of Canada has become increasingly popular for references by certain common law courts such as the South African Constitutional Court.[134] Yet, such popularity has not yet seen in Asia, either for a common law court such as the HKCFA or a civil court such as TCC.

Judge-Initiated v. Litigant-Initiated References

Also noteworthy is who initiates comparative references and what differences that makes. In the HKCFA and TCC, judge-initiated references to Canadian Charter case laws slightly outnumbered references initiated by litigant parties.

---

[129] For example, the HKCFA has foreign judges, and Israel's Supreme Court hires foreign law clerks. For the information of foreign law clerks, see http://elyon1.court.gov.il/eng/Clerking_opportunities/index.html.

[130] See generally S. Dothan, REPUTATION AND JUDICIAL TACTICS (Cambridge University Press, 2014).

[131] Groppi & Ponthoreau, "The use of foreign precedents by constitutional judges," supra note 2, at 414.

[132] Law & Chang, The Limits of Global Judicial Dialogue, supra note 3, at 575; Chang & Yeh, "Judges as discursive agent," supra note 3, at 382–83.

[133] *Town Planning Board v. Society for the Protection of the Harbour,* 7 HKCFAR 1 (2004); JY Interpretation No 577; JY Interpretation No 617.

[134] Groppi & Ponthoreau, "The use of foreign precedents by constitutional judges," supra note 2, at 419.

In the HKCFA, the first reference to Canadian Charter case laws was made by judges in *Secretary for Justice v. Lam Tat Ming & Another* decided in 2000.[135] That reference was quickly followed by references initiated by litigant parties in the four cases between 2001 and 2002. However, as previously shown, in those four cases where the references were made by litigant parties, the HKCFA's majority opinions either found the Canadian Charter case laws unconvincing,[136] distinguished them from local case laws,[137] or found them not interfering with the present doctrine.[138] It was perhaps due to this unfavourable result for litigant-initiated references, there have been no litigant-initiated references to Canadian Charter case laws since 2002. In contrast, references initiated by judges continued to appear in 2002, 2003, 2004 and 2006. In these five cases with judge-initiated reference, a more amiable attitude for Canadian Charter case laws was exhibited. The HKCFA's majority opinions referenced to Canadian Charter case laws either in brief[139] or in detail[140] to support for their own reasoning and found the Charter case laws primarily consistent with their view.

Similar patterns are also found in the TCC. The first – and only – litigant-initiated references to Canadian Charter case laws failed to catch any attention by the majority or separate opinions.[141] Perhaps it was for that reason, there has since been no litigant-initiated reference to Canadian Charter case laws. In contrast, judge-initiated references appeared first in 2006[142] and continued in 2011[143] and 2013.[144] Unlike in the HKCFA, judge-initiated references were not made by the majority opinions in the TCC. Yet, these judge-initiated references also functioned to support – rather than to distinguish – the arguments made by individual justices, which in most cases concurred with the majority opinions.

The study of the HKCFA's and TCC's references to Canadian Charter case laws shows that comparative references are mostly provided by judges rather than litigant parties. More importantly, references initiated by litigant parties

---

[135] *Secretary for Justice v. Lam Tat Ming & Another*, 3 HKCFAR 168 (2000).
[136] *Li Defan & Another v. HKSAR*, 5 HKCFAR 320 (2002).
[137] *HKSAR v. Lee Ming Tee & Another*, 4 HKCFAR 133 (2001); *Lau Cheong & Another v. HKSAR*, 5 HKCFAR 415 (2002).
[138] *Ma Bik Yung v. Ko Chuen*, 9 HKCFAR 888 (2001).
[139] *Secretary for Justice v. Lam Tat Ming & Another*, 3 HKCFAR 168 (2000); *Shum Kwok Sher v. HKSAR*, 5 HKCFAR 381 (2002).
[140] *HKSAR v. Lee Ming Tee & Securities and Futures Commission*, 6 HKCFAR 336 (2003); *Town Planning Board v. Society for the Protection of the Harbour*, 7 HKCFAR 1 (2004); *So Wai Lun v. HKSAR*, 9 HKCFAR 530 (2006).
[141] *JY Interpretation No 577.*   [142] *JY Interpretation No 617.*   [143] *JY Interpretation No 689.*
[144] *JY Interpretation No 708.*

are driven by utility or expected benefits for litigations. Litigant parties lose interests in making comparative references when they find out that comparative references yield no gain for litigation. Although the number of references studied in this chapter is not huge, the present finding is nevertheless consistent with what I have found elsewhere: judges as a key agent for comparative or transnational judicial dialogue.[145] The learned backgrounds of judges – especially those with prior scholarly backgrounds – area intellectually equipped with abundant comparative sources whenever they find their reasoning in need of additional supports.

Openness v. Reticence

Comparative constitutional law scholarship usually divides courts – based upon their attitudes towards foreign or international laws – into two groups: openness v. reticence. A few courts in Asian jurisdictions such as Hong Kong, South Korea or Taiwan have been deemed as more opened to comparative judicial dialogues while others such as Singapore courts rather reticent.[146] Interestingly however, as briefly stated in the previous discussion, the present study of HKCFA's and TCC's referencing to Canadian Charter case laws finds that both attitudes may coexist in the same court, primarily dependent upon who initiates comparative references.

The HKCFA's four cases with litigant-initiated references to Canadian Charter case laws were poorly received by the CFA. In *Li Defan & Another v. HKSAR*, Lord Hoffmann even openly commented the reasoning of a cited Canadian judgment as "unconvincing."[147] In *HKSAR v. Lee Ming Tee & Another*, the CFA emphasized that "the Canadian case law developed in a highly specific context, responding to the peculiar statutory and constitutional needs and values of that jurisdiction" and thus should be distinguished from Hong Kong's own constitutional, legislative and common law context.[148] In *Lau Cheong & Another v. HKSAR*, the CFA bluntly expressed that "we do not accept that view of these Canadian cases"[149] If one reads these cases and concludes that the HKCFA was antagonistic against Canadian Charter case laws, one is surely mistaken.

[145] Chang & Yeh, "Judges as discursive agent" supra note 3.
[146] L.-A. Thio, *Reading Rights Rightly: The UDHR and Its Creeping Influence on the Development of Singapore Public Law*, SINGAPORE JOURNAL OF LEGAL STUDIES 264 (December 2008). *See also* Chang et al, CONSTITUTIONALISM IN ASIA, 432–38.
[147] *Li Defan & Another v. HKSAR*, 5 HKCFAR 320, 330 (2002).
[148] *HKSAR v. Lee Ming Tee & Another*, 4 HKCFAR 133, 179 (2001).
[149] *Lau Cheong & Another v. HKSAR*, 5 HKCFAR 415, 440 (2002).

For, the HKCFA's other five cases with judge-initiated references give a
totally different picture. In *Town Planning Board v. Society for the Protection of
the Harbour*, when the HKCFA was trying to develop the overriding public
need test, it openly stated that "assistance has been derived by way of analogy
from the approach adopted by the Supreme Court of Canada."[150] In *Shum
Kwok Sher v. HKSAR*, before referencing to Canadian Charter case laws, the
CFA expressed an open attitude for foreign and international laws, stating that
in interpreting the Basic Law, it "may consider it appropriate to take account
of the established principles of international jurisprudence as well as the decisions of international and national courts and tribunals."[151] Here, the principle
of legal certainty developed by the Canadian Supreme Court was given such
a referencing status.[152] As above mentioned, the TCC also exhibited such
contrasting attitudes: amiable for references initiated by judges while reticent
against references by litigant parties.

Protecting Rights v. Limiting Rights

Scholars have found that judicial referencing to foreign or international
laws does not necessarily lead to protecting rights or rendering favourable
results for litigant parties.[153] The findings of this chapter confirm, once again,
with such wisdom.

As noted above, the cases of both HKCFA and TCC with references to
Canadian Charter case laws were mostly in criminal context: seven out of
nine in the HKCFA with two civil cases; two out of four in the TCC with one
administrative penalty case and one detention case.

In the HKCFA, all seven criminal cases found unfavourable results for
the defendants with either judge-initiated or litigant-initiated references
to Canadian Charter case laws. In all three cases concerning the criminal
defendant's right against self-incrimination, the HKCFA rejected privileged
claims of the defendants by primarily rejecting or distinguishing from Canadian Charter case laws.[154] In *Shum Kwok Sher v. HKSAR*, the HKCFA made
a brief reference to Canadian Charter case laws to defend for the certainty

---

[150] *Town Planning Board v. Society for the Protection of the Harbour*, 7 HKCFAR 1, 18 (2004).
[151] *Shum Kwok Sher v. HKSAR*, 5 HKCFAR 381, 401 (2002).   [152] *Id.* at 402.
[153] Chang et al., *Constitutionalism in Asia*, 438–39. *See also* W.-C. Chang, *The Convergence
of Constitutions and International Human Rights: Taiwan and South Korea in Comparison*, 36
NORTH CAROLINA JOURNAL OF INTERNATIONAL LAW 593–624 (2011).
[154] *Secretary for Justice v. Lam Tat Ming & Another*, 3 HKCFAR 168 (2000); *HKSAR v. Lee Ming
Tee & Another*, 4 HKCFAR 133 (2001); *Li Defan & Another v. HKSAR*, 5 HKCFAR 320 (2002).

of common law offence.[155] In *HKSAR v. Lee Ming Tee & Securities and Futures Commission*, the HKCFA referenced to Canadian Charter case laws to articulate exceptional tolerance for failed common law duty to disclosure.[156] In *So Wai Lun v. HKSAR*, the HKCFA's references to Canadian Charter case laws were to justify legislative penalization.[157]

Even in the two civil cases, the HKCFA's references to Canadian Charter case laws were not necessarily for the gains of litigant parties. In *Town Planning Board v. Society for the Protection of the Harbour*, the HKCFA's references to the Oakes test was to provide for a less stringent test than the one developed by the lower court that found in favour of the residents against the harbour reclamation.[158] In *Ma Bik Yung v. Ko Chuen*, by referencing to Canadian Charter case laws, the HKCFA concluded with a more dynamic understanding of apology order only to find in favour of the appellee, the taxi driver and in disfavour of the appellant, the paraplegic.[159]

Similar findings are also seen in the TCC's references. Although the references were made in separate opinions, the references to Canadian Charter case laws in *JY Interpretation No 617* were to justify the restriction of sexually explicit speech if all requirements met. In *JY Interpretation No 689*, the brief reference to Canadian constitutional practice was to articulate that the right of privacy was not absolute and must be balanced with freedom of media under the reasonable expectation of privacy test. The exceptions were *JY Interpretation No 708*, in which the right of foreigners was strengthened, and *JY Interpretation No 577*, in which litigant-initiated references to Canadian principle of proportionality caught no judicial attention as discussed above.

CONCLUSION

This chapter has found Canadian Charter's influence – albeit not substantial – on both Hong Kong's Court of Final Appeal and Taiwan's Constitutional Court. The referencing practices of HKCFA and TCC to Canadian Charter case laws has somehow defied a conventional understanding in which legal family or legal tradition is deemed as more influential in determining the direction of transnational judicial dialogues. In both the HKCFA and TCC, referencing to Canadian case laws was rather supplementary, if not

---

[155] *Shum Kwok Sher v. HKSAR*, 5 HKCFAR 381 (2002).
[156] *HKSAR v. Lee Ming Tee & Securities and Futures Commission*, 6 HKCFAR 336 (2003).
[157] *So Wai Lun v. HKSAR*, 9 HKCFAR 530 (2006).
[158] *Town Planning Board v. Society for the Protection of the Harbour*, 7 HKCFAR 1 (2004).
[159] *Ma Bik Yung v. Ko Chuen*, 9 HKCFAR 888 (2001).

insignificant. The references seldom appeared alone, but always with references to other more important jurisdictions such as UK or US.

Also noteworthy was the gap between judge-initiated and litigant-initiated references, and the contrasting judicial attitudes towards them. Both the HKCFA and TCC were open to the references initiated by judges. However, when references were made by litigant parties, they were ignored, distinguished or bluntly rejected. The findings of this chapter also confirms to comparative law wisdom that has found that judicial referencing to foreign or international laws does not necessarily lead to protecting rights or rendering favourable results for litigant parties. In the HKCFA, all seven criminal cases found unfavourable results for the defendants, and comparable results are also witnessed in the TCC. It was perhaps due to this unfavourable result of reverencing to Canadian Charter case laws, such references – especially initiated by litigant parties – have become fewer and fewer, if not entirely disappearing. Litigant parties are surely to lose interests in making comparative references when they realize such efforts yield no returns.

17

The Canadian Charter, South Africa and the Paths of Constitutional Influence

HEINZ KLUG

INTRODUCTION

There can be no doubt that Canadian law and jurisprudence has had a profound impact on the understanding and application of rights in post-apartheid South Africa. This influence has been repeatedly acknowledged, celebrated and at times over claimed. Placing the use of Canadian constitutional ideas in the context of South Africa's democratic transition and subsequent jurisprudence this chapter aims to contextualize this influence and contrast it with the role of United States jurisprudence and foreign law in South Africa more generally. Understanding the contours of this influence requires us to both situate Canada within the South African context as well as to explore more precisely the Constitutional Court's use of Canadian jurisprudence.

Instead of focusing on the identification of specific individual influences this paper argues that Canadian influence has in fact been much broader. Canadian constitutional experience was drawn upon and mobilized for different purposes by a range of groups during the constitution-making process. Subsequently Canadian jurisprudence has been drawn upon in the interpretation of the Constitution in the courts. Adam Dodek is correct to point to the relationship between Canadian anti-apartheid activities and policies and the willingness of South Africans to engage with Canadians and the Canadian example.[1] He also notes the shared common law heritage, having the Privy Council as Court of final appeal and later membership in the Commonwealth. However, it is in these dimensions that a little more specificity might provide a deeper understanding of the ways in which South Africa's

Thank you to my research assistant, David Hollander (J.D. 2017) for his excellent work on this project.

[1] Adam M. Dodek, *Canada as Constitutional Exporter: The Rise of the "Canadian Model" of Constitutionalism*, 36 SUPREME COURT LAW REVIEW (2ND) 309–336 (2007).

openness to the influence of foreign law, and Canadian jurisprudence in particular, might be understood.

As Ran Hirschl argues in *Comparative Matters*[2] it is important to clarify both the goal of a research project as well as being aware of the limits of the methods adopted in pursuit of these goals. This Chapter is part of an ongoing interest in understanding the reception of foreign constitutional ideas. As such it unabashedly seeks to view the exchange of constitutional ideas from the perspective of the importing country rather than from the perspective of the exporter. While the chapter focuses on the influence of Canadian constitutionalism in South Africa, it forms part of a broader comparative project that will seek to understand the reasons why some sources may be more influential and why different sources of foreign law may gain prominence in different places at different times. At this initial stage in the broader project this chapter will describe some of the broad contours the influence Canadian constitutionalism has had on constitutional ideas, constitution-making and constitutional jurisprudence in South Africa. It will also offer some initial comparative observations based on the empirical data collected. More robust conclusions will have to await further analysis of the case law as well as further empirical work, including interviews with members of the Constitutional Court and other participants in this process.

CANADIAN INFLUENCES

Adam Dodek has argued, in his article on *Canada as a Constitutional Exporter* that constitutional influence may be identified in two distinct constitutional phases, in the constitution-making process and in constitutional interpretation.[3] While Dodek focuses primarily on the influence of the Canadian Charter on the making of the "interim" 1993 Constitution in South Africa, his focus on the limitations clause and the specific role of Professor David Beatty demonstrates the dangers of attempting to show influence by identifying overly specific and even individual sources of such influence. There is little question that David Beatty's stay at the University of Cape Town law school in 1992 had a very real impact on his South African colleagues, many of whom would play significant roles in the constitution-making process. However, Dodek's claim that the decision to adopt a general

---

[2] *See,* Ran Hirschl, COMPARATIVE MATTERS: THE RENAISSANCE OF COMPARATIVE CONSTITUTIONAL LAW, (Oxford University Press, 2014).
[3] Dodek, *supra* note 1.

limitations clause similar to section 1 of the Canadian Charter is the direct result of Beatty's enthusiasm for proportionality in constitutional rights inter-pretation fails to appreciate how constitutional ideas achieve the collective recognition and support needed for adoption in a constitution-making process.

A broader and more inclusive description of the role of Canada and Canadians in the development of constitutional ideas in South Africa may provide a more contextual, even if less definitive picture of how constitutional ideas are transmitted. While Dodek is quick to claim the prominence of Prime Minister Mulroney's contribution to the struggle against apartheid, at least within the context of the Commonwealth, a more nuanced understanding would acknowledge both that Mulroney was at times bolder than most Western leaders in his condemnation of apartheid but that it was civil society across Canada that made the most significant contributions to the struggle against apartheid. Despite the strong words, the Canadian government failed to impose the degree of sanctions demanded by the African National Congress (ANC), and even by Mandela after his release from prison, and in fact had a more ambivalent relationship towards the struggle, and particularly armed resistance, than is now acknowledged.[4]

From my own experience I would argue that the relationship between Canadians and those engaged in the debates over constitutional options and then in the constitution-making processes that followed, was fairly extensive. Volunteers in CUSO (now CUSO International) had long built relationships with anti-apartheid activists and even the ANC in the frontline states and in Canada. Prominent Canadian academics, such as John Saul, had relation-ships with liberations movements throughout Southern Africa from the 1960s.[5] At the same time there were numerous South Africans who immigrated to Canada, including a number of academics. Most prominent was Dan O'Meara who also had long established links with the liberation movements in Southern Africa. There were also a number of lawyers and law professors such as David Dyzenhaus at University of Toronto whose sister Carol Lewis would become Dean at the University of the Witwatersrand Law School in the early 1990s and later a Judge of the Supreme Court of Appeal. As a result of these networks a stream of Canadian academics, judges and other legal experts visited South Africa in the first half of the 1990s and came to play different roles in South Africa's constitutional moment.

---

[4]   *See* Gerald Caplan, *Canada and Mandela: The story behind the myth*, THE GLOBE AND MAIL, February 26, 2010.
[5]   *See* John S. Saul, A FLAWED FREEDOM: RETHINKING SOUTHERN AFRICAN LIBERATION, (University of Cape Town Press, 2014).

The best way to get a rough sense of this level of engagement and the different forms that it took is to briefly describe some of the activities and those involved. Among the Canadians who visited South Africa in the early 1990s, presented papers and engaged academic centres and the ANC Constitutional Committee by attending the series of conferences and workshops organized by the ANC included: David Beatty (Professor of Law at the University of Toronto who spent a semester at the University of Cape Town); Donna Greschner (of the Saskatchewan Human Rights Commission and later Dean of the University of Victoria Law School, who participated in the ANC Constitutional Committee's conference on a Bill of Rights outside Durban in 1991); Lorraine Weinrib (Professor of Law at the University of Toronto); Justice Walter Tarnopolsky (of the Ontario Court of Appeal); Richard Bauman (Professor of Law at the University of Alberta); and Richard Simeon (Professor of Political Science at the University of Toronto). While these individuals shared their constitutional ideas and the Canadian experience with lawyers, law teachers and at conferences and workshops, in some cases they briefed political parties and were called upon to present aspects of the Canadian experience that were of particular interest in the continuing South African debates over the future constitutional order. Others, such as plain language writing expert Phil Knight (Director of the Plain Language Institute of British Columbia) and former senior Canadian and Provincial government administrators, such as Dr A. W. Johnson and Rosemary Proctor (South Africa-Canada Program on Governance) would respectively work directly with the Constitutional Assembly to help transpose constitutional drafts into plain English and with the new post-1994 government and provinces to develop new policies and systems of government right through the end of the Mandela government to mid-2000.

Richard Bauman, for example, was specifically asked to come and present a paper on "Property Rights in the Canadian Context" at a conference organized specifically to address issues of land and property rights. His paper was subsequently included in a special issue of the South African Journal on Human Rights and provided an important intellectual basis for the continuing demand that there should be no property clause in the final constitution.[6] Using the Canadian experience as its justification this provided an important constitutional lever for the ultimate reformulation of the property clause that was one of the last issues resolved in the negotiations over the 1996 Constitution. Phil Knight, on the other hand, was brought into the

---

[6] Richard W Bauman, *Property Rights in the Canadian Constitutional Context*, 8 SOUTH AFRICAN JOURNAL ON HUMAN RIGHTS 344–361 (1992).

constitution-making process by Mandela's Minister of Justice, Dullah Omar, to help ensure that the constitution would be intelligible to the public. After the establishment of the Constitutional Court there were reciprocal visits between Justices of the Canadian Supreme Court and South African Constitutional Court who also became acquainted through the increasing network of constitutional justices that met at workshops and conferences around the globe in the new era of global constitutionalism. Finally, senior ANC government officials worked closely with Canadian counterparts in the Canadian Government funded South Africa-Canada Program on Governance on the establishment of constitutional structures such as the Fiscal and Financial Commission and on Nelson Mandela's Presidents Review Commission[7] to reshape the public service and members of provincial governments in South Africa paid visits to Provincial governments in Canada with which they were paired.[8]

In order to understand how these influences may impact outcomes it is instructive to return to the question of the origins of the limitations clause now contained in section 36 of the 1996 Constitution. According to Adam Dodek the idea of a limitations clause was introduced into the South African debate by Professor David Beatty and expressed in a document published by the Department of Public Law at the University of Cape Town in December 1992. While it is true that this document, *A Charter for Social Justice: A contribution to the South African Bill of Rights debate*,[9] authored by a group of prominent Cape Town-based academics and public interest lawyers contained a limitations clause modelled on the Canadian Charter – in that it was contained in Article 1 and stated that "This Bill of rights guarantees the rights and freedoms set out in it subject only to such limits as can be demonstrably justified in a free and open social democracy,"[10] to say that it introduced the notion of a limitations clause would be false. In fact, the ANC Constitutional Committee's own working document, "A bill of Rights for A New South Africa" published by the Centre for Development Studies at the University of the

---

[7]   *See* S.L. Sutherland, SUPPORTING DEMOCRACY: THE SOUTH AFRICA–CANADA PROGRAM ON GOVERNANCE, INTERNATIONAL DEVELOPMENT RESEARCH CENTRE (Ottawa, 1999).

[8]   *See* Rosemary Proctor and Harvey Sims, THE WORK OF THE SOUTH AFRICA/CANADA PROGRAMME ON GOVERNANCE JANUARY 1998 TO JUNE 2000: FINAL REPORT (June 1, 2000).

[9]   Hugh Corder, Steve Kahanovitz, John Murphy, Christina Murray, Kate O'Regan, Jeremy Sarkin, Henk Smith and Nico Steytler, *A Charter for Social Justice: A Contribution to the South African Bill of Rights Debate, Department of Public Law,* University of Cape Town, Department of Public Law, University of the Western Cape and Legal Resources Centre, Cape Town, December 1992.

[10]   *Id.* p. 3.

Western Cape in 1990 and explicitly referenced by the authors of A Charter for Social Justice, contained an elaborate, four part "Limitations" clause.

The ANC Constitutional Committee's limitations clause, which remained unchanged in both the Constitutional Committee's 1990 and subsequent 1993 "preliminary revised text" of a *Bill of Rights for a New South Africa* stated that:

1. Nothing in the Constitution shall be interpreted as implying for any group or person the right to engage in any activity or perform any act aimed at the destruction of any of the rights and freedoms set forth in the Constitution, or at their limitation or suppression to a degree other than is authorized by the Constitution itself.
2. Nothing in this Constitution shall be interpreted as impeding the right of the State to enact legislation regulating the manner in which fundamental rights and freedoms shall be exercised, or limiting such rights, provided that such regulation or limitation is such as might generally be deemed necessary in an open and democratic society.
3. Any restrictions permitted under the Constitution to fundamental rights and freedoms shall not be applied to or used as a cover for any purpose other than that for which they have been expressly or by necessary implication authorized.
4. Any law providing for any regulation or limitation of any fundamental right or freedom shall:
    i.   be of general application;
    ii. not negate the essential content of the right, but simply qualify the way that right is to be exercised or the circumstances in which derogation from the right is permitted;
    iii. as far as practicable, identify the specific clauses of the Constitution relied upon for the limitation of the right and the specific clauses of the Constitution affected by the legislation;
    iv. specify as precisely as possible the exact reach of the limitation and the circumstances in which it shall apply.[11]

Significantly, in first presenting this text, Zola Skweyiya, chairperson of the Committee argued in his introduction to the *Working Document* that "the limitations clause does not set out in detail the limitations that might be imposed in relation to the exercise of rights. Instead, the formula is used for permitting legislation to regulate or limit the exercise of rights to the extent

---

[11] ANC Constitutional Committee, *A Bill of Rights for a New South Africa: A Working Document by the ANC Constitutional Committee*, Center for Development Studies: Bellville, South Africa, 1990 [hereinafter ANC Bill of Rights].

that such limitations would be acceptable in democratic societies."[12] In the *preliminary revised text* published in 1993 the Committee noted that:

> These provisions follow the basic format of limitation clauses used in the European Convention of Human Rights and other similar documents. A general clause like this is needed so as to avoid cluttering up the Bill of Rights with detailed exceptions to each and every clause. Thus, it would be inconvenient to have to spell out such generally accepted limitations on freedom of speech as restrictions on reporting the names of minors in court proceedings, or on speech designed to put pressure on judges during a trial.[13]

Furthermore, it was noted in the introduction to *A Charter for Social Justice* that that group "departed from the ANC Bill in three important ways" including their introduction of "a general circumscription clause at the beginning of the Bill of Rights which provides that limitations of rights contained in the Bill will be legitimate if such limitation would 'be justified in a free and open social democracy.'"[14] The document also acknowledges that its approach was "derived directly from the practice of the Canadian Supreme Court, as expressly articulated in *R v. Oakes*."[15] Furthermore, in their discussion of their proposal the authors of *A Charter for Social Justice* were clearly influenced by Professor David Beatty's concern with proportionality in discussing the justification of any legislative measure that is held to infringe the Bill of Rights, arguing that:

> [o]nce the objective sought by the impugned measure is found to be legitimate, the party defending it must show that the means chosen are proportional to the attainment of the objective – i.e., they are reasonable and demonstrably justified. Important indicators of proportionality were identified in *R v. Oakes*: the measures adopted must be carefully designed to achieve the objective in question, so they must not be arbitrary, unfair or based on irrational considerations and they must be rationally connected to the objective; the means should impair the right or freedom in question as little as possible; and there must be a proportionality between the effects of the measures and the objective which has been identified as of sufficient importance. The more invasive a measure, the more important the objective must be if the measure is to be reasonable and demonstrably justified in a free and open social democracy.[16]

[12] Zola Skweyiya, *Introductory Note: A Bill of Rights for a New South Africa – Working Document*, in ANC Bill of Rights, xiv–xv.
[13] ANC Constitutional Committee, *A Bill of Rights for a New South Africa, Preliminary Revised Text*, February 1993, Note to Article 16: Limitations.
[14] Hugh Corder et al., *A Charter for Social Justice, supra* note 9, at 13.   [15] *Id.* at 14.
[16] *Id.* at 15–16.

While this description of proportionality was clearly drawn from the Canadian model and shows Professor David Beatty's influence on the group, it is significant that the most basic element, that any limitation be "justified in a free and open social democracy" is in fact quite a different standard when compared to section 1 of the Canadian Charter which states that "[t]he *Canadian Charter of Rights and Freedoms* guarantees the rights and freedoms set out in it subject only to such reasonable limits prescribed by law as can be demonstrably justified in a free and democratic society."[17] While some, including myself, might hope that there would be little difference between a "free and democratic society" and a "free and open social democracy" others may beg to differ.

Although Adam Dodek is correct to note that Professor Hugh Corder, one of the primary authors of *A Charter for Social Justice* went on to serve on the committee that drafted the Bill of Rights for the "interim" 1993 Constitution,[18] the more significant point about constitutional influence I would argue is that the introduction of the Canadian experience deepened an approach to the limitation of rights that was already acceptable to the ANC who saw it as both a part of the international human rights framework represented by the European Convention of Human Rights as well as a means to address concerns within the ANC that the adoption of rights would empower the judiciary and frustrate a future government's attempts to address the legacies of apartheid.[19] This acceptance is evident in the limitations clause adopted in the 1993 "interim" Constitution which states in section 33(1)(a) that the "rights entrenched in [the Bill of Rights] ... may be limited by law of general application, provided that such limitation – (a) shall be permissible only to the extent that it is – (i) reasonable and (ii) justifiable in an open and democratic society based on freedom and equality."[20] Instead of the simpler Canadian version or the requirement that any limitation be "justified in a free and open social democracy" the version acceptable to the parties in the negotiations attempts to define the nature of an "open and democratic society" as one which will be based on "freedom and equality."

The reformulation of the limitations clause in the "final" 1996 Constitution brings this discussion a full circle with the Constitutional Assembly turning

---

[17] Constitution Act 1982, enacted as Schedule B to the *Canada Act 1982*, 1982, c. 11 (UK), which came into force on April 17, 1982.
[18] *See* Hugh Corder and Lourens Du Plessis, *Understanding South Africa's Transitional Bill of Rights*, Juta, Cape Town, 1994.
[19] Heinz Klug, CONSTITUTING DEMOCRACY: LAW, GLOBALISM AND SOUTH AFRICA'S POLITICAL RECONSTRUCTION (Cambridge University Press, 2000), 71–85.
[20] Constitution of the Republic of South Africa Act 200 of 1993, section 33(1)(a).

to the early jurisprudence of the Constitutional Court for its guidance. The Constitutional Assembly explicitly incorporated not just some of the Canadian language but also the Constitutional Court's elaboration of a balancing approach based in part on the *Oakes* decision of the Canadian Supreme Court as well as the approaches of the German Constitutional Court and the European Court of Human Rights.[21] Instead of requiring any limitation to be justifiable in an "open and democratic society based on freedom and equality" the new formulation requires that a limitation be "reasonable and justifiable in an open and democratic society based on human dignity, equality and freedom" and then proceeds to specify an open list of five "relevant factors," including:

(a) the nature of the right;
(b) the importance of the purpose of the limitation;
(c) the nature and extent of the limitation;
(d) the relation between the limitation and its purpose; and
(e) less restrictive means to achieve the purpose.[22]

These factors stem not from the language of section 1 of the Canadian Charter of Rights but rather from the application and interpretation of that section in the jurisprudence of the Supreme Court of Canada.[23] While Justice Kentridge may have explicitly declined to adopt the Canadian approach in the Constitutional Court's first case, *S v. Zuma*,[24] the limitations analysis in *Makwanyane* implicitly relies on the *Oakes* analysis even as it also cites to the German and European jurisprudence.

In fact the German Constitution and jurisprudence is referenced mainly to address section 33(b) of the 1993 "interim" Constitution which stated that any limitation of a right "shall not negate the essential content of the right in question." Here the Constitutional Court noted that the German Constitutional Court "apparently avoids making use of this provision."[25] Discussing the inclusion of this provision in the limitations clause the Constitutional Court expressed its concern that "[t]here is uncertainty in the literature concerning the meaning of this provision," and concluded that "[a]t the very least the provision evinces concern that, under the guise of limitation, rights should not be taken away altogether."[26] Significantly, the Constitutional

---

[21] *S v. Makwanyane and Another*, 1995 (3) SA 391, paras 103–110.
[22] Constitution of the Republic of South Africa Act 108 of 1996, section (1)(a)–(e).
[23] *See S v. Makwanyane and Another*, 1995 (3) SA 391, para 107.
[24] *S v. Zuma and Others*, 1995 (2) SA 642, para 35.
[25] *S v. Makwanyane and Another*, 1995 (3) SA 391, para 108.   [26] *Id.* paras 132–134.

Court also noted that this concern "was presumably the same concern that influenced Dickson CJC to say in *R v. Oakes* that rights should be limited 'as little as possible'".[27] Taking its cue from the Constitutional Court's uncertainty about the meaning of the "essential content of the right" the Constitutional Assembly proceeded to remove this provision from the "final" Constitution.

Thus, while it is clear that the South African constitution reflects, in quite specific detail, the impact of Canadian influences on the limitations clause, the precise path of that influence and how it gained acceptance among constitution-makers is rather complex. On the one hand, it was only through repeated iterations of the general idea of limitations on rights that the need for a general limitations clause became acceptable. On the other hand, it was only with the introduction of a sophisticated means of applying a limitations clause, through the Constitutional Court's adoption of a proportionality analysis in its early jurisprudence, that we see the Constitutional Assembly embracing a fully elaborated limitations clause in the "final" Constitution. Significantly too, while it might have been of great interest to those South Africans who continued to be concerned about the "counter-majoritarian difficulty" implicit in a robust system of judicial review, there was no attempt to introduce that other significant aspect of the Canadian model – the notwithstanding clause.

USES OF FOREIGN JURISPRUDENCE IN THE CONSTITUTIONAL COURT

If Canadian constitutionalism was a significant source of inspiration and influence in South Africa's constitution-making and early post-apartheid governing processes, it has been in the jurisprudence of the Constitutional Court that Canada's contribution may be most clearly observed. Before exploring the specific contributions made by Canadian jurisprudence – and the jurisprudence of the Canadian Supreme Court in particular – it is important that we place the use of Canadian jurisprudence in context. This requires understanding exactly how foreign jurisprudence is incorporated in the decisions of the Constitutional Court in South Africa and how this usage has changed over time. To get a sense of the parameters of this reliance and how it has changed we can look at the use of foreign jurisprudence in the court's jurisprudence over its first twenty years – 1995–2015.

---

[27] *Id.* para 134.

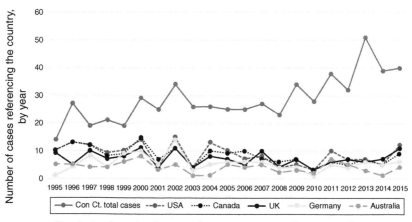

FIGURE 1. Constitutional court's reference to foreign countries: top five countries by year

Following the Constitution's invitation in the 1993 "interim" Constitution for interpreters of the Bill of Rights to "have regard to comparable foreign case law"[28] and the proviso in s39 of the "final" 1996 Constitution that a "court, tribunal or forum ... may consider foreign law" in interpreting the Bill of Rights, the Constitutional Court has embraced the task. The Constitutional Court has referenced and discussed foreign law in approximately 50.3 per cent of the court's 602 decisions during its first twenty years. While the ten countries and courts most discussed in the Constitutional Court's decisions were predominantly from North America, Europe and Australasia, India, Namibia and Zimbabwe also made the list. An additional eleven countries, including Botswana, Israel, Nigeria, Ireland, Tanzania, Kenya, Mauritius, Cyprus, Malaysia, Sri Lanka and Ghana were referenced at least five times. However, four countries, the United States, Canada, the United Kingdom and Germany were referenced over 100 times. Even among these four it was the United States with 182 references and Canada with 173 references that dominated the comparative discussion. Australia, the fifth most referenced jurisdiction was only cited 83 times over this period. If we graph these patterns over the twenty year period a number of other patterns emerge (see Figure 1).

What is immediately obvious from this overview – done using an electronic search by country of all Constitutional Cases over this period[29] – is that the

---

[28] Constitution of the Republic of South Africa, Act 200 of 1993, s.35(1).

[29] These numbers represent a very broad definition of reference or citation since they are based on a general electronic search of the court's cases and include any reference to the particular jurisdiction, not only case citations.

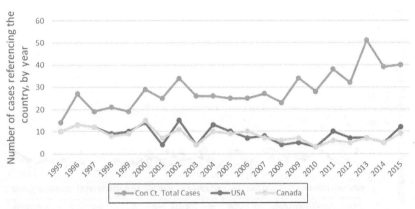

FIGURE 2. Number of constitutional court court cases referencing Canada and the United States, by year

discussion and citation of foreign jurisprudence has declined over these two decades as the Constitutional Court has developed its own jurisprudence. Thus, over twenty years references to foreign law and foreign jurisprudence has been discussed in just over one-half of the Court's cases while the number of cases with references to foreign jurisdictions, whether as citations or in the text of the court's decisions has declined from a high of 85.7 per cent in its first year to just 32.5 per cent of cases in 2015. While this general decline is to be expected, the use of foreign jurisprudence at an average rate of 50.3 per cent per year remains relatively high. Within these broader trends it is clear that the Constitutional Court has mostly referenced two jurisdictions – the United States and Canada. These two jurisdictions make up 37.98 per cent of the total references over this period. Furthermore, the Constitutional Court has referenced the United States in approximately 182 cases while Canada has been discussed or cited in 173 cases (see Figure 2).

Just as in the cases of references to foreign jurisdictions in general, references to the United States and Canada have declined over this same period. If in 1995 the Constitutional Court referenced each of these two jurisdictions in 71 per cent of all cases (83 per cent of cases making reference to foreign jurisdictions), by 2010 this had dropped to an average of only 10 per cent of all cases (although still 30 per cent of cases with references to foreign law). By 2015 it had increased a little, with 30 per cent of all cases referencing United States and 22 per cent Canada (see Figure 3).

In order to develop a deeper empirical understanding of how these foreign jurisdictions have been used in the Constitutional Court's jurisprudence the 355 cases identified in the original electronic search were subsequently

FIGURE 3. Percent of constitutional court cases referencing Canada and US, by year

reviewed in order to understand exactly how the case law of the United States and Canada has been used by the Constitutional Court. The new data set produced by this review, includes only the cases that actually cite to some source of Canadian or American law, including constitutions, statutes, common law, regulations, treatises, law journals and other legal authorities. It excludes cases in which the country is referenced only in the facts (for example, when a Canadian company was party to the suit), or where the first search captured the case only because the search term "America" was over-inclusive (for example, "inter-American Human Rights"). As a result, the number of cases that actually cite US law fell from 184 to 139 while in the case of Canadian law the number of cases fell from 179 to 160. This analysis reveals that in fact Canadian law has been the most cited source of foreign law in the Constitutional Court between 1995 and 2015, if even only slightly ahead of the United States (see Figure 4).

IS THERE A SPECIAL ROLE FOR CANADIAN CONSTITUTIONALISM?

Given that the South African constitution and the Constitutional Court have clearly embraced foreign jurisprudence we might wonder if there are any clear similarities or differences in the way the Constitutional Court has engaged with different jurisdictions. Since the raw numerical data shows that the two most referenced jurisdictions are Canada and the United States a good place to start this enquiry is to compare the Court's use of these two sources of foreign jurisprudence. While the numerical relationship might indicate that

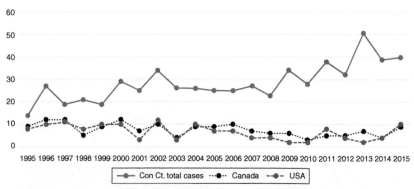

FIGURE 4. Number of South African constitutional court cases that reference Canadian and American law, by year

there is a similar reliance on both of these sources for constitutional ideas and doctrinal arguments a closer look indicates that there is in fact a sharp difference in the way the Constitutional Court has responded to these two jurisdictions.

Despite early concerns that the Court might uncritically follow United States jurisprudence, differences in "constitutional language and structure, as well as history and culture" led the Court to be fairly circumspect.[30] In one of its first cases dealing with the distribution of powers between the national and regional governments, involving a dispute over the National Education Policy Bill which was then before the National Assembly, the Constitutional Court drew heavily on Australian and Canadian jurisprudence yet explicitly warned off the relevance of the federal experience in the United States. In this case, brought as a case of abstract review (in which a law's constitutionality may be challenged on its face by particular constitutionally-defined litigants, such as the President or Premier of a Province, before a specific case arises – similar to a Reference in Canada), the petitioners focused on the claim that the "Bill imposed national education policy on the provinces"[31] and thereby "encroached upon the autonomy of the provinces and their executive authority."[32] They also claimed that the "Bill could have no application in KwaZulu-Natal because it [the province] was in a position to formulate and regulate its own policies."[33] While all parties accepted that education was defined as a

[30] *See* Richard C. Blake, *The Frequent Irrelevance of US Judicial Decisions in South Africa*, 15 SOUTH AFRICAN JOURNAL ON HUMAN RIGHTS 192, 197 (1999).
[31] *Ex Parte Speaker of the National Assembly: In Re Dispute Concerning the Constitutionality of Certain Provisions of the National Education Policy Bill 83 of 1995*, 1996 (3) SA 289, para. 8.
[32] *Id.*   [33] *Id.*

concurrent legislative function under the 1993 "interim" Constitution, the contending parties imagined that different consequences should flow from the determination that a subject matter is concurrently assigned by the Constitution to both provincial and national government.

KwaZulu-Natal and the Inkatha Freedom Party which then held the majority of seats in the regional legislature, assumed a form of preemption doctrine in which the National Assembly and national government would be precluded from acting in an area of concurrent jurisdiction so long as the province was capable of formulating and regulating its own policies. In rejecting this argument the Constitutional Court avoided the notion of pre-emption argued by KwaZulu-Natal altogether and instead argued that the "legislative competences of the provinces and Parliament to make laws in respect of schedule 6 [concurrent] matters do not depend upon section 126 (3)," which the Court argued only comes into operation if it is necessary to resolve a conflict between inconsistent national and provincial laws.[34] The Court's rejection of any notion of preemption is an interpretation of the Constitution which enables both national and provincial legislators to continue to promote and even legislate on their own imagined solutions to issues within their concurrent jurisdiction without foreclosing on their particular options until there is an irreconcilable conflict.

Having avoided siding categorically with either national or provincial authority the Court took a further step arguing that even if a "conflict is resolved in favour of either the provincial or national law the other is not invalidated" it is merely "subordinated and to the extent of the conflict rendered inoperative."[35] Supported by the comparative jurisprudence of Canada and Australia, the Court was able to make a distinction between "laws that are inconsistent with each other and laws that are inconsistent with the Constitution"[36] and thereby argue that "even if the National Education Policy Bill deals with matters in respect of which provincial laws would have paramountcy, it could not for that reason alone be declared unconstitutional."[37]

While the Constitutional Court's approach clearly aimed to reduce the tensions inherent in the continuing conflict between provincial and national governments, particularly in KwaZulu-Natal where tensions were still producing violent confrontations, it also took the opportunity to explicitly preclude an alternative interpretation that was based on the federalism jurisprudence of the United States Supreme Court. Focusing on arguments before the Court based upon the United States Supreme Court's decision in *New York v. United*

---

[34] *Id*. para. 16.   [35] *Id*.   [36] *Id*.   [37] *Id*. para. 20.

States[38] the Court made the point that "[u]nlike their counterparts in the United States of America, the provinces in South Africa are not sovereign states."[39] Furthermore the Court warned that "[d]ecisions of the courts of the United States dealing with state rights are not a safe guide as to how our courts should address problems that may arise in relation to the rights of provinces under our Constitution."[40]

In more general terms the Constitutional Court has repeatedly noted that the legal system, history and culture of South Africa has to be taken into account when interpreting the Constitution. In *S v. Makwanyane* the Court's famous death penalty case Justice Chaskalson emphasized in his opinion for the Court that "[i]n dealing with comparative law" the Court is "required to construe the South African Constitution, and not an international instrument or the constitution of some foreign country, and that this has to be done with due regard to our legal system, our history and circumstances, and the structure and language of our own Constitution" and that the Court may "derive assistance from public international law and foreign case law" but is "in no way bound to follow it."[41]

In comparison to its circumspect approach to United States jurisprudence the Constitutional Court has from its very first opinion embraced the jurisprudence of the Canadian Supreme Court, particularly in regards the interpretation of constitutional rights. In *S v. Makwanyane* Justice Chaskalson noted that in its very first case, *S v. Zuma* the Court had addressed "the approach to be adopted in the interpretation of fundamental rights" and "gave its approval to an approach which, whilst paying due regard to the language that has been used, is 'generous' and 'purposive' and gives expression to the underlying values of the Constitution."[42] He went on to note that in adopting this approach the Court had referred with approval to *R v. Big M Drug Mart Ltd* in which the Canadian Supreme Court had argued that: "The meaning of a right or freedom guaranteed by the Charter was to be ascertained by an analysis of the purpose of such a guarantee; it was to be understood, in other words, in the light of the interests it was meant to protect."[43] The quotation, which comes originally from Justice Dickson (later Chief Justice of Canada) in *Oakes*, continues: "this analysis is to be undertaken, and the purpose of the right or freedom in question is to be sought by reference to the character and

[38] 505 US 144 (1992).
[39] *Ex Parte Speaker of the National Assembly: In Re Dispute Concerning the Constitutionality of Certain Provisions of the National Education Policy Bill 83 of 1995*, 1996 (3) SA 289, para. 23.
[40] *Id.*   [41] *S v. Makwanyane*, 1995 (3) SA 391 (CC), para. 39.   [42] *Id.* para 9.   [43] *Id.*

larger objects of the Charter itself ... [and the] interpretation should be ... a generous rather than legalistic one, aimed at fulfilling the purpose of a guarantee and securing for individuals the full benefit of the Charter's protection."[44]

While the Constitutional Court has continued to rely on this "generous and purposive" approach to the interpretation of rights it is revealing that in *S v. Zuma* the reference to the Canadian approach follows an initial citation by Acting Justice Kentridge to what he terms "judicial dicta"[45] which had been increasingly cited by both regional courts in Southern Africa and lower courts in South Africa. Kentridge, a member of the London Bar and former lawyer for Nelson Mandela who returned to South Africa for a period to serve as Acting Justice stated that: "The first of these is the much-quoted passage from the judgment of Lord Wilberforce in the Privy Council in *Minister of Home Affairs (Bermuda) v. Fisher* ... [who, after] referring to the influence of certain international conventions on the constitutions of former colonies of the British Commonwealth," called for "a generous interpretation ... suitable to give to individuals the full measure of the fundamental rights and freedoms referred to."[46]

Significantly this highlights the relationship between Canadian jurisprudence and the jurisprudence of the Privy Council, which after all was the highest Court of both South Africa and Canada for the first decades of the twentieth century. It may also be seen as a continuing reliance on the common law in the search for basic principles, such as the presumption of innocence. Justice Kentridge notes in his opinion in *S v. Zuma* that: "in both Canada and South Africa the presumption of innocence is derived from the centuries-old principle of English law ... that it is always for the prosecution to prove the guilt of the accused person, and that the proof must be proof beyond a reasonable doubt. Accordingly, I consider that we may appropriately apply the principles worked out by the Canadian Supreme Court."[47]

Apart from basic principles the Constitutional Court also turned to Canadian jurisprudence to interpret the limitations clause in section 33 of the interim Constitution. In *S v. Makwanyane* Justice Chaskalson noted that: "In dealing with this aspect of the case, Mr Trengove placed considerable reliance on the decision of the Canadian Supreme Court in *R v. Oakes* ... [and that the] Canadian Charter of Rights, as our Constitution does, makes provision for the limitation of rights through a general clause."[48] Justice Chaskalson

---

[44] Id.   [45] *S v. Zuma, and Others*, 1995 (2) SA 642, para 13.
[46] Cited in *S v. Zuma, and Others*, SA 642, (1995) para 14.
[47] *S v. Zuma, and Others*, SA 642,(1995) para 25.   [48] *S v. Makwanyane*, para 105.

went on to point out that *"Section* 1 of the Charter permits such reasonable limitations of Charter rights 'as can be demonstrably justified in a free and democratic society' . . . [and that in *Oakes*'case] it was held that in order to meet this requirement a limitation of a Charter right had to be directed to the achievement of an objective of sufficient importance to warrant the limitation of the right in question, and that there had also to be proportionality between the limitation and such objective."[49] He then proceeded to quote Dickson CJC's description of the components of proportionality as:

> First, the measures adopted must be carefully designed to achieve the objective in question. They must not be arbitrary, unfair or based on irrational considerations. In short, they must be rationally connected to the objective. Second, the means, even if rationally connected to the objective in this first sense, should impair "as little as possible" the right or freedom in question . . . [and] Third, there must be a proportionality between the *effects* of the measures which are responsible for limiting the Charter right or freedom, and the objective which has been identified as of "sufficient importance."

Following this reliance on Canadian interpretation of the application of a general limitations clause, Justice Chaskalson proceeded to apply this approach to the question of the death penalty arguing that: "Although there is a rational connection between capital punishment and the purpose for which it is prescribed, the elements of arbitrariness, unfairness and irrationality in the imposition of the penalty, are factors that would have to be taken into account in the application of the first component of this test."[50] Addressing the second component Justice Chaskalson noted that "the fact that a severe punishment in the form of life imprisonment is available as an alternative sentence, would be relevant to the question whether the death sentence impairs the right as little as possible."[51] He also expressed doubts that "if all relevant considerations are taken into account . . . a sentence of capital punishment for murder would satisfy the third component of the *Oakes* test."[52]

Applying the "second requirement of the *Oakes* test, that the limitation should impair the right 'as little as possible,'" Justice Chaskalson argued that it "raises a fundamental problem of judicial review . . . should, an unelected court substitute its own opinion of what is reasonable or necessary for that of an elected legislature?" He then turns to the Canadian Supreme Court's judgment in *R v. Oakes* and argues that the "Canadian Supreme Court has shown that it is sensitive to this tension, which is particularly acute where choices have to be made in respect of matters of policy." Citing the Canadian

[49] *Id.*   [50] *Id.* para 106.   [51] *Id.*   [52] *Id.*

Supreme Court's opinions in *Irwin Toy Ltd v. Quebec (Attorney General)*, *Reference re ss. 193 and 195 (1)(c) of the Criminal Code (Manitoba)*, and *R v. Chaulk*, Justice Chaskalson notes that Canadian jurisprudence holds that "[w]here choices have to be made between "differing reasonable policy options," the courts will allow the government the deference due to legislators, but "[will] not give them an unrestricted licence to disregard an individual's Charter Rights. [and that] Where the government cannot show that it had a reasonable basis for concluding that it has complied with the requirement of minimal impairment in seeking to attain its objectives, the legislation will be struck down."[53]

In his concurring opinion in *President of the RSA v. Hugo* Justice Chaskalson again discussed the Constitutional Courts view of Canadian jurisprudence stating explicitly that the "views of the Canadian Supreme Court are also of assistance" [since] Like the South African Constitution, the Canadian Charter of Rights and Freedoms (the "Canadian Charter") contains a general limitations clause."[54] Furthermore, he noted, the Canadian Supreme Court has "consistently held rules emanating from statute, regulation and common law to be "prescribed by law."[55] This is not to argue that the Constitutional Court uncritically adheres at all times to Canadian jurisprudence. In *S v. Coetzee* involving a challenge to the Criminal Procedure Act, both Justice Langa in his majority opinion[56] and Justice Kentridge in his dissent noted that the challenges relied heavily on Canadian jurisprudence but agreed to distinguish the Canadian jurisprudence. Justice Kentridge noted that he had "referred in some detail to the Canadian authorities because ... they provided the main support for the submission of the applicants" but pointed out "that the Canadian authorities taken as a whole do not provide a sure and unequivocal foundation for the applicants' submissions." In this case Justice Kentridge pointed out that the South African statutory context is very different and although the law in both countries deals with strict liability offences, the "the burden of proof imposed by [the South African statute] ... upon the accused is substantially less than the burdens imposed upon the accused" in the Canadian cases cited.[57]

It is clear from the cases that there is a marked difference between the Constitutional Court's reliance on the jurisprudence of the Canadian Supreme Court when appropriate, and its response to the jurisprudence of the Supreme Court of the United States, which it addresses with much greater circumspection. While there is roughly the same amount of discussion and

---

[53] *Id.* para 107.   [54] *President of the RSA v. Hugo*, 1997 (4) SA 1, para 100.   [55] *Id.*
[56] *S v. Coetzee and Others*, 1997 (3) SA 527, para 34.   [57] *Id.* para 92.

citation of United States law, instead of using this source of legal argument as a model for interpreting the South African Constitution, the Constitutional Court is most likely to note the constitutional, structural, social and legal differences that exist between the United States and South Africa – in effect using United States law and jurisprudence as an anti-model. This point should however not be exaggerated since the majority of citations to both Canadian and United States law are general citations to the laws and legal traditions of developed jurisdictions in which both countries are presented as representative of the constitutional rule of law or common law analysis more generally.

CONCLUSION: CANADIAN JURISPRUDENCE
AS A SPECIAL CASE

While this is only a preliminary study of the influence of Canadian constitutionalism in South Africa, there are three tentative conclusions that may be reached based on the review and analysis of the empirical data. First, the link between Canadians and South Africans, including among lawyers and the legal academy is based on a well-established networks of relationships. Second, the incorporation of a Bill of Rights with a general limitations clause has clearly made Canadian jurisprudence an important source of comparative law for the Constitutional Court, and finally, that among different sources of comparative law the jurisprudence of the Canadian Supreme Court has clearly become the most influential even if it is on par with the United States as the two most referenced foreign jurisdictions more generally.

It is also possible to suggest some tentative reasons for why there is this special relationship between South African and Canadian constitutionalism. First, there is, as Adam Dodek has pointed out the importance of a shared language – which might also explain why four of the top five referenced jurisdictions are all primarily English language jurisdictions. This does not however explain why there is less reliance on India, Botswana, Nigeria or any of the many other commonwealth jurisdictions whose court opinions are published in English. Second, there is the shared common law heritage and method. While both South African and Canadian legal systems have roots in both the common law and civil law systems, their public law is rooted in the public law of the United Kingdom and the Constitutional Courts of civil law jurisdictions provide far leaner sets of reasons for their decisions than is prevalent in common law courts. Third, South Africa and Canada share a constitutional heritage in their former status as Dominions involving an important set of constitutional arrangements from the Colonial Laws Invalidity Act and the Statue of Westminster to the jurisdiction of the Privy Council.

Finally, there are two elements that press against the influence of Canadian constitutionalism that will need further exploration. First, the justices of the Constitutional Court have since its founding had a number of foreign law clerks who have played significant roles in researching and explaining foreign law within the confines of the Court. From my understanding, most of these have come from the United States and one has always come from Germany. It is unclear how many Canadians have served as clerks and whether this has had any impact on either the negative interpretation of United States jurisprudence or the positive influence of Canadian jurisprudence. Second, while Adam Dodek notes that multiculturalism is an important aspect of the Canadian model, it should be noted that this aspect has been interpreted very differently in South Africa, and that along with the notwithstanding clause it has not influenced the direction of South African constitutionalism.

Conclusion
The Court and Constitution in the World

DAVID R. CAMERON

In introducing this volume, Richard Albert noted what US Supreme Court Justice Ruth Bader Ginsburg said in an interview in 2012 on the Egyptian Al-Hayat Television channel. After mentioning that she had met with the elections commission and that everyone agreed the elections for the lower house had been free and fair, she said the next milestone would be the drafting of a constitution – one that should safeguard basic fundamental rights, like the American constitution's First Amendment, the right to speak freely and publish freely without government censorship. She offered some advice about how the Egyptians should go about the constitution-writing task:

> You should certainly be aided by all the constitution-writing that has gone on since the end of World War II. I would not look to the US constitution if I were drafting a constitution in the year 2012. I might look at the constitution of South Africa. That was a deliberate attempt to have a fundamental instrument of government that embraced basic human rights, had an independent judiciary ... Much more recent than the US constitution – Canada has a Charter of Rights and Freedoms. It dates from 1982. You would almost certainly look at the European Convention on Human Rights. Yes, why not take advantage of what there is elsewhere in the world?[1]

As Justice Ginsberg's colleague, Justice Stephen Breyer, argues, her wise advice to take advantage of what others have done extends beyond constitution writing to the decision-making of constitutional courts.[2] For a court that is sworn to interpret and apply the world's oldest written constitution, the notion

[1] Ruth Bader Ginsburg interview on Al-Hayat Television, January 30, 2012, at www.memritv.org/clip_transcript /-en/3295.htm. The *Canadian Charter of Rights and Freedoms* is Part I of the *Constitution Act 1982*, which is annexed as Schedule B to the *Canada Act 1982* (UK).

[2] Stephen Breyer, THE COURT AND THE WORLD: AMERICAN LAW AND THE NEW GLOBAL REALITIES (New York: Alfred A. Knopf, 2015).

that the US Supreme Court should look to the decisions or conclusions of foreign courts is regarded by many, including some of that court's justices, as antithetical to the obligation of applying the written words of the Constitution in accordance with, insofar as they can be ascertained, the original intentions of the Founders and meaning of their words. Nevertheless, Justice Breyer argues, "it is important for Americans to understand and to appropriately apply international and foreign law."[3] For one thing, in an increasingly interdependent world, the Court has been obliged to extend its awareness and understanding of events and places beyond its traditional focus and "must increasingly consider foreign and domestic law together, as if they constituted parts of a broadly interconnected legal web."[4] Since there is, he notes, no Supreme Court of the world, "national courts must act piecemeal, without direct coordination, in seeking interpretations that can dovetail rather than clash with the working of foreign statutes. And so our Court does, and should, listen to foreign voices, to those who understand and can illuminate relevant foreign laws and practices"[5] The purpose, he emphasizes, is not to take on the rulings of the foreign courts but, rather, to achieve "legal harmony" in a variety of matters ranging from commercial statutes pertaining to antitrust, "discovery," securities and copyright to violations of human rights – a harmony that requires "a broader, more worldly-wise understanding and knowledge ... of foreign activities and laws."[6]

But Justice Breyer notes the Court has increasingly looked to the decisions and conclusions of foreign courts not just to understand the relevant foreign laws and practices to achieve "legal harmony" in matters that transcend national boundaries but also, on occasion, to provide guidance or reinforcement, through "cross-referencing," in its own decisions. He notes, for example, that in two highly controversial cases – one involving the application of the death penalty to someone under the age of eighteen, the other involving a state's prohibition of consensual same-sex relations – Justice Anthony Kennedy, writing for the Court, drew upon foreign law and practices to support its decision.[7] Justice Breyer, following the arguments of Jeremy Waldron and others, provides a robust defence of "cross-referencing" on the grounds that, even if references to foreign law are not necessary in order to arrive at a decision, they may "help judges produce better decisions without constraining their decisional autonomy."[8] After all,

---

[3] *Id.* at 7.   [4] *Id.* at 91.   [5] *Id.* at 92.   [6] *Id.* at 92–93.

[7] The cases were *Roper v. Simmons*, 543 US 551 (2005) and *Lawrence v. Texas*, 539 US 558 (2003), cited in Breyer, *Id.* at 238.

[8] Breyer, *Id.* at 239. On cross-referencing see, among many, Jeremy Waldron, "Partly Laws Common to All Mankind": Foreign Law in American Courts (New Haven: Yale University Press, 2012).

if someone with a job roughly like my own, facing a legal problem roughly like the one confronting me, interpreting a document that resembles the one I look to, has written a legal opinion about a similar matter, why not read what the judge has said? I might learn from it, whether or not I end up agreeing with it ... Opinions often note useful law review articles, books of history, statistical studies, and all sorts of other sources ... So why not include foreign court decisions as well? To learn from foreign opinions or to consider their reasoning is to find in them something of use in interpreting *American*, not foreign, law ... The growing complexity of problems, taken together with the need to produce a judgment in a few weeks or months at most, adds value to the experience of other judges who have faced comparable problems. The wheel needn't be reinvented every time.[9]

If openness to the views of other constitutional courts on issues under consideration remains a minority position on the American court, it is widely accepted by justices on other constitutional courts, including the Supreme Court of Canada. Almost twenty years ago, Justice Claire L'Heureux-Dubé noted the existence of an "active and ongoing dialogue among judges" and the fact that "more and more courts, particularly within the common-law world, are looking to the judgments of other jurisdictions, particularly when making decisions on human rights issues."[10] Likewise, in a keynote address several years ago that contrasted the American and Canadian perspectives on the use of foreign law, Chief Justice Beverley McLachlin noted the existence of a "world-wide rights culture" and remarked that "a willingness to look at foreign law is no impediment to developing and maintaining distinctive legal approaches that respond to the particular history, values and needs of a nation."[11]

In her contribution to this volume, Chief Justice McLachlin observes that "Canadian lawyers are comparative lawyers; Canadian judges are comparative judges. It's not a matter of debate; it's simply the way we are, the way our history has made us." Unlike the situation in the United States, where the idea developed that looking at the law of other courts in other countries might "sully the unique and pristine nature of American law," in Canada, perhaps because British law served for so long as its law – she notes that until 1949 the Judicial Committee of the Privy Council served as its final court of appeal – the Court

---

[9]   Breyer, *Id.* at 240.
[10] Claire L'Heureux-Dubé, *The Importance of Dialogue: Globalization and the International Impact of the Rehnquist Court*, 34 Tulsa L. J. 15 (1998).
[11] Chief Justice Beverley McLachlin, *The Use of Foreign Law: A Comparative View of Canada and the United States*, Keynote Address, 104th Annual Meeting, American Society of International Law, Washington, D.C., 24 April 2010, available at www.fora.tv.

remains committed to the idea that we can gain insights and ideas from jurists in countries that possess similar values to our own. To be sure, we do not simply slap foreign law on a Canadian problem. We approach the rulings of other courts on problems we face with respectful caution and with attention to the different history and social context that shaped those decisions. Each nation's law must be true to its own history, context and jurisprudential traditions. Using comparative law involves sophisticated, high-level judging. But used appropriately, it produces richer, better decisions.

The opportunity for and likelihood of cross-referencing has increased dramatically in recent decades, in part because of the dramatic increases in both the number of new constitutions and the number of constitutional systems that provide for judicial review, the rise of a number of new constitutional issues – most notably, issues pertaining to rights, including newly defined rights – and the development of technologies such as the Internet that greatly facilitate the ability of the members of constitutional courts and their clerks to read the rulings of other courts throughout the world.[12] For example, Saunders reports that since 1990 more than ninety new constitutions or constitutional-type instruments for states and other polities have come into force.[13] And Ginsburg reports that, whereas only a handful of constitutions provided for judicial review in the period immediately after World War II, 151 of the 191 constitutional systems now do.[14] As a large number of new constitutional courts exercised their responsibilities, including their powers of judicial review, their justices often found themselves in precisely the situations Justice Breyer and Chief Justice McLachlin describe – and, for the same reason, did what they often do, which is to look at the decisions of other courts that have addressed the same issue.

As that happened, a scholarly literature developed in regard to what Anne-Marie Slaughter called "transjudicial communication" – the emergence of a "global dialogue" among courts and justices who increasingly found themselves looking at and learning from the reasoning and decisions of justices in other constitutional courts and, in the wake of that communication and

[12] See Elaine Mak, JUDICIAL DECISION-MAKING IN A GLOBALISED WORLD: A COMPARATIVE ANALYSIS OF THE CHANGING PRACTICES OF WESTERN HIGHEST COURTS (Oxford and Portland: Hart, 2013).

[13] Cheryl Saunders, *Judicial Engagement with Comparative Law*, in Tom Ginsburg and Rosalind Dixon, eds., COMPARATIVE CONSTITUTIONAL LAW (Cheltenham: Edward Elgar, 2011) at 574.

[14] Tom Ginsburg, *The Global Spread of Constitutional Review*, in Keith E. Whittington et al., eds., THE OXFORD HANDBOOK OF LAW AND POLITICS (Oxford: Oxford University Press, 2008) at 81.

dialogue, the "migration of constitutional ideas" from one court to another.[15] Of course, not all constitutional courts participate in that "global dialogue" to the same degree; Groppi and Ponthoreau report that in the period between 2000 and 2010 the constitutional courts of Austria, Germany, Hungary, Japan, Mexico, Romania, Russia, Taiwan and, notwithstanding the willingness of Justices Ginsburg and Breyer to look at the rulings of foreign courts, the United States only rarely cited foreign precedents. But some courts – those of Australia, Canada, India, Israel, Ireland, Namibia and South Africa – cited foreign precedents frequently.[16] Thus, while less than 3 per cent of the decisions of the German and Hungarian constitutional courts and less than 1 per cent of the decisions of the Austrian, Japanese and American constitutional courts included one or more references to a foreign precedent, more than 50 per cent of the decisions of the Australian and South African courts, 44 per cent of the decisions of the Irish court, 40 per cent of the decisions of the Supreme Court of Canada and 28 per cent of the decisions of Israel's court included one or more references to a foreign precedent.[17]

In his chapter discussing the role of the Supreme Court of Canada as a "giver" and "taker," "exporter" and "importer," of constitutional jurisprudence, Ran Hirschl cites Gentili's finding that from 1982 through 2013 the Court cited the courts of other countries in roughly 40 per cent of its more than 900 decisions in constitutional cases, resulting in a total of more than 1900 citations.[18] That clearly places Canada among the courts that most frequently cite the rulings of other constitutional courts. On the other hand, Gentili's research also demonstrates that the Court is highly selective in the foreign courts it cites. Thus, of its 1944 citations of foreign precedents between 1982 and 2013, almost 1,200 were to decisions of the US Supreme Court and more than 500 were to British decisions. The Australian High Court was a distant third with eighty-seven citations, followed by the European Court of

---

15 Anne-Marie Slaughter, A *Typology of Transjudicial Communication*, 29 U. RICH. L. REV. 99 (1994). See also Anne-Marie Slaughter, A *Global Community of Courts*, 44 HARVARD INT. LAW J. 19 (2003); Anne-Marie Slaughter, A NEW WORLD ORDER (Princeton: Princeton University Press, 2004); and Sujit Choudhry, ed., THE MIGRATION OF CONSTITUTIONAL IDEAS (Cambridge: Cambridge University Press, 2006).

16 Tania Groppi and Marie-Claire Ponthoreau, eds., THE USE OF FOREIGN PRECEDENTS BY CONSTITUTIONAL JUDGES (Oxford and Portland: Hart Publishing, 2013) at 3.

17 *Id.* at 411–12.

18 Gianluca Gentili, *Enhancing Constitutional Self-Understanding through Comparative Law: An Empirical Study of the Use of Foreign Case Law by the Supreme Court of Canada (1982–2013)*, in Mads Andenas and Duncan Fairgrieve, eds., COURTS AND COMPARATIVE LAW (Oxford: Oxford University Press, 2015) at 378–406.

Human Rights with sixty-nine, the New Zealand court with thirty-five and the French court with sixteen. All other courts were in single digits.[19]

No less interesting than the fact that its foreign precedents have come largely from a small number of courts – indeed, largely from only two courts, those of the United States and United Kingdom – is the fact that, while the Court continued to cite roughly the same number of precedents each year from the United Kingdom – generally in the range of one to two dozen – the number of citations each year of decisions of the American court, which was negligible prior to the mid-1980s, increased dramatically from the mid-1980s through the mid-1990s and then dropped markedly after the mid-1990s.[20] The dramatic increase of American citations from the mid-1980s through the mid-1990s undoubtedly reflected the greater propensity of the Court to look at decisions of the American court pertaining to the US Bill of Rights as it began to deal with cases pertaining to rights in the years after the Charter took effect. The subsequent drop in citations to the American court after the mid-1990s may, as Hirschl suggests, reflect the Court's maturation, as it came, with the accumulation of decisions pertaining to rights, to rely more heavily on its own precedents. But as he notes, it may also reflect, alongside the increasing self-confidence of the Canadian Court, "the declining relevance of US jurisprudence as persuasive authority." In that regard, Gentili notes that more than half of the Court's citations of American decisions were to decisions by the Warren (1953–1969) and Burger (1969–1986) courts rather than by the Rehnquist (1986–2005) and Roberts (2005–) courts.[21]

It is of course not surprising that the vast majority of foreign citations by the Canadian Court were to decisions of the American and British courts. During much of the period after Confederation, although the Canadian courts occasionally cited American precedents, the Judicial Committee of the Privy Council, which as Chief Justice McLachlin noted, remained Canada's final court of appeal until 1949, considered only British precedents and disregarded foreign precedents.[22] As a result, interpretation of the British North American Act 1867 was, as Gentili noted, based very largely on domestic – meaning British – precedents rather than foreign precedents, a pattern that continued even after the Supreme Court became the highest court of appeal.[23] However, as noted above, enactment of the Charter dramatically altered the situation

---

[19] *Id.* at 395.   [20] *Id.*   [21] *Id.* at 400.

[22] In September 1949, the Federal government enacted legislation amending the Supreme Court Act to make judgments of the Supreme Court final and conclusive in all cases, thereby terminating the Privy Council's role as the final court of appeal. See Alan C. Cairns, *The Judicial Committee and Its Critics*, CAN. J. POLIT. SCI. 4 (1971).

[23] Gentili, *supra* note 18 at 399.

and made American jurisprudence pertaining to its Bill of Rights relevant. Thus, whereas the Court cited American cases only five times in 1982, not at all in 1983 and six times in 1984, the number of citations increased dramatically thereafter – to 31 in 1985, 70 in 1986, 69 in 1987 and a peak of 74 to 157 in 1989–92.[24]

Drawing on Manfredi, Gentili argues the Charter "brought US and Canadian cultures closer, the latter acquiring a rights-based foundation the former had already experienced for decades, and making US precedents relevant to the interpretation of Canadian laws."[25] As Chief Justice Dickson put it in *R v. Simmons*, "The American courts have the benefit of two hundred years of experience in constitutional interpretation. This wealth of experience may offer guidance to the judiciary in this country."[26] In addition, of course, the two courts share a number of attributes: both exist in countries that were at one time British colonies, both share a common language and a common-law legal tradition that began in England, and both exist in federal systems, which, as systems organized, as Stephen Tierney notes in this volume, on the principle of territorial pluralism, give rise to especially complex jurisdictional and jurisprudential issues between the national and sub-national levels of government and among the latter. On the other hand, it should be noted that, despite the frequency of its citation of American cases, the Court's decisions did not always follow the American decisions; indeed, far from it. Thus, Gentili reports that out of 268 constitutional cases in which the Court cited American precedents between 1982 and 2010, the American decision was followed in only 15 per cent of the cases, the Court reached a different conclusion in 29 per cent of the cases, and in the remaining 56 per cent of the cases the references were simply informative.[27]

While the largest number of citations of foreign precedents by the Court in the period since 1982 involved decisions made in London and Washington, the Court was influenced by other courts as well. One of the most interesting examples involves the use of proportionality tests to determine whether a legislative act adversely affects a right. Adrienne Stone in her chapter on the rulings of the Court in cases involving section 2(b) of the Charter on the

---

[24] *Id.* at 395.

[25] *Id.* at 400. See, also, Christopher P. Manfredi, *Adjudication, Policy-Making and the Supreme Court of Canada: Lessons from the Experience of the United States*, CAN. J. POLIT. SCI. 22 (1989).

[26] *R v. Simmons*, 2 SCR 495 (1988).

[27] Gianluca Gentili, *Canada: Protecting Rights in a "Worldwide Rights Culture". An Empirical Study of the Use of Foreign Precedents by the Supreme Court of Canada (1982–2010)*, in Groppi and Ponthoreau, *supra* note 16 at 63.

freedom of expression notes that proportionality tests have made their way into common-law systems via European law, most directly through decisions of the European Court of Human Rights. But the origin can be traced to Germany, which is, she says, clearly the progenitor of the proportionality approach that has come to be employed most frequently in Canada. The reason, she argues, lies in the Canadian Court's relative openness, in contrast to the American court, not only to the specific rulings of other courts but to approaches that balance the purpose of a legislative act and the infringement of that act on a right.

The reason the Court found that balancing approach helpful is, of course, section 1 of the Charter, the so-called "limitations clause," which states "The Canadian Charter of Rights and Freedoms guarantees the rights and freedoms set out in it subject only to such reasonable limits prescribed by law as can be demonstrably justified in a free and democratic society."[28] In the Court's first decision, in 1985, interpreting section 2 (Fundamental Freedoms) of the Charter, Chief Justice Dickson, writing for the Court in striking down the 1906 *Lord's Day Act*, a statute that prohibited commerce on Sundays, said the limitation on a right must be for an important objective and must be as limited as possible.[29] As Ayelet Shachar notes in this volume, the Court concluded that, while prohibiting businesses from operating on Sundays reflected the preference of a religious majority, doing so imposed that majority's view on those of other religions who did not object to businesses operating on Sundays and on non-believers. That, the Court said, violated section 27 of the Charter, which states that it "shall be interpreted in a manner consistent with the preservation and enhancement of the multicultural heritage of Canadians." Shachar notes that, with that decision, the Court officially enshrined multiculturalism as a constitutional principle, something no other court has done.

In a second decision a year later, again writing for the Court, Chief Justice Dickson formulated what has come to be known as the Oakes Test, in which the objective of the statute infringing upon a right must be one that is related to "concerns which are pressing and substantial in a free and democratic society" and the means for achieving the objective must be "reasonable and demonstrably justified"; carefully designed to achieve the objective in question; fair and not arbitrary, rationally connected to the objective; and impair "as little as possible" the right or freedom in question. Lastly, "there must be a

---

[28] *Constitution Act 1982, Part I. Charter of Rights and Freedoms* at http://laws-lois-justice.gc.ca/eng/Const/page-15.html.

[29] *R v. Big M Drug Mart Ltd*, 1 SCR 295 (1985).

proportionality between the effects of the limiting measure and the objective – the more severe the deleterious effects of a measure, the more important the objective must be."[30]

The balancing of competing rights that underlies proportionality is well illustrated by another decision discussed by Shachar, that in *R. v. N. (S.)* (2012) in which the Court weighed the right of the victim of sexual assault to wear the *niqab* while testifying in court versus the defendant's right to a fair trial that required her face to be visible during cross-examination.[31] In a divided decision, the Court, with Chief Justice McLachlin writing for the majority, ruled that, when faced with a conflict between the freedom of religion and other values, an individual's religious belief should be accommodated if at all possible. That approach, Shachar notes, "places the competing interests in a balancing formula, rather than categorically prioritizing one set of interests over the others, reflecting the preference for proportionality and minimal impairment that has become deeply entrenched in Canada's constitutional jurisprudence." In light of that approach, the Court held that a total ban on the *niqab* was inconsistent with the Charter.

Mark Tushnet in his chapter focuses on the Canadian Court's use of proportionality analysis to determine whether, in the event a statute infringes upon a right, the infringement is justified. In contrast to the United States, where there is a relatively stringent test for justification, the Canadian proportionality review allows the stringency of the test to vary depending on the relative importance of the affected interests. After noting that some have argued that the use of such an analysis inevitably leads to "rights inflation" – a broadening of the application of a right to a wider range of specific activities – he suggests that, although it is difficult to confirm, "rights inflation" has indeed occurred in rulings of the Canadian Court. On the other hand, he notes that the Court recognized in *Baier v. Alberta* that Charter rights, while "usually broad and often overlapping ... are not formless and boundless."[32]

As mentioned earlier, Chief Justice McLachlin notes an important reason why the Canadian court so frequently refers to the decisions of other constitutional courts: Unlike its neighbour to the south, Canada "kept the law of England as its basic law (apart from the Civil Code in Quebec governing private law) until the second half of the twentieth century. Until 1949, the Judicial Committee of the Privy Council was Canada's final court of appeal." "Think of it," she says, "our law was not our own law; it was another country's law. The thought gives comparative law a whole new twist." For more than

[30] *R. v. Oakes*, 1 SCR 103 (1986).   [31] *R. v. N.(S.)*, 3 SCR 726 (2012).
[32] *Baier v. Alberta*, 2 SCR 673 (2007).

200 years, from 1763, when the Treaty of Paris that ended the Seven Years War gave New France to the United Kingdom, to 1982, when the Constitution was patriated, Canada was subject to some form and degree of British legal authority. Indeed, as Jamie Cameron discusses in this volume, even after Canada was granted its independence in the *Statute of Westminster* (1931), the United Kingdom retained – at the request of the federal government, which had been unable to reach agreement with the provinces on an amending formula – the sole authority to amend the constitution until that authority was finally patriated in 1982. At the request of the federal government, the United Kingdom amended the Canadian Constitution nine times between 1931 and 1982.[33]

The importance of the fact that the Judicial Committee of the Privy Council remained as Canada's final court of appeal even after the *Statute of Westminster* and until 1949 cannot be overstated. Throughout the more than eighty years between Confederation and 1949, the Canadian Court was not, as it is today, in a situation in which it could, after perusing a decision of the Privy Council in a particular matter, disregard that decision and reach a different conclusion if it wished. Instead, it was, in juridical terms, subordinate to the Judicial Committee and the decisions of that committee constituted obligatory precedents that were the law of the land. That remained the case until 1949, when the Supreme Court Act was amended and the Court became the final court of appeal in all cases. Given the long period of time during which the Judicial Committee served as the country's de facto supreme court, it is no wonder the Canadian Court is so attentive today to the decisions of other constitutional courts.

Stephen Tierney argues in this volume that "the distinguishing feature of the federal constitutional moment is the explicit or implicit recognition of territorial diversity ... the existence of territories, their significance to the citizens who comprise them, and, accordingly, their role in mediating the

---

[33] Jamie Cameron notes that in four of the nine instances, the federal government obtained unanimous provincial consent for the amendment, but in the other five, it proceeded without provincial consent or with provincial objection. She also notes the federal government unilaterally requested amendment for the last time in 1949 and did not request any amendment after 1964 – until, of course, late 1981 when, after a prolonged dispute between the federal government and some provinces, the federal government requested patriation of the constitution. That conflict gave rise to two Supreme Court references – *Reference Re Resolution to Amend the Constitution* 1 SCR 753 (1981), addressing the question of whether the federal government could unilaterally request the United Kingdom to amend the constitution and *Reference Re Amendment to the Canadian Constitution* 2 SCR 793 (1982), addressing the question of whether Quebec had a veto over any such request. The former is known as the *Patriation Reference*.

relationship between the individual and the state." "The federal constitutional moment is," he says, "therefore the coming together not only of individuals but also of territorial communities in a more complex contractual pact." What made the Canadian pact so complex and at times so contentious, of course, was its inclusion, in a state that was a British dominion, in which the population was predominantly British in heritage, English-speaking and Protestant and in which the British Privy Council was the final court of appeal, of a territory which had been a French colony for more than 150 years prior to the Treaty of Paris and in which the population was predominantly French in heritage, French-speaking and Catholic.[34]

One aspect of the complex territorial pact that has incorporated the diverse and distinctive societies of Canada into a single state has been the recognition, legitimation and accommodation, in a state which adheres to the English common-law legal tradition and in which British law has been the law of the land for most of the past 250 years, of the use of the French Civil Code in Quebec. As both Chief Justice McLachlin and Alain Gagnon note, in 1774, eleven years after obtaining New France, the United Kingdom enacted the *Quebec Act*, which gave those living in what had been New France the right to practice their Catholic faith, omitted any reference to the Protestant faith in the oath of allegiance and restored the use of French civil law. Those rights continued when the Province of Quebec was divided by the 1791 *Constitutional Act* into Upper Canada and Lower Canada. The act recognized the *Coutume de Paris*, which had been the civil law in New France until 1763, as the law pertaining to property, inheritance and other civil matters alongside English common law for matters of public law. The *British North America Act 1867*, which in 1982 became the *Constitution Act 1867*, recognized in section 94 the civil law of Quebec as distinct from that of the other provinces.[35] All of which is to say that the Canadian Court had to be attentive not only to British jurisprudence but also, in some cases involving Quebec, to French civil law as well.

The long juridical relationship between Canada and the United Kingdom, coupled with the presence of French civil law in Quebec, made it entirely natural and indeed often necessary that the Canadian Court would look to, and on occasion be influenced by, the decisions of foreign courts, the British

[34] The 1871 census reported the population of Quebec as 1.2 million and that of Canada as 3.7 million, at www.statcan.gc.ca/access_acces/archive.action?l=eng&loc=A2_14-eng.csv. Samuel de Champlain founded the city of Quebec and New France in 1608.

[35] See *Constitution Act 1867*, 30 & 31 Victoria c 3. As Alain Gagnon notes, section 133 of the *British North America Act 1867* also made French an official language of Canada and made the province of Quebec officially bilingual.

in particular but others as well. And because it was routinely involved in a trans-Atlantic judicial dialogue with the Judicial Committee of the British Privy Council in the latter's role as the final court of appeal in innumerable cases for more than eighty years after Confederation, it was inevitable that it would be influenced not only by the accumulated jurisprudence of the Judicial Committee but also by its view of its proper role in interpreting the Canadian constitution. No decision better illustrates that influence than the committee's 1930 decision in *Edwards v. Canada*, the Persons case. In that decision, Viscount Sankey, the Lord Chancellor, writing for the Privy Council, created what soon became and remains to this day the single most frequently employed metaphor for the Canadian constitution – a "living tree."[36]

The case arose as a reference to the Supreme Court by the Federal government on behalf of Emily Murphy, an Albertan judge, and four other women from that province in regard to whether a woman could be appointed to the Senate. Section 24 of the *British North America Act 1867* stated that "qualified persons" could be appointed to the Senate. The reference asked whether "qualified persons" included "female persons." In 1928, the Court ruled that women were not eligible for appointment because they were not "qualified persons." The decision was appealed to the Judicial Committee of the Privy Council and in 1930 it ruled that women were "qualified persons" and hence eligible for appointment to the Senate by the Governor-General. On behalf of the committee, Viscount Sankey wrote:

> The British North America Act planted in Canada a living tree capable of growth and expansion within its natural limits. The object of the Act was to provide a Constitution to Canada ... Their Lordships do not conceive it to be the duty of this Board – it is certainly not their desire – to cut down the provisions of the Act by a narrow and technical construction, but rather to give it a large and liberal interpretation so that the Dominion to a great extent, but within certain fixed limits, may be mistress in her own house.[37]

In 1984, in *Hunter et al. v. Southam*, the Court issued its first major Charter ruling, striking down a Federal statute pertaining to a search.[38] In the ruling, Chief Justice Dickson elaborated upon what Viscount Sankey had said more than fifty years earlier:

---

[36] *Edwards v. Canada* (AG) A.C. 124 (1930). On the case, see Robert J. Sharpe and Patricia I. McMahon, THE PERSONS CASE: THE ORIGINS AND LEGACY OF THE FIGHT FOR LEGAL PERSONHOOD (Toronto: University of Toronto Press, 2007).

[37] *Edwards v. Canada* (AG), A.C. 124 (1930).

[38] *Hunter et al. v. Southam, Inc.*, 2 SCR 145 (1984).

The task of expounding a constitution is crucially different from that of construing a statute. A statute defines present rights and obligations. It is easily enacted and as easily repealed. A constitution, by contrast, is drafted with an eye to the future. Its function is to provide a continuing framework for the legitimate exercise of governmental power and, when joined by a Bill or a Charter of Rights, for the unremitting protection of individual rights and liberties. Once enacted, its provisions cannot easily be repealed or amended. It must, therefore, be capable of growth and development over time to meet new social, political and historical realities often unimagined by its framers. The judiciary is the guardian of the constitution and must, in interpreting its provisions, bear these considerations in mind.

Continuing, Justice Dickson said, "The need for a broad perspective in approaching constitutional documents is a familiar theme in Canadian constitutional jurisprudence. It is contained in Viscount Sankey's classic formulation in *Edwards v. Attorney General for Canada* cited and applied in countless Canadian cases." He proceeded to quote the Lord Chancellor's words in that case. He also noted that Lord Wilberforce, in a more recent Privy Council decision dealing with the Bermudian Constitution, had reiterated that a constitution is a document "sui generis, calling for principles of interpretation of its own, suitable to its character" and that as such, a constitution incorporating a Bill of Rights calls for "a generous interpretation avoiding what has been called 'austerity of tabulated legalism,' suitable to give individuals the full measure of the fundamental rights and freedoms referred to."[39]

Goldsworthy and Huscroft in this volume argue that the "living tree" metaphor, although articulated more than eighty years ago, has remained under-theorized, is too vague to resolve some issues such as the discovery of new rights and is hard to explain other than by what it is not – originalism. Yet, although the idea of a "living constitution" is philosophically problematic, they conclude the rationale – the need to accommodate growth and development in response to new circumstances – does not differ from contemporary public meaning originalism which allows constitutional law to evolve. But while they do not see a great deal of difference between that form of originalism and Viscount Sankey's metaphor, they do suggest it is important to recognize that a living tree has roots and a trunk that are fixed – and that, in creating the metaphor, Viscount Sankey noted a living tree has "natural limits" and that there are "certain fixed limits" on the "large and liberal interpretation" of the constitution.

---

[39] The Bermuda case was *Minister of Home Affairs v. Fisher*, A.C. 319 (1980).

As Chief Justice McLachlin, the longest-serving Chief Justice in Canadian history, notes in this volume, the "living tree" principle continues to be one of the central tenets of Canadian constitutional interpretation – one that "recognizes the ability of constitutional jurisprudence to be applied to changing social realities in Canadian society" and "has been of great assistance in coming to grips with the tensions and disputes inevitable in a diverse society." She recognizes what Goldsworthy and Huscroft say about the trunk and roots of the "living tree"; as she puts it, "The tree of the constitution stands firm and fixed, rooted in the national soil of the country." But she also notes that the constitution, like a "living tree," "is capable, from time to time, of sprouting a new leaf or even growing a new branch. The constitution lives and adapts through its application to new situations."

Ran Hirschl argues in his chapter that "the most significant development in contemporary comparative constitutionalism is the global spread of constitutional courts, judicial review and bills of rights as the cynosures of the comparative constitutional universe." And

> no single country's constitutional landscape exemplifies this transformation more vividly than Canada, which ... entered the twentieth century embodying the deferential, British-style constitutional tradition and emerged out of it with a robust constitutional culture featuring active judicial review, an acclaimed constitutional bill of rights – the Canadian Charter of Rights and Freedoms – pervasive rights discourse and one of the most frequently cited high courts in the World.

Indeed, in assessing the transformation of Canada's stature into a "giver" of constitutional thought, he argues constitutional innovation has become one of the country's main intellectual exports. Anne-Marie Slaughter has suggested, interestingly, that Canada has become an influential exporter of constitutional jurisprudence at least in part because it has also been an importer of constitutional jurisprudence; other constitutional courts, aware that the Canadian Court is attentive to and informed about the jurisprudential insights and wisdom of other courts in regard to the complex issues that come before it, look to it as a court that is well-informed about current jurisprudence in regard to those issues and often find its decisions helpful as they address the same issues.[40]

That Canadian jurisprudence in the post-Charter era has become an important resource for constitutional courts in other countries has been

---

[40] Anne-Marie Slaughter, *A Brave New Judicial World*, in Michael Ignatieff, ed., AMERICAN EXCEPTIONALISM AND HUMAN RIGHTS (Princeton: Princeton University Press, 2005).

recognized by jurists and scholars alike. Aharon Barak, who served as a justice on the Supreme Court of Israel from 1978 to 1995 and as Chief Justice from 1995 to 2006, has said, "Canadian law serves as a source of inspiration for many countries around the world."[41] Hirschl, in *Comparative Matters*, notes the Canadian Court has not only become a source of inspiration for other high courts; at a time when the British and American courts are declining in influence, the international stature of the Canadian Court, along with that of the German Constitutional Court and the European Court of Human Rights, has been rising.[42] In the same vein, Choudhry notes that in the years since the Charter of Rights was entrenched in the Constitution, it has become the leading alternative to the US Bill of Rights as a model for constitutional-izing rights.[43] Likewise, Tania Groppi has documented the extensive and increasing influence of decisions by the Supreme Court of Canada, which she describes as a "user-friendly court," on those of other constitutional courts over the past three decades.[44]

One of the most noteworthy examples of the Canadian Court's role as a constitutional and jurisprudential "giver" or exporter involves South Africa. In his chapter, Heinz Klug examines both the reception and impact of Canada on the constitution-making that occurred in that country in the 1990s and its constitutional jurisprudence thereafter. He notes that Canadian constitutional ideas had a profound effect on South Africa's post-apartheid constitution and jurisprudence – not only because the countries shared a common-law heri-tage, membership in the Commonwealth and a long common experience of having the British Privy Council serve as their final court of appeal, but also because of a substantial amount of interaction between Canadian and South African academics and lawyers in workshops, conferences and exchanges in the period preceding the actual writing of the latter's constitution.

Klug notes that Canadian constitutionalism influenced both South Africa's 1993 interim and 1996 final constitution. For example, in part because the African National Congress sought to prevent the use of the rights and

---

[41] Aharon Barak, *A Judge on Judging: The Role of a Supreme Court in a Democracy*, 116 Harvard L. R. 19 (2002) at 114.

[42] Ran Hirschl, Comparative Matters: The Renaissance of Comparative Constitutional Law (Oxford: Oxford University Press, 2014) at 8.

[43] Sujit Choudhry, *Globalization in Search of Justification: Toward a Theory of Comparative Constitutional Interpretation*, 74 Indiana L.J. 819 (1999).

[44] Tania Groppi, A User-friendly Court: The Influence of Supreme Court of Canada Decisions Since 1982 on Court Decisions in Other Liberal Democracies, 36 Supreme Court L. R. 37 (2007). See also Groppi and Ponthoreau, *Conclusion: The Use of Foreign Precedents by Constitutional Judges: A Limited Practice, An Uncertain Future*, in Groppi and Ponthoreau, *supra*, at 420, who note at 420 that *R v. Oakes* is especially popular among Canadian precedents.

freedoms guaranteed by the new constitution to block efforts to deal with the legacy of apartheid, South Africa introduced in Section 33 of the interim constitution a "limitations clause" similar to the one specified in Section 1 of the Canadian Charter, which stipulated that the rights and freedoms guaranteed by the constitution were subject only to such reasonable limits prescribed by law as could be demonstrably justified in a free and democratic society. In addition, taking a leaf from the Canadian experience, both the interim and final constitutions formally invited and allowed the use of foreign case law. In that regard, Klug reports the South African constitutional court referenced and discussed foreign law in 50 per cent of all its cases since 1995. Perhaps not surprisingly, given the influence of Canadian ideas in the constitution-writing process, the Canadian court was by far the single most frequently cited foreign court in the South African court's first two decades. Thus, Rautenbach reports that over the period between 1995 and 2010, the South African constitutional court cited foreign precedents in more than 200 decisions. Canadian rulings were cited 860 times, compared with 726 citations of American decisions, 482 citations of UK decisions and 142 citations of European Court of Human Rights decisions.[45]

Kent Roach in this volume describes another constitutional invention that has been exported to other countries and, like the "limitations clause," was incorporated into the South African constitution. In 1980, Manitoba enacted legislation that in effect repealed the constitutional requirement that legislation be published in English and French and allowed it to be published only in English. In 1983, a new government, together with the federal government, agreed to a constitutional amendment that would forgive the translation of many older laws into French in exchange for the recognition of French as an official language. But in the face of substantial public opposition, the legislation was not enacted and the federal government referred the matter to the Supreme Court. The Court rejected Manitoba's defence of its failure to adhere to the constitutional commitment to bilingualism and declared all unilingual acts and regulations null and void.[46] But it also said the unconstitutional laws should have temporary validity for the minimal amount of time required for their translation, thereby inventing the Suspended Declaration of Invalidity. Since that decision, the Court has made

---

[45] Christa Rautenbach, *South Africa: Teaching an "Old Dog" New Tricks? An Empirical Study of the Use of Foreign Precedents by the South African Constitutional Court*, in Groppi and Ponthoreau, *supra* note 16 at 197.

[46] *Manitoba Language Reference*, 1 SCR 721 (1985).

frequent use of the invention and it provided the inspiration for section 172(1) of the 1996 South Africa constitution.

Decisions of the Supreme Court of Canada have been cited frequently by a number of other constitutional courts as well. Thus, Cheryl Saunders and Adrienne Stone report the Australian High Court cited foreign law in 99 of the 193 constitutional cases decided between 2000 and 2008. The Canadian court was cited more than 300 times, considerably less often than the UK court (1,217) and American court (1,103) but considerably more than the New Zealand court (75), the European Court of Human Rights (36) and other courts.[47] Likewise, over the period between 2000 and 2010, the Canadian court was the second-most frequently cited court after the American court by the Israeli court, the third-most frequently cited court after the British and American courts by the Namibian court and the fourth-most frequently cited court after the British, American and Australian courts by the Indian and Irish courts.[48]

Canada exports not only its jurisprudential wisdom as reflected in the decisions of its Supreme Court. Undoubtedly its most influential constitutional innovation is its 1982 *Charter of Rights and Freedoms*. Alison Young in this volume notes the Charter was a response to Canada's first effort to protect rights in its 1960 Bill of Rights, which she says collapsed into a weak parliamentary protection of rights in practice, both because the definition of rights was in effect frozen circa 1960 and because the bill provided the courts no remedy. She argues the Charter was influential in two respects. First, it established what Gardbaum called a commonwealth model of rights protection that was soon emulated in other countries – most notably, in the Australian Capital Territory's Human Rights Act (1984), New Zealand's Bill of Rights Act (1990), the United Kingdom's Human Rights Act (1998) and South Africa's Charter of Human Rights and Responsibilities (2006).[49] Second, it offered a middle ground between strong constitutional protection and weak political protection of rights by creating – for example, through Section 33, the

[47] Cheryl Saunders and Adrienne Stone, *Reference to Foreign Precedents by the Australian High Court: A Matter of Method,* in Groppi and Ponthoreau, *supra* note 16 at 34.

[48] See Suzie Navot, *Israel: Creating a Constitution – The Use of Foreign Precedents by the Supreme Court* (1994–2010); Irene Spigno, *Namibia: The Supreme Court as a Foreign Law Importer;* Christina Fasone, *The Supreme Court of Ireland and the Use of Foreign Precedents: The Value of Constitutional History;* and Valentina Rita Scotti, *India: A "Critical" Use of Foreign Precedents in Constitutional Adjudication* in Groppi and Ponthoreau, *supra* note 16 at 145, 174, 120, 92.

[49] Stephen Gardbaum, THE NEW COMMONWEALTH MODEL OF CONSTITUTIONALISM: THEORY AND PRACTICE (Cambridge: Cambridge University Press, 2012).

"notwithstanding clause," of the Canadian Charter – the possibility of an institutional dialogue between the court and the legislature in which the latter could respond to a judicial determination of rights by overriding for a period of time the right or rights in question.[50]

Young suggests the attraction of the "commonwealth model" is its provision, through its "notwithstanding clause," the general restrictions clause, equality protections and specific non-absolute rights, of an opportunity for the legislature to respond to judicial decisions, thereby tempering the claim that a strong constitutional protection of rights can, in certain circumstances, harm democracy by enabling courts to issue rulings that run counter to the preferences of citizens and legislatures. She suggests that for the United Kingdom and other commonwealth countries, the Canadian Charter was especially attractive because it simultaneously provided stronger protection of human rights while preserving parliamentary sovereignty. But she argues the model is flawed both empirically and normatively and, perhaps for that reason, has collapsed into a strong constitutional protection of rights in all but name, both because the legislature has little ability to respond to a judicial determination of rights and because Section 33 is used so rarely that it has essentially lapsed. That, of course, will not worry those who support the strong constitutional protection of rights and fear the ability of a legislature to use a "notwithstanding clause" to override constitutionally entrenched rights.

There can be no doubt that Canadian jurisprudence has become, in the years since patriation and the *Charter of Rights and Freedoms*, an important source of guidance for courts in other countries. But it is nevertheless important to take note of Wen-Chen Chang's cautionary warning. In her chapter, she examines the impact of case law pertaining to the Charter on Hong Kong's Court of Final Appeal and Taiwan's Constitutional Court. While she notes that Canadian law, especially with respect to rights, has had a substantial effect in other countries, she finds very little effect in East Asia. In Hong Kong, for example, the Charter was cited in only nine cases between 2000 and 2006 and it has not been cited at all in any case since 2006. Litigants referred to the Charter case law in only four courses, one of them civil and three criminal. Likewise, while the Taiwan court did refer to foreign case law in 16 per cent of its cases, the largest numbers of references were to the constitutional courts of Germany (291), the United States (120), Japan (52), the European Court of

---

[50] Section 33 (1) of the Charter states: "Parliament or the legislature of a province may expressly declare in an Act of Parliament or of the legislature, as the case may be, that the Act or a provision thereof shall operate notwithstanding a provision included in section 2 or sections 7 to 15 of this Charter."

Justice and the European Court of Human Rights (23). There were only two references to Canadian Charter law, only one of which was brought to the court by a litigant. In short, however much it is relied upon as a reference by the constitutional courts of some countries, it is largely absent from the transjudicial dialogue in which justices and courts in other countries are involved. As with the Canadian Court's citation of foreign precedents, there is a wide variation in the extent to which other courts import Canadian precedents. As with its imports, it appears that the courts that draw upon Canadian precedents to the greatest extent are those in countries that, like Canada, were, prior to the 1931 *Statute of Westminster*, British colonies and thereafter dominions of the British empire and members of the Commonwealth and that shared a common language, a common-law legal tradition and a common experience of having the British Privy Council and Parliament serve for many years as their ultimate judicial and legislative authorities.

The role of the Canadian Court as an "exporter" of constitutional jurisprudence is not limited to the courts of other countries or, in the case of the Charter, to legislation in other members of the commonwealth. As Lech Garlicki discusses in this volume, one aspect and consequence of the global dialogue among courts is the development of law regarding human rights both in national courts and international judicial bodies such as the European Court of Human Rights (ECtHR). The mutual use of each other's case law has resulted in different forms of judicial borrowing, cross-fertilization and the development of a common body of concepts and rules – both, he suggests, a constitutionalization of international law and an internationalization of constitutional law.

Garlecki argues the key actors in this cross-national and cross-level dialogue are the strong courts in well-established constitutional systems. The ECtHR was created by the Convention for the Protection of Human Rights and Fundamental Freedoms agreed by the member states of the Council of Europe in Rome in 1950. Canada is of course not a member of the council.[51] Nevertheless, the Canadian court has influenced not only the decisions of other national courts but also those of the ECtHR in regard to a variety of human rights issues. Garlecki notes that decisions of the Canadian Court often reach the ECtHR via references in British cases and, through such references, have sometimes influenced the ECtHR. Two prominent instances are the ECtHR's decisions in the *Hirst* cases (2004, 2005) pertaining to prisoners' voting rights, and the *Pretty* cases (2001, 2002), pertaining to the

---

[51] Canada has had official observer status in the Council since 1996.

right to choose assisted suicide in order to avoid an undignified and distressing end of life. Both of those cases came from the United Kingdom and earlier decisions by the Canadian Court in *Sauvé v. Canada* (1993, 2002) and *Rodriguez v. Attorney General of Canada* (1993) were referenced in the UK cases.[52] Indeed, in those decisions, the ECtHR not only mentioned the earlier Canadian decisions but to a considerable extent relied on the argumentation of the Canadian court in its decisions.

Garlecki notes the ECtHR has referenced Canadian decisions in a number of other cases involving human rights – for example, in cases involving the deportation of an alleged terrorist, disproportionately severe sentencing, incriminating statements while in custody, retention of DNA samples and fingerprints and the right to wear religious clothing in a workplace – often because the references are made to the Canadian decisions by the UK courts in earlier stages in the proceedings. He concludes that although the Canadian references are not frequent,

> it seems that the Supreme Court of Canada is quoted more regularly than any other foreign jurisdiction, including the U.S. Supreme Court ... The Canadian references are usually of mostly informative value, sometimes they play also a legitimization function. On two occasions, the judgments of the Supreme Court of Canada played a more prominent role and – to a considerable extent – 'fertilized' the final decisions of the ECtHR.

There are other instances in which Canadian constitutional innovations or Supreme Court decisions influenced supranational or international institutions. Two of the most consequential involved the European Union. One involved the impact of Canada's *Charter of Rights and Freedoms* on the EU's creation of a *Charter of Fundamental Rights* in 2000.[53] The other involved the impact of the Court's 1998 decision in regard to whether Quebec could unilaterally secede on the elaboration of a procedure by which a member state of the EU might withdraw from the Union.[54] As Ran Hirschl notes in his chapter, the Court's decision in the *Secession Reference* has influenced the debate about regional secession in a number of countries, including Spain,

---

[52] *Sauvé v. Canada (Attorney General)* 2 SCR 438 (1993); *Sauvé v. Canada (Chief Electoral Officer)* 3 SCR 519 (2002); *Rodriguez v. British Columbia (Attorney General)* 3 SCR 519 (1993). The Sauvé cases pertained to the voting rights of convicted prisoners. In the Rodriguez decision, the Court refused to decriminalize physician-assisted suicide. In 2015, it reversed that decision in *Carter v. Canada (Attorney General)* 1 SCR 331 (2015).

[53] *Charter of Fundamental Rights of the European Union*, OFFICIAL JOURNAL OF THE EUROPEAN UNION, C 326/2, October 26, 2012, 391–407.

[54] *Reference Re Secession of Quebec*, SCR 217 (1998).

with respect to Catalonia, and the United Kingdom, with respect to Scotland. It influenced as well the EU's elaboration for the first time in its 2004 failed constitutional treaty and then in its 2009 *Treaty of Lisbon* of a procedure by which a member state might withdraw from the Union – a procedure that, in the wake of the UK referendum on 23 June 2016, is now being applied as the United Kingdom moves toward "Brexit."[55]

Considering first the influence of the Canadian *Charter of Rights and Freedoms* on the EU, at their meeting in Cologne in June 1999, the European Council, which consists of the heads of state and government of the EU member states, declared that "the fundamental rights applicable at Union level should be consolidated in a Charter and thereby made more evident" and asked the incoming Presidency to establish the conditions for the implementation of that decision by the time of the council's meeting in Tampere in October of that year. The presidency did so and a body, which called itself the European Convention, began its work in December 1999.[56]

The Convention completed its work in October 2000 and the *Charter of Fundamental Rights of the European Union* was proclaimed two months later by the presidents of the European Parliament, Council and Commission at the meeting in Nice of the European Council.[57] Although not incorporated into the EU treaties and thus having no legal effect, the Charter did, like the Canadian Charter before it, provide an expansive and comprehensive enumeration of rights that all EU citizens possessed by virtue of their country's membership in the EU – one that far exceeded the limited eighteenth-century enumeration found in the US Constitution's Bill of Rights.[58] Thus, it guaranteed the rights to liberty and security, protection of personal data, freedom of thought, conscience, religion, expression, information, assembly, association,

---

[55] In the referendum, in which 72 per cent of the UK electorate participated, voters were asked "Should the United Kingdom remain a member of the European Union or leave the European Union?" 51.9 per cent said "leave."

[56] The Convention consisted of fifteen representatives of the heads of state or government, sixteen members of the European Parliament, thirty members of the national parliaments and one member of the commission. It elected Rainer Herzog as its chair. Herzog served on the German Federal Constitutional Court as a judge from 1983 to 1987 and as its president from 1987 to 1994. In 1994, he was elected President of Germany and served until 1999.

[57] *Charter of Fundamental Rights of the European Union*, OFFICIAL JOURNAL OF THE EUROPEAN UNION, C 326/2, October 26, 2012, 391–407.

[58] The Bill of Rights consists of the first ten amendments to the US Constitution. In 1789, seventeen amendments were drafted by the House of Representatives, twelve of which were approved by the Senate and sent to the states for ratification. Ten were ratified by the states, the last of which was Virginia in 1791. The eleventh was ratified in 1992 and became the 27th amendment. The last of the original twelve, on Congressional apportionment, remains pending.

education, property, work and asylum and protection in the event of removal, expulsion or extradition, full equality before the law, non-discrimination, full equality between women and men, the right to vote and stand as a candidate at local elections and elections to the European Parliament, to be subject to good administration, to have access to documents, to be able to petition the European Parliament, to have freedom of movement and residence and to enjoy diplomatic and consular protection. In the area of criminal justice, it provided the right to an effective remedy and to a fair trial, the right to a presumption of innocence and the right of defence, to proportionality of criminal penalties and to not being tried or punished twice for the same criminal offence.

In December 2001, the European Council announced it was convening another Convention to consider the future of Europe and address a plethora of issues related to a widely perceived "democratic challenge" facing the EU, the allocation of competences between the member states and EU institutions, the imminent enlargement to include most of the formerly Communist-ruled states of central and eastern Europe and the EU's role in the region and the world.[59] Among other things, the Convention, which, like the one that drafted the *Charter of Fundamental Rights*, would be composed of representatives of the governments of the fifteen member states and members of the national parliaments and the European Parliament, was asked to consider whether the Charter should be integrated into the EU treaties and whether the EU should enact a constitution.

Although its mandate with respect to a constitution was ambiguous, the Convention drafted a treaty that established a constitution for the EU. It also adapted the *Charter of Fundamental Rights* to incorporate it into the treaties and give it legal effect. Completed in June 2004 and agreed by all of the member states at an Intergovernmental Conference in October 2004, the treaty was, as with any EU treaty, subjected to ratification by all of the member states. It was defeated in referendums in France and the Netherlands on 29 May and 1 June 2005. After a period of reflection, a greatly downsized version of the treaty – one that, because, unlike the original version, it was limited to amending the existing treaties, would not have to be subjected to referendums in most member states – was prepared by the German presidency in the Spring of 2007 and, after being approved by the European Council in June 2007, was submitted to another Intergovernmental Conference in the autumn of 2007.

---

[59] *Laeken Declaration on the future of the European Union*, Annex I, *Presidency Conclusions, European Council*, 14–15 December 2001, EUROPEAN UNION, SN 300/1/01 REV 1.

At their June meeting, the EU leaders decided the Charter would not be incorporated into the new treaty and would, instead, simply be attached to it as a declaration. The European Parliament vigorously disagreed and insisted that it be incorporated into the EU treaties so the rights described in the Charter would have legal value. After an overwhelming vote of the European Parliament in favour of that course, the member states agreed to add an article to the treaty that would have that effect. Meeting at the European Parliament in Strasbourg on 12 December 2007, the day before the treaty was to be signed in Lisbon, the presidents of the Commission, European Parliament and Council signed and formally proclaimed the *Charter of Fundamental Rights* and announced it would take effect when the *Treaty of Lisbon* took effect.[60] The new article replaced Article 6(1) of the *Treaty on European Union* with the following: "The Union recognises the rights, freedoms and principles set out in the Charter of Fundamental Rights of the European Union of 7 December 2000, as adapted at Strasbourg, on 12 December 2007, which shall have the same legal value as the Treaties."[61] The *Treaty of Lisbon* was signed the next day, ratified by all of the member states, and took effect on 1 December 2009.[62]

Turning to the issue of withdrawal, until the *Treaty of Lisbon* took effect there was no way for a member state to withdraw from the EU. But that possibility was created for the first time by Article 50 of that treaty. Article 50(1) states that "any member state may decide to withdraw from the Union in accordance with its own constitutional requirements." Having decided to withdraw, Article 50(2) directs the member state to notify the European Council of its intention, after which the EU, in light of guidelines provided by the European Council, and the member state "shall negotiate and conclude an agreement ... setting out the arrangements for its withdrawal, taking account of the framework for its future relationship with the Union. That agreement ... shall be concluded on behalf of the Union by the Council, acting by a qualified majority, after obtaining the consent of the European Parliament." Article 50(3) states that "the Treaties shall cease to apply to the

---

[60] *Charter of Fundamental Rights of the European Union*, OFFICIAL JOURNAL OF THE EUROPEAN UNION, 2007/C 303/01, 14 December 2007.

[61] *Consolidated Version of the Treaty on European Union*, OFFICIAL JOURNAL OF THE EUROPEAN UNION, C 326/1, Oct. 26, 2012, 13–390.

[62] Because the Treaty of Lisbon was an amending treaty, France, the Netherlands and most of the other states that ratify EU treaties by referendum ratified it by parliamentary vote. The Irish constitution, however, requires that all international treaties be ratified by referendum and, as happened with the Treaty of Nice several years earlier, Irish voters rejected the Treaty of Lisbon in June 2008. But, as also happened after Irish voters rejected the Treaty of Nice, they subsequently approved the treaty in a second referendum in October 2009.

State in question from the date of entry into force of the withdrawal agreement or, failing that, two years after the notification ... unless the European Council, in agreement with the Member State concerned, unanimously decides to extend this period."[63]

As in the case of the *Charter of Fundamental Rights*, it cannot be said that the EU's creation of a right of withdraw and elaboration of a procedure for doing so would not have happened without the Canadian Supreme Court's decision in the *Secession Reference*. Nevertheless, just as it has provided a constitutional framework for dealing with secessionist claims that has influenced the debate between proponents and opponents of secession in Spain, the United Kingdom and other countries, so too it provided a framework for a procedure by which a member state that wishes to withdraw from the EU may do so.

The reference came about after Quebec refused to support the federal government's request to the United Kingdom that it enact legislation patriating the Canadian constitution, the failures of the efforts undertaken at Meech Lake and Charlottetown to reach a federal-provincial accommodation, and the 30 October 1995 referendum in Quebec, which came very close to producing a majority in favour of sovereignty.[64] In response to the federal government's request for an advisory decision as to whether Quebec's National Assembly or government could unilaterally secede, the Court ruled Quebec could not secede only on the basis of a decision by its Assembly or government to do so, even if the decision was preceded by a clear majority in a referendum in favour of independence. But it did say that such a vote would "confer democratic legitimacy on the secession initiative, which all of the other participants in Confederation would have to recognize."[65] However, because in the years since Confederation "the people of the provinces and territories have created close ties of interdependence (economic, social, political and cultural) based on shared values that include federalism, democracy,

---

[63] *Consolidated Version of the Treaty on European Union, supra* note 59, *Title VI Final Provisions, Article 50.*

[64] See *Reference re: Resolution to Amend the Constitution*, 1 S.C.R. 754 (1981). The 1987 Meech Lake Accord negotiated by the federal and provincial first ministers was opposed by Manitoba and Newfoundland and expired in 1990. The Charlottetown Accord, agreed by the first ministers in August 1992, was defeated by 54 per cent of the voters in a national referendum in October 1992. In the 1995 referendum in Quebec, in which more than 93 per cent of the electorate voted, 50.6 per cent of those voting said "No" in response to the question whether Quebec should become sovereign.

[65] *Reference Re Secession of Quebec*, SCR 217 (1998). For a discussion of such referendums, see Stephen Tierney, CONSTITUTIONAL REFERENDUMS: THE THEORY AND PRACTICE OF REPUBLICAN DELIBERATION (Oxford: Oxford University Press, 2014).

constitutionalism and the rule of law, and respect for minorities" and because "a democratic decision of Quebecers in favour of secession would put those relationships at risk," there would have to be, after a decision by Quebec to pursue secession, negotiations between Quebec and the rest of Canada.

The Court went on to describe those negotiations in some detail:

> The negotiations that followed such a vote would address the potential act of secession as well as its possible terms should in fact secession proceed. There would be no conclusions predetermined by law on any issue. The negotiations would need to address the interests of the other provinces, the federal government and Quebec and indeed the rights of all Canadians both within and outside Quebec, and specifically the rights of minorities. The negotiation process precipitated by a decision of a clear majority of the population of Quebec on a clear question to pursue secession would require the reconciliation of various rights and obligations by the representatives of two legitimate majorities, namely, the clear majority of the population of Quebec, and the clear majority of Canada as a whole, whatever that may be ... In the circumstances, negotiations following such a referendum would undoubtedly be difficult. While the negotiators would have to contemplate the possibility of secession, there would be no absolute legal entitlement to it and no assumption that an agreement reconciling all relevant rights and obligations would actually be reached. It is foreseeable that even negotiations carried out in conformity with the underlying constitutional principles could reach an impasse. We need not speculate here as to what would then transpire. Under the Constitution, secession requires that an amendment be negotiated.[66]

The procedure elaborated in the *Secession Reference* differs in some important ways from the EU's procedure under Article 50. Most notably, the EU procedure requires neither agreement on withdrawal nor on the terms of withdrawal and the future relationship between the EU and the departing member state; if, two years after the state that wishes to withdraw has notified the European Council of its intention, there is no agreement on withdrawal, the treaties cease to apply to the state unless the remaining member states unanimously agree to extend the period of negotiation. In contrast, because secession requires, as the Court said, the "reconciliation of various rights and obligations by the representatives of two legitimate majorities" and "must be considered, in legal terms, to require an amendment to the Constitution," it requires not only negotiation but agreement – and, indeed, not only an agreement that reconciles the various rights and obligations of the parties but

---

[66] *Id.* at paragraphs 93 and 97.

one that, because the Constitution is silent on the matter of secession, amends the Constitution. Given the country's fraught history prior to patriation in regard to obtaining provincial consent to federal government requests to the United Kingdom to amend the constitution, the protracted constitutional crisis prior to and after patriation and the complex two-stage procedure for amending the constitution after passage in 1996 of an act that established a regional veto on the tabling of a constitutional amendment, enacting such an amendment is no easy matter.[67] Nevertheless, in one very important way, the EU procedure resembles the one elaborated by the Court in the Secession Reference: although the obstacles to separation are not as great in the EU as in Canada, or indeed in any long-standing state, both procedures emphasize the fact that, after a territorial unit has expressed its desire to secede or withdraw, rather than a unilateral declaration of independence the next step should be negotiation – a negotiation in which the parties, while adhering to the constitutional principles they hold in common, attempt to reach an agreement to separate themselves from each other. Because it underscores the importance of adhering to constitutional principles, recognizing and accepting the legitimate concerns of the other parties and negotiating in order to reconcile the divergent interests, rights and obligations, the Canadian procedure has become a model for both those advocating and opposing the independence of culturally distinctive regions such as Catalonia and Scotland. For example, the last paragraph of the 2012 memorandum of agreement between the governments of the United Kingdom and Scotland that set the stage for the September 2014 referendum in Scotland on independence stated, "The two governments are committed to continue to work together constructively in light of the outcome, whatever it is, in the best interests of the people of Scotland and the rest of the United Kingdom."[68]

---

[67] The *Constitution Act 1982*, Part V, Article 38(1) states that an amendment may be proclaimed when authorized by resolutions of the Senate and House of Commons and the legislative assemblies of at least two-thirds of the provinces that have at least 50 per cent of the population of all provinces. However, the *Act Respecting Constitutional Amendments* (S.C. 1996, c. 1), known as the regional veto, also requires that, before a constitutional amendment can be tabled in Parliament, the government must obtain the consent of a majority of provinces including, specifically, Ontario, Quebec, British Columbia, two of the Atlantic provinces with at least 50 per cent of that region's population and two of the Prairie provinces with at least 50 per cent of that region's population.

[68] See *Agreement between the United Kingdom government and the Scottish government on a referendum on independence for Scotland*, 15 October 2012 (known as the Edinburgh Agreement) at www.gov.scot/About/Government/concordats/Referendum-on-independence. In the referendum, held on 18 September 2014, 85 per cent of the registered voters in Scotland voted. 44.7 per cent of those voting said Scotland should be an independent country.

As Richard Albert said in introducing this volume, the sesquicentennial of the *British North America Act 1867*, renamed in 1982 the *Constitution Act 1867*, offers an occasion to look back and reflect on the long path Canada has taken to the present. There is of course much to celebrate about what happened in 1867; after all, three colonial provinces of the United Kingdom – Canada, New Brunswick and Nova Scotia – were combined into a single federation of four provinces governed by a constitution modelled largely on the United Kingdom's but modified to reflect the territorial and cultural particularities of the new country.[69] The year 1867 was not a grand constitutional moment in the same sense that 1787 was for Americans.[70] It was not a moment in which an independent people came together and decided how they wished to govern themselves. It was, instead, just one more of the many *British North American Acts* enacted by the British government and parliament as it administered its colonial territories. Nevertheless, 1867 was, as Stephen Tierney argues, a federal constitutional moment, one that recognized and incorporated the territorial and cultural diversity and distinctiveness of the British colonies into a single federation. It would take sixty-four more years before the country obtained its independence with the *Statute of Westminster*, another eighteen years after that before its Supreme Court became the final court of appeal and another thirty-three years after that before it finally completed the long trek to full independence by patriating its constitution and, with it, the power to amend that constitution. Nevertheless, 1867, as Canada's founding moment, deserves to be celebrated.

The sesquicentennial is an appropriate time not only to celebrate the founding of the state and reflect upon the path it has followed over the past 150 years but, also, to celebrate the constitution Canada has today – a constitution that, through the entrenchment of the *Canadian Charter of Rights and Freedoms*, guarantees its citizens an array of rights and freedoms more expansive in range and applicable to more of the issues that arise in their lives than those guaranteed by other states, even states that share Canada's commitment to liberal democratic values and the protection of individual rights and

[69] The *Constitutional Act* of 1791 divided the province of Quebec, created when the United Kingdom obtained New France in 1763, into Upper and Lower Canada ("upper" and "lower" referring to the St. Lawrence River). The *British North America Act 1840* combined Upper and Lower Canada into the province of Canada. The *British North America Act 1867* divided the province of Canada into the provinces of Ontario and Quebec.

[70] On constitutional moments, see Bruce A. Ackerman, *The Storrs Lectures: Discovering the Constitution*, YALE L. J. 93 (6), (1984); Bruce A. Ackerman and Robert E. Charney, *Canada at the Constitutional Crossroads*, UNIVERSITY OF TORONTO L. J. 34 (1984); and Bruce A. Ackerman, WE THE PEOPLE – VOLUME 1: FOUNDATIONS (Cambridge: Harvard University Press, 1991).

liberties. It is a time, also, to celebrate a Supreme Court that regards the constitution not as carved in stone two centuries ago but as a "living tree" – one that, as Chief Justice McLachlin says, "is capable from time to time of sprouting a new leaf or even growing a new branch (and) lives and adapts through its application to new situations." It is a time to celebrate the paradoxical fact that, because the Court was, for so long, juridically subordinate to and hence formally engaged in a trans-Atlantic jurisprudential dialogue with, the Judicial Committee of the British Privy Council, its justices have become accustomed to informing themselves about the insights and wisdom of other courts in regard to issues that come before them. And it is a time to celebrate the fact that, as the Court has come to be recognized as one that is open to the insights and wisdom of other courts and, because of its relatively recent, constitutionally entrenched and expansive *Charter of Rights and Freedoms*, is dealing with a wide range of contemporary issues pertaining to rights, those courts have come to look to it as a source of insight and wisdom as they address similar issues.

But if the sesquicentennial is an opportune time to reflect upon the country's long path to the present and celebrate a constitution that, as a "living tree," can be applied to the contemporary realities of Canadian society and a Court that has become a highly respected participant in the transjudicial dialogue among the constitutional courts of the worlds, it is also an opportune time to recognize the constitutional challenges, some of them long-standing, others the result of recent social and demographic changes in Canadian society, that remain today.

One of those long-standing challenges involves the still-ambiguous place, a quarter-century after the rejection of the Charlottetown Accord, of Quebec in the federation. Stephen Tierney argues that "the ongoing fundamental purpose of the federal polity is the constitutional accommodation of territorial plurality." And, he says, "the consent that underpins the legitimacy of the federal polity is the consent of its constituent territories as well as that of the individual citizens of the state." But patriation without Quebec's consent, coupled with the subsequent failures of Meech Lake and Charlottetown, has meant that Canadian federalism, while taking seriously the role of the provinces, has not taken full account of the country's biculturalism. For Quebec, the result has been, Tierney argues, a concern about its ability to maintain its cultural specificity and identity. Jamie Cameron notes, similarly, that patriation without Quebec's consent and the subsequent failures of Meech Lake and Charlottetown dealt Quebec "an unforgivable insult that largely robbed patriation of legitimacy in that province and radically escalated the danger of separation" – something that Quebec voters very nearly approved in 1995. As Alain Gagnon notes, that has left Quebec with some considerable uncertainty in regard to its identity: Is it one of the country's two founding nations, a "distinct society," a "province state," just one of four original provinces or something else? More than a quarter-century after Charlottetown, that question remains unanswered.

Another long-standing challenge – one that, like Quebec, was present before the creation of Canada in 1867 – involves the place of the Indigenous peoples in the constitutional order. Patrick Macklem notes that since 1665, when France agreed to a peace treaty with four nations of the Iroquois Confederacy, more than 500 treaties have been negotiated with Indigenous peoples. The treaties typically dispossessed them of their ancestral territories and facilitated their relocation in exchange for continued access to the territories for hunting and fishing. In the late nineteenth century, the courts gradually began to interpret the treaties as a type of contract, albeit one that was subject to legislative authority, meaning the rights could be unilaterally regulated or terminated. Macklem notes that section 35(1) of the Constitution Act 1982, which recognized and affirmed the existing aboriginal and treaty rights of the aboriginal peoples, has ushered in significant changes in the constitutional relationship between those peoples and the state. The Court's decision in *R. v. Badger* required that treaty stipulations regarding hunting rights be interpreted in a manner consistent with the Indigenous peoples' understanding.[71] And in *Delgamuukw v. British Columbia*, it confirmed that, as stated in section 35 (1), Aboriginal title was not just common law but a constitutional right.[72] Nevertheless, as important as those decisions were in describing relations between the Indigenous peoples and the state in terms of constitutional pluralism, Macklem argues their relations are not in fact constitutionally plural and won't be until Indigenous governments are recognized as "sovereign within their spheres of authority, capable of exercising exclusive and concurrent lawmaking powers formally equivalent to their federal and provincial counterparts."

One of the most challenging issues in Canadian society and one that has frequently come before the Court and has proven to be especially difficult to resolve, concerns claims in regard to the right to equality under section 15 and to gender equality under section 28 of the *Charter of Rights and Freedoms*. Section 15(1) states that all individuals are equal before and under the law and have the right to the equal protection and benefits of the law without discrimination. Section 28 states that the rights and freedoms referred to in the Charter are guaranteed equally to male and female persons.

---

[71] *R. v. Badger*, SCR 771 (1996).   [72] *Delgamuukw v. British Columbia* 3 SCR 1010 (1997).

Catharine MacKinnon notes in this volume that Canada has taken major strides, more than anywhere else in the world, in equality adjudication over the past two decades; it is, she says, the only country that has approached sex equality principles in criminal cases for sexual assault. Yet the country still has some considerable distance to go. She notes that in *Andrews v. The Law Society of British Columbia*, the first equality decision under the Charter, the Court developed a standard of "substantive equality," as opposed to the more conventional standard of "formal equality." The substantive equality standard subjects a claim to an assessment based on the disadvantage created by an inequality that affected, "in a systematic and cumulative way, dignity, respect, access to sources, physical security, credibility, membership in community, or power," one that is perhaps reflected in a group's "social history of disempowerment, exploitation, and subordination to and by dominant interests."[73] While a pioneering formulation, MacKinnon notes the standard is, as one justice observed, an elusive concept; indeed, in a decision a decade later, the Court said section 15 "is perhaps the Charter's most conceptually difficult provision."[74] But what is most problematic about the concept, MacKinnon believes, and perhaps explains why section 15 has proven to be so difficult to apply, is the Court's failure to recognize that hierarchy is the underlying cause of inequality: "Hierarchy is what is unequal about inequality in substance." The Court's explicit embrace of hierarchy "as the core substantive inequality concept would," she says, "clarify and fortify the existing Canadian constitutional approach." In other words, behind, underlying and giving rise to the disadvantage and indignity of inequality is hierarchy, whether of income, gender, race, cultural heritage or some other attribute. Until the Court explicitly addresses the cause of inequality, it is unlikely to provide an adequate remedy to substantive inequality.

In a similar vein, Ayelet Shachar illustrates, with the interesting case of Zunera Ishaq, the fact that, although Canada is one of the most accommodating jurisdictions in the world of the new constitutionalism – the *Charter of Rights and Freedoms* is the only one in the world that includes explicit and constitutionally entrenched commitments to multiculturalism and gender equality – it has not escaped the charged questions of "who are we" and what values do Canadians share as members of a political community. And, she notes, when gender and minority culture or religion are thrown into the mix, one has the ingredients of a perfect constitutional storm.

---

[73] *Andrews v. Law Society of British Columbia*, 1 SCR 143 (1989).
[74] *Law v. Canada (Minister of Employment and Immigration)*, 1 SCR 497 (1997).

Ishaq is a young woman who immigrated from Pakistan, became a permanent resident in 2008, had her citizenship application approved in 2013 and was looking forward to taking the citizenship oath. In 2011, the federal minister of citizenship and immigration introduced a ban on wearing the *niqab* in the swearing-in ceremony. Ishaq objected to the ban, went to court and won in both the federal court and the court of appeal. But neither decision dealt with the constitutional issue – namely, the ban's breach of the entrenched rights of religious freedom, multiculturalism and gender equality of a person who has completed all of the requirements for citizenship except the oath. The federal government appealed to the Supreme Court but it declined to take the case and has not, as yet, ruled on the issue.[75] But in a country in which more than 20 per cent of the population is foreign-born and a substantial portion of the foreign-born population has arrived in recent years, the issue will no doubt come before the Court in the near future.

In addition to the challenges posed by the still-unresolved place of Quebec in the federation, the failure to empower the governments of the Indigenous peoples, the elusive nature of the Court's standard for assessing claims under section 15 and the absence of a Court ruling in regard to the breach of rights at the intersection of those involving cultural and religious freedom, multiculturalism and gender equality, Canada and its constitution also face a plethora of challenges pertaining to its institutions. As Ran Hirschl notes, the constitutional definitions of Canada's executive branch are imprecise; the Senate remains, in a democratic era, filled by appointment rather than election and plays a less consequential role in policy-making than the upper chamber of the legislature in many countries; the large metropolitan regions do not have an institutional role comparable to their demographic importance; and for all the expansiveness of its catalogue of rights, the Charter omits some obvious ones such as subsistence social rights. And as Richard Albert and Jamie Cameron note, the process of constitutional amendment, so necessary if these and other institutional shortcomings are to be repaired, is so complex and so loaded with potential veto points that there is little likelihood of any amendment pertaining to an important institutional issue being tabled and adopted unless the amending rules themselves are amended – which is undoubtedly even less likely to occur.[76]

---

[75] With the ban lifted, Ishaq took the citizenship oath in October 2015. In November 2015, the newly elected Liberal government of Justin Trudeau withdrew the government's appeal of the decision rejecting the ban on wearing the *niqab* while taking the citizenship oath.

[76] See also Richard Albert, *The Difficulty of Constitutional Amendment in Canada*, ALTA L. REV., 53 (2015); Richard Albert, *Amending Constitutional Amendment Rules*, INT. J. CON. LAW, 13 (2015).

The sesquicentennial is an opportune time to reflect on the long path Canada has taken to the present day and to celebrate the constitution it received in 1867 and patriated, complete with an expansive and constitutionally entrenched *Charter of Rights and Freedoms* in 1982. But it is also an appropriate time to reflect on the challenges that face the country – and to realize that there is still much unfinished business, constitutionally speaking, and that as with any constitution, the one Canada received in 1867 remains, 150 years later, a work-in-progress.

Index

Index